Taking SIDES

Clashing Views on Controversial Psychological Issues

Ninth Edition

Taking
SIDES

Clashing Views on
Controversial
Psychological Issues

Ninth Edition

Taking SIDES

Clashing Views on Controversial Psychological Issues

Ninth Edition

Edited, Selected, and with Introductions by

Brent Slife
Brigham Young University

Dushkin Publishing Group/Brown & Benchmark Publishers
A Times Mirror Higher Education Group Company

To my three garrulous sons, Conor, Nathan, and Jacob

Photo Acknowledgments

Part 1   Elaine M.Ward
Part 2   DPG/B&B
Part 3   Digital Stock
Part 4   DPG/B&B
Part 5   Louis P. Raucci/DPG/B&B
Part 6   Digital Stock

Cover Art Acknowledgment

Charles Vitelli

Manufactured in the United States of America

Ninth Edition

10 9 8 7 6 5 4 3 2 1

Library of Congress Cataloging-in-Publication Data

Main entry under title:
   Taking sides: clashing views on controversial psychological issues/edited, selected, and
with introductions by Brent Slife.—9th ed.
   Includes bibliographical references and index.
   1. Psychology. 2. Human behavior. I. Slife, Brent, *comp.*

0-697-31293-3

150
95-83857

 Printed on Recycled Paper

PREFACE

Critical thinking skills are a significant component of a meaningful education, and this book is specifically designed to stimulate critical thinking and initiate lively and informed dialogue on psychological issues. In this book I present 36 selections, arranged in pro and con pairs, that address a total of 18 different controversial issues in psychology. The opposing views demonstrate that even experts can derive conflicting conclusions and opinions from the same body of information.

A dialogue approach to learning is certainly not new. The ancient Greek philosopher Socrates engaged in it with his students some 2,400 years ago. His point-counterpoint procedure was termed a *dialectic.* Although Socrates and his companions hoped eventually to know the "truth" by this method, they did not see the dialectic as having a predetermined end. There were no right answers to know or facts to memorize. The emphasis in this learning method is on how to evaluate information—on developing reasoning skills.

It is in this dialectical spirit that *Taking Sides: Clashing Views on Controversial Psychological Issues* was originally compiled, and it has guided me through this ninth edition as well. To encourage and stimulate discussion and to focus the debates in this volume, each issue is expressed in terms of a single question and answered with two points of view. But certainly the reader should not feel confined to adopt only one or the other of the positions presented. There are positions that fall between the views expressed, or totally outside them, and I encourage you to fashion your own conclusions.

Some of the questions raised in this volume go to the very heart of what psychology as a discipline is all about and the methods and manner in which psychologists work. Others address newly emerging concerns. In choosing readings I was guided by the following criteria: the readings had to be understandable to newcomers to psychology; they had to have academic substance; and they had to express markedly different points of view.

Plan of the book   Each issue in this volume has an issue *introduction,* which defines each author's position and sets the stage for debate. Also provided is a set of point-counterpoint statements that pertain to the issue—they should help get the dialogue off the ground. Each issue concludes with *challenge questions* to provoke further examination of the issue. The introduction and challenge questions are designed to assist the reader in achieving a critical and informed view on important psychological issues. At the back of the book is a listing of all the *contributors to this volume,* which gives information on the psychologists, psychiatrists, philosophers, professors, and social critics whose views are debated here.

i

Changes to this edition   This edition represents a considerable revision. There are 10 completely new issues: *Is There Evidence that Homosexuality Is Biologically Determined?* (Issue 1); *Do Evolutionary and Genetic Factors Determine Our Sexual Behaviors?* (Issue 2); *Does Viewing Television Increase a Child's Aggression?* (Issue 4); *Is a Child's Development Negatively Affected by a Working Mother?* (Issue 5); *Do Physically Punished Children Become Violent Adults?* (Issue 7); *Is Schizophrenia a Disease?* (Issue 11); *Classic Dialogue: Do Diagnostic Labels Hinder Treatment?* (Issue 13); *Should Psychologists Be Allowed to Prescribe Drugs?* (Issue 14); *Have Antidepressant Drugs Proven to Be Effective?* (Issue 15); and *Does Religious Commitment Improve Mental Health?* (Issue 18). In addition, for the issue on using animals in psychological research (Issue 3), both the YES and NO readings have been changed to bring a fresh perspective to the debate. In all, there are 22 new selections. The issues that were dropped from the previous edition were done so on the recommendation of professors who let me know what worked and what could be improved.

A word to the instructor   An *Instructor's Manual With Test Questions* (multiple-choice and essay) is available through the publisher for the instructor using *Taking Sides* in the classroom. A general guidebook, *Using Taking Sides in the Classroom*, which discusses methods and techniques for integrating the pro-con approach into any classroom setting, is also available.

Acknowledgments   In working on this revision I received useful suggestions from many of the users of the previous edition, and I was able to incorporate many of their recommendations for new issues and new readings. I particularly wish to thank the following professors:

Margaret Bierley
California State
    University–Chico

Marvin Brodsky
University of Manitoba

Robin Frye
Fitchburg State College

Stephen S. Fugita
Santa Clara University

Bryan Gibson
Trenton State College

Steve Hardin
Midlands Technical College

Harold A. Herzog
Western Carolina University

Allen Huffcutt
Bradley University

Patricia Ann Humphreys
Chapman University

Kimberly J. Husenits
Indiana University of
    Pennsylvania

Robert J. Lovinger
Central Michigan University

Louis Manza
Gettysburg College

Jean-Luis Marchand
Chesapeake College

Ralph J. McKenna
Hendrix College

Michael Nielsen
Georgia Southern University

R.A. Selgiman
Chaffey Community College

Harriet Shaklee
Seattle University

George Spilich
Washington College

Richard T. Sponge
High Point University

Donald Spring
Union College

Bruce C. Stockin
Westmont College

Alan Swinkels
St. Edward's University

Judith K. Winters
Dekalb College–North

In addition, special thanks go to Mimi Egan, publisher for the Taking Sides series at Dushkin Publishing Group/Brown & Benchmark Publishers, for her perspicacity.

Brent Slife
Brigham Young University

CONTENTS IN BRIEF

CONTENTS

Simon LeVay and Dean H. Hamer, researchers in neuroanatomy and biochemistry, respectively, contend that evidence points to a biological component for male homosexuality. Neuroscientist William Byne argues that the evidence for innate biological traits in homosexuality is flawed.

Robert Wright, a senior editor of *The New Republic*, claims that sexual behavior is determined by people's genes. Theoretical psychologist Richard N. Williams argues that the philosophy underlying genetic explanations of human behavior is dangerous.

Elizabeth Baldwin, a research ethics officer for the American Psychological Association's Science Directorate, maintains that the benefits of behavioral research with animals are substantial. Professor of educational psychology Alan D. Bowd and Kenneth J. Shapiro, executive director of Psychologists for the Ethical Treatment of Animals, argue that the "benefits" of animal research do not make up for the cruel treatment of the animals.

Brandon S. Centerwall, an epidemiologist, argues that children who see a lot of violence on television display more violent behaviors in adulthood. Brian Siano, a writer and researcher, argues that parental neglect and lack of nurturance are better predictors of aggression than television viewing habits.

Developmental scientists Nazli Baydar and Jeanne Brooks-Gunn assert that maternal employment has detrimental effects on the cognitive and behavioral development of children. Child development researchers Deborah Lowe Vandell and Janaki Ramanan found that a mother's employment during a child's infancy is associated with high achievement test scores.

Clinician Judith S. Wallerstein contends that children of divorced parents are
at greater risk of developing mental and physical problems than are children
of intact families. Sociologists David H. Demo and Alan C. Acock argue that
any negative effects of divorce are short-lived and that divorce often produces
many positive changes.

Murray A. Straus, a social science researcher, finds a relationship between
physical punishment in childhood and violent behavior in the teenage and
adult years. Joan McCord, a professor of criminal justice, concludes that
neglected children, not those who are physically punished, become the most
violent adults.

Ellen Bass and Laura Davis, both counselors of victims of child sexual abuse,
assert that even a faint or vague memory of sexual abuse is prime evidence
that sexual abuse has occurred. Psychiatrist Lee Coleman argues that "memories" of sexual abuse that never occurred can be created in therapy with the
encouragement of mental health professionals.

Bernard Dixon, an editor and writer who specializes in science and health issues, proposes that a positive mental attitude can prevent illness because it reduces psychological stress, which can impair functioning of the immune system. Physician Marcia Angell argues that maintaining a positive attitude will not ward off disease.

Psychologist Robert J. Sternberg argues that intelligence can be taught through training programs, three of which he summarizes. Psychologist Arthur R. Jensen contends that programs designed to increase intelligence have a faulty understanding of the nature of intelligence.

Psychiatrist Eve C. Johnstone contends that schizophrenia is a biological disease. Theodore R. Sarbin, noted researcher and psychologist, argues that schizophrenia is actually a social construct developed to make sense of a variety of behaviors.

Psychotherapists Anne C. Speckhard and Vincent M. Rue argue that abortion has serious psychological consequences for women. Psychologists Nancy E. Adler et al. contend that severe negative psychological reactions following abortion are infrequent.

Psychologist D. L. Rosenhan argues that patients labeled as schizophrenic are seen as such by mental health workers regardless of the true state of the patients' mental health. Psychiatrist Robert L. Spitzer argues that diagnostic labels are necessary and valuable.

Psychologist Patrick H. DeLeon and his colleagues argue that the public would benefit greatly from psychologists' obtaining prescription privileges. Clinical psychologist Garland Y. DeNelsky maintains that prescription privileges for psychologists would harm the discipline's ability to serve the public.

Psychiatrist Peter D. Kramer argues that antidepressant drugs benefit depressed patients with almost no side effects. Professors of psychology Seymour Fisher and Roger P. Greenberg maintain that there is no reliable evidence that antidepressants are safe and effective.

Psychiatrist Raymond R. Crowe argues that not only is electroconvulsive therapy (ECT) safe and effective, but it also acts quickly after many other treatments have failed. Leonard Roy Frank, an outspoken advocate against psychiatric shock therapy, asserts that ECT only seems effective because of the brain damage it causes.

Victor Cline, a professor emeritus of psychology, argues that pornography poses a great harm to viewers because it degrades women and desensitizes males to sexual violence. Professor of philosophy F. M. Christensen contends that there is little evidence that pornography is harmful and that pornography is only a scapegoat for other societal problems.

David B. Larson, president of the National Institute for Healthcare, maintains that religious commitment improves mental health. Albert Ellis, president of the Institute for Rational-Emotive Therapy, asserts that extreme religious commitment, or fanaticism, is mentally unhealthy.

INTRODUCTION

Unresolved Issues in Psychology

Brent Slife
Stephen C. Yanchar

Eminent psychologist Edward Bradford Titchener (1867–1927) once stated that although psychology has a short history, it has a long past. He meant that even though the science of psychology is of relatively recent origin, the subject matter of psychology extends back to ancient history. Unfortunately, this dual history—the short and the long—is rarely treated in psychology texts; most texts focus almost exclusively on the shorter history. This shorter history is thought to be guided by the scientific method, so texts are generally filled with the scientific facts of the discipline. However, we cannot fully understand psychology without also understanding its longer intellectual history, a history of age-old questions that have recently been addressed by science but rarely been completely answered. Some history texts portray this longer intellectual history, but they do not deal with its contemporary implications. *Taking Sides: Clashing Views on Controversial Psychological Issues* is dedicated to the unresolved issues that still plague psychologists from this longer history.

WHY ARE THERE UNRESOLVED ISSUES?

The subject matter of psychology is somewhat different from the subject matter of the natural sciences. In fact, psychology has been termed a "soft" science because it deals with neither the "hard" world of observable entities and physical elements—like zoology, biology, physiology, and chemistry— nor the rigorous computational analyses of mathematics, physics, and astronomy. These hard sciences are disciplines in which the crucial questions can usually be answered through scientific observation and experimentation.

Psychologists, on the other hand, deal with the warm, "soft" world of human beings—the thoughts, attitudes, emotions, and behaviors of people interacting with other people. Psychologists are therefore concerned with many of the philosophical questions that seem so central and unique to humanity. These questions have no quick and simple answers. Indeed, these questions have occupied thinkers—scientists and philosophers alike—since at least the time of the ancient Greeks.

For example, psychologists regularly deal with the topic of mind and matter, or what is sometimes referred to as the mind-body problem. The mind-body problem essentially asks, Does the mind (which is often viewed as *not* being entirely composed of matter) control the body (which *is* entirely composed of matter), or does the brain control the mind? Issue 9 of this volume ("Can Mental Attitude Affect Biological Disease?") is devoted to a contemporary version of this problem. Yet the essence of what we mean by the mind-body problem has been a topic of debate since at least the time of the Greek philosopher Aristotle (Robinson, 1989). Aristotle (384–322 B.C.) believed that the human mind had to be distinct from the crude matter of the human body. While the human body would eventually die and decay, the human mind (or soul) was imperishable. Aristotle accounted for much of human psychology on biological grounds (i.e., in terms of matter), but he still considered the higher rational activities of a human to be aspects of a mind that are independent of the body (Robinson, 1986). However, what is left out of his and other accounts is a precise explanation of how mind and body are connected. That is, if we assume that the mind is *not* composed of matter and is thus intangible, then how can it connect or interact with something material and tangible like the body? If, on the other hand, we decide that the mind *is* tangible and material, then we inherit a host of other problems associated with reductionism (see Slife & Williams, 1995, for details).

The point is that these and other such questions may not be resolved merely through scientific observation and experimentation. Scientific method is helpful for answering certain empirical questions, but its benefits are limited for many philosophical questions. And, for better or worse, psychology is infused with philosophical questions as well as empirical questions. There are basically two reasons for this infusion: the complexity of psychology's subject matter and the methods that psychologists use to study their subject matter.

Human beings—the primary subject matter of psychology—appear to operate with wills of their own within a hopelessly complex network of situations and relationships. This, it would seem, hinders the ability of scientists to attain the kind of certainty with people that they can attain with inanimate objects. Perhaps more important, it is difficult to know *why* persons act in a particular manner because we cannot directly observe their intentions, thoughts, and desires. Thus, there are some aspects of human beings that elude the traditional methods of natural science.

The scientific method itself provides no irrefutable verification of an explanation. This is because data alone do not provide answers. Scientists sometimes talk as if the data from their experiments "tell" them what to believe or "give" them results, but this is somewhat misleading. Data are meaningless until they have been interpreted by the scientist (Slife & Williams, 1995). That is, scientists have a lot to do with their findings. Because there are a number of possible interpreters, there are, in principle, a number of possible interpretations. As some of the issues in this volume show, results that seem to supply indubitable proof for one interpreter might appear quite dubious to another. The reason for this is that the scientific method is set up in a manner that requires interpretation. As many who have studied this method have noted (e.g., Popper, 1959; Rychlak, 1988), the scientific method basically takes the form of a logical if-then statement: *If* my theory is correct, *then* my data will come out as I predict. However, problems can occur when we use this logic inappropriately. What if we know, for example, that we have the "then" portion of our statement, that the data did come out as I predicted? Do we then know that my theory is correct? Of course we cannot know this, because there can be an alternative theory (or many alternatives) that could explain the same data.

Unfortunately, however, this is the way in which science is conducted. We do not know the "if" portion of our logical statement—that my theory is correct; we can only know the "then" portion—that my data came out as I predicted. And our knowledge of our data cannot tell us that our theory is correct. All we can ever do is *interpret* what our data mean because our data can always mean something else.[1]

So, as a little logic has shown, data from human subjects can always be interpreted in different ways. In fact, because of these possible interpretations, there can never be a final and definitive experiment to determine what is really true about human beings (Slife & Williams, 1995). This is what scientists mean when they say that they cannot *prove* a theory but can only *support* it. Unfortunately, this simple distinction leaves many important questions unresolved, such as the mind-body problem. Still, this lack of resolution does not mean that scientists can ignore these issues. Just because certain issues are not amenable to scientific methods does not mean they go away. The issue of whether or not the mind controls matter, for example, is vital to cancer patients who wonder whether or not positive mental attitudes will alter the course of their disease. Such issues require exploration and debate regardless of the state of scientific knowledge. Whatever scientific information is available is important, and the lack of a complete scientific answer cannot prevent us from debating what information we do have, particularly when we may never get a complete scientific answer.

A DIALECTICAL APPROACH

This volume introduces some of the most important contemporary debates in psychology as well as some classical issues that remain unresolved. As mentioned, this volume is different from texts that focus exclusively on what is known scientifically. Most texts with an exclusive scientific focus adopt a "banking conception" of education.

The banking conception of education assumes that students are essentially "banks" in which scientific facts are "deposited." Because psychology is considered a science, there are presumably many scientific psychological facts, derived from experiments, that need to be deposited in students' minds. The banking conception makes teachers and textbooks fact distributors or information transmitters. Lectures are monologues through which the facts of experiments or the findings of method are distributed and transmitted into the mental "banks" of students. At test time, then, teachers make information "withdrawals" to discern how well students have maintained the deposits of educational currency referred to as knowledge.

Since the time of the Greek philosopher Socrates (470–399 B.C.), the banking conception of education has not been considered effective for learning about unresolved conceptual issues. One reason for this is that nestled within the banking conception lies the assumption that knowledge is above reasonable criticism and that the facts of a scholarly discipline are approximations of truth—distilled and ready for distribution to students. This is the notion of education that considers knowledge to be strictly objective. Students are thought to acquire a clear and objective picture of reality—the way things really are. As we have observed, however, it is questionable whether teachers of the "soft" sciences have access to clear and objective facts only. In many cases, the "facts" are not so clear and objective but rather puzzling and debatable. Indeed, interpretations of data are always debatable, in principle.

An alternative to the banking tradition of education is the *dialectical* tradition of education. In this tradition, there can be no meaning (and thus no knowledge) without opposition. For example, there is no way to understand what "beauty" or "upness" means without implicitly understanding what "ugliness" or "downness" is, respectively. To judge the beauty of a work of art, one must have some notion of the contrast to beauty. In other words, opposing notions only make sense when considered at the same time, one complementing the other and together forming a complete concept. In this Greek conception of the dialectic, there are no quick and easy answers to difficult questions, and there are few incontestable facts to present. Instead, there are at least two sides to every issue.

Socrates taught his students that we may begin in error or falsity, but we will eventually arrive at truth if we continue our dialectical conversation. This is because truth, for Socrates, involves uncovering what is already there. Because all conceptions—true or false—supposedly have their dialectical complements implicit within them, truth is itself already implicit and waiting to be revealed. Truth, then, according to Socrates, is uncovered by a rational analysis of the relevant (and perhaps even false) ideas and arguments already under discussion.

The discipline of psychology is often considered to be dialectical, at least in part. Any student who has studied the many different theories of human behavior (e.g., humanism, behaviorism, psychoanalysis) can attest to this. Psychology frequently consists of two or more voices on the same psychological issue. Consequently, many of the ideas of psychology develop through conversation that takes place among psychologists or among the students of psychology. Although this is understandable when we consider the complexity of psychology's subject matter, it can create problems for the banking approach to education. What can be deposited in a mental bank when two or more voices are possible and the conversation among the voices is ongoing? Some information distribution is certainly important. However, information distribution alone cannot capture this type of knowledge in the discipline, because that knowledge is dialectical in nature.

BENEFITS OF A DIALECTICAL APPROACH

The dialectical approach is the focus of this volume: Psychological issues are presented in true dialectical fashion, with two distinct sides. Students are asked to familiarize themselves with both sides of an issue, look at the supporting evidence on both sides, and engage in constructive conversation about possible resolutions. This approach to education requires students to take an active role in making sense of the issues. In so doing, students benefit in several ways.

First, students come to a richer understanding of the subject matter of psychologists. It is important to understand that there is a dialectical, or humanities, side of psychology as well as an informational, or scientific, side of psychology. As necessary as data may be, there will always be a human interpreter of the data that will never permit psychology to dispense with humanities entirely.

Second, students develop a healthy respect for both sides of a debate. There is a natural tendency to underestimate reasonable arguments on one side or the other of a debate. Often, of course, the side one favors is the "most reasonable." Without exception, the issues in this book have reasonable people and reasonable arguments *on both sides.* That is, these issues are issues in psychology precisely because they have reasonable arguments and evidence on either side. This is not to say that both sides are correct (although this too is possible). It is to say, rather, that a proper appreciation of both sides is necessary to understanding what is at issue and thus to begin to find a resolution.

A third benefit of this dialectical approach is that students better understand the nature of psychological knowledge in general. Although contemporary psychologists have taken up the scientific challenge of exploring behavior and mind, many questions are still far from being answered. Psychology's parent, like all sciences, is philosophy. Hence, philosophical (or theoretical) issues always lurk behind the activities of psychologists. Issues such as mind versus body, free will versus determinism, nature versus nurture, and the philosophy of science are both philosophical and psychological questions. Students will necessarily have to entertain and explicate these types of issues as they learn about and advance the discipline.

Fourth, students become more aware of alternative views on controversial psychological issues. People often do not even realize that there is another point of view to an issue or evidence to the contrary. This realization, however, can help students to be more cautious in their knowledge. As the dialectician Socrates once noted, this caution is sometimes the first step toward true wisdom—knowing what it is that you don't know.

Finally, the dialectical approach promotes critical thinking skills. As authorities on critical thinking have noted (e.g., Brookfield, 1987), thinking skills require an awareness of what one *does* believe and a knowledge of alternatives regarding what one *could* believe. *Taking Sides: Clashing Views on*

Controversial Psychological Issues provides both elements. Finely honed critical skills give students a better position from which to examine the psychological literature critically and to select or develop their own positions on important psychological issues.

NOTES

1. Unfortunately, falsifying the consequent—the "then" portion of our logical statement—does not prevent us from needing to interpret either, as Slife and Williams (1995) have shown.

REFERENCES

Brookfield, S. (1987). *Developing critical thinkers: Challenging adults to explore alternative ways of thinking.* San Francisco: Jossey-Bass.

Popper, K. (1959). *The logic of scientific discovery.* New York: Basic Books.

Robinson, D. (1986). *An intellectual history of psychology.* Madison, WI: University of Wisconsin Press.

Robinson, D. (1989). *Aristotle's psychology.* New York: Columbia University Press.

Rychlak, J. F. (1988). *The psychology of rigorous humanism* (2d ed.). New York: New York University Press.

Slife, B. D., & Williams, R. N. (1995). *What's behind the research: Discovering hidden assumptions in the behavioral sciences.* Thousand Oaks, CA: Sage Publications.

PART 1

Biological and Research Issues

No behavioral or mental activity can take place without biology. Biological processes are fundamental to all mental functions, including emotion, perception, and mental health. Does this mean that differences in behavior are essentially the result of biological differences? Are differences between males and females or between thin people and fat people primarily biological?

Research methods allow psychologists to investigate their ideas and subject matter. How psychologists perform their research is often a subject of controversy. For example, sometimes animals are used to test experimental procedures before they are applied to humans. Is this right? Should animals be experimented upon—and sometimes sacrificed—in the service of humans?

■ Is There Evidence that Homosexuality
    Is Biologically Determined?

■ Do Evolutionary and Genetic Factors
    Determine Our Sexual Behaviors?

■ Should Animals Be Used in Psychological
    Research?

ISSUE 1

Is There Evidence that Homosexuality Is Biologically Determined?

YES: Simon LeVay and Dean H. Hamer, from "Evidence for a Biological Influence in Male Homosexuality," *Scientific American* (May 1994)

NO: William Byne, from "The Biological Evidence Challenged," *Scientific American* (May 1994)

ISSUE SUMMARY

YES: Simon LeVay and Dean H. Hamer, researchers in neuroanatomy and biochemistry, respectively, contend that two new pieces of evidence—a structure within the human brain and a genetic link— point to a biological component for male homosexuality.

NO: Neuroscientist William Byne argues that the evidence for innate biological traits in homosexuality is flawed and that causation is far from proved.

Homosexuality has long been a controversial issue in psychology. Before 1973 homosexuality was considered abnormal or a sexual deviance. Homosexuals were thought to have an "arrested development" or interpersonal problems that resulted in their preference for sexual relations with the same sex. In 1973, however, psychology endorsed changes in its diagnostic manual that intentionally omitted homosexuality from the list of possible abnormalities. Homosexuality became, in effect, a normal variation of sexuality.

This diagnostic change, however, did not answer the deeper and perhaps more difficult question: Why are some people homosexual and some people heterosexual? Many psychological, theological, and political issues seem to hinge on the answer to this question. If homosexuality were a learned behavior, then, presumably, homosexuals could *un*learn their sexual orientation. This would mean that a therapeutic change in sexual orientation would be possible, if it was desired. On the other hand, if homosexuality were genetically determined, then no amount of psychotherapy could effect any change.

The importance of this question has led to many psychological and neuroscientific investigations. Two of the more noted researchers in the latter arena, Simon LeVay and Dean H. Hamer, present two major pieces of evidence that they feel indicate that homosexuality is biologically determined. The first piece of evidence suggests that structural differences in the brain arise during fetal development that establish sexual orientation. The second piece of evidence indicates that a genetic link also influences sexual orientation.

Specifically, gene sharing in a genetic region known as Xq28 is significantly greater in homosexual brothers than in the general population. LeVay and Hamer warn against making too much of their findings. However, they do conclude that this is "the strongest evidence to date that human sexuality is influenced by heredity."

William Byne, on the other hand, asserts that "most of the links in the chain of reasoning from biology to sexual orientation and social policy do not hold up under scrutiny." In particular, Byne says, structural and genetic studies suffer from a confounding of nature and nurture. For instance, structural differences in the brains of homosexuals may be the result of social factors, not biological agents. Research on hormones, where males are deficient in androgen, shows no evidence for the biological determination of homosexuality. The findings of LeVay and Hamer, according to Byne, have not been replicated, and the population of gay men used for their study came primarily from men with AIDS. This AIDS factor allows for several alternative explanations of their findings. Furthermore, such studies rarely say anything about how homosexuality could be inherited. Findings to date could as readily indicate how genes influence interpersonal relationships that, in turn, contribute to the social learning of homosexuality.

POINT	COUNTERPOINT
• The cell group INAH3 of the hypothalamus was found to be larger in straight men than in gay men.	• The size of INAH3 was actually caused by hormonal abnormalities associated with AIDS.
• Data suggests a dimorphism related to male sexual orientation that is about as great as that related to sex.	• Sexual orientation is not dimorphic; it has many forms.
• The anterior commissures in women and gay men are comparable in size, while it is smaller in heterosexual men.	• The size of the anterior commissure would say nothing about an individual's sexual orientation.
• Chromosomal region Xq28 contains a gene that influences male sexual orientation.	• No single, specific Xq28 sequence (a putative "gay gene") was identified in all 66 men.
• Brothers of gay men had a 14 percent likelihood of being gay as compared to 2 percent for the men without a gay brother.	• The incidence of homosexuality in the adopted brothers of homosexuals was equal to the rate for biological brothers.

YES   Simon LeVay and Dean H. Hamer

EVIDENCE FOR A BIOLOGICAL
INFLUENCE IN MALE HOMOSEXUALITY

Most men are sexually attracted to women, most women to men. To many people, this seems only the natural order of things—the appropriate manifestation of biological instinct, reinforced by education, religion and the law. Yet a significant minority of men and women—estimates range from 1 to 5 percent—are attracted exclusively to members of their own sex. Many others are drawn, in varying degrees, to both men and women.

How are we to understand such diversity in sexual orientation? Does it derive from variations in our genes or our physiology, from the intricacies of our personal history or from some confluence of these? Is it for that matter a choice rather than a compulsion?

Probably no one factor alone can elucidate so complex and variable a trait as sexual orientation. But recent laboratory studies, including our own, indicate that genes and brain development play a significant role. How, we do not yet know. It may be that genes influence the sexual differentiation of the brain and its interaction with the outside world, thus diversifying its already vast range of responses to sexual stimuli.

The search for biological roots of sexual orientation has run along two broad lines. The first draws on observations made in yet another hunt—that for physical differences between men's and women's brains. As we shall see, "gay" and "straight" brains may be differentiated in curiously analogous fashion. The second approach is to scout out genes by studying the patterns in which homosexuality occurs in families and by directly examining the hereditary material, DNA.

* * *

Researchers have long sought within the human brain some manifestation of the most obvious classes into which we are divided—male and female. Such sex differentiation of the brain's structure, called sexual dimorphism, proved hard to establish. On average, a man's brain has a slightly larger size that goes along with his larger body; other than that, casual inspection does not reveal any obvious dissimilarity between the sexes. Even under a microscope, the architecture of men's and women's brains is very similar. Nor surprisingly, the first significant observations of sexual dimorphism were made in laboratory animals.

Of particular importance is a study of rats conducted by Roger A. Gorski of the University of California at Los Angeles. In 1978 Gorski was inspecting the rat's hypothalamus, a region at the base of its brain that is involved in instinctive behaviors and the regulation of metabolism. He found that one group of cells near the front of the hypothalamus is several times larger in male than in female rats. Although this cell group is very small, less than a millimeter across even in males, the difference between the sexes is quite visible in appropriately stained slices of tissue, even without the aid of a microscope.

Gorski's finding was especially interesting because the general region of the hypothalamus in which this cell group occurs, known as the medial preoptic area, has been implicated in the generation of sexual behavior—in particular, behaviors typically displayed by males. For example, male monkeys with damaged medial preoptic areas are apparently indifferent to sex with female monkeys, and electrical stimulation of this region can make an inactive male monkey approach and mount a female. It should be said, however, that we have yet to find in monkeys a cell group analogous to the sexually dimorphic one occurring in rats.

Nor is the exact function of the rat's sexually dimorphic cell group known. What is known, from a study by Gorski and his co-workers, is that androgens —typical male hormones—play a key role in bringing about a dimorphism during development. Neurons within the cell group are rich in receptors for sex hormones, both for androgens— testosterone is the main representative —and for female hormones known as estrogens. Although male and female rats initially have about the same numbers of neurons in the medial preoptic area, a surge of testosterone secreted by the testes of male fetuses around the time of birth acts to stabilize their neuronal population. In females the lack of such a surge allows many neurons in this cell group to die, leading to the typically smaller structure. Interestingly, it is only for a few days before and after birth that the medial preoptic neurons are sensitive to androgen; removing androgens in an adult rat by castration does not cause the neurons to die.

Gorski and his colleagues at U.C.L.A., especially his student Laura S. Allen, have also found dimorphic structures in the human brain. A cell group named INAH3 (derived from "third interstitial nucleus of the anterior hypothalamus") in the medial preoptic region of the hypothalamus is about three times larger in men than in women. (Notably, however, size varies considerably even within one sex.)

In 1990 one of us (LeVay) decided to check whether INAH3 or some other cell group in the medial preoptic area varies in size with sexual orientation as well as with sex. This hypothesis was something of a long shot, given the prevailing notion that sexual orientation is a "high-level" aspect of personality molded by environment and culture. Information from such elevated sources is thought to be processed primarily by the cerebral cortex and not by "lower" centers such as the hypothalamus.

LeVay examined the hypothalamus in autopsy specimens from 19 homosexual men, all of whom had died of complications of AIDS, and 16 heterosexual men, six of whom had also died of AIDS. (The sexual orientation of those who had died of non-AIDS causes was not determined. But assuming a distribution similar to that of the general populace, no more than one or two of them were likely to have been gay.) LeVay also included specimens from six women whose sexual orientation was unknown.

After encoding the specimens to eliminate subjective bias, LeVay cut each hypothalamus into serial slices, stained these to mark the neuronal cell groups and measured their cross-sectional areas under a microscope. Armed with information about the areas, plus the thickness of the slices, he could readily calculate the volumes of each cell group. In addition to Allen and Gorski's sexually dimorphic nucleus INAH3, LeVay examined three other nearby groups—INAH1, INAH2 and INAH4.

Like Allen and Gorski, LeVay observed that INAH3 was more than twice as large in the men as in the women. But INHA3 was also between two and three times larger in the straight men than in the gay men. In some gay men, as in the example shown at the top of the opposite page, the cell group was altogether absent. Statistical analysis indicated that the probability of this result's being attributed to chance was about one in 1,000. In fact, there was no significant difference between volumes of INAH3 in the gay men and in the women. So the investigation suggested a dimorphism related to male sexual orientation about as great as that related to sex.

A primary concern in such a study is whether the observed structural differences are caused by some variable other than the one of interest. A major suspect here was AIDS. The AIDS virus itself, as well as other infectious agents that take advantage of a weakened immune system, can cause serious damage to brain cells. Was this the reason for the small size of INAH3 in the gay men, all of whom had died of AIDS?

Several lines of evidence indicate otherwise. First, the heterosexual men who died of AIDS had INAH3 volumes no different from those who died of other causes. Second, the AIDS victims with small INAH3s did not have case histories distinct from those with large INAH3s; for instance, they had not been ill longer before they died. Third, the other three cell groups in the medial preoptic area—INAH1, INAH2 and INAH4—turned out to be no smaller in the AIDS victims. If the disease were having a nonspecific destructive effect, one would have suspected otherwise. Finally, after completing the main study, LeVay obtained the hypothalamus of one gay man who had died of non-AIDS causes. This specimen, processed "blind" along with several specimens from heterosexual men of similar age, confirmed the main study: the volume of INAH3 in the gay man was less than half that of INAH3 in the heterosexual men.

One other feature in brains that is related to sexual orientation has been reported by Allen and Gorski. They found that the anterior commissure, a bundle of fibers running across the midline of the brain, is smallest in heterosexual men, larger in women and largest in gay men. After correcting for overall brain size, the anterior commissure in women and in gay men were comparable in size.

* * *

What might lie behind these apparent correlations between sexual orientation and brain structure? Logically, three possibilities exist. One is that the structural differences were present early in life—perhaps even before birth—and helped to establish the men's sexual orientation. The second is that the differences arose in adult life as a result of the men's sexual feelings or behavior. The third possibility is that there is no causal connection, but both sexual orientation and the brain structures in question are linked to some third variable, such as a developmental event during uterine or early postnatal life.

We cannot decide among these possibilities with any certainty. On the basis of animal research, however, we find the second scenario, that the structural differences came about in adulthood, unlikely. In rats, for example, the sexually dimorphic cell group in the medial preoptic area appears plastic in its response to androgens during early brain development but later is largely resistant to change. We favor the first possibility, that the structural differences arose during the period of brain development and consequently contributed to sexual behavior. Because the medial preoptic region of the hypothalamus is implicated in sexual behavior in monkeys, the size of INAH3 in men may indeed influence sexual orientation. But such a causal connection is speculative at this point.

Assuming that some of the structural differences related to sexual orientation were present at birth in certain individuals, how did they arise? One candidate is the interaction between gonadal steroids and the developing brain; this interaction is responsible for differences in the structure of male and female brains. A number of scientists have speculated that atypical levels of circulating androgens in some fetuses cause them to grow into homosexual adults. Specifically, they suggest that androgen levels are unusually low in male fetuses that become gay and unusually high in female fetuses that become lesbian.

A more likely possibility is that there are intrinsic differences in the way individual brains respond to androgens during development, even when the hormone levels are themselves no different. This response requires a complex molecular machinery, starting with the androgens receptors but presumably including a variety of proteins and genes whose identity and roles are still unknown.

At first glance, the very notion of gay genes might seem absurd. How could genes that draw men or women to members of the same sex survive the Darwinian screening for reproductive fitness? Surely the parents of most gay men and lesbians are heterosexual? In view of such apparent incongruities, research focuses on genes that sway rather than determine sexual orientation. The two main approaches to seeking such genes are twin and family studies and DNA linkage analysis.

* * *

Twin and family tree studies are based on the principle that genetically influenced traits run in families. The first modern study on the patterns of homosexuality within families was published in 1985 by Richard C. Pillard and James D. Weinrich of Boston University. Since then, five other systematic studies on the twins and siblings of gay men and lesbians have been reported.

The pooled data for men show that about 57 percent of identical twins, 24 percent of fraternal twins and 13 percent of brothers of gay men are also gay. For women, approximately 50 percent of identical twins, 16 percent of fraternal twins and 13 percent of sisters of lesbians are also lesbian. When these data are compared with baseline rates of homosexuality, a good amount of family clustering of sexual orientation becomes evident for both sexes. In fact, J. Michael Bailey of Northwestern University and his co-workers estimate that the overall heritability of sexual orientation—that proportion of the variance in a trait that comes from genes—is about 53 percent for men and 52 percent for women. (The family clustering is most obvious for relatives of the same sex, less so for male-female paris.)

To evaluate the genetic component of sexual orientation and to clarify its mode of inheritance, we need a systematic survey of the extended families of gay men and lesbians. One of us (Hamer), Stella Hu, Victoria L. Magnuson, Nan Hu and Angela M. L. Pattatucci of the National Institutes of Health [NIH] have initiated such a study. It is part of a larger one by the National Cancer Institute to investigate risk factors for certain cancers that are more frequent in some segments of the gay population.

Hamer and his colleagues' initial survey of males confirmed the sibling results of Pillard and Weinrich. A brother of a gay man had a 14 percent likelihood of being gay as compared with 2 percent for the men without gay brothers. (The study used an unusually stringent definition of homosexuality, leading to the low average rate.) Among more distant relatives, an unexpected pattern showed up: maternal uncles had a 7 percent chance of being gay, whereas sons of maternal aunts had an 8 percent chance. Fathers, paternal uncles and the three other types of cousins showed no correlation at all.

Although this study pointed to a genetic component, homosexuality occurred much less frequently than a single gene inherited in simple Mendelian fashion would suggest. One interpretation, that genes are more important in some families than in others, is borne out by looking at families having two gay brothers. Compared with randomly chosen families, rates of homosexuality in maternal uncles increased from 7 to 10 percent and in maternal cousins from 8 to 13 percent. This familial clustering, even in relatives outside the nuclear family, presents an additional argument for a genetic root to sexual orientation.

*　*　*

Why are most gay male relatives of gay men on the mother's side of the family? One possibility—that the subjects somehow knew more about their maternal relatives—seems unlikely because opposite-sex gay relatives of gay males and lesbians were equally distributed between both sides of the family. Another explanation is that homosexuality, while being transmitted by both parents, is expressed only in one sex—in this case, males. When expressed, the trait reduces the reproductive rate and must therefore be disproportionately passed on by the mother. Such an effect may partially account for the concentration of gay men's gay relatives on the maternal side of the family. But proof of this hypothesis will require finding an appropriate gene on an autosomal chromosome, which is inherited from either parent.

A third possibility is X chromosome linkage. A man has two sex chromosomes: a Y, inherited from his father, and an X, cut and pasted from the two X chromosomes carried by his mother. Therefore, any trait that is influenced by a gene on the X chromosome will tend to be inherited through the mother's side and will be preferentially observed in brothers, maternal uncles and maternal cousins, which is exactly the observed pattern.

To test this hypothesis, Hamer and his colleagues embarked on a linkage study of the X chromosome in gay men. Linkage analysis is based on two principles of genetics. If a trait is genetically influenced, then relatives who share the trait will share the gene more often than is expected by chance—this is true even if the gene plays only a small part. Also, genes that are close together on a chromosome are almost always inherited together. Therefore, if there is a gene that influences sexual orientation, it should be "linked" to a nearby DNA marker that tends to travel along with it in families. For traits affected by only one gene, linkage can precisely locate the gene on a chromosome. But for complex traits such as sexual orientation, linkage also helps to determine whether a genetic component really exists.

To initiate a linkage analysis of male sexual orientation, the first requirement was to find informative markers, segments of DNA that flag locations on a chromosome. Fortunately, the Human Genome Project has already generated a large catalogue of markers spanning all of the X chromosomes. The most useful ones are short, repeated DNA sequences that have slightly different lengths in different persons. To detect the markers, the researchers used the polymerase chain re-action to make several billion copies of specific regions of the chromosome and then separated the different fragments by the method of gel electrophoresis.

The second step in the linkage analysis was to locate suitable families. When scientists study simple traits such as color blindness or sickle cell anemia—which involve a single gene—they tend to analyze large, multigenerational families in which each member clearly either has or does not have the trait. Such an approach was unsuited for studying sexual orientation. First, identifying someone as not homosexual is tricky; the person may be concealing his or her true orientation or may not be aware of it. Because homosexuality was even more stigmatized in the past, multigenerational families are especially problematic in this regard. Moreover, genetic modeling shows that for traits that involve several different genes expressed at varying levels, studying large families can actually decrease the chances of finding a linked gene: too many exceptions are included.

For these reasons, Hamer and his co-workers decided to focus on nuclear families with two gay sons. One advantage of this approach is that individuals who say they are homosexual are unlikely to be mistaken. Furthermore, the approach can detect a single linked gene even if other genes or noninherited factors are required for its expression. For instance, suppose that being gay requires an X chromosome gene together with another gene on an autosome, plus some set of environmental circumstances. Studying gay brothers would give a clear-cut result because both would have the X chromosome gene. In contrast, heterosexual brothers of gay men would sometimes share the X chromosome gene and sometimes not, leading to confusing results.

Genetic analysts now believe that studying siblings is the key to traits that are affected by many elements. Because Hamer and his colleagues were most interested in finding a gene that expresses itself only in men but is transmitted through women, they restricted their search to families with gay men but no gay father–gay son pairs.

Forty such families were recruited. DNA samples were prepared from the gay brothers and, where possible, from their mother or sisters. The samples were typed for 22 markers that span the X chromosome from the tip of the short arm to the end of the long arm. At each marker, a pair of gay brothers was scored as concordant if they inherited identical markers from their mothers or as discordant if they inherited different ones. Fifty percent of the markers were expected to be identical by chance. Corrections were also made for the possibility of the mother's having two copies of the same marker.

The results of this study were striking. Over most of the X chromosome the markers were randomly distributed between the gay brothers. But at the tip of the long arm of the X chromosome, in a region known as Xq28, there was a considerable excess of concordant brothers: 33 pairs shared the same marker, whereas only 7 pairs did not. Although the same size was not large, the result was statistically significant: the probability of such a skewed ratio occurring by chance alone is less than one in 200. In a control group of 314 randomly selected pairs of brothers, most of whom can be presumed to be heterosexual, Xq28 markers were randomly distributed.

The most straightforward interpretation of the finding is that chomosomal region Xq28 contains a gene that influences male sexual orientation. The study provides the strongest evidence to date that human sexuality is influenced by heredity because it directly examines the genetic information, the DNA. But as with all initial studies, there are some caveats.

First, the result needs to be replicated: several other claims of finding genes related to personality traits have proved controversial. Second, the gene itself has not yet been isolated. The study locates it within a region of the X chromosome that is about four million base pairs in length. This region represents less than 0.2 percent of the total human genome, but it is still large enough to contain several hundred genes. Finding the needle in this haystack will require either large numbers of families or more complete information about the DNA sequence to identify all possible coding regions. As it happens, Xq28 is extraordinarily rich in genetic loci and will probably be one of the first regions of the human genome to be sequenced in its entirety.

A third caveat is that researchers do not know quantitatively how important a role Xq28 plays in male sexual orientation. Within the population of gay brothers studied, seven of 40 brothers did not share markers. Assuming that 20 siblings should inherit identical markers by chance alone, 36 percent of gay brothers show no link between homosexuality and Xq28. Perhaps these men inherited different genes or were influenced by nongenetic physiological factors or by the environment. Among all gay men—most of whom do not have gay brothers—the influence of Xq28 is even less clear. Also unknown is the role of Xq28, and other genetic loci, in female sexual orientation.

How might a genetic locus at Xq28 affect sexuality? One idea is that the hypothetical gene affects hormone synthesis or metabolism. A candidate for such a gene was the androgen receptor locus, which encodes a protein essential for masculinization of the human brain and is, moreover, located on the X chromosome. To test this idea, Jeremy Nathans, Jennifer P. Macke, Van L. King and Terry R. Brown of John Hopkins University teamed up with Bailey of Northwestern and Hamer, Hu and Hu of the NIH. They compared the molecular structure of the androgen receptor gene in 197 homosexual men and 213 predominantly heterosexual men. But no significant variations in the protein coding sequences were found. Also, linkage studies showed no correlation between homosexuality in brothers and inheritance of the androgen receptor locus. Most significant of all, the locus turned out to be at Xq11, far from the Xq28 region. This study excludes the androgen receptor from playing a significant role in male sexual orientation.

A second idea is that the hypothetical gene acts indirectly, through personality or temperament, rather than directly on sexual-object choice. For example, people who are genetically self-reliant might be more likely to acknowledge and act on same-sex feelings than are people who are dependent on the approval of others.

Finally, the intriguing possibility arises that the Xq28 gene product bears directly on the development of sexually dimorphic brain regions such as INAH3. At the simplest level, such an agent could act autonomously, perhaps in the womb, by stimulating the survival of specific neurons in preheterosexual males or by promoting their death in females and prehomosexual men. In a more complex model, the gene product could change the sensitivity of a neuronal circuit in the hypothalamus to stimulation by environmental cues—perhaps in the first few years of life. Here the genes serve to predispose rather than to predetermine. Whether this fanciful notion contains a grain of truth remains to be seen. It is in fact experimentally testable, using current tools of molecular genetics and neurobiology.

* * *

Our research has attracted an extraordinary degree of public attention, not so much because of any conceptual breakthrough—the idea that genes and the brain are involved in human behavior is hardly new—but because it touches on a deep conflict in contemporary American society. We believe scientific research can help dispel some of the myths about homosexuality that in the past have clouded the image of lesbians and gay men. We also recognize, however, that increasing knowledge of biology may eventually bring with it the power to infringe on the natural rights of individuals and to impoverish the world of its human diversity. It is important that our society expand discussions of how new scientific information should be used to benefit the human race in its entirety.

NO

William Byne

THE BIOLOGICAL EVIDENCE
CHALLENGED

Human-rights activists, religious organizations and all three branches of the
U.S. government are debating whether sexual orientation is biological. The
discussion has grabbed headlines, but behavioral scientists find it passé.
The salient question about biology and sexual orientation is not whether
biology is involved but how it is involved. All psychological phenomena are
ultimately biological.

Even if the public debate were more precisely framed, it would still be
misguided. Most of the links in the chain of reasoning from biology to sexual
orientation and social policy do not hold up under scrutiny. At the political
level, a requirement that an unconventional trait be inborn or immutable is an
inhumane criterion for a society to use in deciding which of its nonconformists
it will grant tolerance. Even if homosexuality were entirely a matter of choice,
attempts to extirpate it by social and criminal sanctions devalue basic human
freedoms and diversity.

Furthermore, the notion that homosexuality must be either inborn and immutable or freely chosen is in turn misinformed. Consider the white-crowned
sparrow, a bird that learns its native song during a limited period of development. Most sparrows exposed to a variety of songs, including that of their
own species, will learn their species's song, but some do not. After a bird
has learned a song, it can neither unlearn that song nor acquire a new one.
Although sexual orientation is not a matter of mimicry, it is clear that learned
behavior can nonetheless be immutable.

Finally, what evidence exists thus far of innate biological traits underlying homosexuality is flawed. Genetic studies suffer from the inevitable
confounding of nature and nurture that plagues attempts to study heritability of psychological traits. Investigations of the brain rely on doubtful hypotheses about differences between the brains of men and women. Biological
mechanisms that have been proposed to explain the existence of gay men
often cannot be generalized to explain the existence of lesbians (whom studies have largely neglected). And the continuously graded nature of most

biological variables is at odds with the paucity of adult bisexuals suggested by most surveys.

* * *

To understand how biological factors influence sexual orientation, one must first define orientation. Many researchers, most conspicuously Simon LeVay, treat it as a sexually dimorphic trait: men are generally "programmed" for attraction to women, and women are generally programmed for attraction to men. Male homosexuals, according to this framework, have female programming. Some researchers suggest that this programming is accomplished by biological agents, perhaps even before birth; others believe it occurs after birth in response to social factors and subjective experiences. As a function of the brain is undoubtedly linked to its structure and physiology, it follows that homosexuals' brains might exhibit some features typical of the opposite sex.

The validity of this "intersex" expectation is questionable. For one, sexual orientation is not dimorphic; it has many forms. The conscious and unconscious motivations associated with sexual attraction are diverse even among people of the same sex and orientation. Myriad experiences (and subjective interpretations of those experiences) could interact to lead different people to the same relative degree of sexual attraction to men or to women. Different people could be sexually attracted to men for different reasons; for example, there is no a priori reason that everyone attracted to men should share some particular brain structure.

Indeed, the notion that gay men are feminized and lesbians masculinized may tell us more about our culture than about the biology or erotic responsive-ness. Some Greek myths held that heterosexual rather than homosexual desire had intersex origins: those with predominately same-sex desires were considered the most manly of men and womanly of women. In contrast, those who desired the opposite sex supposedly mixed masculine and feminine in their being. Classical culture celebrated the homosexual exploits of archetypally masculine heroes such as Zeus, Hercules and Julius Caesar. Until a decade ago (when missionaries repudiated the practice), boys among the Sambia of New Guinea would form attachments to men and fellate them; no one considered that behavior a female trait. Indeed, the Sambia believed ingesting semen to be necessary for attaining strength and virility.

But there is a more tangible problem for this intersex assumption; the traits of which homosexuals ostensibly have opposite-sex versions have not been conclusively shown to differ between men and women. Of the many supposed sex differences in the human brain reported over the past century, only one has proved consistently replicable: brain size varies with body size. Thus, men tend to have slightly larger brains than women. This situation contrasts sharply with that for other animals, where many researchers have consistently demonstrated a variety of sex differences.

If brains are indeed wired or otherwise programmed for sexual orientation, what forces are responsible? Three possibilities come into play: The direct model of biological causation asserts that genes, hormones or other factors act directly on the developing brain, probably before birth, to wire it for sexual orientation. Alternatively, the social learning model suggests that biology provides a blank slate of neural circuitry on which experience inscribes orientation. In the indirect model, biological factors do not wire the brain for orientation; instead they predispose individuals toward certain personality traits that influence the relationships and experiences that ultimately shape sexuality.

During past decades, much of the speculation about biology and orientation focused on the role of hormones. Workers once thought an adult's androgen and estrogen levels determined orientation, but this hypothesis withered for lack of support. Researchers have since pursued the notion that hormones wire the brain for sexual orientation during the prenatal period.

According to this hypothesis, high prenatal androgen levels during the appropriate critical period cause heterosexuality in men and homosexuality in women. Conversely, low fetal androgen levels lead to homosexuality in men and heterosexuality in women. This hypothesis rests largely on the observation that in rodents early exposure to hormones determines the balance between male and female patterns of mating behaviors displayed by adults. Female rodents that were exposed to androgens early in development show more male-typical mounting behavior than do normal adult females. Males deprived of androgens by castration during the same critical period display a female mating posture called lordosis (bending of the back) when they are mounted.

Many researchers consider the castrated male rat that shows lordosis when mounted by another male to be a homosexual (as is the female rat that mounts others). Lordosis, however, is little more than a reflex: the male will take the same posture when a handler strokes its back. Furthermore, the male that mounts another male is considered to be heterosex-ual, as is the female that displays lordosis when mounted by another female. Applying such logic to humans would imply that of two people of the same sex engaged in intercourse only one is homosexual—and which member of the couple it is depends on the positions they assume.

In addition to determining rodent mating patterns, early hormonal exposure determines whether an animal's brain can regulate normal ovarian function. A male rat's brain cannot respond to estrogen by triggering a chain of events, called positive feedback, that culminates in the abrupt increase of luteinizing hormone in the bloodstream, which in turn triggers ovulation. Some researchers reasoned from this fact to the idea that homosexual men (whose brains they allege to be insufficiently masculinized) might have a stronger positive-feedback reaction that do heterosexual men.

Two laboratories reported that this was the case, but carefully designed and executed studies, most notably those of Luis J. G. Gooren of the Free University in Amsterdam, disproved those findings. Furthermore, the feedback mechanism turns out to be irrelevant to human sexual orientation: workers have since found that the positive-feedback mechanism is not sexually dimorphic in primates, including humans. If this mechanism is indistinguishable in men and women, it is illogical to suggest that it should be "feminized" in gay men.

Moreover, a corollary of the expectation that luteinizing hormone responses should be feminized in homosexual men is that they should be "masculinized" in lesbians. If that were true, homosexual women would neither menstruate nor bear children. The overwhelming proportion of lesbians with normal menstrual cycles and the growing number of openly lesbian mothers attest to the fallacy of that idea.

* * *

If the prenatal hormonal hypothesis were correct, one might expect that a large proportion of men with medical conditions known to involve prenatal androgen deficiency would be homosexual, as would be women exposed prenatally to excess androgens. That is not the case.

Because androgens are necessary for development of normal external genitals in males, the sex of affected individuals may not be apparent at birth. Males may be born with female-appearing genitals, and females with male-appearing ones. These individuals often require plastic surgery to construct normal-appearing genitals, and the decision to raise them as boys or as girls is sometimes based not on genetic sex but on the possibilities for genital reconstruction.

Research into the sexual orientation of such individuals tends to support the social learning model. Regardless of their genetic sex or the nature of their prenatal hormonal exposure, they usually become heterosexual with respect to the sex their parents raise them as, provided the sex assignment is made unambiguously before the age of three.

Nevertheless, some studies report an increase in homosexual fantasies or behavior among women who were exposed to androgens as fetuses. In accordance with the notion of direct biological effects, these studies are often interpreted as evidence that prenatal androgen exposure wires the brain for sexual attraction to women. The neurobiologist and feminist scholar Ruth H. Bleier has offered an alternative interpretation. Rather than reflecting an effect of masculinizing hormones on the sexual differentiation of the brain, the adaptations of prenatally masculinized women may reflect the impact of having been born with masculinized genitalia or the knowledge that they had been exposed to aberrant levels of sex hormones during development. "Gender must seem a fragile and arbitrary construct," Bleier concluded, "if it depends upon plastic surgery."

* * *

Stephen Jay Gould of Harvard University has written of the way that the search for brain differences related to sex and other social categories was for the most part discredited during the past century by anatomists who deluded themselves into believing that their brain measurements justified the social prejudices of their day. The search for sex differences in the human brain was revitalized in the late 1970s, when Roger A. Gorski's team at the University of California at Los Angeles discovered a group of cells in the preoptic part of the rat hypothalamus that was much larger in males than in females. The researchers designated this cell group the sexually dimorphic nucleus of the preoptic area (SDN-POA). The preoptic area has long been implicated in the regulation of sexual behavior.

Like the sex differences in mating behaviors and luteinizing hormone regulatory mechanisms, the difference in the size of the SDN-POA was found to result from differences in early exposure to androgens. Shortly thereafter, Bleier and I, working at the University of Wisconsin at Madison, examined the hypothalamus of several rodent species and found that the SDN-POA is only one part of a sexual dimorphism involving several additional hypothalamic nuclei.

Three laboratories have recently sought sexually dimorphic nuclei in the human hypothalamus. Laura S. Allen, working in Gorski's lab, identified four possible candidates as potential homologues of the rat's SDN-POA and designated them as the interstitial nuclei of the anterior hypothalamus (INAH1-INAH4). Different laboratories that have measured these nuclei, however, have produced conflicting results: Dick F. Swaab's group at the Netherlands Institute for Brain Research in Amsterdam, for example, found INAH1 to be larger in men that in women, whereas Allen found no difference in that nucleus but reported that INAH2 and INAH3 were larger in men. Most recently, LeVay found no sex difference in either INAH1 or INAH2 but corroborated Allen's finding of a larger INAH3 in men. LeVay also reported that INAH3 in homosexual men tends to be small, like that of women. (Neurologist Clifford Saper of Harvard and I are in the process of measuring the interstitial nuclei; at present, we have no definitive results.)

LeVay's study has been widely interpreted as strong evidence that biological factors directly wire the brain for sexual orientation. Several considerations militate against that conclusion. First, his work has not been replicated, and human neuroanatomical studies of this kind have a very poor track record for reproducibility. Indeed, procedures similar to those LeVay used to identify the nuclei have previously led researchers astray.

Manfred Gahr, now at the Max Planck Institute for Animal Physiology in Seewiesen, Germany, used a cell-staining technique similar to LeVay's to observe what appeared to be seasonal variations in the size of a nucleus involved in singing in canaries. Two more specific staining methods, however, revealed that the size of the nucleus did not change. Gahr suggested that the less specific method might have been influenced by seasonal hormonal variations that altered the properties of the cells in the nucleus.

Furthermore, in LeVay's published study, all the brains of gay men came from AIDS patients. His inclusion of a few brains from heterosexual men with AIDS did not adequately address the fact that at the time of death virtually all men with AIDS have decreased testosterone levels as the result of the disease itself or the side effects of particular treatments. To date, LeVay has examined the brain of only one gay man who did not die of AIDS. Thus, it is possible that the effects on the size of INAH3 that he attributed to sexual orientation were actually caused by the hormonal abnormalities associated with AIDS. Work by Deborah Commins and Pauline I. Yahr of the University of California at Irvine supports precisely this hypothesis. The two found that the size of a structure in mongolian gerbils apparently comparable to the SDN-POA varies with the amount of testosterone in the bloodstream.

A final problem with the popular interpretation of LeVay's study is that it is founded on an imprecise analysis of the relevant animal research. LeVay has suggested that INAH3, like the rat's SDN-POA, is situated in a region of the hypothalamus known to participate in the generation of male sexual behavior. Yet studies in a variety of species have consistently shown that the precise hypothalamic region involved in male sexual behavior is not the one occupied by these nuclei. Indeed, Gorski and Gary W. Arendash, now at the University of South Florida, found that destroying the

SDN-POA on both sides of a male rat's brain did not impair sexual behavior.

Jefferson C. Slimp performed experiments in Robert W. Goy's laboratory at the Wisconsin Regional Primate Research Center (shortly before I joined that group) that suggested that the precise region involved in sexual behavior in male rhesus monkeys is located about the area comparable to that occupied by INAH3 in humans. Males with lesions in that region mounted females less frequently than they did before being operated on, but their frequency of masturbation did not change. Although some have taken these observations to mean that the lesions selectively decreased heterosexual drive, their conclusion is unwarranted; male monkeys pressed a lever for access to females more often after their operations than before. Unfortunately, these males had no opportunity to interact with other males, and so the study tells us nothing about effects on homosexual as opposed to heterosexual motivation or behavior.

Interstitial hypothalamic nuclei are not the only parts of the brain to have come under scrutiny for links to sexual orientation. Neuroanatomists have also reported potentially interesting differences in regions not directly involved in sexual behaviors. Swaab and his co-worker Michel A. Hofman found that another hypothalamic nucleus, the suprachiasmatic nucleus, is larger in homosexual than in heterosexual men. The size of this structure, however, does not vary with sex, and so even if this finding can be replicated it would not support the assumption that homosexuals have intersexed brains.

Allen of U.C.L.A., meanwhile, has reported that the anterior commissure, a structure that participates in relaying information from one side of the brain to the other, is larger in women than in men. More recently, she concluded that the anterior commissure of gay men is feminized—that is, larger than in heterosexual men. Steven Demeter, Robert W. Doty and James L. Ringo of the University of Rochester, however, found just the opposite: anterior commissures larger in men than in women. Furthermore, even if Allen's findings are correct, the size of the anterior commissure alone would say nothing about an individual's sexual orientation. Although she found a statistically significant difference in the average size of the commissures of gay men and heterosexual men, 27 of the 30 homosexual men in her study had anterior commissures within the same size range as the 30 heterosexual men with whom she compared them.

* * *

Some researchers have turned to genetics instead of brain structure in the search for a biological link to sexual orientation. Several recent studies suggest that the brothers of homosexual men are more likely to be homosexual than are men without gay brothers. Of these, only the study by J. Michael Bailey of Northwestern University and Richard C. Pillard of Boston University included both nontwin biological brothers and adopted (unrelated) brothers in addition to identical and fraternal twins.

Their investigation yielded paradoxical results: some statistics support a genetic hypothesis, and others refute it. Identical twins were most likely to both be gay; 52 percent were concordant for homosexuality, as compared with 22 percent of fraternal twins. This result would support a genetic interpretation because identical twins share all of their genes, whereas fraternal twins share only half of theirs. Nontwin brothers of homosexuals, however, share the same proportion of genes as fraternal twins; however, only 9 percent of them were concordant for homosexuality. The genetic hypothesis predicts that their rates should be equal.

Moreover, Bailey and Pillard found that the incidence of homosexuality in the adopted brothers of homosexuals (11 percent) was much higher than recent estimates for the rate of homosexuality in the population (1 to 5 percent). In fact, it was equal to the rate for nontwin biological brothers. This study clearly challenges a simple genetic hypothesis and strongly suggests that environment contributes significantly to sexual orientation.

Two of three other recent studies also detected an increased rate of homosexuality among the identical as opposed to fraternal twins of homosexuals. In every case, however, the twins were reared together. Without knowing what developmental experiences contribute to sexual orientation—and whether those experiences are more similar between identical twins that between fraternal twins—the effects of common genes and common environments are difficult to disentangle. Resolving this issue requires studies of twins raised apart.

Indeed, perhaps the major finding of these heritability studies is that despite having all of their genes in common and having prenatal and postnatal environments as close to identical as possible, approximately half of the identical twins were nonetheless discordant for orientation. This finding underscores just how little is known about the origins of sexual orientation.

Dean H. Hamer's team at the National Institutes of Health has found the most direct evidence that sexual orientation may be influenced by specific genes.

The team focused on a small part of the X chromosome known as the Xq28 region, which contains hundreds of genes. Women have two X chromosomes and so two Xq28 regions, but they pass a copy of only one to a son (who has a single X chromosome). The theoretical probability of two sons receiving a copy of the same Xq28 from their mother is thus 50 percent. Hamer found that of his 40 pairs of gay siblings, 33 instead of the expected 20 had received the same Xq28 region from their mother.

Hamer's finding is often misinterpreted as showing that all 66 men from these 33 pairs shared the same Xq28 sequence. That is quite different from what the study showed: Each member of the 33 concordant pairs shared his Xq28 region only with his brother—not with any of the other 32 pairs. No single, specific Xq28 sequence (a putative "gay gene") was identified in all 66 men.

Unfortunately, Hamer's team did not examine the Xq28 region of its gay subjects' heterosexual brothers to see how many shared the same sequence. Hamer suggests that inclusion of heterosexual siblings would have confounded his analysis because the gene associated with homosexuality might be "incompletely penetrant"—that is to say, heterosexual men could carry the gene without expressing it. In other words, inclusion of heterosexual brothers might have revealed that something other than genes is responsible for sexual orientation.

Finally, Neil J. Risch of Yale University, one of the developers of the statistical techniques that Hamer used, has questioned whether Hamer's results are statistically significant. Risch has argued that until we have more details about the familial clustering of homosexuality, the implications of studies such as Hamer's will remain unclear.

* * *

Studies that mark homosexuality as a heritable trait (assuming that they can be replicated) do not say anything about how that heritability might operate. Genes in themselves specify proteins, not behavior or psychological phenomena. Although we know virtually nothing about how complex psychological phenomena are embodied in the brain, it is conceivable that particular DNA sequences might somehow cause the brain to be wired specifically for homosexual orientation. Significantly, however, heritability requires no such mechanism.

Instead particular genes might influence personality traits that could in turn influence the relationships and subjective experiences that contribute to the social learning of sexual orientation. One can imagine many ways in which a temperamental difference could give rise to different orientations in different environments.

The *Achillea* plant serves as a useful metaphor: genetic variations yield disparate phenotypes depending on elevation. The altitude at which a cutting of *Achillea* grows does not have a linear effect on the plant's growth, however, nor is the impact limited to a single attribute. Height, number of leaves and stems, and branching pattern are all affected. If a plant can display such a complex response to its environment, then what of a far more complex organism that can modify its surroundings at will?

The possible interaction between genes and environment in the development of sexual orientation can be sketched here only in the most oversimplified of ways. For example, many researchers believe aversion to rough-and-tumble play in boys is moderately predictive of homosexual development. (Direct-model theorists argue this aversion is merely the childhood expression of a brain that has been wired for homosexuality.) Meanwhile psychoanalysts have noted that of those gay men who seek therapy, many report having had poor rapport with their fathers. They thus suggest that an impaired father-son relationship leads to homosexuality.

One could combine these observations to speculate that a genetically based aversion to rough-and-tumble play in boys could impair rapport with fathers who demand that they adhere to rigid sex-role stereotypes. Fathers who make no much demands would maintain a rapport with their sons. As a result, the hypothetical gene in question could affect sexual orientation in some cases but not in others. Even such a reductionist example (based on traits that reflect cultural stereotypes rather than biology) shows how neither temperament nor family environment might be decisive. Studies focusing on either one or the other would yield inconclusive results.

* * *

These speculations reemphasize how far researchers must go before they understand the factors—both biological and experiential—that contribute to sexual orientation. Even if the size of certain brain structures does turn out to be correlated with sexual orientation, current understanding of the brain is inadequate to explain how such quantitative differences could generate qualitative differences in a psychological phenomenon as complex as sexual orientation. Similarly, confirmation of genetic research purporting to show that homosexuality is heritable makes clear neither what is inherited nor how it influences sexual orientation. For the foreseeable future, then, interpretation of these results will continue to hinge on assumptions of questionable validity.

While attempts to replicate these preliminary findings continue, researchers and the public must resist the temptation to consider them in any but the most tentative fashion. Perhaps more important, we should also be asking ourselves why we as a society are so emotionally invested in this research. Will it—or should it—make any difference in the way we perceive ourselves and others or how we live our lives and allow others to live theirs? Perhaps the answers to the most salient questions in this debate lie not within the biology of human brains but rather in the cultures those brains have created.

CHALLENGE QUESTIONS

Is There Evidence that Homosexuality Is Biologically Determined?

1. What are the implications for psychotherapy for homosexuals if homosexuality is an inherited trait? What if homosexuality is a learned characteristic?

2. Psychological researchers often say, "Correlation does not mean causation." That is, a high or a significant correlational finding does not necessarily prove a causal relation. How does this relate to the dispute between LeVay and Hamer, on the one hand, and Byne, on the other hand?

3. What does Byne mean when he says, "Genetic studies suffer from the inevitable confounding of nature and nurture that plagues attempts to study heritability of psychological traits"? What is it that plagues attempts to study heritability in psychology (such as research on intelligence), and how does Byne contend that this plagues genetic studies?

4. Byne states that genes in themselves specify proteins, not behavior or psychological phenomena. How is this a criticism of LeVay and Hamer's conclusions?

5. How might a social psychologist account for the extraordinary degree of attention paid to LeVay and Hamer's research?

ISSUE 2

Do Evolutionary and Genetic Factors Determine Our Sexual Behaviors?

YES: Robert Wright, from "Our Cheating Hearts," *Time* (August 15, 1994)

NO: Richard N. Williams, from "Science or Story Telling? Evolutionary Explanations of Human Sexuality," An Original Essay Written for this Volume (1995)

ISSUE SUMMARY

YES: Robert Wright, a senior editor of *The New Republic*, claims that it is natural for people to commit adultery because human sexual behavior is determined by their genes.

NO: Theoretical psychologist Richard N. Williams questions the evidence supporting Wright's claim and argues that the philosophy underlying genetic explanations of human behavior is dangerous.

There is perhaps no explanation that has more excited scientists in the last century than that of evolution. The main contribution of Charles Darwin (1809–1882) to this theory is a mechanism for the evolution of species— natural selection. In essence, Darwin proposed that nature, or the environment, "selects" the species that survive and the species that become extinct. Some species are better adapted for some environmental niches, so they thrive and even endow their offspring with genetic advantages that further their adaptability.

As history shows, this mechanism of natural selection allowed the popularity of evolutionary explanations to explode. Suddenly, all types of phenomena were explained as evolutionary processes, including psychological phenomena. For instance, immediate comparisons were made between the evolution of the species and the evolution of a person's behaviors and personality.

What accounts for the popularity of evolutionary explanations? Proponents of evolution will contend that the empirical evidence is strongly supportive of Darwin's theory. However, the evidence and its strength are somewhat in the eye of the beholder. Moreover, history has repeatedly shown that some popular explanations become overly extended to arenas that are inappropriate. Could the connections between evolutionary theory and psychological phenomena, such as human sexuality, be an instance of inappropriate theory extension?

In the following selection, Robert Wright asserts that the connections are appropriate. Indeed, he describes a new and growing subdiscipline called *evolutionary psychology* that argues for just such connection making. Wright argues that the natural, evolved characteristics of men and women determine marital fidelity and contends that lifelong monogamy is not as "natural" as many might think. He argues, instead, that natural selection favors genes that incline men and women to eventually sour on a mate. He suggests that evolution has invented romantic love and also corrupted it.

Richard N. Williams, in an original response, argues that evolutionary explanations have been overextended by Wright and others, perhaps dangerously so. Although Wright seems to be reporting the facts of human sexuality, claims Williams, his evidence is composed primarily of stories and analogies —not scientific data. In addition, a closer look at genetic evidence, according to Williams, shows that our genes are responsible for *physical* structures, not particular *mental* events or behaviors. Although evolutionary theory may make a good story, he says it does not make for good science, at least in this instance.

POINT

- By studying how natural selection shaped the mind, evolutionary psychologists are painting a new portrait of human nature.

- Natural selection indicates that genes incline men and women to sour on a mate after long periods.

- Human beings are designed to fall in love. Unfortunately, they are not designed to stay there.

- Evolutionary psychology can establish how evolution and genetic factors influence psychological factors.

COUNTERPOINT

- Evolutionary accounts of our behavior are not based on scientific findings; they are more storytelling than fact.

- Genes cannot be aware of "outside romantic opportunities" and motivate us to act on them.

- The consequence of such explanations is the loss of our very humanity, because without agency and relationships, there is no humanity in our lives.

- Science has never established that psychological or mental events are produced by genetic material.

YES

Robert Wright

OUR CHEATING HEARTS

The language of zoology used to be so reassuring. Human beings were called a "pair-bonding" species. Lasting monogamy, it seemed, was natural for us, just as it was for geese, swans and the other winged creatures that have filled our lexicon with such labels as "lovebirds" and "lovey-dovey." Family values, some experts said, were in our genes. In the 1967 best seller *The Naked Ape*, zoologist Desmond Morris wrote with comforting authority that the evolutionary purpose of human sexuality is "to strengthen the pair-bond and maintain the family unit."

This picture has lately acquired some blemishes. To begin with, birds are no longer such uplifting role models. Using DNA fingerprinting, ornithologists can now check to see if a mother bird's mate really is the father of her offspring. It turns out that some female chickadees (as in "my little chickadee") indulge in extramarital trysts with males that outrank their mates in the social hierarchy. For female barn swallows, it's a male with a long tail that makes extracurriculars irresistible. The innocent-looking indigo bunting has a cuckoldry rate of 40%. And so on. The idea that most bird species are truly monogamous has gone from conventional wisdom to punctured myth in a few short years. As a result, the fidelity of other pair-bonding species has fallen under suspicion.

Which brings us to the other problem with the idea that humans are by nature enduringly monogamous: humans. Of course, you don't need a Ph.D. to see that till-death-do-we-part fidelity doesn't come as naturally to people as, say, eating. But an emerging field known as evolutionary psychology can now put a finer point on the matter. By studying how the process of natural selection shaped the mind, evolutionary psychologists are painting a new portrait of human nature, with fresh detail about the feelings and thoughts that draw us into marriage—or push us out.

The good news is that human beings are designed to fall in love. The bad news is that they aren't designed to stay there. According to evolutionary psychology, it is "natural" for both men and women—at some times, under some circumstances—to commit adultery or to sour on a mate, to suddenly find a spouse unattractive, irritating, wholly unreasonable. (It may even be natural to *become* irritating and wholly unreasonable, and thus hasten the departure of a mate you've soured on.) It is similarly natural to find some attractive colleague superior on all counts to the sorry wreck of a spouse you're saddled with. When we see a couple celebrate a golden anniversary, one apt reaction is the famous remark about a dog walking on two legs: the point is not that the feat was done well but that it was done at all.

All of this may sound like cause for grim resignation to the further decline of the American family. But what's "natural" isn't necessarily unchangeable. Evolutionary psychology, unlike past gene-centered views of human nature, illuminates the tremendous flexibility of the human mind and the powerful role of environment in shaping behavior. In particular, evolutionary psychology shows how inhospitable the current social environment is to monogamy. And while the science offers no easy cures, it does suggest avenues for change.

* * *

The premise of evolutionary psychology is simple. The human mind, like any other organ, was designed for the purpose of transmitting genes to the next generation; the feelings and thoughts it creates are best understood in these terms. Thus the feeling of hunger, no less than the stomach, is here because it helped keep our ancestors alive long enough to reproduce and rear their young. Feelings of lust, no less than the sex organs, are here because they aided reproduction directly. Any ancestors who lacked stomachs or hunger or sex organs or lust—well, they wouldn't have become ancestors, would they? Their traits would have been discarded by natural selection.

This logic goes beyond such obviously Darwinian feelings as hunger and lust. According to evolutionary psychologists, our everyday, ever shifting attitudes toward a mate or prospective mate —trust, suspicion, rhapsody, revulsion, warmth, iciness—are the handiwork of natural selection that remain with us today because in the past they led to behaviors that helped spread genes.

How can evolutionary psychologists be so sure? In part, their faith rests on the whole data base of evolutionary biology. In all sorts of species, and in organs ranging from brains to bladders, nature's attention to the subtlest aspects of genetic transmission is evident. Consider the crafting of primate testicles—specifically, their custom tailoring to the monogamy, or lack thereof, of females. If you take a series of male apes and weigh their testicles (not recommended, actually), you will find a pattern. Chimpanzees and other species with high "relative testes weight" (testes weight in comparison to body weight) feature quite promiscuous females. Species with low relative testes weight are either fairly monogamous (gibbons, for example) or systematically polygynous (gorillas), with one male monopolizing a harem of females. The explanation is simple. When females breed with many males, male genes can profit by producing lots of semen for their own transportation. Which male succeeds in getting his genes into a given egg may be a question of sheer volume, as competing hordes of sperm do battle.

THE TROUBLE WITH WOMEN

Patterns like these, in addition to showcasing nature's ingenuity, allow a kind of detective work. If testicles evolved to match female behavior, then they are clues to the natural behavior of females. Via men's testicles, we can peer through the mists of prehistory and see how women behaved in the social environment of our evolution, free from the influence of modern culture; we can glimpse part of a pristine female mind.

The relative testes weight of humans falls between that of the chimpanzee and the gorilla. This suggests that women, while not nearly so wild as chimpanzee females (who can be veritable sex machines), are by nature somewhat adventurous. If they were not, why would natural selection divert precious resources to the construction and maintenance of weighty testicles?

There is finer evidence, as well, of natural female infidelity. You might think that the number of sperm cells in a husband's ejaculate would depend only on how long it has been since he last had sex. Wrong. What matters more, according to a recent study, is how long his mate has been out of sight. A man who hasn't had sex for, say, a week will have a higher sperm count if his wife was away on a business trip than if she's been home with the flu. In short, what really counts is whether the woman has had the opportunity to stray. The more chances she has had to collect sperm from other males, the more profusely her mate sends in his own troops. Again: that natural selection designed such an elaborate weapon is evidence of something for the weapon to combat—female faithlessness.

So here is problem No. 1 with the pair-bond thesis: women are not by nature paragons of fidelity. Wanderlust is an innate part of their minds, ready to surface under propitious circumstances. Here's problem No. 2: if you think women are bad, you should see men.

THE TROUBLE WITH MEN

With men too, clues from physiology help uncover the mind. Consider "sexual dimorphism"—the difference between average male and female body size. Extreme sexual dimorphism is typical of a polygynous species, in which one male may impregnate several females, leaving other males without offspring. Since the winning males usually secure their trophies by fighting or intimidating other males, the genes of brawny, aggressive males get passed on while the genes of less formidable males are deposited in the dust-bin of history. Thus male gorillas, who get a whole haremful of mates if they win lots of fights and no mates if they win none, are twice as big as females. With humans, males are about 15% bigger—sufficient to suggest that male departures from monogamy, like female departures, are not just a recent cultural invention.

Anthropology offers further evidence. Nearly 1,000 of the 1,154 past or present human societies ever studied—and these include most of the world's "hunter-gatherer" societies—have permitted a man to have more than one wife. These are the closest things we have to living examples of the "ancestral environment" —the social context of human evolution, the setting for which the mind was designed. The presumption is that people reared in such societies—the !Kung San of southern Africa, the Ache of Paraguay, the 19th century Eskimo—behave fairly "naturally." More so, at least, than people reared amid influences that weren't part of the ancestral environment: TVs, cars, jail time for bigamy.

There are vanishingly few anthropological examples of systematic female polygamy, or polyandry—women monopolizing sexual access to more than one man at once. So, while both sexes are prone under the right circumstances to infidelity, men seem much more deeply inclined to actually acquire a second or third mate—to keep a harem.

They are also more inclined toward the casual fling. Men are less finicky • about sex partners. Prostitution—sex with someone you don't know and don't care to know—is a service sought overwhelmingly by males the world round. And almost all pornography that relies sheerly on visual stimulation— images of anonymous people, spiritless flesh—is consumed by males.

Many studies confirm the more discriminating nature of women. One evolutionary psychologist surveyed men and women about the minimal level of intelligence they would accept in a person they were "dating." The average response for both male and female: average intelligence. And how smart would the potential date have to be before they would consent to sex? Said the women: Oh, in that case, markedly above average. Said the men: Oh, in that case, markedly below average.

There is no dispute among evolutionary psychologists over the basic source of this male open-mindedness. A woman, regardless of how many sex partners she has, can generally have only one offspring a year. For a man, each new mate offers a real chance for pumping genes into the future. According to the *Guinness Book of Records,* the most prolific human parent in world history was Moulay ("The Bloodthirsty") Ismail, the last Sharifian Emperor of Morocco, who died in 1727. He fathered more than 1,000 children.

This logic behind undiscerning male lust seems obvious now, but it wasn't always. Darwin had noted that in species after species the female is "less eager than the male," but he never figured out why. Only in the late 1960s and early 1970s did biologists George Williams and Robert Trivers attribute the raging libido of males to their nearly infinite potential rate of reproduction.

WHY DO WOMEN CHEAT?

Even then the female capacity for promiscuity remained puzzling. For women, more sex doesn't mean more offspring. Shouldn't they focus on quality rather than quantity—look for a robust, clever mate whose genes may bode well for the offspring's robustness and cleverness? There's ample evidence that women are drawn to such traits, but in our species genes are not all a male has to offer. Unlike our nearest ape relatives, we are a species of "high male-parental investment." In every known hunter-gatherer culture, marriage is the norm—not necessarily monogamous marriage, and not always lasting marriage, but marriage of some sort; and via this institution, fathers help provide for their children.

In our species, then, a female's genetic legacy is best amplified by a mate with two things: good genes and much to invest. But what if she can't find one man who has both? One solution would be to trick a devoted, generous and perhaps wealthy but not especially brawny or brainy mate into raising the offspring of another male. The woman need not be aware of this strategy, but at some level, conscious or unconscious, deft timing is in order. One study found that women who cheat on mates tend to do so around ovulation, when they are most likely to get pregnant.

For that matter, cheating during the infertile part of the monthly cycle might have its own logic, as a way (unconsciously) to turn the paramour into a dupe; the woman extracts goods or services from him in exchange for his fruitless conquest. Of course the flowers he buys may not help her genes, but in the ancestral environment, less frivolous gifts—notably food—would have. Nisa, a woman in a !Kung San hunter-gatherer village, told an anthropologist that "when you have lovers, one brings you something and another brings you something else. One comes at night with meat, another with money, another with beads. Your husband also does things and gives them to you."

Multiple lovers have other uses too. The anthropologist Sarah Blaffer Hrdy has theorized that women copulate with more than one man to leave several men under the impression that they might be the father of particular offspring. Then, presumably, they will treat the offspring kindly. Her theory was inspired by langur monkeys. Male langurs sometimes kill infants sired by others as a kind of sexual icebreaker, a prelude to pairing up with the (former) mother. What better way to return her to ovulation—by putting an emphatic end to her breast-feeding—and to focus her energies on the offspring to come?

Anyone tempted to launch into a sweeping indictment of langur morality should first note that infanticide on grounds of infidelity has been acceptable in a number of human societies. Among the Yanomamö of South America and the Tikopia of the Solomon Islands, men have been known to demand, upon marrying women with a past, that their babies be killed. And Ache men sometimes collectively decide to kill a newly fatherless child. For a woman in the ancestral environment, then, the benefits of multiple sex partners could have ranged from their sparing her child's life to their defending or otherwise investing in her youngster.

Again, this logic does not depend on a conscious understanding of it. Male langurs presumably do not grasp the concept of paternity. Still, genes that make males sensitive to cues that certain infants may or may not carry their genes have survived. A gene that says, "Be nice to children if you've had lots of sex with their mothers," will prosper over the long haul.

THE INVENTION AND CORRUPTION OF LOVE

Genes don't talk, of course. They affect behavior by creating feelings and thoughts—by building and maintaining the brain. Whenever evolutionary psychologists talk about some evolved behavioral tendency—a polygamous or monogamous bent, say, or male parental investment—they are also talking about an underlying mental infrastructure.

The advent of male parental investment, for example, required the invention of a compelling emotion: paternal love. At some point in our past, genes that inclined a man to love his offspring began to flourish at the expense of genes that promoted remoteness. The reason, presumably, is that changes in circumstance —an upsurge in predators, say—made it more likely that the offspring of undevoted, unprotective fathers would perish.

Crossing this threshold meant love not only for the child; the first step toward becoming devoted parents consists of the man and woman developing a mutual attraction. The genetic payoff of having two parents committed to a child's welfare seems to be the central reason men and women can fall into swoons over one another.

Until recently, this claim was heresy. "Romantic love" was thought to be the unnatural invention of Western culture. The Mangaians of Polynesia, for instance, were said to be "puzzled" by references to marital affection. But lately anthropologists have taken a second look at purportedly loveless cultures, including the Mangaians, and have discovered what nonanthropologists already knew: love between man and woman is a human universal.

In this sense the pair-bonding label is apt. Still, that term—and for that matter the term love—conveys a sense of permanence and symmetry that is wildly misleading. Evolution not only invented romantic love but from the beginning also corrupted it. The corruption lies in conflicts of interest inherent in male parental investment. It is the goal of maximizing male investment, remember, that sometimes leads a woman to infidelity. Yet it is the preciousness of this investment that makes her infidelity lethal to her mate's interests. Not long for this world are the genes of a man who showers time and energy on children who are not his.

Meanwhile, male parental investment also makes the man's naturally polygynous bent inimical to his wife's reproductive interests. His quest for a new wife could lead him to withdraw, or at least dilute, investment in his first wife's children. This reallocation of resources may on balance help his genes but certainly not hers.

The living legacy of these long-running genetic conflicts is human jealousy— or, rather, human jealousies. In theory, there should be two kinds of jealousy —one male and one female. A man's jealousy should focus on sexual infidelity, since cuckoldry is the greatest genetic threat he faces. A woman, though she'll hardly applaud a partner's strictly sexual infidelity (it does consume time and divert some resources), should be more concerned with emotional infidelity—the sort of magnetic commitment to another woman that could lead to a much larger shift in resources.

David Buss, an evolutionary psychologist at the University of Michigan, has confirmed this prediction vividly. He placed electrodes on men and women and had them envision their mates doing various disturbing things. When men imagined sexual infidelity, their heart rates took leaps of a magnitude typically induced by three cups of coffee. They sweated. Their brows wrinkled. When they imagined a budding emotional attachment, they calmed down, though not quite to their normal level. For women, things were reversed: envisioning emotional infidelity—redirected love, not supplementary sex—brought the deeper distress.

That jealousy is so finely tuned to these forms of treachery is yet more evidence that they have a long evolutionary history. Still, the modern environment has carried them to new heights, making marriage dicier than ever. Men and women have always, in a sense, been designed to make each other miserable, but these days they are especially good at it.

MODERN OBSTACLES TO MONOGAMY

To begin with, infidelity is easier in an anonymous city than in a small hunter-gatherer village. Whereas paternity studies show that 2% of the children in a !Kung San village result from cuckoldry, the rate runs higher than 20% in some modern neighborhoods.

Contraceptive technology may also complicate marriage. During human evolution, there were no condoms or birth-control pills. If an adult couple slept together for a year or two and produced no baby, the chances were good that one of them was not fertile. No way of telling which one, but from their genes' point of view, there was little to lose and much to gain by ending the partnership and finding a new mate. Perhaps, some have speculated, natural selection favored genes inclining men and women to sour on a mate after long periods of sex without issue. And it is true that barren marriages are especially likely to break up.

Another possible challenge to monogamy in the modern world lies in movies, billboards and magazines. There was no photography in the long-ago world that shaped the human male mind. So at some deep level, that mind may respond to glossy images of pinups and fashion models as if they were viable mates —alluring alternatives to dull, monogamous devotion. Evolutionary psychologist Douglas Kenrick has suggested as much. According to his research, men who are shown pictures of *Playboy* models later describe themselves as less in love with their wives than do men shown other images. (Women shown pictures from *Playgirl* felt no such attitude adjustment toward spouses.)

Perhaps the largest modern obstacle to lasting monogamy is economic inequality. To see why, it helps to grasp a subtle point made by Donald Symons, author of the 1979 classic *The Evolution of Human Sexuality*. Though men who leave their wives may be driven by "natural" impulses, that does not mean men have a natural impulse designed expressly to make them leave their wives. After all, in the ancestral environment, gaining a second wife didn't mean leaving the first. So why leave her? Why not stay near existing offspring and keep giving some support? Symons believes men are designed less for opportune desertion than for opportune polygyny. It's just that when polygyny is illegal, a polygynous impulse will find other outlets, such as divorce.

If Symons is right, the question of what makes a man feel the restlessness that leads to divorce can be rephrased: What circumstances, in the ancestral environment, would have permitted the acquisition of a second wife? Answer: possessing markedly more resources, power or social status than the average Joe.

Even in some "egalitarian" hunter-gatherer societies, men with slightly more status or power than average are slightly more likely to have multiple wives. In less egalitarian pre-industrial societies, the anthropologist Laura Betzig has shown, the pattern is dramatic. In Incan society, the four political offices from petty chief to chief were allotted ceilings of seven, eight, 15 and 30 women. Polygyny reaches its zenith under the most despotic regimes. Among the Zulu, where coughing or sneezing at the king's dinner table was punishable by death, his highness might monopolize more than 100 women.

To an evolutionary psychologist, such numbers are just extreme examples of a simple fact: the ultimate purpose of the wealth and power that men seek so ardently is genetic proliferation. It is only natural that the exquisitely flexible human mind should be designed to capitalize on this power once it is obtained.

Thus it is natural that a rising corporate star, upon getting a big promotion, should feel a strong attraction to women other than his wife. Testosterone —which expands a male's sexual appetite —has been shown to rise in nonhuman primates following social triumphs, and there are hints that it does so in human males too. Certainly the world is full of triumphant men—Johnny Carson, Donald Trump—who trade in aging wives for younger, more fertile models. (The multi-wived J. Paul Getty said, "A lasting relationship with a woman is only possible if you are a business failure.")

A man's exalted social status can give his offspring a leg up in life, so it's natural that women should lust after the high-status men who lust after them. Among the Ache, the best hunters also have more extramarital affairs and more illegitimate children than lesser hunters. In modern societies, contraception keeps much of this sex appeal from translating into offspring. But last year a study by Canadian anthropologist Daniel Pérusse found that single men of high socioeconomic status have sex with more partners than lower-status men.

One might think that the appeal of rich or powerful men is losing its strength. After all, as more women enter the work force, they can better afford to premise their marital decisions on something other than a man's income. But we're dealing here with deep romantic attractions, not just conscious calculation, and these feelings were forged in a different environment. Evolutionary psychologists have shown that the tendency of women to place greater emphasis than men on a mate's financial prospects remains strong regardless of the income or expected income of the women in question.

The upshot of all this is that economic inequality is monogamy's worst enemy. Affluent men are inclined to leave their aging wives, and young women —including some wives of less affluent men—are inclined to offer themselves as replacements.

Objections to this sort of analysis are predictable: "But people leave marriages for emotional reasons. They don't add up their offspring and pull out their calculators." True. But emotions are just evolution's executioners. Beneath the thoughts and feelings and temperamental differences marriage counselors spend their time sensitively assessing are the stratagems of the genes—cold, hard equations composed of simple variables: social status, age of spouse, number of children, their ages, outside romantic opportunities and so on. Is the wife really duller and more nagging than she was 20 years ago? Maybe, but maybe the husband's tolerance for nagging has dropped now that she is 45 and has no reproductive future. And the promotion he just got, which has already drawn some admiring glances from a young woman at work, has not helped.

Similarly, we might ask the young, childless wife who finds her husband intolerably insensitive why the insensitivity wasn't so oppressive a year ago, before he lost his job and she met the kindly, affluent bachelor who seems to be flirting with her. Of course, maybe her husband's abuses are quite real, in which case they signal his disaffection and perhaps his impending departure—and merit just the sort of pre-emptive strike the wife is now mustering.

THE FALLOUT FROM MONOGAMY'S DEMISE

Not only does male social inequality favor divorce. Divorce can also reinforce male social inequality; it is a tool of class exploitation. Consider Johnny Carson. Like many wealthy, high-status males, he spent his career dominating the reproductive years of a series of women. Somewhere out there is a man who wanted a family and a pretty wife and, if it hadn't been for Johnny Carson, would have married one of these women. And if this man has managed to find another woman, she was similarly snatched from the clutches of some other man. And so on—a domino effect: a scarcity of fertile females trickles down the social scale.

As theoretical as this sounds, it cannot help happening. There are only about 25 years of fertility per woman. When some men dominate more than 25 years' worth, some man somewhere must do with less. And when, in addition to all the serial husbands, you count the men who live with a woman for five years before deciding not to marry her, and then do it again (perhaps finally at 35 marrying a 28-year-old), the net effect is not trivial. As some Darwinians have put it, serial monogamy is tantamount to polygyny. Like polygyny, it lets powerful men grab extra sexual resources (a.k.a. women), leaving less fortunate men without mates —or at least without mates young enough to bear children. Thus rampant divorce not only ends the marriages of some men but also prevents the marriage of others. In 1960, when the divorce rate was around 25%, the portion of the never married population age 40 or older was about the same for men and women. By 1990, with the divorce rate running at 50%, the portion for men was larger by 20% than for women.

Viewing serial monogamy as polygyny by another name throws a kink into the family-values debate. So far, conservatives have got the most political mileage out of decrying divorce. Yet lifelong monogamy—one woman per man for rich and poor alike—would seem to be a natural rallying cry for liberals.

One other kind of fallout from serial monogamy comes plainly into focus through the lens of evolutionary psychology: the toll taken on children. Martin Daly and Margo Wilson of McMaster University in Ontario, two of the field's seminal thinkers, have written that one of the "most obvious" Darwinian predictions is that stepparents will "tend to care less profoundly for children than natural parents." After all, parental investment is a precious resource. So natural selection should "favor those parental psyches that do not squander it on nonrelatives"—who after all do not carry the parent's genes.

Indeed, in combing through 1976 crime data, Daly and Wilson found that an American child living with one or more substitute parents was about 100 times as likely to be fatally abused as a child living with biological parents. In a Canadian city in the 1980s, a child age two or younger was 70 times as likely to be killed by a parent if living with a stepparent and a natural parent than if living with two natural parents.

Of course, murdered children are a tiny fraction of all children living with stepparents; divorce and remarriage hardly amount to a child's death warrant. But consider the more common problem of nonfatal abuse. Children under 10 were, depending on their age and the study in question, three to 40 times as likely to suffer parental abuse if living with a stepparent and a biological parent instead of two biological parents.

There are ways to fool Mother Nature, to induce parents to love children who are not theirs. (Hence cuckoldry.) After all, people cannot telepathically sense that a child is carrying their genes. Instead they rely on cues that in the ancestral environment would have signaled as much. If a woman feeds and cuddles an infant day after day, she may grow to love the child, and so may the woman's mate. This sort of bonding is what makes adopted children lovable (and is one reason relationships between stepparent and child are often harmonious). But the older a child is when first seen, the less profound the attachment will probably be. Most children who acquire stepfathers are past infancy.

Polygynous cultures, such as the 19th century Mormons, are routinely dismissed as cruelly sexist. But they do have at least one virtue: they do not submit children to the indifference or hostility of a surrogate father. What we have now—serial monogamy, quasi-polygyny—is in this sense worse than true polygyny. It massively wastes the most precious evolutionary resource: love.

IS THERE HOPE?

Given the toll of divorce—on children, on low-income men, and for that matter on mothers and fathers—it would be nice to come up with a magic monogamy-restoration plan. Alas, the importance of this task seems rivaled only by its difficulty. Lifelong monogamous devotion just isn't natural, and the modern environment makes it harder than ever. What to do?

As Laura Betzig has noted, some income redistribution might help. One standard conservative argument against antipoverty policies is their cost: taxes burden the affluent and thus, by lowering work incentive, reduce economic output. But if one goal of the policy is to bolster monogamy, then making the affluent less so would help. Monogamy is threatened not just by poverty in an absolute sense but also by the relative wealth of the rich. This is what lures a young woman to a wealthy married or formerly married man. It is also what makes the man who attracts her feel too good for just one wife.

As for the economic consequences, the costs of soaking the rich might well be outweighed by the benefits, financial and otherwise, of more stable marriages, fewer divorces, fewer abused children and less loneliness and depression.

There are other levers for bolstering monogamy, such as divorce law. In the short run, divorce brings the average man a marked rise in standard of living, while his wife, along with her children, suffers the opposite. Maybe we should not lock people into unhappy marriages with financial disincentives to divorce, but surely we should not reward men for leaving their wives either.

A MORAL ANIMAL

The problem of divorce is by no means one of public policy alone. Progress will also depend on people using the explosive insight of evolutionary psychology in a morally responsible way. Ideally this insight would lead people to subject their own feelings to more acute scrutiny. Maybe for starters, men and women will realize that their constantly fluctuating perceptions of a mate are essentially illusions, created for the (rather absurd, really) purpose of genetic proliferation, and that these illusions can do harm. Thus men might beware the restlessness designed by natural selection to encourage polygyny. Now that it brings divorce, it can inflict great emotional and even physical damage on their children.

And men and women alike might bear in mind that impulses of wanderlust, or marital discontent, are not always a sign that you married the "wrong person." They may just signify that you are a member of our species who married another member of our species. Nor, as evolutionary psychiatrist Randolph L. Nesse has noted, should we believe such impulses are a sign of psychopathology. Rather, he writes, they are "expected impulses that must, for the most part, be inhibited for the sake of marriage."

The danger is that people will take the opposite tack: react to the new knowledge by surrendering to "natural" impulses, as if what's "in our genes" were beyond reach of self-control. They may even conveniently assume that what is "natural" is good.

This notion was common earlier in this century. Natural selection was thought of almost as a benign deity, constantly "improving" our species for the greater good. But evolutionary psychology rests on a quite different world view: recogni-

tion that natural selection does not work toward overall social welfare, that much of human nature boils down to ruthless genetic self-interest, that people are naturally oblivious to their ruthlessness.

George Williams, whose 1966 book *Adaptation and Natural Selection* helped dispel the once popular idea that evolution often works for "the good of the group," has even taken to calling natural selection "evil" and "the enemy." The moral life, in his view, consists largely of battling human nature.

Darwin himself believed the human species to be a moral one—in fact, the only moral animal species. "A moral being is one who is capable of comparing his past and future actions or motives, and of approving or disapproving of them," he wrote.

In this sense, yes, we are moral. We have at least the technical capacity to lead an examined life: self-awareness, memory, foresight and judgment. Still, chronically subjecting ourselves to moral scrutiny and adjusting our behavior accordingly is hardly a reflex. We are potentially moral animals—which is more than any other animal can say—but we are not naturally moral animals. The first step to being moral is to realize how thoroughly we aren't.

NO

Richard N. Williams

SCIENCE OR STORY TELLING? EVOLUTIONARY EXPLANATIONS OF HUMAN SEXUALITY

Robert Wright's article, "Our Cheating Hearts," provides a good example of how genetic explanations of behavior (derived from evolutionary theory) have become popular in the social sciences, and thus, how they have found their way into the mainstream of our culture. Wright introduces his audience to the new field of environmental psychology, which attempts to explain some of our most important and meaningful human behaviors, like sexuality and marital fidelity, in terms of evolutionary and genetic processes. However, a careful analysis of Wright's article illuminates the problems and conceptual gaps found in attempts to explain human behavior as being caused by evolutionary forces or genes.

On the surface of his article, Wright seems to be simply reporting scientific facts that have been discovered about how and why animals engage in sexual behaviors, and how they have evolved in ways that facilitate such behaviors. Wright's article is similar to a great many other articles and books all trying to make the point that human behaviors are governed by genes, and by evolutionary processes, and, therefore, humans are essentially like animals in their sexual and other behaviors. However, the kind of data used to support this kind of explanation is not scientific in the usual sense. It is composed mostly of stories and analogies. On the surface, Wright seems to be merely pointing out the truths of the similarities of animal to human behavior, and then offering the obvious explanation for these similarities—that evolution, through the workings of our genes, has guided, and continues to control our behaviors. A closer look at the so-called evidence that evolutionary psychology uses to explain our sexual behaviors reveals that it is not at all convincing. It is more story telling than it is science.

IS THERE COMPELLING EVIDENCE THAT OUR INTIMATE OR SEXUAL BEHAVIORS ARE DETERMINED BY EVOLUTION OR GENES?

The idea that human sexual behaviors and intimate relationships are governed by biological structures or evolutionary forces is not scientific in the sense in which we usually use that term. We usually consider scientific facts to be those that are discovered through careful experimentation giving rise to unambiguous results. Scientific work on which evolutionary psychology bases its explanations of human behavior is of quite a different sort. To make this point clear, it is important to distinguish between what we might call "evolutionary theory," and genetic biology.

Scientific studies in the field of genetic biology are very sophisticated and careful. They have provided us a convincing picture of what genes are and how they work. Studies in genetics have resulted in hybrid strains of plants and animals, and in new, and even patented, life forms. However, all this work demonstrates only that genetic material is responsible for a number of *physical* structures and attributes. There is little argument that our genetic material plays a major role in such things as eye color, physical stature, and certain diseases. These are physical characteristics and have a recognizably physical and/or chemical foundation. However, the claims of evolutionary psychology are quite different.

There are several important ideas that Wright, and the evolutionary psychologists, take for granted that are not established by hard scientific evidence. What is not established by careful scientific work is: (a) that psychological or mental events and behaviors (such as human intimacy and sexual attraction) can be produced by genetic material; and (b) that *evolution* controls these events and governs their development and their manifestation.[1] Wright, and the evolutionary psychologists, assume that these two points are true. However, before we are willing to accept them, and Wright's explanations for our sexual behavior, these two points need to be clarified and examined more carefully. Because Wright simply accepts these two claims as true, he is able to tell an evolutionary story about us and our sexual behavior. I argue that Wright's account is a creative story about human sexuality and not a report of scientific facts of human sexuality.

Evolutionary Explanation as Story

Evolutionary theory is convincing to many people chiefly because the living world we experience seems to be like evolutionary theory would predict it should be. In other words, evolutionary theory seems to be true because it fits the data. Evolutionary theorists have offered an account or story of the origin of life, how it developed, and how it regulates itself that makes sense. It seems reasonable, and we can think of very few examples of phenomena that evolutionary theory could not explain. However, it should be kept in mind that because a theory or story can be shown to fit the world and explain it reasonably well, it is not necessarily the case that the story is true. Certainly this is not enough to establish the story as scientific fact. To see why this is the case, we need only ask ourselves what people used to think about the world before evolutionary theories became popular. Did they live in a world they could not explain? Did the world not make sense to them? Certainly a study of history reveals that before evolutionary theories as we know them came into vogue as explanations, people had other stories that made sense of the living world, its origins, and its development. The truth or falsity of evolutionary explanations is not a scientific question because it would be impossible to formulate a properly scientific test of these explanations in contrast to other nonevolutionary explanations. Instead, evidence for evolutionary theory is philosophical and conceptual. Evolutionary theorists observe the world and the nature and behavior of various species and then offer a story of what might be the case. Wright's notion of evolutionary psychology thus rests on conceptual and philosophical rather than scientific grounds.

For example, evolutionary theory suggests that humans are motivated above all to insure the survival of their own genes in succeeding generations. This, in turn, suggests that the best way to do this would be to make sure our offspring survive. And this, in turn, suggests that humans will take better care of their own biological children than stepchildren who do not share their genes. Statistics are reported in Wright's article that show that children who live with one or more stepparents are much more likely to be abused than are children who live with both of their biological parents. Evolutionary theorists will claim that this statistic supports evolutionary theory because it is consistent with what an evolutionary story would predict. However, it seems clear that there are more obvious and immediate factors that might explain why children living with stepparents are more likely to be abused. It seems obvious that children living with stepparents are doing so because of some trouble in their birth family. The factors that contributed to the breakup of the birth family in the first place are likely to continue with both parents and children into subsequent family arrangements. These factors include unsatisfactory relationships between parents, stresses from the breakup of the original family, economic troubles, and any number of other social and cultural factors. It seems that the evolutionary account of the abuse of these children is quite far removed from the immediate and compelling circumstances of the case. Evolutionary forces do not seem—even by common sense—to be the most direct or obvious source of the problem of abused stepchildren. There does not seem to be anything obvious that would argue that the evolutionary explanation of the statistics of abuse is the best, or most sensible one. Rather, the evolutionary account of this tragedy seems rather contrived. It should also be noted that there is no scientific test that could possibly separate evolutionary causes from the host of social and personal causes of this sort of child abuse.

Wright's account of the evolutionary origins of human intimacy provides many good illustrations of this sort of story telling. For example, he points out that the size of the testicles (relative to body weight) in various primate species is correlated with the extent to which the species tend to be monogamous or polygynous. The story of evolutionary biology is consistent with this bit of data, however, there is nothing about these data that suggest in the least that some evolutionary process is the *cause* of the correlation. Similarly, Wright reports that nearly 1,000 of 1,154 past or present human societies have at one time or another permitted the practice of polygamy. This is also consistent with evolutionary theory —or, rather, evolutionary theory can fit this bit of information into its story. However, there are many other reasons for which cultures might practice polygamy besides evolutionary forces. Some societies practice it for religious reasons, some for seemingly pragmatic reasons, and some, perhaps, for purely social reasons. The point is that these alternative stories can also "make sense" of this bit of data. The datum itself (i.e., the practice of polygamy) does not demand an evolutionary explanation. Which story we prefer is not based on scientific evidence but on our historical prejudices, and current preferences for some kinds of explanations over others. Evolutionary explanations are currently very popular.

In summary then, evolutionary explanations of our behavior rest not on sound scientific demonstration but on our perceptions that evolutionary accounts, like the one Wright gives, make sense, and fit the data. Support for the story of evolution is grounded in how well the story can be used to make sense of the data of the world.

The Logical Fallacy of Affirming the Consequent

We will leave the specifics of Wright's evolutionary analysis in order to make an important but more general point and then show how this general point applies to Wright's argument. From the analysis of evolutionary theories just given, it can be concluded that the truth or falsity of evolutionary theory as an explanation of human behavior is not a genuinely scientific question because it depends for support not on hard scientific data but on reason and argument and a certain degree of cleverness in making the story fit. Since evolutionary accounts of our behavior stand or fall on the basis of reason and argument, we should be very careful about the kind of reasoning and arguments that are used to support the evolutionary explanation of our actions. From the very beginnings of our Western intellectual tradition, scholars have spent much effort detailing what kinds of reasoning and arguments were valid and trustworthy and what kinds were not. Rules have been established for logical analysis so that we can be confident of the conclusions we reach from our arguments. Likewise, certain kinds of errors have been identified which make our arguments and conclusions invalid —or illogical. This is not the forum to fully discuss the nature of human reason itself, and the power of logic. We need only point out that by the rules scholars have traditionally accepted certain forms of argument are considered invalid, and do not bring us to valid necessary conclusions.[2]

One of the most common and well known logical fallacies is *affirming the consequent*. To see what this fallacy looks like, let us consider one common type of logical argument. It has the following form:

1. *If* Socrates is a man, *then* he is mortal.
2. Socrates is a man.
3. Therefore, he is mortal.

Note that this whole argument hangs on the validity of a very important assumption that is not even stated in the argument—that *all men really are mortal.* If this is not true, then the argument, while still valid according to the rules of logic, is not sensible. Many theoretical arguments, including many of those supporting evolutionary explanations of human behavior, have assumptions that are presumed to be true but are almost never stated, much less examined.

Whenever an argument is presented in the form just presented, it is considered, by the rules of logic, to be valid. That is, the conclusion is reasonable, and we should agree with it and comprehend that it is true. The part of the argument (in statement 1) that follows the word *if* is called the antecedent of the argument. The part following the word *then* is the consequent. In statement 2 the antecedent is restated. That is, it is shown to be true —Socrates really is a man. Whenever we can show that the antecedent is true, then, as we see in statement 3, the consequent follows—it is taken to be true. If he *is* a man—we can show or accept that he is—then he *is* mortal. This classical type of arguing is called affirming the antecedent.

What would have happened, however, if the argument had been made in the following form?

1. *If* Socrates is a man, *then* he is mortal.
2. Socrates *is* mortal.
3. Therefore, he is (must be) a man.

Notice that in this argument we have stated that the consequent is true in statement 2, rather than the antecedent. Then we try to conclude that the antecedent must also be true in statement 3. A moment's reflection is sufficient to show that our conclusion is not valid. Socrates could be a dog—since dogs are mortal. Just because he is mortal, we do not know that he is a man. The conclusion is not valid because the form of the argument is not valid. This is an illustration of a classical logical fallacy called affirming the consequent. Even though this is a commonly understood logical fallacy, it is a commonly employed strategy in arguing for the validity of theories.

In Wright's exposition of the evolutionary basis of human sexuality, there are numerous examples of this fallacy of af-

firming the consequent. For example, as I noted above, Wright uses evidence of sexual dimorphism—the difference in the average size of human males and females —to argue for the validity of his evolutionary account. The argument has the following form:

1. *If* evolution makes humans prone to polygyny, *then* we will find sexual dimorphism in humans (because there is dimorphism in polygynous animals).
2. We do find sexual dimorphism in humans. (The consequent is true.)
3. Therefore, evolution makes humans prone to polygyny. (The antecedent supposedly follows.)

This is, of course, a classic example of affirming the consequent.

Wright's article offers a long string of similar but unsound arguments. In its general form the foundational argument for evolutionary explanations of human behavior is:

1. *If* evolutionary theory is true, *then* we should observe that humans do X (some phenomenon).
2. We observe that humans do X (this phenomenon).
3. Therefore, evolutionary theory is true.

In summary, it should be noted that this style of reasoning by affirming the consequent is not sound scientific practice. Thus, the evidence generally marshalled in favor of evolutionary accounts of human behavior, such as evolutionary psychology, is not genuinely scientific. Rather, it is argument and deduction. And, as has been shown, most often it is not sound argument.

The Criterion of Falsifiability

At least since the publication of the influential work of Karl Popper (1959), a philosopher of science, it has been accepted in most scientific circles that a good theory—a genuinely scientific theory—must be of the type that can be proven false. That is, sound scientific practice demands that a theory must be capable of being tested in such a way that if the results don't turn out to be consistent with the predictions of the theory, then it can be concluded that the theory is false. Theories that cannot be shown to be false are not to be considered genuinely scientific theories. I have already argued in the previous sections of this essay that evolutionary explanations of human behavior are not falsifiable in this sense. There is no experimental test that can settle the question of the validity of these explanations.

However, most proponents of evolutionary theories of human behavior do not even attempt to formulate or explain their theories in a way that can be falsified.[3] While it should be acknowledged that Wright's article is written more for a popular audience than for a professional scientific audience, it nonetheless is illustrative of the approach taken even in more technical and scientific presentations of evolutionary theory. Thus it provides a good example of how the theories are generally presented in unfalsifiable form.

In order to see how evolutionary theories are presented in unfalsifiable form let us pay attention to the way in which Wright reassures his readers that the new evolutionary psychology does not subscribe to the strict and fatalistic theories of previous evolutionary and genetic explanations. He points out that "what's 'natural' isn't necessarily unchangeable."

This is because of the "tremendous flexibility of the human mind and the powerful role of the environment in shaping behavior." Two important points are illustrated in this quotation. The first is that most proponents of evolutionary or genetic explanations of human behavior allow for some determining influence from the environment. However, being caused to behave by our environment does not make for a much better image of our humanity than does being caused by our biology. Acknowledging the causal role of the environment is not much of a corrective to the strict fatalism of biological explanations of our behavior.

The other point, more relevant to the present discussion, is that Wright suggests that the flexibility of the human mind is a source of power to counteract some of the natural processes that might otherwise control us. The problem, however, is that according to Wright's own account of the evolutionary perspective, the human mind is "built and maintained" by genes to serve their (reproductive) purposes. For example, evolutionary theory might predict that since our overriding concern is to get our genes into the next generation, we (especially males) would not care much for one another, especially, for reproductive rivals. We would expect males to be aggressive with all other males. However, as we study societies throughout history, we notice that humans, even males, have tended to be rather civilized and caring, even altruistic. On the surface, this seems to counter evolutionary explanations. However, many evolutionary accounts would claim that our minds (or brains) evolved the capacity to care for others and be kind because being kind and caring had survival value, and actually would help us make sure our genes survived into the next generation, because if we care for others, they are likely to care for us and our children. So, no matter what we observe about the behavior of human males—aggression or cooperation—evolutionary theory can claim the observation as evidence that it is true.

If we take this kind of argument seriously, then, when we see people behaving in accordance with the predictions of evolutionary theory, it is evidence that evolutionary theory is true. And when we see people behaving in a way that seems not to be consistent with evolutionary theory, it is because of the influence of a "tremendously flexible" mind—which, in turn, has evolved according to the dictates of evolutionary theory to serve the ends of evolution itself. So when evolutionary theory seems to work as an explanation we can assume it is true. When it does not seem to work so well it is still true because it is merely *appearing to* work against itself via the evolved human mind. Evolutionary theory is thus unfalsifiable because both observations that confirm predictions, and observations that do not, are counted as evidence for the validity of evolution as an explanation.

Myths of Magic Genes
There is one aspect of evolutionary theory that has a firm foundation of scientific research. This is the structure and function of genes and their role in determining important characteristics of organisms. These are, for the most part, physical characteristics. Very sophisticated research assures us that many important characteristics of organisms have their origins in genetic codes contained in the chromosomes of the tissues of the organism. However, even though we know much about the structure and function of genes, the picture is not at all clear

when we turn attention to the relationship between genes and *psychological*— rather than strictly physical—characteristics and behaviors of organisms, especially humans.[4]

We find in Wright's essay the following:

> Genes don't talk, of course. They affect behavior by creating feelings and thoughts—by building and maintaining... an underlying mental infrastructure.

The claim here is quite clear: genes create mental phenomena. Wright also speaks of "genes that inclined a man to love his offspring," and suggests that the purposes of the genes required "the invention of a compelling emotion: parental love." Not only are genes sophisticated enough to invent emotions, but, according to Wright, also to contradict them. "Evolution not only invented romantic love but from the beginning also corrupted it."

According to evolutionary theory, not only are genes capable of producing particular emotions, they are also capable of predicting and monitoring behavioral outcomes. This portrayal of genes and their activities is problematic for a number of reasons. The description of genes as intelligent and possessing "stratagems" is problematic in that it seems to overlook what genes really are. We need to remind ourselves as we read evolutionary and genetic accounts of our behavior that genes are simply molecules—chemicals—locked away in the nuclei of the cells of our bodies. How, we might ask, could genes as molecules of chemicals be aware of such things as "outside romantic opportunities" in order to motivate us to take advantage of them? The orthodox evolutionary answer, of course, is that the genes are not aware of such things (that would be silly). Rather, the genes give rise to minds, thoughts, feelings, and sophisticated mental capacities for monitoring all of these social factors and deciding what should be done. But here we run headlong into the fundamental and perpetually vexing question of evolutionary and genetic theories of our behavior. The response to this question determines the adequacy and believability of the accounts of our behavior these theories offer. The question is this: How do chemical compounds locked within the nuclei of the cells of the tissues of our bodies give rise to nonchemical and intelligent things like particular ideas, feelings, emotions, and stratagems? Ideas, feelings, emotions, and stratagems are not simply and strictly chemical or physical. "Stratagems," and "romantic opportunities" are not chemical substances, nor substances at all. It is not at all clear how they might arise from molecules of chemicals that compose our genes. There seems to be no answer to this essential question in all the literature on evolutionary and genetic accounts of human behavior. It is simply assumed that it can happen and does because then the theory "fits."

CONCLUSION

This response to "evolutionary psychology" and Wright's treatment of it has centered on the argument that evolutionary and genetic explanations of human behaviors are not based on hard scientific data and that they are really more like story telling than science. However, much more is at stake than a mere disagreement about how certain observations should be interpreted. Simply making the case that there are other and simpler explanations for our behaviors than the evolutionary explanation, or that such evolutionary explanations are not truly scientific, is not in itself a strong enough refutation and is hardly sufficient grounds for rejecting them. The larger issues need to be made clear.

Evolutionary and genetic explanations of human behavior are not just stories about us; they are stories that pretend not to be stories. Furthermore, they ask us to reduce our most human and most meaningful behaviors to the level of simple animal behaviors. They ask us to accept that the same fundamental processes are at work to determine our intimate relationships as determine "mating behaviors" in animal species. Evolutionary psychologists accomplish this reduction subtly by using the same terms to describe both animal and human behaviors. This reduction of the human to the animal and the application of a common vocabulary destroys the meaning of human behavior. If, as evolutionary psychology declares, human and animal sexuality have the same roots, then human intimacy is no more meaningful than the copulatory acts of common breeding stock. Proponents of evolution claim that we are recompensed for the loss of meaning in our lives by scientific credibility. But if, as I argue, there is no convincing scientific base for the evolutionary account of our behaviors, then we are being asked to sacrifice the meaning of human intimacy for nothing.

The end result of evolutionary and genetic accounts of human behavior is a moral vacuum in which we do not engage one another as moral agents at all but as organisms controlled by biological forces beyond our control. Until such time as there is overwhelming scientific evidence that chemicals in our cells can produce morality and human affections, we are morally obligated to resist explanations that destroy the meaning and morality of our lives. The evolutionary story exacts too great a price both in credulity and in humanity.

NOTES

1. Some evolutionary theorists might argue that at some future date when technology has advanced and when they are given permission to manipulate human genes, genuine scientific validation will be available. It is axiomatic in science, however, that one does not rely on nor claim credibility from what might someday be done. To argue in this way moves one from science to science fiction.

2. The interested reader is referred to Slife & Williams (1995) for a fuller account of how logic plays a role in scientific and theoretical work, and how both scientists and theorists too easily fall into the practice of affirming the consequent.

3. The work of most experimental geneticists is sophisticated and scientifically sound. Their experiments are routinely set up so that their *predictions can* be falsified. However, to falsify a prediction derived from a theory such as evolution is not at all the same thing as to falsify the theory itself. Even though it has generated much credible scientific work, evolutionary theory as a world view has never been at risk. Because of the way it is formulated and promulgated it is unfalsifiable.

4. Some would argue that some behavioral characteristics can also be shown to be genetically determined. Whether this is the case depends in large part on how the term "behavior" is defined. For example, is a plant's "growing" a behavior?

REFERENCES

James, W. (1897/1956). The dilemma of determinism. In W. James, *The will to believe and other essays in popular philosophy* (pp. 145–184). New York: Dover.

Popper, K. (1959). *The logic of scientific discovery.* New York: Basic Books.

Slife, B. D., & Williams, R. N. (1995). *What's behind the research? Discovering hidden assumptions in the behavioral sciences.* Newbury Park, CA: Sage Publications.

CHALLENGE QUESTIONS

Do Evolutionary and Genetic Factors Determine Our Sexual Behaviors?

1. Is Williams correct that there is no specified process for nor evidence that genetic materials produce psychological factors? Interview a geneticist to investigate this.

2. Explore the implications of an evolutionary/genetic account of sexuality for your own life. If it were proved true, how would it affect your current and future relationships?

3. Williams describes the importance of falsifiability in scientific explanations. After reading the selections by Wright and Williams, do you believe that the evolutionary theory described by Wright is falsifiable? Why, or why not?

4. Is there evidence other than that cited by Wright that supports claims about the importance of the new field of evolutionary psychology?

5. Wright claims that it is natural for both men and women to commit adultery "at some times, under some circumstances." Under what circumstances is it *not* natural for adultery, according to Wright? How is it that evolutionary theory only operates under certain circumstances?

ISSUE 3

Should Animals Be Used in Psychological Research?

YES: Elizabeth Baldwin, from "The Case for Animal Research in Psychology," *Journal of Social Issues* (vol. 49, no. 1, 1993)

NO: Alan D. Bowd and Kenneth J. Shapiro, from "The Case Against Laboratory Animal Research in Psychology," *Journal of Social Issues* (vol. 49, no. 1, 1993)

ISSUE SUMMARY

YES: Elizabeth Baldwin, a research ethics officer for the American Psychological Association's Science Directorate, maintains that the benefits of behavioral research with animals are substantial and that the animals are being treated humanely.

NO: Professor of educational psychology Alan D. Bowd and Kenneth J. Shapiro, executive director of Psychologists for the Ethical Treatment of Animals, argue that the harm done to animals in this research is not widely known and that the "benefits" are not sufficient to balance this cruelty.

Until relatively recently, humans were thought to be distinctly different from lower animals. Only humans were considered to have self-consciousness, rationality, and language. Today, however, these distinctions appear to have been blurred by modern research. Many scientists, for example, believe that chimpanzees use language symbols and that many animals have some type of consciousness.

This apparent lack of hard and fast distinctions between humans and other animals has many implications. One of these concerns the use of animals in experimental research. For hundreds of years animals have been considered tools of research. In fact, research ethics has demanded that most experimental treatments be tested on animals before they are tested on humans. Another view, however, has come to the fore. Because there is no clear distinction between lower and higher animals, this view asserts that the lower animals should be accorded the same basic rights as humans. Animal experimentation, from this perspective, cannot be taken for granted; it must be justified on the same moral and ethical grounds as research on humans. This perspective has recently gained considerable momentum as supporters have become politically organized.

Elizabeth Baldwin disagrees with this perspective. She argues that animals should be used in psychological research and that although people should be held responsible for the humane treatment of animals, animals do not have the same rights as humans. Baldwin describes the important role that animals have played in improving the human condition through research and how animal research benefits the health and welfare of other animals. Baldwin argues that many people are not aware of the many federal regulations and laws that protect animals from inhumane treatment. Ultimately, she contends, humans and animals cannot be viewed as essentially the same, with the same ethics and rights.

Alan D. Bowd and Kenneth J. Shapiro do not concur with this view. Their case against the use of animals for psychological research hinges on the idea that animals are denied basic rights. Bowd and Shapiro have developed what they call a "scale of invasiveness," which is an index of the suffering and harm done to animals before, during, or after an experimental procedure. Unlike Baldwin, they argue that federal laws and regulations are not sufficient because they do not consider the animals. Bowd and Shapiro also maintain that the research revealing the harm done to animals is not being published and, in turn, is not being sufficiently recognized. Consequently, they suggest that alternatives to the use of animals in laboratory research be found.

POINT	COUNTERPOINT
• Animals do not have the same rights as humans, but people have a responsibility to ensure the humane treatment of animals.	• Those who accord rights to human beings and deny them to other species must show a morally relevant difference between these species.
• There are elaborate federal regulations protecting animals in research, as well as state laws and professional guidelines on the care of animals.	• Many species are not covered by the Animal Welfare Act and are therefore not reported as part of federally mandated inspections.
• Society has made a collective judgment that the benefits derived from animal research far outweigh the costs.	• In contrast to the uncertain benefits of laboratory animal research, the cost to animals is clear and real.
• Animals have played a pivotal role in improving the human condition and, in return, society should strive to treat them well.	• The benefits of animal research are indeterminate because they depend on unknowns, such as human welfare.

YES

Elizabeth Baldwin

THE CASE FOR ANIMAL RESEARCH IN PSYCHOLOGY

Animal liberationists do not separate out the human animal. A rat is a pig is a dog is a boy.

> —Ingrid Newkirk, Director, People for the
> Ethical Treatment of Animals.

The shock value of this quote has made it a favorite of those defending the use of animals in research. It succinctly states the core belief of many animal rights activists who oppose the use of animals in research. Although some activists work for improved laboratory conditions for research animals, recent surveys suggest that most activists would like to eliminate animal research entirely (Plous, 1991). These activists believe animals have rights equal to humans and therefore should not be used as subjects in laboratory research.

The debate over animal research can be confusing unless one understands the very different goals of animal welfare organizations and animal rights groups. People concerned with animal welfare seek to improve laboratory conditions for research animals and to reduce the number of animals needed. These mainstream goals encompass traditional concerns for the humane treatment of animals, and most researchers share these goals. In contrast, the views of animal rights activists are *not* mainstream, since there are few people who would agree with the above quote from Ingrid Newkirk. Indeed, in a national poll conducted by the National Science Foundation, half the respondents answered the following question affirmatively: "Should scientists be allowed to do research that causes pain and injury to animals like dogs and chimpanzees if it produces new information about human health problems?" (National Science Board, 1991). These findings are particularly impressive given the explicit mention of "pain and injury" to popular animals such as dogs and chimpanzees. My own position is that animals do not have rights in the same sense that humans do, but that people have a responsibility to ensure the humane treatment of animals under their care. Animals have played a pivotal role in improving the human condition, and in return, society should strive to treat them well.

From Elizabeth Baldwin, "The Case for Animal Research in Psychology," *Journal of Social Issues*, vol. 49, no. 1 (1993), pp. 121–129. Copyright © 1993 by The Society for the Psychological Study of Social Issues. Reprinted by permission. References omitted.

BACKGROUND

The modern animal rights movement is intellectual and spiritual heir to the Victorian antivivisection movement in Britain (Sperling, 1988). This 19th-century movement was a powerful force in Britain and arose in part from accelerating changes brought about by science and technology (and the resulting challenges to the prevailing view of humanity's relationship to nature).

The British movement peaked in 1876 with the passage of the Cruelty to Animals Act. This compromise legislation required licenses for conducting animal research, but recognized the societal value of continuing to use animals in research. It was about this time that the scientific community began to organize a defense of animal research. Several challenges to animal research were made in the ensuing 20 years, but in the end, the medical and scientific community were able to successfully protect their interests. The Victorian antivivisection movement, however, did bring about the regulation of research and helped prevent outright abuse (Sperling, 1988).

The beginning of the modern animal rights movement is generally dated to the 1975 publication of *Animal Liberation* by philosopher Peter Singer. Although Singer himself is not an advocate of animal "rights," he provided the groundwork for later arguments that animals have rights—including the right not to be used in research. Most animal rights activists believe animals have a right not to be used for research, food, entertainment, and a variety of other purposes. An inordinate amount of attention is devoted to animal research, however, even though far fewer animals are used for research than for other purposes (Nicoll & Russell, 1990).

There has been a phenomenal growth in the animal rights movement since the publication of Singer's book. People for the Ethical Treatment of Animals (PETA), the leading animal rights organization in the United States, has grown from 18 members in 1981 to more than 250,000 members in 1990. (McCabe, 1990). By any standard, the animal rights movement is a force to be reckoned with.

PHILOSOPHICAL ISSUES

There are two basic philosophies that support the animal rights movement, although activists are often unable to articulate them (Sperling, 1988). These two positions are summarized by Herzog (1990) as the *utilitarian* argument and the *rights* argument.

The utilitarian position is that the greatest good is achieved by maximizing pleasure and happiness, and by minimizing suffering and pain. Although traditionally applied only to humans, Singer argues that animals should be included when considering the greatest good. He states, "No matter what the nature of the being, the principle of equality requires that its suffering be counted equally with the like suffering—insofar as rough comparisons can be made—of any other being" (Singer, 1990, p. 8). Utilitarians would thus argue that animals have an interest equal to that of humans in avoiding pain and suffering, and should therefore not be used in experiments that could cause them harm. Two problems with this philosophy are that (1) it is hard to draw a line between creatures that suffer and creatures that do not, and (2) the argument does not address *qualitative* differences in pain and pleasure across species (Herzog, 1990).

The rights position states that animals possess certain rights based on their inherent value. This philosophy, first developed by Tom Regan (1983), argues that animals have a right not to be used by humans in research (and for many other purposes). Major problems with this position arise in deciding just what rights are and in determining who is entitled to hold them (Herzog, 1990).

While the above positions have been developed relatively recently, the alternative view of animals as qualitatively different from humans has a long history in Judeo-Christian thought. Traditionally, humans were believed to have been created in the image of God and to have dominion over animals. Robb (1988) uses this perspective in arguing that humans are unique by virtue of their capacity for moral choice. Because of this capacity, humans can be held responsible for their choices, and can therefore enter into contractual agreements with binding rights and responsibilities for *both* parties. Robb acknowledges that some animals have human capacities in certain areas, but he argues that this does not make them morally equal to humans or give them rights that take precedence over human needs.

The most persuasive argument for using animals in behavioral research, however, is the untold benefit that accrues to both humans and animals. The benefits of behavioral research with animals have been enumerated by such authors as Miller (1985) and King and Yarbrough (1985), and for most people, these benefits are the reason that they support the continued use of animals in research. This argument—which is basically utilitarian—is the one most

often cited by the research community in defense of animal research. In contrast to Singer's utilitarianism, however, animals are not given the same degree of consideration as people.

In conclusion, both sides in the animal rights debate have philosophical underpinnings to support their position, but what often emerges in the rhetoric is not reasoned debate but emotion-laden charges and personal attacks. This is not surprising, given the strong passions aroused in the discussion.

FRAMING THE DEBATE

In the 1980s, activists targeted certain researchers or areas of research that they viewed as vulnerable to attack, and researchers were forced to assume a defensive posture. Unfortunately, activists were right about the vulnerability of individual scientists; little or no institutional defense was mounted against these early attacks. The prevailing attitude was to ignore the activists in hopes that they would go away, and thus attract less attention from the public and the press. This passivity left the early targets of animal rights activists in the position of a man asked, "Why do you beat your wife?" No matter how researchers responded, they sounded defensive and self-serving. It took several years for the research community to realize that animal rights activists were not going away, and that the activists' charges needed to be answered in a systematic and serious manner.

This early failure on the part of the research community to communicate its position effectively left the public with little information beyond what was provided by the animal rights activists. Framing the debate is half the battle, and the research community was left playing catch-up and answering the question, "Why do you abuse your research animals?"

The research community also faced the daunting task of explaining the use of animals in research to a public whose understanding of the scientific method was almost nil. The most difficult misconception to correct was the belief that every research project with animals should produce "useful" results (Orem, 1990). Social scientists who have received Senator William Proxmire's "Golden Fleece Award" are well aware of this line of thinking—a line of thinking that displays a complete misunderstanding of how science works, and ignores the vast amount of basic research that typically precedes each "useful" discovery.

It is difficult for scientific rationales to compete with shocking posters, catchy slogans, and soundbites from the animal rights movement. The most effective response from the scientific community has been to point out innumerable health advances made possible by the use of animals as research models. This approach is something that most people can relate to, since everyone has benefited from these advances.

The early defensive posture of scientists also failed to allay public concerns about the ability of researchers to self-regulate their care and use of research animals. Unlike the participation of humans in research (who are usually able to speak in their own defense and give consent), there seemed to be no one in the system able to "speak" for the animals. Or so people were encouraged to believe by animal rights activists. As discussed below, there are elaborate federal regulations on the use of animals in research, as well as state laws and professional guidelines on the care and use of animals in research.

RESTORING TRUST

Scientists, research institutions, and federal research agencies finally came to realize that the charges being leveled by animal rights activists needed to be publicly —and forcefully—rebutted. Dr. Frederick Goodwin, former Administrator of the Alcohol, Drug Abuse, and Mental Health Administration (ADAMHA), was one of the first federal officials to defend animal research publicly, and point out the difference between animal welfare and animal rights (Booth, 1989). Recently, many more federal officials and respected researchers have publicly spoken on the importance of animal research (Mervis, 1990).

Countering Misinformation

Animal rights literature often uses misleading images to depict animal research —images such as animals grimacing as they are shocked with electricity. These descriptions lead readers to believe animals are routinely subjected to high voltage shocks capable of producing convulsions (e.g., Singer, 1990, pp. 42–45). Such propaganda is far from the truth. In most cases, electric shock (when used at all) is relatively mild—similar to what one might feel from the discharge of static electricity on a cold, dry day. Even this relatively mild use of shock is carefully reviewed by Institutional Animal Care and Use Committees before being approved, and researchers must demonstrate that alternate techniques are not feasible. Stronger shock *is* used in animal research, but it is used to study medical problems such as epilepsy (a convulsive disorder). It is also used to test the effectiveness and side effects of drugs developed to control such disorders. It is not within the scope of this article to refute the myriad charges issued against animal research in general, specific projects, and individual researchers. Suffice it to say that such allegations have been persuasively refuted (Coile & Miller, 1984; Feeney, 1987; Johnson, 1990; McCabe, 1986).

Benefits to Animals
Animal rights activists often fail to appreciate the many benefits to animals that have resulted from animal research. Behavioral research has contributed to improvements in the environments of captive animals, including those used in research (Novak & Petto, 1991). The list of benefits also includes a host of veterinary procedures and the development of vaccines for deadly diseases such as rabies, Lyme disease, and feline leukemia. Research in reproductive biology and captive breeding programs are also the only hope for some animals on the brink of extinction (King et al., 1988).

Regulations and Guidelines
It is clear that many people concerned about the use of animals in research are not aware of the elaborate structure that exists to regulate the care and use of animals in research. This system includes federal regulations under the Animal Welfare Act (U.S. Department of Agriculture, 1989, 1990, 1991), Public Health Service (PHS) policy (Office for Protection from Research Risks, 1986), and state laws that govern the availability of pound animals for research.

The Animal Welfare Act, most recently amended in 1985, is enforced by the USDA's Animal and Plant Health Inspection Service (APHIS). The regulations connected with this law include 127 pages of guidelines governing the use of animals in research. It also includes unannounced inspections of animal research facilities by APHIS inspectors who do nothing but inspect research facilities. Their inspections are conducted to ensure compliance with regulations that include everything from cage size, feeding schedules, and lighting to exercise requirements for dogs and the promotion of psychological well-being among nonhuman primates.

In addition to APHIS inspectors who make unannounced inspections of animal research facilities, there are local Institutional Animal Care and Use Committees (IACUCs) that review each proposed research project using animals. Research proposals must include a justification for the species used and the number of animals required, an assurance that a thorough literature review has been conducted (to prevent unnecessary replication of research), and a consideration of alternatives if available. IACUCs are also responsible for inspecting local animal research facilities to check for continued compliance with state protocols.

Each grant proposal received by a PHS agency (National Institutes of Health, and the Centers for Disease Control) that proposes using animals must contain an assurance that it has been reviewed by an IACUC and been approved. IACUCs must have no less than five members and contain at least one veterinarian, one practicing scientist experienced in research involving animals, one member who is primarily concerned in nonscientific matters (e.g., a lawyer or ethicist), and one member who is not affiliated with the institution in any way and is not an immediate family member of anyone affiliated with the institution (Office for Protection from Research Risks, 1986; USDA, 1989).

Beyond federal animal welfare regulations, PHS policy, and the PHS Guidelines (National Research Council, 1985), there are professional guidelines for the care and use of research animals. Examples include the American Psychological Association's (APA) *Ethical Principles of Psychologists* (1990) and *Guidelines for Ethical Conduct in the Care and Use of Animals* (1993), and the Society for Neuroscience's Handbook (Society for Neuroscience, 1991).

The APA also has a Committee on Animal Research and Ethics (CARE) whose charge includes the responsibility to "review the ethics of animal experimentation and recommend guidelines for the ethical conduct of research, and appropriate care of animals in research." CARE wrote the APA's *Guidelines for Ethical Conduct in the Care and Use of Animals,* and periodically reviews it and makes revisions. These guidelines are widely used by psychologists and other scientists, and have been used in teaching research ethics at the undergraduate and graduate level. The APA's Science Directorate provided support for a conference on psychological well-being of nonhuman primates used in research, and published a volume of proceedings from that conference (Novak & Petto, 1991). The APA also helps promote research on animal welfare by membership in and support for such organizations as the American Association for the Accreditation of Laboratory Animal Care (AAALAC).

AAALAC is the only accrediting body recognized by the PHS, and sets the "gold standard" for animal research facilities. To receive AAALAC accreditation, an institution must go beyond what is required by federal animal welfare regula-

tions and PHS policy. AAALAC accreditation is highly regarded, and those institutions that receive it serve as models for the rest of the research community.

Even with all these safeguards in place, some critics question the ability of the research community to self-regulate its use of animals in research. The system can only be considered self-regulating, however, if one assumes that researchers, institutional officials, members of IACUCs (which must include a member not affiliated with the institution), USDA inspectors, animal care and lab technicians, and veterinarians have identical interests. These are the individuals with the most direct access to the animals used in research, and these are the specialists most knowledgeable about the conditions under which animals are used in research.

In several states, animal rights activists have succeeded in gaining access to IACUC meetings where animal research proposals are discussed. On the whole, however, research institutions have fought—and are still fighting—to keep these meetings closed to the general public. There is a very real fear among researchers that information gleaned from such meetings will be used to harass and target individual researchers. Given the escalating nature of illegal break-ins by such organizations as the Animal Liberation Front, this is a legitimate concern. Indeed, on some campuses "reward posters" offer money to individuals who report the abuse of research animals.

Even though IACUC meetings are generally closed to the public, the elaborate system regulating animal research is by no means a closed one. The most recent animal welfare regulations were finalized after five years of proposals recorded in the *Federal Register;* comments from the public, research institutions, professional associations, animal welfare groups, and animal rights groups; the incorporation of these comments; republication of the revised rules; and so forth. Neither researchers nor animal rights groups were entirely pleased with the final document, but everyone had their say. Although certain elements of the regulatory system rely on researchers, it is hard to imagine a workable system that would fail to use their expertise. The unspoken assumption that researchers cannot be trusted to care for their research animals is not supported by the records of APHIS inspections. Good science demands good laboratory animal care, and it is in a researcher's best interest to ensure that laboratory animals are well cared for.

The Benefits of Behavioral Research With Animals

The use of animals in psychological and behavioral research was an early target of animal rights activists. This research was perceived as a more vulnerable target than biomedical research, which had more direct and easily explained links to specific human health benefits. Psychological and behavioral research also lacked the powerful backing of the medical establishment (Archer, 1986).

There is, of course, a long list of benefits derived from psychological research with animals. These include rehabilitation of persons suffering from stroke, head injury, spinal cord injury, and Alzheimer's disease; improved communication with severely retarded children; methods for the early detection of eye disorders in children (allowing preventive treatment to avoid permanent impairment); control of chronic anxiety without the use of drugs; and improved treatments for alcoholism, obesity, substance abuse, hypertension, chronic migraine headaches, lower back pain, and insomnia (Miller, 1985). Behavioral research with nonhuman primates also permits the investigation of complex behaviors such as social organization, aggression, learning and memory, communication, and growth and development (King et al., 1988).

The nature of psychological and behavioral research makes the development and use of alternatives difficult. It is the behavior of the whole organism, and the interaction among various body systems, that is examined. Computer models may be used, but "research with animals will still be needed to provide basic data for writing computer software, as well as to prove the validity and reliability of computer alternatives" (U.S. Congress, Office of Technology Assessment, 1986). The alternative of using nonliving systems may be possible with epidemiologic data bases for some behavioral research, but chemical and physical systems are not useful for modeling complex behaviors. Likewise, in vitro cultures of organs, tissues, and cells do not display the characteristics studied by psychologists.

CONCLUSION

Research psychologists have been asked to eschew emotionalism, and bring logic and reason to the debate over animal research (Bowd, 1990). This is certainly the style most researchers are comfortable with—yet they have also been advised to quit trying to "apply logic and reason in their responses [to animal rights activists]" (Culliton, 1991). Culliton warns that while "animal rights people go for the heart, the biologists go for the head" and are losing the public in the process.

Which path is best? A reasoned approach draws high marks for civility, but will it help scientists in their trench warfare with animal rights activists?

Do animals have rights that preclude their use in laboratory research? I, and the psychologists I help represent, would say no. But researchers do have responsibilities to the animals they use in their research. These responsibilities include ensuring the humane care of their research animals, using the minimum number of animals necessary, and seeing to it that all laboratory assistants are adequately trained and supervised. As stated in the APA's *Ethical Principles,* "Laws and regulations notwithstanding, an animal's immediate protection depends upon the scientist's own conscience" (APA, 1990).

Researchers and others concerned with animal welfare can engage in a useful dialogue as standards of care and use evolve. This dialogue has proven fruitless with animal rights activists, though, since they seem unwilling to compromise or consider other viewpoints. What is the middle ground for a discussion with someone whose goal is the elimination of all research on animals?

The collective decision society has made is that the benefits derived from animal research far outweigh the costs. As public opinion polls indicate, most people are willing to accept these costs but want assurances that animals are humanely cared for. Yes, I'm "speciesist" in the eyes of Ingrid Newkirk—I will never believe my son is a dog is a pig is a rat.

NO

Alan D. Bowd and
Kenneth J. Shapiro

THE CASE AGAINST LABORATORY ANIMAL RESEARCH IN PSYCHOLOGY

In this article, we will (1) present empirical evidence documenting several serious problems with the use of animals in psychology, (2) consider philosophical objections to the use of animals in invasive research, (3) give an overview of how the research community has responded to these concerns, and (4) suggest directions for change.

THE PROBLEM

The number of nonhuman animals used in psychological research in the United States is difficult to estimate. Many species are not covered by the Animal Welfare Act and are therefore not reported as part of federally mandated inspections (Rowan & Andrutis, 1990). The Animal Legal Defense Fund (a nonprofit animal protection group) is currently challenging this loophole, but at present, rats, mice, and birds—which comprise roughly 90% of all nonhuman research subjects—are not considered "animals" under the Animal Welfare Act. Attempts to arrive at estimates from departmental surveys, analyses of *Psychological Abstracts,* and extrapolations from countries where better records are kept all have their limitations, but integrating these sources of information, we estimate that roughly 1–2 million animals are used in psychological research each year.

Although some laboratory animals are obtained from shelters—a practice that is illegal in 14 states and is abhorred by a majority of the public—most laboratory animals are "purpose bred" for research. This method of procuring subjects is not without problems, however. For example, the legal office of the United States Department of Agriculture is currently investigating a major producer of animals for alleged abuse (Holden, 1990). Other problems with producing animals for laboratory research arise from selective breeding and genetic engineering. Producing animals that are susceptible to audiogenic seizures or cancerous tumors, or that adapt well to confinement, raises significant ethical questions (President's Commission, 1982).

From Alan D. Bowd and Kenneth J. Shapiro, "The Case Against Laboratory Animal Research in Psychology," *Journal of Social Issues,* vol. 49, no. 1 (1993), pp. 133–142. Copyright © 1993 by The Society for the Psychological Study of Social Issues. Reprinted by permission. References omitted.

Invasiveness in Research

In reviewing laboratory practices, it is important to distinguish between the experimental procedure itself and pre- or post-experimental care (i.e., "husbandry"). It is also critical to separate individual cases of abuse from customary practices. The case of the Silver Spring monkeys, for example, is an instance of individual abuse that became a cause célèbre of the animal rights movement. Charges against psychologist Edward Taub centered on abusive husbandry practices—inadequate veterinary care, food, ventilation, and cage space. However, much of the public outcry reflected objections to the experimental procedure (deafferentation) itself (Shapiro, 1989).

An example of a routine experimental procedure under scrutiny is the use of chair restraints. Primates that are chair restrained as part of a study spend a mean time of 5.7 hours confined in the chair each day (Bayne, 1991). An example of a customary husbandry practice under scrutiny is the housing of primates in individual cages. In one survey, 84% of the investigators housed their adult primates singly (Bayne, 1991), despite the importance of social interaction to these animals. Thus, quite apart from any trauma induced by experimental procedures, the animals suffered from routine husbandry practices.

Contrary to what defenders of animal research often say, a good deal of psychological research is highly invasive. Many studies involve stress, pain, punishment, social and environmental deprivation, and induced emotional and intellectual deficits. In their "scale of invasiveness," Field and Shapiro (1988) operationalized the term to encompass suffering and harm before, during, or after an experimental procedure. By this definition, most investigators targeted by the animal rights movement have conducted highly invasive research (e.g., maternal deprivation and drug addiction in macaques, physiology of taste in rats, visual deprivation in kittens). Beyond their invasiveness, these studies have been criticized for their nongeneralizability, redundancy, purely theoretical focus, parametric tinkering, and diversion of funds from treatment programs.

Areas of highly invasive research have shifted over time. In 1947, electroconvulsive shock and audiogenic seizures were prevalent, while in 1967 punishment, brain lesioning, and the administration of curare were more common (Field, 1988). The most frequently cited invasive studies in popular college introductory psychology textbooks (1984–1988 editions) are infant maternal deprivation, perceptual restriction in newborns, brain studies of the eating/satiety center, and learned helplessness (Field, 1990).

As a popular college major, psychology influences thousands of students each year. Typically, psychology coursework includes direct exposure to animal research in laboratories and/or indirect exposure through texts and audiovisual materials that feature animal research. Yet descriptions of invasive research in popular psychology textbooks are often sanitized (Field, 1989). For example, most discussions of Harlow's work on maternal deprivation—the most frequently cited invasive experiment—minimize the suffering involved, present pictures of "cute" animals, and omit reference to the subjective experience of the animals.

ETHICAL ISSUES

The animal rights movement began to have an impact on psychology shortly after the publication of Singer's *Animal Liberation* and Ryder's *Victims of Science* (both in 1975). Both books targeted behavioral research in particular for its painful and unnecessary experiments. The ethical foundation of the animal rights movement has since been broadened to include several other discourses: Regan (1983) provided a theory of rights to complement Singer's utilitarianism, Adams (1990) developed a feminist discourse that linked the subjugation of animals with patriarchy, and several authors provided theological perspectives on the use of animals (Linzey, 1987; McDaniel, 1989; Regenstein, 1991).

Experimental psychologists have been forced to defend their ethical positions with rational arguments. Many psychologists consider ethics a matter of personal preference, a view that exempts individuals from public scrutiny and justifies individual self-regulation. Others have attempted to reduce ethics to science, arguing that ethics is a naturally evolved phenomenon and that regulation from outside the field is inappropriate (e.g., Gallup & Suarez, 1980). However, the burgeoning field of moral philosophy suggests that ethical positions—like any other human beliefs—are subject to logical examination, and may be found to be ambiguous or contradictory.

Following Ryder (1989) and Rollin (1981), here we propose an ethic that draws upon the work of both Singer and Regan. To wit:

Interests and rights are not the sole preserve of the human species, and should be evaluated consistently and with due consideration to an animal's capacity to suffer. Our ethical obligations extend to individuals who are intellectually unable to reciprocate them, within and beyond our own species. Those who would accord rights to human beings but deny them to all other species must make the case that there is a morally relevant difference separating *Homo sapiens* from other creatures. We do not believe such a difference exists.

All creatures capable of experiencing pain and other forms of suffering have an interest in being spared it, and the rights that flow from this interest vary from individual to individual and species to species. Although this point may seem obvious, animal protectionists are often ridiculed for believing all animals are identical or for advocating that farm animals be given the right to vote. Such caricatures (usually based on quotations taken out of context) make easy targets and avoid serious discussion.

Many proponents of invasive research argue that the work is justified by morally relevant differences that exist between the human species and all others. However, by focusing on attributes such as intelligence, empathy, and a sense of moral responsibility (e.g., Fox, 1986; King, 1986), they exclude young children and developmentally delayed adults from moral consideration. Because humans and nonhumans overlap on some of these dimensions (e.g., intelligence, self-awareness), and because young or impaired humans wholly lack other characteristics (e.g., empathy, sense of moral responsibility), there is simply no morally relevant attribute that separates humans from nonhumans. To base ethical decisions on species membership alone in the absence of such an attribute is as arbitrary as relying on skin color or gender in hiring decisions.

The most morally relevant factor in a decision to cause suffering to others is their ability to experience it. Cognitive competence and related abilities are relevant to certain human rights (such as the right to vote), but not to other rights (such as the freedom to move one's limbs or to interact with others). Research justified by consequent human benefit abridges these rights. We feel methods involving inescapable pain, deprivation, or fear are unacceptable because each sentient being, regardless of its other capabilities, has an interest in being spared suffering. Modern-day society rejects the notion of performing painful experiments on humans who are incapable of granting consent, regardless of the benefits which might accrue to others. In the absence of morally relevant distinctions between ourselves and other animals, painful research on sentient nonhumans should be rejected for the same reasons.

THE RESPONSE FROM PSYCHOLOGISTS

Social constructionists and others have recently noted the Western, ethnocentric, and male-dominated agenda of traditional psychological research (Gergen, 1985; Hare-Mustin & Marecek, 1990; Irvine & Berry, 1988). The broad cultural changes represented by the women's movement, environmentalism, and the animal rights movement have been instrumental in fomenting the current debate within psychology regarding animal research, and many analysts now view the practice of invasive laboratory-based research as symptomatic of anthropocentrism in psychology.

Within the psychological community, a growing number of individuals have expressed reservations about animal research on both scientific and ethical grounds (Bowd, 1980, 1990; Fox, 1982; Giannelli, 1985; Segal, 1982; Shapiro, 1991;

Ulrich, 1991). Nonetheless, many psychologists have defended current practices. We will first examine organizational responses and then discuss responses within the professional literature. The focus will be on developments in the United States, though it should be noted that similar debates are taking place among psychologists in Canada, Great Britain, Australia, and other countries.

Organizational Responses

In 1981, the American Psychological Association (APA) amended its Ethics Code to include the treatment of animals (American Psychological Association [APA], 1981). However, the APA Ethics Committee considered only one animal welfare case from 1982 to 1990 (APA, 1991)—a period during which the animal rights movement charged several laboratories with specific animal welfare violations. The Ethics Committee considered the case of Edward Taub, a psychologist who studied deafferentation (the severing of sensory nerves) in macaque monkeys at the Institute for Behavioral Research in Maryland. This case came to light after Alex Pacheco, cofounder of People for the Ethical Treatment of Animals, documented several explicit violations of animal welfare regulations.

According to Principle 10 of the current Ethics Code, researchers must ensure that "The acquisition, care, use and disposal of all animals are in compliance of current Federal, state or provincial, and local laws and regulations" (APA, 1981). After reviewing Pacheco's evidence, the National Institutes of Health (NIH) suspended Taub's grant because of violations in NIH guidelines, and Taub was convicted of cruelty to animals under Maryland law (a verdict that he later appealed). Nevertheless, even though the suspension of funding and the conviction of animal cruelty were known by members of the APA Ethics Committee, the panel cleared Taub of any wrongdoing on a split vote.

A second APA body charged with overseeing animal welfare, the Committee on Animal Research and Ethics (CARE), was established in 1925 "to combat attempts to prevent or restrict [animal experimentation]" (Young, 1928). In fact, the two events that led to the formation of CARE were both legislative efforts, outside APA, to curtail animal research (Young, 1928; Young, 1930). For the first 50 years of its existence, CARE's stated purpose was to defend and protect animal *research*, not *animals*. It was not until the early 1980s that the task of protecting animals was added (CARE, 1980), and even then the meetings continued to focus on the protection of animal research and animal researchers (Bernstein, personal communication, 1990). Furthermore, Field, Shapiro, and Carr (1990) found that the animal research conducted by recent CARE chairs was more invasive than comparable research published in leading journals. Thus, the APA responded to ethical challenges by forming advocacy groups rather than impartial or balanced review panels.

Responses Within the Professional Literature

APA publications have discussed animal welfare with increasing frequency in recent years (Phillips & Sechzer, 1989). However, in its scientific and news publications, the APA often takes a one-sided position (Bowd, 1990). We examined issues of the *APA Monitor* from 1980 to 1986, and found 30 articles and 43 letters dealing with the ethics of animal research. By our estimate, roughly 60% supported animal research and only 10% opposed it explicitly. Similarly, the *American Psychologist* published 17 relevant articles or commentaries during the same period, 10 advocating animal research and 7 opposing it. Of the 5 full-length articles that appeared during this interval, 4 explicitly supported animal research.

A recent article in the *APA Monitor* typifies this slant in coverage. Moses (1991) described how psychology students were upset by a laboratory break-in, but failed to mention a much more widespread source of student concern about animal research—the refusal of faculty to provide alternatives to the laboratory study of animals. In a recent survey of 300 psychology departments, one of the authors (KJS) found that 50% of the departments used animals in education, and of these, only 40% had a policy to accommodate students who objected.

Indeed, not only do APA publications neglect to mention such problems—the APA actively discourages their discussion. For example, the APA refused to sell exhibit space at its 1991 convention to Psychologists for the Ethical Treatment of Animals for the purpose of displaying publications, although other organizations were provided with space to display animal research publications and catalogues of laboratory equipment (Shapiro, 1990).

Turning to the scientific literature, most accounts defend animal research with some version of the following arguments: (1) animal research leads to applications that improve human welfare; (2) the costs to animals are relatively small; (3) whatever harm the animals incur is necessary, because there are no viable alternatives to animal research (Gallup & Suarez, 1985; King, 1984; Miller, 1985).

The tenor of these articles tends to be indignant, adversarial, and defensive. In fact, in their survey of the scientific literature, Phillips and Sechzer (1989) found a marked increase in defensiveness between the 1960s and the 1980s. Gluck and Kubacki (1991) have also described a "strategic defensive posture" assumed by researchers, part of which is to trivialize the issue of animal protection. For example, some researchers trivialize the issue by pointing out that laboratory rats fare better than their uncaged city conspecifics (e.g., Gallup & Suarez, 1987). Typically, there is little empirical evidence offered to support such assertions, and in many cases, the arguments are specious (Shapiro, 1988). For example, Gallup and Suarez (1987) failed to provide evidence about the relative welfare of laboratory and feral rats, although data are available regarding invasiveness of procedures undergone by the former, and Hendrickson (1983) found that rats in urban nonlaboratory settings often proliferate and live quite well. Furthermore, the suffering of laboratory rats is additional; its cost must be added to whatever suffering other rats endure. The argument advanced by Gallup and Suarez (1987) is particularly ironic given their portrayal of scientists as rational and animal activists as illogical and emotional.

Assessment of Costs and Benefits
Miller (1985) and other authors have claimed that animal research generates applications that improve human welfare. However, Kelly (1986) found that in the 1984 volume of the *Journal of Consulting and Clinical Psychology* (a journal devoted to studies of the treatments Miller explicitly linked to animal research), only 0.3% of more than 3,000 citations were of laboratory animal studies. In addition, Giannelli (1985) found that only seven of the 118 citations selected by Miller to demonstrate the value of animal research were listed in the 1985 Association for Advanced Training in the Behavioral Sciences, a well-known and comprehensive course for national licensure in psychology. Even more problematically, the potential benefits of any animal research are indeterminate, for they depend on several unknowns: the applicability of the results to human welfare, the question of whether the study will get published (rejection rates for mainstream psychology journals are over 50%), and more subtly, the *missed benefits of studies not undertaken*. Any research program implies paths not taken.

In contrast to the uncertain benefits from laboratory animal research, the cost to animals is clear and real. Reliable measures of the cost to animals do exist (Field & Shapiro, 1988), yet virtually no published study—or study proposal—presents detailed analyses of the costs of husbandry conditions, experimental procedures, and disposition of the animals. In any case, any analysis of costs to animals presumes they are willing participants. In truth, in the current research enterprise they are commodities produced, confined, and harmed in a system in which they are only incidental beneficiaries. Yet in our Western tradition, individuals have rights that safeguard against their welfare being compromised for the benefit of others. Because of these operational and ethical problems, cost–benefit analyses are an unsatisfactory tool in the assessment of the use of animals in research.

SUGGESTED DIRECTIONS

As an interim strategy, we favor the following: (1) the development of alternatives to laboratory animal research; (2) the specification and prohibition of experimental procedures that are deemed "intrinsically objectionable" (Heim, 1978) —that is, procedures generally agreed to be so invasive that they are objectionable regardless of possible benefits; and (3) a reduced reliance on the search for animal models of complex, culturally generated human phenomena. These practices should replace the hollow, justificatory language of cost–benefit analyses. In the longer term, we favor a shift from laboratory-based invasive research to minimally manipulative research conducted in naturalistic and seminaturalistic settings.

We urge psychologists, individually and through professional societies such as the APA, to (1) establish advocacy committees charged solely with the protection of animals used in psychology-related settings, (2) develop alternatives for students who object to the use of laboratory animals, and (3) include balanced coverage of animal welfare issues and a discussion of ethical issues in professional and textbook publications. Such policies will not only contribute to animal welfare—they will contribute to *human* welfare by broadening the education of tomorrow's psychologists.

CHALLENGE QUESTIONS

Should Animals Be Used in Psychological Research?

1. How and where would you draw the line on the use of animals in research? Even if the use of animals is justified in research that saves human lives, is the use of animals justified in cosmetic or plastic surgery research? Why, or why not?

2. Assuming you were against all instances of animal research, would you turn down medical procedures for yourself or your children because they were developed at the expense of animals? Would there be exceptions, such as vaccinations for your children or a cure for a life-threatening illness?

3. Baldwin makes the case that experimentation with animals has produced many important medical and psychological findings. Are there other types of research that use animals? Is this other research justified? Why, or why not?

4. Baldwin claims that the use of animals in research has been beneficial to animals also. Does this claim change the debate?

5. Locate the federal and state regulations on the use and care of animals in psychological research, and evaluate both authors' claims regarding the sufficiency of those regulations.

PART 2

Human Development

The goal of developmental psychologists is to document the course of our physical, social, and intellectual changes over a life span. Considerable attention has been paid to the childhood part of that life span because this period of development seems to set the stage for later periods. Four potential influences on childhood are debated here: television, formal schooling, parental divorce, and punishment.

- Does Viewing Television Increase a Child's Aggression?

- Is a Child's Development Negatively Affected by a Working Mother?

- Are Children of Divorced Parents at Greater Risk?

- Do Physically Punished Children Become Violent Adults?

ISSUE 4

Does Viewing Television Increase a Child's Aggression?

YES: Brandon S. Centerwall, from "Television and Violent Crime," *The Public Interest* (Spring 1993)

NO: Brian Siano, from "Frankenstein Must Be Destroyed: Chasing the Monster of TV Violence," *The Humanist* (January/February 1994)

ISSUE SUMMARY

YES: Brandon S. Centerwall, an epidemiologist, argues that children act out the violence they see on television and carry the violent behaviors into adulthood.

NO: Brian Siano, a writer and researcher, believes that children with nonnurturing parents, regardless of the children's television viewing habits, tend to be more aggressive than children who closely identified with either parent.

Survey after survey shows that one of the primary concerns of contemporary society is violence. The popular perception is that violence is on the rise. Indeed, some people believe that violence is like some contagious disease that has spread to epidemic proportions. What is the reason for this seeming "epidemic"? Why does the current generation appear to be more prone to violence than previous generations? How is today so different from the "good old days"?

Many people would sum up that difference in one word—television. Television now occupies a place (or two or three) in almost every home in the United States, regardless of the inhabitants' race or level of income. And television has been cited time and again by the U.S. surgeon general, by members of the U.S. Congress, and by psychological researchers as a medium filled with many kinds of violence. It seems only natural for parents to wonder about television's impact on small children, who average over 20 hours of television viewing per week. Indeed, some have suggested that a child witnesses over 100,000 acts of violence on television before graduating from elementary school. How do these acts of violence affect a child's development?

In the following selection, Brandon S. Centerwall asserts that televised violence leads to an increase in a child's aggression, referring to numerous published studies to support this assertion. He theorizes that children have an instinctive desire to imitate behavior. Unfortunately, however, children are not born with an instinct for evaluating the appropriateness of certain actions. This means that children naturally model what they see on television and do not typically think about whether or not they *should* model what they see. Consequently, even when clearly antisocial behaviors are depicted on television, children are still likely to learn and imitate them. Centerwall believes that the danger to a child's development is so great that he advocates making television violence a part of the public health agenda.

In contrast, Brian Siano contends that factors other than television are more influential on a child's tendency for violent actions. He points to research that contradicts Centerwall's views. For example, one study found that boys who watch nonviolent shows tend to be more aggressive than boys who watch violent television. Siano argues that style of parenting is a better indicator of the development of violent behavior. Children of nonnurturing parents and children who do not identify with their parents are the ones most likely to exhibit violence. Although Siano is an advocate of quality programming, he is reluctant to indiscriminately censor all violence from television, particularly when effective parenting can counter any possible ill effects.

POINT	COUNTERPOINT
• Parents who watched more television as children punished their own children more severely.	• Boys who watch nonviolent shows tend to be more aggressive than boys who watch violent shows.
• Children are incapable of discriminating between what they should and should not imitate.	• Good parents teach children how to discriminate among their behaviors.
• Limiting all children's exposure to television violence should become part of the public health agenda.	• Violence can be used in television shows for pro-social reasons.
• Many studies demonstrate a positive relationship between television exposure and physical aggression.	• Parental identification can change the way children interpret physical punishment on television.
• For children to be safe, television violence must be eliminated.	• Indiscriminate censorship of all violence is too high a price to pay for the minimal influence of television.

YES
Brandon S. Centerwall

TELEVISION AND VIOLENT CRIME

Children are born ready to imitate adult behavior. That they can, and do, imitate an array of adult facial expressions has been demonstrated in newborns as young as a few hours old, before they are even old enough to know that they have facial features. It is a most useful instinct, for the developing child must learn and master a vast repertoire of behavior in short order.

But while children have an instinctive desire to imitate, they do not possess an instinct for determining whether a behavior ought to be imitated. They will imitate anything, including behavior that most adults regard as destructive and antisocial. It may give pause for thought, then, to learn that infants as young as fourteen months demonstrably observe and incorporate behavior seen on television.

The average American preschooler watches more than twenty-seven hours of television per week. This might not be bad if these young children understood what they were watching. But they don't. Up through ages three and four, most children are unable to distinguish fact from fantasy on TV, and remain unable to do so despite adult coaching. In the minds of young children, television is a source of entirely factual information regarding how the world works. There are no limits to their credulity. To cite one example, an Indiana school board had to issue an advisory to young children that, no, there is no such thing as Teenage Mutant Ninja Turtles. Children had been crawling down storm drains looking for them.

Naturally, as children get older, they come to know better, but their earliest and deepest impressions are laid down at an age when they still see television as a factual source of information about the outside world. In that world, it seems, violence is common and the commission of violence is generally powerful, exciting, charismatic, and effective. In later life, serious violence is most likely to erupt at moments of severe stress—and it is precisely at such moments that adolescents and adults are most likely to revert to their earliest, most visceral sense of the role of violence in society and in personal behavior. Much of this sense will have come from television.

From Brandon S. Centerwall, "Television and Violent Crime," *The Public Interest*, no. 111 (Spring 1993), pp. 56–71. Copyright © 1993 by National Affairs, Inc. Reprinted by permission.

THE SEEDS OF AGGRESSION

In 1973, a remote rural community in Canada acquired television for the first time. The acquisition of television at such a late date was due to problems with signal reception rather than any hostility toward TV. As reported in *The Impact of Television* (1986), Tannis Williams and her associates at the University of British Columbia investigated the effect of television on the children of this community (which they called "Notel"), taking for comparison two similar towns that already had television.

The researchers observed forty-five first- and second-graders in the three towns for rates of inappropriate physical aggression before television was introduced into Notel. Two years later, the same forty-five children were observed again. To prevent bias in the data, the research assistants who collected the data were kept uninformed as to why the children's rates of aggression were of interest. Furthermore, a new group of research assistants was employed the second time around, so that the data gatherers would not be biased by recollections of the children's behavior two years earlier.

Rates of aggression did not change in the two control communities. By contrast, the rate of aggression among Notel children increased 160 percent. The increase was observed in both boys and girls, in those who were aggressive to begin with and in those who were not. Television's enhancement of noxious aggression was entirely general and not limited to a few "bad apples."

In another Canadian study, Gary Granzberg and his associates at the University of Winnipeg investigated the impact of television upon Indian communities in northern Manitoba. As described in *Television and the Canadian Indian* (1980), forty-nine third-, fourth-, and fifth-grade boys living in two communities were observed from 1973, when one town acquired television, until 1977, when the second town did as well. The aggressiveness of boys in the first community increased after the introduction of television. The aggressiveness of boys in the second community, which did not receive television then, remained the same. When television was later introduced in the second community, observed levels of aggressiveness increased there as well.

In another study conducted from 1960 to 1981, Leonard Eron and L. Rowell Huesmann (then of the University of Illinois at Chicago) followed 875 children living in a semirural U.S. county. Eron and Huesmann found that for both boys and girls, the amount of television watched at age eight predicted the seriousness of criminal acts for which they were convicted by age thirty. This remained true even after controlling for the children's baseline aggressiveness, intelligence, and socioeconomic status. Eron and Huesmann also observed second-generation effects. Children who watched much television at age eight later, as parents, punished their own children more severely than did parents who had watched less television as children. Second- and now third-generation effects are accumulating at a time of unprecedented youth violence.

All seven of the U.S. and Canadian studies of prolonged childhood exposure to television demonstrate a positive relationship between exposure and physical aggression. The critical period is preadolescent childhood. Later exposure does not appear to produce any additional effect. However, the aggression-enhancing effect of exposure in pre-adolescence extends into adolescence and adulthood. This suggests that any interventions should be designed for children and their caregivers rather than for the general adult population.

These studies confirmed the beliefs of most Americans. According to a Harris poll at the time of the studies, 43 percent of American adults believe that television violence "plays a part in making America a violent society." An additional 37 percent think it might. But how important is television violence? What is the effect of exposure upon entire populations? To address this question, I took advantage of an historical accident—the absence of television in South Africa prior to 1975.

THE SOUTH AFRICAN EXPERIENCE

White South Africans have lived in a prosperous, industrialized society for decades, but they did not get television until 1975 because of tension between the Afrikaner- and English-speaking communities. The country's Afrikaner leaders knew that a South African television industry would have to rely on British and American shows to fill out its programming schedule, and they felt that this would provide an unacceptable cultural advantage to English-speaking South Africans. So, rather than negotiate a complicated compromise, the government simply forbade television broadcasting. The entire population of two million whites—rich and poor, urban and rural, educated and uneducated—was thus excluded from exposure to television for a quarter century after the medium was introduced in the United States.

In order to determine whether exposure to television is a cause of violence, I compared homicide rates in South Africa, Canada, and the United States. Since blacks in South Africa live under quite different conditions than blacks in the United States, I limited the comparison to white homicide rates in South Africa and the United States, and the total homicide rate in Canada (which was 97 percent white in 1951).[1] I chose the homicide rate as a measure of violence because homicide statistics are exceptionally accurate.

From 1945 to 1974, the white homicide rate in the United States increased 93 percent. In Canada, the homicide rate increased 92 percent. In South Africa, where television was banned, the white homicide rate declined by 7 percent.

CONTROLLING FOR OTHER FACTORS

Could there be some explanation other than television for the fact that violence increased dramatically in the U.S. and Canada while dropping in South Africa? I examined an array of alternative explanations. None is satisfactory:

- **Economic growth.** Between 1946 and 1974, all three countries experienced substantial economic growth. Per capita income increased by 75 percent in the United States, 124 percent in Canada, and 86 percent in South Africa. Thus differences in economic growth cannot account for the different homicide trends in the three countries.

- **Civil unrest.** One might suspect that anti-war or civil-rights activity was responsible for the doubling of the homicide rate in the United States during this period. But the experience of Canada shows that this was not the case, since Canadians suffered a doubling of the homicide rate without similar civil unrest.

Other possible explanations include changes in age distribution, urbanization, alcohol consumption, capital punishment, and the availability of firearms. As discussed in *Public Communication and Behavior* (1989), none provides a viable explanation for the observed homicide trends.

In the United States and Canada, there was a lag of ten to fifteen years between the introduction of television and a doubling of the homicide rate. In South Africa, there was a similar lag. Since television exerts its behavior-modifying effects primarily on children, while homicide is primarily an adult activity, this lag represents the time needed for the "television generation" to come of age.

The relationship between television and the homicide rate holds *within* the United States as well. Different regions of the U.S., for example, acquired television at different times. As we would expect, while all regions saw increases in their homicide rates, the regions that acquired television first were also the first to see higher homicide rates.

Similarly, urban areas acquired television before rural areas. As we would expect, urban areas saw increased homicide rates several years before the occurrence of a parallel increase in rural areas.

The introduction of television also helps explain the different rates of homicide growth for whites and minorities. White households in the U.S. began acquiring television sets in large numbers approximately five years before minority households. Significantly, the white homicide rate began increasing in 1958, four years before a parallel increase in the minority homicide rate.

Of course, there are many factors other than television that influence the amount of violent crime. Every violent act is the result of a variety of forces coming together—poverty, crime, alcohol and drug abuse, stress—of which childhood TV exposure is just one. Nevertheless, the evidence indicates that if, hypothetically, television technology had never been developed, there would today be 10,000 fewer homicides each year in the United States, 70,000 fewer rapes, and 700,000 fewer injurious assaults. Violent crime would be half what it is.

THE TELEVISION INDUSTRY TAKES A LOOK

The first congressional hearings on television and violence were held in 1952, when not even a quarter of U.S. households owned television sets. In the years since, there have been scores of research reports on the issue, as well as several major government investigations. The findings of the National Commission on the Causes and Prevention of Violence, published in 1969, were particularly significant. This report established what is now the broad scientific consensus: Exposure to television increases rates of physical aggression.

Television industry executives were genuinely surprised by the National Commission's report. What the industry produced was at times unedifying, but physically harmful? In response, network executives began research programs that collectively would cost nearly a million dollars.

CBS commissioned William Belson to undertake what would be the largest and most sophisticated study yet, an investigation involving 1,565 teenage boys. In *Television Violence and the Adolescent Boy* (1978), Belson controlled for one hundred variables, and found that teenage boys who had watched above-average quantities of television violence before adolescence were committing acts of serious violence (e.g., assault, rape, major vandalism, and abuse of animals) at a rate 49 percent higher than teenage boys who had watched below-average quantities of television violence. Despite the large sum of money they had invested, CBS executives were notably unenthusiastic about the report.

ABC commissioned Melvin Heller and Samuel Polsky of Temple University to study young male felons imprisoned for violent crimes (e.g, homicide, rape, and assault). In two surveys, 22 and 34 percent of the young felons reported having consciously imitated crime techniques learned from television programs, usually successfully. The more violent of these felons were the most likely to report having learned techniques from television. Overall, the felons reported that as children they had watched an average of six hours of television per day—approximately twice as much as children in the general population at that time.

Unlike CBS, ABC maintained control over publication. The final report, *Studies in Violence and Television* (1976), was published in a private, limited edition that was not released to the general public or the scientific community.

NBC relied on a team of four researchers, three of whom were employees of NBC. Indeed, the principal investigator, J. Ronald Milavsky, was an NBC vice president. The team observed some 2,400 schoolchildren for up to three years to see if watching television violence increased their levels of physical aggressiveness. In *Television and Aggression* (1982), Milavsky and his associates reported that television violence had no effect upon the children's behavior. However, every independent investigator who has examined their data has concluded that, to the contrary, their data show that television violence did cause a modest increase of about 5 percent in average levels of physical aggressiveness. When pressed on the point, Milavsky and his associates conceded that their findings were consistent with the conclusion that television violence increased physical aggressiveness "to a small extent." They did not concede that television violence actually caused an increase, but only that their findings were consistent with such a conclusion.

The NBC study results raise an important objection to my conclusions. While studies have repeatedly demonstrated that childhood exposure to television increases physical aggressiveness, the increase is almost always quite minor. A number of investigators have argued that such a small effect is too weak to account for major increases in rates of violence. These investigators, however, overlook a key factor.

Homicide is an extreme form of aggression—so extreme that only one person in 20,000 committed murder each year in the United States in the mid-1950s. If we were to rank everyone's degree of physical aggressiveness from the least aggressive (Mother Theresa) to the most aggressive (Jack the Ripper), the large majority of us would be somewhere in the middle and murderers would be virtually off the chart. It is an intrinsic property of such "bell curve" distributions that small changes in the average imply major changes at the extremes. Thus, if exposure to television causes 8 percent of the population to shift from below-average aggression to above-average aggression, it follows that the homicide rate will double. The findings of the NBC study and the doubling of the homicide rate are two sides of the same coin.

After the results of these studies became clear, television industry executives lost their enthusiasm for scientific research. No further investigations were funded. Instead, the industry turned to political management of the issue.

THE TELEVISION INDUSTRY AND SOCIAL RESPONSIBILITY

The television industry routinely portrays individuals who seek to influence programming as un-American haters of free speech. In a 1991 letter sent to 7,000 executives of consumer product companies and advertising agencies, the president of the Network Television Association explained:

> Freedom of expression is an inalienable right of all Americans vigorously supported by ABC, CBS, and NBC. However, boycotts and so-called advertiser "hit lists" are attempts to manipulate our free society and democratic process.

The letter went on to strongly advise the companies to ignore all efforts by anyone to influence what programs they choose to sponsor. By implication, the networks themselves should ignore all efforts by anyone to influence what programs they choose to produce.

But this is absurd. All forms of public discourse are attempts to "manipulate" our free society and democratic process. What else could they be? Consumer boycotts are no more un-American than are strikes by labor unions. The Network Television Association is attempting to systematically shut down all discourse between viewers and advertisers, and between viewers and the television industry. Wrapping itself in patriotism, the television industry's response to uppity viewers is to put them in their place. If the industry and advertisers were to actually succeed in closing the circle between them, the only course they would leave for concerned viewers would be to seek legislative action.

In the war against tobacco, we do not expect help from the tobacco industry. If someone were to call upon the tobacco industry to cut back production as a matter of social conscience and concern for public health, we would regard that person as simple-minded, if not frankly deranged. Oddly enough, however, people have persistently assumed that the television industry is somehow different— that it is useful to appeal to its social conscience. This was true in 1969 when the National Commission on the Causes and Prevention of Violence published its recommendations for the television industry. It was equally true in 1989 when the U.S. Congress passed an anti-violence bill that granted television industry executives the authority to hold discussions on the issue of television violence without violating antitrust laws. Even before the law was passed, the four networks stated that there would be no substantive changes in their programming. They have been as good as their word.

For the television industry, issues of "quality" and "social responsibility" are peripheral to the issue of maximizing audience size—and there is no formula more tried and true than violence for generating large audiences. To television executives, this is crucial. For if advertising revenue were to decrease by just 1 percent, the television industry would stand to lose $250 million in revenue annually. Thus, changes in audience size that appear trivial to most of us are regarded as catastrophic by the industry. For this reason, industry spokespersons have made innumerable protestations of good intent, but nothing has happened. In the more than twenty years that levels of television violence have been monitored, there has been no downward movement. There are no recommendations to make to the television industry. To make any would not only be futile but could create the false impression that the industry might actually do something constructive.

On December 11, 1992, the networks finally announced a list of voluntary guidelines on television violence. Curiously, reporters were unable to locate any network producers who felt the new guidelines would require changes in their programs. That raises a question: Who is going to bell the cat? Who is going to place his or her career in jeopardy in order to decrease the amount of violence on television? It is hard to say, but it may be revealing that when Senator Paul Simon held the press conference announcing the new inter-network agreement, no industry executives were present to answer questions.

MEETING THE CHALLENGE

Television violence is everybody's problem. You may feel assured that your child will never become violent despite a steady diet of television mayhem, but you cannot be assured that your child won't be murdered or maimed by someone else's child raised on a similar diet.

The American Academy of Pediatrics recommends that parents limit their children's television viewing to one to two hours per day. But why wait for a pediatrician to say it? Limiting children's exposure to television violence should become part of the public health agenda, along with safety seats, bicycle helmets, immunizations, and good nutrition. Part of the public health approach should be to promote child-care alternatives to the electronic babysitter, especially among the poor.

Parents should also guide what their children watch and how much. This is an old recommendation that can be given new teeth with the help of modern technology. It is now feasible to fit a television set with an electronic lock that permits parents to preset the channels and times for which the set will be available; if a particular program or time of day is locked, the set will not operate then. Time-channel locks are not merely feasible; they have already been designed and are coming off the assembly line.

The model for making them widely available comes from closed-captioning circuitry, which permits deaf and hard-of-hearing persons access to television. Market forces alone would not have made closed-captioning available to more than a fraction of the deaf and hard-of-hearing. To remedy this problem, Congress passed the Television Decoder Circuitry Act in 1990, which requires that virtually all new television sets be manufactured with built-in closed-captioning circuitry. A similar law should require that all new television sets be manufactured with built-in time-channel lock circuitry—and for a similar reason. Market forces alone will not make this technology available to more than a fraction of households with children and will exclude most poor families, the ones who suffer the most from violence. If we can make television technology available to benefit twenty-four million deaf and hard-of-hearing Americans, surely we can do no less for the benefit of fifty million American children.

A final recommendation: Television programs should be accompanied by a violence rating so that parents can judge how violent a program is without having to watch it. Such a rating system should be quantitative, leaving aesthetic and social judgments to the viewers. This approach would enjoy broad popular support. In a *Los Angeles Times* poll, 71 percent of adult Americans favored the establishment of a TV violence rating system. Such a system would not impinge on artistic freedom since producers would remain free to produce programs with high violence ratings. They could even use high violence ratings in the advertisements for their shows.

None of these recommendations would limit freedom of speech. That is as it should be. We do not address the problem of motor vehicle fatalities by calling for a ban on cars. Instead, we emphasize safety seats, good traffic signs, and driver education. Similarly, to address the problem of television-inspired violence, we need to promote time-channel locks, program rating systems, and viewer education about the hazards of violent programming. In this way we can protect our children and our society.

NOTES

1. The "white homicide rate" refers to the rate at which whites are the victims of homicide. Since most homicide is intra-racial, this closely parallels the rate at which whites commit homicide.

REFERENCES

William A. Belson, *Television Violence and the Adolescent Boy*. Westmead, England: Saxon House (1978).

Brandon S. Centerwall, "Exposure to Television as a Cause of Violence," *Public Communication and Behavior*, Vol. 2. Orlando, Florida: Academic Press (1989), pp. 1–58.

Leonard D. Eron and L. Rowell Huesmann, "The Control of Aggressive Behavior by Changes in Attitudes, Values, and the Conditions of Learning," *Advances in the Study of Aggression*. Orlando, Florida: Academic Press (1984), pp. 139–171.

Gary Granzberg and Jack Steinbring (eds.), *Television and the Canadian Indian*. Winnipeg, Manitoba: University of Winnipeg (1980).

L. Rowell Huesmann and Leonard D. Eron, *Television and the Aggressive Child*. Hillsdale, New Jersey: Lawrence Erlbaum Associates (1986), pp. 45–80.

Candace Kruttschnitt, et al., "Family Violence, Television Viewing Habits, and Other Adolescent Experiences Related to Violent Criminal Behavior," *Criminology*, Vol. 24 (1986), pp. 235–267.

Andrew N. Meltzoff, "Memory in Infancy," *Encyclopedia of Learning and Memory*. New York: Macmillan (1992), pp. 271–275.

J. Ronald Milavsky, et al., *Television and Aggression*. Orlando, Florida: Academic Press (1982).

Jerome L. Singer, et al., "Family Patterns and Television Viewing as Predictors of Children's Beliefs and Aggression," *Journal of Communication*, Vol. 34, No. 2 (1984), pp. 73–89.

Tannis M. Williams (ed.), *The Impact of Television*. Orlando, Florida: Academic Press (1986).

NO

Brian Siano

FRANKENSTEIN MUST BE DESTROYED: CHASING THE MONSTER OF TV VIOLENCE

Here's the scene: Bugs Bunny, Daffy Duck, and a well-armed Elmer Fudd are having a stand-off in the forest. Daffy the rat-fink has just exposed Bugs' latest disguise, so Bugs takes off the costume and says, "That's right, Doc, I'm a wabbit. Would you like to shoot me now or wait until we get home?"

"Shoot him now! Shoot him now!" Daffy screams.

"You keep out of this," Bugs says. "He does not have to shoot you now."

"He does *so* have to shoot me now!" says Daffy. Full of wrath, he storms up to Elmer Fudd and shrieks, "And I *demand* that you shoot me now!"

Now, if you *aren't* smiling to yourself over the prospect of Daffy's beak whirling around his head like a roulette wheel, stop reading right now. This one's for a very select group: those evil degenerates (like me) who want to corrupt the unsullied youth of America by showing them violence on television.

Wolves' heads being conked with mallets in Tex Avery's *Swing Shift Cinderella*. Dozens of dead bodies falling from a closet in *Who Killed Who?* A sweet little kitten seemingly baked into cookies in Chuck Jones' *Feed the Kitty*. And best of all, Wile E. Coyote's unending odyssey of pain in *Fast and Furrious* and *Hook, Line, and Stinker*. God, I love it. The more explosions, crashes, gunshots, and defective ACME catapults there are, the better it is for the little tykes.

Shocked? Hey, I haven't even gotten to "The Three Stooges" yet.

* * *

The villagers are out hunting another monster—the Frankenstein of TV violence. Senator Paul Simon's hearings in early August 1993 provoked a fresh round of arguments in a debate that's been going on ever since the first round of violent kids' shows—"Sky King," "Captain Midnight," and "Hopalong Cassidy"—were on the air. More recently, Attorney General Janet Reno has taken a hard line on TV violence. "We're fed up with excuses," she told the Senate, arguing that "the regulation of violence is constitutionally permissible" and that, if the networks don't do it, "government should respond." ...

Simon claims to have become concerned with this issue because, three years ago, he turned on the TV in his hotel room and was treated to the sight of a man being hacked apart with a chainsaw. ... This experience prompted him to sponsor a three-year antitrust exemption for the networks, which was his way of encouraging them to voluntarily "clean house." But at the end of that period, the rates of TV violence hadn't changed enough to satisfy him, so Simon convened open hearings on the subject in 1993.

If Simon was truly concerned with the content of television programming, the first question that comes to mind is why he gave the networks an antitrust exemption in the first place. Thanks to Reagan-era deregulation, ownership of the mass media has become steadily more concentrated in the hands of fewer and fewer corporations. For example, the Federal Communications Commission used to have a "seven-and-seven" rule, whereby no company was allowed to own more than seven radio and seven television stations. In 1984, this was revised to a "12-and-12-and-12" rule: 12 FM radio stations, 12 AM radio stations, and 12 TV stations. It's a process outlined by Ben Bagdikian in his fine book *The Media Monopoly*. The net result is a loss of dissident, investigative, or regional voices; a mass media that questions less; and a forum for public debate that includes only the powerful.

This process could be impeded with judicious use of antitrust laws and stricter FCC controls—a return to the "seven-and-seven" rule, perhaps. But rather

than hold hearings on this subject—a far greater threat to the nation's political well-being than watching *Aliens* on pay-per-view—Simon gave the networks a three-year *exemption* from antitrust legislation. ...

The debate becomes even more impassioned when we ask how children might be affected. The innocent, trusting little tykes are spending hours bathed in TV's unreal colors, and their fantasy lives are inhabited by such weirdos as Wolverine and Eek the Cat. Parents usually want their kids to grow up sharing their ideals and values, or at least to be well-behaved and obedient. Tell parents that their kids are watching "Beavis and Butt-head" in their formative years and you set off some major alarms.

There are also elitist, even snobbish, attitudes toward pop culture that help to rationalize censorship. One is that the corporate, mass-market culture of TV isn't important enough or "art" enough to deserve the same free-speech protection as James Joyce's *Ulysses* or William Burrough's *Naked Lunch*. The second is that rational, civilized human beings are supposed to be into Shakespeare and Scarlatti, not Pearl Jam and "Beavis and Butt-head." Seen in this "enlightened" way, the efforts of Paul Simon are actually for *our own good*. And so we define anything even remotely energetic as "violent," wail about how innocent freckle-faced children are being defiled by such fare as "NYPD Blue," and call for a Council of Certified Nice People who will decide what the rest of us get to see. A recent *Mother Jones* article by Carl Cannon (July/August 1993) took just this hysterical tone, citing as proof "some three thousand research studies of this issue."

Actually, there aren't 3,000 studies. In 1984, the *Psychological Bulletin* published an overview by Jonathan Freedman of research on the subject. Referring to the "2,500 studies" figure bandied about at the time (it's a safe bet that 10 years would inflate this figure to 3,000), Freedman writes:

> The reality is more modest. The large number refers to the complete bibliography on television. References to television and aggression are far fewer, perhaps around 500.... The actual literature on the relation between television violence and aggression consists of fewer than 100 independent studies, and the majority of these are laboratory experiments. Although this is still a substantial body of work, it is not vast, and there are only a small number of studies dealing specifically with the effects of television violence outside the laboratory.

The bulk of the evidence for a causal relationship between television violence and violent behavior comes from the research of Leonard Eron of the University of Illinois and Rowell Huesmann of the University of Michigan. Beginning in 1960, Eron and his associates began a large-scale appraisal of how aggression develops in children and whether or not it persists into adulthood. (The question of television violence was, originally, a side issue to the long-term study.) Unfortunately, when the popular press writes about Eron's work, it tends to present his methodology in the simplest of terms: *Mother Jones* erroneously stated that his study "followed the viewing habits of a group of children for twenty-two years." It's this sort of sloppiness, and overzealousness to prove a point, that keeps people from understanding the issues or raising substantial criticisms. Therefore, we must discuss Eron's work in some detail.

* * *

The first issue in Eron's study was how to measure aggressiveness in children. Eron's "peer-nominated index" followed a simple strategy: asking each child in a classroom questions about which kids were the main offenders in 10 different categories of classroom aggression (that is, "Who pushes or shoves children?"). The method is consistent with other scales of aggression, and its one-month test/retest reliability is 91 percent. The researchers also tested the roles of four behavioral dimensions in the development of aggression: *instigation* (parental rejection or lack of nurturance), *reinforcement* (punishment versus reward), *identification* (acquiring the parents' behavior and values), and *sociocultural norms*.

Eron's team selected the entire third-grade population of Columbia County, New York, testing 870 children and interviewing about 75 to 80 percent of their parents. Several trends became clear almost immediately. Children with less nurturing parents were more aggressive. Children who more closely identified with either parent were less aggressive. And children with low parental identification who were punished tended to be *more* aggressive (an observation which required revision of the behavioral model).

Ten years later, Eron and company tracked down and re-interviewed about half of the original sample. (They followed up on the subjects in 1981 as well.) Many of the subjects—now high-school seniors—demonstrated a persistence in aggression over time. Not only were the "peer-nominated" ratings roughly consistent with the third-grade ratings, but the more aggressive kids were three times as likely to have a police record by adulthood.

Eron's team also checked for the influences on aggression which they had previously noted when the subjects were eight. The persistent influences were parental identification and socioeconomic variables. Some previously important influences (lack of nurturance, punishment for aggression) didn't seem to affect the subjects' behavior as much in young adulthood. Eron writes of these factors:

> Their effect is short-lived and other variables are more important in predicting later aggression. Likewise, contingencies and environmental conditions can change drastically over 10 years, and thus the earlier contingent response becomes irrelevant.

It's at this stage that Eron mentions television as a factor:

> One of the best predictors of how aggressive a young man would be at age 19 was the violence of the television programs he preferred when he was 8 years old. Now, because we had longitudinal data, we could say with more certainty, on the basis of regression analysis, partial correlation, path analysis, and so forth, that there indeed was a cause-and-effect relation. *Continued research, however, has indicated that the causal effect is probably bidirectional: Aggressive children prefer violent television, and the violence on television causes them to be more aggressive.* [italics added]

Before we address the last comment, I should make one thing clear. Eron's research is sound. The methods he used to measure aggression are used by social scientists in many other contexts. His research does not ignore such obvious factors as the parents' socioeconomic status. And, as the above summary makes clear, Eron's own work makes a strong case for the positive or negative influence of parents in the development of their children's aggressiveness.

Now let's look at this "causal effect" business. Eron's data reveals that aggressive kids who turn into aggressive adults like aggressive television. But this is a correlation; it is not proof of a causal influence. If aggressive kids liked eating strawberry ice cream more often than the class wusses did, that too would be a predictor, and one might speculate on some anger-inducing chemical in strawberries.

Of course, the relation between representational violence and its influence on real life isn't as farfetched as that. The problem lies in determining precisely the nature of that relation, as we see when we look at the laboratory studies conducted by other researchers. Usually, the protocol of these experiments involves providing groups of individuals with entertainment calibrated for violent content, and studying some aspect of behavior after exposure—response to a behavioral test, which toys the children choose to play with, and so forth. But the results of these tests have been somewhat mixed. Sometimes the results are at variance with other studies, and many have methodological problems. For example, which "violent" entertainment is chosen? Bugs Bunny and the "Teenage Mutant Ninja Turtles" present action in very different contexts, and in one study, the Adam West "Batman" series was deemed nonviolent, despite those *Pow! Bam! Sock!* fistfights that ended every episode.

Many of the studies report that children do demonstrate higher levels of interpersonal aggression shortly after watching violent, energetic entertainment. But a 1971 study by Feshbach and Singer had boys from seven schools watch preassigned violent and nonviolent shows for six weeks. The results were not constant from school to school—and the boys watching the *nonviolent* shows tended to be more aggressive. Another protocol, carried out in Belgium as well as the United States, separated children into cottages at an institutional school and exposed certain groups to violent films. Higher aggression was noted in *all* groups after the films were viewed, but it returned to a near-baseline level after a week or so. (The children also rated the less violent films as less exciting, more boring, and sillier than the violent films —indicating that maybe kids *like* a little rush now and then.) Given the criticisms of the short-term-effects studies, and the alternate interpretations of the longitudinal studies, is this matter really settled?

Eron certainly thinks so. Testifying before Simon's committee in August, he declared that "the scientific debate is over" and called upon the Senate to reduce TV violence. His statement did not include any reference to such significant factors as parental identification—which, as his own research indicates, can change the way children interpret physical punishment. And even though Rowell Huesmann concurred with Eron in similar testimony before a House subcommittee, Huesmann's 1984 study of 1,500 youths in the United States, Finland, Poland, and Australia argued that, assuming a causal influence, television might be responsible for 5 percent of the violence in society. At *most*.

This is where I feel one has to part company with Leonard Eron. He is one of the most respected researchers in his field, and his work points to an imperative for parents in shaping and sharing their children's lives. But he has lent his considerable authority to such diversionary efforts as Paul Simon's and urged us to address, by questionable means, what only *might* be causing a tiny portion of real-life violence.

Some of Eron's suggestions for improving television are problematic as well. In his Senate testimony, Eron proposed restrictions on televised violence from 6:00 AM to 10:00 PM—which would exclude pro football, documentaries about World War II, and even concerned layperson Janet Reno's proudest moments. Or take Eron's suggestion that, in televised drama, "perpetrators of violence should not be rewarded for violent acts." I don't know what shows Eron's been watching, but all of the cop shows I remember usually ended with the bad guys getting caught or killed. And when Eron suggests that "gratuitous violence that is not necessary to the plot should be reduced or abandoned," one has to ask just *who* decides that it's "not necessary"? Perhaps most troubling is Eron's closing statement:

> For many years now Western European countries have had monitoring of TV and films for violence by government agencies and have *not* permitted the showing of excess violence, especially during child viewing hours. And I've never heard complaints by citizens of those democratic countries that their rights have been violated. If something doesn't give, we may have to institute some such monitoring by government agencies here in the U.S.A. If the industry does not police itself, then there is left only the prospect of official censorship, distasteful as this may be to many of us.

* * *

The most often-cited measure of just how violent TV programs are is that of George Gerbner, dean of the Annenberg School of Communications at the University of

Pennsylvania. Few of the news stories about TV violence explain how this index is compiled, the context in which Gerbner has conducted his studies, or even some criticisms that could be raised.

Gerbner's view of the media's role in society is far more nuanced than the publicity given the violence profile may indicate. He sees television as a kind of myth-structure/religion for modern society. Television dramas, situation comedies, news shows, and all the rest create a shared culture for viewers, which "communicates much about social norms and relationships, about goals and means, about winners and losers." One portion of Gerbner's research involves compiling "risk ratios" in an effort to discern which minority groups—including children, the aged, and women—tend to be the victims of the aggressors in drama. This provides a picture of a pecking order within society (white males on top, no surprise there) that has remained somewhat consistent over the 20-year history of the index.

In a press release accompanying the 1993 violence index, Gerbner discusses his investigations of the long-term effects of television viewing. Heavy viewers were more likely to express feelings of living in a hostile world. Gerbner adds, "Violence is a demonstration of power. It shows who can get away with what against whom."

In a previous violence index compiled for cable-television programs, violence is defined as a "clear-cut and overt episode of physical violence—hurting or killing or the threat of hurting and/or killing —in any context." An earlier definition reads: "The overt expression of physical force against self or other compelling action against one's will on pain of being hurt or killed, or actually hurting or killing." These definitions have been criticized for being too broad; they encompass episodes of physical comedy, depiction of accidents in dramas, and even violent incidents in documentaries. They also include zany cartoon violence; in fact, the indexes for Saturday-morning programming tend to be substantially higher than the indexes for prime-time programming. Gerbner argues that, since he is analyzing cultural norms and since television entertainment is a deliberately conceived expression of these norms, his definition serves the purposes of his study.

The incidents of violence (total number $= R$) in a given viewing period are compiled by Gerbner's staff. Some of the statistics are easy to derive, such as the percentage of programs with violence, the number of violent scenes per hour, and the actual duration of violence, in minutes per hour. The actual violence index is calculated by adding together the following stats:

$\%P$—the *percentage* of programs in which there is violence;

$2(R/P)$—twice the number of violent episodes per program;

$2(R/H)$—twice the number of violent episodes per *hour*;

$\%V$—percentage of *leading characters* involved in violence, either as victim or perpetrator; and

$\%K$—percentage of leading characters involved in an actual *killing*, either as victim or perpetrator.

But if these are the factors used to compile the violence profile, it's difficult to see how they can provide a clear-cut mandate for the specific content of television drama. For example, two of the numbers used are averages; why are they arbitrarily doubled and then added to percentages? Also, because the numbers are determined by a definition which explicitly separates violence from dramatic context, the index says little about actual television content outside of a broad, overall gauge. One may imagine a television season of nothing but slapstick comedy with a very high violence profile.

This is why the violence profile is best understood within the context of Gerbner's wider analysis of media content. It does not lend itself to providing specific conclusions or guidelines of the sort urged by Senator Paul Simon. (It is important to note that, even though Simon observed little change in prime-time violence levels during his three-year antitrust exemption, the index for all three of those years was *below* the overall 20-year score.)

* * *

Finally, there's the anecdotal evidence—loudly trumpeted as such by Carl Cannon in *Mother Jones*—where isolated examples of entertainment-inspired violence are cited as proof of its pernicious influence. Several such examples have turned up recently. A sequence was edited out of the film *The Good Son* in which McCaulay Culkin drops stuff onto a highway from an overhead bridge. (As we all know, nobody ever did this before the movie came out.) The film *The Program* was re-edited when some kids were killed imitating the film's characters, who "proved their courage" by lying down on a highway's dividing line. Perhaps most notoriously, in October 1993 a four-year-old Ohio boy set his family's trailer on fire, killing his younger sister; the child's mother promptly blamed MTV's "Beavis and Butt-head" for setting a bad example. But a neighbor interviewed on CNN reported that the family didn't even have cable television and that the kid had a local rep as a pyromaniac months before. This particular account was not followed up by the national media, which, if there were no enticing "Beavis and Butt-head" angle, would never have mentioned this fire at a low-income trailer park to begin with.

Numerous articles about media-inspired violence have cited similar stories —killers claiming to be Freddy Kreuger, kids imitating crimes they'd seen on a cop show a few days before, and so forth. In many of these cases, it is undeniably true that the person involved took his or her inspiration to act from a dramatic presentation in the media—the obvious example being John Hinckley's fixation on the film *Taxi Driver*.... But stories of media-inspired violence are striking mainly because they're so *atypical* of the norm; the vast majority of people don't take a movie or a TV show as a license to kill. Ironically, it is the *abnormality* of these stories that ensures they'll get widespread dissemination and be remembered long after the more mundane crimes are forgotten.

Of course, there are a few crazies out there who will be unfavorably influenced by what they see on TV. But even assuming that somehow the TV show (or movie or record) shares some of the blame, how does one predict what future crazies will take for inspiration? What guidelines would ensure that people write, act, or produce something that *will not upset a psychotic*? Not only is this a ridiculous demand, it's insulting to the public as well. We would all be treated as potential murderers in order to gain a hypothetical 5 percent reduction in violence.

* * *

In crusades like this—where the villagers pick up their torches and go hunting after Frankenstein—people often lose sight of what they're defending. I've read reams of statements from people who claim to know what television does to kids; but what do *kids* do with television? Almost none of what I've read gives kids any credit for thinking. None of these people seems to remember what being a kid is like.

When *Jurassic Park* was released, there was a huge debate over whether or not children should be allowed to see it. Kids like to see dinosaurs, people argued, but this movie might scare them into catatonia.... These objections were actually taken seriously. But kids like dinosaurs because they're big, look really weird, and scare the hell out of everything around them. Dinosaurs *kick ass.* What parent would tell his or her child that dinosaurs were *cute*? . . .

Along the same lines, what kid hasn't tried to gross out everyone at the dinner table by showing them his or her chewed-up food? Or tried using a magnifying glass on an anthill on a hot day? Or clinically inspected the first dead animal he or she ever came across? Sixty years ago, adults were terrified of *Frankenstein* and fainted at the premiere of *King Kong.* But today, *Kong* is regarded as a fantasy story, *Godzilla* can be shown without the objections of child psychologists, and there are breakfast cereals called Count Chocula and Frankenberry. Sadly, there are few adults who seem to remember how they identified more with the monsters. Who wanted to be one of those stupid villagers waving torches at Frankenstein? That's what our *parents* were like.

But it's not just an issue of kids liking violence, grossness, or comic-book adventure. About 90 percent of the cartoon shows I watched as a child were the mass-produced sludge of the Hanna-Barbera Studios—like "Wacky Races," "The Jetsons," and "Scooby Doo, Where Are You?" I can't remember a single memorable moment from any of them. But that Bugs Bunny sequence as the beginning of this article (from *Rabbit Seasoning,* 1952, directed by Chuck Jones) was done from memory, and I have no doubt that it's almost verbatim.

I know that, even at the age of eight or nine, I had some rudimentary aesthetic sense about it all. There was something hip and complex about the Warner Bros. cartoons, and some trite, insulting *sameness* to the Hanna-Barbera trash, although I couldn't quite understand it then. Bugs Bunny clearly wasn't made for kids according to some study on social-interaction development. Bugs Bunny was meant to make adults laugh as much as children. Kids can also enjoy entertainment ostensibly created for adults—in fact, that's often the most rewarding kind. I had no trouble digesting *Jaws,* James Bond, and Clint Eastwood "spaghetti westerns" in my preteen years. And I'd have no problems with showing a 10-year-old *Jurassic Park,* because I know how much he or she would love it....

I don't enjoy bad television with lots of violence, but I'd rather not lose *decent* shows that use violence for good reason. Shows like "Star Trek," "X-Men," or the spectacular "Batman: The Animated Series" can give kids a sense of adventure while teaching them about such qualities as courage, bravery, and heroism. Even better, a healthy and robust spirit of irreverence can be found in Bugs Bunny, "Ren and Stimpy," and "Tiny Toons." Some of these entertainments—like adventure stories and comic books of the past—can teach kids how to be really *alive*.

Finally, if we must have a defense against the pernicious influence of the mass media, it cannot be from the Senate's legislation or the pronouncements of social scientists. It must begin with precisely the qualities I described above—especially irreverence. One good start is Comedy Central's "Mystery Science Theater 3000," where the main characters, forced to watch horrendous movies, fight back by heckling them. Not surprisingly, children love the show, even though most of the jokes go right over their curious little heads. They recognize a kindred spirit in "MST 3000." Kids want to stick up for themselves, maybe like Batman, maybe like Bugs Bunny, or even like Beavis and Butt-head—but always against a world made by adults.

You know, *adults*—those doofuses with the torches, trying to burn up Frankenstein in the old mill.

CHALLENGE QUESTIONS

Does Viewing Television Increase a Child's Aggression?

1. Pretend that you have two young children, ages 5 and 7. After reading the selections by Centerwall and Siano, how would you handle television for your youngsters, and why?

2. Centerwall seems to imply that children have no choice but to imitate adults; imitation is instinctive. How does this explanation involve the issues of free choice and determinism? If children are truly determined by their environments and their instincts, can they be held responsible for their actions? Why, or why not?

3. Whose view does most of the research on this issue support, Centerwall's or Siano's? Review the research at your library to help you form a judgment.

4. There is considerable research on children who watch television with their parents. One set of findings indicates that parents who actively comment upon and engage their children in discussions about television programs minimize the impact of television's ill effects. How might such research affect the debate between Centerwall and Siano?

ISSUE 5

Is a Child's Development Negatively Affected by a Working Mother?

YES: Nazli Baydar and Jeanne Brooks-Gunn, from "Effects of Maternal Employment and Child-Care Arrangements on Preschoolers' Cognitive and Behavioral Outcomes: Evidence from the Children of the National Longitudinal Survey of Youth," *Developmental Psychology* (vol. 27, no. 6, 1991)

NO: Deborah Lowe Vandell and Janaki Ramanan, from "Effects of Early and Recent Maternal Employment on Children from Low-Income Families," *Child Development* (vol. 63, 1992)

ISSUE SUMMARY

YES: Developmental scientists Nazli Baydar and Jeanne Brooks-Gunn assert that maternal employment during a child's infancy has detrimental effects on the cognitive and behavioral development of the child.

NO: Child development researchers Deborah Lowe Vandell and Janaki Ramanan found that a mother's employment during a child's infancy was a predictor of higher achievement test scores in elementary school.

Parents and developmental psychologists have long been concerned about the effect of working mothers on children's development. With more mothers than ever choosing to, or having to, work, many children are not being raised in the more "traditional" environment—at home with one parent. Children today see their parents less often at home and spend more time with caretakers in other locations. What effect, if any, does this situation have on the development of the child? Should mothers welcome the opportunity to work because their children will profit from effective caretakers? Or should one parent avoid working at all costs? What about single mothers, who generally have little choice?

Interestingly, developmental psychologists have had a tough time answering these questions. Early in their research, they treated a mother's working as an isolated factor that might have a direct influence on development. Now, however, many developmental investigators believe that the issue of maternal employment is more complex than they first thought. Most now agree that researchers must study this issue in the context of the family system and simultaneously address many other factors. For example, does the mother have to work or want to work? How do the child, siblings, and father feel about her working? How does the family's culture or income level interact with these issues? What methods are best for understanding this complex phenomenon?

In the following selections, both sets of authors use the same database, the National Longitudinal Survey of Youth, in arriving at their opposing conclusions. In their analysis, Nazli Baydar and Jeanne Brooks-Gunn found that maternal employment, while children were infants, had significant negative effects on cognitive and behavioral outcomes in white children, ages three to four years old. Baydar and Brooks-Gunn also refer to analyses indicating that white, middle-class boys whose mothers work are more likely to be insecurely attached to their parents than the same-aged boys whose mothers do not work. For parents and children classified as poor, Baydar and Brooks-Gunn found that mother and grandmother care was the most beneficial for children.

Deborah Lowe Vandell and Janaki Ramanan, on the other hand, report that math and reading achievement scores were higher for children whose mothers were employed than for children whose mothers were not employed. In addition, Vandell and Ramanan found no evidence for increased behavioral problems or limited attention span in connection with maternal employment. The authors contend that mothers from low-income families who stay at home can ultimately hurt their children because with the mother not working, the family's income is lowered even further, resulting in a decrease in the parents' ability to provide for their children.

POINT

- Maternal employment had significant negative effects on cognitive and behavioral outcomes in many ages of white children.

- The cognitive development of children in poverty was negatively affected by poor child care.

- How intensely a mother is involved in her job is associated with cognitive and behavioral deficits.

- Maternal characteristics associated with entry into the labor force also played a role in increasing insecure attachment.

COUNTERPOINT

- Neither early nor recent maternal employment contributed significantly to a child's behavioral problems or attention span.

- Children from low-income families in which the mother worked had higher achievement test scores.

- Black children with single parents benefitted when their mothers were employed.

- Low-income families in which the mother does not work cannot provide as much for the children.

YES

Nazli Baydar and
Jeanne Brooks-Gunn

EFFECTS OF MATERNAL EMPLOYMENT AND CHILD-CARE ARRANGEMENTS ON PRESCHOOLERS' COGNITIVE AND BEHAVIORAL OUTCOMES: EVIDENCE FROM THE CHILDREN OF THE NATIONAL LONGITUDINAL SURVEY OF YOUTH

The dramatic rise in the proportion of working mothers with young children over the past quarter century is well documented. The number of women who were employed and who had children under age 6 increased from 2.3 million in 1960 to 7.1 million in 1988 (U.S. Bureau of the Census, 1989). One half of mothers with infants 1 year of age or younger and almost two thirds of mothers with toddlers (2- to 3-years olds) are in the work force. The percentages are higher for married mothers, for mothers with fewer children, and for mothers with more education, even though the percentages for all subgroups are over one half (Bureau of Labor Statistics, 1988; Hayes, Palmer, & Zaslow, 1990). At the minimum, two thirds of infants and toddlers are expected to have an employed mother by 1995 (Scarr, Phillips, & McCartney, 1989). The increases in the proportion of young children with working mothers over the past 20 years are most pronounced for children in their first year of life: In 1988, more than one half of mothers with babies under 1 year of age were employed, compared with one third of similar mothers in the mid-1970s (Bureau of Labor Statistics, 1988). As a result many, if not the majority, of young children today are cared for, at least part of the time, by someone other than their mother.

These trends have generated research debates on the effects of nonmaternal care and maternal employment on young children and policy debates on the need for high-quality child care, its cost, and its availability (Chase-Lansdale, Michael, & Desai, in press; Clarke-Stewart, 1989; Hayes et al., 1990; Maynard, 1989). Somewhat surprisingly, however, research on the effects of maternal employment has remained separate from research on the effects of various

From Nazli Baydar and Jeanne Brooks-Gunn, "Effects of Maternal Employment and Child-Care Arrangements on Preschoolers' Cognitive and Behavioral Outcomes: Evidence from the Children of the National Longitudinal Survey of Youth," *Developmental Psychology*, vol. 27, no. 6 (1991). Copyright © 1991 by The American Psychological Association. Reprinted by permission. Notes and references omitted.

child-care arrangements, even though the two are clearly intertwined. With the exception of programs aimed at ameliorating the effects of poverty on young children, child care during the first year is used primarily by employed women.

Research on the effects of maternal employment on children grew in part out of a concern for the effects of maternal separation on young children, particularly regarding social and emotional development in the first year (Bowlby, 1969; Bretherton & Waters, 1985; Bronfenbrenner, 1979; Rutter, 1981a; Sroufe, 1979). Few studies address the effects of maternal employment in the first year on children's cognitive functioning (see for exceptions, Hock, 1980; Pedersen, Cain, Zaslow, & Anderson, 1982). The bulk of the research on the effects of maternal separation during infancy is focused on the mother and infant in a laboratory-based setting, using the Strange Situation to assess infants' responses to separation from and reunion with the mother (see Campos, Barrett, Lamb, Goldsmith, & Sternberg, 1983). The studies looking at employment effects tend to have small samples composed of primarily White middle-class families. Many report that 1-year-old White, middle-class boys whose mothers work are more likely to be insecurely attached (as evidenced by avoidant and anxious behavior) than same-age boys whose mothers do not work (Barglow, Vaughn, & Molitor, 1987; Belsky & Rovine, 1988; Chase-Lansdale & Owen, 1987; Doyle & Somers, 1978; Hock & Clinger, 1980; Schwartz, 1983). However, it is not known whether such behavior among boys with employed mothers is associated with later maladjustment. Links between insecure attachment and later social and emotional problems are

reported in studies that do not focus on maternal employment (Farber & Egelan, 1982; Sroufe, 1983; Vaughn, Deane, & Waters, 1985). Research to date has been unable to elucidate possible mechanisms underlying the phenomenon: Insecure attachment may be indicative of problems associated with separation or may be a reflection of earlier independence and autonomy (Clarke-Stewart, 1989). Maternal characteristics associated with entry into the labor force may also play a role in increasing insecure attachment (Clarke-Stewart, 1989; Rutter, 1981b; see study results of Hock, 1980).

Most studies on maternal employment do not consider either the type or the quality of care that infants are receiving, even though the latter is known to be associated with child functioning (Phillips, 1987). The effects of timing of maternal entry into the labor force during the first 3 years have also not been examined, although the significance of the development during the first year suggests that this period might be a particularly vulnerable developmental period.

A separate body of research focuses on the child care received, rather than on maternal employment. Almost no research compares the effects of different types of nonmaternal care. Instead, most of the research to date focuses on center-based care and, more recently, on family-based care (Hayes et al., 1990). One line of research concentrates on children in poverty who receive early educationally oriented intervention services through home visiting, center-based care services, or both (Beller, 1979; Bronfenbrenner, 1975; Bryant & Ramey, 1987; Clarke-Stewart & Fein, 1983; Haskins, 1989; Zigler & Valentine, 1979). For children who participate in center-based intervention, negative effects on social or emotional functioning are not found (Haskins, 1989). On the contrary, more positive mother-infant interaction and infant social development are shown in over one half of the studies evaluating social and emotional outcomes (Benasich, Brooks-Gunn, & Clewell, in press; Haskins, 1989). Almost all program evaluations report enhanced cognitive functioning through the preschool years (Lazar, Darlington, Murray, Royce, & Snipper, 1982). Although the provision of daily center-based care services might facilitate entry into the work force, most of the early intervention programs did not have this as an explicit goal. The studies that investigate maternal employment find it to be higher in the families who participated in these programs than in the families in the control groups (Benasich et al., in press; Clewell, Brooks-Gunn, & Benasich, 1989). These studies have neither looked at differential effects of intervention for children whose mothers were employed versus children whose mothers were not employed nor looked at the effects of child-care arrangements in the comparison groups (many of whom were probably receiving some nonmaternal care).

Two other avenues of research on child care exist. One focuses on the variations in the quality of child care, and the other considers the links between the quality of family and child-care environment (Hayes et al., 1990). To date, these research lines have had center-based child care as their primary focus.

The intersection of maternal employment and child-care type was considered in this article, vis-à-vis its effects on subsequent cognitive and behavioral outcomes in children at preschool ages. Such an analysis requires a large and heterogeneous sample, and the Children of the National Longitudinal Survey of Youth (NLSY) data set is well suited to addressing the outcomes of intersecting life circumstances of children and their families. In keeping with the preceding two articles (Brooks-Gunn, Phelps, & Elder, 1991; Chase-Lansdale, Mott, Brooks-Gunn, & Phillips, 1991), we also considered various methodological issues that arose when using the Children of the NLSY data: How to operationalize child care and employment; whether retrospective and prospective child care data are similar; whether to analyze results for ethnic groups separately; and ways to construct multivariate models to examine differential effects of independent variables on the dependent variable as a function of background characteristics such as sex and poverty status. Although these methodological issues do not constitute an exhaustive list of problems that might be encountered when analyzing the data from the Children of the NLSY, they are illustrative of the issues pertaining to the use of this or other national data sets to address developmental issues.

Three sets of questions were addressed. The first set inquired about the effects of maternal employment in the first 3 years of life on cognitive and behavioral functioning of 3- and 4-year-old children and the factors that possibly mediate these effects. The effects of timing of maternal entry into the labor force were examined by estimating the effects of entry in each of the first 3 years on subsequent child outcomes, controlling for maternal characteristics that are associated with entry into labor force. In keeping with previous studies, we expected maternal entry into the labor force during the first year of life to have a negative effect on cognitive and behavioral functioning of preschoolers (cf. reviews by Chase-

Landsdale, Michael, & Desai, 1991; Hayes et al., 1990). We expected the negative effects of maternal entry into the labor force to decline over the first 3 years with minimal effects of entry in the third year. On the basis of previous studies, effects of maternal employment in the first year were expected to vary by gender, with stronger effects for boys. Another analysis of the NLSY data set (Desai, Chase-Lansdale, & Michael, 1989) found gender variation in maternal employment effects only for high-income families. Hence, we investigated the differential effects of maternal employment by poverty status as well as by gender.

Previous studies have not identified the particular aspects of maternal employment in the first year that might be most detrimental. The second set of questions related to the continuity, intensity, and timing of maternal employment in the first year of life. Among the children whose mothers were employed in the first year, those whose mothers were employed continuously throughout the first 3 years were expected to experience more detrimental effects than those whose mothers remained home during some of those years. Maternal employment was expected to have stronger negative effects with increasing weekly number of hours worked by the mother. A few studies suggested that negative effects appeared when the number of hours worked per week was over 20, although few direct tests of the amount of hours worked per week were made (Barglow et al., 1987; Belsky, 1988; Belsky & Rovine, 1988; Heynes & Catsambis, 1986; Milne, Myers, Rosenthal, & Ginsburg, 1986). In addition, the timing of maternal entry in the labor force during the first year was expected to have substantial impact on children. Children of mothers who en-

ter the work force later in the child's first year could be expected to fare better than children whose mothers enter the work force earlier in the first year, possibly because of the amount of time spent with the mother. We expected more negative effects from maternal entry into the work force during the second and third quarters of the first year than from entry during the first or fourth quarter. This prediction is based on the admittedly speculative premise that infants in the last quarter of their first year have more sophisticated cognitive conceptions of object and person permanence (Harris, 1983; Lewis & Brooks-Gunn, 1979), rendering the older infant less vulnerable to the coming and going of a mother who has been available earlier than infants in the second or third quarters of their first year (Chase-Lansdale & Owen, 1987; Hoffman, 1984). During the first quarter of the first year, person permanence is not yet formed, as such, and maternal entry into the labor force at this time may be less detrimental than later (Hock, 1980), during its formation.

The third set of questions investigated whether the types of child-care arrangements influence child outcomes over and above the expected maternal employment effect. Quality of child care could not be explored with the Children of the NLSY data set because the characteristics of child-care arrangements used in the first, second, and third years of life were not asked. Note that information on child-care type was not used to test hypotheses regarding the effects of quality of child care. Care by relatives was expected to be beneficial for infants of employed mothers when compared with care by nonrelatives in the first year. On the basis of scanty evidence, grandparents and fathers were posited to enhance functioning as compared with other relatives because of their stability (i.e., presence in the child's life even when not performing primary child care) and long-lasting relationship and presumed commitment to the child (Furstenberg, Brooks-Gunn, & Morgan, 1987; Lamb, 1976; Parke, 1979; Tinsley & Parke, 1984). Whether care by other relatives operates in a similar beneficial fashion is not known. Nonrelative care in the first year was expected to have particularly negative effects for poor children, because the quality of paid care that is affordable for families in poverty is likely to be low. Hence, the comparative advantage of relative child care as compared with paid child care was expected to be larger for children in poverty than for children not in poverty....

RESULTS

Intersection of Maternal Employment and Child-Care Arrangements

Of the children whose mothers were employed, 48.6% were employed for the child's first year, 56.6% for the child's second year, and 59.7% for the child's third year. These percentages are similar to those from other nationally representative samples (Bureau of Labor Statistics, 1988; see Figures 2 and 3 in Hayes et al., 1990)....

During the first year, grandmother care was the most prevalent type of nonmaternal care for all employment status groups, and the most common child-care arrangement for the children of employed mothers. During the second year, nonrelative care was the most prevalent nonmaternal care type for the children of employed mothers irrespective of the intensity of employment. For the children of mothers who were not employed, grandmother care remained the most prevalent nonmaternal care type during the second year. During the third year, center-based care gained prevalence for all children and became the type of nonmaternal care most frequently used for the children of mothers who were not employed. For the children of part-time employed mothers, grandmother care was the most common nonmaternal care type in the third year of life. For the children of mothers who were employed more than an average of 20 hr per week, nonrelative care was the most common care type. Employment status and the intensity of employment of the mothers were clearly associated with the type of child-care arrangements that the children experienced....

Effects of Child-Care Arrangements in Infancy

Before presenting results pertaining to the effects of infancy-care arrangements on cognitive and behavioral outcomes in preschool children, it is important to reiterate that very few children whose mothers were not employed during the first year of their life received nonmaternal care. Hence, during infancy, nonmaternal care was closely linked with maternal employment, and it was not possible to compare the effects of most forms of nonmaternal care between children whose mothers were employed and children whose mothers were not employed. Two regression models were estimated to quantify the effects of various child-care arrangements on preschoolers whose mothers were employed during infancy. The first model includes the main effects of having experienced various child-care arrangements during infancy. The second model includes a set of interaction effects allowing the effects of child-care arrangements to vary by sex and poverty status. These models are presented in Table 1.

... The main effects of child-care arrangements on the BPI scores were significant. Model 1 for the BPI (Table 1, column 3) indicates that for the children of employed mothers, baby-sitter care, grandmother care, and mother care in infancy resulted in significantly lower BPI scores than father (or father figure) care. Similar to the results of the effects of child care on the PPVT–R, the effects of various forms of child care on the BPI depended on the sex of the child. The beneficial effects of baby-sitter care or grandmother care were stronger for girls than for boys. The size of the interaction effect of sex and maternal care was relatively small. The interaction effect of mother care with poverty status on the BPI scores was not significant, indicating no poverty status differentials in the beneficial effects of maternal care in infancy.

Table 2 shows the predicted mean PPVT–R and BPI scores of children in each care type during infancy, classified by sex and poverty status. These predicted means pertain to the children whose mothers were employed during infancy. When the PPVT–R was considered, it was seen that mother and grandmother care were the most beneficial types of care for children in poverty. For children who were not in poverty, relative care for boys and baby-sitter care for girls appeared to be the most beneficial. When the BPI was considered, mother care emerged as the most beneficial type of care for boys, and baby-sitter care emerged as the most beneficial type of care for girls.

Mother and grandmother care were the only two care types for which effects can be compared between the children whose mothers had different employment statuses. Grandmother care was received by 5.4% of children whose mothers were not employed as well as 22.9% of children whose mothers were employed during the first year of life. For all children who were cared for either by their grandmothers or by their mothers, we estimated models that quantified the effects of these care types and the interactions of these effects with the maternal employment status (results not shown). These models did not support the hypothesis that the effects of maternal and grandmother care differed by maternal employment status. Hence, grandmother care was not more beneficial to the children of employed mothers than to the children of mothers who were not working in this sample.

DISCUSSION

As the Children of the NLSY data set demonstrates, maternal employment and child-care choices are closely linked during the first 3 years of life, especially during infancy. Very few infants whose mothers are not employed receive nonmaternal care. Very large proportions of infants whose mothers work more than half time receive care from relatives and nonrelatives, though the proportion of children who receive center-based care during the first year of life is negligibly small. Because maternal employment leads to profound changes in an infant's experiences and interactions, it is important to know if maternal employment has any negative effects on children. Our analyses indicate that maternal employment in infancy had significant negative

Table 1

The Effects of Child-Care Arrangements on the Cognitive and Behavioral Outcomes of 3–4-Year-Old White Children Whose Mothers Were Employed in Infancy: Unstandardized Regression Coefficients

Variable	PPVT–R[a]		BPI[b]	
	Model 1	Model 2	Model 1	Model 2
Controls				
Male	−2.382	−11.134	−0.863	−5.491
In poverty	−2.982	−13.117	2.375*	3.022
Mother employed 10–19 hr	−4.807*	−3.599	–	–
Mother employed 20+ hr	−4.043†	−4.400	–	–
Mother's AFQT score	0.030*	0.030	–	–
Child-care arrangements[c]				
Mother care	1.219	−4.545	−3.076*	−4.106
Father care	−3.663	−3.176	CC	CC
Grandmother care	4.901	−4.076	−3.483*	−6.431
Baby-sitter care	5.462	3.404	−4.383*	−8.494
Relative care	3.495	−5.366	EX	EX
Center-based care	CC	CC	EX	EX
Interaction of child care and poverty status[d]				
Mother care × In poverty[e]	–	13.692[F]	–	−0.372
Grandmother care × In poverty	–	14.698	–	–
Interaction of child-care and sex				
Mother care × male	–	6.988[F]	–	1.975[F]
Grandmother care × male	–	14.758	–	6.248
Baby-sitter care × male	–	3.667	–	9.207
Relative care × male	–	20.859	–	–
r^2	0.159	0.218	0.081	0.175

Note: PPVT–R = Peabody Picture Vocabulary Test—Revised; BPI = Behavioral Problems Index; AFQT = Armed Forces Qualification Test; CC = comparison category; EX = excluded from the analysis. [a]Models are based on 252 3–4-year-old White children of mothers who were employed during their 1st year of life. [b]Models are based on 116 4-year-old White children of mothers who were employed during their 1st year of life, excluding those children who were in center-based or relative care. [c]The comparison categories are center-based care for the models of PPVT–R and father (figure) care for the models of BPI. [d]The significance of the interaction effects are shown by a superscript *F* when the sum of squares accounted by that group of interaction effects are significant at $p < .05$. The significance of each coefficient cannot be tested due to the multicollinearity of dummy variables representing the main effects and interaction effects. [e]The interaction effects are estimated only if the category of interest is represented by at least 10 observations. Consequently, for children in poverty, only the differential effects of mother and grandmother care could be estimated.
†$p < .10$ *$p < .05$.

effects on cognitive and behavioral outcomes in White children of age 3 to 4 years. Once maternal employment was postponed to the second or third years, it had negligible effects. At the same time, continuous employment throughout the first 3 years was not more detrimental than intermittent employment following the first year. Because the trends in maternal employment are socially and economically driven, factors that might counteract its possible negative effects need to be identified....

The association of the timing of maternal entry into the labor force during the first year with cognitive and behavioral development is a question that has not been studied before. Postponement of labor-force entry to the last quarter of infancy compared with the first 3 quarters had beneficial effects for White preschoolers' cognitive and behavioral development. A variety of factors may have accounted for this beneficial effect, such as the amount of time spent with the mother, the cognitive and emotional developmental level of the child at the time of separation, or some unmeasured differences in the characteristics of mothers who entered the work force late in the child's life (although our findings controlled for the usual socioeconomic factors, other differences might exist; Hock, Christman, & Hock, 1980; Rutter, 1981b). These analyses suggest that the former (i.e., the amount of time) is not the only factor; returning to the labor force in the second quarter was associated with lower preschool cognitive scores than was returning in the first quarter. What factors might render the second quarter (and possibly the third quarter) of the first year the most vulnerable to the effects of maternal employment and render the fourth quarter the least vulnerable? It is possible that in the second (and third) quarter, children are forming representations of their parents vis-à-vis dimensions such as constancy, consistency, and differentiation (Bell, 1970; Decarie, 1965; Mahler, Pine, & Bergman, 1975; Stern, 1977). Separation from the mother during this period may be more detrimental than earlier or later separation. If the mother returns to the labor force before the second quarter,

Table 2

Predicted Scores of the PPVT–R and BPI by Infancy-Care Arrangements for the Children of Mothers Who Were Employed During the First Year of Life

Child-care arrangement	Not in poverty		In poverty	
	Boys	Girls	Boys	Girls
	PPVT–R			
Mother	69.4	73.6	70.0	74.2
Father	63.8	75.0	50.7	61.8
Grandmother	77.7	74.1	79.3	75.6
Relative	82.5	72.8	69.4	59.7
Baby-sitter	74.1	81.5	61.0	68.4
Center	67.0	78.1	53.9	65.0
	BPI			
Mother	8.1	11.6	10.7	14.2
Father	10.2	15.7	13.2	18.7
Grandmother	10.0	9.3	13.0	12.3
Baby-sitter	10.9	7.2	13.9	10.2

Note: PPVT–R = Peabody Picture Vocabulary Test —Revised; BPI = Behavioral Problems Index. The predicted PPVT–R scores were computed on the basis of the regression equations given in Table 1 (Model 2). It was assumed that the mother's Armed Forces Qualifications Test score was 39.2 (the mean value for the sample concerned), that the child in question was a first-born and that the mother worked more than 20 hr per week. Expected scores are given by sex and poverty status, because characteristics were shown to interact with the type of child care to affect cognitive development. Only sex of the child interacted with the type of child care to determine behavioral development; however, poverty status had a significant independent effect. Hence, a two-way breakdown is given for the expected behavioral problem scores as well.

a child might develop a notion of maternal constancy that includes regular absence. If the mother returns to the labor force during the fourth quarter, maternal representations may be better established and changes in maternal routine may be more easily incorporated into maternal representations.

This study shows that the intensity of maternal employment during infancy is associated with later cognitive and behavioral outcomes. However, the effects of intensity of maternal employment on cognitive and behavioral outcomes are not linear. Under 10 hr of employment is the least detrimental, whereas 10–20 hr and more than 20 hr of employment a week exhibit negative effects on cognitive and behavioral outcomes. We found slightly larger detrimental effects for 10–20 hr of employment than for more than half-time employment. Children whose mothers were employed less than 10 hr per week could still receive maternal care for substantial proportions of time. Our data do not allow for a detailed look at the processes that account for differential effects of 10- to 20-hr versus more than 20-hr maternal employment. We speculate that children whose mothers are more than half-time employed may be more likely to be placed into more stable and possibly higher quality child-care arrangements because the mother knows that the child will spend a substantial number of hours every day in that care type and because the mother might be able to afford higher quality care. Furthermore, children of mothers who are employed more than half-time might develop an attachment to their caregiver (Hayes et al., 1990; Howes, Rodning, Galluzzo, & Myers, 1988). Children whose mothers are employed 10–20 hr a week might be placed in more ad hoc care, less stable arrangements, or lower quality care arrangements than children of more intensively employed mothers.

Type of child-care arrangements may alter the effects of maternal employment on children in the first year of life. Our results suggest that types of child-care arrangements have different effects on cognitive development as compared with behavioral development. The cognitive development of boys and children in poverty was vulnerable to child-care effects. The behavioral problems of all children were influenced by child-care arrangements regardless of the poverty status of the family and sex of the child. Mother care and grandmother care were more beneficial for the cognitive development of children in poverty than for children of nonpoverty families. Grandmother care was found to be associated with preschoolers' cognitive functioning in two studies of Black, mostly poor children (Furstenberg et al., 1987; Kellam, Adams, Brown, & Ensnubger, 1982). However, these studies did not focus on care in the first year or on working mothers. Our findings on the beneficial effects of grandmother care were not solely due to residence with the grandmother, because 75% of the children in grandmother care were not residing with her. The care that poor families could afford (or that is available in their communities) might not be of high quality, or poor children may be especially vulnerable to the low-quality care provided in many paid (nonrelative) care arrangements. Each of these hypotheses needs to be tested because the mechanisms through which child care influences cognitive development will determine the policy formulations. For example, if children in poverty receive low-quality care because their families cannot afford better care, child-care subsidies might alleviate the problem. On the other hand, if children in poverty are especially vulnerable to the care provided by nonrelatives (i.e., baby-sitter and center-based care), then programs such as those developed by the early intervention field might be necessary compensation for the negative effects of poverty.

Among the children of employed mothers, boys were found to be more sensitive to the type of care provided than were girls. Boys were likely to have higher PPVT–R scores if they were cared for by their grandmother or a relative other than their father. Perhaps as others have speculated, boys are more vulnerable to a variety of factors, such as low-quality care, less attentive or less attached caregivers (presuming relatives are more attentive or attached), and lack of stability. Negative effects of maternal employment found by the earlier studies might be because of the heightened vulnerability of boys to unstable care arrangements or less attentive caregivers in infancy.

We found that types of infancy-care arrangements are predictive of behavioral outcomes in preschoolers and that these associations are mediated by child gender. For the children of mothers who were employed in infancy, baby-sitter care for girls and mother care for boys are the most beneficial in terms of behavioral outcomes. These results point to the particular significance of child-care arrangements, especially for boys.

Father care appears to be associated with low cognitive scores and high behavioral problem scores in all children. This is contrary to our hypothesis that father care would be similar to grandmother and other relative care in its effects on early development. One could speculate that the fathers who were the main care providers were probably unemployed, with associated problems in emotional well-being and self-esteem....

The Children of the NLSY data set allowed us to examine maternal employment and child-care effects on children simultaneously, which, to our knowledge, has not been done previously. The size of the NLSY sample facilitated the examination of possible differential effects by gender and poverty status. Children in poverty are known to be at risk of delays in cognitive development irrespective of child-care arrangements (McLoyd, 1990). On the other hand, families in poverty are targeted by numerous policies for increased female labor-force participation. Hence, it is crucial to accumulate evidence regarding the effects of child-care arrangements on children in poverty. However, this data set does not allow for process-oriented studies of effects of the quality of child-care arrangements and the relationship between the caregiver and the child. Both types of studies are necessary to understand the mechanisms underlying maternal employment and child-care effects and to inform policy on child care.

NO

Deborah Lowe Vandell
and Janaki Ramanan

EFFECTS OF EARLY AND RECENT MATERNAL EMPLOYMENT ON CHILDREN FROM LOW-INCOME FAMILIES

The norm in the United States is for mothers to be employed outside the home. Recent U.S. Bureau of Labor Statistics figures (1988) indicate that 73% of the married mothers of school-age children and 57% of the married mothers of infants and preschoolers are employed. Employment figures for single mothers are even higher: 84% of the single mothers of school-age children and 70% of the single mothers of children under 6 years are employed. In part because of this high level of labor force participation by mothers of young children, researchers, policymakers, and families are asking whether and in what ways maternal employment affects children's development.

There are considerable difficulties in trying to ascertain the effects of maternal employment on children. One difficulty is that mothers who are employed may differ a priori from mothers who are not employed. There is accumulating evidence that employed mothers have less traditional views about child rearing (McCartney, 1984), are less anxious about separating from their children (Hock, DeMeis, & McBride, 1988), and are more committed to their careers (Greenberger & Goldberg, 1989) than are women who are not employed or who resume employment later. In addition to these psychological differences, there are demographic differences associated with the likelihood that women are employed. Women who return to the workforce more quickly following the birth of their children are more likely to be black (as opposed to Hispanic or white) and to have higher family incomes (Garrett, Lubeck, & Wenk, 1991) than do women who resume employment more slowly. If these demographic and psychological characteristics contribute to differences in children's development, it is necessary to control for them when studying maternal employment. Unfortunately, many studies examining the effects of maternal employment on children do not have longitudinal designs that adequately permit the consideration of selection factors.

From Deborah Lowe Vandell and Janaki Ramanan, "Effects of Early and Recent Maternal Employment on Children from Low-Income Families," *Child Development*, vol. 63 (1992). Copyright © 1992 by The Society for Research in Child Development, Inc. Reprinted by permission.

The study of maternal employment is further complicated by the possibility that its effects may depend on the child's age when the mother is employed. Belsky (1988) and others (Bogenschneider, 1990; Heyns & Catsambis, 1986; Vandell & Corasaniti, 1990) have argued that maternal employment during infancy and early childhood is a more powerful influence on children's later development than is subsequent maternal employment. Historically, however, researchers (see the review by Hoffman, 1989) have focused on the concurrent effects of maternal employment on older preschool and elementary school children. Typically, researchers have not simultaneously examined early and subsequent maternal employment in order to determine which is the better predictor of children's development.

Yet another difficulty in studying maternal employment is a growing awareness that the effects of maternal employment may be moderated by child and family characteristics (Belsky & Eggebeen, 1991; Desai, Chase-Lansdale, & Michael, 1989). Because of the possibility that maternal employment affects families differentially, it is risky to assume a priori that results from studies involving maternal employment within middle-class white families are generalizable to low-income, single-parent, and racial minority households.

The current study seeks to examine further this complicated question of the effects of maternal employment by focusing on children from economically disadvantaged families. Analyses were conducted on a national data set, the National Longitudinal Survey of Youth (NLSY). The current study focuses on the second-grade children within the 1986 NLSY data set. These were the oldest children for whom detailed maternal employment histories from birth were available in sufficient numbers for analysis.

This study differs in significant ways from other recent papers that have used the NLSY to examine questions relating to maternal employment. Both Desai et al. (1989) and Belsky and Eggenbeen (1991) used the NLSY to examine the effects of early maternal employment on preschoolers. These preschool-age children had mothers who were older at their birth, were better educated, and were more affluent than the mothers of the second-grade children examined in the current study. Recent work by Brooks-Gunn (personal communication) using the NLSY also examines younger children than those in the current study and does not include the array of child outcomes examined within the current study.

Two conflicting hypotheses concerning the effects of maternal employment on children from economically disadvantaged families can be proposed. One is that maternal employment, poverty, and single-parent status act as cumulative stresses on families, thereby resulting in poorer social and academic outcomes in low-income children when their mothers are employed. An alternative hypothesis is that the financial and emotional benefits associated with maternal employment are so substantial that children whose mothers are employed demonstrate better developmental progress than low-income children whose mothers are not employed. Recent efforts at welfare reform in the United States, as exemplified by the JOBS and New Chance programs, are based on the assumption that maternal employment has positive effects in low-income families and children, but this assumption is largely untested.

Several studies conducted 20 years ago are consistent with the assumption of advantageous effects of maternal employment on low-income children. Within a group of low-income, black fifth graders, IQ scores were highest when mothers were employed full time (Woods, 1972). Similarly, within a sample of single-parent families living in poverty, Rieber and Womack (1968) reported children having higher achievement test scores when mothers were employed rather than not employed. More recently, others (Cherry & Eaton, 1977; Milne, Myers, Rosenthal, & Ginsburg, 1986) have found that black children whose mothers were single parents scored higher on standardized cognitive assessments when their mothers were employed rather than not employed.

The current study is a notable improvement over these earlier investigations. First, it utilizes a longitudinal data set to examine possible self-selection differences associated with maternal employment. These selection factors include mother's mental aptitude, self-esteem, and attitudes about employment and child rearing. The earlier studies of low-income families have not typically included the consideration of selection effects. A second improvement is that the current study utilizes a national data set rather than the small convenience samples that were typically used in the past. A third improvement is that the effects of both early and subsequent maternal employment were tested, whereas the previous work has focused only on the effects of concurrent maternal employment.

Another difference between this study and previous studies examining economically disadvantaged children is that several potential moderators of maternal employment are examined. Given evidence that middle-class boys and girls react differently to maternal employment (Bogenschneider, 1990; Desai et al., 1989; Gold & Andres, 1978; Montemayor, 1984), interactions between maternal employment and child gender are tested. Also, family marital composition and child race/ethnicity are examined as possible moderators of the effects of maternal employment in accordance with suggestions (Brooks-Gunn, personal communication; Scarr, Lande, & McCartney, 1989) that these factors can result in maternal employment differentially affecting children.

A final difference between the current study and other studies involving economically disadvantaged families is that we examine possible processes and experiences by which maternal employment affects children. Maternal employment can provide families with greater financial resources, thereby reducing the likelihood that the family is living in poverty. It can change the emotional climate in the family by either reducing (or increasing) family stress and emotional support. Consequently, we examined ways in which family functioning might vary as a result of maternal employment in order to ascertain possible mechanisms by which maternal employment exerts effects on children.

METHOD

Subjects

One hundred eighty-nine second-grade children whose mothers were part of the National Longitudinal Survey of Youth served as subjects. The children ranged in age from 80 to 100 months

(M = 7 years 9 months). The sample consisted of 104 girls. Forty-six percent of the children were African-American; the remainder were white. Hispanic children were not included in the analyses because all 1986 assessments were conducted in English, and the data set does not specify how many of the Hispanic children had sufficient English skills to complete the tasks. Forty-one percent of the children lived in households whose incomes fell below the poverty line. Forty-eight percent lived in single-parent households. Most of the children (80%) were born to adolescent mothers (M mother age at the child's birth was 18 years). Seventy-five percent of the children resided in urban areas. Maternal education, on average, was 11.3 years.

Procedures...

Family Characteristics.
The 1986 NLSY data set includes information collected from the children's mothers beginning in 1979. These measures include yearly updates on demographic variables such as mothers' age, education, marital status, family income, and child race. During 1980, measures of maternal attitudes, values, and aptitudes were collected when the focal children in the current study were infants and toddlers. The 1980 assessment included the Armed Forces Qualification Test [AFQT], Rosenberg's (1965) Self-Esteem Scale, and the women's attitudes about women's roles.

The Armed Forces Qualification Test is a general measure of the mothers' intellectual aptitude and trainability (Baker & Mott, 1989). It consists of the sum of raw scores from the following sections of the Armed Services Vocational Battery (ABVAB): Section 2—Arithmetic Reason-

ing; Section 3—Word Knowledge; Section 4—Paragraph Comprehension; and one-half of the score from Section 5—Numerical Operations.

Women's self-esteem was assessed using 4-point ratings for the 10 items that make up Rosenberg's (1965) Self-Esteem Scale. Cronbach's alpha for this scale within the current data set was .82.

The traditionality of attitudes about women's roles was measured using 5-point scales in response to four statements previously used in NLS studies: (*a*) "A woman's place is in the home, not in the office or shop," (*b*) "A wife who carries out her full family responsibilities doesn't have time for outside employment," (*c*) "It is much better for everyone concerned if the man is the achiever outside the home and the woman takes care of the family," and (*d*) "Women are much happier if they stay at home and take care of their children." Cronbach alpha within the current sample for these four items was .75.

During 1986, observers completed the standard NLSY. In addition, observers completed a shortened form of Caldwell and Bradley's HOME [Home Observation for Measurement of the Environment] scale. Ratings of the quality of the home environment were determined by mothers' responses to questions and by direct observations. The HOME scale assessed the extent to which children's home environment provided cognitive stimulation (14 items) and emotional support (12 items). Cronbach's alpha was .70 for the total scale.

Child Assessments.
During the 1986 interview, mothers also completed a questionnaire describing their children's behavior using a revised form of the Behavior Problems Index

(Pedersen & Zill, 1986). These 28 questions assessed six domains (peer conflicts, hyperactivity, anxiety, dependence, antisociability, and headstrong). A total behavior problems score standardized with a mean of 100 has been established using data from the National Health Survey. A higher score on this measure designates more behavior problems. For the NLSY children, Cronbach's alpha for the total behavior problems score was .87.

A battery of cognitive assessments was completed by the children during 1986. Subscales from the Peabody Individual Achievement Test (PIAT) were administered to measure children's mathematics and reading achievement. The Peabody Picture Vocabulary Test (PPVT) was used as an indicator of the children's verbal functioning, while the Digit Span Subscale of the WISC-R was used to assess children's short term memory and attentiveness. Standardized scores for each child were provided for the PIAT, PPVT, and digit span attention. The Digit Span was normed against a distribution with a mean of 10 and a standard deviation of 3. The PIAT and PPVT were standardized on a mean of 100.

RESULTS...

Associations Between Early and Recent Maternal Employment and Child Outcomes

... Duncan post hoc analyses revealed that both math and reading achievement scores were higher for those low-income children whose mothers were employed both early and recently in comparison to those low-income children whose mothers were not employed during either period ($p < .05$) or those children whose mothers were only recently employed

($p < .05$). PPVT scores were higher for children whose mothers were employed both early and recently in contrast to those children whose mothers were not employed during either period ($p < .05$). There were no associations between maternal employment and child behavior problems or child attention.

Maternal Selection Factors Associated With Early and Recent Maternal Employment

... Extent of maternal employment during the children's first 3 years was positively correlated with mothers' mental aptitude scores on the 1980 AFQT, $r(182) = .25$, $p < .001$. Selection factors were also indicated for mothers' employment during the previous 3 years (i.e., recent employment).... [R]ecent maternal employment hours were positively correlated with the mothers' 1980 AFQT scores, $r(180) = .23$, $p < .001$, and mothers' level of education, $r(183) = .21$, $p < .01$. These analyses suggest that economically disadvantaged women who were more intellectually competent and more highly educated were more likely to be employed than were economically disadvantaged women who were less intellectually competent.

Associations Between Maternal Employment and Family Functioning

A third set of analyses examined associations between maternal employment and the children's current home environment.... [M]aternal employment hours during the children's first 3 years was related to current family conditions in the second graders' homes. Early maternal employment hours were correlated with the quality of the second graders' home environment as assessed using the HOME, $r(156) = .17$, $p < .03$, and with the family being a two-parent household, $r(185) = -.16$, $p < .03$. Early maternal employment was negatively correlated with the second graders' families living in poverty, $r(170) = -.24$, $p < .001$. Significant correlations were also apparent between mothers' recent employment hours (i.e., employment during the previous 3 years) and current family conditions. Recent employment hours was negatively correlated with family poverty, $r(170) = -.38$, $p < .0001$, and positively correlated with quality of the HOME environment, $r(155) = .19$, $p < .01$, and with family income, $r(155) = .18$, $p < .05$.

Mothers' Employment During the First Three Years and Recently as Predictors of Child Development

The next question was whether maternal employment predicted children's development after controlling for selection factors. To test this question, a series of hierarchical multiple regressions were conducted. Within the first equation, maternal factors assessed in 1980 (AFQT, self-esteem, and traditional values) and implicated significantly or marginally significantly in differential rates of maternal employment were used in conjunction with child demographic variables (age and race) to predict the children's behaviors. In the second, third, and fourth regression equations (respectively), the increments of variance explained by the additions of (a) hours of early maternal employment, (b) hours of recent employment, and (c) both early and recent employment to the family selection variables were tested.

The first regression equation composed of the selection variables was a significant predictor of the children's math achievement, adjusted $R^2 = .32$, $p < .0001$, reading achievement adjusted $R^2 = .33$, $p < .0001$, attention, adjusted $R^2 = .10$, $p < .005$, and PPVT, adjusted $R^2 = .27$, $p < .0001$. Within these regressions, inspection of the individual betas indicated that mother's AFQT score was a significant positive predictor of children's reading achievement ($b = .51$, $p < .01$), math achievement ($b = .56$, $p < .01$), and PPVT ($b = .26$, $p < .05$) scores. Child age was a significant negative predictor of the PPVT ($b = -.17$, $p < .05$), reading ($b = -.36$, $p < .01$), and math achievement ($b = -.18$, $p < .05$) scores.

The second, third, and fourth equations tested the increments to the R^2 for the first equation provided by (a) early maternal employment hours, (b) recent employment hours, and (c) both early and recent employment. Early maternal employment contributed a significant increment to the R^2 for children's math achievement scores over and above the selection factors. The adjusted R^2 for selection factors alone was .32; the adjusted R^2 after adding early maternal employment was .35. This increment was a significant increase in R^2, $p < .05$. The addition of recent maternal employment did not improve the prediction of math achievement.

Recent maternal employment did contribute a significant increment to the R^2 for children's reading achievement ($p < .02$). The adjusted R^2 for selection factors alone was .33. The adjusted R^2 after adding recent maternal employment was .36. Recent maternal employment also contributed a significant increment ($p < .05$) to the prediction of the children's PPVT. The adjusted R^2 for the selection factors was .27. The addition of recent maternal employment increased the adjusted R^2 to .29. Early maternal employment did not contribute significant increments to the R^2's for these variables.

Neither early nor recent maternal employment contributed significantly to the variance explained for the children's behavior problems or attention span.

The next set of hierarchical regressions used as its first equation both selection factors and measures of current family conditions (poverty, marital status, HOME score) as predictors of child outcomes. The increments to R^2 provided by (a) early maternal employment, (b) recent maternal employment, and (c) both early and recent maternal employment were then tested. Thus, this set of hierarchical regressions enabled us not only to control for selection factors when examining the effects of maternal employment but also to determine if current family conditions might serve as mediators of maternal employment effects.

... [T]he addition of early maternal employment to the initial selection factors and the current family measures significantly improved the prediction of the children's math achievement ($p < .05$). The R^2 for the first equation consisting of family selection factors and current family functioning was .31. The addition of early maternal employment improved the prediction to .34. Recent maternal employment significantly improved the prediction of reading achievement ($p < .01$) and the PPVT ($p < .05$) over and above that predicted by the selection factors and current family conditions.

Tests for Moderating Factors

Because of suggestions that maternal employment effects are moderated by child gender, child race, and family marital composition, regression equations in which these interactions were added to the models... were tested. In no case did these interactions add a significant increment to R^2.

Tests for First Year and Current Year Effects

A final issue was whether single year employment records would be better predictors of child behaviors than the 3-year cumulative employment records. For these analyses, hierarchical regressions were conducted in which first year maternal employment and current year maternal employment were substituted for the 3-year cumulative scores. Results using a single year of data paralleled the 3-year cumulative data, but the adjusted R^2 and betas for the cumulative employment hours were higher in every case.

DISCUSSION

This study underscores the importance of several factors that make the study of the effects of maternal employment on children complicated: (1) self-selection results in maternal employment not being randomly distributed across families, (2) maternal employment contributes to differences in family environments that should be considered as possible mediators of maternal employment effects, (3) the timing of maternal employment must be considered because early employment and recent maternal employment predict different aspects of low-income children's development, and (4) the effects of maternal employment on children and families must be placed within a broader ecological context. Each of these points is discussed in turn.

Controlling for Self-Selection Effects

The longitudinal design of the NLSY allowed for a better test of selection effects than has typically been the case for research concerning maternal employment. In the current study, early maternal employment was associated with a number of maternal characteristics. In comparison to low-income women who were not employed during their children's first 3 years, low-income employed women (*a*) scored higher on a measure of mental aptitude (the Armed Forces Qualification Test) and (*b*) were more highly educated. These associations suggest that maternal employment is not randomly distributed across economically disadvantaged families but occurs selectively, resulting in more competent women being employed.

The nature of these associations underscores the importance of controlling for selection factors when studying the effects of maternal employment. Before taking at face value the better performance of low-income children with employed mothers on the math, reading, and language tests, it was necessary to control for selection effects. To this end, hierarchical regressions were conducted that controlled for selection factors. From these hierarchical regressions, it appeared that children from low-income families benefited from maternal employment. Children's math achievement scores were positively predicted by early maternal employment, even after controlling for the maternal and demographic selection factors such as AFQT, maternal self-esteem and attitudes, and child race. Reading achievement and PPVT scores were positively predicted by recent maternal employment, after controlling for selection factors. Within these analyses, it did not appear that the positive effects of maternal employment on the children were solely an artifact of self selection. Although one might argue that we failed to include the "right" selection factors as controls, the number of potential selection factors that were considered was large and diverse. Conse-

quently, we turn to aspects of the children's current family environment for possible processes that contribute to differences in child behavior.

Associations Between Maternal Employment and Current Family Conditions

The longitudinal design of the NLSY permitted an examination of the associations between early maternal employment and family functioning over time. In comparison to families in which mothers were employed, unemployed mothers were more likely to have families that were living in poverty when the children were in second grade. Maternal employment, on the other hand, was associated with the second graders having higher quality home environments as assessed by the HOME scale. These associations are counter to one cultural ideal in the United States, namely, that young children should be cared for in their own homes by their own mothers. This ideal could be a costly one for economically disadvantaged families. Staying home with mother can deprive families of the financial wherewithal to escape from poverty. Staying home can result in low-income families being less able, because of their economic or emotional circumstances, to provide their children with an environment that fosters development.

Although the associations between family conditions and maternal employment are important in their own right, the primary reason for including them in the current study was to use them to aid in the interpretation of the associations between maternal employment and child development. Consequently, a second set of hierarchical regressions were conducted in which both selection factors and measures of current family conditions were used as "controls." While current family conditions such as poverty were negatively associated with maternal employment and other family conditions such as quality of the HOME environment and a two-parent household were positively associated with maternal employment, it does not appear that these factors alone explain why maternal employment positively predicted children's behaviors. Early maternal employment continued to be a positive predictor of math achievement, and recent maternal employment continued to be a positive predictor of reading achievement, even after controlling for these measures of current family functioning.

It appears, then, that the study of maternal employment must turn to other child experiences in order to understand the processes by which maternal employment influences children's development. One critical aspect of children's experience not directly measured in the NLSY are children's experiences in alternate forms of child care. Interestingly, Field (1991) has reported higher math grades for children who attended high-quality infant day-care programs in contrast to children who began high-quality day-care programs later; and Andersson (1989) reported similar beneficial effects of early day-care experiences on Swedish children's math performance. The results of the current study are consistent with the contention that alternative forms of child care can be a positive force in the lives of young, low-income children. Unfortunately, the retrospective early child care questions and the limited questions about current after-school care administered as part of the NLSY do not include adequate measures of the nature of quality of the alternate child care experiences

in order for us to ascertain if the children's child care experiences were the mechanism by which maternal employment was associated with positive effects on low-income children.

Importance of Both Early and Recent Maternal Employment

Although the current study was unable to test for the potential contribution of alternate child care experiences, the results of the current study are quite clear on another issue. Whereas some (Belsky, 1988) have emphasized the importance of early experiences for child development, others have highlighted the role of recent experiences for children (Hoffman, 1989). The results of the current study point to the independent contributions of both early and recent experiences within the context of maternal employment for children's development. These differential contributions highlight the importance of including measures of both early and recent maternal employment in any study of school-age and adolescent children.

Ecological Context of Maternal Employment

Finally, the results of this study should be placed within a broader ecological context. The children observed in the current study were from economically disadvantaged families. Most had adolescent mothers who had limited education. Many of the children lived in single parent households. Within this ecological context, maternal employment was a significant positive predictor of children's math, reading, and language scores. Interestingly, these positive effects were not moderated by child gender, child race, or family marital composition.

It is premature, however, to assume that maternal employment inevitably affects low-income families in positive ways. Effects of maternal employment may be quite different for families in which mothers choose to be employed as opposed to those families in which mothers are forced by either personal circumstances or governmental regulations to be employed during their children's early years. Observations of middle-class mothers (Gold & Andres, 1978; Hock et al., 1988) suggest that the congruence between actual employment situation and preferred employment situation is a significant predictor of mothers' and children's reactions to maternal employment. Congruence may be an important moderator of the effects of maternal employment in low-income households as well.

Caution must also be taken in generalizing these results to children from middle-class or affluent families. The balance of trade-offs between financial needs, employment preferences, job stresses, and availability of child care may shift in families with different economic resources. Maternal employment may have a different meaning and different consequences for middle-class families and children.

REFERENCES

Andersson, B. E. (1989). Effects of public day-care: A longitudinal study. *Child Development, 60,* 857–866.

Baker, P. C., & Mott, F. L. (1989). *NLSY child handbook: 1989.* Columbus: Center for Human Resource Research, Ohio State University.

Belsky, J. (1988). The "effects" of infant day care reconsidered. *Early Childhood Research Quarterly, 3,* 235–272.

Belsky, J., & Eggebeen, D. (1991). Early and extensive maternal employment and young children's socioemotional development: Children of the National Longitudinal Survey of Youth. *Journal of Marriage and the Family, 53,* 1083–1110.

Bogenschneider, K. (1990). *Maternal employment and adolescent academic achievement: Mediating, moderating and developmental influences.* Unpublished doctoral dissertation, Department of Child and Family Studies, University of Wisconsin—Madison.

Cherry, F. F., & Eaton, E. L. (1977). Physical and cognitive development in children of low-income mothers working in the child's early years. *Child Development, 48,* 158–166.

Desai, S., Chase-Lansdale, P. L., & Michael, R. T. (1989). Mother or market? Effects of maternal employment on the intellectual ability of 4-year-old children. *Demography, 26,* 545–561.

Field, T. (1991). Quality infant day-care and grade school behavior and performance. *Child Development, 62,* 863–870.

Garrett, P., Lubeck, S., & Wenk, D. (1991). Childbirth and maternal employment: Data from a national longitudinal survey. In J. S. Hyde & M. J. Essex (Eds.), *Parental leave and child care.* Philadelphia: Temple University Press.

Gold, D., & Andres, D. (1978). Developmental comparisons between 10-year-old children with employed and nonemployed mothers. *Child Development, 49,* 75–84.

Greenberger, E., & Goldberg, W. A. (1989). Work, parenting, and the socialization of children. *Developmental Psychology, 25,* 22–35.

Heyns, B., & Catsambis, S. (1986). Mother's employment and children's achievement: A critique. *Sociology of Education, 59,* 140–151.

Hock, E., DeMeis, D., & McBride, S. (1988). Maternal separation anxiety: Its role in the balance of employment and motherhood in mothers of infants. In A. E. Gottfried & A. W. Gottfried (Eds.), *Maternal employment and children's development: Longitudinal research* (pp. 191–230). New York: Plenum.

Hoffman, L. W. (1989). Effects of maternal employment in the two-parent family. *American Psychologist, 44,* 283–292.

McCartney, K. (1984). Effects of quality of day care environment on children's language development. *Developmental Psychology, 20,* 244–260.

Milne, A. M., Myers, D. E., Rosenthal, A. S., & Ginsburg, A. (1986). Single parents, working mothers, and the educational achievement of school children. *Sociology of Education, 59,* 125–139.

Montemayor, R. (1984). Maternal employment and adolescent's relations with parents, siblings, and peers. *Journal of Youth and Adolescence, 13,* 543–557.

Pedersen, J. L., & Zill, N. (1986). Marital disruption, parent-child relationship, and behavioral problems in children. *Journal of Marriage and the Family, 48,* 295–307.

Rieber, M., & Womack, M. (1968). The intelligence of preschool children as related to ethnic and demographic variables. *Exceptional Children, 34,* 609–614.

Rosenberg, M. (1965). *Society and the adolescent self-image.* Princeton, NJ: Princeton University Press.

Scarr, S., Lande, J., & McCartney, K. (1989). Child care and the family: Cooperation and interaction. In J. Lande, S. Scarr, & N. Gunzenhauser (Eds.), *Caring for children: The future of child care in the United States* (pp. 1–21). Hillsdale, NJ: Erlbaum.

U.S. Bureau of Labor Statistics (1988). *Special labor force reports.* Nos. 13, 130, and 134. Washington, DC: Government Printing Office.

Vandell, D. L., & Corasaniti, M. A. (1990). Child care and the family: Complex contributors to child development. In K. McCartney (Ed.), *New directions in child development research* (pp. 23–37). San Francisco: Jossey-Bass.

Woods, M. B. (1972). The unsupervised child of the working mother. *Developmental Psychology, 6,* 14–25.

CHALLENGE QUESTIONS

Is a Child's Development Negatively Affected by a Working Mother?

1. Describe how the seemingly opposing conclusions of Baydar/Brooks-Gunn and Vandell/Janaki (on the same database) can be made compatible. Did the two sets of authors attend to differing factors?

2. Describe what you would do with your own young children under various circumstances (e.g., poor, rich, black, white). Justify your answer using the selections by Baydar/Brooks-Gunn and Vandell/Janaki.

3. How might the concept of developmental stages (e.g., Piaget's cognitive theory of development) be important to the issue of maternal employment effects?

4. Determine your own position on this issue, and support it using developmental research other than that cited in either of the selections.

ISSUE 6

Are Children of Divorced Parents at Greater Risk?

YES: Judith S. Wallerstein, from "Children of Divorce: The Dilemma of a Decade," in Elam W. Nunnally, Catherine S. Chilman, and Fred M. Cox, eds., *Troubled Relationships* (Sage Publications, 1988)

NO: David H. Demo and Alan C. Acock, from "The Impact of Divorce on Children," *Journal of Marriage and the Family* (August 1988)

ISSUE SUMMARY

YES: Judith S. Wallerstein, a clinician, researcher, and the senior consultant to the Marin County Community Mental Health Center, contends that children of divorced parents are at greater risk of developing mental and physical problems than are children of intact families.

NO: Sociologists David H. Demo and Alan C. Acock question the idea that intact, two-parent families are always best for children. They argue that any negative effects of divorce are short-lived and that divorce often produces many positive changes.

Over half of all marriages now end in divorce. What effect do these divorces have on the young children involved? Many people assume that the changes involved in divorce would naturally lead to some emotional problems, with potentially permanent ramifications. Hidden in this view, however, is the assumption that the traditional, two-parent family is the most appropriate environment in which to raise children. Indeed, most research on children of divorce has been based on this assumption.

Several developmental psychologists have begun to question this assumption. They suggest that nontraditional families—single-parent families, for example—can also produce happy, emotionally stable children. This could mean that divorce is not always negative. In fact, the effects of living in a highly conflictual environment—such as the environment of a couple contemplating divorce—could be more damaging than the actual act of divorce itself. In this sense, the level of family conflict would have more to do with a child's adjustment than would the number of parents he or she has.

Judith S. Wallerstein, while acknowledging certain limitations on the relevant research, contends that children of divorce are at great risk of developing problems. She argues that increased attention to education, treatment, and prevention programs is needed for this special population of children. She identifies three broad stages in the divorcing process along with the effects each stage has on the children. Wallerstein also chronicles changes in the parent-child relationship that occur during the divorce process. These include a diminished capacity of adults to parent their children, a decline in emotional sensitivity and support for the children, decreased pleasure in the parent-child relationship, and less interaction with the children. All these changes, she concludes, have a negative impact on the development of the children. She asserts that for most children, divorce is "the most stressful period of their lives."

David H. Demo and Alan C. Acock, on the other hand, argue that "it is simplistic and inaccurate to think of divorce as having uniform consequences for children." They contend that most current research is based upon Freudian or social learning concepts, which emphasize that both parents are necessary for a child to develop normally. Demo and Acock, however, question the necessity of the traditional, two-parent family. They cite evidence showing that parental separation is actually beneficial for children when the alternative is continued familial conflict. Other studies reveal that factors such as maternal employment and social support are more important than the actual divorce in determining how successfully a child develops following a family breakup. Unfortunately, most studies do not distinguish between the effects of family structure (one- versus two-parent families, for example) and the effects of divorce. Demo and Acock maintain that studies that make this distinction are required before any final conclusions can be drawn about the effects of divorce on children.

POINT	COUNTERPOINT
• Children of divorce are at greater risk of developing problems than are children in traditional, two-parent families.	• Nontraditional families can also produce healthy, emotionally stable children.
• Children experience parental separation and its aftermath as the most stressful period of their lives.	• Children who experience divorce indicate that it is preferable to living in conflict.
• There are significant negative changes in the parent-child relationship during the divorce process.	• There are positive outcomes of divorce, such as greater assumption of responsibility and internal locus of control.
• A child's age and developmental stage appear to be the most important factors affecting his or her response to divorce.	• These factors are not as important as family characteristics in understanding the effects of divorce.

YES

Judith S. Wallerstein

CHILDREN OF DIVORCE:
THE DILEMMA OF A DECADE

It is now estimated that 45% of all children born in 1983 will experience their parents' divorce, 35% will experience a remarriage, and 20% will experience a second divorce (A. J. Norton, Assistant Chief, Population Bureau, United States Bureau of the Census, personal communication, 1983)....

Although the incidence of divorce has increased across all age groups, the most dramatic rise has occurred among young adults (Norton, 1980). As a result, children in divorcing families are younger than in previous years and include more preschool children....

Although many children weather the stress of marital discord and family breakup without psychopathological sequelae, a significant number falter along the way. Children of divorce are significantly overrepresented in outpatient psychiatric, family agency, and private practice populations compared with children in the general population (Gardner, 1976; Kalter, 1977; Tessman, 1977; Tooley, 1976). The best predictors of mental health referrals for school-aged children are parental divorce or parental loss as a result of death (Felner, Stolberg, & Cowen, 1975). A national survey of adolescents whose parents had separated and divorced by the time the children were seven years old found that 30% of these children had received psychiatric or psychological therapy by the time they reached adolescence compared with 10% of adolescents in intact families (Zill, 1983).

A longitudinal study in northern California followed 131 children who were age 3 to 18 at the decisive separation. At the 5-year mark, the investigators found that more than one-third were suffering with moderate to severe depression (Wallerstein & Kelly, 1980a). These findings are especially striking because the children were drawn from a nonclinical population and were accepted into the study only if they had never been identified before the divorce as needing psychological treatment and only if they were performing at age-appropriate levels in school. Therefore, the deterioration observed in these children's adjustment occurred largely following the family breakup....

Divorce is a long, drawn-out process of radically changing family relationships that has several stages, beginning with the marital rupture and its immediate aftermath, continuing over several years of disequilibrium, and finally coming to rest with the stabilization of a new postdivorce or remarried family unit. A complex chain of changes, many of them unanticipated and unforeseeable, are set into motion by the marital rupture and are likely to occupy a significant portion of the child or adolescent's growing years. As the author and her colleague have reported elsewhere, women in the California Children of Divorce study required three to three-and-one-half years following the decisive separation before they achieved a sense of order and predictability in their lives (Wallerstein & Kelly, 1980a). This figure probably underestimates the actual time trajectory of the child's experience of divorce. A prospective study reported that parent–child relationships began to deteriorate many years prior to the divorce decision and that the adjustment of many children in these families began to fail long before the decisive separation (Morrison, 1982). This view of the divorcing process as long lasting accords with the perspective of a group of young people who reported at a 10-year follow-up that their entire childhood or adolescence had been dominated by the family crisis and its extended aftermath (Wallerstein, 1978).

Stages in the Process

The three broad, successive stages in the divorcing process, while they overlap, are nevertheless clinically distinguishable. *The acute phase* is precipitated by the decisive separation and the decision to divorce. This stage is often marked by steeply escalating conflict between the adults, physical violence, severe distress, depression accompanied by suicidal ideation, and a range of behaviors reflecting a spilling of aggressive and sexual impulses. The adults frequently react with severe ego regression and not unusually behave at odds with their more customary demeanor. Sharp disagreement in the wish to end the marriage is very common, and the narcissistic injury to the person who feels rejected sets the stage for rage, sexual jealousy, and depression. Children are generally not shielded from this parental conflict or distress. Confronted by a marked discrepancy in images of their parents, children do not have the assurance that the bizarre or depressed behaviors and moods will subside. As a result, they are likely to be terrified by the very figures they usually rely on for nurturance and protection.

As the acute phase comes to a close, usually within the first 2 years of the divorce decision, the marital partners gradually disengage from each other and pick up the new tasks of reestablishing their separate lives. *The transitional phase* is characterized by ventures into new, more committed relationships; new work, school, and friendship groups; and sometimes new settings, new lifestyles, and new geographical locations. This phase is marked by alternating success and failure, encouragement and discouragement, and it may also last for several years. Children observe and participate in the many changes of this period. They share the trials and errors and the fluctuations in mood. For several years life may be unstable, and home may be unsettled.

Finally, *the postdivorce phase* ensues with the establishment of a fairly stable single-parent or remarried household. Eventually three out of four divorced women and four out of five divorced men reenter wedlock (Cherlin, 1981). Unfortunately, though, remarriage does not bring immediate tranquility into the lives of the family members. The early years of the remarriage are often encumbered by ghostly presences from the earlier failed marriages and by the actual presences of children and visiting parents from the prior marriage or marriages. Several studies suggest widespread upset among children and adolescents following remarriage (Crohn, Brown, Walker, & Beir, 1981; Goldstein, 1974; Kalter, 1977). A large-scale investigation that is still in process reports long-lasting friction around visitation (Jacobson, 1983).

Changes in Parent–Child Relationships

Parents experience a diminished capacity to parent their children during the acute phase of the divorcing process and often during the transitional phase as well (Wallerstein & Kelly, 1980a). This phenomenon is widespread and can be considered an expectable, divorce-specific change in parent–child relationships. At its simplest level this diminished parenting capacity appears in the household disorder that prevails in the aftermath of divorce, in the rising tempers of custodial parent and child, in reduced competence and a greater sense of helplessness in the custodial parent, and in lower expectations of the child for appropriate social behavior (Hetherington, Cox, & Cox, 1978; 1982). Diminished parenting also entails a sharp decline in emotional sensitivity and support for the child; decreased pleasure in the parent–child relationship; decreased attentiveness to the child's needs and wishes; less talk, play, and interaction with the child; and a steep escalation in inappropriate expression of anger. One not uncommon component of the parent–child relationship coincident with the marital breakup is the adult's conscious or unconscious wish to abandon the child and thus to erase the unhappy marriage in its entirety. Child neglect can be a serious hazard.

In counterpoint to the temporary emotional withdrawal from the child, the parent may develop a dependent, sometimes passionate, attachment to the child or adolescent, beginning with the breakup and lasting throughout the lonely post-separation years (Wallerstein, 1985). Parents are likely to lean on the child and turn to the child for help, placing the child in a wide range of roles such as confidante, advisor, mentor, sibling, parent, caretaker, lover, concubine, extended conscience or ego control, ally within the marital conflict, or pivotal supportive presence in staving off depression or even suicide. This expectation that children should not only take much greater responsibility for themselves but also should provide psychological and social support for the distressed parent is sufficiently widespread to be considered a divorce-specific response along with that of diminished parenting. Such relationships frequently develop with an only child or with a very young, even a preschool, child. Not accidentally, issues of custody and visitation often arise with regard to the younger children. While such disputes, of course, reflect the generally unresolved anger of the marriage and the divorce, they may also reflect the intense emotional need of one or both parents for the young child's constant presence (Wallerstein, 1985).

Parents may also lean more appropriately on the older child or adolescent. Many youngsters become proud helpers, confidantes, and allies in facing the difficult postdivorce period (Weiss, 1979b). Other youngsters draw away from close involvement out of their fears of engulfment, and they move precipitously out of the family orbit, sometimes before they are developmentally ready....

CHILDREN'S REACTIONS TO DIVORCE

Initial Responses

Children and adolescents experience separation and its aftermath as the most stressful period of their lives. The family rupture evokes an acute sense of shock, intense anxiety, and profound sorrow. Many children are relatively content and even well-parented in families where one or both parents are unhappy. Few youngsters experience any relief with the divorce decision, and those who do are usually older and have witnessed physical violence or open conflict between their parents. The child's early responses are governed neither by an understanding of issues leading to the divorce nor by the fact that divorce has a high incidence in the community. To the child, divorce signifies the collapse of the structure that provides support and protection. The child reacts as to the cutting of his or her lifeline.

The initial suffering of children and adolescents in response to a marital separation is compounded by realistic fears and fantasies about catastrophes that the divorce will bring in its wake. Children suffer with a pervasive sense of vulnerability because they feel that the protective and nurturant function of the family has given way. They grieve over the loss of the noncustodial parent, over the loss of the intact family, and often over the multiple losses of neighborhood, friends, and school. Children also worry about their distressed parents. They are concerned about who will take care of the parent who has left and whether the custodial parent will be able to manage alone. They experience intense anger toward one or both parents whom they hold responsible for disrupting the family. Some of their anger is reactive and defends them against their own feelings of powerlessness, their concern about being lost in the shuffle, and their fear that their needs will be disregarded as the parents give priority to their own wishes and needs. Some children, especially young children, suffer with guilt over fantasied misdeeds that they feel may have contributed to the family quarrels and led to the divorce. Others feel that it is their responsibility to mend the broken marriage (Wallerstein & Kelly, 1980a).

The responses of the child also must be considered within the social context of the divorce and in particular within the loneliness and social isolation that so many children experience. Children face the tensions and sorrows of divorce with little help from anybody else. Fewer than 10% of the children in the California Children of Divorce study had any help at the time of the crisis from adults outside the family although many people, including neighbors, pediatricians, ministers, rabbis, and family friends, knew the family and the children (Wallerstein & Kelly, 1980a). Thus, another striking feature of divorce as a childhood stress is that it occurs in the absence of or falling away of customary support.

Developmental factors are critical to the responses of children and adolescents at the time of the marital rupture. Despite significant individual differences in the child, in the family, and in parent–child relations, the child's age and developmental stage appear to be the most important factors governing the initial response. The child's dominant needs, his or her capacity to perceive and understand family events, the central psychological preoccupation and conflict, the available repertoire of defense and coping strategies, and the dominant patterning of relationships and expectations all reflect the child's age and developmental stage.

A major finding in divorce research has been the common patterns of response within different age groups (Wallerstein & Kelly, 1980a). The age groups that share significant commonalities in perceptions, responses, underlying fantasies, and behaviors are the preschool ages 3 to 5, early school age or early latency ages 5 1/2 to 8, later school age or latency ages 8 to 11, and, finally, adolescent ages 12 to 18 (Kelly & Wallerstein, 1976; Wallerstein, 1977; Wallerstein & Kelly, 1974; 1975; 1980a). These responses, falling as they do into age-related groupings, may reflect children's responses to acute stress generally, not only their responses to marital rupture.

Observations about preschool children derived from longitudinal studies in two widely different regions, namely, Virginia and northern California, are remarkably similar in their findings (Hetherington, 1979; Hetherington et al., 1978; 1982; Wallerstein & Kelly, 1975, 1980a). Preschool children are likely to show regression following one parent's departure from the household, and the regression usually occurs in the most recent developmental achievement of the child. Intensified fears are frequent and are evoked by routine separations from the custodial parent during the day and at bedtime. Sleep disturbances are also frequent, with preoccupying fantasies of many of the little children being fear of abandonment by both parents. Yearning for the departed parent is intense. Young children are likely to become irritable and demanding and to behave aggressively with parents, with younger siblings, and with peers.

Children in the 5- to 8-year-old group are likely to show open grieving and are preoccupied with feelings of concern and longing for the departed parent. Many share the terrifying fantasy of replacement. "Will my daddy get a new dog, a new mommy, a new little boy?" were the comments of several boys in this age group. Little girls wove elaborate Madame Butterfly fantasies, asserting that the departed father would some day return to them, that he loved them "the best." Many of the children in this age group could not believe that the divorce would endure. About half suffered a precipitous decline in their school work (Kelly & Wallerstein, 1979).

In the 9- to 12-year-old group the central response often seems to be intense anger at one or both parents for causing the divorce. In addition, these children suffer with grief over the loss of the intact family and with anxiety, loneliness, and the humiliating sense of their own powerlessness. Youngsters in this age group often see one parent as the "good" parent and the other as "bad," and they appear especially vulnerable to the blandishments of one or the other parent to engage in marital battles. Children in later latency also have a high potential for assuming a helpful and empathic role in the care of a needy parent. School performances and peer relationships suffered a decline in approximately one-half of these children (Wallerstein & Kelly, 1974).

Adolescents are very vulnerable to their parents' divorce. The precipitation of acute depression, accompanied by suicidal preoccupation and acting out, is frequent enough to be alarming. Anger can be intense. Several instances have been reported of direct violent attacks on custodial parents by young adolescents who had not previously shown such behavior (Springer & Wallerstein, 1983). Preoccupied with issues of morality, adolescents may judge the parents' conduct during the marriage and the divorce, and they may identify with one parent and do battle against the other. Many become anxious about their own future entry into adulthood, concerned that they may experience marital failure like their parents (Wallerstein & Kelly, 1974). By way of contrast, however, researchers have also called attention to the adolescent's impressive capacity to grow in maturity and independence as they respond to the family crisis and the parents' need for help (Weiss, 1979a)....

Long-Range Outcomes

The child's initial response to divorce should be distinguished from his or her long-range development and psychological adjustment. No single theme appears among all of those children who enhance, consolidate, or continue their good development after the divorce crisis has finally ended. Nor is there a single theme that appears among all of those who deteriorate either moderately or markedly. Instead, the author and her colleague (Wallerstein & Kelly, 1980a) have found a set of complex configurations in which the relevant components appear to include (a) the extent to which the parent has been able to resolve and put aside conflict and anger and to make use of the relief from conflict provided by the divorce (Emery, 1982; Jacobson, 1978 a, b, c); (b) the course of the custodial parent's handling of the child and the resumption or improvement of parenting within the home (Hess & Camara, 1979); (c) the extent to which the

child does not feel rejected by the noncustodial or visiting parent and the extent to which this relationship has continued regularly and kept pace with the child's growth; (d) the extent to which the divorce has helped to attenuate or dilute a psychopathological parent–child relationship; (e) the range of personality assets and deficits that the child brought to the divorce, including both the child's history in the predivorce family and his or her capacities in the present, particularly intelligence, the capacity for fantasy, social maturity, and the ability to turn to peers and adults; (f) the availability to the child of a supportive human network (Tessman, 1977); (g) the absence in the child of continued anger and depression; and (h) the sex and age of the child....

FUTURE DIRECTIONS

Despite the accumulating reports of the difficulties that many children in divorced families experience, society has on the whole been reluctant to regard children of divorce as a special group at risk. Notwithstanding the magnitude of the population affected and the widespread implications for public policy and law, community attention has been very limited; research has been poorly supported; and appropriate social, psychological, economic, or preventive measures have hardly begun to develop. Recently the alarm has been sounded in the national press about the tragically unprotected and foreshortened childhoods of children of divorce and their subsequent difficulties in reaching maturity (Winn, 1983). Perhaps this reflects a long-overdue awakening of community concern.

The agenda for research on marital breakdown, separation, divorce, and remarriage and the roads that families travel between each of these way stations [are] long and [have] been cited repeatedly in this [article]. The knowledge that we have acquired is considerable but the knowledge that we still lack is critical. More knowledge is essential in order to provide responsible advice to parents; to consult effectively with the wide range of other professionals whose daily work brings them in contact with these families; to design and mount education, treatment, or prevention programs; and to provide guidelines for informed social policy.

AUTHOR'S NOTE: The Center for the Family in Transition, of which the author is the Executive Director, is supported by a grant from the San Francisco Foundation. The Zellerback Family Fund supported the author's research in the California Children of Divorce Project, one of the sources for this [article]. A slightly different version of this paper has been published in *Psychiatry Update: The American Psychiatric Association Annual Review, Vol. III*. L. Grinspoon (Ed.), pp. 144–158, 1984.

REFERENCES

Cherlin, A. J. (1981). *Marriage, divorce, remarriage.* Cambridge, MA: Harvard University Press.

Crohn, H., Brown, H., Walker, L., & Beir, J. (1981). Understanding and treating the child in the remarried family. In I. R. Stuart & L. E. Abt (Eds.), *Children of separation and divorce: Management and treatment.* New York: Van Nostrand Reinhold.

Emery, R. E. (1982). Interparental conflict and children of discord and divorce. *Psychological Bulletin, 92,* 310–330.

Felner, R. D., Stolberg, A. L., & Cowen, E. L. (1975). Crisis events and school mental health referral patterns of young children. *Journal of Consulting and Clinical Psychology, 43,* 303–310.

Gardner, R. A. (1976). *Psychotherapy and children of divorce.* New York: Jason Aronson.

Goldstein, H. S. (1974). Reconstructed families: The second marriage and its children. *Psychiatric Quarterly, 48,* 433–440.

Hess, R. D., & Camara, K. A. (1979). Postdivorce relationships as mediating factors in the consequences of divorce for children. *Journal of Social Issues, 35,* 79–96.

Hetherington, E. (1979). Divorce: A child's perspective. *American Psychology, 34,* 79–96.

Hetherington, E., Cox, M., & Cox, R. (1978). The aftermath of divorce. In H. Stevens & M. Mathews (Eds.), *Mother–child relations.* Washington, DC: National Association for the Education of Young Children.

Hetherington, E. M., Cox, M., & Cox, R. (1982). Effects of divorce on parents and children. In M. E. Lamb (Ed.), *Nontraditional families: Parenting and child development.* Hillsdale, NJ: Lawrence Erlbaum Associates.

Jacobson, D. (1978a). The impact of marital separation/divorce on children: I. Parent–child separation and child adjustment. *Journal of Divorce, 1,* 341–360.

Jacobson, D. (1978b). The impact of marital separation/divorce on children: II. Interparent hostility and child adjustment. *Journal of Divorce, 2,* 3–20.

Jacobson, D. (1978c). The impact of marital separation/divorce on children: III. Parent–child communication and child adjustment, and regression analysis of findings from overall study. *Journal of Divorce, 2,* 175–194.

Jacobson, D. S. (1983). *Conflict, visiting and child adjustment in the stepfamily: A linked family system.* Paper presented at annual meeting of the American Orthopsychiatric Association, Boston.

Kalter, N. (1977). Children of divorce in an outpatient psychiatric population. *American Journal of Orthopsychiatry, 47,* 40–51.

Kelly, J. B., & Wallerstein, J. S. (1976). The effects of parental divorce: Experiences of the child in early latency. *American Journal of Orthopsychiatry, 46,* 20–32.

Kelly, J. B., & Wallerstein, J. S. (1979). The divorced child in the school. *National Principal, 59,* 51–58.

Morrison, A. L. (1982). *A prospective study of divorce: Its relation to children's development and parental functioning.* Unpublished dissertation, University of California at Berkeley.

Norton, A. J. (1980). The influence of divorce on traditional life cycle measures. *Journal of Marriage and the Family, 42,* 63–69.

Springer, C., & Wallerstein, J. S. (1983). Young adolescents' responses to their parents' divorces. In L. A. Kurdek (Ed.), *Children and divorce.* San Francisco: Jossey-Bass.

Tessman, L. H. (1977). *Children of parting parents.* New York: Jason Aronson.

Tooley, K. (1976). Antisocial behavior and social alienation post divorce: The "man of the house" and his mother. *American Journal of Orthopsychiatry, 46,* 33–42.

Wallerstein, J. S. (1977). Responses of the pre-school child to divorce: Those who cope. In M. F. McMillan & S. Henao (Eds.), *Child psychiatry: Treatment and research.* New York: Brunner/Mazel.

Wallerstein, J. S. (1978). Children of divorce: Preliminary report of a ten-year follow-up. In J. Anthony & C. Chilland (Eds.), *The child in his family* (Vol. 5). New York: Wiley.

Wallerstein, J. S. (1985). Parent–child relationships following divorce. In E. J. Anthony & G. Pollock (Eds.), *Parental influences in health and disease* (pp. 317–348). Boston: Little, Brown.

Wallerstein, J. S., & Kelly, J. B. (1974). The effects of parental divorce: The adolescent experience. In J. Anthony & C. Koupernik (Eds.), *The child in his family: Children at psychiatric risk* (Vol. 3). New York: Wiley.

Wallerstein, J. S., & Kelly, J. B. (1975). The effects of parental divorce: The experiences of the preschool child. *American Journal of Orthopsychiatry, 46,* 256–269.

Wallerstein, J. S., & Kelly, J. B. (1980a). *Surviving the breakup: How children and parents cope with divorce.* New York: Basic Books.

Weiss, R. S. (1979a). *Going it alone: The family life and social situation of the single parent.* New York: Basic Books.

Weiss, R. S. (1979b). Growing up a little faster. *Journal of Social Issues, 35,* 97–111.

Winn, M. (8 May 1983). The loss of childhood. *The New York Times Magazine.*

Zill, N. (22 March 1983). *Divorce, marital conflict, and children's mental health: Research findings and policy recommendations.* Testimony before Subcommittee on Family and Human Services, United States Senate Subcommittee on Labor and Human Resources.

NO

David H. Demo and
Alan C. Acock

THE IMPACT OF DIVORCE
ON CHILDREN

With the acceleration of the divorce rate from the mid-1960s to the early 1980s, the number of nontraditional families (such as single-parent families and reconstituted families) have increased relative to intact, first-time nuclear families. This article reviews empirical evidence addressing the relationship between divorce, family composition, and children's well-being. Although not entirely consistent, the pattern of empirical findings suggests that children's emotional adjustment, gender-role orientation, and antisocial behavior are affected by family structure, whereas other dimensions of well-being are unaffected. But the review indicates that these findings should be interpreted with caution because of the methodological deficiencies of many of the studies on which these findings are based. Several variables, including the level of family conflict, may be central variables mediating the effect of family structure on children.

The purpose of this article is to review and assess recent empirical evidence on the impact of divorce on children, concentrating on studies of nonclinical populations published in the last decade. We also direct attention to a number of important theoretical and methodological considerations in the study of family structure and youthful well-being. We begin by briefly describing some of the theoretical propositions and assumptions that guide research in this area.

THEORETICAL UNDERPINNINGS

Consistent with the Freudian assumption that a two-parent group constitutes the minimal unit for appropriate sex-typed identification, anthropologists, sociologists, and social psychologists have long maintained the necessity of such a group for normal child development. Representative of structural-functional theorizing, Parsons and Bales argued that one of the basic functions of the family is to serve as a stable, organically integrated "factory" in which human personalities are formed.

From David H. Demo and Alan C. Acock, "The Impact of Divorce on Children," *Journal of Marriage and the Family*, vol. 50, no. 3 (August 1988). Copyright © 1988 by The National Council on Family Relations, 3989 Central Avenue, NE, Suite #550, Minneapolis, MN 55421. Reprinted by permission. Notes and references omitted.

Similarly, social learning theory emphasizes the importance of role models, focusing on parents as the initial and primary reinforcers of child behavior (Bandura and Walters, 1963). Much of the research adopting this perspective centers on parent-child similarities, analyzing the transmission of response patterns and the inhibitory or disinhibitory effect of parental models. The presence of the same-sex parent is assumed to be crucial in order for the child to learn appropriate sex-typed behavior. This assumption is shared by developmental and symbolic interactionist theories, various cognitive approaches to socialization, and confluence theory, as well as anthropological theories.

It logically follows that departures from the nuclear family norm are problematic for the child's development, especially for adolescents, inasmuch as this represents a crucial stage in the developmental process. Accordingly, a large body of research literature deals with father absence, the effects of institutionalization, and a host of "deficiencies" in maturation, such as those having to do with cognitive development, achievement, moral learning, and conformity. This focus has pointed to the crucial importance of both parents' presence but also has suggested that certain causes for parental absence may accentuate any negative effects....

Divorce and Family Structure

In examining [the] research, ... it is important to distinguish between studies investigating the effects of family structure and those investigating the effects of divorce. Most studies compare intact units and single-parent families, guided by the assumption that the latter family structure is precipitated by divorce. Of course, this is not always the case. Single-parent families consist of those with parents who have never married, those formed by the permanent separation of parents, and those precipitated by the death of a parent. Simple comparisons between one- and two-parent families are also suspect in that *two*-parent families are not monolithic. First-time or nondivorced units differ from divorced, remarried units in which stepparents are involved. In addition, little recognition has been given to the fact that families of different types may exhibit varying levels of instability or conflict, a potentially confounding variable in establishing the effects of family structure. In short, most investigations of the linkage between family structure and youthful well-being have failed to recognize the complexity of present-day families....

Bearing in mind these conceptual distinctions, we now move to a systematic review of recent evidence on the impact of divorce on children and adolescents.

EXISTING RESEARCH

A substantial amount of research has examined the effects of family structure on children's social and psychological well-being. Many studies document negative consequences for children whose parents divorce and for those living in single-parent families. But most studies have been concerned with limited dimensions of a quite complex problem. Specifically, the research to date has typically (a) examined the effects of divorce or father absence on children, ignoring the effects on adolescents; (b) examined only selected dimensions of children's well-being; (c) compared intact units and single-parent families but not recognized important variations (e.g., levels of marital instability and conflict) within these structures;

and (d) relied on cross-sectional designs to assess developmental processes.

Social and psychological well-being includes aspects of personal adjustment, self-concept, interpersonal relationships, antisocial behavior, and cognitive functioning....

Personal Adjustment

Personal adjustment is operationalized in various ways by different investigators but includes such variables as self-control, leadership, responsibility, independence, achievement orientation, aggressiveness, and gender-role orientation....

On the basis of her review of research conducted between 1970 and 1980, Cashion (1984: 483) concludes: "The evidence is overwhelming that after the initial trauma of divorce, the children are as emotionally well-adjusted in these [female-headed] families as in two-parent families." Investigations of long-term effects (Acock and Kiecolt, 1988; Kulka and Weingarten, 1979) suggest that, when socioeconomic status is controlled, adolescents who have experienced a parental divorce or separation have only slightly lower levels of adult adjustment....

While their findings are not definitive, Kinard and Reinherz speculate that either "the effects of parental divorce on children diminish over time; or that the impact of marital disruption is less severe for preschool-age children than for school-age children" (1986: 291). Children's age at the time of disruption may also mediate the impact of these events on other dimensions of their well-being (e.g., self-esteem or gender-role orientation) and thus will be discussed in greater detail below.... But two variables that critically affect children's adjustment to divorce are marital discord and children's gender.

Marital discord. ... [E]xtensive data on children who had experienced their parents' divorce indicated that, although learning of the divorce and adjusting to the loss of the noncustodial parent were painful, children indicated that these adjustments were preferable to living in conflict. Many studies report that children's adjustment to divorce is facilitated under conditions of low parental conflict—both prior to *and* subsequent to the divorce (Guidubaldi, Cleminshaw, Perry, Nastasi, and Lightel, 1986; Jacobson, 1978; Lowenstein and Koopman, 1978; Porter and O'Leary, 1980; Raschke and Raschke, 1979; Rosen, 1979).

Children's gender. Children's gender may be especially important in mediating the effects of family disruption, as most of the evidence suggests that adjustment problems are more severe and last for longer periods of time among boys (Hess and Camara, 1979; Hetherington, 1979; Hetherington, Cox, and Cox, 1978, 1979, 1982; Wallerstein, 1984; Wallerstein and Kelly, 1980b). Guidubaldi and Perry (1985) found, controlling for social class, that boys in divorced families manifested significantly more maladaptive symptoms and behavior problems than boys in intact families. Girls differed only on the dimension of locus of control; girls in divorced households scored significantly higher than their counterparts in intact households....

While custodial mothers provide girls with same-sex role models, most boys have to adjust to living without same-sex parents. In examining boys and girls living in intact families and in different custodial arrangements, Santrock and Warshak (1979) found that few effects could be attributed to family structure per se, but that children living with opposite-sex parents (mother-custody boys and father-custody girls) were not as well adjusted on measures of competent social behavior....

Along related lines, a number of researchers have examined gender-role orientation and, specifically, the relation of father absence to boys' personality development. Most of the evidence indicates that boys without adult male role models demonstrate more feminine behavior (Biller, 1976; Herzog and Sudia, 1973; Lamb, 1977a), except in lower-class families (Biller, 1981b). A variety of studies have shown that fathers influence children's gender role development to be more traditional because, compared to mothers, they more routinely differentiate between masculine and feminine behaviors and encourage greater conformity to conventional gender roles (Biller, 1981a; Biller and Davids, 1973; Bronfenbrenner, 1961; Heilbrun, 1965; Lamb, 1977b; Noller, 1978).... But it should be reiterated that these effects have been attributed to father absence and thus would be expected to occur among boys in all female-headed families, not simply those that have experienced divorce....

[M]ost of the research on boys' adjustment fails to consider the quality or quantity of father-child contact or the availability of alternative male role models (e.g., foster father, grandfather, big brother, other male relatives, coach, friend, etc.), which makes it difficult to assess the impact of changing family structure on boys' behavior. There are also limitations imposed by conceptualizing and measuring masculinity-femininity as a bipolar construct (Bem, 1974; Constantinople, 1973; Worell, 1978), and there

is evidence that boys and girls in father-absent families are better described as androgynous (Kurdek and Siesky, 1980a).

Positive outcomes of divorce. ... [T]he tendency of children in single-parent families to display more androgynous behavior may be interpreted as a beneficial effect. Because of father absence, children in female-headed families are not pressured as strongly as their counterparts in two-parent families to conform to traditional gender roles. These children frequently assume a variety of domestic responsibilities to compensate for the absent parent (Weiss, 1979), thereby broadening their skills and competencies and their definitions of gender-appropriate behavior. Divorced parents also must broaden their behavioral patterns to meet increased parenting responsibilities, thereby providing more androgynous role models. Kurdek and Siesky (1980a: 250) give the illustration that custodial mothers often "find themselves needing to acquire and demonstrate a greater degree of dominance, assertiveness, and independence while custodial fathers may find themselves in situations eliciting high degrees of warmth, nurturance, and tenderness."

Aside from becoming more androgynous, adolescents living in single-parent families are characterized by greater maturity, feelings of efficacy, and an internal locus of control (Guidubaldi and Perry, 1985; Kalter, Alpern, Spence, and Plunkett, 1984; Wallerstein and Kelly, 1974; Weiss, 1979). For adolescent girls this maturity stems partly from the status and responsibilities they acquire in peer and confidant relationships with custodial mothers....

There is evidence (Kurdek et al., 1981) that children and adolescents with an internal locus of control and a high level of interpersonal reasoning adjust more easily to their parents' divorce and that children's divorce adjustment is related to their more global personal adjustment.

Self-Concept...

Marital discord. ... [F]amily structure is unrelated to children's self-esteem (Feldman and Feldman, 1975; Kinard and Reinherz, 1984; Parish, 1981; Parish, Dostal, and Parish, 1981), but parental discord is negatively related (Amato, 1986; Berg and Kelly, 1979; Cooper, Holman, and Braithwaite, 1983; Long, 1986; Raschke and Raschke, 1979; Slater and Haber, 1984). Because this conclusion is based on diverse samples of boys and girls of different ages in different living arrangements, the failure to obtain effects of family structure suggests either that family composition really does not matter for children's self-concept or that family structure alone is an insufficient index of familial relations. Further, these studies suggest that divorce per se does not adversely affect children's self-concept. Cashion's (1984) review of the literature indicates that children living in single-parent families suffer no losses to self-esteem, except in situations where the child's family situation is stigmatized (Rosenberg, 1979)....

Cognitive Functioning

... Many ... studies find that family conflict and disruption are associated with inhibited cognitive functioning (Blanchard and Biller, 1971; Feldman and Feldman, 1975; Hess and Camara, 1979; Kinard and Reinherz, 1986; Kurdek, 1981; Radin, 1981).... In this section we summarize the differential effects of family disruption on academic performance by gender and social class and offer some insights as to the mechanisms by which these effects occur.

Children's gender. Some studies suggest that negative effects of family disruption on academic performance are stronger for boys than for girls (Chapman, 1977; Werner and Smith, 1982), but most of the evidence suggests similar effects by gender (Hess and Camara, 1979; Kinard and Reinherz, 1986; Shinn, 1978). While females traditionally outscore males on standardized tests of verbal skills and males outperform females on mathematical skills, males who have experienced family disruption generally score higher on verbal aptitude (Radin, 1981). Thus, the absence of a father may result in a "feminine" orientation toward education (Fowler and Richards, 1978; Herzog and Sudia, 1973). But an important and unresolved question is whether this pattern results from boys acquiring greater verbal skills in mother-headed families or from deficiencies in mathematical skills attributable to father absence. The latter explanation is supported by evidence showing that father-absent girls are disadvantaged in mathematics (Radin, 1981).

Children's race. ... [M]ost studies show academic achievement among black children to be unaffected by family structure (Hunt and Hunt, 1975, 1977; Shinn, 1978; Solomon, Hirsch, Scheinfeld, and Jackson, 1972). Svanum, Bringle, and McLaughlin (1982) found, controlling for social class, that there are no significant effects of father absence on cognitive performance for white or black children. Again, these investigations focus on family composition and demonstrate that the effects of family structure on academic performance do not vary as much by race as by social class, but race differences in the impact of divorce remain largely unexplored....

Family socioeconomic status. ... When social class is controlled, children in female-headed families fare no worse than children from two-parent families on measures of intelligence (Bachman, 1970; Kopf, 1970), academic achievement (Shinn, 1978; Svanum et al., 1982), and educational attainment (Bachman, O'Malley, and Johnston, 1978).... In order to disentangle the intricate effects of family structure and SES [socioeconomic status] on children's cognitive performance, family researchers need to examine the socioeconomic history of intact families and those in which disruption occurs, to examine the economic resources available to children at various stages of cognitive development, and to assess changes in economic resources and family relationships that accompany marital disruption.

Family processes. ... First, family disruption alters daily routines and work schedules and imposes additional demands on adults and children living in single-parent families (Amato, 1987; Furstenberg and Nord, 1985; Hetherington et al., 1983; Weiss, 1979). Most adolescents must assume extra domestic and child care responsibilities, and financial conditions require some to work part-time. These burdens result in greater absenteeism, tardiness, and truancy among children in single-parent households (Hetherington et al., 1983). Second, children in recently disrupted families are prone to experience emotional and behavioral problems such as aggression, distractibility, dependency, anxiety, and withdrawal (Hess

and Camara, 1979; Kinard and Reinherz, 1984), factors that may help to explain problems in school conduct and the propensity of teachers to label and stereotype children from broken families (Hess and Camara, 1979; Hetherington et al., 1979, 1983). Third, emotional problems may interfere with study patterns, while demanding schedules reduce the time available for single parents to help with homework....

Interpersonal Relationships ...

Peer relations. Studies of preschool children (Hetherington et al., 1979) and preadolescents (Santrock, 1975; Wyman, Cowen, Hightower, and Pedro-Carroll, 1985) suggest that children in disrupted families are less sociable: they have fewer close friends, spend less time with friends, and participate in fewer shared activities. Stolberg and Anker (1983) observe that children in families disrupted by divorce exhibit psychopathology in interpersonal relations, often behaving in unusual and inappropriate ways. Other studies suggest that the effects are temporary. Kinard and Reinherz (1984) found no differences in peer relations among children in intact and disrupted families, but those in recently disrupted families displayed greater hostility. Kurdek et al. (1981) conducted a two-year follow-up of children whose parents had divorced and showed that relationships with peers improved after the divorce and that personal adjustment was facilitated by opportunities to discuss experiences with peers, some of whom had similar experiences....

Dating patterns. Hetherington (1972) reported that adolescent girls whose fathers were absent prior to age 5 had difficulties in heterosexual relations, but Hainline and Feig's (1978) analyses of female college students indicated that early and later father-absent women could not be distinguished on measures of romanticism and heterosexual attitudes.

An examination of dating and sexual behavior among female college students found that women with divorced parents began dating slightly later than those in intact families, but women in both groups were socially active (Kalter, Riemer, Brickman, and Chen, 1985). Booth, Brinkerhoff, and White (1984) reported that, compared to college students with intact families, those whose parents were divorced or permanently separated exhibited higher levels of dating activity, and this activity increased further if parental or parent-child conflict persisted during and after the divorce. . . . Regarding adolescent sexual behavior, the findings consistently demonstrate that males and females not living with both biological parents initiate coitus earlier than their counterparts in intact families (Hogan and Kitagawa, 1985; Newcomer and Udry, 1987). But Newcomer and Udry propose that, because parental marital status is also associated with a broad range of deviant behaviors, these effects may stem from general loss of parental control rather than simply loss of control over sexual behavior. Studies of antisocial behavior support this interpretation.

Antisocial Behavior

Many studies over the years have linked juvenile delinquency, deviancy, and antisocial behavior to children living in broken homes (Bandura and Walters, 1959; Glueck and Glueck, 1962; Hoffman, 1971; McCord, McCord, and Thurber, 1962; Santrock, 1975; Stolberg and Ank-

er, 1983; Tooley, 1976; Tuckman and Regan, 1966). Unfortunately, these studies either relied on clinical samples or failed to control for social class and other factors related to delinquency. However, . . . a number of studies involving large representative samples and controlling for social class provide similar findings (Dornbusch, Carlsmith, Bushwall, Ritter, Leiderman, Hastorf, and Gross, 1985; Kalter et al., 1985; Peterson and Zill, 1986; Rickel and Langner, 1985). Kalter et al. (1985) studied 522 teenage girls and found that girls in divorced families committed more delinquent acts (e.g., drug use, larceny, skipping school) than their counterparts in intact families. Dornbusch et al. (1985) examined a representative national sample of male and female youth aged 12–17 and found that adolescents in mother-only households were more likely than their counterparts in intact families to engage in deviant acts, partly because of their tendency to make decisions independent of parental input. The presence of an additional adult (a grandparent, an uncle, a lover, a friend) in mother-only households increased control over adolescent behavior and lowered rates of deviant behavior, which suggests that "there are functional equivalents of two-parent families—nontraditional groupings that can do the job of parenting" (1985: 340). . . .

A tentative conclusion based on the evidence reviewed here is that antisocial behavior is less likely to occur in families where two adults are present, whether as biological parents, stepparents, or some combination of biological parents and other adults. Short-term increases in antisocial behavior may occur during periods of disruption, however, as children adjust to restructured relationships and parents struggle to maintain consistency in disciplining (Rickel and Langner, 1985).... Peterson and Zill (1986) demonstrated that, when social class was controlled, behavior problems were as likely to occur among adolescents living in intact families characterized by persistent conflict as among those living in disrupted families.... Peterson and Zill found that "poor parent-child relationships lead to more negative child behavior, yet maintaining good relationships with parents can go some way in reducing the effects of conflict and disruption" (1986: 306). Hess and Camara's (1979) analyses of a much smaller sample yielded a similar conclusion: aggressive behavior in children was unrelated to family type but was more common in situations characterized by infrequent or low-quality parent-child interaction and parental discord....

CONCLUSIONS

There is reason to question the validity of the family composition hypothesis. Theoretically, it has been assumed that the nuclear family is the norm and, by implication, that any departure from it is deviant and therefore deleterious to those involved. Even if this were the case, no theoretical perspective recognizes that these effects may be short-lived or otherwise mitigated by compensatory mechanisms and alternative role models. In the absence of a parent, it is possible that developmental needs are met by other actors.

It is simplistic and inaccurate to think of divorce as having uniform consequences for children. The consequences of divorce vary along different dimensions of well-being, characteristics of children (e.g., predivorce adjustment, age at the time of disruption) and charac-

teristics of families (e.g., socioeconomic history, pre- and postdivorce level of conflict, parent-child relationships, and maternal employment). Most of the evidence reviewed here suggests that some sociodemographic characteristics of children, such as race and gender, are not as important as characteristics of families in mediating the effects of divorce. Many studies report boys to be at a greater disadvantage, but these differences usually disappear when other relevant variables are controlled. At present, there are too few methodologically adequate studies comparing white and black children to conclude that one group is more damaged by family disruption than the other.

Characteristics of families, on the other hand, are critical to youthful well-being. Family conflict contributes to many problems in social development, emotional stability, and cognitive skills (Edwards, 1987; Kurdek, 1981), and these effects continue long after the divorce is finalized. Slater and Haber (1984) report that ongoing high levels of conflict, whether in intact or divorced homes, produce lower self-esteem, increased anxiety, and a loss of self-control. Conflict also reduces the child's attraction to the parents (White, Brinkerhoff, and Booth, 1985). Rosen (1979) concludes that parental separation is more beneficial for children than continued conflict.... Such conflict and hostility may account for adolescent adjustment problems whether the family in question goes through divorce or remains intact (Hoffman, 1971). The level of conflict is thus an important dimension of family interaction that can precipitate changes in family structure and affect children's well-being.

Maternal employment is another variable mediating the consequences of divorce for children. Divorced women often find the dual responsibilities of provider and parent to be stressful (Bronfenbrenner, 1976). But studies indicate that women who work prior to the divorce do not find continued employment problematic (Kinard and Reinherz, 1984); the problem occurs for women who enter the labor force after the divorce and who view the loss of time with their children as another detriment to the children that is caused by the divorce (Kinard and Reinherz, 1984). As a practical matter, the alternative to employment for single-parent mothers is likely to be poverty or, at best, economic dependency. The effects of maternal employment on children's well-being need to be compared to the effects of nonemployment and consequent poverty.

Other bases of social support for single-parent mothers and their children must also be examined. The presence of strong social networks may ease the parents' and, presumably, the child's adjustment after a divorce (Milardo, 1987; Savage et al., 1978). However, women who are poor, have many children, and must work long hours are likely to have limited social networks and few friends. Typically, the single mother and her children are also isolated from her ex-husband's family (Anspach, 1976). By reuniting with her family of origin, the mother may be isolated from her community and new social experiences for herself and her children (McLanahan, Wedemeyer, and Adelberg, 1981). Kinship ties are usually strained, as both biological parents and parents-in-law are more critical of the divorce than friends are (Spanier and Thompson, 1984). Little has been done to relate these considerations about kinship relations and social networks of divorced women to the well-being of children and adolescents. We believe that these social relations are important, but empirical verification is needed.

CHALLENGE QUESTIONS

Are Children of Divorced Parents at Greater Risk?

1. How should parents help their children adjust to divorce? What types of educational and treatment programs should be established to support children of divorce?

2. Which do you feel is more damaging to children, divorce or living in a conflictual environment? Give reasons (and possibly research) to support your stance.

3. What do you feel is the most significant factor affecting children's adjustment following divorce? Why? How would this affect treatment strategies for children?

4. Demo and Acock list several positive outcomes of divorce. Why do you think these occur, and can you think of other possible positive outcomes?

ISSUE 7

Do Physically Punished Children Become Violent Adults?

YES: Murray A. Straus, from "Discipline and Deviance: Physical Punishment of Children and Violence and Other Crime in Adulthood," *Social Problems* (May 1991)

NO: Joan McCord, from "Questioning the Value of Punishment," *Social Problems* (May 1991)

ISSUE SUMMARY

YES: Murray A. Straus, a social science researcher, finds a relationship between the physical punishment that young children receive and the violent acts that they commit during their teenage and adult years.

NO: Joan McCord, a professor of criminal justice, concludes that children who are rejected and neglected, not those who are physically punished, become the most violent adults.

Using physical means to punish children (e.g., spanking or slapping) is a time-honored and, some would say, infamous tradition. Even ancient biblical texts warn of "sparing the rod and spoiling the child."

Interestingly, 1994 was one of the first years on record in which a survey (commissioned by the National Committee for the Prevention of Child Abuse) indicated that a majority of parents reported *not* physically punishing their children. Why have parents begun to question physical punishment? Many of us have "survived" such punishment, but is it actually "good" for us? Does it help or hinder a child's development? Do many parents go too far, and are many children unalterably damaged by a switch or a paddle? What role do such practices play in child abuse?

These and many other questions are currently being considered by psychologists. Unfortunately, the experts seem to differ almost as much as parenting traditions and practices. Some psychologists, such as James Dobson in his book *Dare to Discipline* (Bantam Books, 1982), favor the use of punishment such as spanking, as long as parenting also includes encouragement and affection. In contrast, child development professionals Lee Salk and T. Berry Brazelton contend that physical punishment is not appropriate for behavior problems. Physical punishment, they argue, has too many negative, long-term consequences, including leading the children to become violent.

This is the position taken by Murray A. Straus in the following selection. Straus describes an explanatory model for understanding how violence begets violence—his Cultural Spillover Theory. This theory holds that violence in one sphere of life engenders violence in other spheres, regardless of how "legitimate" that violence is. In other words, even though the spanking of children is itself lawful, the fact that it is violent inevitably increases the probability of other types of violence, including those of the unlawful variety. As evidence for his theory, Straus cites correlational studies that indicate that the more an adult experienced physical punishment as a child, the higher the probability that he or she will assault his or her spouse.

Joan McCord, in opposition, asserts that the correlational nature of such evidence allows for all types of explanations. McCord emphasizes that any negative life experience can lead to crime and violence, not just physical punishment. Parental neglect of children is also highly associated with violent crime as well as physical abuse. McCord offers an alternative explanation, which she terms Construct Theory. This theory suggests that discipline, including nonphysical punishment and even the use of rewards, teaches children to focus on their own pains and pleasures, and thus teaches them to be egocentric. This egocentricity, or concern primarily for one's self, means that the welfare of others is secondary, increasing the probability that violence toward others will occur.

POINT	COUNTERPOINT
• Adults who were physically punished as children engaged in more violent crime and property crime.	• Children who were physically punished *and* given parental affection were less likely to become criminals.
• The more physical punishment experienced as a child, the higher the probability of assaulting a spouse as an adult.	• Neglect and sexual abuse were in fact more likely than physical abuse to lead to violence.
• "Legitimate violence" tends to spill over to illegitimate violence and other crimes.	• The children of criminals are likely to be criminals themselves because of a variety of factors.
• Use of physical punishment is associated with an increased risk of child abuse.	• Poor socialization, not punishment per se, contributes to inappropriate behavior.

YES

Murray A. Straus

DISCIPLINE AND DEVIANCE: PHYSICAL PUNISHMENT OF CHILDREN AND VIOLENCE AND OTHER CRIME IN ADULTHOOD

In this paper I present a theoretical model intended to aid research on physical punishment of children and its consequences. The model focuses primarily on the hypothesis that while physical punishment by parents or teachers may produce conformity in the immediate situation, in the long run it tends to *increase* the probability of deviance, including delinquency in adolescence and wife-beating, child abuse, and crime outside the family (such as robbery, assault, and homicide) as an adult. This hypothesis involves considerable irony since the intent of physical punishment is to increase socially *conforming* rather than deviant behavior. As shown below, almost all parents and a majority of teachers believe that physical punishment is an appropriate and effective form of discipline. . . .

DEFINITIONS

Physical Punishment
Exploring such issues as the legitimacy of physical punishment requires some definition of terms. Physical punishment is a legally permissible physical attack on children. The most common forms are spanking, slapping, grabbing, and shoving a child "roughly"—with more force than is needed to move the child. Hitting a child with an object is also legally permissible and widespread (Wauchope and Straus 1990). Parents in the United States and most countries have a legal right to carry out these acts, as do teachers in most U.S. states and most nations; whereas, the same act is a criminal assault if carried out by someone not in a custodial relationship to the child.

The section on "General Justification" of violence in the Texas Penal Code, for example (9.61, West Publishing Company 1983), declares that the use of force, but not deadly force, against a child younger than 18 years is justified

(1) when the actor is the child's parent or step-parent or is acting in *loco parentis* to the child, and (2) when and to the degree that the actor reasonably believes that force is necessary to discipline the child or to safeguard or promote welfare.

The New Hampshire Criminal Code (627.6:I, Equity Publishing 1985) similarly declares that "A parent, guardian, or other person responsible for the general care and welfare of a minor is justified in using force against such a minor when and to the extent that he reasonably believes it necessary to prevent or punish such a minor's misconduct." Both these statutes cover parents and teachers, and neither sets any limit except "not deadly."

Is Physical Punishment Violence?

Since the concept of violence is used in this paper as often as physical punishment, it also needs to be defined. Though the lack of a standard definition or consensus on its meaning results in considerable confusion, the following definition makes clear the conceptual framework of this paper, even though it will not be accepted by all readers: *Violence* is an act carried out with the intention, or perceived intention, of causing physical pain or injury to another person.

This definition and alternative definitions are examined in detail in Gelles and Straus (1979). As defined, violence is synonymous with the term "physical aggression" as used in social psychology (Bandura 1973; Berkowitz 1962). This definition overlaps with but is not the same as the legal concept of "assault." The overlap occurs because the definition of assault, like the definition of violence, refers to an *act*, regardless of whether injury occurred as a result of that act. However, the concept of assault is more narrow than that of violence because not all acts of violence are crimes, including acts of self-defense and physical punishment of children. Some violent acts are required by law—for example, capital punishment.[1]

The fact that physical punishment is legal is not inconsistent with the definition of violence just given, since, as noted, there are many types of legal violence. An examination of the definition shows that physical punishment of children fits every element of the definition of violence given. Thus, from a theoretical perspective, physical punishment and capital punishment are similar, despite the vast difference in level of severity.

PHYSICAL PUNISHMENT OF CHILDREN AS THE PRIMORDIAL VIOLENCE

Incidence of Physical Punishment by Parents

Ninety-nine percent of the mothers in the classic study of *Patterns of Child Rearing* (Sears, Maccoby, and Levin 1957) used physical punishment as defined above on at least some occasions, and 95 percent of students in a community college sample reported having experienced physical punishment at some point (Bryan and Freed 1982).... [T]he National Family Violence Surveys (Straus 1983; Wauchope and Straus 1990), studies of large and nationally representative samples of American children conducted in 1975 and 1985 ... found that almost all parents in the United States use physical punishment with young children—over 90 percent of parents of children age 3 and 4. A remarkable correspondence exists between the results of these four surveys in the near universality with which physical punishment was used on children age 2 to 6; and also between the two national surveys in showing that physical punishment was still being used on one out of three children at age 15.

Despite the widespread use of physical punishment, there is nontheless considerable variation—more than enough to enable empirical study of the correlates of physical punishment. First, we see that the percentage of people experiencing physical punishment drops off rapidly with age so that by age 13 there are nearly equal numbers of children who are and who are not punished. Second, at each age, there is enormous variation in how often a specific child experiences physical punishment (Wauchope and Straus 1990).

Incidence of Physical Punishment in Schools

In 1989 all but eleven states permitted physical punishment of children by school employees. A 1978–79 national survey of schools found an annual incidence of 2.5 instances of physical punishment per 100 children. Only five states reported no instances of physical punishment (calculated from Hyman 1990: Appendix B). These figures are probably best interpreted as "lower bound" estimates, and the reported absence of physical punishment in five states must also be regarded with some caution.

A THEORETICAL MODEL

In the light of the above incidence rates and the previously listed reasons for the importance of research on physical punishment, a framework is needed to help stimulate and guide research. This section presents such a framework in the form of a causal model. The model was created on the basis of previous theoretical and empirical research.

Cultural Spillover Theory

An important component of the theoretical model to be presented is what I have called "Cultural Spillover Theory" (Baron and Straus 1987; Baron, Straus, and Jaffee 1988; Straus 1985), which holds that violence in one sphere of life tends to engender violence in other spheres, and that *this carry-over process transcends the bounds between legitimate and criminal use of force.* Thus, the more a society uses force to secure socially desirable ends (for example, to maintain order in schools, to deter criminals, or to defend itself from foreign enemies) the greater the tendency for those engaged in illegitimate behavior to also use force to attain their own ends.

Cultural Spillover Theory was formulated as a macro-sociological theory to explain society-to-society differences in violence rates, such as the huge differences between societies in the incidence of murder and rape. My colleagues and I tested this theory using a 12 indicator index to measure the extent to which violence was used for socially legitimate purposes ranging from physical punishment of children to capital punishment of criminals. We found that the higher the score of a state on the Legitimate Violence Index, the higher the rate of criminal violence such as rape (Baron and Straus 1987, 1989; Baron, Straus, and Jaffee 1988) and murder (Baron and Straus 1988).

We must also understand the individual-level processes which underlie the macro-level relationship. These can be illustrated by considering the hypothesis that use of physical punishment by teachers tends to increase the rate of violence by children in schools. The individual level aspect of this hypothesis is based on two assumptions: (1) that children often mistreat other children, (2) that teachers are important role models. Therefore, if children frequently misbehave toward other children, and if teachers who serve as role models use violence to correct misbehavior, a larger proportion of children will use violence to deal with other children whom they perceive as having mistreated them than would be the case if teachers did not provide a model of hitting wrongdoers.

The Cultural Spillover Theory overlaps with the "Brutalization" Theory of capital punishment (Bowers 1984; Hawkins 1989), and the "Cultural Legitimation" Theory of homicide (Archer and Gartner 1984). All three of these theories can be considered a variant of what Farrell and Swigert (1988:295) identify as "social and cultural support" theories of crime, including the Differential Association Theory, the Delinquent Subculture Theory, and the Social Learning Theory. Each of these theories seeks to show that crime is not just a reflection of individual deviance (as in psycho-pathology theories of crime) or the absence of social control (as in Social-Disorganization Theory). Rather, crime is also engendered by social integration into groups which share norms and values that support behavior which the rest of society considers to be criminal. Thus, the processes which produce criminal behavior are structurally parallel to the processes which produce conforming behavior, but the cultural content differs.[2]

The Model

The theoretical model diagramed in Figure 1 depicts the causes and consequences of physical punishment and suggests salient issues for empirical investigation. It is a "system model" because it assumes that the use of physical punishment is a function of other characteristics of the society and its members and that physical punishment in turn influences the society and its members....

Each of the blocks in Figure 1 should also have arrows between the elements within each block; except for Block II at the center of the model, they were omitted to provide a clear picture. The arrows within Box II posit a mutually reinforcing relationship between physical punishment in the schools and by parents. It seems highly plausible that a society which approves of parents hitting children will also tend to approve of teachers doing the same, and that when physical punishment is used in the schools, it encourages parents to also hit children....

ANTECEDENTS OF PHYSICAL PUNISHMENT BY PARENTS

Block I at the left of the model identifies characteristics of the society, of the schools, of families, and of individual parents which are hypothesized to influence the extent to which physical punishment is used. This list is far from exhaustive, as are the hypotheses to be tested. Both are intended only to illustrate some of the many factors which might influence use of physical punishment.[3]

Societal Norms

Physical punishment is deeply rooted in Euro-American religious and legal traditions (Foucault 1979; Greven 1990). It would be difficult to find someone who could not recite the biblical phrase "spare the rod and spoil the child." The common law of every American state permits parents to use physical punishment. These are not mere vestiges of ancient but

Figure 1
System Model of Causes and Consequences of Physical Punishment

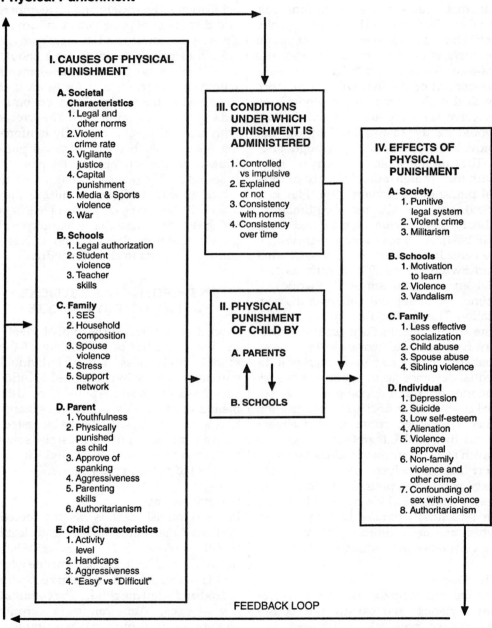

no longer honored principles. In addition to defining and criminalizing "child abuse," the child abuse legislation which swept through all 50 states in the late 1960s often reaffirmed cultural support for physical punishment by declaring that nothing in the statute should be construed as interfering with the rights of parents to use physical punishment. There is a certain irony to this legislation because, as will be suggested below, use of physical punishment is associated with an *increased* risk of "child abuse."[4]

Approval of physical punishment.
Attitude surveys have repeatedly demonstrated high approval of physical punishment. Ninety percent of the parents in the 1975 National Family Violence Survey expressed at least some degree of approval of physical punishment (Straus, Gelles, and Steinmetz 1980:55). Other studies report similar percentages. For example, a 1986 NORC national survey found that 84 percent agreed or strongly agreed that "It is sometimes necessary to discipline a child with a *good, hard spanking* (italics added). Moreover, this approval does not apply only to small children. The New Hampshire Child Abuse Survey (described in the Methodological Appendix and in Moore and Straus 1987) found that less than half of the parents interviewed (47 percent) strongly disagree with the statement "Parents have a right to slap their teenage children who talk back to them." When asked whether "Spanking children helps them to be better people when they grow up," only one out of six disagreed (16.7 percent).

Approval of hitting and actual hitting.
There is evidence that, as hypothesized by the path going from Block I.D2 of the theoretical model to Block II.A, parents who approve of physical punishment do it more often. Parents who approve of slapping a teenager who talks back reported hitting their teenager an average of 1.38 times during the year, about four times more often than the average of .33 for the parents who did not approve. For younger children, the frequency of physical punishment was much greater (an average of 4.9 times for preschool children and 2.9 times for 6-12 year old children), but the relationship between approval and actual hitting was almost identical.

Role Modeling

The path in Figure 1 from I.D2 to II.A, and from II.A to IV.C2 is based on the assumption that children learn by example, and we have seen that over 90 percent of parents provide examples of physical punishment. However, as noted above, there is a great deal of variation in how long physical punishment continues to be used and in the frequency with which it is used. This variation made it possible to test the hypothesis that the more a person experienced physical punishment, the more likely such persons are to use physical punishment on their own children. ...

EFFECTS OF PHYSICAL PUNISHMENT BY PARENTS

Block IV on the right side of Figure 1 illustrates the hypothesized effects of physical punishment on individuals, schools, families, and the society. The empirical analyses to be reported are all derived from the proposition that the "legitimate violence" of physical punishment tends to spill over to illegitimate violence and other crime. If subsequent research supports these effects, the next step will be research to identify the processes which produce them.

Physical Punishment and Physical Abuse

The basic tenant of Cultural Spillover Theory—that legitimate violence tends to increase the probability of criminal violence—is represented by the path going from II.A (physical punishment by parents) to IV.C2 (physical abuse by parents).

Analysis of the New Hampshire Child Abuse Survey (Moore and Straus 1987) shows that parents who believe in physical punishment not only hit more often, but they more often go beyond ordinary physical punishment and assault the child in ways which carry a greater risk of injury to the child such as punching and kicking. Specifically, parents who approved of physical punishment had a child abuse rate of 99 per 1,000, which is four times the rate for parents who did not approve of physical punishment (28 per 1,000).

Assaults on Siblings and Spouses

From the 1975 National Family Violence Survey (Straus 1983), we know that children who were physically punished during the year of that survey have almost three times the rate of severely and repeatedly assaulting a sibling three or more times during the year. Though it is likely that many of these children were physically punished precisely because of hitting a sibling, it is also clear that the physical punishment did not serve to reduce the level of assaults to the rate for children who were not physically punished.

Similarly, findings from the 1975 National Family Violence Survey (Straus 1983) clearly show that for both men

Figure 2

Juvenile Assault and Theft Rate by Physical Punishment

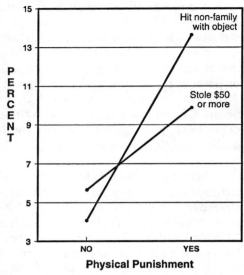

and women the more physical punishment a respondent experienced as a child, the higher the probability of assaulting a *spouse* during the year of the survey. These findings are consistent with the hypothesized path from Box II.A to IV.C3.

Physical Punishment and Street Crime

The theoretical model predicts that ordinary physical punishment increases the probability of "street crime" (path from Box II.A to IV.D.4). Evidence consistent with that hypothesis is presented in Figure 2 for juveniles and Figures 3 and 4 for adults.

The juvenile crime data are from a 1972 survey of 385 college students (Straus 1973, 1974, 1985) who completed a questionnaire referring to events when they were high school seniors. The questionnaire included an early version of the Conflict Tactics Scales and also a self-report delinquency scale. Figure 2

Figure 3
Non-Family Assaults of Adults by Physical Punishment as a Teen

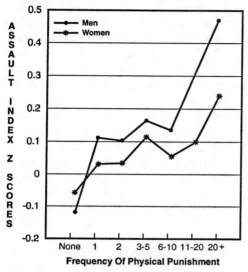

Frequency Of Physical Punishment

shows that significantly more children who were physically punished engaged in both violent crime and property crime.

The findings on crime by adults were obtained by an analysis of covariance of the 1985 National Family Violence Survey sample, controlling for socioeconomic status. Figure 3 shows that the more physical punishment experienced by the respondent as a child, the higher the proportion who as adults reported acts of physical aggression *outside the family* in the year covered by this survey. This relationship is highly significant after controlling for SES. The results are parallel when physical punishment by the father is the independent variable.

Although the arrest rate of respondents in the 1985 National Family Violence Survey was very low (1.1 percent or 1,100 per 100,000 population), this is very close to the 1,148 per 100,000 rate for the entire U.S. population (Federal Bureau of In-

vestigation 1985). Consequently, despite the low rate, we examined the relationship of arrests to physical punishment experienced during the teenage years. Although the differences overall are statistically significant (F = 3.75, p < .001), the graph does not show the expected difference between those who were and were not hit as a teen. Instead, only respondents who were hit extremely often (eleven or more times during the year) had the predicted higher arrest rates. It is possible that these erratic results occur because the base rate for arrests is so low. A statistical analysis based on a characteristic which occurs in such a small percentage of the population is subject to random fluctuations unless the sample is much larger than even the 6,002 in the 1985 survey. . . .

SUMMARY AND CONCLUSIONS

This paper formulated a theoretical model of the links between physical punishment of children and crime and also presented preliminary empirical tests of some of the paths in the model. Although the empirical findings are almost entirely consistent with the theory, they use data which cannot prove the theory because they do not establish the causal direction. Nevertheless, the fact that so many analyses which could have falsified the theory did not strengthens the case for the basic proposition of the theory: that although physical punishment may produce short term conformity, over the longer run it probably also creates or exacerbates deviance.

The Causal Direction Problem
The causal direction problem can be illustrated at the macro level by the correlation between laws authorizing

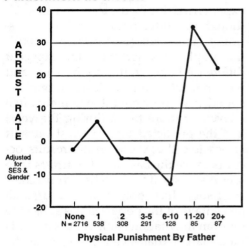

Figure 4
Arrests Per 1,000 by Physical Punishment as a Teen

physical punishment in schools and the homicide rate. It is likely that at least part of this relationship occurs because both physical punishment and crime are reflections of an underlying violent social climate. When crime and violence flourish, even ordinarily law-abiding citizens get caught up in that milieu. When crime rates are high, citizens tend to demand "getting tough" with criminals, including capital punishment and laws such as those recently enacted in Colorado and other states. These laws added protection of property to self-defense as a circumstance under which a citizen could use "deadly force." The question from the perspective of Cultural Spillover Theory is whether such laws, once in effect, tend to legitimize violence and, therefore, further increase rather than reduce violent crime.

The causal direction problem in the individual-level findings is even more obvious because it is virtually certain that part of the linkage between phys-

ical punishment and crime occurs because "bad" children are hit, and these same bad children go on to have a higher rate of criminal activity than other children.[5] However, the question is not whether misbehaving children are spanked but whether spanking for misbehavior, despite immediate compliance, tends to have longer term negative effects. Research by Nagaraja (1984), Patterson (1982), and Patterson and Bank (1987) suggests that this is the case. This research found an escalating feedback loop which is triggered by attempts to use physical punishment or verbal aggression to control deviant behavior of the child. These processes together with the hypothesized legitimation of violence are modeled in Figure 5.

It should be noted that physical punishment usually does not set in motion the deviation amplifying process just discussed, at least not to the extent that it produces seriously deviant behavior. We must understand the circumstances or branching processes which produce these different outcomes. The variables identified in Box III of Figure 1 ("Conditions Under Which Punishment is Administered") and by the diagonal path in Figure 5, are likely to be crucial for understanding this process. Three examples can illustrate this process. (1) If physical punishment is administered "spontaneously" and as a means of relieving tension, as advocated by a number of child care "experts" (e.g., Ralph 1989), it may increase the risk of producing a person who as an adult will be explosively violent, as compared to physical punishment is administered under more controlled circumstances. The latter is assumed to provide a model of controlled use of force. (2) If physical punishment is accompanied by verbal assaults, it may

Figure 5
Process Model of Effects of Corporal Punishment

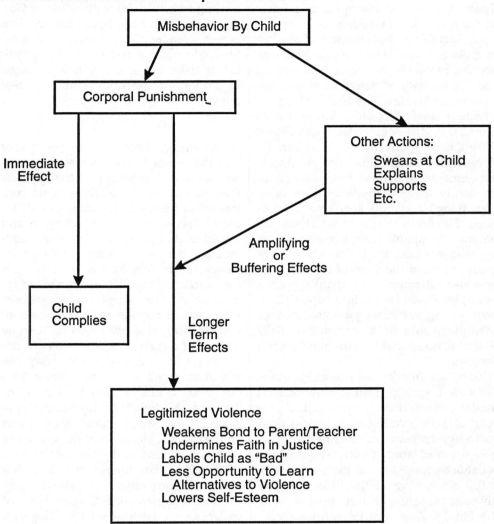

increase the risk of damage to the child's self-esteem compared to physical punishment administered in the context of a supportive relationship. (3) If physical punishment is administered along with reasoned explanations, the correlation between physical punishment and child's aggressiveness may be reduced.

A study by Larzelere (1986) found such a reduction, but also found that despite the lowered relationship, a statistically significant relationship remains.

Research Implications
Both the overall theoretical model (Figure 1) and the micro-process model (Figure

5) can only be adequately investigated with longitudinal and experimental data. There are already examples of studies at the macro-level which meet these criteria, including the research of Archer and Gartner (1984) on the effects of war on the homicide rate and research on the "brutalization" effect of executions (Bowers 1984; Hawkins 1989). At the individual level, McCord's follow up of the Cambridge-Somerville Youth Study (1988) sample illustrates what can be done with a longitudinal design. As for experiments, it would be unethical to randomly assign groups of parents to "spanking" and "no spanking" conditions. However, the fact that almost all parents do spank makes a number of experiments possible because the treatment can be in the form of helping parents use alternatives to spanking. One example would be an interrupted time series using volunteer parents. Another example would be a randomized field trial of a "no-spanking" parent education program.

There are hundreds of research questions that spring from the theoretical model presented in this paper. The process of transforming that model into meaningful research can be aided if criminologists and family violence researchers collaborate more than in the past to seek a full accounting of the links between physical punishment and crime outside the family. There are no serious structural or theoretical barriers to discourage such mutually informed work, but there is a set of beliefs that continues to define "family violence" in ways which inhibit research on physical punishment. Among family violence researchers, but especially those concerned with wife-beating, there has been a reluctance, and sometimes even condemnation, of considering ordinary physical punishment as part of the same continuum as wife-beating and child abuse (Breines and Gordon 1983: 505, 511). Spanking children is not seen as "real family violence." Similarly, among criminologists, physical punishment of children is not seen as important for understanding "real crime."

The theory developed in this paper and the research evidence so far available on that theory support the opposite formulation. However, there is no contradiction between the idea that all violence has something in common and the idea that there are important differences between various types of violence. Both propositions can be correct, and both approaches are needed for research on this complex phenomenon. Whether one focuses on the common elements in all violence or on the unique aspects of a certain type of violence depends on the purpose of the study. Research intended to inform interventions designed to aid "battered women" or "abused children," or to deter "wife-beating" or "street crime" must focus on the specific situation of those specific types of victims and offenders (Straus 1990c). However, for research intended to inform programs of "primary prevention" (Caplan 1974; Cowen 1984) of violent crime such as wife beating and homicide, it is essential to understand the social structural and social psychological process by which violence becomes an integral part of both legitimate and criminal behavior. The theoretical model presented in this paper suggests that the almost universal use of physical punishment in child rearing is part of the process.

NOTES

1. This brief discussion shows that the fact of a physical assault having taken place is not sufficient for understanding violence. Several other dimensions also need to be considered. It is also important that each of these other dimensions be measured separately so that their causes and consequences and joint effects can be investigated. Other dimensions include the seriousness of the assault (ranging from a slap to shooting), whether a physical injury was produced (from none to death), the motivation (from a concern for a person's safety, as when a child is spanked for going into the street, to hostility so intense that the death of the person is desired), and whether the act of violence is normatively legitimate (as in the case of slapping a child) or illegitimate (as in the case of slapping a spouse), and which set of norms are applicable (legal, ethnic or class norms, couple norms, etc.). See Gelles and Straus (1979) for further analyses of these issues.

2. There are a number of other theories relevant to the issues discussed in this paper. The larger theoretical task will be to integrate Cultural Spillover Theory and the theories just listed with theories such as Control Theory (Hirshi 1969), Labeling Theory (Scheff 1966; Straus 1973), Social Learning Theory (Bandura 1973; Berkowitz 1962; Eron, Walder, and Lefkowitz 1971; Gelles and Straus 1979; McCord 1988), and a variety of personality mediated theories. Although space limitations required deletion of my initial attempts to specify some of the interrelationships, the concluding theoretical discussion is a small step in that direction. I argue that physical punishment might bring about changes in personality, such as lowered self-esteem or increased powerlessness and alienation. These personality variables can, by themselves, serve as "risk factors" for violence. At the empirical level, it will require a "competing theories" research design and triangulation via several different types of research to adequately investigate these issues.

3. Moreover, due to space limitations, I will only discuss the paths for which I carried out empirical tests. However, since a reader of an earlier draft of the paper questioned the hypothesized paths and feedback loop running from use of corporal punishment back to low teacher and parental skill (I.C3 and I.D5), the reasoning needs to be summarized: It is simply that to the extent parents and teachers use corporal punishment as a means of inducing appropriate behavior, they get less practice in using other means of inducing appropriate behavior and, therefore, do not enhance their skills in those techniques, thus further increasing the probability of using corporal punishment.

4. A study of the reasons for including reaffirmation of corporal punishment in the child abuse legislation might provide important insights on American attitudes about children and violence. Such a study could be undertaken by analysis of the proceedings of state legislatures. For the moment, I would like to suggest two scenarios, both of which may have been operating. The first reason is that both spring from a concern about the welfare of children, and specifically the idea that children need to be protected from abuse but also need "strong discipline" (including physical punishment "when necessary") if they are to become responsible law-abiding citizens. The second reason is that the combination reflects a political compromise which the advocates of "child protection" needed to make in order to have the legislation pass. However, these two reasons overlap to a certain extent because conservative members of the legislatures who needed to be placated favor physical punishment because they deeply believe it is in the best interests of children.

5. I emphasize "a higher *rate*" because most "bad" children, regardless of whether they have been physically punished, do not become criminals. The theory put forth in this paper does not assert that corporal punishment is a necessary and sufficient cause of violence and other crime. On the contrary, crime is a multiply determined phenomenon, and corporal punishment is assumed to be only one of these many causes. Consequently, many individuals who have not been assaulted as children engage in crime, just as many who have been assaulted by teachers or parents avoid criminal acts.

NO

Joan McCord

QUESTIONING THE VALUE
OF PUNISHMENT

The author critically examines and rejects the claim that physical punishments lead to aggression through the acceptance of norms of violence. She proposes an alternate theory to account for how children acquire norms and why they become violent. The proposed Construct Theory explains why abused, neglected, and rejected children—as well as those who are punished—tend to become anti-social.

"Spare the rod and spoil the child," many have argued. "No," say others, as they refer to evidence that physical punishment leads to, rather than prevents, violent behavior. Yet only a few, it seems, have whispered that we should question the value of every type of punishment, including psychological punishments and deprivation of privileges as well as physical punishments.

When attention has been focused only on physical punishment, critics typically note that such discipline provides a model for the use of force, thereby teaching people to use force. Murray Straus, for example, argues that corporal punishment contributes to a cycle of violence that includes violent crime, child abuse, spouse abuse, non-violent crimes, ineffective family socialization, and ineffective schooling. Straus accounts for correlations between the use of physical punishment, on the one hand, and antisocial or dysfunctional behaviors on the other by means of Cultural Spillover Theory. This theory is an amalgam of explanations that consider behavior to be learned through imitation of models and adoption of norms supported by groups with whom an individual associates. In this view, individuals come to accept the use of violence—and to be violent—because they see violence as legitimated through its use by role models, and they generalize the behavioral norm to include illegitimate uses of violence.

While Straus is correct that physical punishments tend to increase aggression and criminal behavior, I believe he takes too narrow a view about the mechanisms that account for the relationships. My conclusion is grounded in evidence from longitudinal studies about the transmission of violence from

From Joan McCord, "Questioning the Value of Punishment," *Social Problems*, vol. 38, no. 2 (May 1991), pp. 167–176. Copyright © 1991 by The Society for the Study of Social Problems. Reprinted by permission.

one generation to the next. I offer a competing theory, one that merges evidence from experimental studies designed by psychologists to understand the conditions under which children learn and that considers critical issues related to the learning of language. The competing theory, which I call the Construct Theory, suggests how the same mechanism that links physical punishment to aggression can be triggered by nonphysical punishments and neglect. Before turning to the competing theory, I present empirical evidence that physical punishment leads to aggression and criminal behavior and then show that the Cultural Spillover Theory inadequately explains the relationship.

PROBLEMS WITH THE CULTURAL SPILLOVER EXPLANATION

Much of the research to which Straus refers in his analysis of the relationship between physical punishment and misbehavior is cross-sectional. With such data, as Straus acknowledges, one cannot determine whether punishments were a cause or an effect of the behavior. Three longitudinal studies that measured discipline prior to the age serious antisocial behavior began, however, suggest temporal priority for punitive discipline. Comparing children whose parents depended on physical punishments with those whose parents did not in Finland (Pulkkinen 1983), Great Britain (Farrington 1978), and in the United States (McCord 1988), researchers found that those whose parents used harsh physical punishments had greater probabilities for subsequently committing serious crimes. Longitudinal studies of victims of child abuse, too, suggest that violence tends to increase the probability that victims will

commit serious crimes (McCord 1983; Widom 1989).

The theory of Cultural Spillover, like similar theories that attempt to explain pockets of violence, postulates acceptance of norms exhibited by the subculture using violence. Although longitudinal studies suggest that violence in the family precedes violence in society, they contain data incongruent with a theory that explains the causal mechanism as socialization into norms that legitimize violence.

One incongruence is revealed in my study of long-term effects of child abuse in which I compared abused sons with neglected and rejected and loved sons (McCord 1983). The classifications were based on biweekly observations in the homes when the boys were between the ages of 8 and 16 years and living in high-crime areas. Records of major (FBI Index) crime convictions were collected thirty years after the study ended. Twenty-three percent of those reared in loving families and 39 percent of those reared in abusing families had been convicted; but the conviction rate was 35 percent for the neglected and 53 percent for the rejected boys. That is, the data show almost as much violence produced from neglect as from abuse, and greater violence from rejection without abuse than from abuse. Because neglect and rejection typically lead to socialization failure, these results raise doubts that acceptance of norms of violence account for transmission of violence. It would be an anomaly if the very conditions that undermine acceptance of other types of norms promoted norms of violence.

One might argue that Cultural Spillover Theory accounts for violence among the abused and some other theory accounts for violence among neglected and rejected children. Yet neglect and rejection have enough in common with abuse to suggest that a more parsimonious account would be desirable. Furthermore, as will be shown, when neglect is combined with abuse, the result is not increased violence as one would expect were there different causes involved.

My data from the Cambridge-Somerville Youth Study records permitted further checks on the Cultural Spillover Theory. The data include parental criminal records as well as coded descriptions of family life between 1939 and 1945. Sons' criminal records had, as noted, been collected in 1978, when the sons were middle-aged. Among the 130 families containing two natural parents, 22 included a father who had been convicted for an Index crime. Fifty-five percent (12) of their sons were convicted for an Index crime. In comparison, twenty-five percent (27) of the 108 sons of noncriminal men had been convicted ($X^2_{(1)}$ = 7.60, P = .006). The criminal fathers were more likely to use physical punishment: 73 percent compared with 48 percent ($X^2_{(1)}$ = 4.43, P = .035). Further, the combined impact of a criminal father using physical punishment appeared to be particularly criminogenic.

These data support the view that use of physical punishment increases the likelihood that sons of criminals will be criminals. Cultural Spillover Theory suggests that the increase comes about because sons adopt the norms displayed through physical punishments. If the theory were correct, then the transmission of norms of violence should be particularly effective under conditions that promote acceptance of other types of norms as well. The evidence, however, gives another picture.

Many studies have shown that warmth or affection facilitates acceptance of social norms (e.g., Austin 1978; Bandura and Huston 1961; Bandura and Walters 1963; Baumrind 1978; Bender 1947; Bowlby 1940; Glueck and Glueck 1950; Goldfarb 1945; Hirschi 1969; Liska and Reed 1985; Maccoby 1980; McCord 1979; Olson, Bates, and Bayles 1990; Patterson 1976). Parental affection for the child should increase concordance if a similar mechanism for acceptance of norms accounts for a connection between parents' and children's aggression. To test this hypothesis, the 130 families were divided into three groups: those not using physical punishment, those using physical punishment and also expressing affection for the child, and those using physical punishment and not expressing affection for the child.

The data show that parental affection did not increase acceptance of norms of violence, but the opposite. For individuals reared with physical punishment, those whose parents were affectionate were *less* likely to become criminals. This result does not easily fit an assumption that normative acquisition accounts for the violence.

Another inconsistency is apparent in a longitudinal study that at first glance might appear to support the Cultural Spillover Theory. Widom (1989) retraced children reported to have been victims of abuse or neglect prior to the age of 11. Using records from elementary schools and hospitals at birth, Widom was able to match 667 of 908 children on sex, race, and age with children not known to have been either abused or neglected. Widom's analyses, based either on aggregate data combining abuse with neglect or matched and unmatched cases, have led her to conclude that violence breeds violence.

I reanalyzed her data (Widom 1990) to differentiate effects of neglect from effects of violence.

The matched pairs were divided into those in which the child had experienced sexual abuse (85 females, 15 males), neglect but not physical abuse (205 females, 254 males), physical abuse but not neglect (14 females, 35 males), and both physical abuse and neglect (29 females, 30 males). Assuming that acceptance of a norm of violence accounts for the high rates of crime that Widom found to follow abuse, crime would be considerably more prevalent among those who had been physically abused than among those who had been neglected but not abused.

Using Widom's codes of the individuals' criminal records, I compared each case with the matched control to see which had the worse criminal record. If both had been convicted of at least one crime, the one convicted for more crimes was counted as being worse.

The data show that neglect is about as criminogenic as sexual abuse and physical abuse. Moreover, the combined effects of neglect and abuse are not worse than those of either alone as would be expected if each had separate causal impact. Comparisons of cases and controls for crimes of violence (e.g., assault, murder, attempted murder) produced similar results.

These comparisons again suggest that continuity in violence among abusing families has been mistakenly attributed to transmission of norms of violence. Among males, neglect and sexual abuse were in fact more likely than physical abuse to lead to violence. Yet if transmission of social norms accounts for violence, physical abuse should create more. The reanalysis of these data suggest that one ought to search for a common cause, for something shared by neglect and abuse that might lead to violence.

In sum, violence seems to beget violence, but studies of child abuse and of family socialization undermine the argument that violence begets violence *through acceptance of family (subcultural) norms of violence.* Because neglect, rejection, and physical abuse result in similarly high rates of crime, it seems appropriate to search for a cause in terms of what they have in common.

A sound understanding of the way children learn can explain why physical abuse, neglect, and rejection lead to antisocial behavior. Below I develop such an understanding to show that a norm of self-interest, rather than a norm of violence, underlies the education shared by those who are rejected, neglected, and abused. It is the norm of self-interest that leads to violence in some circumstances.

UNDERMINING SOME ASSUMPTIONS

Side stepping the issue of how infants learn, many psychologists have simply assumed that babies are completely self-centered. In contrast, the evidence shows that how much children care about their own pleasures and pains and what they will consider pleasurable and painful is largely a function of the way are taught.

It may, for instance, be tempting to believe that an infant "instinctively" cries for food, to be held, or to have dirty diapers removed, but evidence points to large contributions from experience. In a study of neonates, Thoman, Korner, and Benson-Williams (1977) randomly assigned primiparous healthy newborns to conditions in which one third were held when they awakened. As anticipated by the authors, the babies who were held spent more time with their eyes open and cried less vigorously while being held; unexpectedly, however, they spent more time crying during non-stimulus periods. The babies had been equated for pretrial behaviors, so the authors suggest that the infants had come to associate their crying with being picked up during the 48 hour training period.

In another study also showing that neonates learn from their environments, Riese (1990) compared 47 pairs of monozygotic twins, 39 pairs of dizygotic twins of the same sex, and 72 pairs of dizygotic twins of the opposite sex. Using standardized tests for irritability, resistance to soothing, activity level when awake, activity level when asleep, reactivity to a cold disk on the thigh and to a pin prick, and response to cuddling, she found significant correlations for the dizygotic twins (both same and opposite sex), indicating shared environmental influences, but no significantly larger correlations among the monozygotic pairs. Riese concluded that "environment appears to account for most of the known variance for the neonatal temperament variables" (1236).

Just as neonates can learn to cry in order to be picked up, children learn what to consider painful. Variability in recognizing sensations as painful has been dramatically evidenced through studies of institutionalized infants, who received serious injuries without seeming to notice (Goldfarb 1958). During the period of observation, one child caught her hand in the door, injuring a finger so severely that it turned blue; yet the child did not cry or otherwise indicate pain. Another child sat on a radiator too hot for the teacher to touch. Observed injuries also included a child who was cutting the palm of his own hand with sharp scissors and another who had removed from her cornea a steel splinter that had been imbedded for two days without any report of pain. All the children, however, gave pain responses to a pin prick, dispelling the hypotheses that they had a higher than normal threshold for pain. Goldfarb reasonably concluded: "The perception of pain and the reaction to pain-arousing stimuli are episodes far more complex than is implied in the concept of pure, unencumbered sensation" (1945: 780–781).

Often, children show no signs of pain after a fall until adults show that they expect a "pained" response. Studies with college students that feeling pain is influenced by pain exhibited by models (Craig and Theiss 1971), role playing as calm or upset (Kopel and Arkowitz 1974), and feedback from one's own responsive behavior (Bandler, Madaras, and Bem 1968). My personal experience and reports from students suggest that children whose mothers do not respond to their cuts with anxious concern do not exhibit such pain-behavior as crying when they fall.

Not only do children learn what is painful, but they attach pleasure to circumstances intended to result in pain. Solomon (1980) demonstrated that over a range of behaviors, pain-giving consequences acquire positive value through repetition (see Shipley 1987; Aronson, Carlsmith, and Darley 1963; Walster, Aronson, and Brown 1966). Studies showing that children learn to repeat behaviors that result in "reinforcement" through negative attention demonstrate that expectations are only one basis for the attraction of "pain-giving" stimuli (Gallimore, Tharp, and Kemp 1969; Witte and Grossman 1971).

Children also learn without extrinsic reinforcement. Curious about why so many young children appeared to increase their aggressiveness in experimental situations, Siegel and Kohn (1959) measured aggression both with and without an adult in the room. Only when adults were present did escalation occur. The authors drew the sensible conclusion that young children assume that what is not forbidden is permitted.

The egocentric motivational assumption that underlies classic theories of socialization has been subjected to a series of criticism, most notably by Butler (1726) and Hume (1960 [1777]). These authors pointed out that the plausibility of the egocentric assumption rests on circular reasoning. The fact that a voluntary action must be motivated is confused with an assumption that voluntary actions must be motivated by desire to benefit from them. Often the only evidence for self-interest is the occurrence of the act for which a motive is being sought.

Raising further questions about the assumption of egocentrism in children, some studies indicate that altruistic behavior is not always egoistic behavior in disguise (Batson et al. 1988; Grusec and Skubiski 1970). In fact, altruistic behavior turns up at very young ages (Rheingold and Emery 1986; Zahn-Waxler and Radke-Yarrow 1982; Zahn-Waxler et al. 1988) suggesting that even babies are not exclusively interested in themselves.

The prevalent view that children require punishment in order to learn socialized behavior rests on three erroneous assumptions. The first two—that children are motivated by self-interest and that what gives them pain is "fixed"—have been shown to lack support in empirical research. The third—that unless there are punishments rules have no power—

is addressed in my proposal of Construct Theory.

AN ALTERNATIVE: CONSTRUCT THEORY

Construct Theory states that children learn what to do and what to believe in the process of learning how to use language. In simplest form, Construct Theory claims that children learn by constructing categories organized by the structure of the language in their culture. These categories can be identified by descriptions, much as one might identify a file, for example, "accounting," "things to do," "birthdays," "Parsons, T.," "true." Some categories are collections of objects, but others are actions that can be identified by such descriptions as "to be done" or "to be believed" or "to be doubted."

Learning a language requires learning more than concepts. Children learn not only what to count as tables and chairs, cars and trucks, but also what to count as painful or pleasant, undesirable or desirable, and worth avoiding or pursuing. In learning labels, in learning how to name and to re-identify objects, children are constructing classifications. The classification systems they develop will permeate what they notice and how they act as well as what they say.

Construct Theory explains the fact that different people consider similar events to have different affective characteristics —for example, as undesirable and desirable—because individuals construct different classifications of the events. This theory can account for relations between knowledge and action that have led many theorists to conjure "pro-attitudes" as the means by which some knowledge sometimes changes behavior (e.g.,

Kenny 1963; Milligan 1980; Müller 1979; Nowell-Smith 1954). According to Construct Theory, those reasons that move one to action are classified as "reasons worth acting upon"; no special entity need also be attached to them.[1] Construct Theory also explains how language can be learned and how people can communicate, for it shows the way in which meanings can be made public through the categories that are constructed.[2]

Learning a language involves learning to formulate sentences as well as learning how to use words. At its most fundamental level, sentences involve stringing together what logicians call "predicates" (which can be thought of as classes) and functional relations among them. Perhaps no component of a sentence is so critical to understanding how punishment works as the connective "if . . . then," for on this connective punishments rely. This connective also gives linguistic expression to what the neonates described above learned when they cried and were picked up (if I cry, then I will be picked up), what an infant learns by pushing a ball (if I push, then it will roll), and what the child learns when discovering natural consequences in the physical world.

Both natural and artificial contingencies provide information to the child who is learning about consequences. When a child is credibly threatened with punishment, the information conveyed extends beyond the intended message that the child ought not do something. A punishment is designed to give pain. Unless the chosen event is thought by the punisher to be painful, it would not be selected as a means for controlling the child's behavior. What is selected as a punishment, then, shows what the punisher thinks to be painful.[3]

A child also perceives the intention of the punisher to give pain (and may attempt to thwart the intention by saying such things as "I didn't like the dessert anyway" or "There's nothing good on TV anyhow"). So the use of punishment shows the child that the punisher is willing to hurt the threatened or punished child. This knowledge may decrease the child's desire to be with the punisher or to care how the punisher feels, thereby reducing the socializing agent's influence.

An interesting study illustrated another feature of punishment: it conveys information about what (according to the punisher) is valuable, thus potentially enhancing the value of the forbidden. Aronson and Carlsmith (1963) asked preschool children, individually, to compare five toys until they established stable transitive preferences. The experimenter then said he had to leave the room for a few minutes and placed on a table the toy ranked second-favorite by the child. The child was told not to play with that toy but that playing with the others was permissible. Half of the 44 children were randomly assigned to each of two conditions. In the "mild threat" condition, the experimenter said he would be annoyed if the child played with the forbidden toy. In the "severe threat" condition, the experimenter said that if the child played with the forbidden toy, the experimenter would be very angry and would take all the toys and never come back. The experimenter left the child for 10 minutes. Approximately 45 days later, the children were again asked to rank the five toys. For this ranking, 4 of the children from the mild threat condition ranked the forbidden toy as a favorite whereas 14 of those in the severe threat condition regarded the forbidden toy as the favorite. Conversely, 8 of those who were merely told that the experimenter would be annoyed had decreased their preference for the forbidden toy whereas none of the children who were threatened with punishment had they played with the toy decreased their preference for it.

In a near replication, Lepper (1973) found that, two weeks later, children from his stronger threat condition were more likely to cheat in a game. There are two explanations for this. Lepper explained the findings by suggesting that the children who resisted with severe threat reasoned: "I am the sort of person who would break the rules except for the fact that I would be punished." In contrast, according to this self-referential theory, the children under mild threat defined themselves as the sorts of people who generally conform to rules and requests.

I suggest an alternative explanation: The different exposures in the experiment taught the children something about the world and about other people—not primarily something about themselves. The more severe threats taught the children that they ought to orient their behavior around estimates of consequences *to themselves*. In the process of assessing their self-interests, the children looked for attractive features of that which had been forbidden. The "mild threat" condition in both experiments, however, implied only that the child should be concerned about how the experimenter might feel.

Punishments are invoked only when rules are disobeyed, so that telling a child about rules in conjunction with information about punishments for infractions informs a child that he or she has a choice: obey, or disobey-and-accept-the-consequences named as punishment.

Negative correlations between a parent's use of punishments and insistence that rules be followed were so strong in their study of misbehavior that Patterson, Dishion, and Bank (1984) could not use both measures in their model. Believing that punishments were more important, they dropped the follow-through measure. The data, however, show equally that a parent who insists that rules be followed need not use punishments to socialize children.

It might be tempting to argue that rewards circumvent the unwanted effects of punishment as a means for teaching norms. That would be a mistake. Although using rewards does not hazard rejection of the purveyor, rewarding shares many of the characteristics of punishing. Rewards as well as punishments employ the "if ... then" relationship. Laboratory studies have demonstrated, as predicted from the Construct Theory, that contingent reinforcements sometimes interfere with the discovery of general rules (Schwartz 1982). Studies have demonstrated, also as predicted from Construct Theory, that incentives larger than necessary to produce an activity sometimes result in devaluation of the activity being rewarded (Greene and Lepper 1974; Lepper, Greene, and Nisbett 1973; Lepper et al. 1982; Ross 1975; Ross, Karniol, and Rothstein 1976).

Like those involved in punishments, contingencies that use rewards convey more information than intended when a socializing agent uses them to convince a child to do something. A reward is designed to be attractive, so rewards contain information about what the rewarder believes to be valuable. When a reward is clearly a benefit to the person being promised the reward, rewarding teaches the child to value his or her own benefit.[4]

In addition to learning that whatever requires reward is probably considered unpleasant, children learn that the reward is something considered valuable by the reward-giver. That children *learn* to perceive rewards as valuable has been demonstrated in the laboratory (Lepper et al. 1982). Children were told a story about a mother giving her child two supposed foods; children in the study were asked which the child in the story would prefer: "hupe" or "hule." Children in the experimental group were told that the mother explained to her child that (s)he could have one ("hupe" or "hule" for different children) if (s)he ate the other. In this condition, the contingent relation led the children to suppose that the second food was a reward for eating the first. The children overwhelmingly thought the second food would be preferred—and gave grounds for the choice in terms of its tasting better. The experiment showed that the continguent relation, rather than the order of presentation, influenced preference because children in the control condition who were told only that the child's mother gave the child first one and then the other food either refused to make a choice or gave no reason for a selection (which they equally distributed between the two). In other experiments with preschool children, play objects have been manipulated similarly, showing that an activity that is arbitrarily selected as the one to be rewarded will be "discounted" whereas the arbitrarily selected inducement gains value (e.g., Lepper et al. 1982; Boggiano and Main 1986). These studies show that children learn what to value as well as how to act from perceiving the ways in which rewards are used.[5]

The Construct Theory explains why punishments tend to increase the attraction of activities punished—and why extrinsic rewards tend to reduce the value of activities rewarded. The categorizing that children learn as they learn sentences in a language can be schematically represented by formal logic. When children become aware of the logical equivalence between the conditional (if x then y) and the disjictive (either not-x or y), they learn that *rewards and punishments weaken the force of a rule by introducing choices.* If rewards are designed to give pleasure to the child and punishments are designed to give the child pain, then their use teaches children that they ought to value their own pleasure and to attempt to reduce their own pain.

CONCLUSION

Rewards and punishments are used to manipulate others. They often result in short-term gains, but their use teaches children to look for personal benefits. Like rewards and punishments, neglect and rejection teach egocentrism. Children brought up among adults who do not attend to their well-being are given no grounds for learning to consider the welfare of others.

Using punishment seems particularly short-sighted. Punishments may increase the attraction of forbidden acts. They also risk desensitizing children both to their own pains and to the pains of others (Cline, Croft, and Courrier 1973; Pearl 1987; Thomas et al. 1977). Although severe penalties may force compliance in specific instances, the behavior being punished is actually more likely to occur at a time or place when opportunities for detection are reduced (Bandura and Walters 1959).

No increase in punishment or in reward can guarantee that children will make the choices adults wish them to make. Several studies show, however, that children are more likely to want to do what an adult wishes if the adult generally does as the child desires. In one study, randomly selected mothers of preschoolers were trained to respond to their children's requests and to avoid directing them during a specified period of time each day for one week. Their children complied with more of the mother's standardized requests in the laboratory than the comparison group of children whose mothers used contingency training (Papal and Maccoby 1985). The results are mirrored in a natural setting with the discovery that children reared at pre-school age in a consensual environment were among the most likely to value autonomy, intellectual activity, and independence as well as to have high educational aspirations ten years later (Harrington, Block, and Block 1987).

In another study, mothers and children were observed at home for three months when the children were between 9 and 12 months in age. Mothers were rated for their sensitivity to their babies, a rating based on their perceived ability to see things from the baby's perspective, positive feelings expressed toward the baby, and adaptations favoring the baby's arrangements of his or her own behavior. Discipline was rated for verbal commands as well as for frequency of any physical interventions. The baby's compliance was a simple measure of the proportion of verbal commands the baby obeyed without further action by the mother. Compliance turned out to be practically unrelated to discipline, although it was strongly related to the mother's responsiveness. The authors note: "The findings suggest that a disposition toward obedience emerges in a responsive, accommodating social environment without extensive training, discipline or other massive attempts to shape the infant's course of development" (Stayton, Hogan, and Ainsworth 1971:1065).

Punishments—nonphysical as well as physical—teach children to focus on their own pains and pleasures in deciding how to act. If parents and teachers were to substitute non-physical punishments for physical ones, they might avoid teaching children to hit, punch, and kick; yet, they would nevertheless perpetuate the idea that giving pain is a legitimate way to exercise power. If the substitute for physical punishment were to be non-physical punishments, the consequences could be no less undermining of compassion and social interests.

Children do not require punishments if their teachers will guide them consistently, and they do not require rewards if intrinsic values of what they ought to do are made apparent to them. I am not suggesting that a child will be constantly obedient or agree completely with the values of those who do not punish. No techniques will guarantee a clone. Rather, I do suggest that children can be taught to follow reasonable rules and to be considerate—and that the probabilities for their learning these things are directly related to the use of reason in teaching them and to the consideration they see in their surroundings.

Straus turns a spotlight on physical punishment, suggesting that by using violence to educate, adults legitimize the use of violence. I paint a broader canvas, suggesting that by using rewards and punishments to educate, adults establish self-interest as the legitimate grounds for choice.

NOTES

1. This interpretation of language provides a modification of the Aristotelian notion that action is the conclusion of a practical syllogism; it adds a proviso that the syllogism must correctly represent the classification system of the actor, and then "straightway action follows." The interpretation also reflects the Humean claim that reason alone cannot account for action. It does so by including motivational classifications as separate from purely descriptive classifications.

2. Wittgenstein (1958) demonstrated the implausibility of accounting for language through private identification of meanings.

3. Thus, there is the irony that when teachers use school work, parents use performing chores, and both use being by oneself as punishments, they are likely to create distaste for learning, doing chores, and being alone.

4. One could, of course, reward a child by permitting some action beneficial to others or by permitting the child a new challenge.

5. The phenomenon is well enough known to have produced several theories, ranging from balance theory (Heider 1946) and Theory of Cognitive Dissonance (Festinger 1957) to Psycholoical Reactance (Brehm 1966; Brehm and Brehm 1981). None to my knowledge has tied the phenomenon with language.

REFERENCES

Aronson, Elliot, and J. Merrill Carlsmith 1963 "Effect of the severity of threat on the devaluation of forbidden behavior." Journal of Abnormal and Social Psychology 66:584–588.

Aronson, Elliot, J. Merrill Carlsmith, and John M. Darley 1963 "The effects of expectancy on volunteering for an unpleasant experience." Journal of Abnormal and Social Psychology 6:220–224.

Austin, Roy L. 1978 "Race, father-absence, and female delinquency." Criminology 15:487–504.

Bandler, Richard J., George R. Madaras, and Daryl J. Bem 1968 "Self-observation as a source of pain perception." Journal of Personality and Social Psychology 9:205–209.

Bandura, Albert and Aletha C. Huston 1961 "Identification as a process of incidental learning." Journal of Abnormal and Social Psychology 63:311–318.

Bandura, Albert and Richard H. Walters 1959 Adolescent Aggression. New York: Ronald. 1963 Social Learning and Personality Development. New York: Holt, Rinehart, and Winston.

Batson, C. Daniel, Janine L. Dyck, J. Randall Brandt, Judy G. Batson, Anne L. Powell, M. Rosalie McMaster, and Cari Griffitt 1988 "Five studies testing two new egoistic alternatives to the empathy-altruism hypothesis." Journal of Personality and Social Psychology 55:52–77.

Baumrind, Diana 1978 "Parental disciplinary patterns and social competence in children." Youth and Society 9:239–276.

Bender, Loretta 1947 "Psychopathic behavior disorders in children." In Handbook of Correctional Psychology, ed. R. Lindner and R. Seliger, 360–377. New York: Philosophical Library.

Boggiano, Ann K., and Deborah S. Main 1986 "Enhancing children's interest in activities used as rewards: The bonus effect." Journal of Personality and Social Psychology 31:1116–1126.

Bowlby, John 1940 "The influence of early environment on neurosis and neurotic character." International Journal of Psychoanalysis 21:154–178.

Brehm, Jack W. 1940 A Theory of Psychological Reactance. New York: Academic Press.

CHALLENGE QUESTIONS

Do Physically Punished Children Become Violent Adults?

1. How would you manage your own children's behavior? Would you use punishment, rewards, or neither? Why?

2. Why do you think parents elect to use physical punishment in their child-rearing practices?

3. What other research in developmental psychology is relevant to this issue? Cite the research and describe how it pertains to the issue.

4. McCord argues that the people who only (or primarily) care for themselves are more prone to violence. How would McCord advocate that parents raise their children?

5. How would you characterize McCord's main criticism of Straus's Cultural Spillover Theory? How does McCord's own theory account for her criticism of Straus's theory?

PART 3

Cognitive Processes

The nature and limitations of our mental (or cognitive) processes pose fundamental questions for psychologists. Are mental capacities, such as intelligence, determined at birth, or can they be increased with the proper form of education? Also, how reliable is memory? For example, are memories of early sexual abuse always reliable? Can they be trusted enough to bring alleged abusers to trial? And to what extent can cognitive processes work for an individual? Can they help a person have a healthier life? Can they fight disease?

■ Are Memories of Sex Abuse Always Real?

■ Can Mental Attitude Affect Biological Disease?

■ Can Intelligence Be Increased?

ISSUE 8

Are Memories of Sex Abuse Always Real?

YES: Ellen Bass and Laura Davis, from *The Courage to Heal: A Guide for Women Survivors of Child Sexual Abuse* (Harper & Row, 1988)

NO: Lee Coleman, from "Creating 'Memories' of Sexual Abuse," *Issues in Child Abuse Accusations* (vol. 4, no. 4, 1992)

ISSUE SUMMARY

YES: Ellen Bass and Laura Davis, both counselors of victims of child sexual abuse, assert that even a faint or vague memory of sexual abuse is prime evidence that sexual abuse has occurred.

NO: Psychiatrist Lee Coleman argues that individual memories of sexual abuse are susceptible to manipulation by laypersons and mental health professionals and that "memories" of sexual abuse that never occurred can be created in therapy.

It is hard to imagine a more heinous crime than sexual abuse. Yet, perhaps surprisingly, it is a crime that often goes unpunished. Frequently, sexual abusers are family members and their victims are children who are too young to protest or to know that they are being violated. This is part of the reason why memories have become so significant to the sexual abuse issue. Often, it is not until the victims become adults that they realize they were abused.

The problem is that the reliability of memory itself has come into question. Some cognitive psychologists have expressed doubt about the accuracy of memories when people are formally questioned (such as on the witness stand). Another issue is whether or not memory is subject to manipulation. People under hypnosis, for example, tend to be susceptible to the hypnotist's suggestions as to what they "should" remember. Do therapists of alleged victims of sexual abuse make similar suggestions? Could these therapists be unconsciously or consciously "shaping" through therapeutic suggestion the memories of the people they treat?

In the following selections, Ellen Bass and Laura Davis argue that memories of sexual abuse and what they identify as symptoms of sexual abuse are sufficient evidence that a person was abused. They provide a list of experiences that, if remembered, indicate that a person was probably abused. They also describe a number of the symptoms that they contend are commonly experienced by those who have been abused. Bass and Davis emphasize that a lack of explicit memories about sexual abuse does not mean that abuse did not occur.

Lee Coleman refutes the claims of those who place faith in all memories of sexual abuse. He argues that people can be led to believe that they were sexually abused when, in fact, they were not. Coleman presents a case to show that so-called recovered memories of sexual abuse can be created in therapy with the encouragement of mental health professionals. He holds that professionals who consider themselves specialists in sexual abuse recovery tend to accept without question that sexual abuse has occurred if a client says it has, to encourage as many memories as possible, and to accept all allegations of sexual abuse as real. Coleman views these professionals as manipulative and often without awareness.

POINT	COUNTERPOINT
• If someone says that they believe they were sexually abused, they probably were.	• People can be made to believe that they have been sexually abused when, in fact, they have not.
• Memories for traumatic events are likely to be repressed, so they must be "helped" to be recovered.	• "Helping" memories to be recovered can unintentionally create them.
• Mental health professionals do not create people's memories for them.	• Mental health professionals sometimes create false memories for their patients.
• Memory is like a videotape that records things exactly as they occur.	• Evidence shows that memory is not infallible and can be distorted and inaccurate.

YES

Ellen Bass and Laura Davis

THE COURAGE TO HEAL

If you have been sexually abused, you are not alone. One out of three girls, and one out of seven boys, are sexually abused by the time they reach the age of eighteen. Sexual abuse happens to children of every class, culture, race, religion, and gender. Children are abused by fathers, stepfathers, uncles, brothers, grandparents, neighbors, family friends, baby-sitters, teachers, strangers, and sometimes by aunts and mothers.[1] Although women do abuse, the vast majority of abusers are heterosexual men.

All sexual abuse is damaging, and the trauma does not end when the abuse stops. If you were abused as a child, you are probably experiencing long-term effects that interfere with your day-to-day functioning.

However, it is possible to heal. It is even possible to thrive. Thriving means more than just an alleviation of symptoms, more than band-aids, more than functioning adequately. Thriving means enjoying a feeling of wholeness, satisfaction in your life and work, genuine love and trust in your relationships, pleasure in your body.

Until now, much of the literature on child sexual abuse has documented the ravages of abuse, talking extensively about "the tragedy of ruined lives," but little about recovery. This [reading] is about recovery—what it takes, what it feels like, how it can transform your life.

People say "time heals all wounds," and it's true to a certain extent. Time will dull some of the pain, but deep healing doesn't happen unless you consciously choose it. Healing from child sexual abuse takes years of commitment and dedication. But if you are willing to work hard, if you are determined to make lasting changes in your life, if you are able to find good resources and skilled support, you can not only heal but thrive. We believe in miracles and hard work.

HOW CAN I KNOW IF I WAS A VICTIM OF CHILD SEXUAL ABUSE?

When you were a young child or teenager, were you:

- Touched in sexual areas?

- Shown sexual movies or forced to listen to sexual talk?
- Made to pose for seductive or sexual photographs?
- Subjected to unnecessary medical treatments?
- Forced to perform oral sex on an adult or sibling?
- Raped or otherwise penetrated?
- Fondled, kissed, or held in a way that made you uncomfortable?
- Forced to take part in ritualized abuse in which you were physically or sexually tortured?
- Made to watch sexual acts or look at sexual parts?
- Bathed in a way that felt intrusive to you?
- Objectified and ridiculed about your body?
- Encouraged or goaded into sex you didn't really want?
- Told all you were good for was sex?
- Involved in child prostitution or pornography?[2]

If you are unable to remember any specific instances like the ones mentioned above but still have a feeling that something abusive happened to you, it probably did.…

Children often cope with abuse by forgetting it ever happened. As a result, you may have no conscious memory of being abused. You may have forgotten large chunks of your childhood. Yet there are things you do remember. When you are touched in a certain way, you feel nauseated. Certain words or facial expressions scare you. You know you never liked your mother to touch you. You slept with your clothes on in junior high school. You were taken to the doctor repeatedly for vaginal infections.

You may think you don't have memories, but often as you begin to talk about what you do remember, there emerges a constellation of feelings, reactions, and recollections that add up to substantial information. To say "I was abused," you don't need the kind of recall that would stand up in a court of law.

Often the knowledge that you were abused starts with a tiny feeling, an intuition. It's important to trust that inner voice and work from there. Assume your feelings are valid. So far, no one we've talked to thought she might have been abused, and then later discovered that she hadn't been. The progression always goes the other way, from suspicion to confirmation. If you think you were abused and your life shows the symptoms, then you were.…

* * *

I've looked the memories in the face and smelled their breath. They can't hurt me anymore.

For many survivors, remembering is the first step in healing. To begin with, you may have to remember that you *were* abused at all. Second come specific memories.… The third kind of remembering is the recovery of the feelings you had at the time the abuse took place. Many women have always remembered the physical details of what happened but have forgotten the emotions that went with it. One survivor explained, "I could rattle off the facts of my abuse like a grocery list, but remembering the fear and terror and pain was another matter entirely."

Remembering is different for every survivor. If, as a young woman, you turned your abuser in to the police and testified against him in court, there's not much chance you forgot. Likewise, if you had to raise your abuser's child, or abort it, you've probably always remembered. Or the abuse may have been so present in the daily texture of your life that there was no way to forget.

One woman who'd kept a vivid image of what had happened to her said she sometimes wished she *had* forgotten: "I wish I could have gotten shock treatments like my mother. She had forgotten huge segments of her life, and I used to envy her." On the other hand, this woman said she was glad she'd always known just how bad things were: "At least I knew why I was weird! Knowing what had happened allowed me to work on the damn problem."

You may not have forgotten entirely, but coped by having selective memories.

I always knew that we had an incestuous relationship. I remember the first time I heard the word "incest," when I was seventeen. I hadn't known there was a word for it. I always remembered my father grabbing my breasts and kissing me.

I told my therapist, "I remember every miserable thing that happened to me." It seemed like I remembered so much, how could there be more? I didn't remember anything *but* abuse. But I didn't remember being raped, even though I knew I had been. I categorically told my therapist, "I don't want to remember being raped." We talked about the fact that I didn't want to remember that for months. Yet I knew my father had been my first lover.

There is no right or wrong when it comes to remembering. You may have multiple memories. Or you may just have one. Years of abuse are sometimes telescoped into a single recollection. When you begin to remember, you might have new images every day for weeks on end. Or you may experience your memories in clumps, three or four of them coming in a matter of days, then not again for months. Sometimes survivors remember one abuser, or a specific kind of abuse, only to remember, years later, a second abuser or a different form of abuse.

There are many women who show signs of having been abused without having any memories. You may have only a vague feeling that something happened but be unable to remember what it was. There are reasons for this, and to understand them, we have to first look at the way early memories are stored.

ABOUT MEMORIES

The process of storing memories is complex. We store different experiences in the right and left halves of our brain. The left brain stores sequential, logical, language-oriented experience; the right stores perceptual, spatial experiences. When we try to retrieve right-brain information through left-brain techniques, such as logic and language, we sometimes hit a blank. There are some experiences that we are simply not going to remember in an orderly, precise way.

If you were abused when you were preverbal, or just as you were learning to talk, you had no way of making sense of what was happening to you. Babies don't know the difference between touching someone's penis and touching someone's leg. If a penis is put in their mouth, they will suck it, much as they would a breast or a bottle. Young children are aware of sensations but cannot come up with a name or a concept—like "sexual abuse" —for what is being done to them.

Another thing that makes remembering difficult is the simple fact that you are trying to remember details of something that happened a long time ago. If you ask friends who weren't abused, you will find that most of them also don't remember a great number of details from their childhood. It is even more difficult to remember the times when we were hurt, humiliated, or otherwise violated.

If the abuse happened only once, or if it was an abuse that is hard to name (inappropriate boundaries, lewd looks, subtler forms of abuse), it can be even harder to remember. For others, the constancy of the abuse prevents detailed naming. As one survivor put it, "Do you remember every time you sat down to eat? What you had for dinner the Tuesday you turned six? I remember the flavor. It was a constant, like eating. It was always there."

WHAT REMEMBERING IS LIKE

Recovering occluded memories (those blocked from the surface) is not like remembering with the conscious mind. Often the memories are vague and dreamlike, as if they're being seen from far away.

The actual rape memories for me are like from the end of a tunnel. That's because I literally left my body at the scene. So I remember it from that perspective—there's some physical distance between me and what's going on. Those memories aren't as sharp in focus. It's like they happened in another dimension.

Other times, memories come in bits and pieces.

I'd be driving home from my therapist's office, and I'd start having flashes of things—just segments, like bloody sheets, or taking a bath, or throwing away my nightgown. For a long time, I remembered all the things around being raped, but not the rape itself.

If memories come to you in fragments, you may find it hard to place them in any kind of chronological order. You may not know exactly when the abuse began, how old you were, or when and why it stopped. The process of understanding the fragments is a lot like putting together a jigsaw puzzle or being a detective.

Part of me felt like I was on the trail of a murder mystery, and I was going to solve it. I really enjoyed following all the clues. "Okay, I was looking at the clock. It was mid-afternoon. Why was it mid-afternoon? Where could my mother have been? Oh, I bet she was at..." Tracing down the clues to find out exactly what had happened was actually fun.

Ella is a survivor who remembered in snatches. To make sense of her memories, she began to examine some of her own strange ways of coping. She started to analyze certain compulsive behaviors, like staring at the light fixture whenever she was making love:

I'd be making love and would think, "Why would somebody lay here, when they're supposed to be having a pleasurable experience, and concentrate on a light fixture?" I remember every single lighting fixture in every single house we ever lived in! Why have I always been so obsessed with light under doors, and the interruption of light? That's a crazy thing for an adult woman to be obsessive about —that someone walks past and cracks the light. What's that about?

What it was about was watching to see if her father's footsteps stopped outside her door at night. If they stopped, that meant he'd come in and molest her. Once Ella started to pay attention to these kinds of details, the memories started to fit in place.

Flashbacks

In a flashback, you reexperience the original abuse. Flashbacks may be accompanied by the feelings you felt at the time, or they may be stark and detached, like watching a movie about somebody else's life.

Frequently flashbacks are visual: "I saw this penis coming toward me," or "I couldn't see his face, just the big black belt he always wore." First-time visual memories can be very dramatic:

> My husband was beginning to initiate some lovemaking. I had a flash in my mind. The closest way I can describe it is that it was much like viewing slides in a slide show, when the slide goes by too fast, but slow enough to give you some part of the image. It was someone jamming their fingers up my vagina. It was very vivid, and enough of the feelings came sneaking in that I knew it wasn't a fantasy. There was an element of it that made me stop and take notice. I lay there and let it replay a couple of times.
>
> I felt confused. I was aware that it was something that happened to me. I even had a recollection of the pain. I scrambled around in my mind for an explanation. "Was that a rough lover I had?" Immediately I knew that wasn't the case. So I went back into the flash again. Each time I went back, I tried to open it up to see a little more. I didn't see his face, but I could sense an essence of my father.

Sometimes visual memories are more complete. A survivor who's had them both ways explained the difference:

A flashback is like a slide compared to a film. It's the difference between getting one shot or one look into a room and getting the expanded version. A full memory is more like panning over the whole scene, with all the details, sound, feeling, and visuals rolled into one.

But not everyone is visual. One woman was upset that she couldn't get any pictures. Her father had held her at knifepoint in the car, face down in the dark, and raped her. She had never seen anything. But she had heard him. And when she began to write the scene in Spanish, her native language, it all came back to her—his threats, his brutality, his violation.

Regression

Another way to regain memory is through regression. Under the guidance of a trustworthy therapist, it is possible to go back to earlier times. Or you may find yourself going back on such a journey on your own, with only the prompting of your own unconscious.

> Most of the regressions I experienced felt almost like going on a ride. They'd last maybe three or four hours at a time. One of the most vivid physical regressions I went through was late one evening, when Barbara and I were talking about her going to visit a friend. All of a sudden, I felt like I was being sucked down a drain. And then I felt like a real baby. I started crying and clinging and saying, "You can't go! You have to stay with me!" And I began to talk in a five-year-old's voice, using words and concepts that a five-year-old might use.
>
> All of a sudden I thought I was just going to throw up. I ran to the bathroom, and then I really started to sob. I saw lots of scenes from my childhood. Times I felt rejected flashed by me, almost in slides.

Barb held me, and kind of coached me through it. "It's okay. You can get through this." Having her just sit there and listen really helped me. I just kept crying, and described to Barbara all these slides that were going by. After about twenty minutes, I fell into the deepest sleep I'd had for months. The next morning when I woke up, I felt a million pounds lighter.

Sense Memory

Often it is a particular touch, smell, or sound that triggers a memory. You might remember when you return to the town, to the house, to the room, where the abuse took place. Or when you smell a certain aftershave the abuser wore.

Thirty-five-year-old Ella says, "It's all real tactile, sensory things that have brought memories back. Textures. Sounds. The smell of my father's house. The smell of vodka on somebody."

Ella had a magic purple quilt when she was a little girl. Her grandmother made it for her. It was supposed to keep her safe— nothing bad could happen to her as long as she was under it. The quilt had been lost for many years, but when Ella finally got it back at twenty-one, it triggered a whole series of memories.

Touch can also reopen memories. Women have had images come up while they were being massaged. You may freeze up and see pictures when you're making love. Your lover breathes in your ear just as your abuser once did, and it all comes spilling back:

Sometimes when we're making love, I feel like my head just starts to float away somewhere. I feel like I literally split off at my shoulders, and I get very lightheaded and dizzy. It's as if someone was blowing a fan down on top of my head. There's a lot of movement down past my hair. It's like rising up out of my head. I get really disoriented.

The other thing I experience is a lot of splitting right at the hips. My legs get very heavy and really solid. They just feel like dead weight, like logs. No energy is passing through them. Then I get real sick to my stomach, just violently ill. I find the minute I get nauseous, whatever it is is very close to me. And if I pay attention to it, I can see it, and move on.

The Body Remembers What the Mind Chooses to Forget

It is also possible to remember only feelings. Memories are stored in our bodies, and it is possible to physically reexperience the terror of the abuse. Your body may clutch tight, or you may feel the screams you could not scream as a child. Or you may feel that you are suffocating and cannot breathe.

I would get body memories that would have no pictures to them at all. I would just start screaming and feel that something was coming out of my body that I had no control over. And I would usually get them right after making love or in the middle of making love, or right in the middle of a fight. When my passion was aroused in some way, I would remember in my body, although I wouldn't have a conscious picture, just this screaming coming out of me.

WAYS TO REMEMBER

Memories come up under many different circumstances. You might remember because you're finally in a relationship that feels safe. Or because you've just been through a divorce and everything in your life is unraveling. Women often remember childhood abuse when they are raped or attacked in adult life.

Memories don't always surface in such dramatic ways. While talking with her friend, one woman suddenly heard herself saying something she didn't realize she knew. "It's as though I always knew it," she explained. "It's just that I hadn't thought about it in twenty or thirty years. Up until that moment, I'd forgotten."

You may remember seemingly out of the blue. Or because you're having persistent nightmares that reach up through sleep to tell you:

I'd always had a dream about my brother assaulting me. It was a foggy dream, and I had it over and over again. I'd wake up thinking it was really disgusting because I was enjoying it in the dream. I'd think, "You're sick. Why are you having this dream? Is that what you want?" I'd give myself all those kinds of guilt messages, 'cause it was still a dream. It wasn't history yet.

Then, six months ago, I was sitting in a training meeting for working with sexual assault prevention. I don't even remember what the trainer said, but all of a sudden, I realized that it wasn't a dream, and that it had really happened. I can't tell you anything about the rest of the meeting. I was just in shock.

The fact that this woman remembered in the middle of a training session for sexual assault is significant. As the media focus on sexual abuse has increased, more and more women have had their memories triggered.

Media Coverage of Sexual Abuse

Jennierose, who remembered in her mid-forties, was sitting with her lover one night, watching a TV program about sexual offenders in prison. The therapist running the group encouraged the offenders to get very emotional, at which time they'd remember the traumatic events in their own childhoods.

In the middle of the program, Jennierose turned to her lover and said, "I wish there was a therapist like that I could go to, because I know there's something I'm not remembering." As soon as she said that, Jennierose had a vision of the first time her father sodomized her, when she was four and a half and her mother had gone to the hospital to have another baby. "It was a totally detailed vision, to the point of seeing the rose-colored curtains blowing in the window."

Sobbing, Jennierose said to her lover, "I think I'm making something up." Her lover simply said, "Look at yourself! Look at yourself! Tell me you're making it up." And Jennierose couldn't. She knew she was telling the truth.

This kind of memory is common. Often women become very uncomfortable (nauseated, dizzy, unable to concentrate, emotional) when they hear another survivor's story and realize that what's being described happened to them too.

When You Break an Addiction

Many survivors remember their abuse once they get sober, quit drugs, or stop eating compulsively. These and other addictions can effectively block any recollection of the abuse, but once you stop, the memories often surface. Anna Stevens explains:

At the point I decided to put down drinking, I had to start feeling. The connection to the abuse was almost immediate. And I've watched other people come to AA and do the same thing. They have just enough time to get through the initial shakes, and you watch them start to go through the memories. And you know what's coming, but they don't....

When You Become a Mother

Mothers often remember their own abuse when they see their children's vulnerability, or when their children reach the age they were when their own abuse began. Sometimes they remember because their child is being abused. Dana was court-ordered to go for therapy when her three-year-old daughter, Christy, was molested. Dana first remembered when she unconsciously substituted her own name for her daughter's:

I was in therapy talking about Christy, and instead of saying "Christy," I said "I." And I didn't even catch it. My therapist did. She had always suspected that I was abused too, but she hadn't said anything to me.

She told me what I had said, and I said, "I did? I said 'I?' I hadn't even heard myself. It was really eerie.

What came out was that I was really dealing with Christy's molestation on a level of my own. The things that I was outraged at and that hurt me the most were things that had happened to me, not things that had happened to Christy. Part of the reason I fell apart and so much came back to me when I found out about Christy was because my husband was doing the same things to her that my father had done with me.

After a Significant Death

Many women are too scared to remember while their abusers are still alive. One woman said, "I couldn't afford to remember until both my parents were dead, until there was nobody left to hurt me." A forty-seven-year-old woman first remembered a year and a half after her mother died: "Then I could no longer hurt my mother by telling her."

FEELING THE FEELINGS

Although some remembering is emotionally detached, when you remember with feeling, the helplessness, terror, and physical pain can be as real as any actual experience. You may feel as if you are being crushed, ripped open, or suffocated. Sexual arousal may also accompany your memories, and this may horrify you, but arousal is a natural response to sexual stimulation. There is no reason to be ashamed.

You might remember feeling close and happy, wrapped in a special kind of love. Disgust and horror are not the only way to feel when you have memories. There is no *right* way to feel, but you must feel, even if it sends you reeling:

When I first remembered, I shut down emotionally right away. I climbed all the way up into my mind and forgot about the gut level. That's how I protected myself. For a long time it was just an intellectual exercise. "Oh, that's why I have trouble with men and authority. That's why I might not have remembered much about growing up." It took nine months after I first remembered for the feelings to start bubbling up.

I found myself slipping into the feelings I'd had during the abuse, that hadn't been safe to feel at the time. The first was this tremendous isolation. From there, I moved into absolute terror. I got in touch with how frightening the world is. It was the worst of the fear finally coming up. I felt like it was right at the top of my neck all the time, just ready to come out in a scream.

I was right on the edge. I had an encounter with my boss, who said that my performance had been poor. I finally told him what had happened, which was really heavy—telling some male authority figure that you remembered incest in your family. He is a kind and caring person. The best he could do was back off and leave me alone.

I was then carrying around all this external pressure—my job was in jeopardy, my life was falling apart, and I was having all these feelings I didn't know what to do with. In order to keep myself in control, I started compulsively eating. Finally I decided I didn't want to go through this stuff by myself anymore." I got myself into therapy.

Having to experience the feelings is one of the roughest parts of remembering. "It pisses me off that I have to survive it twice, only this time with feelings," one woman said. "This time it's worse. I'm not so effective at dissociating anymore."

Another woman said, "I started off very butch [tough] about remembering. I kicked into my overachiever thing. I was going to lick this thing. I believed getting the pictures was what was important. I got a ton of memories, all on the intellectual level. It was kind of like I was going to 'do' incest, just like I might take up typing."

It was only after a year of therapy that this woman began to realize that *she* was the one who'd been abused. "I finally realized, I finally *felt*, that this was something that had happened to me, and that it had been damaging. I had to realize that just getting the memories was not going to make it go away. *This was about me!*"

LETTING MEMORIES IN

Few survivors feel they have control over their memories. Most feel the memories have control of them, that they do not choose the time and place a new memory will emerge. You may be able to fight them off for a time, but the price—

headaches, nightmares, exhaustion—is not worth staving off what is inevitable.

Not everyone will know a memory is coming, but many survivors do get warnings, a certain feeling or series of feelings, that clue them in. Your stomach may get tight. You may sleep poorly, have frightening dreams. Or you may be warned in other ways:

I always know when they're coming. I get very tense. I get very scared. I get snappy at things that ordinarily wouldn't make me angry. I get sad. Usually it's anger and anxiety and fear that come first. And I have a choice. It's a real conscious choice. It's either I want it or I don't want it. And I said "I don't want it" a lot. And when I did that, I would just get sicker and sicker. I'd get more depressed. I'd get angry irrationally.

Now I don't say I don't want it. It's not worth it. My body seems to need to release it. The more I heal, the more I see these memories are literally stored in my body, and they've got to get out. Otherwise I'm going to carry them forever.

REMEMBERING OVER TIME

Often when you've resolved one group of memories, another will make its way to the surface.

The more I worked on the abuse, the more I remembered. First I remembered my brother, and then my grandfather. About six months after that I remembered my father. And then about a year later, I remembered my mother. I remembered the "easiest" first and the "hardest" last. Even though it was traumatic for me to realize that everyone in my family abused me, there was something reassuring about it. For a long time I'd felt worse than the initial memories should have made me feel, so remembering the rest of the abuse was actually one of the most grounding things to happen. My life suddenly made sense.

The impact new memories have will shift over time. One woman who has been getting new memories for the past ten years says remembering has become harder over time:

My first flood of memories came when I was twenty-five. The memories I get now are like fine-tuning—more details, more textures. Even though there was more of a feeling of shock and catharsis at first, remembering is harder now. I believe them now. It hurts more. I have the emotions to feel the impact. I can see how it's affected my life.

Laura also says new memories are harder:

Just when I felt that my life was getting back to normal and I could put the incest aside, I had another flashback that was much more violent than the earlier pictures I'd seen. I was furious. I wanted to be finished. I didn't want to be starting in with incest again! And my resistance made the remembering a lot more difficult.

Other survivors say memories have gotten easier to handle:

As I've come to terms with the fact that I was abused, new pictures, new incidents, don't have the same impact. The battle of believing it happened is not one I have to fight each time another piece falls into place. Once I had a framework to fit new memories into, my recovery time got much faster. While my first memories overwhelmed me for weeks, now I might only cry for ten minutes or feel depressed for an hour. It's not that I don't have new memories. It's just that they don't devastate me.

And new memories don't take anything away from the healing you've already done. Paradoxically, *you are already healing from the effects of the things you have yet to remember.*

"BUT I DON'T HAVE ANY MEMORIES"

If you don't remember your abuse, you are not alone. Many women don't have memories, and some never get memories. This doesn't mean they weren't abused.

If you don't have any memory of it, it can be hard to believe the abuse really happened. You may feel insecure about trusting your intuition and want "proof" of your abuse. This is a very natural desire, but it is not always one that can be met. The unconscious has its own way of unfolding that does not always meet your demands or your timetable.

One thirty-eight-year-old survivor described her relationship with her father as "emotionally incestuous." She has never had specific memories of any physical contact between them, and for a long time she was haunted by the fact that she couldn't come up with solid data. Over time, though, she's come to terms with her lack of memories. Her story is a good model if you don't have specific pictures to draw from:

Do I want to know if something physical happened between my father and me? Really, I think you have to be strong enough to know. I think that our minds are wonderful in the way they protect us, and I think that when I'm strong enough to know, I'll know.

I obsessed for about a year on trying to remember, and then I got tired of sitting around talking about what I couldn't remember. I thought, "All right, let's act as if." It's like you come home and your home has been robbed, and everything has been thrown in the middle of the room, and the window is open and the curtain is blowing in the wind, and the cat is gone. You know somebody robbed you, but you're never going to know who. So what are you going to do? Sit there and try to figure it out while your stuff lies around? No, you start to clean it up. You put bars on the windows. You assume somebody was there. Somebody could come along and say, "Now how do you know someone was there?" You don't know.

That's how I acted. I had the symptoms. Every incest group I went to I completely empathized. It rang bells all the time. I felt like there was something I just couldn't get to, that I couldn't remember yet. And my healing was blocked there.

Part of my wanting to get specific memories was guilt that I could be accusing this man of something so heinous, and what if he didn't do it? How horrible for me to accuse him! That's why I wanted the memories. I wanted to be sure. Societally, women have always been accused of crying rape.

But I had to ask myself, "Why would I be feeling all of this? Why would I be feeling all this anxiety if something didn't happen?" If the specifics are not available to you, then go with what you've got.

I'm left with the damage. And that's why I relate to that story of the burglar.

I'm owning the damage. I want to get better. I've been very ill as a result of the damage, and at some point I realized, "I'm thirty-eight years old. What am I going to do—wait twenty more years for a memory?" I'd rather get better.

And then maybe the stronger I am, the more the memories will come back. Maybe I'm putting the cart before the horse. Maybe I've remembered as much as I'm able to remember without breaking down. I don't want to go insane. I want to be out in the world. Maybe I should go with that sense of protection. There is a survivor in here and she's pretty smart. So I'm going with the circumstantial evidence, and I'm working on healing myself. I go to these incest groups, and I tell people, "I don't have any pictures," and then I go on and talk all about my father, and nobody ever says, "You don't belong here."

NOTES

1. For sources on the scope of child sexual abuse, see the "About Sexual Abuse" section of the Resource Guide. A number of these books cite recent studies to which you can refer for more complete statistics.

2. Between 500,000 and 1,000,000 children are involved in prostitution and pornography in this country; a high percentage of them are victims of incest. See *Sex Work: Writings by Women in the Industry*, edited by Frédérique Dellacoste and Priscilla Alexander (Pittsburgh: Cleis Press, 1987).

NO

Lee Coleman

CREATING "MEMORIES" OF SEXUAL ABUSE

ABSTRACT: An analysis of a case of alleged recovered memories of sexual abuse is presented to illustrate how such mental images can be created in therapy. The memories, although believed by the woman to be of actual events, were the result of suggestions from both lay persons and professionals.

While, just a few years ago, students of child sexual abuse accusations thought they had seen every imaginable brand of irresponsibility on the part of certain mental health professionals, something new and equally terrible has emerged. To the growing number of children trained to say and believe things which never happened is now added a growing number of adults, usually women, being trained to say and believe that they have suddenly "unblocked" memories of childhood sexual abuse.

Just like allegations coming from children, concern about biased and unprofessional methods of eliciting statements from adults should in no way cast doubt on the reality of sexual abuse. There are countless numbers of adults who were molested as children, who did not speak of it, but who now may reveal their experiences as part of our society's belated recognition of such abuse. But to acknowledge the reality of sexual abuse, and the reality of the silence kept by some of the victims, does nothing to mitigate the harm being done by those therapists who are convincing patients that even if sexual abuse is not remembered, it probably happened anyway.

In this article, I will illustrate the process by which a young woman, moderately depressed and unsure of her life goals, but in no way out of touch with reality (psychotic), came to make allegations which were so bizarre that they might easily be thought to be the product of [a] major mental disorder. In such cases, I have repeatedly seen the falsely accused and their closest family and friends make this assumption. This case will show, as have the others I have studied, that the source is not a disorder in the patient, but a "disorder" in the therapist. The problem is the irresponsible adoption by some therapists of a new fad which will be clarified below.

From Lee Coleman, "Creating 'Memories' of Sexual Abuse," *Issues in Child Abuse Accusations*, vol. 4, no. 4 (1992), pp. 169–176. Copyright © 1992 by The Institute for Psychological Therapies. Reprinted by permission of *Issues in Child Abuse Accusations*.

Here, then, is a report I submitted to the Court hearing the civil lawsuit filed by this woman against her cousin. All names and identifying information have been changed.

*   *   *

Judge John Q. Smith
Superior Court, All American County
Anywhere, USA

The following report concerns the suit between Susan Q. Smith and John V. Public. The opinions expressed are based on a study of the Amended List of Documents of the Plaintiff, dated April 6, 1992, Additional Documents (such as police records and Children's Services Records), Examination for Discovery transcripts of Mrs. Smith and Mr. Public, and my examination of Mrs. Smith on May 4, 1992, which lasted somewhat over three hours. I have also studied several videotapes pertinent to the case, enumerated below.

Based upon all this information, as well [as] my prior professional experience, it is my opinion that the alleged "memories" of Mrs. Smith, relating a variety of sexual and abusive acts perpetrated upon her by Mr. Public and others, are not memories at all. They are, instead, mental images which, however sincerely felt by her to be memories of past events, are nonetheless the result of a series of suggestions from both lay persons and professionals.

That Mrs. Smith has succumbed to these influences in no way implies that she suffers from any mental disorder. By her own account, she has had problems of low self-esteem, depression, and bulimia in her past. She has, however, never suffered and does not now suffer a mental disorder which would imply a loss of contact with reality. If the reliability of her claims are to be best evaluated by the Court, it should be understood that there is another way that a person may say things that may not be true, yet be entirely sincere.

Suggestibility is something we all share as part of our being human, with some persons obviously being more suggestible than others. In this case, Mrs. Smith has been involved with individuals and groups, over a period of years, the end result of which has been to promote a process of accepting the false idea that whatever mental image is conjured up, especially if part of "therapy," is necessarily a valid retrieval of past experience, i.e. a "memory."

Let me now document the evidence which has led me to the above conclusions.

1. Mrs. Smith's Suspicions About John Public and His Daughter Alice.

From several sources, such as her deposition, my interview, and investigative interviews, it seems clear that Mrs. Smith suspected for several years that her cousin John Public was engaging in sexual behavior with his daughter Alice. When asked for examples which led to these suspicions, she mentioned alleged comments from him that "a child's hands" felt so good. She also mentioned that no other adults seemed to be concerned about such comments.

Seeing Mr. Public and Alice (approximately eight years old at the time) lying in bed together, in their underwear, reinforced her suspicion, as did the alleged comment from Mr. Public to Mr. Smith (not heard by Mrs. Smith), that his (Smith's) daughter would make him horny. Mrs. Smith also noted that, until age 18 months, her own daughter would cry if Mr. Public attempted to pick her up or get close to her, and Mrs. Smith noted to herself, "She's a smart child." (It should be noted that such behavior in infants of this age is perfectly normal.)

Mrs. Smith told me that she had informed family members on several occasions of her suspicions, but no one else apparently shared her opinions, or felt anything needed to be reported.

The 1986 video of a family Halloween party was the event that convinced Mrs. Smith she should report her suspicions. It is quite important that the Court view this video, in order to judge for itself whether the material could reasonably lead a person to believe something untoward was taking place. My own opinion is there was nothing happening that was unusual or abnormal. It was Alice who first struck a somewhat playful and seductive pose, and such displays are hardly abnormal for a teenage girl. Police investigators likewise saw nothing untoward on this tape.

The question raised, then, is whether Mrs. Smith had for her own personal reasons, upon which I will not attempt to speculate, developed an obsession about Mr. Public and his daughter, one which was leading her (Smith) to overinterpret ordinary behaviors.

It is not surprising, then, that when the report was investigated by Children's Services, no evidence of abuse was uncovered. Mrs. Smith tells me, however, that she was not reassured, and only felt that she had fulfilled an obligation to report something.

2. Early Influences Promoting in Mrs. Smith a Belief That Prior Sexual Abuse Might Have Occurred but Not Be Remembered.

From numerous sources (deposition, my interview, journals, therapy records), it is clear that Mrs. Smith was strongly influenced by a statement she says Dr. Gwen Olson made to her regarding bulimia, a problem Mrs. Smith had suffered from to one degree or another since early adolescence.

Mrs. Smith states that Dr. Olson told her, sometime in early 1987 (the records indicate this was in December 1986), that "one hundred percent of my patients with bulimia have later found out that they were sexual abuse victims." Whether these words were actually spoken by Dr. Olson, or instead interpreted this way by Mrs. Smith, I of course do not know. But in either case, the words Mrs. Smith took away with her are extremely important, because the words "found out" would imply that a person could have been sexually abused, not be aware of it, and later recover such an awareness. I will later on be discussing the lack of evidence for, and major evidence against, any such phenomenon being genuine.

Mrs. Smith told me she was seriously affected by this, experiencing crying and feelings of fear. She began to wonder if she might have been sexually abused. When I asked her if she had ever before that time had such a question, she said that she "had no memories" of any such abuse. She had, in fact, told Children's Services shortly before, during the investigation of Alice, that John Public had "never before abused me...I was relying on my memory."

At this time, Mrs. Smith was being seen in psychotherapy, first by Edna Johnson, and then by Dr. Abraham, for what seems to have been feelings of anxiety and depression. Sexual abuse was apparently not an issue in this therapy. Instead, Mrs. Smith states that her self-esteem was low, and that she was "not functioning" well as a housewife, even though she felt good about her marriage. Both she and Dr. Abraham apparently felt she was "a bored housewife." She decided to start her own business, but this never happened because events leading to the current accusations against John Public interceded.

Mrs. Smith explains that she went to an Entrepreneurs Training Camp in the Fall of 1987, was doing extremely well, but then "sabotaged myself" by performing poorly despite knowing correct answers on an examination. She felt, after the camp, that she needed to work on herself.

In addition, she saw an Oprah Winfrey program on the subject of child abuse. Mrs. Smith told me that she cried as she watched this program, "for me and not for them... I wondered at my feelings and where they were coming from."

Mrs. Smith confirms that it was shortly after seeing this program, with all of the above background in place, that she called the Women's Sexual Assault Center (WSAC) on September 3, 1987.

After a telephone intake, she had a face-to-face contact with Joan Oliver, and told her that "I had concerns, feelings, but no memory of being sexually assaulted.... I thought it would be better to wait (for therapy) until I had a memory. They said OK, and put me on a waiting list."

The records of WSAC generally confirm this account which I received from Mrs. Smith on May 4, 1992. During the first telephone contact, Mrs. Smith related

> ... strong feelings of abuse as a child came up... She can't remember specific things... her GP told her most bulimics have been sexually abused as children...

A second telephone contact, September 16, include[d]

> ... occluded memories. Sister was abused by neighborhood man as a child. Susan gets very retriggered by this and by shows about child abuse. Her doctor told her that close to 100% of bulimics have been sexually abused. This really brought up a lot of feelings and some images but not really a memory.

Yet another important event happened around Christmas 1987, before Mrs. Smith had entered the treatments (with Mary Brown and Veronica Erickson) where the mental images alleged to be "memories" started. This was something I had not discovered from any written materials, and learned about for the first time from Mrs. Smith on May 4, 1992.

Mrs. Smith had a friend, Valerie White, who told her about her treatments for back problems. Biofeedback was used at the pain and stress clinic she attended, and Ms. White told Mrs. Smith that she had started to remember being abused. When I asked Mrs. Smith how she reacted to this, she said, "I felt... that if she was in therapy, remembering, maybe I should start as well. I had no memory, but if she was in therapy..."

To summarize, then, the suggestive influences to this point: Mrs. Smith is still not reassured that Alice is not being abused by John Public; Dr. Olson either says or Mrs. Smith believes she says that in her experience all bulimics are sexual abuse victims; finally, after she decides she shouldn't go into therapy "until she has a memory" of sexual abuse, a friend tells her "the remembering" can wait, and Mrs. Smith concludes she should give it a try.

It is my opinion, based on the above material, that Mrs. Smith was at this point being victimized by lay persons and professionals who were representing to her that sexual abuse might not be remembered, when in truth there is no evidence to support such a claim. While Mrs. Smith may have had her own personal problems and/or motivations for claiming abuse at the hands of Mr. Public (something I will not speculate upon) she was being profoundly influenced by unsound information. It is my opinion that this has persisted to this day.

3. Suggestive and Unprofessional Therapy Creates the "Memories."

In March 1988, Mrs. Smith started seeing Mary Brown for individual psychotherapy, and also had interviews with Veronica Erickson, a student who was writing a thesis on "Recovering Memories of Childhood Sexual Abuse." On March 9, 1988, Ms. Erickson commented that Mrs. Smith had done

> ... a lot of great body work. Worked on her anger, hurt about being sexually abused. Has a few memories about it and wants more.

On March 28, the WSAC records show that the

> "memory recovery process" was getting into high gear: ... had lots of memories come to her which she feels good about; 2 "rapes," 9 sodomies, and 2 oral sex (she has remembered both rapes and 1 sodomy and oral sex), 8 sodomies and 1 oral sex to go. Can't wait.

Further WSAC records of Ms. Erickson show just as clearly that she has lost all professional objectivity.... The June 14, 1988 note gives an insight as to the position Ms. Erickson was taking with regard to whether Mrs. Smith's

increasingly severe claims should be automatically assumed to be accurate:

> ... trying to remember a memory that was just beginning to flash... really scared that this memory is made up... I told her I believed her.

If there is any doubt about the stance being adopted by Ms. Erickson, i.e. that whatever Mrs. Smith "recovers" from week to week is a reliable statement about past events, a reading of her Ph.D. thesis makes it abundantly clear that it was simply a given for her and the selected sources she relies on, that the patient's claims must be taken at face value. She writes, for example:

> Validation, feeling believed, was seen as essential for incest survivors struggling to reconcile their memories.

Nowhere in the thesis is mention made of any concern that false claims may arise in therapy specifically aimed at such "uncovering." Next, she speaks of

> ... the ability of counselor... to facilitate the survivor's recall of the abuse... which of course assumes that abuse has taken place.

Just how broadly based is the source of these allegedly reliable "memories," is indicated by her quoting the book, *The Courage to Heal*, which has been influential in promoting the very ideas at the center of this case:

> "Occluded" memories are vague flashbacks, triggered by touches, smells, sounds, body memories, bodily sensations as "warning signs." Some women just intuitively knew that they had been sexually abused and were struggling to trust their intuition.

It is also clear that the proper role for the therapist, according to Ms. Erickson, is not only to accept all images as "memories," but to actively encourage this process. She writes of her method which

> ... serves to continually promote an atmosphere in which the researcher is spontaneously both receptive and actively stimulating the recollection of the participant.... The participants and researcher... create the world within which this study is revealed.

Ms. Erickson says of "Victoria" (pseudonym for Mrs. Smith),

> She thought about who might have abused her and when she said his name, she knew who the offender was but she still had no memories as proof (p. 56 of Erickson thesis).

Let me now turn to her other therapist, Mary Brown. Ms. Brown in her intake notes of March 1, 1988 refers to Mrs. Smith having

> ... flashbacks of childhood sexual abuse experiences, she believes by this same cousin.

Ms. Brown's treatment plan was to "assist Susan express and release the emotions associated with the sexual abuse experience." This is important, because it shows that Ms. Brown, from the beginning, assumed the truth of the allegations.

It wasn't too long after this, the night of March 12/13, that Mrs. Smith's calendar indicates she had a "nightmare," and her "first memories." When I asked Mrs. Smith about this, she said it was

> ... the nightmare which triggered the memory.... In the nightmare, the neighbor had shot her husband in the chest. Her cleaning up his blood, I recalled John blotting up my blood after raping me.

There are, of course, no reputable data which would indicate that a patient or therapist can use dream material to reliably "recover memories" of real events. Ms. Brown, however, seems to have utter confidence in the process, for she wrote to the police on August 3, 1988:

> The treatment methods I use enable clients to express and release the very deepest feelings that may have been stifled.... It is precisely because the emotional intensity of sexual abuse in childhood is greater than what most children can integrate that these experiences are quickly lost to memory. The ensuing, forgetting and denial are the mind's way of protecting the individual from total disruption of their cognitive functioning. This was particularly true of survivors of sexual abuse whose experiences occurred more than ten years ago. The reason for this is that there was not the social awareness nor the professional expertise for dealing with these problems at that time. Children instinctively know when the adults around them are going to be able to help them. When they find themselves in situations where they may either be disbelieved... this forgetting and denial comes into play even more strongly....

> Memories tend to return in fragments and to be unclear or non-specific in the beginning... the blocks in the way of memory are gradually removed.... This is precisely what occurred... with Susan Smith. It is my clinical judgment that Susan had reached a point in her healing process when the memories that were returning were completely reliable.... She was unprepared to report until she herself was certain and until she received validation from me that I was in agreement that the memories could be trusted...

NO Lee Coleman / 177

That Ms. Brown was not only accepting all statements as real events, but actively encouraging them, is seen by the following passage from the same letter:

> Susan herself questioned any inconsistency.... It took some education on my part for her to... understand the whole process of how it is that the recall process works...

Ms. Brown was even willing to assure the police that the other persons that Mrs. Smith was gradually naming as victims during that Spring and Summer of 1988 would also need "help" in remembering.

> ... It is highly likely that most or all of the children that Susan remembers... will be unable to remember these experiences. This does not mean they did not occur any more than Susan's former amnesia means that these events had not happened to her. One of these (youngsters) may be precipitated to remember and recapture the experiences through a process similar to what occurred for Susan.

There is, of course, absolutely no evidence that this whole process has anything to do with memory, or a recall of past events. The only professionals who advocate these ideas are those making up a small, fringe group who hold themselves out as "specialists in treating sexual abuse," but who (as this case shows) seem to assume that it is permissible to pass off wild theories, like the ones above, to both patients, families, and investigative agencies.

Most important, however, is that outsiders evaluate the possible impact of such ideas on persons like Mrs. Smith. The evidence is clear that she has raised doubts from time to time, but each time, these "specialists" have told her that her mental images must represent real events. In this sense, I believe the professionals (Brown, Erickson, and others to be mentioned) are most responsible for creating the unreliable information in this case.

Not only do the ideas promoted by Brown and Erickson hold great potential to contaminate information coming from such counseling, but the techniques used with Mrs. Smith would likely heighten this possibility. Mrs. Smith described pounding pillows and being encouraged to express her anger in sessions with Ms. Erickson, and in individual and group sessions with Ms. Brown, she described exercises in which she was using hyperventilation or bending from the waist. The many group sessions she has attended, focusing on "recovery from sexual abuse," have a potentially profound influence on the participants.

In addition, Ms. Brown had a technique, which she called the "denial game," that was used when Mrs. Smith expressed caution about whether her mental images were reliable. This process had the intended effect of causing Mrs. Smith to once more *assume that whatever she could think of had actually happened.*

The police investigation was dropped for lack of evidence, for lack of corroboration from any of the many alleged victims named by Mrs. Smith, and because an outside consultant told the police that the impact of the therapy might be contaminating the information....

Mrs. Smith's statements to police include "trying to see" alleged events, having

> a flash... (a) visual memory of a spirit part of me coming out of me via my mouth and sitting on a head board. I now understand this to be dissociation....

The police, quite understandably, wondered whether this might be a sign of major mental disorder, like a psychosis. Instead, such statements reflect not that Mrs. Smith was suffering a major mental disorder, but simply that she was absorbing unsupported ideas from her therapists. I have studied the process by which some mental health professionals are passing these ideas to patients, via articles, speeches, and in therapy sessions. Many, if not most, patients, will accept these ideas as accepted scientific information, coming as they do from a professional therapist.

Just how much Mrs. Smith had come to believe in this process, already by April, 1988, is seen by her telling the police on April 20, 1988 that

> These are not complete memories at this point but there are bits and pieces of which I would like to tell you now and when I have the complete memory back I will talk to you again.... I would like to add that I expect to have further recall of incidents as I have just begun to have recall in the last five weeks or so....

4. The Growth of the Allegations.
The process described above will often lead to a virtual flood of allegations which grow and grow. Particularly if there are emotional rewards for producing more claims, the sky is the limit. In this case, it ultimately led to claims of ritual abuse, animal killings, gang rape, multiple personalities, etc. which Mrs. Smith now seems to disavow but which she at the time was claiming as legitimate memory. A brief review of these developments offers important perspective on the unreliable nature of this entire process.

Dr. Wagner saw Mrs. Smith from May 20, 1988 to January 27, 1989. He used a method Mrs. Smith describes as "regression," and which she now does not trust. She feels that some of the things she said as a result of these methods may not have happened.

For example, Dr. Wagner's notes of November 24, 1988 speak of "... memory of John and 'Joe.' Tying her up—raping her. Two others came in, Evan and [unreadable]." Mrs. Smith says she doesn't recall saying this to Dr. Wagner, doesn't believe she said it to him, believes his records are incorrect, and believes she talked about "Sam."

Dr. Wagner, while nowhere in his records expressing any doubt about the reality of these statements, did mention at the outset (June 3, 1988) that he thought Mrs. Smith was: "I suspect getting a lot of mileage out of sexual abuse. Attention and support from home she never got from mom and dad?"

When I questioned Mrs. Smith about other examples of statements drawn from the notes of the many therapists she saw in the coming months, I noted an interesting pattern. Whenever a statement in therapy records referred to events which she now says may not have happened, like seeing a boy with slits for eyes and no face, she says that she cannot recall saying any of this. She repeatedly said it was only her study of the therapy records which allows her to remember what she might have said in therapy.

However, when I asked her about a note from Morton Hunt's evaluation of January 15, 1991, she was quite clear that she did not say the following "... Then had nightmare. Chose John. Just knew it was him (reviewed possible men)."

Such selective "memory" merely reinforces my opinion that these multiple therapy contacts, of the nature described, make a mockery of the idea that claims growing out of the sessions, or growing out of the mental images of a patient between such sessions, are reliable.

The fact that Mrs. Smith was in much more therapy than I have yet summarized, only deepens the dilemmas. She was in group therapy with Ms. Summers, for 32 sessions, from March 21, 1989 to December 1, 1989, and Ms. Summers, who is another of those who specialize in "working mainly with women recovering from childhood sexual abuse," wrote in her records that "Susan's abuse was the most cruel and degrading I have encountered."

Once again, unquestioning acceptance seems to be the *sine qua non* of many of the therapists in this case. Sadly, such an attitude may be quite destructive to patients. A review of her journals, which I will highlight, shows that (as Dr. Wagner had indicated) Mrs. Smith was getting a lot of positive feedback from more and more "memories." A patient might feel good at the time of such feedback, but the encouragement of this process does not bode well for the long-term welfare of such patients.

May 24, 1988—"Another memory came back—arms tied,... I know there are things I can't even imagine yet that they did to me. I know I still have a lot of memories to go... I know I'll have the strength to handle them... I'm on my way to a happy successful life... I love my strength.

May 26, 1988—This morning at the Mom's Group... another memory came back.... I called WSAC. The more I discover about what I've been through the more I wonder how I ever survived.... You're so strong Susan, so wonderful. You're capable of whatever you believe in. You're OK, Susan Smith. You're strong, you're a survivor, and a winner, you're going straight to the top, head of the class. You're OK, you're a winner. I'm really truly beginning to like myself and I really like that—all these years I hated myself.

May 27—I begin my workshop with my therapist. (Mary Brown)

May 28—... we did rapid breathing... I went to my sexual abuse... my body was twitching and squirming just as if it were tied up by the hands... I started getting these vague recollections of this blond male being Warren and some occurrence happening.... I wasn't ready to look at it until I could intellectually figure out how this could be...

May 31—Describes Dave* meeting with Smith—He explained to him that these memories had been undisturbed for twenty years and had not been distorted... and that I was not making it up... I knew Dave was not ready to look at his abuse... at WSAC I went into denial mode... Veronica played the denial game with me just to show me that I was crazy to believe I was making this up.

June 14, 1988—Saw Veronica, talked about Yellowstone incident with Gretchen involved, how I was blocking everything because I had no proof John was in Yellowstone and the fact that Gretchen must have repressed and that she would probably deny remembering such an incident... so she had me "hang" and it took a much longer time for the feelings to come, but they did, I cried, pound pillows, yelled, and got back more memories... so much doesn't make sense. Where is everyone else?

Nov. 9, 1988—What I learned in therapy today: When I was abused it happened to my body. It happened to a part of me that I dissociated from. I have separated from and disowned the part of

---

*A cousin of Mrs. Smith, and one of the other alleged victims, none of whom had any memories of abuse.

me that it happened to. ... I am ashamed of my body ... so I abuse it.

April 18, 1989—I love myself and that's something I couldn't have said a year ago. I've come a long way.... Signed Terrific Susan.

May ?, 1989—... I let my little girls talk ... etc.

June 8, 1989—attended Conference on Child Sexual Abuse... I learned a lot... talked to Gretchen two weeks ago. More about her "other personalities."... Memories, memories. Where are they. I want to remember all the mean sadistic things John did to me.

July 5, 1989—I know I am going to go on and achieve great things in my life... speak out against abuse of children, especially sexual abuse. l know I'm strong, a survivor, and a successeder. (sic)

Oct. 16, 1989—I got back memories of what happened after John gave my body to the two "tough men" in exchange for drugs.

October 29, 1989—I don't think this can happily, successfully end for me unless I have power over him.

Nov. 29, 1989—Cousin Joe called and told me Warren had memories of being sexually assaulted by John. The memories are just beginning... I told Warren... I was really proud of him.

Nov. 27, 1990—... I don't want any more memories!!! ... I called WSAC this afternoon and bits of memories came up. One was John beside me, and about 5 men, in black robes, or gowns—full length with hoods on their heads.... These men had swordlike daggers in their hands... a memory of John slitting the throat of a cat with a knife... telling us that this is what would happen to us if we ever told about him.

Dec. 16, 1990—I think I might have multiple personalities. It is something I've wondered about before, but believed you only developed multiples if you

were severely abused before age 8.... My first day with Veronica there was this other part of me talking. She named herself Julie... it was really weird cause I knew what was happening... I'm going to get to the other side of this—new and improved. But in the mean time, I'm a nuttsy basketcase.

Dec. 25, 1990—I started back in therapy mid-December, I could no longer contain the memories within me.... I want to write about and keep track of my memories. I've had a feeling for several months now that there might have been ritual abuse. When I started having flashes of white candles, lots of them, burning, I thought well, this is probably just an image I've seen on TV.... My 2nd day in therapy (3rd time I'd seen June) I had this memory—a faceless boy,... he had no nose and only slits for eyes.... They told us if we didn't behave, or if we ever told they would burn our faces with an iron.... They told the girls they use their genitals as eyes, then when they grow older they'd have furry, hairy eyes and everyone would laugh.

Toward the end of our meeting, I asked Mrs. Smith how she distinguished between the many allegations which she insists took place, and the many allegations which she made but now says she cannot remember saying and isn't sure they are real. The gist of her answer (the tape is of course available) was that "memories" which were like a "videotape," where a picture is complete, from start to finish, and which occurred to her sometimes in therapy but often by herself, are reliable. Brief images, or "flashes," which are incomplete, and which were often in response to therapeutic techniques she now is critical of, like those of June Schreiber and others, she distrusts.

I find this distinction, which I must assume to be sincere on Mrs. Smith's part, to be utterly unreliable. First, the therapy from the beginning has been manipulative, even though I have no doubt that all the therapists were sincere in wanting to help. They all, nonetheless, adopted the position that "the more memory the better."

While this might be interpreted to mean that this is standard practice in the therapeutic community, since so many therapists in this case acted in this manner, it is instead an artifact which resulted when Mrs. Smith sought out or was referred to a selected group of therapists who "specialize in recovery from sexual abuse." Amongst this group, whose work and education I have studied intensively, it is common practice to assume abuse occurs if anyone claims it has, common practice to encourage as many "memories" as possible, common practice to encourage anger and "empowerment," and common practice to accept all allegations, however unlikely, as being real.

All this is terribly unscientific, without general agreement from the mental health community, and in my view highly destructive to many patients. Perhaps most important here, in the context of litigation, is the fact that these techniques absolutely fly in the face of reliable fact-finding.

I cannot emphasize strongly enough how important it is for the Court, in studying this case and deciding what is reliable and what is not, to understand that if commonsense leads to one conclusion about where the truth lies, the use of psychiatric labels and esoteric explanations should not cause the Court to abandon what the facts otherwise seem to show.

* * *

As of this writing, the Court has yet to render a verdict. But whatever is decided in this case, it should be clear that our society is about to experience yet another wave of unreliable sexual abuse allegations. Once again, it is the promulgation of faulty ideas by a small segment of the mental health community (see for example Bass & Davis, 1988; Blume, 1990; Briere & Conte, in press; Cozolino, 1989; Maltz, 1990; Herman & Schatzow, 1987; Summit, 1987; Young, Sachs, Braun, & Watkins, 1991), coupled with the apathy of the bulk of the mental health community, which promises to create a new form of abuse of patients, families, and the falsely accused. The moral and economic costs are incalculable, and the promotion of pseudoscientific ideas which confuse memory with mental imagery is already confusing the scientific literature.

Fortunately, clearer heads are also in evidence (see Ganaway, 1991; Lanning, 1989 and 1992; Mulhern, 1991a, 1991b, 1991c; Nathan, 1989, 1990, 1991; Passantino, Passantino, & Trott, 1989; Price, 1992; Putnam, 1991; Wakefield & Underwager, 1992 and undated). Given our society's tendency to become infatuated with all manner of fads, it should be obvious that this latest development in the child sexual abuse circus is not going to go away quickly or easily. It will take insight and perseverance to counteract the tendency of the media and most lay persons to uncritically accept the "blocked memory" claims now emerging with increasing regularity. If our society is serious about responding to the reality of childhood sexual abuse, a critical ingredient is the avoidance of irresponsible empire-building by some mental health professionals who have abandoned both science and reason.

REFERENCES

Bass, E., & Davis, L. (1988). *The courage to heal.* New York, Harper & Row.

Blume, E. (1990). *Secret survivors: Uncovering incest and its aftereffects in women.* New York: J. Wiley & Sons.

Briere, J., & Conte, J. (in press). Self reported amnesia for abuse in adults molested as children. *Journal of Traumatic Stress.*

Cozolino, L. (1989). The ritual abuse of children: Implications for clinical practice and research, *The Journal of Sex Research, 26(1),* 131–138.

Ganaway, G. K. (1991, August 19). *Alternate hypotheses regarding satanic ritual abuse memories.* Presented at the 99th Annual Convention of the American Psychological Association, San Francisco.

Herman, J. L., & Schatzow, E. (1987). Recovery and verification of memories of childhood sexual trauma. *Psychoanalytic Psychology, 4(1),* 1–14.

Lanning, K. V. (1989, October). *Satanic, occult, ritualistic crime: A law enforcement perspective.* National Center for the Analysis of Violent Crime, FBI Academy, Quantico, VA.

Lanning, K. V. (1992). *Investigator's guide to allegations of "ritual" child abuse.* National Center for the Analysis of Violent Crime: Quantico, VA.

Maltz, W. (1990, December). Adult survivors of incest: How to help them overcome the trauma. *Medical Aspects of Human Sexuality,* 42–47.

Mulhern, S. (1991a). *Ritual abuse: Defining a syndrome v. defending a belief.* Unpublished manuscript.

Mulhern, S. (1991b). [Letter to the Editor]. *Child Abuse & Neglect, 15,* 609–610.

Mulhern, S. (1991c). Satanism and psychotherapy: A rumor in search of an inquisition. In J. T. Richardson, J. Best, & D. G. Bromley (Eds.), *The Satanism scare* (pp. 145–172). New York: Aldine de Gruyter.

Nathan, D. (1989, June 21). The Devil and Mr. Mattox, *Texas Observer,* pp. 10–13.

Nathan, D. (1991). Satanism and child molestation: Constructing the ritual abuse scare. In J. T. Richardson, J. Best, & D. G. Bromley (Eds.), *The Satanism scare* (pp. 75–94). New York: Aldine de Gruyter.

Nathan, D. (1990, June 20). The ritual sex abuse hoax, *Village Voice,* pp. 36–44.

Passantino, G., Passantino, B., & Trott, J. (1989). Satan's sideshow. *Cornerstone, 18(90),* 23–28.

Price, L. (1992, April 20). Presentation at the Midwest Regional False Memory Syndrome Foundation Meeting. Benton Harbor, Michigan.

Putnam, F. (1991). The satanic ritual abuse controversy. *Child Abuse & Neglect, 15,* 175–179.

Summit, R. (1987, July). Declaration of Roland Summit, MD, Regarding *People v. Dill.*

Wakefield, H., & Underwager, R. (1992, June 20). *Recovered memories of alleged sexual abuse: Lawsuits against parents.* Presentation at 4th Annual Convention of the American Psychological Society, San Diego, CA. (Also, *Behavioral Sciences and the Law,* in press.)

Wakefield, H., & Underwager, R. (undated). Magic, mischief, and memories: Remembering repressed abuse. Unpublished manuscript. (Also see *Issues in Child Abuse Accusations,* 1991, Vol. 3, No. 3.)

Young, W. C., Sachs, R. G., Braun, B. G., & Watkins, R. (1991). Patients reporting ritual abuse in childhood: A clinical syndrome of 37 cases. *Child Abuse & Neglect, 15,* 181–189.

CHALLENGE QUESTIONS

Are Memories of Sex Abuse Always Real?

1. Can a psychologist or other mental health professional lead a patient to believe something that is not true? If so, how can this happen?

2. Can you think of any explanations for the "instances" described by Bass and Davis other than prior sexual abuse?

3. How would you go about "proving" that someone had been sexually abused? What evidence would you need?

4. What are your beliefs about how memories are stored and retrieved?

ISSUE 9

Can Mental Attitude Affect Biological Disease?

YES: Bernard Dixon, from "Dangerous Thoughts," *Science86 Magazine,* a publication of the American Association for the Advancement of Science (April 1986)

NO: Marcia Angell, from "Disease as a Reflection of the Psyche," *The New England Journal of Medicine* (June 13, 1985)

ISSUE SUMMARY

YES: Bernard Dixon, an editor and writer who specializes in science and health issues, proposes that a positive mental attitude can prevent illness because it reduces psychological stress, which can impair functioning of the immune system.

NO: After reviewing the available research, Marcia Angell, a physician and the executive editor of the *New England Journal of Medicine,* concludes that maintaining a positive attitude will not ward off disease.

Does our mood and self-esteem influence our physical health? Many scientists, from medical professionals to psychologists, are attempting to answer this provocative question. Proponents of holistic medicine believe in relying to some degree on oneself and one's own mood and attitude for physical health. This is the basis on which support groups for people who are battling diseases are developed. These groups try to empower members and improve their attitudes toward themselves and toward their disease in order to improve their health. Are these groups effective in promoting health? If so, what elements of the groups might be responsible?

The fields of health psychology and behavioral medicine attempt to answer questions such as these. Health psychologists study how psychological factors might influence the health and well-being of people, while professionals who study behavioral medicine are concerned with the "behaviors" of health, illness, and related dysfunctions. Persons in these fields consult with medical professionals regarding the effect of illness on a patient's psychological state and vice versa. Psychologists also involve themselves in support groups, bringing to these groups their knowledge of the relation between attitude and physical health. How is the *psyche* (mind) and *soma* (body) connected? Does a mind-body connection help explain recovery from disease?

In the selections that follow, Bernard Dixon presents some human and animal research indicating that psychological stressors (such as anxiety or bereavement) have a negative impact on the immune system, which is a crucial part of the body's defense against illness and disease. Additionally, he argues that mood disorders, such as depression, also negatively affect the immune system.

Marcia Angell criticizes the available research on the connection between mental state and disease. She states that most of this research is anecdotal or methodologically flawed, the biggest flaws being design problems and interpretive bias. Angell also describes research indicating that there is no effect of psychosocial factors on certain illnesses (such as cancer). Although she concedes that a *belief* that attitude can affect disease may have both negative and positive effects, she maintains that individuals should not be made to feel responsible for developing diseases.

POINT	COUNTERPOINT
• In addition to organic components, illness has strong psychological components.	• Illness is governed by physiological processes almost exclusively.
• Research shows that mental state can profoundly affect physical health and illness.	• Research indicating that mental state can cause or cure illnesses is flawed.
• Improving mood and attitude can improve recovery from and future avoidance of physical illness.	• The belief that mental state determines physical health can be harmful.

YES

Bernard Dixon

DANGEROUS THOUGHTS

HOW WE THINK AND FEEL CAN MAKE US SICK

Until recently, Ellen hadn't seen a physician in years. When other people got a bug, she was the one who invariably stayed healthy. But then her luck seemed to change. First she caught a bad cold in January, then had a bout of flu in February, followed by a nasty cough that still lingers. What an infuriating coincidence that these ailments hit as her career was faltering—months of unemployment following companywide layoffs.

But is it a coincidence? Intuition may suggest that we have fewer colds when we are content with our lives, more when we are under stress. That the mind can influence the body's vulnerability to infection in an insidious but potent way is a perennial theme of folklore and literature. Now even scientists are beginning to take that idea seriously. An alliance of psychiatrists, immunologists, neuroscientists, and microbiologists, specialists who rarely look beyond their own disciplines, are beginning to work together in a field so new that it goes under a variety of names, including behavioral immunology, psychoimmunology, and neuroimmunomodulation. Behind these polysyllables lies the challenge of understanding the chemical and anatomical connections between mind and body and eventually, perhaps, even preventing psychosomatic illness.

Just 10 years ago, most specialists in communicable disease would have scoffed at any suggestion that the mind can influence the body in this way. Textbooks portrayed infection as the simple, predictable outcome whenever a disease causing microbe encountered a susceptible host. Various factors such as old age, malnutrition, and overwork could make a disease more severe. But there was no place for the fanciful notion that elation, depression, contentment, or stress could affect the course of disease.

Today, that once-conventional wisdom is being revised by scientists around the world. Playing a major role in these investigations are researchers at England's Medical Research Council Common Cold Unit near Salisbury. Their work shows that even this relatively trivial infection is affected by the psyche. And the lessons learned may apply to more serious diseases, including cancer.

For nearly four decades now, volunteers at the Common Cold Unit have helped test the efficacy of new antiviral drugs and have proven that colds are caused by rhinoviruses and a few related viruses. In 1975 psychologist Richard Totman at Nuffield College, Oxford, and Wallace Craig and Sylvia Reed of the Common Cold Unit conducted the first psychological experiments. The scientists infected 48 healthy volunteers by dribbling down their nostrils drops containing two common cold viruses. The researchers then offered 23 of their subjects the chance to take a new "drug," actually a placebo, that would presumably prevent colds. The investigators warned these subjects that if they accepted this treatment, they would have to have their gastric juices sampled with a stomach tube. The scientists had no intention of doing this; the warning was simply a ruse to put the volunteers under stress. The other half of the group was neither offered the drug nor cautioned about the stomach tube. Totman and his colleagues theorized that the 23 offered the placebo would experience either mild anxiety or regret, depending on the decision they made. This might cause them to allay their state of mind by justifying to themselves their decision—as a theory called cognitive dissonance predicts —which would result in greater bodily resistance and milder colds.

The experts were wrong. When an independent physician assessed the volunteers' symptoms, he found that the 23 offered the choice had cold symptoms that were significantly more severe than those given no option. Apparently anxiety generated by contemplating some-thing unpleasant or refusing to help a worthy cause had a tangible influence on the course of the illness.

Totman's group also made some intriguing observations about the way stress affects people outside the laboratory. Volunteers were interviewed by a psychologist, received rhinoviruses, caught colds, and were monitored. Individuals who during the previous six months had experienced a stressful event, such as death of a loved one, divorce, or a layoff, developed worse colds than the others, and introverts had more severe colds than extroverts. Not only were the introverts' symptoms worse than those of their peers, their nasal secretions contained more rhinovirus, confirming that their illnesses were worse.

The Common Cold Unit is now trying to find out how stress affects people with strong social networks compared with their more introverted colleagues.

But how could an individual's mental state encourage or thwart the development of a cold? Research at several centers in the United States supports the most plausible explanation—that psychological stress impairs the effectiveness of the immune system, which has the dual role of recognizing and eliminating microbes from outside the body as well as cancer cells originating within.

The first line of defense of the immune system is the white blood cells called lymphocytes. These include B cells, which manufacture antibodies against microbes; helper T cells, which aid the B cells in making the right kind of antibodies; and killer T cells, which wipe out invading organisms if they have been exposed to them before. Another kind of lymphocyte, the natural killer cell, has received a lot of attention lately for its ability to detect and destroy harmful cells, including malignant ones, even if it hasn't encountered the invaders previously. Together with scavenging white blood cells that gobble up dead cells and debris, the various types of lymphocytes work in complex, coordinated ways to police the body's tissues.

Researchers can measure the efficiency of the immune system by measuring how well a patient's lymphocytes respond to foreign substances. For instance, they can grow the patient's lymphocytes in glassware and expose them to substances called mitogens, which mimic the behavior of microorganisms by stimulating the white cells to divide. Since a rapid increase in the number of white cells is a crucial early stage in the defense against invasion, patients whose white cells don't proliferate may have malfunctioning immune systems.

But most researchers are cautious about generalizing from the results obtained from a single technique of this sort, since the immune system has complicated backups to keep us healthy even when our lymphocytes aren't proliferating. Nevertheless, reports of stress reducing the efficiency of the immune system have been accumulating on such a scale —and with such variety—that it is becoming difficult to resist the conclusion that anxiety increases our vulnerability to disease.

In one landmark study, for example, Steven Schleifer and his colleagues at Mt. Sinai School of Medicine in New York sought help from spouses of women with advanced breast cancer. They persuaded 15 men to give blood samples every six to eight weeks during their wives' illnesses and for up to 14 months after the women died. While none of the men showed depressed lymphocyte response while their wives were ill, their white cell response was significantly lowered as early as two weeks after their wives died and for up to 14 months later. Schleifer believes he has shown, contrary to earlier studies, that it was bereavement, not the experience of the spouses' illness, that lowered immunity.

Prompted by his observations of the bereaved widowers, Schleifer wondered if serious, debilitating depression would also show up as weakened immunity. When he took blood samples from 18 depressed patients at Mt. Sinai and the Bronx Veterans Administration Hospital, he found their lymphocytes were significantly less responsive to mitogens than those of healthy individuals from the general population matched for age, sex, and race.

We sometimes think humans are uniquely vulnerable to anxiety, but stress seems to affect the immune defenses of lower animals too. In one experiment, for example, behavioral immunologist Mark Laudenslager and colleagues at the University of Denver gave mild electric shocks to 24 rats. Half the animals could switch off the current by turning a wheel in their enclosure, while the other half could not. The rats in the two groups were paired so that each time one rat turned the wheel it protected both itself and its helpless partner from the shock. Laudenslager found that the immune response was depressed below normal in the helpless rats but not in those that could turn off the electricity. What he has demonstrated, he believes, is that lack of control over an event, not the experience itself, is what weakens the immune system.

Other researchers agree. Jay Weiss, a psychologist at Duke University School of Medicine, has shown that animals who are allowed to control unpleasant stimuli don't develop sleep disturbances, ulcers, or changes in brain chemistry typical of stressed rats. But if the animals are confronted with situations they have no control over, they later behave passively when faced with experiences they can control. Such findings reinforce psychiatrists' suspicions that the experience or perception of helplessness is one of the most harmful factors in depression.

One of the most startling examples of how the mind can alter the immune response was discovered by chance. In 1975 psychologist Robert Ader at the University of Rochester School of Medicine and Dentistry conditioned mice to avoid saccharin by simultaneously feeding them the sweetener and injecting them with a drug that while suppressing their immune systems caused stomach upsets. Associating the saccharin with the stomach pains, the mice quickly learned to avoid the sweetener. In order to extinguish the taste aversion, Ader reexposed the animals to saccharin, this time without the drug, and was astonished to find that those rodents that had received the highest amounts of sweetener during their earlier conditioning died. He could only speculate that he had so successfully conditioned the rats that saccharin alone now served to weaken their immune systems enough to kill them.

If you can depress the immune system by conditioning, it stands to reason you can boost it in the same way. Novera Herbert Spector at the National Institute of Neurological and Communicative Disorders and Stroke in Bethesda, Maryland, recently directed a team at the University of Alabama, Birmingham, which confirmed that hypothesis. The researchers injected mice with a chemical that enhances natural killer cell activity while simultaneously exposing the rodents to the odor of camphor, which has no detectable effect on the immune system. After nine sessions, mice exposed to the camphor alone showed a large increase in natural killer cell activity.

What mechanism could account for these connections between the psyche and the immune system? One well-known link is the adrenal glands, which the brain alerts to produce adrenaline and other hormones that prepare the body to cope with danger or stress. But adrenal hormones cannot be the only link between mind and body. Research by a group under Neal Miller, professor emeritus of psychology at the Rockefeller University in New York City, has shown that even rats whose adrenal glands have been removed suffer depressed immunity after being exposed to electric shocks.

Anxiety, it seems, can trigger the release of many other hormones, including testosterone, insulin, and possibly even growth hormone. In addition, stress stimulates secretion of chemicals called neuropeptides, which influence mood and emotions. One class of neuropeptides known as endorphins kills pain and causes euphoria. Endorphins have another interesting characteristic: they fit snugly into receptors on lymphocytes, suggesting a direct route through which the mind could influence immunity.

This idea is borne out in the lab, where one of the natural pain-killers, beta-endorphin, can impair the response of lymphocytes in test tubes. Evidence from cancer studies shows that chemicals blocking the normal functions of endorphins can slow the growth of tumors. And other work suggests that tumor cells may be attracted to certain neuropeptides, providing a route for cancer to spread all over the body.

Neuropeptides are turning out to be extraordinarily versatile in their interaction with the immune system. At the National Institutes of Health in Bethesda, Maryland, Michael Ruff has found neuropeptides that attract scavenging white cells called macrophages to the site of injured or damaged tissue. There the macrophages regulate and activate other immune cells as well as gobble up bacteria and debris. What is even more surprising, however, is that the macrophages themselves actually release neuropeptides. This has led Ruff to speculate that these scavenging white cells may also serve as free-floating nerve cells able to communicate with the brain.

But why should that two-way communication sometimes have the effect of allowing stress to upset the body's defenses? One answer may lie in evolution. When early man was attacked by a sabertoothed tiger, for example, it may have been more important from a survival standpoint for his immune system to turn off briefly. In its zeal to get rid of foreign matter and damaged tissue, a revved-up immune system can also attack healthy tissue. Shutting down the immune system for a short time would avert any damage to the body's healthy tissues and would cause no harm, since it takes a while for infection to set in. As soon as the danger had passed, the immune system was able to rebound—perhaps stronger than before—and go about its main business of fighting invading organisms. But the kind of stress we modern humans suffer is of a different kind: it is rarely life threatening and often lasts a long time, weakening our immune defenses for long periods and making us vulnerable to infections and cancer.

The immune system is extraordinarily complex, and the mind is even more so. As Nicholas Hall of George Washington University School of Medicine says, "We're putting together two kinds of black boxes and trying to make sense of what happens."

In the process, researchers are wrestling with three issues of scientific and social import. First, what can be done to protect people at vulnerable times in their lives from a potentially catastrophic failure of their immune defenses? Second, should counseling and psychological support become as important as traditional therapeutic measures in the treatment of disease? And finally, what are the corresponding benefits to health of the positive emotions of hope, affection, love, mirth, and joy?

NO

Marcia Angell

DISEASE AS A REFLECTION OF THE PSYCHE

Is cancer more likely in unhappy people? Can people who have cancer improve their chances of survival by learning to enjoy life and to think optimistically? What about heart attacks, peptic ulcers, asthma, rheumatoid arthritis, and inflammatory bowel disease? Are they caused by stress in certain personality types, and will changing the personality change the course of the disease? A stranger in this country would not have to be here very long to guess that most Americans think the answer to these questions is yes.

The popular media, stirred by occasional reports in the medical literature, remind us incessantly of the hazards of certain personality types. We are told that Type A people are vulnerable to heart attacks, repressed people (especially those who have suffered losses) are at risk of cancer, worry causes peptic ulcers, and so on. The connection between mental state and disease would seem to be direct and overriding. The hard-driving executive has a heart attack *because* he is pushing for promotion; the middle-aged housewife gets breast cancer *because* she is brooding about her empty nest.

Furthermore, we are told that just as mental state causes disease, so can changes in our outlook and approach to life restore health. Books, magazines, and talk shows abound in highly specific advice about achieving the necessary changes, as well as in explanations about how they work. Norman Cousins, for example, tells us how he managed to achieve a remission of his ankylosing spondylitis by means of laughter and vitamin C—the former, he assumes, operating through reversal of "adrenal exhaustion."[1] Carl and Stephanie Simonton prescribe certain techniques of relaxation and imagery as an adjunct to the conventional treatment of cancer.[2] The imagery includes picturing white cells (strong and purposeful) destroying cancer cells (weak and confused).

Clearly, this sort of postulated connection between mental state and disease is not limited to the effect of mood on our sense of physical well-being. Nor are

From Marcia Angell, "Disease as a Reflection of the Psyche," *The New England Journal of Medicine,* vol. 312, no. 24 (June 13, 1985), pp. 1570–1572. Copyright © 1985 by The Massachusetts Medical Society. Reprinted by permission.

we talking about relaxation as a worthy goal in itself. Cousins, the Simontons, and others of their persuasion advocate a way of thinking not as an end, but rather as a means for defeating disease. The assumption is that mental state is a major factor in causing and curing specific diseases. Is it, and what is the effect of believing that it is?

The notion that certain mental states bring on certain diseases is not new. In her book, *Illness as Metaphor*, Susan Sontag describes the myths surrounding two mysterious and terrifying diseases—tuberculosis in the 19th century and cancer in the 20th.[3] Tuberculosis was thought to be a disease of excessive feeling. Overly passionate artists "consumed" themselves, both emotionally and through the disease. In contrast, cancer is seen today as a disease of depletion. Emotionally spent people no longer have the energy to battle renegade cells. As Sontag points out, myths like these arise when a disease of unknown cause is particularly dreaded. The myth serves as a form of mastery—we can predict where the disease will strike and we can perhaps ward it off by modifying our inner life. Interestingly, when the cause of such a disease is discovered, it is usually relatively simple and does not involve psychological factors. For example, the elaborate construct of a tuberculosis-prone personality evaporated when tuberculosis was found to be caused by the tubercle bacillus.

The evidence for mental state as a cause and cure of today's scourges is not much better than it was for the afflictions of earlier centuries. Most reports of such a connection are anecdotal. They usually deal with patients whose disease remitted after some form of positive thinking, and there is no attempt to determine the frequency of this occurrence and compare it with the frequency of remission without positive thinking. Other, more ambitious studies suffer from such serious flaws in design or analysis that bias is nearly inevitable.[4] In some instances, the bias lies in the interpretation. One frequently cited study, for example, reports that the death rate among people who have recently lost their spouses is higher than that among married people.[5] Although the authors were cautious in their interpretation, others have been quick to ascribe the finding to grief rather than to, say, a change in diet or other habits. Similarly, the known physiologic effects of stress on the adrenal glands are often overinterpreted so that it is a short leap to a view of stress as a cause of one disease or another. In short, the literature contains very few scientifically sound studies of the relation, if there is one, between mental state and disease.

In this issue of the *Journal*, Cassileth et al. report the results of a careful prospective study of 359 cancer patients, showing no correlation between a number of psychosocial factors and progression of the disease.[6] In an earlier prospective study of another disease, Case et al. found no correlation between Type A personality and recurrence of acute myocardial infarction.[7] The fact that these well-designed studies were negative raises the possibility that we have been too ready to accept the venerable belief that mental state is an important factor in the cause and cure of disease.

Is there any harm in this belief, apart from its lack of scientific substantiation? It might be argued that it is not only harmless but beneficial, in that it allows patients some sense of control over their disease. If, for example, patients believe that imagery can help arrest cancer, then they feel less helpless; there is something they can do.

On the other hand, if cancer spreads, despite every attempt to think positively, is the patient at fault? It might seem so. According to Robert Mack, a surgeon who has cancer and is an adherent of the methods of the Simontons, "The patients who survive with cancer or with another catastrophic illness, perhaps even in the face of almost insurmountable odds, seem to be those who have developed a very strong will to live and who value each day, one at a time."[8] What about the patients who *don't* survive? Are they lacking the will to live, or perhaps self-discipline or some other personal attribute necessary to hold cancer at bay? After all, a view that attaches credit to patients for controlling their disease also implies blame for the progression of the disease. Katherine Mansfield described the resulting sense of personal inadequacy in an entry in her journal a year before her death from tuberculosis: "A bad day ... horrible pains and so on, and weakness. I could do nothing. The weakness was not only physical. I must *heal my Self* before I will be well.... This must be done alone and at once. It is at the root of my not getting better. My mind is not *controlled*."[3] In addition to the anguish of personal failure, a further harm to such patients is that they may come to see medical care as largely irrelevant, as Cassileth et al. point out, and give themselves over completely to some method of thought control.

The medical profession also participates in the tendency to hold the patient responsible for his progress. In our desire to pay tribute to gallantry and grace in the face of hardship, we sometimes credit these qualities with cures, not realizing that we may also be implying blame when there are reverses. William Schroeder, celebrated by the media and his doctors as though he were responsible for his own renascence after implantation of an artificial heart, was later gently scolded for slackening. Dr. Allan Lansing of Humana Heart Institute worried aloud about Schroeder's "ostrich-like" behavior after a stroke and emphasized the importance of "inner strength and determination."[9]

I do not wish to argue that people have no responsibility for their health. On the contrary, there is overwhelming evidence that certain personal habits, such as smoking cigarettes, drinking alcohol, and eating a diet rich in cholesterol and saturated fats, can have great impact on health, and changing our thinking affects these habits. However, it is time to acknowledge that our belief in disease as a direct reflection of mental state is largely folklore. Furthermore, the corollary view of sickness and death as a personal failure is a particularly unfortunate form of blaming the victim. At a time when patients are already burdened by disease, they should not be further burdened by having to accept responsibility for the outcome.

REFERENCES

1. Cousins N. Anatomy of an illness as perceived by the patient. New York: WW Norton, 1979.

2. Simonton OC, Matthews-Simonton S, Creighton J. Getting well again: a step-by-step, self-help guide to overcoming cancer for patients and their families. Los Angeles: JP Tarcher, 1978.

3. Sontag S. Illness as metaphor. New York: Farrar, Straus and Giroux, 1977.

4. Fox BH. Premorbid psychological factors as related to cancer incidence. J Behav Med 1978; 1:45–133.

5. Kraus AS, Lilienfeld AM. Some epidemiologic aspects of the high mortality rate in the young widowed group. J Chronic Dis 1959; 10:207–17.
6. Cassileth BR, Lusk EJ, Miller DS, Brown LL, Miller C. Psychosocial correlates of survival in advanced malignant disease. N Engl J Med 1985; 312:1551–5.
7. Case RB, Heller SS, Case NB, et al. Type A behavior and survival after acute myocardial infarction. N Engl J Med 1985; 312:737–41.
8. Mack RM. Lessons from living with cancer. N Engl J Med 1985; 311:1640–4.
9. McLaughlin L. Schroeder kin, doctors try to lift his spirits. Boston Globe. December 17, 1984:1.

CHALLENGE QUESTIONS

Can Mental Attitude Affect Biological Disease?

1. When you are ill, what is your typical course of action? What assumptions is this action based on?

2. Under what circumstances, if any, do you feel that people's state of mind affects their physical health?

3. If you were diagnosed with a serious illness, would improving your mental attitude be part of your treatment regimen? Why, or why not?

4. How do stress and anxiety affect a person's quality of life and vice versa?

ISSUE 10

Can Intelligence Be Increased?

YES: Robert J. Sternberg, from "How Can We Teach Intelligence?" *Educational Leadership* (September 1984)

NO: Arthur R. Jensen, from "Compensatory Education and the Theory of Intelligence," *Phi Delta Kappan* (April 1985)

ISSUE SUMMARY

YES: Psychologist Robert J. Sternberg presents his view that intelligence is a changeable and multifaceted characteristic, and he suggests that intelligence can be taught through training programs, three of which he summarizes.

NO: Psychologist Arthur R. Jensen contends that efforts to increase intelligence have not resulted in any appreciable gains and that programs designed for this purpose are based on a faulty understanding of the nature of intelligence.

Are we born with all the intelligence we will ever have? To what extent can we ensure that all healthy people will be able to cope with the increasing complexities of our society? As we become increasingly dependent upon our educational systems, these questions assume special importance.

If intelligence is a capacity fixed by the time of birth, then an efficient educational system should not waste the time, space, money, and resources that teach beyond each student's capacity. It might be appropriate for each individual's educational track to be determined in advance through extensive intelligence testing.

The 1960s in America can be characterized in part by the conviction that the educational disadvantages of poverty could be overcome by special "head start" programs early in a child's life. Early outcomes provided some evidence that intelligence could be increased. However, the long-term results were less encouraging. The question of an unchangeable intelligence is still open.

Robert J. Sternberg complains that psychologists' traditional preoccupation with the measurement of intelligence has prevented them from understanding the nature of intelligence. The most serious error, he says, has been the assumption "that intelligence is, for the most part, a fixed and immutable characteristic of the individual." Sternberg alleges that a vested interest in intelligence tests with stable scores has interfered with the view that intelligence is changeable.

Sternberg asserts that his own research findings suggest that intelligence *can* be trained and focuses on the question of *how* it can be trained. He presents his own theory of what intelligence is, then he reviews three programs that train aspects of intelligence specified by his theory. Finally, he discusses the variables to be considered by educational administrators who are in the position of choosing programs for their specific school systems.

Arthur R. Jensen claims, "The plain truth is that compensatory programs have not resulted in any appreciable, durable gains in IQ or scholastic achievement for those youngsters who have taken part in them." He points out that these programs have produced positive gains in care, involvement, and attitudes but not in intelligence or academic achievement.

Jensen says that the specialists responsible for these compensatory programs were wrong in their understanding of what intelligence is and what IQ tests measure. He argues that their error was in their view of intelligence as "consisting of a general learning ability of almost unlimited plasticity plus the 'knowledge contents' of memory."

POINT	COUNTERPOINT
• Existing intelligence tests are inadequate.	• Existing intelligence tests have high validity.
• Intelligence is plastic.	• Intelligence is fixed.
• Intelligence can be trained.	• Intelligence is not subject to manipulation.

YES

Robert J. Sternberg

HOW CAN WE TEACH INTELLIGENCE?

For most of the century, psychologists studying intelligence have been pre-occupied with a single question, "How can we measure intelligence?" In retrospect, this preoccupation has turned out to be a grave mistake for several reasons. First, it has led to neglect of the more important question, "What is intelligence?" If intelligence tests have not improved much over the years —and the evidence suggests that they haven't (Sternberg, 1979, 1980)—one can scarcely be surprised. Better tests of intelligence could arise only from better ideas of what intelligence is; curiously enough, few psychologists have sought better tests through better understanding. Rather, they have sought better tests through small refinements of existing technology, which is limited by the inadequacies of the meager theory underlying it (Sternberg, 1977).

Second, the preoccupation with testing has been based on certain assumptions, at least one of which is seriously in error. This assumption is that intelligence is, for the most part, a fixed and immutable characteristic of the individual. After all, if intelligence is constantly changing, or even potentially changeable, what good could tests be? With scores constantly changing, the usefulness of the tests as measures to rank individuals in a stable way over time would be seriously challenged.

Third, and most important for concerned educators, both the preoccupation with testing and the assumption that intelligence is a fixed entity have led to neglect of an even more productive question, "Can intelligence be trained, and if so, how?" My research findings suggest that intelligence *can* be trained. Thus, the focus of this article is the question of "How?"

Because there is no unanimous agreement among psychologists as to the exact nature of intelligence, my own views are necessarily somewhat idiosyncratic. Nevertheless, they are accepted in large part by many specialists in the field, and especially those who have set their goal to train intelligence rather than merely to measure it (Brown, 1983; de Bono, 1983; Resnick, 1976; Detterman and Sternberg, 1982).

My "componential" theory of intelligence seeks to understand intelligence in terms of the component processes that make up intelligence performance (Sternberg, 1979). I will briefly describe the theory, then review three

From Robert J. Sternberg, "How Can We Teach Intelligence?" *Educational Leadership* (September 1984). Copyright © 1984 by The Association for Supervision and Curriculum Development and funded by The National Institute of Education. Reprinted by permission.

programs that train aspects of intelligence as specified by the theory. Then I will conclude with general remarks and suggestions on the adoption of an intellectual or thinking skills training program.

COMPONENTS OF INTELLIGENCE

The view of intelligence as comprising, in part, a set of processes differs in a fundamental way from the view that led to IQ tests. At the turn of the century, the traditional or psychometric view was (and for some continues to be) that intelligence comprises one or more stable, fixed entities (Cattell, 1971; Guilford, 1967; Vernon, 1971). These entities, called *factors*, were alleged to give rise to the individual differences we observe both in IQ test performance and in students' performances at school. The problem with this view is that it does little to suggest how intelligence can be modified. But if intelligence can be broken down into a set of underlying processes, then it is clear what we can do to improve it: we can intervene at the level of the mental process and teach individuals what processes to use when, how to use them, and how to combine them into workable strategies for task solution.

What exactly are these processes? My research suggests they can be divided into three types (Sternberg, 1984). The first type, *metacomponents*, are the higher order or executive processes that we use to plan what we are going to do, monitor what we are doing, and evaluate what we have done. Deciding on a strategy for solving an arithmetic problem or organizing a term paper are examples of metacomponents at work. The second type of processes are *performance components*.

Whereas metacomponents decide what to do, performance components actually do it. So the actual steps we use in, say, solving an analogy or an arithmetic problem, whether on an IQ test or in everyday life, would be examples of sets of performance components in action. The third type of processes are *knowledge-acquisition components*. Processes of this kind are used in learning new material; for example, in first learning how to solve an analogy or a given type of arithmetic problem.

This may seem very abstract, so let's take a concrete example: an analogy. An analogy provides a particularly apt example because virtually everyone who has ever studied intelligence has found the ability to see and solve analogies to be fundamental to intelligent performance. According to the traditional psychometric view, the ability to solve an analogy would be attributed to a static underlying factor of intelligence. Charles Spearman, a famous psychometrician around the turn of the century, called this factor "g," or general intelligence. Some years later, Louis Thurstone, another psychometrician, called the factor "reasoning." The problem with such labels is that they tell us little either about how analogies are solved, or about how the ability to solve analogous problems can be taught.

In contrast, a process-based approach seeks to identify the mental processes used to solve the analogy or other problem. Consider the processes one might use in solving an analogy such as, "*Washington* is to *one* as *Lincoln* is to (a) five, (b) 15, (c) 20, (d) 50." First, we must decide what processes to use, a decision that is metacomponential in nature. Next we must decide how to sequence these processes so as to form a workable strategy for analogy solution, another metacomponential decision. Then we must use the performance components and strategy we have selected to actually solve the problem. It appears, through experimental data we have collected, that what people do is to *encode*, as they need them, relevant attributes of the terms of the analogy: that Washington was the first President of the United States, that he was a Revolutionary War general, and that his is the portrait that appears on a one-dollar bill. Next they *infer* the relation between the first two terms of the analogy, perhaps in this case recognizing that the basis of the analogy might be either Washington as first president or Washington as the portrait on the one-dollar bill. Then they *map* the relation they have inferred in the first part of the analogy to the second part of the analogy (that is, from the Washington part to the Lincoln part), perhaps recognizing that the topic of the analogy is some property of U.S. presidents. Next people *apply* the relation they inferred in the first part of the analogy, as mapped to the second part of the analogy, to the third term so as to select the best alternative. In this case, "five" is the preferred alternative, because it enables one to carry through the relation of portraits on currency (that is, Lincoln's portrait is on the five-dollar bill just as Washington's is on the one-dollar bill). Although this account is a simplification of my model of reasoning by analogy (Sternberg, 1977), it represents the kind of theorizing that goes into a process-based account of intelligent performance.

Now, how can the metacomponents and performance components of intelligence be taught? How can we make students better at structuring and then solving problems than they would be on their own? I recommend three widely dissem-inated programs, each of which has a unique set of strengths and weaknesses.

INSTRUMENTAL ENRICHMENT

The first training program, Reuven Feuerstein's (1980) *Instrumental Enrichment (IE)* program, was originally proposed for use with children showing retarded performance; it has since been recognized by Feuerstein and others to be valuable for children at all levels of the intellectual spectrum. It is based on Feuerstein's theory of intelligence, which emphasizes what I refer to as metacomponential and performance-componential functioning.

Instrumental Enrichment is intended to improve cognitive functioning related to the input, elaboration, and output of information. Feuerstein has compiled a long list of cognitive deficits his program is intended to correct. This list includes:

- Unplanned, impulsive, and unsystematic exploratory behavior. When presented with a number of cues to problem solving that must be scanned, the individual's approach is disorganized, leaving the individual unable to select those cues whose specific attributes make them relevant for a proper solution to the problem at hand.

- Lack of or impaired capacity for considering two sources of information at once, reflected in dealing with data in a piecemeal fashion rather than as a unit of organized facts.

- Inadequacy in experiencing the existence of an actual problem and subsequently in defining it.

- Lack of spontaneous comparative behavior or limitation of its appearance to a restricted field of needs.

- Lack of or impaired strategies for hypothesis testing.
- Lack of orientation toward the need for logical evidence.
- Lack of or impaired planning behavior.
- Episodic grasp of reality. The individual is unable to relate different aspects of his or her experience to one another. Feuerstein seeks to correct these deficits and, at the same time, to increase the student's intrinsic motivation and feeling of personal competence and self-worth.

What are some of the main characteristics of the Feuerstein program? The materials themselves are structured as a series of units, or instruments, each of which emphasizes a particular cognitive function and its relationship to various cognitive deficiencies. Feuerstein defines an instrument as something by means of which something else is effected; hence, performance on the materials is seen as a means to an end, rather than as an end in itself. Emphasis in analyzing *IE* performance is on processes rather than products. A student's errors are viewed as a source of insights into how the student solves problems. *Instrumental Enrichment* does *not* attempt to teach either specific items of information or formal, operational, abstract thinking by means of a well-defined, structured knowlege base. To the contrary, it is as content-free as possible....

What are the strengths and weaknesses of the *IE* program? On the positive side, it (a) can be used for children in a wide age range (from the upper grades of elementary school to early high school) and for children of a wide range of ability levels (from the retarded to the above average) and socioeconomic groups; (b) is well liked by children and appears

to be effective in raising their intrinsic motivation and self-esteem; (c) is well packaged and readily obtainable; and (d) appears effective in raising children's scores on ability tests. Indeed, most of the training exercises contain items similar or identical to those found on intelligence and multiple aptitude tests, so that it should not be totally surprising that intensive practice and training on such items should raise these test scores.

On the more negative side: (a) the program requires extensive teacher training, which must be administered by a designated training authority for the duration of the program; (b) the isolation of the problems from any working knowledge or discipline base (such as social studies or reading, for example) raises questions regarding the transferability of the skills to academic and real-world intellectual tasks, especially over the long term; and (c) despite Feuerstein's aversion to IQ tests, the program trains primarily those abilities that IQ tests tap rather than a broader spectrum of abilities that go beyond intelligence as the tests test it.

To sum up, then, Feuerstein's *Instrumental Enrichment* program is an attractive package in many respects, although with limitations in regard to breadth of skills taught and potential power for generalization. Nevertheless, it is among the best of the available programs that emphasize thinking skill training. Probably it has been the most widely used and field-tested program, both in this country and abroad. As a result, it can be recommended both for members of the majority culture and for members of other cultures and subcultures as well.

PHILOSOPHY FOR CHILDREN

Matthew Lipman's *Philosophy for Children* program is about as different from *Instrumental Enrichment* as it could be (Lipman, Sharp, and Oscayan, 1980). Yet it seeks to foster many of the same intellectual skills, albeit in a very different manner.

Philosophy for Children consists of a series of texts in which fictional children spend a considerable portion of their time thinking about thinking and about ways in which better thinking can be distinguished from poorer thinking. The keys to learning presented in the program are identification and simulation: through reading the texts and engaging in classroom discussions and exercises that follow the reading, the author's objective is for students to identify with the characters and to join in the kinds of thinking depicted in the program.

Lipman has listed 30 thinking skills that *Philosophy for Children* has intended to foster in children of the upper elementary school, generally grades 5–8. A representative sampling of these skills includes the following:

Concept development. Students clarify their understanding of concepts by applying them to specific cases, learning to identify those cases that are within the boundaries and those that are outside. For example, when considering the concept of friendship, children are asked whether people have to be the same age to be friends, whether two people can be friends and not like each other very much, and whether it is possible for friends ever to lie to one another.

Generalizations. Given a set of facts, students are to note uniformities or regularities and to generalize these regularities from given instances to similar ones. For example, children might be asked to consider generalizations that can be drawn from a set of given facts such as, "I get sick when I eat raspberries; I get sick when I eat strawberries; I get sick when I eat blackberries."

Formulating cause-effect relationships. Students should discern and construct formulations indicating relationships between causes and effects. For example, students might be given a statement such as "He threw the stone and broke the window," and then be asked whether the statement necessarily implies a cause-effect relationship.

Drawing syllogistic inferences. Students should draw correct conclusions from valid syllogisms and recognize invalid syllogisms when they are presented. For example, they might be given the premises, "All dogs are animals; all collies are dogs," and be asked what valid inference they can draw from these premises.

Consistency and contradictions. Students should recognize internal consistencies and inconsistencies within a given set of statements or other data. For example, they might be asked to ponder whether it is possible to eat animals if one genuinely cares about them.

Identifying underlying assumptions. Students should recognize the often hidden assumptions that underlie statements. For example, they might be given the following sentences: "I love your hair that way, Peg. What beauty parlor did you go to?" and be asked to identify the hidden assumption underlying the question.

Grasping part-whole and whole-part connections. Students should recognize relations between parts and wholes and avoid mistakes in reasoning based on identification of the part with the whole, or vice versa. For example, students might be asked to identify the part-whole fallacy underlying the statement, "If Mike's face has handsome features, Mike must have a handsome face."

Working with analogies. Students should form and identify analogies. For example, they should be able to solve an analogy such as Germ is to Disease as Candle is to (a) Wax, (b) Wick, (c) White, (d) Light.

The skills trained through the *Philosophy for Children* program are conveyed through a series of stories about children. Consider, for example, the first chapter of *Harry Stottlemeier's Discovery*, the first book in the program series. In this chapter about the consequences of Harry's not paying attention in science class, children are introduced to a wealth of thinking skills. For instance:

Problem formulation. Harry says, "All planets revolve about the sun, but not everything that revolves about the sun is a planet." He realizes that he had been assuming that just because all planets revolve about the sun, everything that revolves about the sun must be a planet.

Nonreversibility of logical "all" statements. Harry says that "a sentence can't be reversed. If you put the last part of a sentence first, it'll no longer be true." For example, he cannot convert "all model airplanes are toys" into "all toys are model airplanes."

Reversibility of logical "no" statements. Lisa, a friend of Harry's, realizes that logical "no" statements can be reversed. "No submarines are kangaroos," for example, can be converted to "No kangaroos are submarines."

Application of principles to real-life situations. Harry intervenes in a discussion between two adults, showing how a principle he had deduced earlier can be applied to disprove one of the adult's argument....

The nature of the *Philosophy for Children* program may be further elucidated by comparing it to Feuerstein's program. The notable similarity between the two programs is that both seek to teach thinking skills, especially what was referred to earlier as executive processes (metacomponents) and nonexecutive processes (performance components). But given the basic similarity of goals, the differences between the programs are striking.

First, whereas Feuerstein's program minimizes the role of knowledge base and customary classroom content, Lipman's program maximizes such involvement. Although the introductory volume, *Harry Stottlemeier's Discovery*, is basically philosophical in tone, the subsequent volumes—*Mark, Pixie, Suki,* and *Lisa*—emphasize infusion of thinking skills into different content areas: the arts, social studies, and science.

Second, whereas the material in Feuerstein's program minimizes the use of written language, the material in Lipman's program is conceptually abstract but is presented through wholly verbal text that deals with highly concrete situations.

Third, although both programs involve class discussion, there is much more emphasis on discussion and interchange in Lipman's program than in Feuerstein's. Similarly, the written exercises are less important in Lipman's program.

Fourth, Feuerstein's program was originally designed for retarded learners, although it has since been extended to children at all points along the continuum of intellectual ability. Lipman's program seems oriented toward children of at least average ability on a scale of national norms. Moreover, the reading in *Philosophy for Children* can be a problem for children much below grade level in reading.

What are the strengths and weaknesses of *Philosophy for Children*? The program has outstanding strengths. First, the stories are exciting and highly motivating to upper elementary school children. Second, it is attractively packaged and easily obtainable. Third, tests of the program have shown it to be effective in raising the level of children's thinking skills. Fourth, the infusion of the thinking skills into content areas should help assure durability and at least some transferability of learning attained through the program. Finally, the thinking skills taught are clearly the right ones to teach for both academic and everyday information processing—no one could possibly complain that the skills are only relevant for IQ tests, although, in fact, the skills are also relevant for performance on such tests....

In summary, although it is limited somewhat by the range of students for whom it is appropriate, no program I am aware of is more likely to teach durable and transferable thinking skills than *Philosophy for Children*.

CHICAGO MASTERY LEARNING READING PROGRAM

Whereas *Instrumental Enrichment* and *Philosophy for Children* emphasize thinking skills (metacomponents and performance components), the *Chicago Mastery Learning Reading Program* emphasizes learning strategies and study skills (knowledge-acquisition [Jones, 1982] components)—a fuzzy but nevertheless useful distinction.

The *Chicago* program, developed by Beau Fly Jones in collaboration with others, equips students with the learning strategies and study skills they need to succeed in school and in their everyday lives. Like *Philosophy for Children*, this program is written for children roughly in grades five through eight. There are four books (tan, purple, silver, and gold), each of which teaches somewhat different skills. The emphasis in all four books, however, is on learning to learn. Within each grade (color) level, there are two kinds of units: comprehension and study skills.

Consider, for example, the purple (Grade 7) sequence. The comprehension program contains units on using sentence context, mood in reading and writing, comprehending complex information, comprehending comparisons, analyzing characters, and distinguishing facts from opinions. The study skills program contains units on parts of a book, graphs and charts, preview-question-read, studying textbook chapters, major and minor ideas, and outlining with parallel structure. The silver (Grade 8) sequence for comprehension contains units of figurative language, word meaning from context, reasoning from facts to complex inferences, analyzing stories and plays, completing a story or a play, signs, and symbols. The sequence for study skills contains units on supporting facts, research aids, notetaking in outline form, summaries and generalizations, comprehending road maps, and understanding forms and directions.

The *Chicago* program is based on the belief that almost all students can learn what only the best students currently learn, if only the more typical or less able students are given appropriate learning opportunities. Mastery learning is described as differing from traditional instruction primarily in the systematic and frequent use of formative and diagnostic testing within each of the instructional units. Instruction is done in groups, with individual assistance and remediation as necessary. Because students typically enter the classroom situation with differing skills and levels of proficiency in the exercise of these skills, instructional units begin with simple, concrete, literal, and familiar material and proceed gradually to the more complex, abstract, inexplicit, and unfamiliar material.

Each instructional unit in the *Chicago* program contains several distinct parts: student activities, optional teaching activities, formative tests, additional activities, enrichment activities, retests, and subject-related applications. Students and teachers are thus provided with a wide variety of materials.

The number and variety of exercises is so great as to rule out the possibility of giving a fair sample of materials in the program. Thus, I can make no claim that the following few examples are representative of the program as a whole:

Using sentence context. In one type of exercise, students read a sentence containing a new word for them to learn. They are assisted in using cues in the sentence to help them determine the word's meaning.

Mood in reading and writing. Students are given a sentence from either expository or fictional text. They are asked to choose which of three words or phrases best describes the mood conveyed by the sentence.

Comprehending comparisons. Students are taught about different kinds of comparisons. They are then given some sample comparisons and asked to elaborate on the meanings, some of which are metaphorical.

Facts and opinions. Students are taught how to distinguish facts from opinions. They are given a passage to read, along with some statements following the passage. Their task is to indicate which statements represent facts and which opinions.

The *Chicago* program is similar to the *Instrumental Enrichment* and *Philosophy for Children* programs in its direct teaching of cognitive skills. The program differs in several key respects, however. First, it resembles typical classroom curriculum more than either of the other two programs. Whereas implementation of either of the others would almost certainly have to follow an explicit policy decision to teach thinking skills as an additional part of the curriculum, the *Chicago* program could very well be implemented as part of an established program, such as the reading curriculum. Second, the program does fit into a specific curriculum area that is common in schools, namely, reading. The Lipman program would fit into a philosophy curriculum, if any school offered such instruction. The Feuerstein program would be unlikely to fit into any existing curricular program, except those explicitly devoted to teaching thinking skills. Third, the *Chicago* program emphasizes learning strategies, whereas the emphasis of the other two programs tends to be on thinking skills. Finally, the *Chicago* program seems most broadly applicable to a wide range of students, including those who are above and below grade level.

Like all programs, the *Chicago* program has both strengths and weaknesses. Its most notable strengths are (1) the wide range of students to whom it can be administered, both in terms of intellectual levels and socio-economic backgrounds; (2) the relatively lesser amount of teacher training required for its implementation; (3) the ease with which the program can be incorporated into existing curricula; and (4) the immediate applicability of the skills to school and other life situations. Students in the program have shown significant pretest to pretest gains in achievement from the program (Jones, 1982).

As for weaknesses, or at least limitations, compared to the *IE* and Lipman's programs, (1) the materials applied are less likely to be intrinsically motivating to students; (2) the skills trained by the *Chicago* program are within a non-limited domain (reading and performing verbal comprehension) than in some other programs; and (3) the program is less clearly based on a psychological theory of cognition.

In conclusion, the *Chicago Mastery Learning Program* offers an attractive means for teaching learning skills, in the context of a reading program. The materials are carefully prepared to be wide ranging and should meet the needs of a wide variety of schools.

CHOOSING THE RIGHT PROGRAM

Do we really need intervention programs for teaching students intellectual skills? The answer is clearly "yes." During the last decade or so we have witnessed an unprecedented decline in the intellec-

tual skills of our school children (Wigdor and Garner, 1982). This is evident, of course, from the decline in scores on tests such as the Scholastic Aptitude Test (SAT); but college professors don't need SAT scores to be apprised of the decline: they can see it in poorer class performance and particularly in the poorer reading and writing of their students. Moreover, thinking skills are needed by more than the college-bound population. Perhaps intellectual skills could be better trained through existing curricula than they are now. But something in the system is not working, and I view programs such as those described here as exciting new developments for reversing the declines in intellectual performance we have witnessed in recent years.

How does one go about choosing the right program for one's particular school and student needs? I believe that wide-ranging research is needed before selecting any one of several programs for school or districtwide implementation. Which program to select will depend on the grade level, socioeconomic level, and intellectual level of the students; the particular kinds of skills one wishes to teach; the amount of time one can devote to training students; one's philosophy of intellectual skills training (that is, whether training should be infused into or separated from regular curricula); and one's financial resources, among other things. Clearly, the decision of which program to use should be made only after extensive deliberation and outside consultation, preferably with people who have expertise, but not a vested interest, in the implementation of one particular program or another.

The following general guidelines can be applied in selecting a program (see also Sternberg, 1983):

- The program should be based on a psychological theory of the intellectual processes it seeks to train and on an educational theory of the way in which the processes will be taught. A good pair of theories should state what processes are to be trained, how the processes work together in problem solving, and how the processes can be taught so as to achieve durability and transfer of training. Innumerable programs seek to train intelligence, but most of them are worth little or nothing. One can immediately rule out large numbers of the low-value programs by investigating whether they have any theoretical basis. The three programs described here are both strong psychological and educational foundations.

- The program should be socioculturally appropriate. It should be clear from the examples described here that programs differ widely in terms of the student populations to whom they are targeted. The best intentions in such a program may be thwarted if the students cannot relate the program both to their cognitive structures and to the world in which they live.

- The program should provide explicit training both in the mental processes used in task performance (performance components and knowledge-acquisition components) and in self-management strategies for using these components (metacomponents). Many early attempts at process training did not work because investigators assumed that just teaching the processes necessary for task performance would result in improved performance on intellectual tasks. The problem was that students often did not learn when to use the processes or how to implement them in tasks differing even slightly from the ones on which they had been trained. In order to achieve durable and transferable learning, it is essential that students be taught not only how to perform tasks but also when to use the strategies they are taught and how to implement them in new situations.

- The program should be responsive to the motivational as well as the intellectual needs of the students. A program that does not adequately motivate students is bound not to succeed, no matter how excellent the cognitive component may be.

- The program should be sensitive to individual differences. Individuals differ greatly in the knowledge and skills they bring to any educational program. A program that does not take these individual differences into account will almost inevitably fail to engage large numbers of students.

- The program should provide explicit links between the training it provides and functioning in the real world. Psychologists have found that transfer of training does not come easily. One cannot expect to gain transfer unless explicit provisions are made in the program so as to increase its likelihood of occurrence.

- Adoption of the program should take into account demonstrated empirical success in implementations similar to one's own planned implementation. Surprisingly, many programs have no solid data behind them. Others may have data that are relevant only to school or student situations quite different from one's own. A key to success is choosing a program with a demonstrated track record in similar situations.

* The program should have associated with it a well-tested curriculum for teacher training as well as for student training. The best program can fail to realize its potential if teachers are insufficiently or improperly trained.
* Expectations should be appropriate for what the program can accomplish. Teachers and administrators often set themselves up for failure by setting expectations that are inappropriate or too high.

Programs are now available that do an excellent, if incomplete, job of improving children's intellectual skills. The time has come for supplementing the standard curriculum with such programs. We can continue to use intelligence tests, but we will provide more service to children by developing their intelligence than by testing it.

REFERENCES

Brown, A. L. "Knowing When, Where, and How to Remember: A Problem of Metacognition." In Advances in Instructional Psychology, Vol 1. Edited by R. Glaser. Hillsdale, N.J.: Erlbaum, 1978.

Brown, J. L. "On Teaching Thinking Skills in the Elementary and Middle Schools." Phi Delta Kappan 64 (1983): 709–714.

Cattell, R. B. Abilities: Their Structure, Growth, and Action. Boston: Houghton-Mifflin, 1971.

de Bono, E. "The Direct Teaching of Thinking as a Skill." Phi Delta Kappan 64 (1983): 703–08.

Detterman, D. K., and Sternberg, R. J., eds. How and How Much Can Intelligence Be Increased? Norwood, N.J.: Ablex, 1982.

Feuerstein, R. Instrumental Enrichment: An Intervention Program for Cognitive Modifiability. Baltimore: University Park Press, 1980.

Guilford, J. P. The Nature of Intelligence. New York: McGraw-Hill, 1967.

Jones, B. F. Chicago Mastery Learning: Reading. 2nd ed. Watertown, Mass.: Mastery Education Corporation, 1982.

Lipman, M.; Sharp, A. M.; and Oscanyan, F. S. Philosophy in the Classroom. 2nd ed. Philadelphia: Temple University Press, 1980.

Resnick, L. B. The Nature of Intelligence. Hillsdale, N.J.: Erlbaum, 1976.

Sternberg, R. J. Intelligence, Information Processing, and Analogical Reasoning: The Componential Analysis of Human Abilities. Hillsdale, N.J.: Erlbaum, 1977.

Sternberg, R. J. "The Nature of Mental Abilities." American Psychologist 34 (1979): 214–230.

Sternberg, R. J. "The Construct Validity of Aptitude Tests: An Information-Processing Assessment." In Construct Validity in Psychological Measurement. Princeton, N.J.: Educational Testing Service, 1980.

Sternberg, R. J. "Criteria for Intellectual Skills Training." Educational Researcher 12 (1983): 6–12, 26. Sternberg, R. J. Beyond IQ: A Triarchic Theory of Human Intelligence. New York: Cambridge University Press, 1984.

Vernon, P. E. The Structure of Human Abilities. London: Methuen, 1971.

Wigdor, A. K., and Garner, W. R., eds. Ability Testing: Uses, Consequences, and Controversies (2 volumes). Washington, D.C.: National Academy Press, 1982.

NO

Arthur R. Jensen

COMPENSATORY EDUCATION AND THE THEORY OF INTELLIGENCE

The past 20 years have been a period of unparalleled affluence for public education and educational research in the U.S. When the history of this era is written, two features will stand out prominently: racial desegregation of the schools and large-scale experimentation with compensatory education.

The nation focused its educational resources during this period primarily on extending the benefits of education to every segment of the population —especially to those groups that historically have derived the least benefit from the traditional system of schooling. During the past 20 years more young people have gone to school for more years and have obtained more diplomas, per capita, in the U.S. than in any other nation. Fifty percent of U.S. high school graduates in the 1970s went on to college.

These proud facts are one side of the picture. The other side is much less complimentary and should shake any complacency we Americans might feel. The past 20 years, which have brought the most energetic large-scale innovations in the history of U.S. education, have also brought an accelerating decline in Scholastic Aptitude Test scores. And there are other signs of malaise as well. On objective measures of the average level of educational achievement, the U.S. falls below all other industrialized nations, according to the International Association for the Evaluation of Educational Achievement.[1] In fact, average levels of educational achievement lower than that of the U.S. are found only in the industrially under-developed nations of the Third World.

Illiteracy in the U.S. has been grossly underestimated. Until recently, the U.S. Census Bureau routinely estimated the rate of illiteracy as the percentage of Americans with fewer than six years of schooling. The 1980 Census found that only two-tenths of 1% (0.2%) of the U.S. population between the ages of 14 and 24 met this definition of illiteracy—a rate that was the same for both black and white Americans.

Simple tests of actual reading ability reveal a much less rosy picture, however. According to lawyer and psychologist Barbara Lerner, evidence collected by the National Assessment of Educational Progress shows that "the overall rate of illiteracy for cohorts reaching their 18th birthday in the 1970s

From Arthur R. Jensen, "Compensatory Education and the Theory of Intelligence," *Phi Delta Kappan* (April 1985). Copyright © 1985 by Arthur R. Jensen. Reprinted by permission.

can safely be estimated to have been at least 20%.... [Moreover, the] black-white gap was still dramatic: 41.6% of all black 17-year-olds still enrolled in school in 1975 were functionally illiterate."[2] Lerner goes on to emphasize the broad implications of this finding:

On this basis, it would have seemed reasonable to predict serious shortages of literate workers throughout the 1980s and perhaps beyond, along with high levels of structural unemployment, particularly among younger black workers, and increasing difficulty in meeting economic competition from foreign countries with more literate work forces.[3]

Clearly, those conditions that originally gave rise to the aims and aspirations of compensatory education are as relevant today as they were 20 years ago. Of the many lessons that can be learned from assessments and meta-analyses of the results of 20 years of compensatory education, I intend to dwell in this article on what seems to me to be one of the most important. Because the lesson on which I will dwell is one of the clearest and seemingly least-debatable findings of studies of compensatory education programs of all kinds and because this lesson has important implications for both theory and practice, it is peculiar that this lesson has been soft-pedaled in most published summaries of compensatory education outcomes.

The lesson to which I refer is this: compensatory education has made its least impressive impact on just those variables that it was originally intended (and expected) to improve the most: namely, I.Q. and scholastic achievement. The plain truth is that compensatory programs have not resulted in any appreciable, durable gains in I.Q. or scholastic

achievement for those youngsters who have taken part in them. This is an important discovery, and the fact that we do not like this outcome or that it is not what we expected neither diminishes its importance nor justifies downplaying it. Rather, we are challenged to try to understand its theoretical implications for the study of intelligence and its practical implications for the practice of education.

Let us not be distracted from trying to understand the discrepancy between the expected and the actual outcomes of compensatory education programs by the too-easy response of retroactively revising our original expectations. We should gain more from our 20 years of experience than just a list of excuses for the disappointing discrepancy between our expectations and the actual results.

To be sure, Head Start and other compensatory education programs have produced some positive gains. The fact that the bona fide benefits of compensatory education have not been primarily cognitive in nature and not strongly reflected in academic achievement per se should not detract from the social importance of these gains. The positive outcomes of Head Start and similar programs include such things as the improvement of participants' nutrition and of their medical and dental care. The list of positive outcomes also includes greater involvement of parents in their children's schooling, noticeable improvement in the children's attitude toward school and in their self-esteem, fewer behavioral problems among participants, fewer retentions in grade, and a smaller percentage of special education placements.[4]

These socially desirable outcomes have not been accompanied by marked or lasting improvement in either I.Q. or academic performance, however. Even the smaller percentage of special education placements may be attributable to teachers' and administrators' knowledge that certain children have taken part in Head Start or other compensatory education programs, because such children are less apt than nonparticipating peers to be labeled as candidates for special education. Gene Glass and Mary Ellwein offer an insightful observation on this point in their review of *As the Twig Is Bent*, a book on 11 compensatory education programs and their outcomes, as assessed by the Consortium for Longitudinal Studies. According to Glass and Ellwein:

[T]hose whose ideas are represented in *As the Twig Is Bent* see themselves as developmental psychologists molding the inner, lasting core of the individual —one can almost visualize the cortical wiring they imagine being rearranged by ever-earlier intervention. And yet the true lasting effects of a child's preschool experiences may be etched only in the attitudes of the professionals and in the records of the institutions that will husband his or her life after preschool.[5]

Even studies of those compensatory programs that involve the most intensive and prolonged educational experience show the effects of such programs on I.Q. to be relatively modest and subject to "fadeout" within one to three years. The highly publicized "Miracle in Milwaukee" Study by Rick Heber and Howard Garbert appears to be a case in point. In that study, the researchers gave intensive training designed to enhance cognitive development to children who were deemed at risk for mental retardation because of their family backgrounds. The training lasted from birth until the participants entered school. Unfortunately, no detailed account of the conduct of the Milwaukee Study or of its long-term out-

comes has yet appeared in any refereed scientific journal. Because the data are not available for full and proper critical review, I cannot legitimately cite this study with regard to the effects of early intervention on subsequent intelligence and scholastic achievement.

Fortunately, a similar study—the Abecedarian Project,[6] currently under way in North Carolina—is being properly reported in the appropriate journals, and the researchers conducting this study promise the kind of evaluation that Heber and Garber have failed to deliver. From infancy to school age, children in the Abecedarian Project spend six or more hours daily, five days a week, 50 weeks a year, in a cognitive training program. Their I.Q. gains, measured against a matched control group at age 3, look encouraging. However, the possibility exists that the program has merely increased participants' I.Q. scores and not the underlying factor of intelligence that the I.Q. test is intended to measure and upon which its predictive and construct validity depend.[7]

Probably the most scholarly, thorough, and up-to-date examination of the variety of experimental attempts to improve intelligence and other human abilities is *How and How Much Can Intelligence Be Increased?* edited by Douglas Detterman and Robert Sternberg.[8] In a review of this book, I said:

What this book may bring as something of a surprise to many psychologists who received their education in the 1950s and '60s, in the heyday of what has been termed "naive environmentalism" in American educational psychology, is the evident great difficulty in effecting practically substantial and durable gains in individuals' intelligence. In terms of some conceptions of human intelligence as predominantly a product of cultural learning, this fact should seem surprising.... The sum total of the wide-ranging information provided in this book would scarcely contradict the conclusion that, as yet, investigators have not come up with dependable and replicable evidence that they have discovered a psychological method by which they can increase "intelligence" in the sense of Spearman's g.[9]

Thus current claims regarding the plasticity of human intelligence are notably more subdued than were the promises of only 20 years ago. Edward Zigler, one of the founders of and leaders in compensatory education, and his colleague, Winnie Berman, have recently warned that workers in the field "must be on guard never again to make the errors of overpromising and overselling the positive effects of early childhood intervention."[10]

Despite their personal enthusiasm for compensatory education, Zigler and Berman have surveyed the history and developments of this field with critical objectivity. Of the beginning of preschool intervention in the 1960s, they say:

It was widely believed that a program of early environmental enrichment would give lower SES [socioeconomic status] children the boost they needed to perform on a par with their middle SES peers. Intervention was supposed to impart immediate benefits so that class differences would be eliminated by the time of school entry. Furthermore, many expected that the brief preschool experience would be so potent a counteraction to the deficits in poor children's lives that it could prevent further attenuation in age-appropriate performance and a recurrence of the gap between social classes in later grades.... What we witnessed in the 1960s was the belief that

intelligence quotients can be dramatically increased with minimal effort.... Unfortunately, "knowing more" was easily translated into "becoming smarter."[11]

Elsewhere, Zigler describes the thinking in the early days of Head Start, a program that he helped to initiate:

... J. McV. Hunt, Benjamin Bloom, and others constructed for us a theoretical view that conceptualized the young child as possessing an almost unlimited degree of plasticity. Joe Hunt continued to assert that the norm of reaction for intelligence was 70 I.Q. points... and that relatively short-term intervention efforts could result in I.Q. gains of 49 or 63 points. With such environmental sugarplums dancing in our heads, we actually thought we could compensate for the effects of several years of impoverishment as well as inoculate the child against the future ravages of such impoverishment, all by providing a six- or eight-week summer Head Start experience.[12]

This theoretical view of human intelligence—a view that governed the design and expectations of compensatory education programs in the 1960s—has been put to the test during the past 20 years. And the outcome seems remarkably clear. It turns out that the prevailing views of most psychologists and educators in the 1960s were largely wrong with regard to such questions as, What is the nature of intelligence? What is it that our I.Q. tests measure primarily? Why is the I.Q. so highly predictive of scholastic performance?

The error lay in believing that the disadvantage with which many poor or culturally different children entered school —and the disadvantage that compensatory education was intended to remedy —was mainly a deficiency in *knowledge*.

Implicit in this belief was a view of intelligence as consisting of a general learning ability of almost unlimited plasticity plus the "knowledge contents" of memory, particularly those kinds of knowledge that serve to improve scholastic performance. Holders of this view saw the information content of I.Q. tests as an arbitrary sample of the specific items of knowledge and skill normally acquired by members of the white middle and upper classes.

In this highly behavioristic conception of intelligence, which I have elsewhere termed the *specificity doctrine*,[13] intelligence is erroneously identified with the content of the test items that psychologists have devised for assessing intelligence. These test items cover such things as general information, vocabulary, arithmetic, and the ability to copy certain geometric figures, to make block designs, and to work puzzles. To acquire the knowledge and skills to do these things—or to learn other, similar things that would have positive transfer to performance on I.Q. tests or in coursework—is to become more intelligent, according to this deceptive view of intelligence. As Zigler and Berman have put it, "knowing more" is erroneously translated into "becoming smarter."

Striking findings from two recent lines of research—that on test bias and that on mental chronometry—clearly contradict the view of individual and group differences in intelligence as differences primarily in knowledge.

The research on test bias has shown that the level of difficulty of I.Q. and achievement test items is consistent across all American-born, English-speaking ethnic and social-class groups. Moreover, I.Q. and achievement tests do not differ in their predictive validity for these groups. These findings are highly inconsistent with the hypothesis that cultural differences exist in the knowledge base that these tests sample. Available evidence from studies of test bias makes it extremely implausible that racial and social-class differences can be explained by cultural differences in the knowledge base or by differential opportunity for acquiring the knowledge that existing tests sample.[14] For every American-born social class and racial group, highly diverse test items maintain the same relative standing on indices of item difficulty, regardless of the culture loadings of the items. This phenomenon requires that we find some explanation for group differences on I.Q. and achievement tests other than cultural differences in exposure to the various kind of knowledge sampled by the tests.

We must seek the explanation, I believe, at the most basic level of information processing. In recent years, both the theory and the technology of research on cognitive processes have afforded powerful means for analyzing individual and group differences in abilities. Within the framework of cognitive processes research, the kinds of questions that we can investigate are quite different and more basic than those we can study through traditional psychometric tests and factor analysis. Mental chronometry, or measurement of the time required for various mental events in the course of information processing, permits us to investigate individual differences at the level of elementary cognitive processes—those processes through which individuals attain the complex learning, knowledge, and problem-solving skills that I.Q. tests sample.

Researchers devise the tasks used to measure individual differences in various elementary cognitive processes in such a way as to rule out or greatly minimize individual differences in knowledge. These tasks are so simple, and the error rates on them are so close to zero, that individual differences can be studied only by chronometric techniques. For example, the cognitive tasks that we use in our laboratory are so easy that they typically require less than one second to perform.[15] Yet these very brief response latencies, derived from a number of elementary processing tasks, together can account for some 70% of the variance in scores on untimed standard psychometric tests of intelligence. Very little of the true score variance on such tests can be attributed to the knowledge covered by the tests' content per se.

It is important to understand that the items of standardized psychometric tests are mainly vehicles for reflecting the past and present efficiency of mental processes. That these items usually include some knowledge content is only an incidental and nonessential feature. The fact is that individual differences on these content-laden tests correlate with response latencies on elementary cognitive-processing tasks that have minimal intellectual content. This means that our standard I.Q. tests—and the scholastic achievement tests with which these I.Q. tests are highly correlated—reflect individual differences in the speed and efficiency of basic cognitive processes more than they reflect differences in the information content to which test-takers have been exposed. In fact, we can account for a substantial portion of the variance in I.Q. scores by measuring the evoked electrical potentials of the brain, using an electrode attached to the scalp—a measure that is not only free of any knowledge content but that is not even dependent on any voluntary or overt behavior by the subject.[16]

Thus I suggest that the design of compensatory education and the assessment of its effects should be informed by the recent studies on information processing. The variables that have been measured by researchers in this field to date have correlated not only with I.Q., but with scholastic achievement as well.[17] An important question for future research is, What proportions of the variance in I.Q. and in scholastic achievement are associated with elementary cognitive processes and with meta-processes respectively? A second but equally important question is, What possible effects can various types of compensatory training have on these two levels of cognitive processes?

Elementary cognitive processes include such variables as perceptual speed, stimulus scanning, stimulus encoding, mental rotation or transformation of visual stimuli, short-term memory capacity, efficiency of information retrieval from long-term memory, generalization, discrimination, comparison, transfer, and response execution. *Meta-processes* include those planning and executive functions that select and coordinate the deployment of the elementary cognitive processes to handle specific situations, e.g., strategies for problem recognition, for selecting and combining lower-order cognitive processes, for organizing information, for allocating time and resources, for monitoring one's own performance, and the like.

Meta-processes are thought to be more amenable than elementary processes to improvement through training, but no solid evidence currently exists on this question. And, though much is already known about social-class and racial-group differences in I.Q. and scholastic achievement, psychologists have scarcely begun to try to understand the nature and locus of these differences in terms of the cognitive processes and meta-processes involved.[18] As yet, virtually nothing is known about the effects of compensatory education on the various levels of cognitive processing or about the extent to which the levels of cognitive processing can be influenced by training especially designed for that purpose.

I suspect that a substantial part of the individual variance in I.Q. and scholastic achievement—probably somewhere between 50% and 70%, according to the best evidence on the heritability of I.Q.—is not subject to manipulation by any strictly psychological or educational treatment. The reason for this, I assume, is that the main locus of control of that unyielding source of variance is more biological than psychological or behavioral.

At an even more fundamental level, we might ask why variance in intelligence should be so surprisingly resistant to experimental manipulation. As I have suggested elsewhere,[19] this apparent resistance to manipulation seems less surprising if we view human intelligence as an outcome of biological evolution. Genetic variation is the one absolutely essential ingredient to enable evolution to occur. If intelligence has evolved as a fitness characteristic in the Darwinian sense—that is, as an instrumentality for the survival of humankind —it is conceivable that the biological basis of intelligence has a built-in stabilizing mechanism, rather like a gyroscope, that safeguards the individual's behavioral capacity for coping with the exigencies of survival. If that were the case, mental development would not be wholly at the mercy of often erratic environmental happenstance. A too-malleable fitness trait would afford an organism too little protection against the vagaries of its environment. Thus, as humanity evolved, processes may also have evolved to buffer intelligence from being pushed too far in one direction or another, whether by adventitiously harmful or by intentionally benevolent environmental forces.

NOTES

1. Barbara Lerner, "Test Scores as Measures of Human Capital," in Raymond B. Cattell, ed., *Intelligence and National Achievement* (Washington, D.C.: Cliveden Press, 1983).

2. Ibid., p. 73.

3. Ibid., p. 74.

4. Consortium for Longitudinal Studies, *As the Twig Is Bent . . . Lasting Effects of Preschool Programs* (Hillsdale, N.J.: Erlbaum, 1983); and Edward Zigler and Jeanette Valentine, *Project Head Start* (New York: Free Press, 1979).

5. Gene V. Glass and Mary C. Ellwein, review of *As the Twig Is Bent . . .*, by the Consortium for Longitudinal Studies, in *Science*, 20 January 1984, p. 274.

6. Craig T. Ramey et al., "The Carolina Abecedarian Project: A Longitudinal and Multidisciplinary Approach to the Prevention of Developmental Retardation," in Theodore D. Tjossem, ed., *Intervention Strategies for High Risk Infants and Young Children* (Baltimore: University Park Press, 1976).

7. Craig T. Ramey and Ron Haskins, "The Modification of Intelligence Through Early Experience," *Intelligence*, January/March 1981, pp. 5–19; and Arthur R. Jensen, "Raising the I.Q.: The Ramey and Haskins Study," *Intelligence*, January/March 1981, pp. 29–40.

8. Douglas K. Detterman and Robert J. Sternberg, eds., *How and How Much Can Intelligence Be Increased?* (Norwood, N.J.: Ablex, 1982).

9. Arthur R. Jensen, "Again, How Much Can We Boost I.Q.?" review of *How and How Much Can Intellignce Be Increased?* edited by Douglas K. Detterman and Robert J. Sternberg, in *Contemporary Psychology*, October 1983, p. 757.

10. Edward Zigler and Winnie Berman, "Discerning the Future of Early Childhood Intervention," *American Psychologist*, August 1983, p. 897.

11. Ibid., pp. 895–96.

12. Quoted in Peter Skerry, "The Charmed Life of Head Start," *Public Interest*, Fall 1983, pp. 18–39.

13. Arthur R. Jensen, "Test Validity: g Versus the Specificity Doctrine," *Journal of Biological Structures*, vol. 7, 1984, pp. 93–118.

14. Arthur R. Jensen, *Bias in Mental Testing* (New York: Free Press, 1980); and Cecil R. Reynolds and Robert T. Brown, *Perspectives on Bias in Mental Testing* (New York: Plenum, 1984).

15. Arthur R. Jensen, "Chronometric Analysis of Intelligence," *Journal of Social and Biological Structures*, April 1980, pp. 103–22; idem, "The Chronometry of Intelligence," in Robert J. Sternberg, ed., *Advances in the Psychology of Human Intelligence* (Hillsdale, N.J.: Erlbaum, 1982); and idem, "Reaction Time and Psychometric *g*," in Hans J. Eysenck, ed., *A Model for Intelligence* (Heidelberg: Springer-Verlag, 1982).

16. Donna E. Hendrickson and Alan E. Hendrickson, "The Biological Basis of Individual Differences in Intelligence," *Personality and Individual Differences*, January 1980, pp. 3–34.

17. Jerry S. Carlson and C. Mark Jensen, "Reaction Time, Movement Time, and Intelligence: A Replication and Extension," *Intelligence*, July/September 1982, pp. 265–74.

18. John G. Borkowski and Audrey Krause, "Racial Differences in Intelligence: The Importance of the Executive System," *Intelligence*, October/December 1983, pp. 379–95; Arthur R. Jensen, "Race Differences and Type II Errors: A Comment on Borkowski and Krause," *Intelligence*, in press; and Philip A. Vernon and Arthur R. Jensen, "Individual and Group Differences in Intelligence and Speed of Information Processing," *Personality and Individual Differences*, in press.

19. Jensen, "Again, How Much Can We Boost I.Q.?" p. 758.

CHALLENGE QUESTIONS

Can Intelligence Be Increased?

1. If you had a child about to enter school and you had the choice between one administered by Jensen and one administered by Sternberg, which school would you choose? Why?

2. If you were a school administrator with the task of efficiently using the school's resources to make the most of each student's potential, would you give each student an intelligence test to determine which classes are most appropriate for him or her? Why, or why not?

3. If programs for improving the thinking skills of students are successful, has the intelligence of the students been increased? Explain your answer.

4. Should it be taken for granted that college students already have mature thinking skills? Why, or why not?

5. Should programs with goals similar to those described by Sternberg be a part of a college education? If so, should they be separate courses or part of all courses?

PART 4

Mental Health

A mental disorder is often defined as a pattern of thinking or behaving that is either disruptive to others or uncomfortable for the person with the disorder. This definition seems straightforward; however, is it universally applicable? Certain patterns of social behavior fit this definition, but does this make them "diseases" in the medical sense? Some researchers have recently argued that stress related to abortion is often severe enough to be labeled a disorder—specifically, "postabortion syndrome." Is this a legitimate disease requiring treatment? We usually think of diagnosis as an important prerequisite to treatment. But when we apply it to behavior we run the risk of prejudicing the way we think about that behavior. How great is that risk for competent treatment?

- Is Schizophrenia a Disease?

- Does Abortion Have Severe Psychological Effects?

- Classic Dialogue: Do Diagnostic Labels Hinder Treatment?

ISSUE 11

Is Schizophrenia a Disease?

YES: Eve C. Johnstone, from "A Concept of Schizophrenia," *Journal of Mental Health* (vol. 2, 1993)

NO: Theodore R. Sarbin, from "Toward the Obsolescence of the Schizophrenia Hypothesis," *The Journal of Mind and Behavior* (vol. 11, nos. 3 and 4, 1990)

ISSUE SUMMARY

YES: Psychiatrist Eve C. Johnstone contends that schizophrenia is a biological disease, both in the sense of a medical syndrome and in the sense of a physical lesion.

NO: Theodore R. Sarbin, noted researcher and psychologist, argues that schizophrenia is a social construct developed by scientists and practitioners to make sense of a variety of behaviors.

The condition known as "schizophrenia" has been a puzzle ever since it was first labeled. Considered a "thought disorder" or a type of "psychosis," its symptoms typically include hallucinations, delusions, and a general lack of perception about what is real or actual. Why do people act and think this way? What causes schizophrenia?

Until about the fourth century B.C., schizophrenics were thought to be the victims of demons that required exorcising. It was then that the Greek physician Hippocrates suggested a medical model of abnormality, a model that has dominated the understanding of schizophrenia until the present. The medical model assumes that schizophrenics have some kind of "badness" in them. Recently, the medical model has attempted to locate this badness—this disease—in the properties (or physiology) of the body.

A historical and a modern reaction to this dominant disease model has been termed "social constructionism." Social constructionists have traditionally called attention to the "social" elements of schizophrenia. That is, schizophrenia is not merely an objective condition; it is a moral judgment, based upon the ethics of the society in which the judgment occurs. In some cultures, schizophrenics are seen as especially close to God or exceptionally enlightened. Because this is a different social construction of schizophrenia (i.e., it is not bad), there is no need to find its physiological "cause." Although physiological differences between "normals" and "schizophrenics" occur, it is not known whether these differences are the cause of the schizophrenics' behavior or the result of ethical judgments and societal treatment as a consequence of such judgments.

Psychiatrist Eve C. Johnstone supports the former explanation. She carefully examines the notion of "disease" in the medical sense and finds that the concept of schizophrenia fits it in two major respects. First, Johnstone cites evidence to show that the symptoms of schizophrenia form a "syndrome picture" with a characteristic outcome. Second, she attempts to demonstrate that the disorder is based on a physical condition. Johnstone concludes that even if the disease concept is false, the medical model of schizophrenia still has practical value to patients and clinicians.

In contrast, Theodore R. Sarbin finds little of value in the medical model of schizophrenia; he considers the disease "construction" to be no longer tenable. Sarbin describes how this disease notion originated from its social and historic origins, implying that schizophrenia is not an objective thing but a cultural invention. He also attempts to demonstrate that there is no valid biological or psychological distinction between schizophrenics and normals. According to Sarbin, eight decades of research has shown that such distinctions produce an unacceptable number of misdiagnoses, and this research has also failed to differentiate schizophrenic problems from other, more normal problems.

POINT	COUNTERPOINT
• The scientific evidence is sufficient to conclude that schizophrenia is a biological disease.	• Decades of research have failed to produce a reliable distinction between schizophrenia and normalcy.
• The symptoms of schizophrenia form a syndrome picture that has a characteristic outcome.	• The symptoms of schizophrenia originate from social and moral judgments, not from the disease itself.
• Schizophrenics cannot help that they have this disease.	• To make a pattern of behavior such as schizophrenia into a disease is to make a person into an object.
• The medical model of schizophrenia has practical value for patients.	• When behaviors and thoughts are "modeled" medically, it means that *all* our thoughts and behaviors are not chosen but determined.

YES

Eve C. Johnstone

A CONCEPT OF SCHIZOPHRENIA

SCHIZOPHRENIA AS A DISEASE

It is twenty-seven years since as a medical student I saw my first schizophrenic patient. She was about my own age. I remember her name, her face, her perplexity and fear. Her mother was interviewed for the benefit of the students and she described her bewilderment and grief over the inexplicable change in her daughter, who had previously functioned effectively, working successfully in the local textile industry.

I was given to understand that really nothing was known about the cause of this condition, although it was certainly sometimes familial, that the pathogenesis was not understood at all, that although the treatment was relatively successful in the short term, it was entirely empirical and there was no understanding of its mechanism. I was told that in the longer term treatment was not successful, that relapse was usual and most patients suffered a general deterioration of function and could not work, make social relationships or achieve independence.

In the West of Scotland among the deprived individuals who formed the majority of the patients in the big infirmaries, rheumatic heart disease was still common enough for there to be several affected patients in every medical ward that I saw, cases of chronic bronchitis, emphysema and respiratory failure packed the wards every winter, tuberculosis was not yet a disease of the past, and as now cancers and cardiovascular disease were very common. Like many of the idealistic medical students that I now teach, I was fascinated by serious illness and I wanted to look after people who were really very ill, to the best standard possible. To me, at that time, schizophrenia was the worst disease that I had ever seen. It seemed to come from nowhere to strike the young, affect them with bizarre, frightening and non-understandable symptoms, to progressively blunt their abilities and warp their personalities and probably forever destroy their promise and potential. No-one knew why, and not a great deal could be done about it—certainly not about the loss of potential. I could identify all too readily with that situation and could imagine no worse fate.

From Eve C. Johnstone, "A Concept of Schizophrenia," *Journal of Mental Health*, vol. 2 (1993). Copyright © 1993 by Eve C. Johnstone. Reprinted by permission. References omitted.

Research did not seem to be being performed in the way that it was in other specialties. This was, of course, in the 1960s. 'The Divided Self' had been published only a few years before by the Glaswegian psychiatrist Dr. R. D. Laing, and his later work 'Sanity, Madness and the Family' had just reached the shelves. Ideas that schizophrenia was in some way the result of flawed interpersonal interactions within the patients's family and home were widely discussed. I found the acceptance of such ideas very hard to understand, although then, as now, I found that some of the descriptions of the patients' symptomatology and suffering that appear in 'The Divided Self' very perceptive.

At that time I did not appreciate the lack of experimental support that there was for these ideas, and of course they have not stood the test of time, but I could not understand how it could be believed that imperfect interactions that could not really be defined could possibly have such devastating and lasting effects upon some people, when others in the same family were not affected and when there was evidence all around us in that vibrant but often deprived and sometimes violent city, that people could and did triumph over interpersonal difficulties of every kind.

To his credit, the then Professor of Psychiatry in Glasgow, Professor T. Ferguson Rodger, who had at one time been Dr. R. D. Laing's Head of Department, taught his students that although the work of Laing & Esterson was very popular and that Ronnie Laing was in many ways gifted and wrote in a very compelling style, schizophrenia was a disease. I remember him saying, "schizophrenia is a disease like multiple sclerosis or cancer. We do not know its cause, but it will be found one day". I agreed with him then and essentially I agree with him now, although I have given a good deal more thought to the issue than I had when I first accepted the idea.

As a student and in my early years as a psychiatrist, I believed wholeheartedly that in my own lifetime I would see the unravelling of the principal elements of the causation of schizophrenia. After so many years I should perhaps have more sense, but in fact I believe it still, although I would have to concede that the odds I would suggest to a bookmaker are not quite so overwhelming as they would have been at one time. When I was told and readily accepted that schizophrenia was a disease, that concept was not defined. I came across these issues when I was being taught to be a doctor by other doctors, and of course as Kendell pointed out in 1975 in his book, 'The Role of Diagnosis in Psychiatry', most doctors give little thought to the meaning of concepts of illness and disease, and tend to take it for granted that their meaning is self-evident and unambiguous. This is far from the case, and an adequate definition that globally covers the situation of all disorders that physicians would regard as diseases is hard to find. Disease may be defined in various ways (Kendell, 1975); as suffering, by the presence of a lesion, as an imperfection, or indeed it may be defined statistically as in Scadding's (1967) definition, 'the sum of the abnormal phenomena displayed by a group of living organisms in association with a specified common characteristic or set of characteristics by which they differ from the norm for their species in such a way as to place them at a biological disadvantage'. It is not difficult to advance the view that in these terms schizophrenia is a disease, but this is not really what I mean when I express that opinion.

Part of the difficulty about defining what we mean by disease as a general concept is our need to find an all-embracing definition. The concept becomes clearer when individual diseases are considered, because we can then see that there is no consistent defining characteristic. Tuberculosis and syphilis are defined by their bacteriological cause, ulcerative colitis and tumors are defined by histology, porphyria is defined by biochemistry and prion disease by molecular biology, but some other conditions, for example migraine and most psychiatric disorders, are defined as a constellation of symptoms with a characteristic course (i.e. to resolve, to remit or to persist).

This uncertainty, as Kendell (1975) points out, relates to the historical development of our concepts of disease. In the ancient world, symptoms and signs, e.g. fever, asthma, rashes, joint pains, were themselves regarded as diseases to be studied separately, and it was really only with Sydenham's work in the 17th century that the idea of disease as a syndrome and constellation of symptoms having a characteristic prognosis became established (Sydenham, 1696). With the increasing popularity of post-mortem examination in the 19th century, disease became defined by pathological findings rather than by the clinical picture, and later technological development has allowed diseases to be defined in bacteriological, biochemical and molecular biological terms. As these new methods of definition of disease have developed, the older ones have persisted to some extent, so that any medical textbook will list diseases defined in terms of varied concepts

which may have little or no relationship to one another.

The principal model of disease in psychiatry is still the syndrome model —i.e. a cluster of symptoms and signs which are associated with a characteristic course over time—and that is partly, but not entirely, what was meant by the idea of schizophrenia as a disease, as it was first discussed with me in the 1960s. While the disorder was regarded as a cluster of symptoms and signs with a characteristic course, part of the idea of its being a disease came from the view that it was like other diseases that we as doctors were familiar with; i.e. like them, although originally defined as a syndrome, it would eventually be found to have a biological cause, be that demonstrated by biochemical, histological or some yet undiscovered means. Furthermore, in accepting the idea of schizophrenia as a disease, we were essentially rejecting the concept of the disorder as a response to imperfect interpersonal interactions within the patient's family. Therefore in terms of the classification of concepts of disease described by Kendell (1975) the concept that was being put forward was a combination of disease as a syndrome and disease as a lesion.

The development of morbid anatomy and histology in the 19th century and later physiology and biochemistry showed that many diseases defined as syndromes were in fact associated with identifiable lesions. This led to the view that the demonstration of such an identifiable lesion was the defining characteristic of disease. There are many problems with this clear-cut and initially appealing view, and as far as much of psychiatry is concerned, there is the very considerable problem that no physical basis has been defined for most of the major syndromes. For some psychiatrists this has not seemed to be the overwhelming difficulty that one might expect. Emil Kraepelin, who defined dementia praecox (1896) (which came to be known as schizophrenia) on the basis of the characteristic course and outcome of a cluster of symptoms and signs, stated that this was a disorder in which if "every detail" were known a specific anatomical pathology with a specific aetiology would be found. Kurt Schneider (1950) saw no difficulty in accepting the idea that the word illness should only be used in situations in which 'some actual morbid change' or 'defective structure' was present in the body. In this context he stated that he did not regard either neurotic states or personality disorders as illness, but simply as 'abnormal varieties of sane mental life'. He still, however, considered schizophrenia and manic-depressive psychosis as illness, along with organic and toxic psychoses, on the basis of the assumption that in time they would prove to have an "underlying morbid physical condition." ...

DEFINING THE SYNDROME

Since the time the concept of dementia praecox, later known as schizophrenia, was first defined, there has a times been controversy about the symptoms and signs which formed the syndrome. In defining dementia praecox, Kraepelin had drawn together catatonia as described by Kahlbaum (1874), hebephrenia described by Hecker (1871) and his own dementia paranoides, and regarded them as manifestations of the same disorder of which he considered delusions, hallucinations and catatonic features to be important characteristics. In 1911 Eugen

Bleuler published his 'Dementia Praecox or the Group of Schizophrenias.' He considered that he was developing Kraepelin's concept, but in fact changed it substantially. Bleuler was influenced by psychoanalytic schools of thought and saw schizophrenia in terms different from the neuropathological ones envisaged by Kraepelin. His term schizophrenia, meaning split mind, was intended to describe a loosening of the association between the different functions of the mind so that thoughts became disconnected and coordination between emotional, cognitive and volitional processes became poor. He considered thought disorder, affective disturbance, autism and ambivalence to be the fundamental symptoms of schizophrenia, and that the more clear-cut phenomena of hallucinations, delusions and catatonic features emphasised by Kraepelin were secondary phenomena. Bleuler's ideas became influential in some centres, particularly in the United States, but Kraepelin's concept of dementia praecox, although that name was no longer used, never lost its domination in many European countries.

The lack of common ground between these two concepts was illustrated by the findings of the US-UK diagnostic project (Cooper et al, 1972). In this comparative study, 250 consecutive admissions between the ages of 20 and 59 were studied in New York and London. Information was obtained from patients and their relatives by structured interviews and a diagnosis using nomenclature from the International Classification of Disease (ICD) (WHO, 1967) was assigned to each patient. The project diagnoses obtained in this way were compared with the diagnoses given independently to the same patients by the hospital staff. In the New

York series 61.5% of the patients were given a hospital diagnosis of schizophrenia, whereas in the London series the proportion was 33.9%. However, in terms of the project diagnoses the percentages were 29.2 and 35.1, i.e. clearly similar. By contrast, 31.5% of the London sample received a hospital diagnosis of manic-depressive disorder, but only 5.2% of the New York sample were given such a diagnosis. Clearly therefore, the concept of schizophrenia in New York at that time was wider than that employed in London. These findings and others encouraged the formulation of operational rules for defining schizophrenia; examples of these are the St. Louis criteria (Feighner et al, 1972) and DSM III R (American Psychiatric Association, 1987).

It is obvious that schizophrenia defined according to the very different concepts used in New York and London might well have different characteristic courses. Problems of definition for diagnosis are not the only issue here, as outcome may also be difficult to define. Stephens (1978) has pointed out that outcome should include at least four areas of function: severity of symptomatology, duration of hospitalization after diagnostic evaluation, employment, and social function. While this is so, studies where this is done (and there are relatively few) are difficult to compare because of variability of clinical practices, employment possibilities, and social circumstances....

The introduction of operational definitions of schizophrenia has clarified the syndrome picture of the disorder, but it adds an additional problem to outcome studies. This is the fact that the St. Louis criteria and DSM III both include a six-month period without return to the previous level of function as an obligatory criterion of diagnosis. As far as most of medicine is concerned, there is no better predictor of what will happen in the future as examination of what has happened, and an illness which has been associated with six months of impaired function of whatever kind is relatively likely to be associated with impairment in the future. The fact that a substantial proportion of people with schizophrenia defined by the St. Louis (Feighner et al, 1972) criteria showed a course of remission and relapse, continuing symptomatology, and social impairments occurred in a substantial proportion of patients—be this judged in long-stay in-patients (Owens & Johnstone, 1980) or in those discharged to the community (Johnstone et al, 1981; Johnstone, 1984; 1991)—does not fully answer the question of whether the syndrome of schizophrenia has a characteristic outcome. This issue is better dealt with by studies that have used diagnostic definitions of schizophrenia which do not include an element of chronicity. The Present State Examination (PSE) (Wing et al, 1974) is a system of diagnostic categorisation which relies upon the features of the mental state detected at a detailed standardized interview. It is conducted in conjunction with a computer programme, CATEGO, which relies substantially upon the presence of Schneider's (1957) first rank symptoms in the diagnosis of schizophrenia. The PSE categorisation can be reliably used in diverse countries and cultures, and was employed in the International Pilot Study of Schizophrenia (WHO, 1975). In that study patients with a schizophrenic categorisation had a poorer outcome than a small group of non-schizophrenic patients in the same investigation. Some studies in which I have been involved are relevant to these issues. The Northwick Park Study of First

Episodes of Schizophrenia (Johnstone et al, 1986) used PSE criteria to identify cases of first episode schizophrenia. Four hundred and sixty-two patients were assessed over a period of 28 months and 253 were considered to have first episodes of schizophrenia. Most of the PSEs were conducted by my former colleague Dr. Fiona Macmillan, although I did some of them, and I do not think that Dr. Macmillan would object to my saying that they were conducted in circumstances that were sometimes less than ideal, on patients who were often unable to cooperate fully and were sometimes suspicious of interviewers that they had only just met.

I suspected when this study was designed that our criteria for first schizophrenic episode, referring clinician's diagnosis of at least possible schizophrenia, categorisation within S (schizophrenia), P (paranoid) or O (other non-affective) categories on application of the CATEGO programme to the PSE (Wing et al, 1974) profiles in patients requiring admission for at least one week with no prior history of psychosis or possible psychosis, and the absence of organic disease, might include patients with brief psychotic episodes who would do well. In fact this was not so. Outcome at two years in terms of relapse, employment, marriage and child care was far from reassuring, and only 13 of 253 cases made educational, occupational or social achievements. Thus the clusters of symptoms fulfilling the PSE (Wing et al, 1974) concept of schizophrenia did indeed appear to predict a characteristically poor outcome, even when the symptoms were detected under less than ideal circumstances. The first episodes study only concerned patients with schizophrenia and the outcome is classed as poor in comparison with the patients' premorbid

function and expectations of the function of well people in the same circumstances, rather than as compared with any group of patients with a different mental illness. This issue was addressed in the follow-up phase of the Northwick Park 'Functional' Psychosis Study (Johnstone et al, 1992). This investigation addresses the relationship between classification within the broad category of functional psychosis and outcome two and a half years later. We examined the outcome in social, clinical and cognitive terms of a cohort of over 200 psychotic patients who were not selected by diagnosis within the broad category of functional psychosis (Johnstone et al, 1991). We considered whether or not outcome in these terms could appropriately be used as a validation of the specific diagnostic categories of schizophrenia, affective disorder and schizoaffective psychosis as derived by the later application of the diagnostic systems of DSM III (American Psychiatric Association, 1980) and the PSE/CATEGO (Wing et al, 1974). The deterioration in occupational and hospital careers demonstrated at follow-up were worse in patients with diagnostic classifications of schizophrenia; and positive and negative features were also worse in patients with a classification of schizophrenia (Johnstone et al, 1992). Although no differences in cognitive test performance were found between the groups based upon diagnostic classification, there was no outcome variable in which cases classed as affective achieved a worse score than cases classed as schizophrenic, and there were several clinical and historical measures which showed a significantly worse outcome for schizophrenic patients. This study therefore provides strong support for the view that the symptoms and signs regarded as typical of schizophrenia form a syndrome picture which has a characteristic outcome.

BIOLOGICAL CONSIDERATIONS

I shall now consider the evidence that there is 'an underlying morbid physical condition', i.e. a biological basis, to schizophrenia. This may conveniently be considered under the headings listed in Table 1.

(1) It has long been known that there is a familial predisposition to schizophrenia. This, of course, suggests that there is a genetic factor in the production of the disorder, but the possibility of shared environment has also to be considered. The matter was elegantly dealt with by the adoption studies of Kety and colleagues (1975), who found high rates of schizophrenia in the biological relatives of schizophrenics who had been adopted away at birth and high rates of the later development of schizophrenia in children of schizophrenic mothers who had been adopted away at birth. This clear genetic predispostion to schizophrenia and the development of molecular genetic techniques are the basis of the intensive genetic studies of schizophrenia which are currently being undertaken.

(2) Certain organic diseases which could not result from any of the social or environmental disadvantages of the disorder occur in association with schizophrenia more often than would be expected by chance (Davison & Bagley, 1969). The disorders are varied and the main common thread between them is that they tend to involve the temporal lobe of the brain, although this is by no means always so. In the great majority of schizophrenic patients no underlying organic disease is found. One of the few studies in which a defined cohort of

Table 1
Areas of Evidence for the Biological Basis of Schizophrenia

1.	Familial tendency of the condition
2.	Occurrence of schizophrenia-like psychoses
3.	Mechanism of the antipsychotic effect of neuroleptics
4.	Miscellaneous effects relating to perinatal events
5.	Structural brain changes
6.	Changes in functional imaging related to neuropsychological performance

patients was examined was carried out in connection with the Northwick Park Study of First Episodes of Schizophrenia (Johnstone, Macmillan & Crow, 1987); this showed underlying organic disease of at least possible aetiological significance in 15 of 268 cases. This frequency of about 6% is in keeping with what other work there is. The tantalising possibility that other organic cases are missed is obvious, but in this cohort no additional relevant illnesses are known to have become evident over the next five years.

(3) In 1952 Delay and Deniker introduced chlorpromazine for the treatment of schizophrenia. This discovery of a new class of drugs which relieved the fundamental psychotic symptoms of schizophrenia was a significant advance, and indeed it revolutionised the management of the disorder. A very substantial research effort was subsequently devoted to understanding how phenothiazines and other anti-schizophrenic drugs act upon the brain. This effort was motivated by the idea that such knowledge might not only lead to a more rational basis for the development of new drugs, but also perhaps give some clue to the nature of the abnormalities which underlie schizophrenic illness. On the one

hand this field of endeavour has been a great success, and it is widely accepted that the mechanism of action of typical anti-schizophrenic drugs is blockade of D, dopamine receptors, but on the other hand the effects of these drugs are seen in all psychotic illnesses, so that they are not specific to schizophrenia. And there is no good evidence of abnormality in dopamine function in schizophrenia. Thus in spite of high hopes at times in the last 15 years, study of the mechanism of action of antipsychotic agents has not provided compelling evidence about the biological basis of schizophrenia. The recent demonstration of additional dopamine receptors, together with the efficacy of 'atypical' antipsychotics has raised hopes that these drugs may derive their antipsychotic effects from actions upon D_3, D_4 or D_5 receptors and that this may provide valuable evidence of the mechanisms underlying schizophrenia. At present this is speculation (Johnstone, 1993).

(4) There is a well documented tendency for individuals who later develop schizophrenia to have been born in the winter months of the year (Hare & Walter, 1978; Hafner et al, 1987). This suggests the possibility that some seasonal variable, possibly infective or dietary, acting before or around the time of birth, may be relevant. Recent evidence that second generation Afro-Caribbean immigrants to the United Kingdom have a substantial increase in the incidence of schizophrenia as compared to the indigenous population, might be interpreted in a similar way. Thus the mothers of such patients might have lacked immunity to some relevant infection and contracted it when they arrived in Britain. Perhaps because of these findings there has been recent interest in pre- or perinatal factors such as birth injury (Murray, Lewis & Revely, 1985) or maternal influenza in pregnancy (O'Callaghan et al, 1991). I was involved with colleagues (Done et al, 1991) in a study which identified and obtained details concerning all individuals in the National Child Development Study (Shepherd, P.M.) who came to require inpatient psychiatric care. The frequency of perinatal and birth complications in various diagnostic groups was compared with that of the total sample. There was no significant increase in perinatal events in schizophrenia, but there was in certain other psychoses of early onset, and some of the patients may well turn out to have schizophrenia in the end. The only specific association with schizophrenia was that the mothers of babies who later developed schizophrenia were of significantly lower weight than other mothers. These results, like so very many findings in schizophrenia research, are not clear-cut. It looks unlikely that perinatal events account for the majority of schizophrenia, but they could perhaps account for some of it.

(5) The morbid anatomy of schizophrenia was studied in Kraepelin's time (Kraepelin, 1919), but this early work was conducted when histological techniques were in their infancy and the need to control for fixation and staining artefacts was not appreciated. It is therefore not surprising that these findings were not confirmed by later workers, and in 1976 Corsellis felt forced to conclude that present histological methods are not adequate to demonstrate any convincing structural substrate for the subtle and often reversible mental aberrations that go to make up the 'functional' psychoses. Nonetheless, in that same year, my colleagues and I, using computed tomography (CT) detected

a significant enlargement of the lateral ventricles in a group of patients with chronic schizophrenia (Johnstone et al, 1976). This result has been widely but not invariably replicated, and it has stimulated further work among post-mortem material (Bogerts, Meertes & Schonfeldt-Bausch, 1985; Jellinger, 1985; Jakob & Beckman, 1986; Bruton et al, 1990). Although the findings of the studies are not entirely consistent, there is increasing evidence of smaller lighter brains and abnormalities of neuronal architecture in schizophrenia.

(6) Our CT scan study (Johnstone et al, 1976) showed not only that the lateral ventricles of the schizophrenics were enlarged, but that the degree of this enlargement was significantly related to the degree of cognitive impairment. Poor performance on cognitive tests in schizophrenia had long been noted, following Bleuler's (1911) early writings; however, the view held sway that in spite of their *performance* deficits the cognitive *abilities* of schizophrenic patients did not decline. It was believed that patients did not do the tests well—did not seem to know their own age, their date of birth, or occasionally even their own name—because of lack of volition rather than lack of ability. The idea was that through lack of interest and drive the patients did not try to do the tests, but that if this veil of apathy could be lifted the abilities that lay behind it could be discovered, unimpaired. However, once the poor performance could be related to structural changes, the idea of preserved abilities behind a veil became less credible and extensive studies of cognitive ability in schizophrenia have shown that in a proportion of patients with schizophrenia cognitive impairments are definite and may be severe and crippling (Frith, 1992). The cognitive neuropsychology of schizophrenia has been increasingly widely studied (Frith, 1992) and the introduction of functional imaging has made it possible to relate neuropsychological performance to measures of cerebral blood flow and metabolism (Berman & Weinberger, 1990; Frith et al, 1991; Berman et al, 1993). Again, the findings are not entirely consistent and they do not in themselves demonstrate a clear biological basis, but if the results in all of the areas described are taken together, it appears that while these findings do not amount to proof, the evidence is sufficient to persuade me that schizophrenia is almost certainly a biological disease, that we must continue to seek its causes, and indeed that these will be found.

NO

Theodore R. Sarbin

TOWARD THE OBSOLESCENCE OF THE SCHIZOPHRENIA HYPOTHESIS

Any effort to criticize or clarify the concept of schizophrenia must begin from the position that "schizophrenia" is a hypothetical construct. Notwithstanding the use of the term to denote a firm diagnostic entity by most textbook writers and clinical practitioners, investigators by the hundreds are still trying to establish the empirical validity of the construct. The output of published and unpublished research directed toward establishing empirical validity has been enormous, yet schizophrenia remains an unconfirmed hypothesis. A great deal of the research is directed to the task of breaking out of the circular reasoning in which "schizophrenia" appears on both sides of a causality equation: unwanted behaviors are taken to be symptoms of schizophrenia; schizophrenia is the cause of unwanted behaviors.

Historical accounts of psychiatry and psychology make clear that the core hypothesis—schizophrenia as a disease entity—continues to serve as an implicit guide to the construction of current versions of the schizophrenia concept. The schizophrenia construction continues to be employed in spite of the well-documented fact that it has been submitted to repeated empirical tests and has been found wanting. My thesis is that decades of research have not provided determinate findings that justify continuing the use of schizophrenia-nonschizophrenia as an independent variable. Having voiced this claim, I quickly add that my judgment of the failure of the schizophrenia hypothesis is in no way a disclaimer to the observation that some people, under some conditions, engage in conduct that others might identify as mad, insane, bizarre, foolish, irrational, psychotic, deluded, inept, unwanted, absurd, or plain crazy.

The focus of my paper is that schizophrenia is a construction put forth by nineteenth century physicians and elaborated within an epistemological context that supported the notion that unwanted conduct was caused by disease processes. Historical forces in the nineteenth century influenced doctors to regard perplexing conduct as the outcome of a subtle brain disease. The opacity of the term "schizophrenia" directed scientists and practitioners to employ a prototype when writing their own definitions or when labelling putative

From Theodore R. Sarbin, "Toward the Obsolescence of the Schizophrenia Hypothesis," *The Journal of Mind and Behavior,* vol. 11, nos. 3 and 4 (1990), pp. 259–261, 264–269, 273–280. Copyright © 1990 by The Institute of Mind and Behavior. Reprinted by permission. Notes and references omitted.

patients. The contemporary construction of schizophrenia is consistent with the prototype of a person with an infectious brain disease. The crude diagnostic efforts of the late nineteenth and early twentieth centuries failed to differentiate patients with organic brain disease from patients employing atypical conduct to solve their identity and existential problems. Because so many diagnosed schizophrenics did not fit the specifications of the prototype, some authorities, notably Eugen Bleuler, suggested the employment of the plural, "the schizophrenias." This stratagem has not been productive, but has preserved schizophrenia as a sacred emblem of psychiatry when experiments have yielded indeterminate results. "The schizophrenias" and its modern equivalent "schizophrenia spectrum disorders" have also been employed to increase the size of an experimental sample in order to achieve statistical significance. Such miscellaneous categories do little more than supply Greek or Latin labels to formalize the lay concept that "people can be crazy in different ways and for different causes or reasons."

Nearly 50 years ago, when I had my first encounters with hospitalized patients, I was confronted with the official lore that schizophrenia was a disease. I did not accept, however, the official lore without reservation. Day to day interactions with inmates of a mental hospital influenced me to be tentative about adopting the prevailing doctrine. In the course of working with men and women who had been diagnosed as schizophrenic by appropriately-qualified psychiatrists, I became aware of the multifarious actions that were interpreted as "presenting symptoms"—actions that family members or employers could not readily as-similate into their constructions of acceptable conduct.

My first patient was a middle-aged women who held the belief that agents of a foreign power were conspiring to kidnap her; the second was a man who believed that his neighbor was directing magnetic rays to the nails in his shoes so that walking was a great effort; a third was a 40 year-old man who argued with an absent opponent about metaphysical propositions; a fourth inmate behaved as if he had lost all power of speech; a fifth would not leave his room, even for meals, afraid that he would be the object of massive microbial invasions; a sixth, a seminary student, claimed to be a saint of the thirteenth century; a seventh, a retired baker, held friendly conversations in the privacy of his room with two long-dead religious figures....

In most cases, these actions were so specific to the individual's life story that it was difficult for me to accept the explanation that some brain anomaly could account for the heterogeneity. The notion of a common cause for such an assortment of human actions can be entertained only if, in Procrustean fashion, we reduce the interesting array of polymorphous actions to a small number of categories, for example, delusions, flattened affect, and hallucinations, and further, if we arbitrarily redefine the categories as "symptoms" of a still-to-be-discovered disease entity. Such a redefinition obliterates the specificity, the individuality, and the problem-solving features of each person's conduct. Further, the acceptance of the redefinition renders irrelevant the search for intentions and meanings behind perplexing interpersonal acts....

SEARCH STRATEGIES

... My preliminary excursions called for a more systematic analysis of the published literature. Professor James Mancuso joined me in a project to review every research article on schizophrenia published in the *Journal of Abnormal Psychology* for the 20-year period beginning in 1959 (Sarbin and Mancuso, 1980).... We found 374 reports of experiments designed to illuminate the concept of schizophrenia. By any standard, the published research on schizophrenia during the 20-year period represented a prodigious effort. It is abundantly clear that in the period under review, students of deviant conduct focused on the central problem: to identify a reliable diagnostic marker, psychological or somatic, that would replace subjective (and fallible) diagnosis. The discovery of such a marker would establish the long sought-for validity for the postulated entity, schizophrenia.

In nearly all the studies, schizophrenia/nonschizophrenia was the independent variable. To accomplish their mission, investigators compared the *average* responses of "schizophrenics" on experimental tasks with the *average* responses of persons who were not so diagnosed. It is no exaggeration to say that the experimental tasks devised by creative investigators numbered in the hundreds. All were constructed for the purpose of rigorously testing miniature hypotheses, the origins of which were linked to the postulate that schizophrenia was an identifiable mental disease or disorder. The choice of these variables was influenced by the lore of schizophrenia, beliefs that could be traced to Kraepelin's and Bleuler's claims that schizophrenics were cognitively or linguistically flawed;

perceptually inefficient; affectively dysfunctional; and psychophysiologically impaired. The experimental hypotheses were formulated from the expectation that whatever the task, the schizophrenics would perform poorly when compared with the performance of a control group. The range and variety of the experimental tasks suggests that the formulators of these experimental hypotheses shared the conviction that "schizophrenics" were persons who were basically flawed, that the putative disease affected all somatic and psychological systems.

Mancuso and I analyzed 374 studies on several dimensions. We drew a number of conclusions, among them, that the criteria for selecting subjects were less than satisfactory. The unreliability for psychiatric diagnosis notwithstanding, the experimenters were satisfied to accept diagnoses made by "two staff psychiatrists," "by a psychiatrist and a psychologist," "by consensus in diagnostic staff conference," etc. It is unknown to what extent the diagnosticians employed the *Diagnostic and Statistical Manual-II*, although it is likely that the lore contained in the *Manual* provided the diagnostic criteria. The dependent variables were assessed with great precision, sometimes to two decimal places. In contrast, the independent variable, schizophrenia/nonschizophrenia, was assessed either by the subjective and fallible judgments of clinicians, or by a vote taken in a diagnostic staff conference....

About 80 percent of the studies reported that schizophrenics performed poorly when compared to control subjects. Variability in performance was the rule. Although the published studies reported mean differences between groups as statistically significant, the differences were small. In those studies where it was possible to reconstruct distributions, it was immediately clear that the performances of the schizophrenic samples and the normal samples overlapped considerably. An examination of a number of such distributions points to an unmistakable conclusion: that most schizophrenics cannot be differentiated from most normals on a wide variety of experimental tasks. If one were to employ the dependent variable as a marker for schizophrenia in a new sample, the increase in diagnostic accuracy would be infinitesimal.

That so many studies showed small mean differences has been taken to mean that the schizophrenia hypothesis has earned a modicum of credibility. The degree of credibility dissolves when we consider a number of hidden variables that could account for the observed differences. A large number of reports noted that the schizophrenic subjects were on neuroleptic medication. It is appropriate to ask whether the small mean differences could be accounted for by the drugged status of the experimental subjects and the non-drugged status of the controls. Other hidden variables are socioeconomic status and education. At least since 1855, it has been noted that the diagnosis of insanity (later dementia praecox and schizophrenia) has been employed primarily as a diagnosis for poor people (Dohrenwend, 1990). Many of the experimental tasks called for cognitive skills. The mean difference in performance on such tasks could well be related to cognitive skills, a correlate of education and socioeconomic status. Some experimenters noted the difficulty in recruiting control subjects whose educational level matched the low levels of schizophrenic samples, in many instances, about tenth grade.

Not assessed in these studies were the effects of patienthood. At the time the hospitalized patients were recruited to be subjects, they had been the objects of legal, medical, nursing, and in some cases, police procedures, not to mention mental hospital routines and their effects on personal identity. As mentioned before, only cooperative, i.e., docile, patients were recruited. It would be instructive to investigate to what degree docility influences the subjects' approach to experimental tasks.

Any of the hidden variables could account for the small mean differences observed in experimental studies. One conclusion is paramount: the 30 years of psychological research covered in our analyses has produced no marker that would establish the validity of the schizophrenia disorder. The argument could be made that psychological variables are too crude to identify the disease process. Biochemical, neurological, and anatomical studies, some would argue (e.g., Meehl, 1989), are more likely to reveal the ultimate marker for schizophrenia. However, reported findings employing somatic dependent variables follow the same pattern as for psychological studies. Variation is the rule. For example, one variable of interest for those who would locate the seat of schizophrenia in the brain is the size of the hemispheric ventricles. Several studies employed computer tomography to measure the size of the ventricles. Homogenizing the results of measurement, they found that the schizophrenic group had larger ventricles than the controls. The degree of variation, however, was such as to preclude using the ventricular size as a diagnostic instrument (Nasrallah, Jacoby, McCalley-Whitters, and Kuperman, 1982; Weinberger, Torrey, Neophytides, and Wyatt, 1979). Another set of investigators, presumably employing a more refined method for measuring the scans, reported no differences between schizophrenics and controls (Jernigan, Zatz, Moses, and Berger, 1982a, 1982b). Another hypothesis, disarray of pyramidal cells in the hippocampus, was advanced by several researchers as a potential marker for schizophrenia. Christison, Casanova, Weinberger, Rawlings, and Kleinman (1989) conducted precise measurements on brains stored in the Yakovlev collection. They found no differences in hippocampal measurements when the brains of schizophrenics were compared to the brains of controls.

It is important to note the high degree of variability in biomedical and psychological measurements. To isolate the elusive marker, investigators must discover indicators that cluster near the mean for the experimental sample and at the same time do not overlap with the control sample or with other presumed diagnostic entities. None of the studies we reviewed met this requirement.

SCHIZOPHRENIA AS DISEASE: A SOCIAL CONSTRUCTION

The prevailing mechanistic framework directs practitioners to perceive crazy behavior as caused ultimately by anatomical or biochemical anomalies. An alternative framework is available, one not dependent on the notion that human beings are passive objects at the mercy of biochemical forces. The starting point in this framework is the observation that candidates for the diagnosis of schizophrenia are seldom people who seek out doctors for the relief of pain or discomfort. Rather, they are persons who undergo a prediagnostic phase in which moral judgments are made on their nonconforming or perplexing actions by family members, employers, police officers, or neighbors. In the absence of reliable tests to demonstrate that the unwanted conduct is caused by anatomical or biochemical distortions, diagnosticians unwittingly join in the moral enterprise. They confirm the initial prediagnostic judgment that the deviant behavior belongs to a class of behaviors that are unwanted. After appropriate rituals, diagnosticians can confirm the moral verdict and encode it with a proper medical term, schizophrenia.

The foregoing remarks are preliminary to my argument that schizophrenia is a social construction initially put forth as a hypothesis by medical scientists and practitioners. A social construction is an organized set of beliefs that has the potential to guide action. The construction is communicated and elaborated by means of linguistic and rhetorical symbols. The categories are vicariously received, passed on from generation to generation through symbolic action. Like any construction, the schizophrenia hypothesis serves certain purposes and not others. A pivotal purpose for schizophrenia is diagnosis—professional practice requires diagnosis before treatment can be rationally prescribed. It is important to remind ourselves that any social construction can be abandoned when alternate constructions are put forth that receive symbolic and rhetorical support from scientific and political communities.

To find the origin of the schizophrenia construction, one must refer to historical sources. Because of space limitations, a full historical account is not possible. Instead I point to some pertinent observations. Ellard (1987), an Australian psychiatrist, has contributed a provocative argument under the title "Did Schizophrenia Exist Before the Eighteenth Century?" Ellard's historical analysis begins from a skeptical posture, namely, to "reflect on the question whether or not there has ever been an entity of any kind at all that stands behind the word, 'schizophrenia', and if so, what its true nature might be" (p. 306). Citing well-known authorities, Ellard points to significant changes in the description of schizophrenia over the past 50 or 60 years. He cites the common observation that contemporary clinicians seldom encounter patients who fit the prototype advanced by Kraepelin and Bleuler. If the nosological criteria for schizophrenia changed so radically in a half-century, is it not conceivable that the criteria changed significantly in the half-century before Kraepelin and Bleuler?—and in the half-century before that? Ellard makes clear that schizophrenia is a construction of medical scientists that is historically-bound.

As a point of departure, Ellard takes the construction and eventual abandonment of the nineteenth century diagnosis, masturbatory psychosis. Medical orthodoxy posited a psychosis characterized by restlessness, silliness, intellectual deterioration, and inappropriate affect. The entrenched belief in the association between biological activities and crazy behavior nurtured the idea of masturbatory insanity well into the twentieth century. Although at one time professionally acceptable, it was ultimately abandoned as an empty if not counterproductive hypothesis.

Employing the vaguely-defined "thought disorder" as the criterion of schizophrenia, Ellard searched the literature for evidence of cases noted by physicians and historians. His reading of

case histories and medical records led to the conclusion that insanities involving "thought disorders" were identified in the eighteenth and nineteenth centuries, but such cases were exceedingly rare in the seventeenth century. It remains for future historians to identify the social, political, and professional conditions that brought about the creation of a diagnosis centered on ambiguously-defined "thought disorder." ...

Intrinsic and Extrinsic Support for the Disease Construction

Despite its failure when examined by empirical methods, the social construction of schizophrenia has persisted. Its persistence is a function of the support it has received. Two classes of support can be identified: support intrinsic to the biomedical model; and support extrinsic to the model in the form of social practices and unarticulated beliefs.

Biological research has served as intrinsic support for the schizophrenia construction. I need but mention the names of hypotheses that have been subjected to laboratory and clinical testing: taraxein, CPK (creatine phosphokinase), serotonin, and dopamine, among others. The composite impact of all this research activity is that an entity exists, waiting for refined methods and high technology to identify the causal morphological, neuro-transmission, or biochemical factor.... [C]ountless studies have not identified the disease entity. Nevertheless, the profession and the public have interpreted the sustained research activity by responsible scientists as evidence that the schizophrenia construction is a tenable one.

Guided by the mechanistic paradigm (that behavior is *caused* by antecedent physico-chemical conditions) and operating within the medical variant of that paradigm (that the causes of atypical conduct are to be found in disease entities), research scientists employed a number of broad categories as the defining criteria of schizophrenia. Such categories as cognitive slippage, anhedonia, social withdrawal, ambivalence, thought disorder, loosening of associations, delusions, inappropriate affect, and hallucinations, among others, have been employed for classifying the observed or reported conduct of persons brought to diagnosticians by concerned relatives or by forensic or social agencies. The diagnostic process involved locating the putative patient's conduct in one or more of these broad categories, and then inferring the diagnosis of schizophrenia. Thus, immediate and remote origins of the *meanings* of an individual's atypical conduct become irrelevant to the objective of the diagnosis. A scientist interested in the *person* would have little to go on from reading research reports. Readers of these reports are frustrated if they search for connections between a particular instance of unwanted conduct—the presumed basis for the diagnosis—and some dependent variable assessed after a diagnosis has been made. No causal link can be postulated to account, for example, for a schizophrenic patient's anomalous brain scan and his specific claims to having daily conversations with St. Augustine.

Typically, journal articles provide statements of statistically significant associations between such variables and *diagnoses*, not between such variables and *conduct*. Since heterogeneous acts are lumped together into homogenized diagnoses, experimental results cannot provide information that would allow inferences about the relation between the experimental variable and specific behav-

iors. The conventional publication style facilitates the illusory conclusion that a cause, or partial cause, of schizophrenia has been discovered. Because distributions of the dependent variable are not usually published, the reader cannot calculate the proportions of false positives and false negatives that would be generated if the dependent variable were to be used as a diagnostic instrument. Not reporting the proportion of cases contrary to the hypothesis, like the employment of diagnoses as the independent variable, facilitates the belief that some enduring property of schizophrenia has been isolated....

In addition to direct biological research, the genetic transmission hypothesis has been advanced to support the construction of schizophrenia. Highly visible scientists have reported a heritability factor for schizophrenia. Wide publicity, both within the profession and outside, has been given to studies of twins and to studies of children of schizophrenics who were reared by adoptive parents (see, for example, Gottesman and Shields, 1972; Kety, Rosenthal, Wender, and Shulsinger, 1968; Kety, Rosenthal, Wender, Shulsinger, and Jacobsen, 1975). Current textbooks cite these investigations as revealed truth, but the extensive critiques of the studies are seldom noted. That the reported studies are riddled with methodological, statistical and interpretational errors has been repeatedly demonstrated (see especially, Abrams and Taylor, 1983; Benjamin, 1976; Kringlen and Cramer, 1989; Lewontin, Kamin, and Rose, 1984; Lidz, 1990; Lidz and Blatt, 1983; Lidz, Blatt, and Cook, 1981; Marshall, 1986; Sarbin and Mancuso, 1980). The extent of these criticisms suggests that establishing the validity of "schizophrenia" should have had logical priority over the identification of its genetic features.

My aim is not to rehash the arguments pro and con of the heredity thesis, rather to show that the wide publicity given genetic studies has served as additional support to maintain the schizophrenia construction. My thesis holds for genetic research as it does for psychological and biological research: that no firm ontological basis has been established for schizophrenia. In the absence of determinate criteria, investigators direct their efforts toward discovering intergenerational similarities—not of identifiable behavior but of *diagnosis*, a far cry from the subject matter of behavior genetics in which intergenerational similarities of *behavior* are studied.

In addition to intrinsic supports, it is possible to identify a number of extrinsic supports that help explain the tenacity of the schizophrenia construction. Although constructions that are congruent with the concurrent scientific paradigm may appear self-supporting, they are in great measure sustained by forces external to the scientific enterprise.

A vast bureaucratic network at federal, state, and local levels legitimizes biochemical conceptions of deviant conduct, including schizophrenia. Federal agencies that control research grants advocate studies the aim of which is the understanding and ultimately the control of "the dread disease" schizophrenia....

In addition to bureaucratic advocacy, in recent decades the pharmaceutical industry has been instrumental in furthering the schizophrenia doctrine. Pharmaceutical companies support countless research enterprises in which medications are clinically tested on patients, many of whom are diagnosed as schizophrenic. The psychiatric journals are to a great extent subsidized by pharmaceutical advertising, such advertising being directed to physicians who are legally empowered to prescribe medications.

The implicit power of bureaucracy and the commercial goals of pharmaceutical companies would be minimal if the schizophrenia messages fell on deaf ears. A readiness to believe the schizophrenia story follows from the unwitting acceptance of an ideology—a network of historically-conditioned premises....

One strand in the texture of the schizophrenia ideology is the creation of the mental hospital institution. The transformation of the asylum to a mental hospital, in the context of preserving order, paved the way for regarding inmates as objects. The hospital and its medical climate were legitimated through legislative acts and judicial rulings. The courts, usually acting on the advice of physicians, granted almost unlimited power to physicians to employ their skills and their paradigms in the interest of protecting society. Because of culturally-enscripted roles for physicians and patients, once the physician made the diagnosis, the patient became a figure in an altered social narrative. The power of physicians relative to patients created a condition in which physicians could distance themselves from patients—a necessary precondition for the draconian surgical and medical treatments mentioned previously....

A parallel premise is that "certain types of people are more dangerous than other types of people" (Sarbin and Mancuso, 1980). The origins of the connection between being schizophrenic and being dangerous are obscure. Several strands in the fabric of this premise can be identified, among them, the Calvinistic equation of being poor and being damned, and the attribution "dangerous classes" to the powerless poor. "Dangerous to self or other" remains as a criterion for commitment in most jurisdictions.

The overrepresentation of poor people in the class "schizophrenics" has been repeatedly documented. In addition, Pavkov, Lewis, and Lyons (1989) have shown that being black and coming to the attention of mental health professionals is predictive of a diagnosis of schizophrenia.... Landrine (1989) has concluded on the basis of research evidence that the social role of poor people is a stereotype in the epistemic structure of middle-class diagnosticians. The linguistic performances and social interactions of poor people are of the same quality as the performances of men and women diagnosed as schizophrenics, particular of the "negative type" (Andreasen, 1982), those social failures who have adopted a strategy of minimal action.

With the renewed emphasis on the Kraepelinian construction, interest in studying the relations between socioeconomic status (SES) and psychiatric diagnoses has declined. This decline in interest is not due to any change in the demographics. Schizophrenia is primarily a diagnosis for poor people. The advent of neo-Kraepelinian models, especially the diathesis-stress construction, turned attention to genetics research and to the study of stress. But SES has not figured prominently in stress research. Dohrenwend (1990), a leading epidemiologist, has noted that "... relations between SES or social class and psychiatric disorders have provided the most challenging cues to the role of adversity in the development of psychiatric disorders. The problem remains what it has always been: how to unlock the riddle that low SES

can be either a cause or a consequence of psychopathology" (p. 45). The adversity thesis might be illuminated through an examination of the observation that the outcome of "schizophrenia" varies with economic and social conditions (Warner, 1985). Landrine's research, cited above, adds to the puzzle another dimension: lower class stereotypes held by middle class diagnosticians....

CONCLUSION

To recapitulate: my thesis is that schizophrenia is a social construction, generated to deal with people whose conduct was not acceptable to more powerful others. During the heyday of nineteenth century science, the construction was guided by metaphors drawn from mechanistic biology. Physicians formulated their theories and practices from constructions that grew out of developing knowledge in anatomy, chemistry and physiology. The construction has an ideological cast —its proponents were blind to the possibilities that the absurdities exhibited by mental hospital patients were efforts at sense-making. Instead proponents followed the tenets of mechanistic science: that social misconduct, like rashes, fevers, aches, pains, and other somatic conditions, was caused by disease processes. Reliable and sustained empirical evidence—a cardinal requirement of mechanistic science—has not been put forth to validate the schizophrenia hypothesis. Despite the absence of empirical support, the schizophrenia construction continues its tenacious hold on theory and practice.

My recommendation is that we banish schizophrenia to the musty historical archives where other previously-valued scientific constructions are stored, among them, phlogiston, the luminiferous ether, the geocentric view of the universe, and closer to home, monomania, neurasthenia, masturbatory insanity, lycanthropy, demon possession, and mopishness.

I emphasize that I am not recommending formulating a new descriptive term to replace schizophrenia. It is too late for that. The referents for schizophrenia are too diverse, confounded, changing, and ambiguous (Bentall, Jackson, and Pilgrim, 1988; Carpenter and Kirkpatrick, 1988). The fact that two persons (or 200) who exhibit no absurdities in common may be tagged with the same label demonstrates the emptiness of the concept.

Abandoning the schizophrenia hypothesis, however, will not solve the societal and interpersonal problems generated when persons engage in absurd, nonconforming, perplexing conduct. The first step in solving such problems calls for critical examination of the societal and political systems that support the failing biomedical paradigm. Such examination would be instrumental in replacing the mechanistic world view with a framework that would regard persons as agents trying to solve existential and identity problems....

Understanding the interpersonal or existential themes in the stories of troubled persons is hampered when we rely on the customary vocabulary of pathology: toxins, tumors, traumata, dysfunctional traits, or defective genes. Understanding is more likely to be facilitated if we follow the lead of poets, dramatists, and biographers, and focus on the language of social relationships.

CHALLENGE QUESTIONS
Is Schizophrenia a Disease?

1. What would a social constructionist's view of schizophrenia imply for psychological diagnosis? for psychotherapy?

2. What would a medical model (disease) view of schizophrenia imply for psychological diagnosis? for psychotherapy?

3. If, according to the social constructionist, the diagnosis of schizophrenia is to some degree an ethical or moral judgment, and if our ethics depend upon our particular culture, does this mean that *any* cultural ethic is acceptable? What implications does this *relativity* of ethic have for diagnosis and psychotherapy?

4. Why does Sarbin say that physiological differences between normals and schizophrenics do not necessarily support a disease conception?

5. What would a social constructionist say about Johnstone's reliance on the scientific method? Could the scientific method itself be a social construction of some type? Why, or why not?

ISSUE 12

Does Abortion Have Severe Psychological Effects?

YES: Anne C. Speckhard and Vincent M. Rue, from "Postabortion Syndrome: An Emerging Public Health Concern," *Journal of Social Issues* (vol. 48, no. 3, 1992)

NO: Nancy E. Adler et al., from "Psychological Responses After Abortion," *Science* (April 6, 1990)

ISSUE SUMMARY

YES: Psychotherapists Anne C. Speckhard and Vincent M. Rue argue that abortion has serious psychological consequences for women, including what they term "postabortion syndrome" (PAS).

NO: Psychologists Nancy E. Adler et al. contend that severe negative psychological reactions following abortion are infrequent.

Despite the controversy that induced abortion regularly raises, the procedure is still performed frequently. Currently, almost one-quarter of all pregnancies in the United States are terminated by legal, induced abortion, which equals 1.6 million annual abortions. Twenty-four percent of American women who abort are teenagers, 57 percent are younger than 25 years old, and almost 80 percent of these women are unmarried. Most abortions are performed sometime during the first trimester (the first three months), but a small percentage —about 10 percent—are performed later on in the pregnancy, when the fetus is more developed. Regardless of when a woman chooses to terminate a pregnancy, what psychological effects might be attached to abortion?

For many people, the subject of abortion is not just a psychological issue; it is also a moral and political issue. Those who consider themselves pro-life often claim that women who abort suffer many negative effects. They view abortion as a trauma with many permanent consequences. Those who consider themselves pro-choice, on the other hand, usually argue that any negative effects of abortion are minimal. Indeed, from the pro-choice perspective, abortion offers relief from the stress of pregnancy and the burden of caring for an unwanted child.

In the selections that follow, Anne C. Speckhard and Vincent M. Rue describe the sociopolitical context of abortion research. They argue that "there is a reluctance to call attention to the negative effects of abortion for fear of providing support to anti-abortion groups." They criticize research showing few negative effects of abortion as methodologically flawed and not representative of most women who undergo abortions. Speckhard and Rue maintain that women suffer negative psychological consequences after undergoing abortion much more often than people believe and that, in fact, many women experience symptoms of postabortion syndrome (PAS), including flashbacks, "anniversary reactions," and guilt.

Nancy E. Adler and her colleagues, basing their conclusions on a review of what they feel are methodologically sound studies, argue that psychological distress for women is usually greatest *before* an abortion and that the actual incidence of severe negative responses to abortion is quite low. Adler et al. claim that "the weight of the evidence ... indicates that legal abortion of an unwanted pregnancy in the first trimester does not pose a psychological hazard for most women." The authors also describe some of the risk factors that may contribute to any distress that is experienced following abortion, but they suggest that this distress reflects typical strategies for coping with normal life stress.

POINT	COUNTERPOINT
• Abortion is a stressor that often has severe negative consequences.	• Distress is generally greater before abortion; thus, abortion is a stress reliever.
• Some psychological consequences of abortion can be permanent.	• Any negative psychological consequences are infrequent and limited in duration.
• The research on the effects of abortion is methodologically flawed.	• Methodologically sound studies do exist.
• Certain groups of women are underrepresented in the available research.	• The amount of bias from underrepresentation is minor.
• Psychology needs postabortion recovery treatment centers.	• Counseling and support is more useful before abortion, when the stress is greatest.

YES

Anne C. Speckhard
and Vincent M. Rue

POSTABORTION SYNDROME: AN EMERGING PUBLIC HEALTH CONCERN

Elective abortion, the most common surgical procedure in the United States, continues to generate considerable moral, legal, medical, and psychological controversy. This article reviews the pertinent literature, defines and describes postabortion syndrome (PAS) as a type of Post-Traumatic Stress Disorder. . . .

In the United States, prior to the liberalization and legalization of abortion, permission for an abortion sometimes required psychiatric determination of individual psychopathology (Stotland, 1989). When abortion became decriminalized and liberalized in the U.S. in 1973, psychiatric indications for abortion were eliminated. Today the abortion decision is private and requires no evidence of psychological impairment. In fact, psychiatric illness may be a contraindication (Moseley, Follingstad, & Harley, 1981; Ney & Wickett, 1989; Zakus & Wilday, 1987). In the current context, it is paradoxical but possible that the decision to elect abortion can generate significant resulting psychosocial distress (Rue, 1986; Speckhard, 1987b).

Clinical reports and recent studies have indicated that men, women, families, and even health care providers can sometimes experience negative psychological responses following abortion that do not appear to be linked back to individual pathology (Michels, 1988; Rue, 1986, 1987; Selby, 1990; Speckhard, 1987a, 1987b; Stanford-Rue, 1986). On the other hand, when psychopathology is present preabortion, increasing evidence suggests that abortion does not ameliorate individual dysfunction, but may worsen it (DeVeber, Ajzenstat, & Chisholm, 1991; Mall & Watts, 1979; Ney & Wickett, 1989).

Other recent studies have reported, however, minimal negative outcomes and even relief following abortion (Adler et al., 1990; David, 1985; Major, Mueller, & Hildebrandt, 1985). Not usually examined however, is the question of whether abortion may function in a dual role—as both coping mechanism *and* stressor. While abortion may indeed function as a stress reliever by eliminating an unwanted pregnancy, other evidence suggests that it may also

From Anne C. Speckhard and Vincent M. Rue, "Postabortion Syndrome: An Emerging Public Health Concern," *Journal of Social Issues*, vol. 48, no. 3 (1992), pp. 95–106. Copyright © 1992 by The Society for the Psychological Study of Social Issues. Reprinted by permission.

simultaneously or subsequently be experienced by some individuals as a psychosocial stressor, capable of causing posttraumatic stress disorder (PTSD)— (Barnard, 1990; Rue, 1985, 1986, 1987; Selby, 1990; Speckhard, 1987a, 1987b; Vaughan, 1991). We suggest that this constellation of dysfunctional behaviors and emotional reactions should be termed "postabortion syndrome" (PAS).

SOCIOPOLITICAL CONTEXT OF ABORTION RESEARCH

Like the decision to abort, the scientific study of the stress effects of abortion does not occur in a vacuum. The politicization of abortion has significantly restricted scientific investigation of the effects of abortion, and has produced a profound interpersonal and interprofessional schism in American society, including media reporting biases and public misinformation (Shaw, 1990).

There is a reluctance to call attention to negative consequences of abortion for fear of providing support to anti-abortion groups. Minimizing acknowledgment and discussion of postabortion trauma may result in women feeling abandoned by their counselors and isolated from other women experiencing similar difficulties. This may discourage women from revealing their postabortion feelings and may result in labeling women with emotional difficulties after their abortion as deviant and in need of psychotherapy (Lodl, McGettigan, & Bucy, 1985).

Ironically, the politicization of abortion research may be leading us to stigmatize and label women who experience postabortion stress as pathological. This would indeed be unfortunate given the many years of feminist-oriented research

that attempted to remedy the "a priori" definition of women who choose abortion as pathological. Neither should those who experience abortion as traumatic now be defined as pathological without first considering the potential of abortion to act as a trauma even for some healthy women. Steinberg (1989) has cautioned, "We must examine the impact on these women because their numbers are so great and because the political and social volatility of this issue locks so many of them into silence" (p. 483).

Additionally, there is a danger of professional denial concerning the negative effects of abortion (Mester, 1978). The prevailing opinion espoused by the American Psychological Association (APA) is characteristic of the position held by most national and international mental health associations—i.e., that abortion, "particularly in the first trimester, does not create psychological hazards for most women undergoing the procedure" (Fox, 1990, p. 843); that "psychological sequelae [complications or conditions resulting from the event] are usually mild and tend to diminish over time without adversely affecting general functioning"; and that "severe emotional responses are rare" (American Psychological Association, 1987, p. 25). In the authors' opinion, the APA's position is an unwarranted overgeneralization that cannot be logically supported because it is based on a body of research that is methodologically flawed. David (1987) acknowledged,

Regardless of personal convictions about abortion, there is general agreement that uncertainty persists about the psychological sequelae of terminating pregnancies. Inconsistencies of interpretation stem from lack of consensus regarding the symptoms, severity, and duration of mental disorder; from opinions based on individual case studies; and from the lack of a national reporting system for adequate follow-up monitoring.... The literature abounds with methodological problems, lack of controls, and sampling inadequacies.... (p. 1)

Similarly, Adler et al. (1990) cautioned consumers of abortion regarding the psychological health risks by noting that "no definitive conclusions can be drawn about longer effects," and that "women who are more likely to find the abortion experience stressful may be underrepresented in volunteer samples" (p. 43).

Having gone "on record" supporting abortion, it may now be difficult for these professional groups to be open to reexamining their position. This has certainly been true of the American Psychological Association in its abortion advocacy positions, clearly stated in its U.S. Supreme Court amicus curiae briefs (i.e., in *Thornburgh v. ACOG, Hartigan v. Zbaraz*, and *Hodgson v. Humphrey*). In our opinion, the APA has been correctly criticized for overly extending the weight of scientific authority with respect to its statements and generalizations regarding adolescents and abortion (Gardner, Sherer, & Tester, 1989). On balance, Wilmoth (1988) concluded, "The most scientific conclusion about the psychological sequelae of abortion would be that the research permits no conclusions" (p. 9).

In 1989, U.S. Surgeon General Koop reported on his findings from meetings with scientists and clinicians, and from reviewing over 250 articles pertaining to the health risks of abortion. He concluded, "all these studies were reviewed ... the data do not support the premise that abortion does or does not cause or contribute to psychological

problems" (Koop, 1989a, p. 2). Later Koop testified in the U.S. House of Representatives: "there is no doubt about the fact that there are those people who do have severe psychological problems after abortion" (Koop, 1989b, p. 232), and stated, "if you study abortion the way many people have and see how well women feel about their decision 3 months after the actual procedure, you can be very badly misled" (p. 241).

RECENT ABORTION RESEARCH

Some recent reviews of the literature corroborate Koop's assessment (APA, 1987; Huckeba & Mueller, 1987), though others do not (Adler et al., 1990). Rue, Speckhard, Rogers, and Franz (1987) made an empirical assessment of the literature presented to Surgeon General Koop, which included (a) clinical evidence describing PAS; (b) a systematic analysis by Rogers that quantified threats to validity in 239 postabortion studies; and (c) a meta-analysis by Rogers of the controlled studies. (Excluding the meta-analysis, these data were later refined and published by Rogers, Stoms, & Phifer, 1989). In the paper by Rue et al. (1987), after excluding anecdotal and review articles, there remained 13 postpartum control-group studies, which were meta-analyzed, and 31 prospective and 32 retrospective uncontrolled studies, which were systematically analyzed.

The incidence of 20 methodological shortcomings in the above-mentioned 76 studies is presented in Table 1. For instance, in 69 of 76 studies insufficient sample size was evident (an $N \leq 385$), and in 33 studies substantial sample attrition was evident. Of the total number of studies, 49% used no baseline measurement and 25% had unclear outcome

Table 1

Percentage of Methodological Shortcomings in Comparison, Prospective, and Retrospective Studies of Abortion

Limitations in studies	Comparison studies ($N = 13$)	Prospective studies ($N = 31$)	Retrospective studies ($N = 32$)	Total ($N = 76$)
Sample size ($N \leq 385$)	77	94	94	91
Sample attrition	31	45	47	43
Selection bias	23	35	28	30
No baseline measurement	31	35	69	49
No demographics	8	19	19	17
Abortion granted on psychiatric grounds	69	52	47	53
History of psychiatric instability	54	65	34	50
No/low instrument reliability	8	35	41	33
No/low interrater reliability	38	19	6	17
Interviewer bias	23	39	56	43
Recall distortion	15	3	59	29
Indirect data	31	16	13	17
Incomplete data	38	52	44	46
Contradiction	0	29	16	18
Unclear outcome criteria	23	29	22	25
Recovery room follow-up	0	16	0	7
Follow-up varies	15	10	38	22
Concomitant sterilization	31	32	28	30
No incidence data	23	26	0	15
Multiple abortions	23	39	38	36

Note. Unpublished table from data set of James Rogers originally used in Rue et al. (1987). Data set later refined and published in Rogers, Stroms, and Phifer (1989).

criteria. The mean number of methodological shortcomings per uncontrolled study was 6.9. It was also found that those uncontrolled studies with the greatest methodological weaknesses were more likely to report higher rates of positive experiences after abortion (Rue et al., 1987)....

After considering (a) prospective and retrospective studies, (b) postpartum control-group studies, and (c) the study that appeared to have used the best methodology of the various investigations reviewed (David, Rasmussen & Holst, 1981), Rue et al. (1987) concluded

the following: (1) that the abortion literature is largely flawed as to design and methodology, (2) that all psychological studies of abortion display some negative outcomes for at least a proportion of those women studied, (3) that the clinical literature and experience with postabortion trauma are convergent in suggesting the need for the diagnostic category of PAS, and (4) that the types of errors found in the many studies examined *underestimate* the negative responses to abortion.

After reviewing the conclusions of the authors, Dr. Koop directed that the paper by Rue et al. (1987) be peer reviewed by health scientists within the federal government. Various anonymous criticisms of it were later reluctantly and unofficially provided to us (the identity of these reviewers was subsequently revealed in a congressional hearing and published in the committee report; the published versions are cited here). Some of the reviewers' criticisms displayed considerable bias: "Abortion is a moral issue (although all may not agree on this point either) and it must be removed from academic exercises of proof and disproof" (Dever, 1989, p. 165). Other reviewers concurred with the authors "that the issue could have important implications for public health" (Kleinman, 1989, p. 157). Some reviewers objected to the appropriateness of the meta-analytic technique. Meta-analysis, however, is now widely used and generally accepted as a means to obtain a numerical estimate of the overall effect size of a particular variable on a defined outcome. Indeed, in 1988 the authors conducted a computer search of the psychological, medical, health, biological, sociological, and family relations abstracts from 1980 to 1988, and found 895 citations, including approximately 528 meta-analyses that were reported in article titles. More recently, Posavac and Miller (1990) conducted a meta-analysis of the literature on the psychological effects of abortion and concurred that existing research is flawed methodologically, and that comparison group designs may tend to show more negative outcomes for abortion.

Perhaps the methodologically best-designed study completed to date is the Danish study reported by David et al. (1981), and David (1985). In it, admissions to psychiatric hospitals were tracked for a three-month period after either delivery or abortion for all Danish women under the age of 50, and then compared with the three-month admission rate to psychiatric hospitals for all Danish women of similar age. The authors found, "at all parities, women who obtained abortions are at higher risk for admission to psychiatric hospitals than are women who delivered" (David, 1985, p. 155). For abortion women, the psychiatric admission rate was 18.4 per 10,000 compared to 12.0 for delivering women and 7.5 for all Danish women aged 15–49. Of even more concern were the findings pertaining to women who were divorced, separated, or widowed at the time of abortion or delivery. The corresponding rates of psychiatric admission were 63.8 per 10,000 for these women aborting vs. 16.9 for these women [undergoing] delivery.

Four points require emphasis regarding this study (David et al., 1981): (1) it was relatively short-term and provided no long-term assessment of differences between women who aborted vs. those who delivered; (2) it most likely underreported the incidence and degree of postabortion traumatization because women may often be in denial for a considerable period of time after their abortion...; (3) the outcome measure used was admission to a psychiatric hospital, the worst-case circumstance—one could expect substantial quantitative differences between these two groups if less-severe dependent variables like depressive symptomatology or outpatient treatment in psychotherapy were used; and (4) women who elected abortion at all ages, parities, and relationship strata (except women aged 35–39, those with five pregnancies, and those who were married) had higher rates of admission to psychiatric hospitals than women who delivered.

An example of a methodologically unsound study is one in which 60% of 247 women surveyed failed to complete the study protocol three weeks postabortion (Major et al., 1985). Yet the authors concluded that the majority of women felt relief postprocedure. They did, however, caution:

> Of course, the possibility that women who returned to the clinic for their check-up were coping more successfully three weeks later than women who did not return cannot be ruled out, because we were unable to contact the women who did not return. (p. 594)

This high attrition rate could be attributed to avoidant behavior due to an abortion trauma, and it conforms to the view that women who are more likely to find the abortion experience stressful may be underreported in volunteer samples (Adler et al., 1990).

In 1987, Reardon conducted an exploratory survey of 252 high-stress, postabortion women. Although nonrandomly chosen and self-selected from 42 states, his sample compared favorably to national incidence data on women obtaining abortions by age, family size, race, marital status, and number of previous abortions. He found the majority of respondents experienced some of 28 negative outcomes including the following: flashbacks (61%), anniversary reactions (54%), suicidal ideation (33%), feelings of having less control of their lives (78%), difficulty in maintaining and developing relationships (52%), first use or increased use of drugs (49%), and delayed onset of stress, with most reporting their worst reactions as occurring one year or more postabortion (62%).

Likewise, Speckhard (1987b) found that all of the 30 women in her self-selected descriptive sample had long-term grief reactions, some lasting for over five years. Participants were women who described themselves as experiencing high-stress reactions, recruited through referrals from clinicians and other participants. In structured telephone interviews, the majority reported feelings of depression (100%), anger (92%), guilt (92%), fears that others would learn of the abortion (89%), preoccupation with the aborted child (81%), feelings of low self-worth (81%), discomfort around small children (73%), frequent crying (81%), flashbacks (73%), sexual dysfunction (69%), suicidal thoughts (65%), and increased alcohol usage (61%). The majority of the women studied reported being surprised at such intense reactions to their abortions.

These studies, though done with small, nonrandom groups, show that high-stress postabortive women can be doubly stigmatized by themselves—first by their fear of sharing their abortion experiences with one another and/or being viewed as deviant, and second by feeling that their negative reactions are a sign of maladjustment to what appears a relatively simple, common, and benign procedure (Speckhard, 1987a, 1987b). Koop (1989b) noted that in U.S. government reproductive surveys, the rate at which women reported having had an abortion was only half that expected based on abortion statistics.

Assessing the impact of abortion on the psychological health of women and men may not be as simple as some have suggested. In her book, *Parental Loss of a Child*, Rando included a chapter on the loss from induced abortion. In it, Harris (1986) described three obstacles to the clinical identification of negative responses following abortion: (1) masking of emotional responses may occur both at the time of the abortion and in later contacts with professionals; (2) if grief persists, it may surface in disguised form and be expressed behaviorally or in psychosomatic complaints; and (3) if the caregiver has ambivalent or unresolved feelings about abortion, this may interfere with the accurate assessment of postabortion trauma and the establishment of trust and the ability to be patient and empathic. Because of the self-insulation associated with the abortion experience, it is important that the caregiver be aware of the potential for grief, and take the initiative in exploring the client's perceptions and reactions. Joy (1985) stressed the need to be alert to women who are requesting counseling for depression resulting from unresolved grief over a prior abortion, i.e., a delayed grief reaction.

Vaughan (1991) studied 232 women from 39 states who by self-report suffered stress, guilt, grief, depression, and anger, which were defined as symptoms of PAS. The sample was purposive and was recruited primarily through a national network of crisis pregnancy centers affiliated with the Christian Action Council. The mean length of time since the abortion was 11 years. Vaughan employed the technique of canonical correlation between antecedent variables and postabortion variables. She found the following: (1) two different profiles of anger, guilt, and stress; (2) postabortion, 45% of respondents reported negative feelings toward subsequent pregnancies, difficulty bonding, and obsessive thoughts of having a replacement child; (3) only 5.9% of those not married but in a relationship at the time of the abortion continued their relationship postabortion; (4) 24% of the postabortive women had medical problems perceived as having been caused by the abortion; (5) 36% were suicidal postabortion; (6) 42% indicated negative interaction with the abortion clinic staff and felt the counseling received there was misleading and deceptive—this dissatisfaction was significantly related to high anger and guilt scores; and (7) the onset of the symptoms suggested as indicative of PAS was often several years postprocedure.

Mattinson (1985) reported on case studies from the Tavistock Institute in London. She found that, for some patients, the existence of postabortion grief placed interpersonal relationships at risk. Delayed grief reactions causing interpersonal stress took many different forms. Some were mild but persistent; others of a more extreme nature were triggered many years later by a loss of a different nature. Sometimes husbands were more affected than wives.

The first study to use standardized outcome measures of PTSD compared to the diagnostic criteria for PAS developed by Rue was conducted by Barnard (1990). She randomly selected 984 women from a Maryland abortion clinic for a follow-up questionnaire. Interestingly, 60% apparently gave the wrong telephone number at the time of their abortion. After administering a 48-item questionnaire designed to measure PAS (the Impact of Event Scale) and the Millon Clinical Multiaxial Inventory, Barnard reported 45% of her sample of 80 women had symptoms of avoidance and intrusion, and 19% met the full diagnostic criteria for PTSD three to five years following an abortion. She also noted that 68% of these women had little or no religious involvement at the time of the abortion.

Even representatives of Planned Parenthood, an organization that has historically denied the legitimacy of postabortion traumatization and the idea that abortion involves a human death experience, has affirmed that

> women can have a variety of emotions following an abortion (grief, depression, anger, guilt, relief, etc.). It is important to give her the opportunity to air these feelings and be reassured that her feelings are normal. The counselor can also help by letting the woman know that a sense of loss or depression following an abortion is common, due to both the end of the pregnancy as well as the physical and hormonal changes that occur after a pregnancy is over. (Saltzman & Policar, 1985, p. 94)

Because there has never been a national epidemiological study of the psychological health risks of abortion in this country, it is impossible to estimate with any accuracy the incidence of negative abortion sequelae. Lodl et al. (1985) estimated a range of 10%–50% experiencing distress following abortion. A recent APA task force on women and depression (McGrath, Keita, Strickland, & Russo, 1990) concluded that "abortion's relative risk of mental disorder compared with other reproductive events has not been fully ascertained" (p. 12).

Symptoms of traumatization have also been documented in populations of women aborting for genetic reasons, suggesting that the wantedness of the pregnancy at the time of the abortion may not be the key issue in whether or not a woman is traumatized by her abortion, as some have suggested. In a study of couples who elected prostaglandin induction abortion for genetic reasons, i.e., fetal anomalies, Magyari, Wedehase, Ifft, and Callanan (1987) reported negative psychological sequelae in their sample. Interestingly, the psychological intervention protocol developed by Magyari et al.

(1987) for these parents of wanted children identified the following: (1) the need for grief counseling that is anticipatory in nature, individualized, and emphasizes the normalcy of feelings; and (2) facilitation of the mourning process by affirming the pregnancy and providing memories central to the grief process. The latter included the options of seeing or holding the fetus, knowing the sex of the fetus, viewing a photo of the fetus, and naming the fetus. The majority of couples elected to see their aborted offspring.

As is often the case with abortion for nongenetic reasons, common feelings in these couples after abortion for genetic reasons included relief and a sense of conclusion to the crisis. Yet Magyari et al. (1987) cautioned, "We tell them that they face a difficult time and that recovery may not be as smooth as their friends and family may assume it will be" (p. 78). At six to eight weeks postabortion, the intervention team discussed unmet grief reactions thus far and assisted the couple by discussing future events including anniversary reactions. Immediate reproductive replacement was discouraged and the couple was warned "not to pursue a subsequent pregnancy as a replacement for the lost child" (Magyari et al., 1987, p. 80). Even with this intervention protocol in operation, within one year of the abortion, two out of three couples were pregnant again, suggesting the existence of a "replacement child phenomenon." Peppers (1987) has corroborated that grief over a perinatal loss, including abortion can occur irrespective of the wantedness of the pregnancy. In his study, 80 women having abortions at a clinic in Atlanta completed a 13-item grief scale. . . .

ABORTION EXPERIENCED AS A STRESSOR

"Researchers tend to agree that, at some level, abortion is a stressful experience for all women" (APA, 1987, p. 18). The American Psychiatric Association (1987), in its *Diagnostic and Statistical Manual of Mental Disorders* (3rd ed., rev.; DSM-III-R), listed abortion as an example of a psychosocial stressor, but has not included the category of PAS. As a psychosocial stressor, abortion may lead some women to experience reactions ranging from mild distress to severe trauma, creating a continuum that we conceptualize as progressing in severity from postabortion distress (PAD), to PAS, to postabortion psychosis (PAP).

The concept of PAS is in the formative stages of understanding and operationalization (Wilmoth, 1988). It took the American Psychiatric Association over a decade to officially recognize posttraumatic stress disorder (PTSD). PAD, PAS, and PAP may currently be making a similar transition, though none of them are currently recognized even as subtypes or examples in the DSM-III-R. The following definitions are proposed:

Postabortion Distress

PAD may be defined as the manifestation of symptoms of discomfort following an abortion, resulting from three aspects: (a) the perceived physical pain and emotional stress of the pregnancy and abortion; (b) the perception of a loss from the abortion (i.e., loss of a role, dream, relationship, parts or perception of self, potential life, etc.); and (c) the conflict in personality, roles, values, and relationships that results from a changed perception of the appropriateness of the abortion decision.

PAD might be categorized as an adjustment disorder when impairment in occupational functioning or in usual social activities occurs. In order for it to be considered an adjustment disorder, the onset of distress must occur within three months of the abortion and persist no longer than six months, and persistent reexperience of the abortion stressor cannot be present (American Psychiatric Association, 1987).

Postabortion Psychosis

PAP is suggested as a generic designation for major affective or thought disorders not present before an abortion, and directly and clinically attributable to the induced abortion. PAP is characterized by chronic and severe symptoms of disorganization and significant personality and reality impairment, including hallucinations, delusions, and severe depression. Decompensation occurs when the individual becomes aware of, overwhelmed by, and unable to communicate the feelings of guilt, grief, fear, anger, and responsibility for the traumatic death of her/his unborn child. Other manifestations may include intolerable levels of affect, self-condemnation, anxiety, and terror at feeling unable to face the trauma, and also paranoia about being found out. Although PAP is not a commonly encountered reaction to abortion traumatization, clinical evidence of it has been reported (Sim & Neisser, 1979; Spaulding & Cavenar, 1978; Speckhard & Rue, in press).

Postabortion Syndrome

PAS is proposed as a type of PTSD that is characterized by the chronic or delayed development of symptoms resulting from impacted emotional reactions to the perceived physical and emotional trauma of abortion. We propose four basic components of PAS as a variant of PTSD: (1) exposure to or participation in an abortion experience, i.e., the intentional destruction of one's unborn child,[1] which is perceived as traumatic and beyond the range of usual human experience; (2) uncontrolled negative reexperiencing of the abortion death event, e.g., flashbacks, nightmares, grief, and anniversary reactions; (3) unsuccessful attempts to avoid or deny abortion recollections and emotional pain, which result in reduced responsiveness to others and one's environment; and (4) experiencing associated symptoms not present before the abortion, including guilt about surviving.

The proposed diagnostic criteria for PAS... were developed from the diagnostic assessment of PTSD in the DSM-III-R (American Psychiatric Association, 1987). The course of PAS conforms to the diagnostic criteria for PTSD—i.e., the symptoms of reexperience, avoidance, and associated symptoms must persist more than one month, or the onset may be delayed (i.e., greater than six months after the abortion). Clinical experience suggests that spontaneous recovery from PAS is not characteristic. Although PAS is categorized here as a type of PTSD, additional diagnoses including anxiety, depressive, or organic mental disorder may concurrently be made.

More than an accidental grab bag of isolated symptoms, PAS is conceptualized here as a clustering of related and unsuccessful attempts to assimilate and gain mastery over an abortion trauma. The resulting lifestyle changes involve partial to total cognitive restructuring and behavioral reorganization.

Wilmoth, Bussell, and Wilcox (1991) argue that PAS is not a type of PTSD because abortion is volitional. Peterson, Prout, and Schwarz (1991) have pointed out, however, that there are situations when patients suffering with PTSD in fact have reasons to feel guilty. They identify among many pathological identifications a "killer self" (p. 90). We submit that the volitional nature of the abortion decision is largely responsible for the perceived degree of traumatization. On the other hand, some women with PAS perceive their abortions as less than totally volitional. Some women feel their abortion was coerced, forced, or the only option available to them (Luker, 1975), and others feel their consent was not informed (Reardon, 1987; Speckhard, 1987b). Moreover, the DSM-III-R does not preclude volitional stressors in the criteria for PTSD (e.g., divorce and accidental homicide). In fact, it clearly indicates that PTSD is apparently more severe and longer lasting when the stressor is of human design (American Psychiatric Association, 1987, p. 248). We hold that abortion, intentionally caused and yielding unintended consequences, is one such example.

CONCLUSION

The psychological impact of abortion trauma on women, men, and children is far more complex than previously realized. Flawed studies and political pressure have produced an informational deficit concerning postabortion trauma. It is essential that the aftereffects of abortion be thoroughly reexamined. Failure to do so may lead women into making decisions about abortion that could be detrimental to them, decisions lacking in informed consent and free choice. Even critics like Wilmoth (1988, p. 12) have conceded that "after further study, PAS may become an accepted diagnostic category."

In addition to the need for improved research on this topic, the authors believe there is a growing need for specialized postabortion recovery treatment models and services—for example, postabortion counseling centers, peer support groups, and educational workshops for both the general public and professionals. A growing need is evident; the resistance to this viewpoint, however, may be formidable.

NOTES

1. The term fetal or unborn child is used throughout this article to indicate the differing stages of development, embryo to fetus, at which abortion occurs. This term is used in deference to the perceptions of women and men distressed by the loss of their psychological attachment to what they often refer to as "our baby."

REFERENCES

Adler, E., David, H., Major, B., Roth, S., Russo, N., & Wyatt, G. (1990). Psychological responses after abortion. *Science, 248,* 41–44.

American Psychiatric Association. (1987). *Diagnostic and statistical manual of mental disorders* (3rd ed., rev.). Washington, DC: Author.

American Psychological Association (1987). *Research review: Psychological sequelae of abortion.* Unpublished testimony presented to the Office of the U.S. Surgeon General. Washington, DC: Author.

Barnard, C. A. (1990) *The long-term psychosocial effects of abortion.* Portsmouth, NH: Institute for Pregnancy Loss.

David, H. (1985). Post-abortion and post-partum psychiatric hospitalization. *Ciba Foundation Symposium, 115,* 150–164.

David, H. (1987). Post-abortion syndrome? *Abortion Research Notes, 16,* 1–6.

David, H., Rasmussen, N., & Holst, E. (1981). Postpartum and postabortion psychotic reactions. *Family Planning Perspectives, 13,* 88–91.

DeVeber, L., Ajzenstat, J., & Chisholm, D. (1991). Postabortion grief: Psychological sequelae of induced abortion. *Humane Medicine, 7,* 203–209.

Dever, G. (1989, March 16). A report on *The psychological aftermath of abortion: An evaluation.*

Written testimony submitted to the Human Resources and Intergovernmental Relations Subcommittee of the Committee on Government Operations, U.S. House of Representatives. In *Medical and psychological impact of abortion* (pp. 162–173). Washington, DC: U.S. Government Printing Office.

Fox, R. (1990). Proceedings of the American Psychological Association, Incorporated for the year 1989: Minutes of the annual meeting of the Council of Representatives. *American Psychologist, 45,* 817–847.

Gardner, W., Sherer, D., & Tester, M. (1989). Asserting scientific authority. *American Psychologist, 44,* 895–902.

Huckeba, W., & Mueller, C. (1987). *Systematic analysis of research on psycho-social effects of abortion reported in refereed journals 1966–1985.* Unpublished manuscript. Washington, DC: Family Research Council.

Kleinman, J. (1989, March 16). Written testimony submitted to the Human Resources and Intergovernmental Relations Subcommittee of the Committee on Government Operations, U.S. House of Representatives. In *Medical and psychological impact of abortion* (pp. 156–157). Washington, DC: U.S. Government Printing Office.

Koop, C. (1989a, January 9). Letter to President Ronald Reagan concerning the health effects of abortion. In *Medical and psychological impact of abortion* (pp 68–71). Washington, DC: U.S. Government Printing Office.

Koop, C. (1989b, March 16). Testimony before the Human Resources and Intergovernmental Relations Subcommittee of the Committee on Government Operations, U.S. House of Representatives. In *Medical and psychological impact of abortion* (pp. 193–203, 218, 223–250). Washington, DC: U.S. Government Printing Office.

Lodl, K., McGettigan, A., & Bucy, J. (1985). Women's responses to abortion: Implications for postabortion support groups. *Journal of Social Work and Human Sexuality, 3,* 119–132.

Magyari, P., Wedehase, B., Ifft, R., & Callanan, N. (1987). A supportive intervention protocol for couples terminating a pregnancy for genetic reasons. *Birth Defects, 23,* 75–83.

Mall, D., & Watts, W. (Eds.). (1979). *The psychological aspects of abortion.* Washington, DC: University Publications of America.

Major, B., Mueller, P., & Hildebrandt, K. (1985). Attributions, expectations and coping with abortion. *Journal of Personality and Social Psychology, 48,* 585–599.

Mattinson, J. (1985). The effects of abortion on a marriage. *Ciba Foundation Symposium, 115,* 165–177.

McGrath, E., Keita, G., Strickland, B., & Russo, N. (Eds.). (1990). *Women and depression: Risk factors and treatment issues.* Washington, DC: American Psychological Association.

Mester, R. (1978). Induced abortion in psychotherapy. *Psychotherapy and Psychosomatics, 30,* 98–104.

Michels, N. (1988). *Helping women recover from abortion.* Minneapolis: Bethany House.

Moseley, D., Follingstad, D., & Harley, H. (1981). Psychological factors that predict reaction to abortion. *Journal of Clinical Psychology, 37,* 276–279.

Ney, P., & Wickett, A. (1989). Mental health and abortion: Review and analysis. *Psychiatric Journal of the University of Ottawa Press, 14,* 506–516.

Peppers, L. (1987). Grief and elective abortion: Breaking the emotional bond? *Omega, 18,* 1–12.

Peterson, K., Prout, M., & Schwarz, R. (1991). *Post-traumatic stress disorder: A clinician's guide.* New York; Plenum.

Posavac, E., & Miller, T. (1990). Some problems caused by not having a conceptual foundation for health research: An illustration from studies of the psychological effects of abortion. *Psychology and Health, 5,* 13–23.

Rando, T. (Ed.). (1986). *Parental loss of a child.* Champaign, IL: Research Press.

Reardon, D. (1987). *Aborted women: Silent no more.* Chicago: Loyola University Press.

Rogers, J., Stomis, G., & Phifer, J. (1989). Psychological impact of abortion. *Health Care for Women International, 10,* 347–376.

Rue, V. (1985). Abortion in relationship context. *International Journal of Natural Family Planning, 9,* 95–121.

Rue, V. (1986, August). *Post-abortion syndrome.* Paper presented at Conference on Post-Abortion Healing, University of Notre Dame.

Rue, V. (1987, August). *Current trends and status of post-abortion syndrome.* Paper presented at Conference on Post Abortion Healing, University of Notre Dame.

Rue, V., Speckhard, A., Rogers, J., & Franz, W. (1987). *The psychological aftermath of abortion: A white paper.* Testimony presented to the Office of the Surgeon General, U.S. Department of Health and Human Services, Washington, DC.

Saltzman, L., & Policar, M. (Eds.). (1985). *The complete guide to pregnancy testing and counseling.* San Francisco: Planned Parenthood of Alameda/San Francisco.

Selby, T. (1990). *The mourning after: Help for post-abortion syndrome.* Grand Rapids, MI: Baker Book House.

Shaw, D. (1990). Abortion bias seeps into news. Investigative series. *Los Angeles Times.* July 1, pp. 1, A30, A50; July 2, pp. 1, A20; July 3, pp. 1, A22, A23; July 4, pp. 1, A28, A38.

Sim, M., & Neisser, R. (1979). Post-abortive psychoses: A report from two centers. In D. Mall & W. Watts (Eds.), *The psychological aspects of abortion* (pp. 1–14). Washington, DC: University Publications of America.

Spaulding, J., & Cavenar, J. (1978). Psychoses following therapeutic abortion. *American Journal of Psychiatry, 135,* 364–365.

Speckhard, A. C. (1987a). *Post-abortion counseling.* Portsmouth, NH: Institute for Pregnancy Loss.

Speckhard, A. C. (1987b). *Psycho-social stress following abortion.* Kansas City, MO: Speed & Ward.

Speckhard, A., & Rue, V. (in press). Complicated mourning: Dynamics of impacted post-abortion grief. *Pre- & Peri-natal Psychology Journal.*

Stanford-Rue, S. (1986). *Will I cry tomorrow: Healing post-abortion trauma.* Old Tappan, NJ: Fleming Revell.

Steinberg, T. (1989). Abortion counseling: To benefit maternal health. *American Journal of Law and Medicine, 15,* 483–517.

Stotland, N. (1989). Psychiatric issues in abortion, and the implications of recent legal changes for psychiatric practice. In N. Stotland (Ed.), *Psychiatric aspects of abortion* (pp. 1–16). Washington, DC: American Psychiatric Press.

Vaughan, H. (1991). *Canonical variates of post-abortion syndrome.* Portsmouth, NH: Institute for Pregnancy Loss.

Wilmoth, G. (1988). Depression and abortion: A brief review. *Population and Environmental Psychology News, 14,* 9–12.

Wilmoth, G., Bussell, D., & Wilcox, B. (1991). Abortion and family policy: A mental health perspective. E. A. Anderson & R. C. Hula (Eds.), *The reconstruction of family policy* (pp. 111–127). New York: Greenwood

Zakus, G., & Wilday, S. (1987). Adolescent abortion option. *Social Work in Health Care, 12,* 77–91.

NO

Nancy E. Adler et al.

PSYCHOLOGICAL RESPONSES
AFTER ABORTION

A review of methodologically sound studies of the psychological responses of U.S. women after they obtained legal, nonrestrictive abortions indicates that distress is generally greatest before the abortion and that the incidence of severe negative responses is low. Factors associated with increased risk of negative response are consistent with those reported in research on other stressful life events.

Abortion has been a legal medical procedure throughout the United States since the 1973 Supreme Court decision in *Roe v. Wade*, with 1.5 million to 1.6 million procedures performed annually. U.S. abortion patients reflect all segments of the population. In 1987, almost 60% of abortion patients were under 25 years of age. Most (82%) were not married, and half had no prior births. Nearly 69% of women obtaining abortions were white (1). Abortions are most often performed in the first trimester; the median gestational age is 9.2 weeks; 97% of abortions are performed by instrumental evacuation (2).

Although much literature exists on the psychological consequences of abortion, contradictory conclusions have been reached. Disparate interpretations are due in part to limitations of the research methods and in part to political, value, or moral influences. In this review of studies with the most rigorous research designs, we report consistent findings on the psychological status of women who have had legal abortions under nonrestrictive circumstances (3). This article is limited to U.S. studies; however, results from a study in Denmark are also relevant because of the existence of a uniform national population registration system not available in the United States (4).

RESPONSES AFTER ABORTION

Responses after abortion reflect the entire course of experiencing and resolving an unwanted pregnancy. Although there may be sensations of regret, sadness, or guilt, the weight of the evidence from scientific studies (3) indi-

From Nancy E. Adler, Henry P. David, Brenda N. Major, Susan H. Roth, Nancy F. Russo, and Gail E. Wyatt, "Psychological Responses After Abortion," *Science*, vol. 248 (April 6, 1990), pp. 41–44. Copyright © 1990 by The American Association for the Advancement of Science. Reprinted by permission.

cates that legal abortion of an unwanted pregnancy in the first trimester does not pose a psychological hazard for most women.

Descriptive studies have shown the incidence of severe negative responses after abortion to be low (5–10). After first-trimester abortion, women most frequently report feeling relief and happiness. In a study by Lazarus (5), 2 weeks after first-trimester abortions, 76% of women reported feeling relief, while the most common negative emotion, guilt, was reported by only 17%. Negative emotions reflecting internal concerns, such as loss, or social concerns, such as social disapproval, typically are not experienced as strongly as positive emotions after abortion (5–8). For example, Adler (6) obtained ratings of feelings over a 2- to 3-month period after abortion on Likert-type scales, with 5 representing strongest intensity. Mean ratings were 3.96 for positive emotions, 2.26 for internally based negative emotions, and 1.89 for socially based negative emotions.

Women show little evidence of psychopathology after abortion. For example, on the short form of the Beck Depression Inventory, scores below 5 are considered nondepressed (11). In a sample of first-trimester patients, Major et al. (9) obtained mean scores of 4.17 (SD* = 3.92) immediately after the abortion and 1.97 (SD = 2.93) 3 weeks later.

Measures used in most studies were not designed to assess psychopathology, but, rather, emotional distress within normal populations. These indicators show significant (12) decreases in distress from before abortion to immediately after and from before abortion or immediately after to several weeks later (9, 10). For

*[SD = standard deviation.—Ed.]

example, Cohen and Roth (10) found a drop in the depression subscale of the Symptom Checklist 90 (SCL-90) from a mean of 24.1 (SD = 11.8) at the time of arrival at a clinic to a mean of 18.4 (SD = 12.2) in the recovery room. Similar drops were shown on the anxiety scale of the SCL-90 and on the Impact of Events scale, an indicator of distress.

Only two studies compared responses after abortion with those after birth. Athanasiou et al. (13) studied women after early (suction) abortion, late (saline) abortion, and term birth. Starting with 373 women, researchers matched 38 patients in each group for ethnicity, age, parity, and marital and socioeconomic status. Thirteen to sixteen months after abortion or delivery, women completed the Minnesota Multiphasic Personality Inventory (MMPI) and the SCL. None of the groups had a mean score on any subscales of the MMPI above 70, the cutoff indicating psychopathology. Few differences among groups were shown (14), and the authors concluded that the three groups were "startlingly similar."

Zabin et al. (15) interviewed 360 adolescents seeking pregnancy tests and compared those who had negative results, those who were pregnant and carried to term, and those who were pregnant and aborted. All three groups showed higher levels of state (transient) anxiety at base line than they did 1 or 2 years later (for example, for the abortion group $\bar{X} = 74.6$ at base line versus 45.6 and 43.6 at 1 and 2 years later). Two years after the initial interview, the abortion group showed, if anything, a more positive psychological profile than either of the other two groups. There were no differences on state anxiety, but the abortion group was significantly lower on trait anxiety than either of the other two groups, was higher on self-esteem than the negative pregnancy group, and had a greater sense of internal control than the childbearing group.

FACTORS RELATING TO PSYCHOLOGICAL RESPONSES

Although most women do not experience negative psychological responses after abortion, case studies document some negative experiences. Various aspects of the abortion experience may contribute to distress. Ambivalence about the wantedness of the pregnancy may engender a sense of loss. Conflict about the meaning of abortion and its relation to deeply held values or beliefs, perceived social stigma, or lack of support may also induce negative reactions.

The decision process. The greater the difficulty of deciding to terminate a pregnancy, the more likely there will be negative responses after abortion (6–8, 16). For example, Adler (6) found that the difficulty of deciding to abort, reported several days before abortion, was positively associated with the experience of negative emotions reflecting loss 2 to 3 months after abortion ($r = 0.37$), but was not related to a statistically significant extent to the experience of positive emotions or of negative emotions reflecting social disapproval.

Although most women do not find the decision to abort difficult, some do (16), and it appears to be more difficult for women seeking termination later in pregnancy. Whereas only 7% of 100 first-trimester patients studied by Osofsky et al. (17) reported initial indecision and 12% reported difficulty in deciding about abortion, corresponding figures among 200 second-trimester patients were 36 and 51%. Women undergoing second-trimester abortions also report more emotional distress after abortion than do those terminating first-trimester pregnancies (17–19).

Women who perceive more support for the decision to abort are more satisfied with their decision (7, 20). Those with fewer conflicts over abortion are also more satisfied; in a sample of adolescents, Eisen and Zellman (21) found that satisfaction with the decision 6 months after an abortion was associated with a favorable opinion of abortion in general as well as for themselves.

The more a pregnancy is wanted and is viewed as personally meaningful by the woman, the more difficult abortion may be. Major et al. (9) found that among 247 first-trimester abortion patients, women who described their pregnancy as being "highly meaningful" compared to those who found their pregnancy to be less personally meaningful reported more physical complaints immediately after the abortion and anticipated more negative consequences. Three weeks after the abortion, women who had indicated having had no intention to become pregnant scored significantly lower on the Beck Depression Inventory ($\bar{X} = 1.68$, SD $= 2.33$) than did the minority of women who had at least some intention to become pregnant ($\bar{X} = 3.71$, SD $= 5.03$).

In summary, women who report little difficulty in making their decision, who are more satisfied with their choice, and who are terminating pregnancies that were unintended and hold little personal meaning for them show more positive responses after abortion. Women with negative attitudes toward abortion and who perceive little support for their decision have more difficulty deciding about abortion. These factors may also contribute to delay in obtaining abortions (19), potentially subjecting women to the greater stress of second-trimester procedures (17–19).

Perceived social support. Perceived social support can buffer some adverse effects of stressful life events (22). However, social support is complex. Support for having the abortion needs to be differentiated from support in general; the former is associated with more favorable outcomes; the latter may not be.

Women with greater support for their abortion from parents and the male partner generally show more positive responses after abortion (8, 23, 24). Intimacy with and involvement of the male partner was a significant predictor of emotional reaction in two samples (8). Together with satisfaction with the decision and the woman's initial emotional response to becoming pregnant, partner support accounted for almost 40% of the variance in psychological response 2 to 3 weeks after abortion. Moseley et al. (24) found that having negative feelings toward one's partner, making the abortion decision alone, and experiencing opposition from parents were associated with greater emotional distress on the Multiple Affective Adjective Check List both before a first-trimester abortion and immediately after. However, Robbins (25) found that single women who maintained a strong relationship with their partner reported more negative change on the MMPI 6 weeks after abortion and more regret 1 year later than those whose relationships deteriorated.

In a study of actual social support, Major et al. (9) recorded whether women were accompanied to the clinic by a male partner. Out of 247 women, 83 were accompanied. Compared to unaccompanied women, those with partners were younger and expected to cope less well beforehand; women who were more distressed about the abortion may have expressed a greater need for their partners to accompany them. Accompanied women were significantly more depressed and reported more physical complaints immediately after abortion than unaccompanied women. Differences in depression after abortion remained after controlling for age and coping expectations, but they did not remain in a 3-week follow-up of a subset of women.

Coping processes and expectancies. Generalized positive outcome expectancies and situation-specific coping expectancies and processes have been linked to a variety of health-relevant outcomes (26). Major et al. (9) found that among abortion patients, those who expected to cope well scored lower on the Beck Depression Inventory than those with more negative expectations ($\bar{X} = 2.98$, SD $= 3.04$ versus $\bar{X} = 5.93$, SD $= 4.41$, respectively). Those expecting to cope well also showed more positive mood, anticipated fewer negative consequences, and had fewer physical complaints both immediately after abortion and 3 weeks later.

Cohen and Roth (10) examined coping styles and levels of anxiety and depression before and immediately after abortion. As noted earlier, anxiety and depression decreased significantly from before the abortion to afterwards for all women, but those who used approach strategies (for example, thinking about the procedure, talking about it) showed a greater decrease in anxiety from before to after abortion than those not using these strategies. Women who used denial scored significantly higher in depression and anxiety than did those who did not deny.

LIMITATIONS OF RESEARCH AND FUTURE DIRECTIONS

Although each study has methodological shortcomings and limitations, the diversity of methods used provides strength in drawing general conclusions. Despite the diversity, the studies are consistent in their findings of relatively rare instances of negative responses after abortion and of decreases in psychological distress after abortion compared to before abortion. However, weaknesses and gaps found among studies provide challenges for future research.

First, samples of well-defined populations and information on subjects who choose not to participate are needed. Studies have sampled women from specific clinics or hospitals. Both public and private clinics have been used, and samples have varied in their ethnic and socioeconomic character. Women whose abortions are performed by private physicians are not represented; they are estimated to be about 4% of women having abortions (27).

Of more concern is the necessary use of volunteers, which can introduce bias if women who agree to participate in research differ from those who do not on characteristics linked to more positive or negative outcomes. An analysis of studies that provide data on characteristics of research participants versus the population from which the sample was drawn suggests that women who are more likely to find the abortion experience stressful may be underrepresented in volunteer samples. However, the amount of bias introduced by this underrepresentation appears to be minor and unlikely to influence the general conclusions (28).

Second, the timing of measurement has been limited. Many studies lack base-line date from before the abortion. We know of no studies with data collected before the pregnancy, making it impossible to control for variables that may be associated with the initial occurrence of the pregnancy and which could influence responses after abortion. One of the best predictors of a woman's psychological status after abortion is likely to be her functioning before the occurrence of the unwanted pregnancy (29). Former Surgeon General C. Everett Koop has called for a prospective study of a nationally representative sample of women of childbearing age (30). Such a study would address both issues of representativeness and of base-line measurement.

Timing of assessment after abortion has also been limited. Some studies obtained measures within a few hours after the procedure, while the woman was still in the clinic. Responses at this time may not be indicative of longer term response. A few studies have obtained measures a few weeks or months after abortion; the longest follow-up is 2 years. Therefore, no definitive conclusions can be drawn about longer term effects. Although individual case studies have identified instances in which individuals develop severe problems that they attribute to an earlier abortion experience (31), the number of such cases is comparatively small. Moreover, research on other life stresses suggests that women who do not experience severe negative responses within a few months after the event are unlikely to develop future significant psychological problems related to the event (32). Longer term studies are needed to confirm this observation and to ascertain the influence of other life events attributed retrospectively to the abortion experience.

Finally, in studying psychological responses after abortion, it is important to separate the experience of abortion from the characteristics of women seeking abortion and from the context of resolving an unwanted pregnancy. A useful comparison would be women who carry an unwanted pregnancy to term and surrender the child for adoption; this would control both for the unwantedness of the pregnancy and the experience of loss. The study by Athanasiou *et al.* (13) matched women who were terminating pregnancies with those carrying to term on key demographic variables, but they were not matched on "wantedness" of the pregnancy. Similarly, the comparison used in the Danish study (4) for women aborting their pregnancies was women carrying to term, most of whom were likely to be delivering wanted pregnancies. One would expect more adverse outcomes for women carrying unwanted pregnancies to term (33).

A number of questions can be addressed without a comparison group. Theoretically grounded studies testing conditional hypotheses about factors that may put women at relatively greater risk for negative responses are particularly important. Such studies can address critical questions about the nature of the abortion experience and its aftermath, and can point the way to interventions if needed.

CONCLUSION

Scientific studies on psychological responses to legal, nonrestrictive abortion in the United States suggest that severe negative reactions are infrequent in the immediate and short-term aftermath, particularly for first-trimester abortions. Women who are terminating pregnancies that are wanted and personally meaningful, who lack support from their partner or parents for the abortion, or who have more conflicting feelings or are less sure of their decision beforehand may be at relatively higher risk for negative consequences.

Case studies have established that some women experience severe distress or psychopathology after abortion and require sympathetic care. As former Surgeon General C. Everett Koop testified before Congress regarding his review of research on psychological effects of abortion, such responses can be overwhelming to a given individual, but the development of significant psychological problems related to abortion is "minuscule from a public health perspective" (34).

Despite methodological shortcomings of any single study, in the aggregate, research with diverse samples, different measures of response, and different times of assessment have come to similar conclusions. The time of greatest distress is likely to be before the abortion. Severe negative reactions after abortions are rare and can best be understood in the framework of coping with a normal life stress.

NOTES

1. S. K. Henshaw and J. Silverman, *Fam. Plann. Perspect.* **20,** 158 (1988).

2. S. Henshaw, *ibid.* **19,** 5 (1987); C. Tietze and S. K. Henshaw, *Induced Abortion: A World Review* (Alan Guttmacher Institute, New York, 1986); E. Powell-Griner, *Mon. Vital Stat.* **36** (no. 5), 1 (1987).

3. Studies included in this article had to meet the following three criteria: (i) the research was empirical and based on a definable sample; (ii) the sample was drawn from the United States; and (iii) the women studied had undergone abortions under legal and nonrestrictive conditions (for example, women did not have to qualify for the procedure on the basis of threat to physical or mental health). These criteria allow for maximal generalizability to U.S. women under current conditions.

4. Through the use of computer linkages to national abortion and birth registers, the admissions register to psychiatric hospitals was tracked for women 3 months after abortion (n = 27,234) or delivery (n = 71,370) and for all women 15 to 49 years of age residing in Denmark (n = 1,169,819). To determine incidence rates, only first admissions to psychiatric hospitals were recorded, excluding women who had been admitted within the 15 previous months. The key finding was that for both never-married women and currently married women, the psychiatric admission rate after pregnancy was roughly the same for abortions or deliveries—about 12 per 10,000 compared to 7 per 10,000 for all women of reproductive age. Among the much smaller group of separated, divorced, or widowed women, those who had terminated pregnancies (which perhaps were originally intended) experienced a fourfold higher admissions rate (64 per 10,000) than the group of separated, divorced, or widowed women who delivered (17 per 10,000). However, because there may be a bias against hospitalizing a new mother, particularly if she is nursing, the relative psychological risk of delivery may be underestimated [H. P. David, N. Rasmussen, E. Holst, Fam. Plann. Persect. 13, 88 (1981)].

5. A. Lazarus, J. Psychosom. Obstet. Gynaecol. 4, 141 (1985).

6. N. E. Adler, Am. J. Orthopsychiatry 45, 446 (1975).

7. J. D. Osofsky and H. Osofsky, ibid. 42, 48 (1972).

8. L. R. Shusterman, Soc. Sci. Med. 13A, 683 (1979).

9. B. Major, P. Mueller, K. Hildebrandt, J. Pers. Soc. Psychol. 48, 585 (1985). Means for 3-week follow-up interviews reported here do not match means published in the original article. Due to an error in the original publication, standard deviations were reported instead of means, but all tests of significance were accurate. The correct means are reported here.

10. L. Cohen and S. Roth, J. Hum. Stress. 10, 140 (1984).

11. A. T. Beck and R. W. Beck, Postgrad. Med. 52, 81 (1972).

12. In this article, significance is used in terms of statistical significance and may not represent clinically significant changes or associations.

13. R. Athanasiou, W. Oppel, L. Michaelson, T. Unger, M. Yager, Fam. Plann. Persect, 5, 227 (1973).

14. The only statistically significant differences found were as follows: (i) women who had experienced term birth scored higher on the paranoia subscale of the MMPI ($\bar{X}$ = 61.7, SD = 14.6) than did women in either abortion group ($\bar{X}$ = 58.9, SD = 12.2 for suction patients and $\bar{X}$ = 54.6, SD = 9.4 for saline patients) and (ii) suction abortion patients reported fewer somatic complaints on the SCL ($\bar{X}$ = 10.6, SD = 8.0) than either the saline abortion or delivery patients ($\bar{X}$ = 14.7, SD = 8.1 and $\bar{X}$ = 14.8, SD =9.3, respectively).

15. L. S. Zabin, M. B. Hirsch, M. R. Emerson, Fam. Plann. Persect. 21, 248 (1989).

16. M. B. Bracken, Soc. Psychiatry 13, 135 (1978).

17. J. D. Osofsky, H. J. Osofsky, R. Rajan, D. Spitz, Mt. Sinai J. Med. 42, 456 (1975).

18. J. B. Rooks and W. Cates, Jr., Fam. Plann. Persect. 9, 276 (1977); N. B. Kaltreider, S. Goldsmith, A. Margolis, Am. J. Obstet. Gynecol. 135, 235 (1979).

19. M. Bracken and S. Kasl, ibid. 121, 1008 (1975).

20. M. B. Bracken, L. V. Klerman, M. Bracken, ibid. 130, 251 (1978).

21. M. Eisen and G. L. Zellman, J. Gen. Psychol. 145, 231 (1984).

22. S. Cohen and T. A. Wills, Psychol. Bull. 98, 310 (1985); R. C. Kessler and J. D. McLeod, Social Support and Health, S. Cohen and S. L. Syme, Eds. (Academic Press, Orlando, FL, 1985), pp. 219–240.

23. M. B. Bracken, M. Hachamovitch, G. Grossman, J. Nerv. Ment. Dis. 158, 154 (1974).

24. D. T. Moseley et al., J. Clin. Psychol. 37, 276 (1981).

25. J. M. Robbins, Soc. Probl. 31, 334 (1984).

26. M. F. Scheier and C. S. Carver, J. Pers. 55, 169 (1987); A. Bandura, Psychol. Rev. 84, 191 (1977).

27. S. K. Henshaw, J. D. Forrest, J. Van Vort, Fam. Plann. Persect. 19, 63 (1987).

28. N. E. Adler, J. Appl. Soc. Psychol. 6, 240 (1976); E. W. Freeman, Am. J. Orthopsychiatry 47, 503 (1977).

29. E. C. Payne, A. R. Kravitz, M. T. Notman, J. V. Anderson, Arch. Gen. Psychiatry 33, 725 (1976); E. M. Belsey, H. S. Greer, S. Lal, S. C. Lewis, R. W. Beard, Soc. Sci. Med. 11, 71 (1977).

30. C. E. Koop, letter to R. W. Reagan, 9 January 1989.

31. A. C. Speckhard, The Psycho-Social Aspects of Stress Following Abortion (Sheed and Ward, Kansas City, MO, 1987).

32. C. B. Wortman and R. C. Silver, J. Consult. Clin. Psychol. 57, 349 (1989).

33. One may also find more adverse consequences for the children born as a result of unwanted pregnancy [H. P. David. Z. Dytrych, Z. Matejcek, V. Schuller, *Born Unwanted: Developmental Effects of Denied Abortion* (Springer, New York, 1988)].

34. Committee on Government Operations, House of Representatives, *The Federal Role in Determining the Medical and Psychological Impact of Abortions on Women*, 101st Cong., 2d sess., 11 December 1989, House Report 101-392, p. 14.

35. This article is based on a review conducted by a panel convened by the American Psychological Association. The authors were members of the panel. We thank J. Gentry and B. Wilcox for contributions to the manuscript and G. Markman and A. Schlagel for manuscript preparation.

CHALLENGE QUESTIONS

Does Abortion Have Severe Psychological Effects?

1. If someone you know were considering terminating a pregnancy, what advice would you offer? Why?

2. What potential problems do you see in research on abortion effects? How would you design an experiment to minimize these problems?

3. Is abortion a moral, psychological, or political issue? What is the basis of your conclusion? How does this answer affect your position regarding whether abortion is harmful or not?

4. What are the strengths and weaknesses of Speckhard and Rue's proposal that postabortion syndrome occurs in some women following abortion?

ISSUE 13

Classic Dialogue: Do Diagnostic Labels Hinder Treatment?

YES: D. L. Rosenhan, from "On Being Sane in Insane Places," *Science* (January 13, 1973)

NO: Robert L. Spitzer, from "On Pseudoscience in Science, Logic in Remission and Psychiatric Diagnosis: A Critique of 'On Being Sane in Insane Places,'" *Journal of Abnormal Psychology* (vol. 84, 1975)

ISSUE SUMMARY

YES: Psychologist D. L. Rosenhan describes an experiment that, he contends, demonstrates that once a patient is labeled as schizophrenic, his behavior is seen as such by mental health workers regardless of the true state of the patient's mental health.

NO: Psychiatrist Robert L. Spitzer argues that diagnostic labels are necessary and valuable and that Rosenhan's experiment has many flaws.

Traditionally, the first step in treating a disorder is to diagnose it. When a disorder is diagnosed, presumably the most effective treatment can then be applied. But diagnosis often involves classifying the person and attaching a label. Could such a label do more harm than good?

How would you think and behave if you were introduced to someone described as a high school dropout? A heroin addict? A schizophrenic? What would you think and how would you behave if, having recently taken a series of personality tests, you were told by an expert that you were schizophrenic?

Some people believe that diagnostic labels may actually serve as self-fulfilling prophecies. Labels seem to have a way of putting blinders on the way a problem is seen. Those who are labeled may behave differently toward others or develop self-concepts consistent with the diagnosis—and thereby exaggerate, or even create anew, behavior considered to be "abnormal."

In the following selections, D. L. Rosenhan asks the question, "If sanity and insanity exist, how shall we know them?" He then describes an experiment that he conducted to help answer this question. Rosenhan interprets the results of his investigation as demonstrating that "the normal are not detectably sane" by a mental hospital staff because "having once been labeled schizophrenic, there is nothing the [patient] can do to overcome this tag." He believes that mental institutions impose a specific environment in which the meaning of even normal behaviors can be construed as abnormal. If this is so, Rosenhan wonders, "How many people are sane . . . but not recognized as such in our psychiatric institutions?"

Robert L. Spitzer criticizes Rosenhan's experiment on many grounds and, in fact, contends that "a correct interpretation of his own [Rosenhan's] data contradicts his conclusions." Rosenhan's data, Spitzer contends, show that in "a psychiatric hospital, psychiatrists are remarkably able to distinguish the 'sane' from the 'insane.' " Although Spitzer recognizes some of the dangers of diagnostic classification, he believes that Rosenhan has not presented fairly the purpose and necessity of diagnoses. The misuse of diagnoses, he maintains, "is not a sufficient reason to abandon their use because they have been shown to be of value when properly used." They "enable mental health professionals to communicate with each other . . . , comprehend the pathological processes involved . . . , and control psychiatric disorders," says Spitzer.

POINT	COUNTERPOINT
• Psychiatric diagnoses are in the minds of the observers and do not reflect the behavior of the patients.	• A diagnosis based on real or false symptoms *is* based on a patient's behavior.
• A diagnosis can become a self-fulfilling prophecy for the doctor or the patient.	• Competent diagnoses derive from a necessary classification of the symptoms of disorder.
• In the setting of a mental institution, almost any behavior could be considered abnormal.	• Mental patients *do* eventually get discharged when they continue to show no symptoms of behavior pathology.
• Diagnostic labels serve no useful purpose, especially in view of the harm they do.	• Diagnoses enable psychiatrists to communicate, comprehend, and control disorders.

YES

D. L. Rosenhan

ON BEING SANE IN INSANE PLACES

If sanity and insanity exist, how shall we know them?

The question is neither capricious nor itself insane. However much we may be personally convinced that we can tell the normal from the abnormal, the evidence is simply not compelling. It is commonplace, for example, to read about murder trials wherein eminent psychiatrists for the defense are contradicted by equally eminent psychiatrists for the prosecution on the matter of the defendant's sanity. More generally, there are a great deal of conflicting data on the reliability, utility, and meaning of such terms as "sanity," "insanity," "mental illness," and "schizophrenia." Finally, as early as 1934, Benedict suggested that normality and abnormality are not universal. What is viewed as normal in one culture may be seen as quite aberrant in another. Thus, notions of normality and abnormality may not be quite as accurate as people believe they are.

To raise questions regarding normality and abnormality is in no way to question the fact that some behaviors are deviant or odd. Murder is deviant. So, too, are hallucinations. Nor does raising such questions deny the existence of the personal anguish that is often associated with "mental illness." Anxiety and depression exist. Psychological suffering exists. But normality and abnormality, sanity and insanity, and the diagnoses that flow from them may be less substantive than many believe them to be.

At its heart, the question of whether the sane can be distinguished from the insane (and whether degrees of insanity can be distinguished from each other) is a simple matter: do the salient characteristics that lead to diagnoses reside in the patients themselves or in the environments and contexts in which observers find them? From Bleuler, through Kretchmer, through the formulators of the recently revised *Diagnostic and Statistical Manual* of the American Psychiatric Association, the belief has been strong that patients present symptoms, that those symptoms can be categorized, and, implicitly, that the sane are distinguishable from the insane. More recently, however, this belief has been questioned. Based in part on theoretical and anthropological considerations, but also on philosophical, legal, and therapeutic ones, the view has grown that psychological categorization of mental illness is useless at best and downright harmful, misleading, and pejorative at worst. Psychiatric diagnoses, in this view, are in the minds of the observers and are not valid summaries of characteristics displayed by the observed.

Gains can be made in deciding which of these is more nearly accurate by getting normal people (that is, people who do not have, and have never suffered, symptoms of serious psychiatric disorders) admitted to psychiatric hospitals and then determining whether they were discovered to be sane and, if so, how. If the sanity of such pseudopatients were always detected, there would be prima facie evidence that a sane individual can be distinguished from the insane context in which he is found. Normality (and presumably abnormality) is distinct enough that it can be recognized wherever it occurs, for it is carried within the person. If, on the other hand, the sanity of the pseudopatients were never discovered, serious difficulties would arise for those who support traditional modes of psychiatric diagnosis. Given that the hospital staff was not incompetent, that the pseudopatient had been behaving as sanely as he had been outside of the hospital, and that it had never been previously suggested that he belonged in a psychiatric hospital, such an unlikely outcome would support the view that psychiatric diagnosis betrays little about the patient but much about the environment in which an observer finds him.

This article describes such an experiment. Eight sane people gained secret admission to 12 different hospitals. Their diagnostic experiences constitute the data of the first part of this article; the remainder is devoted to a description of their experiences in psychiatric institutions. Too few psychiatrists and psychologists, even

those who have worked in such hospitals, know what the experience is like. They rarely talk about it with former patients, perhaps because they distrust information coming from the previously insane. Those who have worked in psychiatric hospitals are likely to have adapted so thoroughly to the settings that they are insensitive to the impact of the experience. And while there have been occasional reports of researchers who submitted themselves to psychiatric hospitalization, these researchers have commonly remained in the hospitals for short periods of time, often with the knowledge of the hospital staff. It is difficult to know the extent to which they were treated like patients or like research colleagues. Nevertheless, their reports about the inside of the psychiatric hospital have been valuable. This article extends those efforts.

PSEUDOPATIENTS AND THEIR SETTINGS

The eight pseudopatients were a varied group. One was a psychology graduate student in his 20s. The remaining seven were older and "established." Among them were three psychologists, a pediatrician, a psychiatrist, a painter, and a housewife. Three pseudopatients were women, five were men. All of them employed pseudonyms, lest their alleged diagnoses embarrass them later. Those who were in mental health professions alleged another occupation in order to avoid the special attentions that might be accorded by staff, as a matter of courtesy or caution, to ailing colleagues. With the exception of myself (I was the first pseudopatient and my presence was known to the hospital administrator and chief psychologist and, so far as I can tell, to them alone), the presence of pseudopatients and the nature of the research program was not known to the hospital staffs.

The settings were similarly varied. In order to generalize the findings, admission into a variety of hospitals was sought. The 12 hospitals in the sample are located in five different states on the East and West coasts. Some were old and shabby, some were quite new. Some were research-oriented, others not. Some had good staff-patient ratios, others were quite understaffed. Only one was a strictly private hospital. All the others were supported by state or federal funds or, in one instance, by university funds.

After calling the hospital for an appointment, the pseudopatient arrived at the admissions office complaining that he had been hearing voices. Asked what the voices said, he replied that they were often unclear, but as far as he could tell they said "empty," "hollow," and "thud." The voices were unfamiliar and were of the same sex as the pseudopatient. The choice of these symptoms was occasioned by their apparent similarity to existential symptoms. Such symptoms were alleged to arise from painful concerns about the perceived meaninglessness of one's life. It is as if the hallucinating person were saying, "My life is empty and hollow." The choice of these symptoms was also determined by the *absence* of a single report of existential psychoses in the literature.

Beyond alleging the symptoms and falsifying name, vocation, and employment, no further alterations of person, history, or circumstances were made. The significant events of the pseudopatient's life history were presented as they had actually occurred. Relationships with parents and siblings, with spouse and children, with people at work and in school, consistent with the aforementioned exceptions, were described as they were or had

been. Frustrations and upsets were described along with joys and satisfactions. These facts are important to remember. If anything, they strongly biased the subsequent results in favor of detecting sanity, since none of their histories or current behaviors were seriously pathological in any way.

Immediately upon admission to the psychiatric ward, the pseudopatient ceased simulating *any* symptoms of abnormality. In some cases, there was a brief period of mild nervousness and anxiety, since none of the pseudopatients really believed that they would be admitted so easily. Indeed their shared fear was that they would be immediately exposed as frauds and greatly embarrassed. Moreover, many of them had never visited a psychiatric ward; even those who had, nevertheless had some genuine fears about what might happen to them. Their nervousness, then, was quite appropriate to the novelty of the hospital setting, and it abated rapidly.

Apart from that short-lived nervousness, the pseudopatient behaved on the ward as he "normally" behaved. The pseudopatient spoke to patients and staff as he might ordinarily. Because there is uncommonly little to do on a psychiatric ward, he attempted to engage others in conversation. When asked by staff how he was feeling, he indicated that he was fine, that he no longer experienced symptoms. He responded to instructions from attendants, to calls for medication (which was not swallowed), and to dining-hall instructions. Beyond such activities as were available to him on the admissions ward, he spent his time writing down his observations about the ward, its patients, and the staff. Initially these notes were written "secretly," but as it soon became clear that no one much cared, they were subsequently written on standard tablets of paper in such public places as the day-room. No secret was made of these activities.

The pseudopatient, very much as a true psychiatric patient, entered a hospital with no foreknowledge of when he would be discharged. Each was told that he would have to get out by his own devices, essentially by convincing the staff that he was sane. The psychological stresses associated with hospitalization were considerable, and all but one of the pseudopatients desired to be discharged almost immediately after being admitted. They were, therefore, motivated not only to behave sanely, but to be paragons of cooperation. That their behavior was in no way disruptive is confirmed by nursing reports, which have been obtained on most of the patients. These reports uniformly indicate that the patients were "friendly," "cooperative," and "exhibited no abnormal indications."

THE NORMAL ARE NOT DETECTABLY SANE

Despite their public "show" of sanity, the pseudopatients were never detected. Admitted, except in one case, with a diagnosis of schizophrenia each was discharged with a diagnosis of schizophrenia "in remission." The label "in remission" should in no way be dismissed as a formality, for at no time during any hospitalization had any question been raised about any pseudopatient's simulation. Nor are there any indications in the hospital records that the pseudopatient's status was suspect. Rather, the evidence is strong that, once labeled schizophrenic, the pseudopatient was stuck with that label. If the pseudopatient was to be discharged, he must naturally be "in remission"; but he was

not sane, nor, in the institution's view, had he ever been sane.

The uniform failure to recognize sanity cannot be attributed to the quality of the hospitals, for, although there were considerable variations among them, several are considered excellent. Nor can it be alleged that there was simply not enough time to observe the pseudo-patients. Length of hospitalization ranged from 7 to 52 days, with an average of 19 days. The pseudopatients were not, in fact, carefully observed, but this failure clearly speaks more to traditions within psychiatric hospitals than to lack of opportunity.

Finally, it cannot be said that the failure to recognize the pseudopatients' sanity was due to the fact that they were not behaving sanely. While there was clearly some tension present in all of them, their daily visitors could detect no serious behavioral consequences— nor, indeed, could other patients. It was quite common for the patients to "detect" the pseudopatients' sanity. During the first three hospitalizations, when accurate counts were kept, 35 of a total of 118 patients on the admissions ward voiced their suspicions, some vigorously. "You're not crazy. You're a journalist, or a professor [referring to the continual note-taking]. You're checking up on the hospital." While most of the patients were reassured by the pseudopatient's insistence that he had been sick before he came in but was fine now, some continued to believe that the pseudopatient was sane throughout his hospitalization. The fact that the patients often recognized normality when staff did not raises important questions.

Failure to detect sanity during the course of hospitalization may be due to the fact that physicians operate with a strong bias toward what statisticians call the type 2 error. This is to say that physicians are more inclined to call a healthy person sick (a false positive, type 2) than a sick person healthy (a false negative, type 1). The reasons for this are not hard to find: it is clearly more dangerous to mis-diagnose illness than health. Better to err on the side of caution, to suspect illness even among the healthy.

But what holds for medicine does not hold equally well for psychiatry. Medical illnesses, while unfortunate, are not commonly pejorative. Psychiatric diagnoses, on the contrary, carry with them personal, legal, and social stigmas. It was therefore important to see whether the tendency toward diagnosing the sane insane could be reversed. The following experiment was arranged at a research and teaching hospital whose staff had heard these findings but doubted that such an error could occur in their hospital. The staff was informed that at some time during the following 3 months, one or more pseudopatients would attempt to be admitted into the psychiatric hospital. Each staff member was asked to rate each patient who presented himself at admissions or on the ward according to the likelihood that the patient was a pseudopatient. A 10-point scale was used, with a 1 and 2 reflecting high confidence that the patient was a pseudopatient.

Judgments were obtained on 193 patients who were admitted for psychiatric treatment. All staff who had had sustained contact with or primary responsibility for the patient—attendants, nurses, psychiatrists, physicians, and psychologists—were asked to make judgments. Forty-one patients were alleged, with high confidence, to be pseudopatients by at least one member of the staff. Twenty-three were considered suspect by

at least one psychiatrist. Nineteen were suspected by one psychiatrist *and* one other staff member. Actually, no genuine pseudopatient (at least from my group) presented himself during this period.

The experiment is instructive. It indicates that the tendency to designate sane people as insane can be reversed when the stakes (in this case, prestige and diagnostic acumen) are high. But what can be said of the 19 people who were suspected of being "sane" by one psychiatrist and another staff member? Were these people truly "sane," or was it rather the case that in the course of avoiding the type 2 error the staff tended to make more errors of the first sort—calling the crazy "sane"? There is no way of knowing. But one thing is certain: any diagnostic process that lends itself so readily to massive errors of this sort cannot be a very reliable one.

THE STICKINESS OF PSYCHODIAGNOSTIC LABELS

Beyond the tendency to call the healthy sick—a tendency that accounts better for diagnostic behavior on admission than it does for such behavior after a lengthy period of exposure—the data speak to the massive role of labeling in psychiatric assessment. Having once been labeled schizophrenic, there is nothing the pseudopatient can do to overcome this tag. The tag profoundly colors others' perceptions of him and his behavior.

From one viewpoint, these data are hardly surprising, for it has long been known that elements are given meaning by the context in which they occur. Gestalt psychology made this point vigorously, and Asch demonstrated that there are "central" personality traits (such as "warm" versus "cold") which are so powerful that they markedly color the meaning of other information in forming an impression of a given personality.

"Insane," "schizophrenic," "manic-depressive," and "crazy" are probably among the most powerful of such central traits. Once a person is designated abnormal, all of his other behaviors and characteristics are colored by that label. Indeed, that label is so powerful that may of the pseudopatients' normal behaviors were overlooked entirely or profoundly misinterpreted. Some examples may clarify this issue.

Earlier I indicated that there were no changes in the pseudopatient's personal history and current status beyond those of name, employment, and, where necessary, vocation. Otherwise, a veridical description of personal history and circumstances was offered. Those circumstances were not psychotic. How were they made consonant with the diagnosis of psychosis? Or were those diagnoses modified in such a way as to bring them into accord with the circumstances of the pseudopatient's life, as described by him?

As far as I can determine, diagnoses were in no way affected by the relative health of the circumstances of a pseudo-patient's life. Rather, the reverse occurred: the perception of his circumstances was shaped entirely by the diagnosis. A clear example of such translation is found in the case of a pseudopatient who had had a close relationship with his mother but was rather remote from his father during his early childhood. During adolescence and beyond, however, his father became a close friend, while his relationship with his mother cooled. His present relationship with his wife was characteristically close and warm.

Apart from occasional angry exchanges, friction was minimal. The children had rarely been spanked. Surely there is nothing especially pathological about such a history. Indeed, many readers may see a similar pattern in their own experiences, with no markedly deleterious consequences. Observe, however, how such a history was translated in the psychopathological context, this from the case summary prepared after the patient was discharged:

This white 39-year-old male... manifests a long history of considerable ambivalence in close relationships, which begins in early childhood. A warm relationship with his mother cools during his adolescence. A distant relationship to his father is described as becoming very intense. Affective stability is absent. His attempts to control emotionality with his wife and children are punctuated by angry outbursts and, in the case of the children, spankings. And while he says that he has several friends, one senses considerable ambivalence embedded in these relationships also....

The facts of the case were unintentionally distorted by the staff to achieve consistency with a popular theory of the dynamics of a schizophrenic reaction. Nothing of an ambivalent nature had been described in relations with parents, spouse, or friends. To the extent that ambivalence could be inferred, it was probably not greater than is found in all human relationships. It is true the pseudopatient's relationships with his parents changed over time, but in the ordinary context that would hardly be remarkable —indeed, it might very well be expected. Clearly, the meaning ascribed to his verbalizations (that is, ambivalence, affective instability) was determined by the diagnosis: schizophrenia. An entirely different meaning would have been ascribed if it were known that the man was normal.

All pseudopatients took extensive notes publicly. Under ordinary circumstances, such behavior would have raised questions in the minds of observers, as, in fact, it did among patients. Indeed, it seemed so certain that the notes would elicit suspicion that elaborate precautions were taken to remove them from the ward each day. But the precautions proved needless. The closest any staff member came to questioning these notes occurred when one pseudopatient asked his physician what kind of medication he was receiving and began to write down the response. "You needn't write it," he was told gently. "If you have trouble remembering, just ask me again."

If no questions were asked of the pseudopatients, how was their writing interpreted? Nursing records for three patients indicate that the writing was seen as an aspect of their pathological behavior. "Patient engages in writing behavior" was the daily nursing comment on one of the pseudopatients who was never questioned about his writing. Given that the patient is in the hospital, he must be psychologically disturbed. And given that he is disturbed, continuous writing must be a behavioral manifestation of that disturbance, perhaps a subset of the compulsive behaviors that are sometimes correlated with schizophrenia.

One tacit characteristic of psychiatric diagnosis is that it locates the sources of aberration within the individual and only rarely within the complex of stimuli that surrounds him. Consequently, behaviors that are stimulated by the environment are commonly misattributed to the patient's disorder. For example, one kindly nurse found a pseudopatient pacing the long hospital corridors. "Nervous, Mr. X?" she asked. "No, bored," he said.

The notes kept by pseudopatients are full of patient behaviors that were misinterpreted by well-intentioned staff. Often enough, a patient would go "berserk" because he had, wittingly or unwittingly, been mistreated by, say, an attendant. A nurse coming upon the scene would rarely inquire even cursorily into the environmental stimuli of the patient's behavior. Rather, she assumed that his upset derived from his pathology, not from his present interactions with other staff members. Occasionally, the staff might assume that the patient's family (especially when they had recently visited) or other patients had stimulated the outburst. But never were the staff found to assume that one of themselves or the structure of the hospital had anything to do with a patient's behavior. One psychiatrist pointed to a group of patients who were sitting outside the cafeteria entrance half an hour before lunchtime. To a group of young residents he indicated that such behavior was characteristic of the oral-acquisitive nature of the syndrome. It seemed not to occur to him that there were very few things to anticipate in a psychiatric hospital besides eating.

A psychiatric label has a life and an influence of its own. Once the impression has been formed that the patient is schizophrenic, the expectation is that he will continue to be schizophrenic. When a sufficient amount of time has passed, during which the patient has done nothing bizarre, he is considered to be in remission and available for discharge. But the label endures beyond discharge, with the unconfirmed expectation that he will behave as a schizophrenic again. Such labels, conferred by mental health professionals, are as influential on the patient as they are on his relatives and friends, and it should not surprise anyone that the diagnosis acts on all of them as a self-fulfilling prophecy. Eventually, the patient himself accepts the diagnosis, with all of its surplus meanings and expectations, and behaves accordingly.

The inferences to be made from these matters are quite simple. Much as Zigler and Phillips have demonstrated that there is enormous overlap in the symptoms presented by patients who have been variously diagnosed, so there is enormous overlap in the behaviors of the sane and the insane. The sane are not "sane" all of the time. We lose our tempers "for no good reason." We are occasionally depressed or anxious, again for no good reason. And we may find it difficult to get along with one or another person—again for no reason that we can specify. Similarly, the insane are not always insane. Indeed, it was the impression of the pseudopatients while living with them that they were sane for long periods of time—that the bizarre behaviors upon which their diagnoses were allegedly predicated constituted only a small fraction of their total behavior. If it makes no sense to label ourselves permanently depressed on the basis of an occasional depression, then it takes better evidence than is presently available to label all patients insane or schizophrenic on the basis of bizarre behaviors or cognitions. It seems more useful, as Mischel has pointed out, to limit our discussions to *behaviors*, the stimuli that provoke them, and their correlates.

It is not known why powerful impressions of personality traits, such as "crazy" or "insane," arise. Conceivably, when the origins of and stimuli that give rise to a behavior are remote or unknown, or when the behavior strikes us as immutable, trait labels regarding the *behaver* arise. When, on the other hand, the origins and stimuli are known and available, discourse is limited to the behavior itself. Thus, I may hallucinate because I am sleeping, or I may hallucinate because I have ingested a peculiar drug. These are termed sleep-induced hallucinations, or dreams, and drug-induced hallucinations, respectively. But when the stimuli to my hallucinations are unknown, that is called craziness, or schizophrenia—as if that inference were somehow as illuminating as the others.

THE EXPERIENCE OF PSYCHIATRIC HOSPITALIZATION

The term "mental illness" is of recent origin. It was coined by people who were humane in their inclinations and who wanted very much to raise the station of (and the public's sympathies toward) the psychologically disturbed from that of witches and "crazies" to one that was akin to the physically ill. And they were at least partially successful, for the treatment of the mental ill *has* improved considerably over the years. But while treatment has improved, it is doubtful that people really regard the mentally ill in the same way that they view the physically ill. A broken leg is something one recovers from, but mental illness allegedly endures forever. A broken leg does not threaten the observer, but a crazy schizophrenic? There is by now a host of evidence that attitudes toward the mentally ill are characterized by fear, hostility, aloofness, suspicion, and dread. The mentally ill are society's lepers.

That such attitudes infect the general population is perhaps not surprising, only upsetting. But that they affect the professionals—attendants, nurses, physicians, psychologists, and social workers —who treat and deal with the mentally ill is more disconcerting, both because such attitudes are self-evidently pernicious and because they are unwitting. Most mental health professionals would insist that they are sympathetic toward the mentally ill, that they are neither avoidant nor hostile. But it is more likely that an exquisite ambivalence characterizes their relations with psychiatric patients, such that their avowed impulses are only part of their entire attitude. Negative attitudes are there too and can easily be detected. Such attitudes should not surprise us. They are the natural offspring of the labels patients wear and the places in which they are found.

Consider the structure of the typical psychiatric hospital. Staff and patients are strictly segregated. Staff have their own living space, including their dining facilities, bathrooms and assembly places. The glassed quarters that contain the professional staff, which the pseudopatients came to call "the cage," sit out on every dayroom. The staff emerge primarily for caretaking purposes—to give medication, to conduct a therapy or group meeting, to instruct or reprimand a patient. Otherwise, staff keep to themselves, almost as if the disorder that afflicts their charges is somehow catching.

So much is patient-staff segregation the rule that, for four public hospitals in which an attempt was made to measure the degree to which staff and patients mingle, it was necessary to use "time out of the staff cage" as the operational measure. While it was not the case that all time spent out of the cage was spent mingling with patients (attendants, for example, would occasionally emerge to watch television in the dayroom), it was the only way in which one could gather reliable data on time for measuring.

The average amount of time spent by attendants outside of the cage was 11.3 percent (range, 3 to 52 percent). This figure does not represent only time spent mingling with patients, but also includes time spent on such chores as folding laundry, supervising patients while they shave, directing ward clean-up, and sending patients to off-ward activities. It was the relatively rare attendant who spent time talking with patients or playing games with them. It proved impossible to obtain a "percent mingling time" for nurses, since the amount of time they spent out of the cage was too brief. Rather, we counted instances of emergence from the cage. On the average, daytime nurses emerged from the cage 11.5 times per shift, including instances when they left the ward entirely (range, 4 to 39 times). Late afternoon and night nurses were even less available, emerging on the average 9.4 times per shift (range, 4 to 41 times). Data on early morning nurses, who arrived usually after midnight and departed at 8 a.m., are not available because patients were asleep during most of this period.

Physicians, especially psychiatrists, were even less available. They were rarely seen on the wards. Quite commonly, they would be seen only when they arrived and departed, with the remaining time being spent in their offices or in the cage. On the average, physicians emerged on the ward 6.7 times per day (range 1 to 17 times). It proved difficult to make an accurate estimate in this regard, since physicians often maintained hours that allowed them to come and go at different times.

The hierarchical organization of the psychiatric hospital has been commented on before, but the latent meaning of that kind of organization is worth noting again. Those with the most power have least to do with patients, and those with the least power are most involved with them. Recall, however, that the acquisition of role-appropriate behaviors occurs mainly through the observation of others, with the most powerful having the most influence. Consequently, it is understandable that attendants not only spend more time with patients than do any other members of the staff—that is required by their station in the hierarchy —but also, insofar as they learn from their superiors' behavior, spend as little time with patients as they can. Attendants are seen mainly in the cage, which is where the models, the action, and the power are.

I turn now to a different set of studies, these dealing with staff response to patient-initiated contact. It has long been known that the amount of time a person spends with you can be an index of your significance to him. If he initiates and maintains eye contact, there is reason to believe that he is considering your requests and needs. If he pauses to chat or actually stops and talks, there is added reason to infer that he is individuating you. In four hospitals, the pseudopatient approached the staff member with a request which took the following form: "Pardon me, Mr. [or Dr. or Mrs.] X, could you tell me when I will be eligible for grounds privileges?" (or "... when I will be presented at the staff meeting?" or "... when I am likely to be discharged?"). While the content of the question varied according to the appropriateness of the target and the pseudopatient's (apparent) current needs, the form was always a courteous and relevant request for information. Care was taken never to approach a particular member of the staff more than once a day, lest the staff member become suspicious or irritated. In examining these data, remember that the behavior of the pseudopatients was neither bizarre nor disruptive. One could indeed engage in good conversation with them.

The data for these experiments are shown in Table 1, separately for physicians (column 1) and for nurses and attendants (column 2). Minor differences between these four institutions were overwhelmed by the degree to which staff avoided continuing contacts that patients had initiated. By far, their most common response consisted of either a brief response to the question offered while they were "on the move" and with head averted, or no response at all.

The encounter frequently took the following bizarre form: (pseudopatient) "Pardon me, Dr. X. Could you tell me when I am eligible for grounds privileges?" (physician) "Good morning Dave. How are you today?" (moves off without waiting for a response).

It is instructive to compare these data with data recently obtained at Stanford University. It has been alleged that large and eminent universities are characterized by faculty who are so busy that they have no time for students. For this comparison, a young lady approached individual faculty members who seemed to be walking purposefully to some meeting or teaching engagement and asked them the following questions.

1. "Pardon me, could you direct me to Encina Hall?" (at the medical school: "... to the Clinical Research Center?").

Table 1

Self-Initiated Contact by Pseudopatients With Psychiatrists and Nurses and Attendants, Compared With Other Groups

Contact	Psychiatric hospitals		University campus (nonmedical)	University medical center Physicians		
	(1) Psychiatrists	(2) Nurses and attendants	(3) Faculty	(4) "Looking for a psychiatrist"	(5) "Looking for an internist"	(6) No additional comment
Responses						
Moves on, head averted (%)	71	88	0	0	0	0
Makes eye contact (%)	23	10	0	11	0	0
Pauses and chats (%)	2	2	0	11	0	0
Stops and talks (%)	4	0.5	100	78	100	90
Mean number of questions answered (out of 6)	*	*	6	3.8	4.8	4.5
Respondents (No.)	13	47	14	18	15	10
Attempts (No.)	185	1283	14	18	15	10

*Not applicable

2. "Do you know where Fish Annex is?" (there is no Fish Annex at Stanford).
3. "Do you teach here?"
4. "How does one apply for admission to the college?" (at the medical school: "... to the medical school?").
5. "Is it difficult to get in?"
6. "Is there financial aid?"

Without exception, as can be seen in Table 1 (column 3), all of the questions were answered. No matter how rushed they were, all respondents not only maintained eye contact, but stopped to talk. Indeed, many of the respondents went out of their way to direct or take the questioner to the office she was seeking, to try to locate "Fish Annex," or to

discuss with her the possibilities of being admitted to the university.

Similar data, also shown in Table 1 (columns 4, 5, and 6), were obtained in the hospital. Here too, the young lady came prepared with six questions. After the first question, however, she remarked to 18 of her respondents (column 4), "I'm looking for a psychiatrist," and to 15 others (column 5), "I'm looking for an internist." Ten other respondents received no inserted comment (column 6). The general degree of cooperative responses is considerably higher for these university groups than it was for pseudopatients in psychiatric hospitals. Even so, differences are apparent with the medical school setting. Once having indicated that she was looking for a psychiatrist, the degree of cooperation elicited was less than when she sought an internist.

POWERLESSNESS AND DEPERSONALIZATION

Eye contact and verbal contact reflect concern and individuation: their absence, avoidance and depersonalization. The data I have presented do not do justice to the rich daily encounters that grew up around matters of depersonalization and avoidance. I have records of patients who were beaten by staff for the sin of initiating verbal contact. During my own experience, for example, one patient was beaten in the presence of other patients for having approached an attendant and told him, "I like you." Occasionally, punishment meted out to patients for misdemeanors seemed so excessive that it could not be justified by the most radical interpretations of psychiatric canon. Nevertheless, they appeared to go unquestioned. Tempers were often short. A patient who had not heard a call for medication would be roundly excoriated, and the morning attendants would often wake patients with, "Come on, you m—— f——s, out of bed!"

Neither anecdotal nor "hard" data can convey the overwhelming sense of powerlessness which invades the individual as he is continually exposed to the depersonalization of the psychiatric hospital. It hardly matters *which* psychiatric hospital —the excellent public ones and the very plush private hospital were better than the rural and shabby ones in this regard, but again, the features that psychiatric hospitals had in common overwhelmed by far their apparent differences.

Powerlessness was evident everywhere. The patient is deprived of many of his legal rights by dint of his psychiatric commitment. He is shorn of credibility by virtue of his psychiatric label. His freedom of movement is restricted. He cannot initiate contact with the staff, but may only respond to such overtures as they make. Personal privacy is minimal. Patient quarters and possessions can be entered and examined by any staff member, for whatever reason. His personal history and anguish are available to any staff member (often including the "grey lady" and "candy striper" volunteer) who chooses to read his folder, regardless of their therapeutic relationship to him. His personal hygiene and waste evacuation are often monitored. The water closets may have no doors.

At times, the depersonalization reached such proportions that pseudopatients had the sense that they were invisible, or at least unworthy of account. Upon being admitted, I and other pseudopatients took the initial physical examination in a semipublic room, where staff members went about their own business as if we were not there.

On the ward, attendants delivered verbal and occasionally serious physical abuse to patients in the presence of other observing patients, some of whom (the pseudopatients) were writing it all down. Abusive behavior, on the other hand, terminated quite abruptly when other staff members were known to be coming. Staff are credible witnesses. Patients are not.

A nurse unbuttoned her uniform to adjust her brassiere in the presence of an entire ward of viewing men. One did not have the sense that she was being seductive. Rather, she didn't notice us. A group of staff persons might point to a patient in the dayroom and discuss him animatedly, as if he were not there.

One illuminating instance of depersonalization and invisibility occurred with regard to medications. All told, the pseudopatients were administered nearly 2100 pills, including Elavil, Stelazine, Compazine, and Thorazine, to name but a few. (That such a variety of medications should have been administered to patients presenting identical symptoms is itself worthy of note.) Only two were swallowed. The rest were either pocketed or deposited in the toilet. The pseudopatients were not alone in this. Although I have no precise records on how many patients rejected their medications, the pseudopatients frequently found the medications of other patients in the toilet before they deposited their own. As long as they were cooperative, their behavior and the pseudopatients' own in this matter, as in other important matters, went unnoticed throughout.

Reactions to such depersonalization among pseudopatients were intense. Although they had come to the hospital as participant observers and were fully aware that they did not "belong," they nevertheless found themselves caught up in and fighting the process of depersonalization. Some examples: a graduate student in psychology asked his wife to bring his textbooks to the hospital so he could "catch up on his homework"—this despite the elaborate precautions taken to conceal his professional association. The same student, who had trained for quite some time to get into the hospital, and who had looked forward to the experience, "remembered" some drag races that he had wanted to see on the weekend and insisted that he be discharged by that time. Another pseudopatient attempted

a romance with a nurse. Subsequently, he informed the staff that he was applying for admission to graduate school in psychology and was very likely to be admitted, since a graduate professor was one of his regular hospital visitors. The same person began to engage in psychotherapy with other patients—all of this as a way of becoming a person in an impersonal environment.

THE SOURCES OF DEPERSONALIZATION

What are the origins of depersonalization? I have already mentioned two. First, are attitudes held by all of us toward the mentally ill—including those who treat them—attitudes characterized by fear, distrust, and horrible expectations on the other. Our ambivalence leads us, in this instance as in others, to avoidance.

Second, and not entirely separate, the hierarchical structure of the psychiatric hospital facilitates depersonalization. Those who are at the top have least to do with patients, and their behavior inspires the rest of the staff. Average daily contact with psychiatrists, psychologists, residents, and physicians combined ranged from 3.9 to 25.1 minutes, with an overall mean of 6.8 (six pseudopatients over a total of 129 days of hospitalization). Included in this average are time spent in the admissions interview, ward meetings in the presence of a senior staff member, group and individual psychotherapy contacts, case presentation conferences, and discharge meetings. Clearly, patients do not spend much time in interpersonal contact with doctoral staff. And doctoral staff serve as models for nurses and attendants.

There are probably other sources. Psychiatric installations are presently in serious financial straits. Staff shortages are pervasive, staff time at a premium. Something has to give, and that something is patient contact. Yet, while financial stresses are realities, too much can be made of them. I have the impression that the psychological forces that result in depersonalization are much stronger than the fiscal ones and that the addition of more staff would not correspondingly improve patient care in this regard. The incidence of staff meetings and the enormous amount of record-keeping on patients, for example, have not been as substantially reduced as has patient contact. Priorities exist, even during hard times. Patient contact is not a significant priority in the traditional psychiatric hospital, and fiscal pressures do not account for this. Avoidance and depersonalization may.

Heavy reliance upon psychotropic medication tacitly contributes to depersonalization by convincing staff that treatment is indeed being conducted and that further patient contact may not be necessary. Even here, however, caution needs to be exercised in understanding the role of psychotropic drugs. If patients were powerful rather than powerless, if they were viewed as interesting individuals rather than diagnostic entities, if they were socially significant rather than social lepers, if their anguish truly and wholly compelled our sympathies and concerns, would we not *seek* contact with them, despite the availability of medications? Perhaps for the pleasure of it all?

THE CONSEQUENCES OF LABELING AND DEPERSONALIZATION

Whenever the ratio of what is known to what needs to be known approaches zero, we tend to invent "knowledge" and assume that we understand more than we actually do. We seem unable to acknowledge that we simply don't know. The needs for diagnosis and remediation of behavioral and emotional problems are enormous. But rather than acknowledge that we are just embarking on understanding, we continue to label patients "schizophrenic," "manic-depressive," and "insane," as if in those words we had captured the essence of understanding. The facts of the matter are that we have known for a long time that diagnoses are often not useful or reliable, but we have nevertheless continued to use them. We now know that we cannot distinguish insanity from sanity. It is depressing to consider how that information will be used.

Not merely depressing, but frightening. How many people, one wonders, are sane but not recognized as such in our psychiatric institutions? How many have been needlessly stripped of their privileges of citizenship, from the right to vote and drive to that of handling their own accounts? How many have feigned insanity in order to avoid the criminal consequences of their behavior, and, conversely, how many would rather stand trial than live interminably in a psychiatric hospital—but are wrongly thought to be mentally ill? How many have been stigmatized by well-intentioned, but nevertheless erroneous, diagnoses? On the last point, recall again that a "type 2 error" in psychiatric diagnosis does not have the same consequences it does in medical diagnosis. A diagnosis of cancer that has been found to be in error is cause for celebration. But psychiatric diagnoses are rarely found to be in error. The label sticks, a mark of inadequacy forever.

Finally, how many patients might be "sane" outside the psychiatric hospital but seem insane in it—not because craziness resides in them, as it were, but because they are responding to a bizarre setting, one that may be unique to institutions which harbor nether people? Goffman calls the process of socialization to such institutions "mortification"—an apt metaphor that includes the processes of depersonalization that have been described here. And while it is impossible to know whether the pseudopatients' responses to these processes are characteristic of all inmates—they were after all, not real patients—it is difficult to believe that these processes of socialization to a psychiatric hospital provide useful attitudes or habits of response for living in the "real world."

SUMMARY AND CONCLUSIONS

It is clear that we cannot distinguish the sane from the insane in psychiatric hospitals. The hospital itself imposes a special environment in which the meanings of behavior can easily be misunderstood. The consequences to patients hospitalized in such an environment—the powerlessness, depersonalization, segregation, mortification, and self-labeling—seem undoubtedly countertherapeutic.

I do not, even now, understand this problem well enough to perceive solutions. But two matters seem to have some promise. The first concerns the proliferation of community mental health facilities, of crisis intervention centers, of the human potential movement, and of behavior therapies that, for all of their own problems, tend to avoid psychiatric labels, to focus on specific problems and behaviors, and to retain the individual in a relatively nonpejorative environment.

Clearly, to the extent that we refrain from sending the distressed to insane places, our impressions of them are less likely to be distorted. (The risk of distorted perceptions, it seems to me, is always present, since we are much more sensitive to an individual's behaviors and verbalizations than we are to the subtle contextual stimuli that often promote them. At issue here is a matter of magnitude. And, as I have shown, the magnitude of distortion is exceedingly high in the extreme context that is a psychiatric hospital).

The second matter that might prove promising speaks to the need to increase the sensitivity of mental health workers and researchers to the *Catch-22* position of psychiatric patients. Simply reading materials in this area will be of help to some such workers and researchers. For others, directly experiencing the impact of psychiatric hospitalization will be of enormous use. Clearly, further research into the social psychology of such total institutions will both facilitate treatment and deepen understanding.

I and the other pseudopatients in the psychiatric setting had distinctly negative reactions. We do not pretend to describe the subjective experiences of true patients. Theirs may be different from ours, particularly with the passage of time and the necessary process of adaptation to one's environment. But we can and do speak to the relatively more objective indices of treatment within the hospital. It could be a mistake, and a very unfortunate one, to consider that what happened to us derived from malice or stupidity on the part of the staff. Quite the contrary, our overwhelming impression of them was of people who really cared, who were committed and who were uncommonly intelligent. Where they failed, as they sometimes did painfully, it would be more accurate to attribute those failures to the environment in which they too, found themselves than to personal callousness. Their perceptions and behavior were controlled by the situation, rather than being motivated by a malicious disposition. In a more benign environment, one that was less attached to global diagnosis, their behaviors and judgments might have been more benign and effective.

NO

Robert L. Spitzer

ON PSEUDOSCIENCE IN SCIENCE, LOGIC IN REMISSION AND PSYCHIATRIC DIAGNOSIS

Some foods taste delicious but leave a bad aftertaste. So it is with Rosenhan's study, "On Being Sane in Insane Places" (Rosenhan, 1973a), which, by virtue of the prestige and wide distribution of *Science*, the journal in which it appeared, provoked a furor in the scientific community. That the *Journal of Abnormal Psychology*, at this late date, chooses to explore the study's strengths and weaknesses is a testament not only to the importance of the issues that the study purports to deal with but to the impact that the study has had in the mental health community.

Rosenhan apparently believes that psychiatric diagnosis is of no value. There is nothing wrong with his designing a study the results of which might dramatically support this view. However, "On Being Sane in Insane Places" is pseudoscience presented as science. Just as his pseudopatients were diagnosed at discharge as "schizophrenia, in remission," so a careful examination of this study's methods, results, and conclusions leads me to a diagnosis of "logic, in remission."

Let us summarize the study's central question, the methods used, the results reported, and Rosenhan's conclusions. Rosenhan (1973a) states the basic issue simply: "Do the salient characteristics that lead to diagnoses reside in the patients themselves or in the environments and contexts in which observers find them?" Rosenhan proposed that by getting normal people who had never had symptoms of serious psychiatric disorders admitted to psychiatric hospitals "and then determining whether they were discovered to be sane" was an adequate method of studying this question. Therefore, eight "sane" people, pseudopatients, gained secret admission to 12 different hospitals with a single complaint of hearing voices. Upon admission to the psychiatric ward, the pseudopatients ceased simulating any symptoms of abnormality.

The diagnostic results were that 11 of the 12 diagnoses on admission were schizophrenia and 1 was manic-depressive psychosis. At discharge, all of the patients were given the same diagnosis, but were qualified as "in remission."[1]

From Robert L. Spitzer, "On Pseudoscience in Science, Logic in Remission and Psychiatric Diagnosis: A Critique of 'On Being Sane in Insane Places,'" *Journal of Abnormal Psychology*, vol. 84 (1975). Copyright © 1975 by The American Psychological Association. Reprinted by permission.

Despite their "show of sanity" the pseudopatients were never detected by any of the professional staff, nor were any questions raised about their authenticity during the entire hospitalization.

Rosenhan (1973a) concluded: "It is clear that we cannot distinguish the sane from the insane in psychiatric hospitals" (p. 257). According to him, what is needed is the avoidance of "global diagnosis," as exemplified by such diagnoses as schizophrenia or manic-depressive psychosis, and attention should be directed instead to "behaviors, the stimuli that provoke them, and their correlates."

THE CENTRAL QUESTION

One hardly knows where to begin. Let us first acknowledge the potential importance of the study's central research question. Surely, if psychiatric diagnoses are, to quote Rosenhan, "only in the minds of the observers," and do not reflect any characteristics inherent in the patient, then they obviously can be of no use in helping patients. However, the study immediately becomes confused when Rosenhan suggests that this research question can be answered by studying whether or not the "sanity" of pseudopatients in a mental hospital can be discovered. Rosenhan, a professor of law and psychology, knows that the terms "sane" and "insane" are legal, not psychiatric, concepts. He knows that no psychiatrist makes a diagnosis of "sanity" or "insanity" and that the true meaning of these terms, which varies from state to state, involves the inability to appreciate right from wrong—an issue that is totally irrelevant to this study.

DETECTING THE SANITY OF A PSEUDOPATIENT

However, if we are forced to use the terms "insane" (to mean roughly showing signs of serious mental disturbance) and "sane" (the absence of such signs), then clearly there are three possible meanings to the concept of "detecting the sanity" of a pseudopatient who feigns mental illness on entry to a hospital, but then acts "normal" throughout his hospital stay. The first is the recognition, when he is first seen, that the pseudopatient is feigning insanity as he attempts to gain admission to the hospital. This would be detecting sanity in a sane person simulating insanity. The second would be the recognition, after having observed him acting normally during his hospitalization, that the pseudopatient was initially feigning insanity. This would be detecting that the currently sane never was insane. Finally, the third possible meaning would be the recognition, during hospitalization, that the pseudopatient, though initially appearing to be "insane," was no longer showing signs of psychiatric disturbance.

These elementary distinctions of "detecting sanity in the insane" are crucial to properly interpreting the results of the study. The reader is misled by Rosenhan's implication that the first two meanings of detecting the sanity of the pseudopatient to be a fraud, are at all relevant to the central research question. Furthermore, he obscures the true results of his study—because they fail to support his conclusion—when the third meaning of detecting sanity is considered, that is, a recognition that after their admission as "insane," the pseudopatients were not psychiatrically disturbed while in the hospital.

Let us examine these three possible meanings of detecting the sanity of the pseudopatient, their logical relation to the central question of the study, and the actual results obtained and the validity of Rosenhan's conclusions.

THE PATIENT IS NO LONGER "INSANE"

We begin with the third meaning of detecting sanity. It is obvious that if the psychiatrists judged the pseudopatients as seriously disturbed while they acted "normal" in the hospital, this would be strong evidence that their assessments were being influenced by the context in which they were making their examination rather than the actual behavior of the patient, which is the central research question. (I suspect that many readers will agree with Hunter who, in a letter to *Science* (Hunter, 1973), pointed out that, "The pseudopatients did *not* behave normally in the hospital. Had their behavior been normal, they would have walked to the nurses' station and said, 'Look, I am a normal person who tried to see if I could get into the hospital by behaving in a crazy way or saying crazy things. It worked and I was admitted to the hospital, but now I would like to be discharged from the hospital'" [p. 361].)

What were the results? According to Rosenhan, all the patients were diagnosed at discharge as "in remission."[2] The meaning of "in remission" is clear: It means without signs of illness. Thus, all of the psychiatrists apparently recognized that all of the pseudopatients were, to use Rosenhan's term, "sane." However, lest the reader appreciate the significance of these findings, Rosenhan (1973a) quickly gives a completely incorrect interpretation: "If the pseudopatient was

to be discharged, he must naturally be 'in remission'; but he was not sane, nor, in the institution's view, had he ever been sane" (p. 252). Rosenhan's implication is clear: The patient was diagnosed "in remission" not because the psychiatrist correctly assessed the patient's hospital behavior but only because the patient had to be discharged. Is this interpretation warranted?

I am sure that most readers who are not familiar with the details of psychiatric diagnostic practice assume, from Rosenhan's account, that it is common for schizophrenic patients to be diagnosed "in remission" when discharged from a hospital. As a matter of fact, it is extremely unusual. The reason is that a schizophrenic is rarely completely asymptomatic at discharge. Rosenhan does not report any data concerning the discharge diagnoses of the real schizophrenic patients in the 12 hospitals used in his study. However, I can report on the frequency of a discharge diagnosis of schizophrenia "in remission" at my hospital, the New York State Psychiatric Institute, a research, teaching, and community hospital where diagnoses are made in a routine fashion, undoubtedly no different from the 12 hospitals of Rosenhan's study. I examined the official book that the record room uses to record the discharge diagnoses and their statistical codes for all patients. Of the over 300 patients discharged in the last year with a diagnosis of schizophrenia, not one was diagnosed "in remission." It is only possible to code a diagnosis of "in remission" by adding a fifth digit (5) to the 4-digit code number for the subtype of schizophrenia (e.g., paranoid schizophrenia is coded as 295.3, but paranoid schizophrenia "in remission" is coded as 295.35). I therefore realized that a psychiatrist might intend to make a discharge diagnosis of "in remission" but fail to use the fifth digit, so that the official recording of the diagnosis would not reflect his full assessment. I therefore had research assistants read the discharge summaries of the last 100 patients whose discharge diagnosis was schizophrenia to see how often the term "in remission," "recovered," "no longer ill," or "asymptomatic" was used, even if not recorded by use of the fifth digit in the code number. The result was that only one patient, who was diagnosed paranoid schizophrenia, was described in the summary as being "in remission" at discharge. The fifth digit code was not used.

To substantiate my view that the practice at my hospital of rarely giving a discharge diagnosis of schizophrenia "in remission" is not unique, I had a research assistant call the record room librarians of 12 psychiatric hospitals, chosen catch as catch can.[3] They were told that we were interested in knowing their estimate of how often, at their hospital, schizophrenics were discharged "in remission" (or "no longer ill" or "asymptomatic"). The calls revealed that 11 of the 12 hospitals indicated that the term was either never used or, at most, used for only a handful of patients in a year. The remaining hospital, a private hospital, estimated that the terms were used in roughly 7 percent of the discharge diagnoses.

This leaves us with the conclusion that, because 11 of the 12 pseudopatients were discharged as "schizophrenia in remission," a discharge diagnosis that is rarely given to real schizophrenics, the diagnoses given to the pseudopatients were a function of the patients' behaviors and not of the setting (psychiatric hospital) in which the diagnoses were made. In

fact, we must marvel that 11 psychiatrists all acted so rationally as to use at discharge the category of "in remission" or its equivalent, a category that is rarely used with real schizophrenic patients.

It is not only in his discharge diagnosis that the psychiatrist had an opportunity to assess the patient's true condition incorrectly. In the admission mental status examination, during a progress note or in his discharge note the psychiatrist could have described any of the pseudopatients as "still psychotic," "probably still hallucinating but denies it now," "loose associations," or "inappropriate affect." Because Rosenhan had access to all of this material, his failure to report such judgments of continuing serious psychopathology strongly suggests that they were never made.

All pseudopatients took extensive notes publicly to obtain data on staff and patient behavior. Rosenhan claims that the nursing records indicate that "the writing was seen as an aspect of their pathological behavior." The only datum presented to support this claim is that the daily nursing comment on one of the pseudopatients was, "Patient engaged in writing behavior." Because nursing notes frequently and intentionally comment on nonpathological activities that patients engage in so that other staff members have some knowledge of how the patient spends his time, this particular nursing note in no way supports Rosenhan's thesis. Once again, the failure of Rosenhan to provide data regarding instances where normal hospital behavior was categorized as pathological is remarkable. The closest that Rosenhan comes to providing such data is his report of an instance where a kindly nurse asked if a pseudopatient, who was pacing the long hospital corridors because of boredom, was "nervous." It was, after all, a question and not a final judgment.

Let us now examine the relation between the other two meanings of detecting sanity in the pseudopatients: the recognition that the pseudopatient was a fraud, either when he sought admission to the hospital or during this hospital stay, and the central research question.

DETECTING "SANITY" BEFORE ADMISSION

Whether or not psychiatrists are able to detect individuals who feign psychiatric symptoms is an interesting question but clearly of no relevance to the issue of whether or not the salient characteristics that lead to diagnoses reside in the patient's behavior or in the minds of the observers. After all, a psychiatrist who believes in a pseudopatient who feigns a symptom *is* responding to the pseudopatient's behavior. And Rosenhan does not blame the psychiatrist for believing the pseudopatient's fake symptom of hallucinations. He blames him for the diagnosis of schizophrenia. Rosenhan (1973b) states:

> The issue is not that the psychiatrist believed him. Neither is it whether the pseudopatient should have been admitted to the psychiatric hospital in the first place.... The issue is the diagnostic leap that was made between the single presenting symptom, hallucinations, and the diagnosis schizophrenia (or in one case, manic-depressive psychosis). Had the pseudopatients been diagnosed "hallucinating," there would have been no further need to examine the diagnosis issue. The diagnosis of hallucinations implies only that: no more. The presence of hallucinations does not itself define

the presence of "schizophrenia." And schizophrenia may or may not include hallucinations. (p. 366)

Unfortunately, as judged by many of the letters to *Science* commenting on the study (Letters to the editor, 1973), many readers, including psychiatrists, accepted Rosenhan's thesis that it was irrational for the psychiatrists to have made an initial diagnosis of schizophrenia as *the most likely condition* on the basis of a single symptom. In my judgment, these readers were wrong. Their acceptance of Rosenhan's thesis was aided by the content of the pseudopatients' auditory hallucinations, which were voices that said "empty," "hollow," and "thud." According to Rosenhan (1973a), these symptoms were chosen because of "their apparent similarity to existential symptoms [and] the *absence* of a single report of existential psychoses in the literature" (p. 251). The implication is that if the content of specific symptoms has never been reported in the literature, then a psychiatrist should somehow know that the symptom is fake. Why then, according to Rosenhan, should the psychiatrist have made a diagnosis of hallucinating? This is absurd. Recently I saw a patient who kept hearing a voice that said, "It's O.K. It's O.K." I know of no such report in the literature. So what? I agree with Rosenhan that there has never been a report of an "existential psychosis." However, the diagnoses made were schizophrenia and manic-depressive psychosis, not existential psychosis.

DIFFERENTIAL DIAGNOSIS OF AUDITORY HALLUCINATIONS

Rosenhan is entitled to believe that psychiatric diagnoses are of no use and therefore should not have been given to the pseudopatients. However, it makes no sense for him to claim that within a diagnostic framework it was irrational to consider schizophrenia seriously as the most likely condition without his presenting a consideration of the differential diagnosis. Let me briefly give what I think is a reasonable differential diagnosis, based on the presenting picture of the pseudopatient when he applied for admission to the hospital.

Rosenhan says that "beyond alleging the symptoms and falsifying name, vocation, and employment, no further alterations of person, history, or circumstances were made" (p. 251). However, clearly the clinical picture includes not only the symptom (auditory hallucinations) but also the desire to enter a psychiatric hospital, from which it is reasonable to conclude that the symptom is a source of significant distress. (How often did the admitting psychiatrist suggest what would seem to be reasonable care: outpatient treatment? Did the pseudopatient have to add other complaints to justify inpatient treatment?) This, plus the knowledge that the auditory hallucinations are of 3 weeks duration,[4] establishes the hallucinations as significant symptoms of psychopathology as distinguished from so-called "pseudohallucinations" (hallucinations while falling asleep or awakening from sleep, or intense imagination with the voice heard from inside of the head).

Auditory hallucinations can occur in several kinds of mental disorders. The absence of a history of alcohol, drug abuse, or some other toxin, the absence of any signs of physical illness (such as high fever), and the absence of evidence of distractibility, impairment in concentration, memory or orientation, and a negative neurological examination all make an organic psychosis extremely unlikely. The absence of a recent precipitating stress rules out a transient situational disturbance of psychotic intensity or (to use a nonofficial category) hysterical psychosis. The absence of a profound disturbance in mood rules out an effective psychosis (we are not given the mental status findings for the patient who was diagnosed manic-depressive psychosis).

What about simulating mental illness? Psychiatrists know that occasionally an individual who has something to gain from being admitted to a psychiatric hospital will exaggerate or even feign psychiatric symptoms. This is a genuine diagnostic problem that psychiatrists and other physicians occasionally confront and is called "malingering." However, with the pseudopatients there was no reason to believe that any of them had anything to gain from being admitted into a psychiatric hospital except relief from their alleged complaint, and therefore no reason to suspect that the illness was feigned. Dear Reader: There is only one remaining diagnosis for the presenting symptom of hallucinations under these conditions in the classification of mental disorders used in this country, and that is schizophrenia.

Admittedly, there is a hitch to a definitive diagnosis of schizophrenia: Almost invariably there are other signs of the disorder present, such as poor premorbid adjustment, affective blunting, delusions, or signs of thought disorder. I would hope that if I had been one of the 12 psychiatrists presented with such a patient, I would have been struck by the lack of other signs of the disorder, but I am rather sure that having no reason to doubt the authenticity of the patients' claim of auditory hallucinations, I also would have been fooled into noting schizophrenia as the most likely diagnosis.

What does Rosenhan really mean when he objects to the diagnosis of schizophrenia because it was based on a "single symptom"? Does he believe that there are real patients with the single symptom of auditory hallucinations who are misdiagnosed as schizophrenic when they actually have some other condition? If so, what is the nature of that condition? Is Rosenhan's point that the psychiatrist should have used "diagnosis deferred," a category that is available but rarely used? I would have no argument with this conclusion. Furthermore, if he had presented data from real patients indicating how often patients are erroneously diagnosed on the basis of inadequate information and what the consequences were, it would have been a real contribution.

Until now, I have assumed that the pseudopatients presented only one symptom of psychiatric disorder. Actually, we know very little about how the pseudopatients presented themselves. What did the pseudopatients say in the study reported in *Science*, when asked as they must have been, what effect the hallucinations were having on their lives and why they were seeking admission into a hospital? The reader would be much more confident that a single presenting symptom was involved if Rosenhan had made available for each pseudopatient the actual admission work-up from the hospital record.

DETECTING SANITY AFTER ADMISSION

Let us now examine the last meaning of detecting sanity in the pseudopatients, namely, the psychiatrist's recognition, *after* observing him act normally during

his hospitalization, that the pseudopatient was initially feigning insanity and its relation to the central research question. If a diagnostic condition, by definition, is always chronic and never remits, it would be irrational not to question the original diagnosis if a patient were later found to be asymptomatic. As applied to this study, if the concept of schizophrenia did not admit the possibility of recovery, then failure to question the original diagnosis when the pseudopatients were no longer overtly ill would be relevant to the central research question. It would be an example of the psychiatrist allowing the context of the hospital environment to influence his diagnostic behavior. But neither any psychiatric textbook nor the American Psychiatric Association's *Diagnostic and Statistical Manual of Mental Disorders* (American Psychiatric Association, 1968) suggests that mental illnesses endure forever. Oddly enough, it is Rosenhan (1973a) who, without any reference to the psychiatric literature, says: "A broken leg is something one recovers from, but mental illness allegedly endures forever" (p. 254). Who, other than Rosenhan, alleges it?

As Rosenhan should know, although some American psychiatrists restrict the label of schizophrenia to mean chronic or process schizophrenia, most American psychiatrists include an acute subtype. Thus, the *Diagnostic and Statistical Manual*, in describing the subtype, acute schizophrenic episode, states that "in many cases the patient recovers within weeks."

A similar straw man is created when Rosenhan (1973a) says,

> The insane are not always insane...
> the bizarre behaviors upon which their
> (the pseudopatients) behaviors were

allegedly predicated constituted only a small fraction of their total behavior. If it makes no sense to label ourselves permanently depressed on the basis of an occasional depression, then it takes better evidence than is presently available to label all patients insane or schizophrenic on the basis of behaviors or cognitions. (p. 254)

Who ever said that the behaviors that indicate schizophrenia or any other diagnostic category comprise the total of a patient's behavior? A diagnosis of schizophrenia does not mean that all of the patient's behavior is schizophrenic anymore than a diagnosis of carcinoma of the liver means that all of the patient's body is diseased.

Does Rosenhan at least score a point by demonstrating that, although the professional staff never considered the possibility that the pseudopatient was a fraud, this possibility was often considered by other patients? Perhaps, but I am not so sure. Let us not forget that all of the pseudopatients "took extensive notes publicly." Obviously this was highly unusual patient behavior and Rosenhan's quote from a suspicious patient suggests the importance it had in focusing the other patients' attention on the pseudopatients: "You're not crazy. You're a journalist or a professor (referring to the continual note-taking). You're checking up on the hospital." (Rosenhan, 1973a, p. 252)

Rosenhan presents ample evidence, which I find no reason to dispute, that the professional staff spent little time actually with the pseudopatients. The note-taking may easily have been overlooked, and therefore they developed no suspicion that the pseudopatients had simulated illness to gain entry into the hospital. Because there were no pseudopatients who did not engage in such unusual behaviors, the reader cannot assess the significance of the patients' suspicions of fraud when the professional staff did not. I would predict, however, that a pseudopatient in a ward of patients with mixed diagnostic conditions would have no difficulty in masquerading convincingly as a true patient to both staff and patients if he did nothing unusual to draw attention to himself.

Rosenhan presents one way in which the diagnosis affected the psychiatrist's perception of the patient's circumstances: Historical facts of the case were often distorted by the staff to achieve consistency with psychodynamic theories. Here, for the first time, I believe Rosenhan has hit the mark. What he described happens all the time and often makes attendance at clinical case conferences extremely painful, especially for those with a logical mind and a research orientation. Although his observation is correct, it would seem to be more a consequence of individuals attempting to rearrange facts to comply with an unproven etiological theory than a consequence of diagnostic labeling. One could as easily imagine a similar process occurring when a weak-minded, behaviorally-oriented clinician attempts to rewrite the patient's history to account for "hallucinations reinforced by attention paid to patient by family members when patient complains of hearing voices." Such is the human condition.

One final finding requires comment. In order to determine whether "the tendency toward diagnosing the sane insane could be reversed," the staff of a research and teaching hospital was informed that at some time during the following three months, one or more pseudopatients would attempt to be admitted. No such attempt was actually made. Yet approximately 10 percent of the 193 real patients were suspected by two or more staff members (we are not told how many made judgments) to be pseudopatients. Rosenhan (1973a) concluded: "Any diagnostic process that lends itself so readily to massive errors of this sort cannot be a very reliable one" (p. 179). My conclusion is that this experimental design practically assures only one outcome.

ELEMENTARY PRINCIPLES OF RELIABILITY OF CLASSIFICATION

Some very important principles that are relevant to the design of Rosenhan's study are taught in elementary psychology courses and should not be forgotten. One of them is that a measurement or classification procedure is not reliable or unreliable in itself but only in its application to a specific population. There are serious problems in the reliability of psychiatric diagnosis as it is applied to the population to which psychiatric diagnoses are ordinarily given. However, I fail to see, and Rosenhan does not even attempt to show, how the reliability of psychiatric diagnoses applied to a population of pseudopatients (or one including the threat of pseudopatients). The two populations are just not the same. Kety (1974) has expressed it dramatically:

> If I were to drink a quart of blood and, concealing what I had done, come to the emergency room of any hospital vomiting blood, the behavior of the staff would be quite predictable. If they labeled and treated me as having a bleeding peptic ulcer, I doubt that I could argue convincingly that medical science does not know how to diagnose that condition. (p. 959)

(I have no doubt that if the condition known as pseudopatient ever assumed epidemic proportions among admittants to psychiatric hospitals, psychiatrists would in time become adept at identifying them, though at what risk to real patients, I do not know.)

ATTITUDES TOWARD THE INSANE

I shall not dwell on the latter part of Rosenhan's study, which deals with the experience of psychiatric hospitalization. Because some of the hospitals participated in residency training programs and were research oriented, I find it hard to believe that conditions were quite as bad as depicted, but they may well be. I have always believed that psychiatrists should spend more time on psychiatric wards to appreciate how mind dulling the experience must be for patients. However, Rosenhan does not stop at documenting the horrors of life on a psychiatric ward. He asserts, without a shred of evidence from his study, that "negative attitudes [toward psychiatric patients] are the natural offspring of the labels patients wear and the places in which they are found." This is nonsense. In recent years large numbers of chronic psychiatric patients, many of them chronic schizophrenics and geriatric patients with organic brain syndromes, have been discharged from state hospitals and placed in communities that have no facilities to deal with them. The affected communities are up in arms not primarily because they are mental patients labeled with psychiatric diagnoses (because the majority are not recognized as ex-patients) but because the behavior of some of them is sometimes incomprehensible, deviant, strange, and annoying.

There are at least two psychiatric diagnoses that are defined by the presence of single behaviors, much as Rosenhan would prefer a diagnosis of hallucinations to a diagnosis of schizophrenia. They are alcoholism and drug abuse. Does society have negative attitudes toward these individuals because of the diagnostic label attached to them by psychiatrists or because of their behavior?

THE USES OF DIAGNOSIS

Rosenhan believes that the pseudopatients should have been diagnosed as having hallucinations of unknown origin. It is not clear what he thinks the diagnosis should have been if the pseudopatients had been sufficiently trained to talk, at times, incoherently, and had complained of difficulty in thinking clearly, lack of emotion, and that their thoughts were being broadcast so that strangers knew what they were thinking. Is Rosenhan perhaps suggesting multiple diagnoses of (a) hallucinations, (b) difficulty thinking clearly, (c) lack of emotion, and (d) incoherent speech... all of unknown origin?

It is no secret that we lack a full understanding of such conditions as schizophrenia and manic-depressive illness, but are we quite as ignorant as Rosenhan would have us believe? Do we not know, for example, that hallucinations of voices accusing the patient of sin are associated with depressed affect, diurnal mood variation, loss of appetite, and insomnia? What about hallucinations of God's voice issuing commandments, associated with euphoric affect, psychomotor excitement, and accelerated and disconnected speech? Is this not also an entirely different condition?

There is a purpose to psychiatric diagnosis (Spitzer & Wilson, 1975). It is to enable mental health professionals to (a) communicate with each other about the subject matter of their concern, (b) comprehend the pathological processes involved in psychiatric illness, and (c) control psychiatric disorders. Control consists of the ability to predict outcome, prevent the disorder from developing, and treat it once it has developed. Any serious discussion of the validity of psychiatric diagnosis, or suggestions for alternative systems of classifying psychological disturbance, must address itself to these purposes of psychiatric diagnosis.

In terms of its ability to accomplish these purposes, I would say that psychiatric diagnosis is moderately effective as a shorthand way of communicating the presence of constellations of signs and symptoms that tend to cluster together, is woefully inadequate in helping us understand the pathological processes of psychiatric disorders, but does offer considerable help in the control of many mental disorders. Control is possible because psychiatric diagnosis often yields information of value in predicting the likely course of illness (e.g., an early recovery, chronicity, or recurrent episodes) and because for many mental disorders it is useful in suggesting the best available treatment.

Let us return to the three different clinical conditions that I described, each of which had auditory hallucinations as one of its manifestations. The reader will have no difficulty in identifying the three hypothetical conditions as schizophrenia, psychotic depression, and mania. Anyone familiar with the literature on psychiatric treatment will know that there are numerous well-controlled studies (Klein

& Davis, 1969) indicating the superiority of the major tranquilizers for the treatment of schizophrenia, of electroconvulsive therapy for the treatment of psychotic depression and, more recently, of lithium carbonate for the treatment of mania. Furthermore, there is convincing evidence that these three conditions, each of which is often accompanied by hallucinations, are influenced by separate genetic factors. As Kety (1974) said, "If schizophrenia is a myth, it is a myth with a strong genetic component."

Should psychiatric diagnosis be abandoned for a purely descriptive system that focuses on simple phenotypic behaviors before it has been demonstrated that such an approach is more useful as a guide to successful treatment or for understanding the role of genetic factors? I think not. (I have a vision. Traditional psychiatric diagnosis has long been forgotten. At a conference on behavioral classification, a keen research investigator proposes that the category "hallucinations of unknown etiology" be subdivided into three different groups based on associated symptomatology. The first group is characterized by depressed affect, diurnal mood variation, and so on, the second group by euphoric mood, psychomotor excitement....)

If psychiatric diagnosis is not quite as bad as Rosenhan would have us believe, that does not mean that it is all that good. What is the reliability of psychiatric diagnosis prior to 1972 (Spitzer & Fleiss, 1974) revealed that "reliability is only satisfactory for three categories: mental deficiencies, organic brain syndrome, and alcoholism. The level of reliability is no better than fair for psychosis and schizophrenia, and is poor for the remaining categories." So be it. But where did Rosenhan get the idea that

psychiatry is the only medical specialty that is plagued by inaccurate diagnosis? Studies have shown serious unreliability in the diagnosis of pulmonary disorders (Fletcher, 1952), in the interpretation of electrocardiograms (Davis, 1958), in the interpretation of X-rays (Cochrane & Garland, 1952; Yerushalmy, 1947), and in the certification of causes of death (Markush, Schaaf, & Siegel, 1967). A review of diagnostic unreliability in other branches of physical medicine is given by Garland (1960) and the problem of the vagueness of medical criteria for diagnosis is thoroughly discussed by Feinstein (1967). The poor reliability of medical diagnosis, even when assisted by objective laboratory tests, does not mean that medical diagnosis is of no value. So it is with psychiatric diagnosis.

Recognition of the serious problems of the reliability of psychiatric diagnosis has resulted in a new approach to psychiatric diagnosis—the use of specific inclusion and exclusion criteria, as contrasted with the usually vague and ill-defined general descriptions found in the psychiatric literature and in the standard psychiatric glossary of the American Psychiatric Association. This approach was started by the St. Louis group associated with the Department of Psychiatry of Washington University (Feighner, Robins, Guze, Woodruff, Winokur, & Munoz, 1972) and has been further developed by Spitzer, Endicott, and Robins (1974) as a set of criteria for a selected group of functional psychiatric disorders, called the Research Diagnostic Criteria (RDC). The Display shows the specific criteria for a diagnosis of schizophrenia from the latest version of the RDC.[5]

DIAGNOSTIC CRITERIA FOR SCHIZOPHRENIA FROM THE RESEARCH DIAGNOSTIC CRITERIA

1. At least two of the following are required for definite diagnosis and one for probable diagnosis:

   a. Thought broadcasting, insertion, or withdrawal (as defined in the RDC).

   b. Delusions of control, other bizarre delusions, or multiple delusions (as defined in the RDC), of any duration as long as definitely present.

   c. Delusions other than persecutory or jealousy, lasting at least 1 week.

   d. Delusions of any type if accompanied by hallucinations of any type for at least 1 week.

   e. Auditory hallucinations in which either a voice keeps up a running commentary on the patient's behaviors or thoughts as they occur, or two or more voices converse with each other (of any duration as long as definitely present).

   f. Nonaffective verbal hallucinations spoken to the subject (as defined in this manual).

   g. Hallucinations of any type throughout the day for several days or intermittently for at least 1 month.

   h. Definite instances of formal thought disorder (as defined in the RDC).

   i. Obvious catatonic motor behavior (as defined in the RDC).

2. A period of illness lasting at least 2 weeks.

3. At no time during the active period of illness being considered did the patient meet the criteria for either probable or definite manic or depressive syndrome (Criteria 1 and 2 under Major Depressive or Manic Disorders) to such a degree that it was a prominent part of the illness.

Reliability studies using the RDC with case record material (from which all cues as to diagnosis and treatment were removed), as well as with live patients, indicate high reliability for all of the major categories and reliability coefficients generally higher than have ever been reported (Spitzer, Endicott, Robins, Kuriansky, & Garland, in press). It is therefore clear that the reliability of psychiatric diagnosis can be greatly increased by the use of specific criteria. (The interjudge reliability [chance corrected agreement, K] for the diagnosis of schizophrenia using an earlier version of RDC criteria with 68 newly admitted psychiatric inpatients at the New York State Psychiatric Institute was .88, which is a thoroughly respectable level of reliability). It is very likely that the next edition of the American Psychiatric Association's *Diagnostic and Statistical Manual* will contain similar specific criteria.

There are other problems with current psychiatric diagnosis. The recent controversy over whether or not homosexuality per se should be considered a mental disorder highlighted the lack of agreement within the psychiatric profession as to the definition of a mental disorder. A definition has been proposed by Spitzer (Spitzer & Wilson, 1975), but it is not at all clear whether a consensus will develop supporting it.

There are serious problems of validity. Many of the traditional diagnostic categories, such as some of the subtypes of schizophrenia and of major affective illness, and several of the personality disorders, have not been demonstrated to be distinct entities or to be useful for prognosis or treatment assignment. In addition, despite considerable evidence supporting the distinctness of such conditions as schizophrenia and manic-depressive illness, the boundaries separating these conditions from other conditions are certainly not clear. Finally, the categories of the traditional psychiatric nomenclature are of least value when applied to the large numbers of outpatients who are not seriously ill. It is for these patients that a more behaviorally or problem-oriented approach might be particularly useful.

I have not dealt at all with the myriad ways in which psychiatric diagnostic labels can be, and are, misused to hurt patients rather than to help them. This is a problem requiring serious research which, unfortunately, Rosenhan's study does not help illuminate. However, whatever the solutions to that problem the misuse of psychiatric diagnostic labels is not a sufficient reason to abandon their use because they have been shown to be of value when properly used.

In conclusion, there are serious problems with psychiatric diagnosis, as there are with other medical diagnoses. Recent developments indicate that the reliability of psychiatric diagnosis can be considerably improved. However, *even with the poor reliability of current psychiatric diagnosis, it is not so poor that it cannot be an aid in the treatment of the seriously disturbed psychiatric patient.* Rosenhan's study, "On Being Sane in Insane Places," proves that pseudopatients are not detected by psychiatrists as having simulated signs of mental illness. This rather remarkable finding is not relevant to the real problems of the reliability and validity of psychiatric diagnosis and only serves to obscure them. A correct interpretation of his own data contradicts his conclusions. In the setting of a psychiatric hospital, psychiatrists are remarkably able to distinguish the "sane" from the "insane."

NOTES

1. The original article only mentions that the 11 schizophrenics were diagnosed "in remission." Personal communication from D. L. Rosenhan indicates that this also applied to the single pseudopatient diagnosed as manic-depressive psychosis.

2. In personal communication D. L. Rosenhan said that "in remission" referred to a use of that term or one of its equivalents, such as recovered or no longer ill.

3. Rosenhan has not identified the hospitals used in this study because of his concern with issues of confidentiality and the potential for ad hominem attack. However, this does make it impossible for anyone at those hospitals to corroborate or challenge his account of how the pseudopatients acted and how they were perceived. The 12 hospitals used in my mini-study were: Long Island Jewish-Hillside Medical Center, New York; Massachusetts General Hospital, Massachusetts; St. Elizabeth's Hospital, Washington, D.C.; McLean Hospital, Massachusetts; UCLA, Neuropsychiatric Institute, California; Meyer-Manhattan Hospital (Manhattan State), New York; Vermont State Hospital, Vermont; Medical College of Virginia, Virginia; Emory University Hospital, Georgia; High Point Hospital, New York; Hudson River State Hospital, New York, and New York Hospital-Cornell Medical Center, Westchester Division, New York.

4. This was not in the article but was mentioned to me in personal communication by D. L. Rosenhan.

5. For what it is worth, the pseudopatient would have been diagnosed as "probable" schizophrenia using these criteria because of 1(f). In personal communication, Rosenhan said that when the pseudopatients were asked how frequently the hallucinations occurred, they said "I don't know." Therefore, Criterion 1(g) is not met.

REFERENCES

American Psychiatric Association. *Diagnostic and statistical manual of mental disorders* (2nd ed.). Washington, D.C.: American Psychiatric Association, 1968.

Cochrane, A. L., & Garland, L. H. Observer error in interpretation of chest films: International Investigation. *Lancet*, 1952, 2, 505–509.

Davies, L. G. Observer variation in reports on electrocardiograms. *British Heart Journal*, 1958, 20, 153–161.

Feighner, J. P., and Robins, E., Guze, S. B., Woodruff, R. A., Winokur, G., & Munoz, R. Diagnostic criteria for use in psychiatric research. *Archives of General Psychiatry*, 1972, 26, 57–63.

Feinstein, A. *Clinical judgment*. Baltimore, Md.: Williams & Wilkins, 1967.

Fletcher, C. M. Clinical diagnosis of pulmonary emphysema—an experimental study. *Proceedings of the Royal Society of Medicine*, 1952, 45, 577–584.

Garland, L. H. The problem of observer error. *Bulletin of the New York Academy of Medicine*, 1960, 36, 570–584.

Hunter, F. M. Letters to the editor. *Science*, 1973, 180, 361.

Kety, S. S. From rationalization to reason. *American Journal of Psychiatry*, 1974, 131, 957–963.

Klein, D., & Davis, J. *Diagnosis and drug treatment of psychiatric disorders*. Baltimore, Md.: Williams & Wilkins, 1969.

Letters to the editor. *Science*, 1973, 180, 356–365.

Markush, R. E., Schaaf, W. E., & Siegel, D. G. The influence of the death certifier on the results of epidemiologic studies. *Journal of the National Medical Association*, 1967, 59, 105–113.

Rosenhan, D. L. On being sane in insane places. *Science*, 1973, 179, 250–258. (a)

Rosenhan, D. L. Reply to letters to the editor. *Science*, 1973, 180, 365–369. (b)

Spitzer, R. L., Endicott, J., & Robins, E. *Research diagnostic criteria*. New York: Biometrics Research, New York State Department of Mental Hygiene, 1974.

Spitzer, R. L., Endicott, J., Robins, E., Kuriansky, J., & Garland, B. Preliminary report of the reliability of research diagnostic criteria applied to psychiatric case records. In A. Sudilofsky, B. Beer, & S. Gershon (Eds.), *Prediction in psychopharmacology*, New York: Raven Press, in press.

Spitzer, R. L. & Fleiss, J. L. A reanalysis of the reliability of psychiatric diagnosis. *British Journal of Psychiatry*, 1974. 125, 341–347.

Spitzer, R. L., & Wilson, P. T. Nosology and the official psychiatric nomenclature. In A. Freedman & H. Kaplan (Eds.), *Comprehensive textbook of psychiatry*. New York: Williams & Wilkins, 1975.

Yerushalmy, J. Statistical problems in assessing methods of medical diagnosis with special reference to X-ray techniques. *Public Health Reports*, 1947, 62, 1432–1449.

CHALLENGE QUESTIONS

Classic Dialogue: Do Diagnostic Labels Hinder Treatment?

1. Would society be better off if there were no names (such as "normal" or "abnormal") for broad categories of behavior? Why, or why not?

2. Who would you consider best qualified to judge a person's mental health: a parent, a judge, or a doctor? Why?

3. If a person at any time displays symptoms of a mental disorder, even fraudulently, is it helpful to consider that the same symptoms of disorder may appear again? Why, or why not?

4. Is there any danger in teaching the diagnostic categories of mental behavior to beginning students of psychology? Explain.

PART 5

Psychological Treatment

Psychotherapists have always been concerned about the safety and effectiveness of their treatments. But not all therapists are in agreement about which treatments are the safest and most effective. For example, some people have argued that electroconvulsive therapy, which is often used to treat depression, has significant, lasting physical side effects. Other treatments, while not always as physically invasive, can nevertheless be emotionally harmful or simply a waste of time. For example, is the treatment of depression with drug therapy effective? And, looking at the bigger picture, should psychologists be given the power to prescribe drugs?

■ Should Psychologists Be Allowed to Prescribe Drugs?

■ Have Antidepressant Drugs Proven to Be Effective?

■ Is Electroconvulsive Therapy Safe?

ISSUE 14

Should Psychologists Be Allowed to Prescribe Drugs?

YES: Patrick H. DeLeon et al., from "The Case for Prescription Privileges: A Logical Evolution of Professional Practice," *Journal of Clinical Child Psychology* (vol. 20, no. 3, 1991)

NO: Garland Y. DeNelsky, from "The Case Against Prescription Privileges for Psychologists," *Psychotherapy in Private Practice* (vol. 11, no. 1, 1992)

ISSUE SUMMARY

YES: Psychologist and lawyer Patrick H. DeLeon and his colleagues argue that psychologists and the public would benefit greatly from psychologists' obtaining prescription privileges.

NO: Clinical psychologist Garland Y. DeNelsky opposes prescription privileges for psychologists on the grounds that they are likely to harm the discipline of psychology and its ability to serve the public.

A recent and highly controversial proposal to expand the role of the psychologist entails the prescribing of drugs. Drugs have been increasingly recognized as contributing to the effective treatment of mental disorders. Because such treatment has traditionally been the province of psychology, many psychologists have advocated that they should be allowed to use all the effective treatments available, including prescription medications.

The most controversial aspect of this proposal, however, is that within the mental health field, only psychiatrists (and a few other allied professions) are currently permitted to prescribe drugs. With this proposal, the psychologist would be moving into the professional and economic "turf" of the psychiatrist. Psychiatrists are medical doctors who have their primary training in the anatomy and physiology of the human body. Psychologists, on the other hand, are trained in human relations. Although some psychologists receive considerable education in pharmacology (the study of medications) and related topics, few have the training necessary to enable them to competently prescribe drugs. However, the question arises: What if an appropriate level of training were obtained? Couldn't psychologists, then, prescribe drugs to their patients?

Patrick H. DeLeon and his colleagues, in the following selection, answer this question affirmatively. The authors cite research as well as their own personal experiences to demonstrate that psychologists can successfully and competently prescribe medications. The federal government has allowed some psychologists under certain circumstances to assume the role of drug prescriber; DeLeon et al. argue that these experiences should be reviewed to determine whether or not psychologists should in general assume this role. Almost without exception, the authors argue, these experiences have been positive. The unique perspective of the psychologist, the authors contend, provides an important complement to the perspective of other drug prescribers.

Garland Y. DeNelsky contends that giving psychologists prescription privileges would mean the downfall of the field of psychology. Currently, many consumers find psychology attractive because it successfully treats people without the use of potentially dangerous drugs. This attractiveness would be undermined by prescription privileges. Thus, instead of psychology increasing its role in the treatment of mental disorders, DeNelsky asserts, psychology could find itself without a role at all.

POINT

- The vast majority of child psychologists feel that prescription privileges should be granted with specialized training.

- Psychologists will do a better job of prescribing than the general practitioners who now prescribe psychoactive drugs.

- Prescription privileges will more effectively address the public's mental health needs.

- The profession of psychology has now matured sufficiently to responsibly administer psychotropic medications.

- The unique perspective of the psychologist will complement that of other drug prescribers.

COUNTERPOINT

- Recent surveys indicate that a majority of practicing psychologists do not favor obtaining prescription privileges.

- Psychologists will likely be held to higher standards, leading to more liability problems.

- Prescription privileges will make psychology less attractive to the public it serves.

- Drugs can detract from psychotherapeutic efforts by implying that benefits come from external agents.

- The "war" with psychiatry will detract from the development of other distinctively psychological treatments.

YES

Patrick H. DeLeon et al.

THE CASE FOR PRESCRIPTION PRIVILEGES: A LOGICAL EVOLUTION OF PROFESSIONAL PRACTICE

As psychology has become more intimately involved in addressing society's pressing needs and has begun to conceptualize itself
as a health care profession, it has become necessary collectively
to rethink earlier self-imposed limits on its fundamental "scope of
practice." Under our constitutional framework, psychologists employed within federal and state systems are not bound by the pa-
rameters of the various state practice acts, and certain psychologists
have been able to demonstrate that, like their colleagues in a wide
range of other professions, they can accept the clinical responsibility of utilizing psychoactive medications responsibly. To date,
the profession's traditional training institutions have not accepted
their responsibility of systematically providing relevant training experiences. Further, there is considerable disagreement within the
practice community as to whether the profession should enter the
prescription arena. However, recent legislative developments at
the federal and state level would seem to ensure that this evolution will proceed....

THE FEDERAL GOVERNMENT AS A PROVIDER OF CARE

One of the fundamental roles the federal government currently fulfills in
our society is to provide health services to various legislatively specified
beneficiary populations (DeLeon & VandenBos, 1980)....

In the prescription arena, it has historically been the federal government's
responsibility to determine which medications require prescriptions, and the
responsibility of the various states to determine which health care practitioners would be authorized to prescribe and under what conditions (Burns,
DeLeon, Chemtob, Welch, & Samuels, 1988). However, under our constitutional system of distinct federal–state responsibilities (powers), within

From Patrick H. DeLeon, Raymond A. Folen, Floyd L. Jennings, Diane J. Willis, and Rogers
H. Wright, "The Case for Prescription Privileges: A Logical Evolution of Professional Practice,"
Journal of Clinical Child Psychology, vol. 20, no. 3 (1991), pp. 254–258, 262–265. Copyright © 1991
by Lawrence Erlbaum Associates, Inc. Reprinted by permission. References omitted.

federal health care institutions the various disciplines are not limited by the constraints of their particular state "scope of practice" acts, unless either the administration or the Congress has specifically so designated. Similarly, with the rare exception of overtly grievous or heinous incidents of malfeasance, it has historically been extraordinarily difficult to sue any governmental entity successfully for alleged "malpractice." Thus, from a health policy frame of reference, the federal system presents an excellent laboratory in which to test out new models of care (DeLeon, 1986, 1988b). And, we would further point out that the same flexibility is inherent within our various state governmental systems.

INNOVATIVE HEALTH MANPOWER DEMONSTRATIONS

In addition to providing direct care, another of the responsibilities of government has been to explore the development of innovative health human resources and service delivery initiatives. For example, the need of the VA for ready access to quality mental health care following World War II led to a major influx of training funds to our nation's clinical and counseling psychology programs (Cranston, 1986; Larson, 1986). Similarly, the health manpower interests of the then-Department of Health, Education, and Welfare (HEW) lead to the establishment of the nurse practitioner (NP) initiatives of the mid-1960s. In this context, we feel that as the various facets of psychology debate whether or not our profession should seek to obtain prescription privileges, it is important that the field as a whole step back and collectively look at the broader picture. In essence, we are proposing that

organized psychology learn from the experiences of the other nonphysician, or alternative, health care providers in this arena (DeLeon, 1988a; DeLeon, Kjervik, Kraut, & VandenBos, 1985; DeLeon, Wakefield, Schultz, Williams, & VandenBos, 1989).

In the mid-1970s, the state of California utilized its health human resources demonstration power to test out whether nonphysicians might be properly authorized to utilize prescriptive authority. On July 1, 1973 the state of California's Health Manpower Pilot Project Program became operational. Its *Final Report to the Legislature, State of California and to the Healing Arts Licensing Boards: Prescribing and Dispensing Pilot Projects* (State of California, 1982) was submitted in November, 1982. The authors reported that:

> None of the projects, to date, have received the intense scrutiny that these 10 prescribing and dispensing projects have received. Over one million patients have been seen by these prescribing and dispensing trainees over the past three years. At least 50% of these patients have had drugs prescribed for them or dispensed to them by these professionals. (p. i)

The report noted that the health professionals participating in the pilot projects received additional educational experiences provided by project staff. The principal teaching methods were lectures and seminars, varying from 16 hr to 95 hr in length. It was further noted that only 56% of the trainees had graduated from academic programs with a bachelors degree or higher; that is, they possessed considerably less educational training than doctoral-level psychologists.

Most of the patients seen were female (96%). They were clearly comfortable with the trainees' performance (99.5%), and 84% indicated that they received more information from the trainees than from physicians. The supervising physicians were similarly consistent in their judgment that permitting these physician associates to prescribe and dispense drugs had increased the availability of care and was cost effective. In fact, the state of California's (1982) final report concluded that: "Even when the cost of having physician supervision and pharmacist consultation... is computed, the annual savings to the health care delivery system is at least $2 million per year" (p. ii). Not surprisingly, the California Office of Statewide Health Planning and Development specifically recommended that clear statutory authority be enacted for the prescribing and dispensing of drugs by appropriately prepared registered nurses, physician assistants, and pharmacists.

Psychology should understand that this particular demonstration project was not conducted in a health policy vacuum. The state of California's report also cited literature on nurse practitioner prescription practices, which had found that there was total agreement between the recommendations of pediatric nurse practitioners and consulting pediatricians in 86% of the cases reviewed, and further, that in only two instances, or 0.7% of the cases, was the difference between the nurse and the physician assessment considered significant (Duncan, Smith, & Silver, 1971). Another study cited reported that nurse practitioners in primary care settings could handle two-thirds of the patient care episodes without consulting a physician and that there was no significant difference found in patient physi-

cal capacity, social function, or emotional function (Spitzer et al., 1974).

Independent reviews conducted by the Office of Technology Assessment (OTA; U.S. Congress, OTA, 1981, 1986c), which is the scientific policy arm of the Congress, have reached similar positive conclusions:

> the quality of care provided by NPs functioning within their areas of training and expertise tends to be as good as or better than care provided by physicians.... researchers found that NPs prescribe and use medications less frequently than do physicians, and that NPs tend to prescribe only well-known and relatively simple drugs. (U.S. Congress, OTA, 1986c, p. 19)

And, as one concrete example, we would point out that currently our nation's Certified Registered Nurse Anesthetists (CRNAs) provide care to more than 65% of all patients undergoing surgical or other medical intervention that necessitates the services of an anesthetist. CRNAs are the sole anesthesia provider in approximately 33% of the hospitals in the U.S., and they provide between 80% and 90% of the anesthesia received by Medicare beneficiaries (Jordan, 1990). Although most psychologists are not aware of the legislative struggles that CRNAs experience with their anesthesiologist (MD) colleagues, we would suggest that these are probably only second in intensity to those that our optometrist colleagues experienced with opthamologists (MDs) during their over 50-year successful struggle to obtain prescription privileges.

As we indicated earlier, we feel that it is important that psychology's practice and educational leadership take a careful look at what already exists in the health care (health manpower) literature, rather than allow themselves to enter into hypothetical and/or emotional debates as to whether our practitioners can (or should) be appropriately trained to accept this important clinical responsibility. And, we would further suggest that because our current training programs do not effectively control their own clinical facilities (e.g., we do not possess "teaching nursing homes" or administer "model in-patient wards"), most of our educational leadership does not currently possess sufficient clinical expertise to reach appropriate policy conclusions without consultation with other health care disciplines (Raymond, DeLeon, VandenBos, & Michael, in press).

PSYCHOLOGISTS WITHIN THE INDIAN HEALTH SERVICE

One of the authors (Floyd L. Jennings) served in the Indian Health Service (IHS) from May 1988 through May 1989; while in that capacity he was granted the legal authority to prescribe. In 1986 the IHS Santa Fe Indian Hospital and Service Unit had modified its hospital bylaws to specifically provide authority for qualified psychologists to prescribe under standing orders from a specified limited formulary (i.e., from a predetermined listing of approved medications). This approach (model) is common within the professional nursing community. Its application to psychology was at the behest of physicians in that particular hospital, had the active and enthusiastic support of the IHS area psychiatrist, and received cautious agreement from those in the psychology field! . . .

During the period from August 1, 1988 thru May 3, 1989, when Jennings kept detailed records of his prescription pro-

tocols, 46% of his patient contacts were on an inpatient basis, and 25% of the patient contacts involved psychotropic medication (total number of patient contacts was 378). The vast majority of the prescriptions he ordered were for antidepressants, either tricyclics or second generation antidepressants such as trazodone, as 28% of all patient contacts involved a diagnosis of depression. There were significant sex differences in medications prescribed. For the 37 medication contacts with males, 51% involved neuroleptics. The medications he utilized included: amitriptyline, desipramine, doxepin, imipramine, trazodone, chlorpromazine, haldol, haldol decanoate, prolixin decanoate, stelazine, and thioridazine. Throughout this period the bottom line was that no major adverse experiences were encountered! Further, significant time was spent alleviating problems created by "less than appropriate treatment" provided by his physician colleagues.

Interestingly, when our colleague requested a ruling from the New Mexico Psychological Association as to whether he was functioning in an ethical manner when prescribing, the committee responded, in part, that:

It appears from your statements that you are practicing within relevant APA [American Psychological Association] ethical principles in your employment by the Indian Health Service. The Ethics Committee, however, believes that it is unable to make a definitive statement about the ethics of psychologists, or any particular psychologist, prescribing medication because psychology has not adopted any standards of education or practice as reference criteria. We recognize that general standards exist within the medical profession but we cannot assume that these standards represent criteria for psychologists as another profession. (J. P. Cardillo, personal communication, fall 1988)

From a health policy frame of reference, one might suggest that when Jennings prescribed, he was writing orders trading on the license and supervision (collaboration) of the hospital medical staff in general, and the clinical director, in particular....

From a purely interprofessional/political frame of reference, it is interesting to note that when the fact of Jennings' prescribing practice came to the attention of psychiatry's political leadership, they worked closely with their colleagues throughout organized medicine and in the administration to stop this practice, notwithstanding the fact that there had not been a single incident of adverse care reported. On December 9, 1988 a memorandum was sent out to the field from the associate director, Office of IHS Health Programs, noting that:

> In a limited number of service units, clinical psychologists have been allowed by medical staff by-laws to prescribe psychotropic medications independent of physician supervision.... Therefore ... I am hereby advising you that effective with the date of this letter, it is IHS policy that no psychologist may be permitted to prescribe medications independent of physician supervision. Operationally, this policy means at a minimum that any order for medication written for inpatients or outpatients by psychologists must be countersigned by a physician, preferably a psychiatrist.

For psychology, the IHS has already provided an operational answer to the question "Can we responsibly prescribe?"—We already have! And, it clearly remains IHS Policy that our practitioners can legally prescribe. The policy debate has moved to the issue of "under what conditions." ...

THE CURRENT DEBATE WITHIN PSYCHOLOGY

A number of articles presenting opinions (Adams, 1986; Brandsma & Frey, 1986a, 1986b; Fox, 1986; Gay, 1978; Handler, 1988; Jones, 1984; Kotler-Cope, 1989) and opinion surveys (Bascue & Zlotowski, 1981; Folen, 1989; Massoth, McGrath, Bianchi, & Singer, 1990; Piotrowski, 1989; Piotrowski & Lubin, 1989) have recently been published within the psychological literature, and they generally report that significant numbers of psychologists have strong views on both sides of the policy issue of whether or not our profession should seek prescription privileges. Articles are also beginning to surface that raise the more fundamental question as to whether any profession (including psychology) should utilize psychotropic medications (Greenberg & Fisher, 1990; Klosko, Barlow, Tassinari, & Cerny, 1990). Some of the generic issues raised have been whether malpractice premiums would escalate needlessly versus whether the absence of prescription authority might result in greater liability (Dorken, 1990); whether as a practical matter it is possible to provide adequate training in medications without radically altering professional psychology's current training programs; and whether as a profession we would be in danger of losing our uniqueness (behavioral science and/or humanism) if we obtained this particular clinical responsibility (Platman, Dorgan, & Gerhard, 1976; Wiggins, 1980). And, of course, the issue of whether the political price required for eventual success would be worth it (DeLeon, 1986, 1988b).

The Section on Clinical Child Psychology of Division 12 (Section 1) experienced the same diversity of opinion among its executive committee and recently decided to form a task force to study the issue comprehensively. The committee agreed to explore the advantages and disadvantages of prescription privileges, to discuss the issues involved in the debate, and to survey clinical child psychologists about their opinions concerning the issue. Under the leadership of then-Section 1 President Russell Barkley, the task force reviewed the relevant literature, surveyed the Section membership, and concluded its work by issuing a report on the role of clinical child psychologists in the prescribing of psychoactive medication for children (Barkley et al., 1990). Barkley et al. sent out surveys to 950 Section members, of whom 56.2% responded. Results of the survey suggested that a majority of clinical child psychologists are consulted by, or consult with, a physician on medication issues, and a majority assist in evaluating, or monitoring, the effects of medications. Slightly more than 65% of the respondents felt that prescription privileges should be granted with specialized training in psychopharmacology at a postdoctoral level. Over 80% of those surveyed felt that services to underserved children, or children in rural areas, would improve if psychologists had such prescription privileges.

Clinical child psychologists, by the nature of their training in child development, behavioral assessment/intervention, and research are indeed involved in medication issues in a variety of ways as the Section 1 survey demonstrated (Conners, 1988). Research by Barkley et al. demonstrates the roles psychologists already play in monitoring behavioral effects of medication. In one of these studies the response of aggressive and nonaggressive attention deficit hyperactivity disorder (ADHD) children to two doses of methylphenidate was explored (Barkley, McMurray, Edelbrock, & Robbins, 1989). In another study, Barkley, Fischer, Newby, and Breen (1988) developed a multimethod clinical protocol for assessing stimulant drug responding in attention deficit disorder (ADD) children. The use of psychostimulant medication in treating ADHD children has been studied extensively, and the results demonstrate both the efficacy of treatment by medication (Barkley, 1977; Gadow, 1986; Gadow & Pomeroy, 1990) and the important role played by psychologists in monitoring medication effects.

Paralleling the debate on prescription privileges is the debate on whether children should be medicated. There are a variety of justifiable reasons for medicating children as indicated in the Barkley et al. (1990) report. Medication certainly may eliminate or decrease seizure activity in a child, thus modifying a dysfunctional neurological problem that may contribute to atypical behavior. Drugs used to treat anxiety or depression in children and adolescents may prevent them from harming themselves or others. Drugs for children also may suppress disrupting and embarrassing behavior such as seen in selected cases of Tourette's syndrome. Children who are diagnosed as having ADHD often are socially and behaviorally disruptive, and medication permits them to be placed in regular classrooms or at least in less restrictive environments (Barkley, 1990).

If medication is to be used with children, care must be taken in deciding what conditions indicate the appropriate use of medication. The Barkley et al. (1990) report provides a brief overview of changes in psychopathology and the special considerations in assessing the child prior to the decision to medicate. For example, one special consideration is to determine who the client might be. Parents who report that they cannot manage the child's behavior may be reflecting their own stress levels and not the activity level of the child. Thus, one cannot over-rely on one set of observations. Secondarily, one must be assured of the correct clinical diagnosis (e.g., one would not use medication with oppositional defiant disorder with anxious features and one might with ADHD children; Carlson, 1990). Clinical child psychologists generally have the training and knowledge to make these differential diagnoses. Training in psychopharmacology is a logical extension of working with children and would round out our care of a particular child.

Research is needed to further our knowledge about the appropriate use of medication with children. Clinical child and pediatric psychologists are in a unique position, not only in the assessment area but in the research area. Clinical child psychologists could initiate and collaborate in the pediatric psychopharmacology field. Areas woefully understudied include medication effects with adolescents and the mentally retarded (Campbell & Spencer, 1988). Because many studies dealing with these populations, especially with the mentally retarded, are already conducted by psychologists, a new field of research could be, and should be, initiated. But to be involved in this type of research clinical child psychologists must know something about medications, such as special considerations in pharmacokinetics, the efficacy of child psychoactive drugs, and issues to consider in deciding to medicate children. Barkley et al. (1990) clearly suggested that clinical child psychologists will seek retraining in psychopharmacology when this becomes a viable option, with over 45% responding affirmatively. With this new clinical authority, undoubtedly additional treatment will be provided to underserved populations, and important new research studies on the efficacy of child psychoactive drugs will be undertaken.

Depending on the particular clinical needs of the beneficiary population that one plans to serve, the context of the debate, and the necessary training model required, appear to differ substantially. For example, those working with the chronically mentally ill would have different needs than those working within comprehensive medical centers with the physically handicapped. Similarly, those working in rural America, where there is the necessity for truly comprehensive services (DeLeon et al., 1989) would have different requirements than those specializing in the unique needs of children, where behavior is such a predominant concern (Campbell & Spencer, 1988; U.S. Congress OTA, 1986a; Werry, 1982). Those interested in our nation's elderly are faced with statistics suggesting that (a) mental health problems are significant (U.S. Senate Special Committee on Aging, 1986, 1988) and are overlooked by general physicians in about 50% of elderly patients; (b) the American Medical Association (AMA) has publicly criticized general physicians' ability to prescribe psychotropic medications appropriately; and (c) the Inspector General of the U.S. has referred to the overmedication of the elderly as "our country's other drug problem." Each year drug overdoses cause 32,000 fractured hips from falls, 60,000 cases of Parkinson symptoms, and 15,000 cases of memory loss and dementia, not to mention 250,000 hospital admissions annually for adverse drug reactions (Office of the Inspector General, 1989; Welch, 1989b).

Notwithstanding the range of views that may exist within psychology on the underlying issue, it is clear that the elected political leadership of psychology is becoming increasingly supportive (Fox, 1988a; Graham, 1990a). A number of the practice division presidents have spoken out in favor of the movement (DeLeon, 1987d, 1987b, 1987c, 1987a, 1987e; Samuels, 1985; Wright, 1988), and arrangements have been made to increase significantly the presence of drug companies at relevant state association and divisional meetings. In November 1989 the APA Board of Professional Affairs (BPA) focused its fall retreat meeting on the issue of prescription privileges. After extensive consultation with relevant experts and deliberation, BPA (1989, p. 15) concluded that:

> ... BPA strongly endorses the immediate research and study intervention feasibility and curricula development in psychopharmacology for psychologists in order to provide broader service to the public and to address more effectively the public's psychological and mental health needs. And BPA strongly recommends moving to the highest APA priority a focused attention to the responsibility of preparing the profession of psychology to address the current and future needs of the public for psychologically managed psychopharmacological interventions.

During its August 1990 meeting, the APA Council of Representatives (the association's highest policy body) voted 118–2 to establish a prescription privilege task force.

In the most comprehensive survey conducted to date, the Practice Directorate arranged for an independent telephone interview of 1,505 APA members to be conducted by Frederick/Schneiders, Inc. (1990) between December 7 and December 22, 1990. Their key findings were:

1. There is very strong support for prescription privileges for psychologists (68%).
2. The proposition that psychologists could do a better job of prescribing than the general practitioners who now prescribe most psycho-active drugs is the most effective argument in support of prescription privileges (71%). A potential rise in malpractice rates is the strongest argument against the proposal (58%).
3. There is overwhelming support for a demonstration project on prescription privileges (78%). Even among opponents of the general proposal, a majority support the demonstration project (54%).

The authors concluded that: "There is nothing in these data to suggest that APA is getting too far out in front of the troops on this issue" (p. 28). They further concluded that: "This is overwhelming support for the only proposition that is currently on the table (the demonstration project). Supporting only the demonstration project at this time would be a very cautious and, certainly, very safe position for APA" (p. 23).

In our judgment, the next crucial development in this evolution will be the active participation of our educational training institutions. There can be little doubt that psychologists within the federal sector have (and will continue to) demonstrate that it is possible (and practical) to obtain this clinical privilege. Further, as the prescription privilege debate continues, those seriously interested in serving various underserved segments of our society (e.g., the chronically mentally ill, those in rural America, the elderly, and our nation's children) will come to appreciate the importance of this clinical modality to their collective goals. For some beneficiary populations, it is especially significant that: "the power to prescribe is also the power not to utilize medications" (B. F. Riess, personal communication).

To date, the missing component in the dialogue has been the practical one of how those who desire to obtain this clinical responsibility can obtain the necessary and appropriate training. Currently, at least 28 states authorize nurse practitioners/nurse clinical specialists to prescribe—including psychiatric nurses (American Nurses' Association [ANA], personal communication). Perhaps in one of these states we will soon find the state psychological association serving as a broker with a local nursing school in order to arrange the appropriate summer institute or continuing education courses, so that those of their membership who complete the training will have equivalent expertise to their nursing colleagues who can legally prescribe. Or perhaps the various state associations will pursue the route that Hawaii has chosen; that is, they will first seek legislative authority to prescribe and then develop appropriate training modules. In any case, however, it

is clear that the APA Practice Directorate has already begun the process of making prescription privileges a state association legislative priority (Welch, 1989a).

SUMMARY

As Fox (1988b) pointed out, it may have been prudent and politically expedient 45 years ago, when efforts were directed to passing the first psychology licensing law, to adopt a dualism that placed all "hands-on" (i.e., physical) interventions beyond the scope of the practice of psychology. However, times (and knowledge) have changed dramatically since then, and in our judgment, the profession of psychology has now matured sufficiently to responsibly utilize psychotropic medications (BPA, 1981, 1986). Psychologists within the federal sector have demonstrated that our profession can prescribe and efforts are currently under way to develop appropriate training modules. Historically, the decision as to which health care professions should prescribe, and under which circumstances, has been a state responsibility. Psychologists in the state of Hawaii have been the first in the nation to attempt to modify their "scope of practice" act to allow prescription authority. Not surprisingly, Hawaii was not entirely successful during its first legislative attempt; however, notwithstanding strongly held divergent views within the broader psychological community, there are growing signs that Hawaii will soon be joined by other states in this quest (Brentar & McNamara, 1991; Wickramasekera, 1984).

NO

Garland Y. DeNelsky

THE CASE AGAINST PRESCRIPTION PRIVILEGES FOR PSYCHOLOGISTS

Several leading psychologists have spoken out strongly in favor of psychologists seeking prescription privileges. This paper presents the arguments against this position, including the potentially negative effects prescription privileges could have on the future course of the profession, the training of psychologists, the marketing of psychological services, and other issues of importance to psychology. It is concluded that attempting to obtain the right to prescribe psychoactive medications would involve an extremely expensive struggle that could change professional psychology in many ways, some of which might actually make it less attractive to the public is serves.

Several respected and visible psychologists have argued forcefully in favor of prescription privileges for psychologists (DeLeon, 1988; Fox, 1988a; Burns, DeLeon, Chemtob, Welch, & Samuels, 1988). APA's [American Psychological Association] Board of Professional Affairs recently endorsed the concept. APA's legislative body, the Council of Representatives, recently approved creation of a special Task Force on Psychopharmacology. There is movement toward psychologists getting prescription training through the Department of Defense (Buie, 1989b). Only a few writers have opposed this movement, despite the fact that recent surveys indicate that a majority of practicing psychologists are *not* in favor of psychologists obtaining prescription privileges (Piotrowski & Lubin, 1989; Boswell, Litwin & Kraft, 1988). The purpose of this paper is to provide a reasonably comprehensive exposition of the arguments against psychologists obtaining prescription privileges.

THE INFLUENCE OF PRESCRIPTION PRIVILEGES UPON THE FUTURE DIRECTIONS OF PSYCHOLOGY

If psychologists gained the right to prescribe psychoactive medications a shift is likely to occur in the direction in which professional psychology is evolving. Psychology could move from a predominantly behavioral field toward one increasingly similar to a medical specialty—psychiatry.

From Garland Y. DeNelsky, "The Case Against Prescription Privileges for Psychologists," *Psychotherapy in Private Practice*, vol. 11, no. 1 (1992), pp. 15–23. Copyright © 1992 by The Haworth Press, Inc., Binghamton, NY. Reprinted by permission. References omitted.

No consensus has yet emerged as to a single definition of professional psychology. One definition which has been widely circulated comes from Fox, Barclay, and Rodgers (1982). They proposed that "professional psychology is that profession which is concerned with enhancing the effectiveness of human functioning" (Fox, Barclay, & Rodgers, 1982, p. 307). Congruent with this definition, psychology has been producing a large number of well-trained practitioners who spend a substantial portion of their professional lives practicing psychotherapy and other types of psychological and behavioral interventions. Psychiatry, too, emphasized the practice of psychotherapy before the widespread use of psychoactive drugs. As psychiatry increased its reliance upon the use of medications it turned more and more away from psychotherapy. Psychoactive medications often produce "quick fixes"—reductions in symptoms, with little or no lasting changes in behavior or perception. In the short run, medications may be quicker, easier, and more profitable than the demanding work of psychotherapy. When a patient reports a symptom such as anxiety, depression, an obsessive-compulsive disorder, or a sleep problem, it is both easier and quicker to turn to a prescription pad than to those behavioral and psychotherapeutic interventions which have been demonstrated to be equally (or more) effective. The therapist feels he/she is doing something immediately, and the patient gains some quick symptomatic relief.

This rapid reinforcement of both therapist and patient can begin a pattern with far-ranging implications. For the therapist the message may become that medications provide a quick way to produce some symptomatic relief. It is possible that some therapists may gradually become influenced by another pattern of reinforcement: that regularly utilizing medications yields greater profits since shorter appointments are possible and hence more appointment times per day become available. The result could become a "short circuiting" of psychotherapeutic efforts, an effect that appears to have already influenced many within the field of psychiatry.

Medications also have some significant meanings for the patient, some of which may actually run counter to the processes of personal change and growth. Medications can subtly detract from psychotherapeutic efforts by implying that benefit comes from external agents, not from one's own efforts. As noted by Handler (1988, p. 47), "medication is a temporary solution which has powerful and sometimes peculiar control over consciousness; it teaches the patient little or nothing enduring about self control." The use of medications by psychologists could indeed change the direction in which psychology is evolving.

THE INFLUENCE OF PRESCRIPTION PRIVILEGES ON TRAINING

If training to prescribe becomes a routine part of the training of psychologists, it is highly likely that the educational process would have to be substantially longer than it is now. Training to prescribe medications will require a good deal more than providing a basic understanding of dosage and side effects, information that many practicing psychologists currently need to know. Education will have to focus a great deal more upon basic physiology, pharmacology, and physical diseases. This would result in increasing the length of graduate study, perhaps by a full year or more. Although one advocate of prescription privileges asserts that "addition of a special tract (to teach medications) would neither seriously distort our basic education in psychology nor necessarily require an extension in the length of time to earn the doctorate" (Fox, 1988b, p. 27), it is difficult to imagine how this goal could be realized unless there is a great deal of unessential material in current doctoral programs.

It should be noted that psychologists who prescribe medications will be held responsible for any and all complications that might arise from their use. Medication education will need to impart expertise regarding the potential interactions between medications and various medical conditions (e.g., hypertension, cardiac conditions, hormone therapy, diabetes, etc.). Although the majority of patients may present few if any such complications, psychologists will still have to learn how to deal with the difficult, medically complex patient. Because psychology will be "the new kid on the block," and a non-medical one at that, psychologists will likely be held to higher standards than is customary for physicians. Those standards can be expected to carry over to the courts. They will also be reflected in substantially higher malpractice rates for psychologists who prescribe and those who train others to prescribe; psychiatric malpractice rates currently range from three to 24 times higher than psychological malpractice coverage, depending on the state (Dorken, 1990).

The basic emphasis in our graduate education would likely change. The current emphasis is (or should be) upon psychologists becoming the preeminent specialists in human behavior change and psychotherapy. If psychology incorporates medication training into its graduate education, its training would shift from a primary emphasis upon behavioral change and personal growth through psychological interventions to, at best, a dual emphasis upon psychological and medical interventions. This dual emphasis could be expected to carry over into our postgraduate continuing education programs, too. Since there seems to be a new batch of medications each year or so, it is likely that the preponderance of continuing education programs would be devoted to medication, rather than behavioral change, psychotherapy, assessment, or other psychologically oriented topics. Practicing psychologists would be devoting less time to keeping up with new developments in psychology and more to acquiring new information about medications.

POLITICAL CONSIDERATIONS: A MAJOR WAR AHEAD?

Even the strongest proponents of prescription privileges for psychologist acknowledge that the struggle to secure such privileges would be a formidable one (Fox, 1988b). While it may be correctly argued that an independent profession does not allow other professions to determine its boundaries, the political implications and the potential costs involved in expanding those boundaries must be considered.

Seeking medication privileges would plunge psychology into a full-scale war with both psychiatry and medicine. In all likelihood, all of the previous conflicts psychology is engaged in now or in the past would be eclipsed—battles over licensure, third-party reimbursement, freedom of choice statutes, inclusion in Medicare, even hospital privileges. Medicine seems more than ever grimly committed to resisting all efforts to "encroach" on what it defines as its territory. It is true that other professionals such as dentists, optometrists, pharmacists, podiatrists, nurse practitioners, and physician assistants have been able to secure prescription privileges (Burns, DeLeon, Chemtob, Welch, & Samuels, 1988). However, these professions obtained prescription privileges at a time when organized medicine was not as rigidly committed to resisting further incursions into what it defined as its "turf." Perhaps even more significantly, psychologists with prescription privileges would *not* be viewed as "limited practitioners" such as those other providers with prescription privileges. If psychologists become able to prescribe medications, they will be capable of duplicating virtually everything that psychiatrists do-or at least that is how psychiatry and organized medicine would probably perceive them. None of the other nonmedical professions that have obtained prescription privileges pose such a complete threat to their corresponding medical specialties. In short, if organized psychology decides to push ahead for the right to prescribe, it will undoubtedly find itself locked in an immense struggle.

The financial cost of such a struggle would be overwhelming. It has been estimated that in one state alone—Massachusetts—upwards of four million dollars would be needed to finance the battle for prescription privileges (Tanney, 1987). Expand that figure to estimate the cost if all 50 states seek prescription privileges and it is not an overstatement to estimate that these battles could exhaust all of psychology's current assets and probably sink us deeply into debt.

In addition to the issue of financial cost is the matter of energy expenditure. If organized psychology decides to seriously pursue prescription privileges other issues will almost certainly receive diminished emphasis (Kovacs, 1988). Issues such as inclusion of psychological services in HMO's, hospital privileges, minimum mental health benefits, closing the ERISA loopholes, and marketing of psychological services will all have to assume reduced priority. When a profession is fighting a major war that requires all of its resources and more there is an obvious limit to how many other battles can be undertaken concurrently.

The war for prescription privileges might even cost psychology many of its hard earned gains of the past quarter century. All current psychology licensing laws are written in such a way as to preclude prescription of medications; they would have to be revised or amended (Fox, 1988b). These licensing laws would need to be "opened up" in the state legislatures at a time when psychology's opponents were mobilized against it. It is easy to imagine attempts to cripple existing psychology licensing laws in such a manner as to remove many of the significant gains of the past. Psychology could find itself with much less than it possessed before it sought prescription privileges.

Much greater divisiveness within psychology could also be an outcome if psychology actually obtained prescription privileges. If psychology gains prescription privileges, there would be some psychologists legally permitted to prescribe and some who could not. In view of the strong feelings likely to emerge on both sides of this issue, considerable discord is likely. For example, after having fought so hard and at such cost to earn the right to prescribe, it is easy to imagine that at least some psychologists will prescribe a great deal. That behavior is likely to draw considerable denunciation from others within the field. It is also possible that those psychologists who gain the right to prescribe may consider themselves "full practitioners" in comparison with their peers who are unable to prescribe, resulting in tensions within psychology not unlike those which frequently emerge between psychologist and psychiatrists. If gaining the right to prescribe really does lead those who have it to broader third-party reimbursement and easier access to hospital privileges (as has been argued by some proponents of prescription privileges) will those psychologists unable to prescribe feel relegated to a second-class status within their own profession?

MARKETING OF PSYCHOLOGY: EASIER OR MORE DIFFICULT?

The argument has been made by some that not securing the right to prescribe keeps psychology at a competitive disadvantage with psychiatry (Fox, 1988a). While this may be true in some cases, the overall record of psychology in the marketplace does not support this assertion. Recent figures from CHAMPUS indicate that in 1987 psychologists provided service for 34 percent of outpatient behavioral health visits compared with less than 22 percent for psychiatrists (Buie, 1989a). Five years earlier the figures had been reversed with psychiatrists providing service for 36 percent of the visits and psychologists for 28 percent. Without prescription privileges, psychology seems to be becoming the leading provider of outpatient mental health services. Psychiatry, with prescription privileges, has been steadily losing its market share over the past five years.

It has been asserted that the main reason clinical psychology has prospered is that it has built a reputation as being *different* from psychiatry (Handler, 1988). Handler further points out that there has been a steady increase averaging over ten percent each year in the number of clinical psychologists from 1966 to 1983. He attributes these increases to psychology being "independent and innovative in our training, our research, and in our service delivery ... to ape psychiatry in providing biological answers when our psychologically based answers are far more adequate for psychotherapeutic intervention is ill-advised" (Handler, 1988, p. 45).

Psychology is a vigorous, growing field that is perceived by many as a most viable alternative to the increasingly biological orientation of organized psychiatry. Instead of attempting to blur the differences between psychology and psychiatry in the public's mind, which gaining prescription privileges is likely to do, the argument can be made that psychology needs to sharpen the essential distinctions between the two fields. Practicing psychologists strive to help people learn about themselves and acquire more effective means of coping with stressors in their lives, since symptoms such as depression and anxiety frequently are indications of a mismatch between the demands of the environment and the individual's ability to cope with these demands (DeNelsky & Boat, 1986). Even where there may be biologic predisposing factors, such as with major mental disorders such as schizophrenia, appropriate psychological interventions can be quite effective (Paul & Lentz, 1977; Karon and VandenBos, 1981). It would certainly seem to be curious logic to engage in a monumental struggle to acquire a technique—prescription privileges—which seems to be leading those who have it to a diminishing share of the market which they once dominated!

THE FUTURE OF PRESCRIPTION PRIVILEGES

Without prescription privileges, and despite increasing competition from other disciplines such as social work and counseling, professional psychology has prospered. Psychologists today represent the largest pool of doctoral-level trained mental health practitioners in the United States. They have been steadily gaining in market share to where they now deliver more outpatient mental health care within CHAMPUS than any other group of providers (Dorken, 1989). Whatever some psychologists may perceive as a therapeutic deficiency because they lack prescription privileges is apparently not recognized as such by the general public. Although there is no clear evidence one way or the other on this issue, a case can be made that we have flourished *because* we offer a clear and distinct choice from psychiatry. To quote Handler (1988, p. 48): "I am not worried that we will be replaced by psychiatry if we cannot write prescriptions. I worry instead that we might sell our birthright by failing to value our professional individuality and our professional distinctiveness."

Gaining prescription privileges would likely change the trajectory of the profession of psychology from a field which relies primarily upon strategies of learning, adapting, and growing to a domain similar to the medical specialty of psychiatry. Approximately 20 years ago, psychiatry made a conscious decision to "medicalize." Since then there has been a noteworthy growth in non-medical mental health professions, while psychiatry itself has shown negligible growth. Might psychology fall prey to a similar fate if it turned away from its heritage and toward the prescription pad?

Gaining prescription privileges might help solve some problems for some psychologists, but seeking them is likely to create major ones for the field as a whole. The quest for such privileges would undoubtedly plunge psychology into a major war. At this time, when there is not even a clear majority of practicing psychologists in favor of psychology pursuing the right to prescribe, the quest for prescription privileges could become a costly, no-win situation—a "Viet Nam War" for professional psychology. And if psychology did manage to win the many battles and secure prescription privileges, would it gradually evolve into a field indistinguishable from psychiatry? If so, would such a metamorphose be in the interest of either the public or psychology? In the long run, winning the battles for prescription privileges might turn out to be infinitely less desirable than not going to war at all.

CHALLENGE QUESTIONS

Should Psychologists Be Allowed to Prescribe Drugs?

1. If psychologists were to obtain the privilege of prescribing medications, how would they be different from the profession of psychiatry? How might your answer affect psychology's future?

2. Underlying this issue is what some theorists call reductionism. Reductionism is the notion that all psychological entities (e.g., mind, feelings, unconscious) can be ultimately reduced to biological entities. How might this theoretical notion affect the current controversy, and how might one's stance on reductionism affect one's stance on this issue?

3. How does a profession like psychology balance the sometimes competing interests of its marketability and the good of the public?

4. DeNelsky claims that many people prefer a nonmedication treatment when they experience emotional disturbances. Would you prefer to be treated without medication if you were to experience emotional problems? Why, or why not?

5. How much should the issue of psychiatry's "turf" enter into this debate? That is, should the traditional boundaries between psychology and psychiatry be respected for any reason, or is this irrelevant?

ISSUE 15

Have Antidepressant Drugs Proven to Be Effective?

YES: Peter D. Kramer, from *Listening to Prozac: A Psychiatrist Explores Antidepressant Drugs and the Remaking of the Self* (Viking Penguin, 1993)

NO: Seymour Fisher and Roger P. Greenberg, from "Prescriptions for Happiness?" *Psychology Today* (September/October 1995)

ISSUE SUMMARY

YES: Psychiatrist Peter D. Kramer argues that antidepressant drugs such as Prozac can transform depressed patients into happy people with almost no side effects.

NO: Professors of psychology Seymour Fisher and Roger P. Greenberg claim that the studies that demonstrate the effectiveness of antidepressants are seriously flawed.

Antidepressants are drugs that are "anti-" or "against" depression. The use of antidepressants has recently risen dramatically. However, the relatively high number of people who report serious depression (10 percent of the population) does not account for this increase. The increasing use of antidepressants is due to the fact that more and more physicians and psychiatrists are prescribing them for psychological problems other than clinical depression. Antidepressants are now prescribed for people with "the blues," stress, obsessions, compulsions, and a host of other personal and social difficulties.

A major reason for this widespread use is that antidepressant drugs, especially Prozac, seem to work well with few side effects. Popular news magazines, such as *Newsweek* and *Time*, have heralded the supposed "miracle" power of these drugs: Not only do such drugs help cure what psychologically ails you (e.g., depression), but they are also able to "transform" your personality to a new and better you! In the past, the promise of such benefits was always balanced by the potential side effects of the drugs. People who take traditional antidepressants can experience a variety of symptoms, including dry mouth, a lack of energy, and weight gain. However, with the new types of antidepressants, such as Prozac, there appear to be very few side effects. Why not take antidepressants if they will make us better, happier people without the worry of side effects?

This is the sentiment of Peter D. Kramer, who wrote his best-selling book *Listening to Prozac* after successfully prescribing antidepressant medications to his patients. In the following selection, Kramer tells of one of his patient's experiences with Prozac: the drug not only ameliorated her depressive symptoms, but it also "reshaped [her] identity." Kramer wrestles with the implications of this success. Should such medications be prescribed more widely and more often? Is it acceptable for certain people to be on Prozac for life? These issues need to be addressed, according to Kramer, by "listening" to what drugs like Prozac have to teach us.

Seymour Fisher and Roger P. Greenberg contend that none of the issues that Kramer struggles with are relevant if antidepressants such as Prozac are not effective to begin with. After carefully reviewing the research, Fisher and Greenberg found that fully two-thirds of all the cases did as well with placebos (inert or nonactive pills) as they did with antidepressants. The authors also maintain that studies that do show some benefits of antidepressant medications have "crucial problems" in the methods used to evaluate such drugs.

POINT	COUNTERPOINT
• Antidepressant medications are amazingly effective.	• The effectiveness of antidepressant medications is mixed at best.
• The newer antidepressants, such as Prozac, are more effective than the older antidepressants.	• Many drug researchers and manufacturers are biased in favor of new drug development.
• Some patients who take antidepressant drugs report improvement not only in their depression but in their personalities as well.	• Such testimonials are not as reliable a measure of a drug's effectiveness as controlled studies.
• Research and experience have overwhelmingly indicated the effectiveness and safety of antidepressants.	• Much research is tainted by procedural and researcher biases.
• Many patients do not feel as well when they are off the medication as when they are on it.	• Research has shown that this may actually be a placebo effect.

YES

Peter D. Kramer

MAKEOVER

My first experience with Prozac involved a woman I worked with only around issues of medication. . . .

Tess was the eldest of ten children born to a passive mother and an alcoholic father in the poorest public-housing project in our city. She was abused in childhood in the concrete physical and sexual senses which everyone understands as abuse. When Tess was twelve, her father died, and her mother entered a clinical depression from which she had never recovered. Tess—one of those inexplicably resilient children who flourish without any apparent source of sustenance—took over the family. She managed to remain in school herself and in time to steer all nine siblings into stable jobs and marriages. . . .

Meanwhile, Tess had made a business career out of her skills at driving, inspiring, and nurturing others. . . .

That her personal life was unhappy should not have been surprising. Tess stumbled from one prolonged affair with an abusive married man to another. As these degrading relationships ended, she would suffer severe demoralization. The current episode had lasted months, and, despite a psychotherapy in which Tess willingly faced the difficult aspects of her life, she was now becoming progressively less energetic and more unhappy. It was this condition I hoped to treat, in order to spare Tess the chronic and unremitting depression that had taken hold in her mother when she was Tess's age. . . .

*   *   *

What I found unusual on meeting Tess was that the scars were so well hidden. Patients who have struggled, even successfully, through neglect and abuse can have an angry edge or a tone of aggressive sweetness. They may be seductive or provocative, rigid or overly compliant. A veneer of independence may belie a swamp of neediness. Not so with Tess.

She was a pleasure to be with, even depressed. I ran down the list of signs and symptoms, and she had them all: tears and sadness, absence of hope, inability to experience pleasure, feelings of worthlessness, loss of sleep and appetite, guilty ruminations, poor memory and concentration. Were it not for her many obligations, she would have preferred to end her life. And yet I felt comfortable in her presence. . . .

Tess had . . . done poorly in her personal life. She considered herself unattractive to men and perhaps not even as interesting to women as she would have liked. For the past four years, her principal social contact had been with a married man —Jim—who came and went as he pleased and finally rejected Tess in favor of his wife. Tess had stuck with Jim in part, she told me, because no other men approached her. She believed she lacked whatever spark excited men; worse, she gave off signals that kept men at a distance.

Had I been working with Tess in psychotherapy, we might have begun to explore hypotheses regarding the source of her social failure: masochism grounded in low self-worth, the compulsion of those abused early in life to seek out further abuse. . . . For the moment, my function was to treat my patient's depression with medication.

* * *

I began with imipramine, the oldest of the available antidepressants and still the standard by which others are judged. Imipramine takes about a month to work, and at the end of a month Tess said she was substantially more comfortable. She was sleeping and eating normally—in fact, she was gaining weight, probably as a side effect of the drug. "I am better," she told me. "I am myself again."

She did look less weary. And as we continued to meet, generally for fifteen minutes every month or two, all her overt symptoms remitted. Her memory and concentration improved. She regained the vital force and the willpower to go on with life. In short, Tess no longer

met a doctor's criteria for depression. She even spread the good word to one of her brothers, also depressed, and the brother began taking imipramine.

But I was not satisfied.

* * *

It was the mother's illness that drove me forward. Tess had struggled too long for me to allow her, through any laxness of my own, to slide into the chronic depression that had engulfed her mother.

Depression is a relapsing and recurring illness. The key to treatment is thoroughness. If a patient can put together a substantial period of doing perfectly well— five months, some experts say; six or even twelve, say others—the odds are good for sustained remission. But to limp along just somewhat improved, "better but not well," is dangerous. The partly recovered patient will likely relapse as soon as you stop the therapy, as soon as you taper the drug. And the longer someone remains depressed, the more likely it is that depression will continue or return.

Tess said she was well, and she was free of the signs and symptoms of depression. But doctors are trained to doubt the report of the too-stoical patient, the patient so willing to bear pain she may unwittingly conceal illness. And, beyond signs and symptoms, the recognized abnormalities associated with a given syndrome, doctors occasionally consider what the neurologists call "soft signs," normal findings that, in the right context, make the clinical nose twitch.

I thought Tess might have a soft sign or two of depression.

She had begun to experience trouble at work—not major trouble, but something to pay attention to. The conglomerate she worked for had asked Tess to take over a company beset with labor problems. Tess always had some difficulty in situations that required meeting firmness with firmness, but she reported being more upset by negotiations with this union than by any in the past. She felt the union leaders were unreasonable, and she had begun to take their attacks on her personally. She understood conflict was inevitable; past mistakes had left labor-management relations too strained for either side to trust the other, and the coaxing and cajoling that characterized Tess's management style would need some time to work their magic. But, despite her understanding, Tess was rattled.

As a psychotherapist, I might have wondered whether Tess's difficulties had a symbolic meaning. Perhaps the hectoring union chief and his foot-dragging members resembled parents— the aggressive father, the passive mother —too much for Tess to be effective with them. In simpler terms, a new job, and this sort especially, constitutes a stressor. These viewpoints may be correct. But what level of stress was it appropriate for Tess to experience? To be rattled even by tough negotiations was unlike her.

And I found Tess vulnerable on another front. Toward the end of one of our fifteen-minute reviews of Tess's sleep, appetite, and energy level, I asked about Jim, and she burst into uncontrollable sobs. Thereafter, our meetings took on a predictable form. Tess would report that she was substantially better. Then I would ask her about Jim, and her eyes would brim over with tears, her shoulders shake. People do cry about failed romances, but sobbing seemed out of character for Tess.

These are weak reeds on which to support a therapy. Here was a highly competent, fully functional woman who no longer considered herself depressed and who had none of the standard overt indicators of depression. Had I found her less remarkable, considered her less capable as a businesswoman, been less surprised by her fragility in the face of romantic disappointment, I might have declared Tess cured. My conclusion that we should try for a better medication response may seem to be based on highly subjective data—and I think this perception is correct. Pharmacotherapy, when looked at closely, will appear to be as arbitrary—as much an art, not least in the derogatory sense of being impressionistic where ideally it should be objective —as psychotherapy. Like any other serious assessment of human emotional life, pharmacotherapy properly rests on fallible attempts at intimate understanding of another person.

* * *

When I laid out my reasoning, Tess agreed to press ahead. I tried raising the dose of imipramine; but Tess began to experience side effects—dry mouth, daytime tiredness, further weight gain— so we switched to similar medications in hopes of finding one that would allow her to tolerate a higher dose. Tess changed little.

And then Prozac was released by the Food and Drug Administration. I prescribed it for Tess, for entirely conventional reasons—to terminate her depression more thoroughly, to return her to her "premorbid self." My goal was not to transform Tess but to restore her.

* * *

But medications do not always behave as we expect them to.

Two weeks after starting Prozac, Tess appeared at the office to say she was no longer feeling weary. In retrospect, she said, she had been depleted of energy for as long as she could remember, had almost not known what it was to feel rested and hopeful. She had been depressed, it now seemed to her, her whole life. She was astonished at the sensation of being free of depression.

She looked different, at once more relaxed and energetic—more available—than I had seen her, as if the person hinted at in her eyes had taken over. She laughed more frequently, and the quality of her laughter was different, no longer measured but lively, even teasing.

With this new demeanor came a new social life, one that did not unfold slowly, as a result of a struggle to integrate disparate parts of the self, but seemed, rather, to appear instantly and full-blown.

"Three dates a weekend," Tess told me. "I must be wearing a sign on my forehead!"

Within weeks of starting Prozac, Tess settled into a satisfying dating routine with men. She had missed out on dating in her teens and twenties. Now she reveled in the attention she received. She seemed even to enjoy the trial-and-error process of learning contemporary courtship rituals, gauging norms for sexual involvement, weighing the import of men's professed infatuation with her.

I had never seen a patient's social life reshaped so rapidly and dramatically. Low self-worth, competitiveness, jealousy, poor interpersonal skills, shyness, fear of intimacy—the usual causes of social awkwardness—are so deeply ingrained and so difficult to influence that ordinarily change comes gradually if at all. But Tess blossomed all at once.

"People on the sidewalk ask me for directions!" she said. They never had before.

The circle of Tess's women friends changed. Some friends left, she said, because they had been able to relate to her only through her depression. Besides, she now had less tolerance for them. "Have you ever been to a party where other people are drunk or high and you are stone-sober? Their behavior annoys you, you can't understand it. It seems juvenile and self-centered. That's how I feel around some of my old friends. It is as if they are under the influence of a harmful chemical and I am all right—as if I had been in a drugged state all those years and now I am clearheaded."

The change went further: "I can no longer understand how they tolerate the men they are with." She could scarcely acknowledge that she had once thrown herself into the same sorts of self-destructive relationships. "I never think about Jim," she said. And in the consulting room his name no longer had the power to elicit tears.

This last change struck me as most remarkable of all. When a patient displays any sign of masochism, and I think it is fair to call Tess's relationship with Jim masochistic, psychiatrists anticipate a protracted psychotherapy. It is rarely easy to help a socially self-destructive patient abandon humiliating relationships and take on new ones that accord with a healthy sense of self-worth. But once Tess felt better, once the weariness lifted and optimism became possible, the masochism just withered away, and she seemed to have every social skill she needed....

* * *

There is no unhappy ending to this story. It is like one of those Elizabethan dramas —Marlowe's *Tamburlaine*—so foreign to modern audiences because the Wheel of Fortune takes only half a turn: the patient recovers and pays no price for the recovery. Tess did go off medication, after about nine months, and she continued to do well. She was, she reported, not quite so sharp of thought, so energetic, so free of care as she had been on the medication, but neither was she driven by guilt and obligation. She was altogether cooler, better controlled, less sensible of the weight of the world than she had been.

After about eight months off medication, Tess told me she was slipping. "I'm not myself," she said. New union negotiations were under way, and she felt she could use the sense of stability, the invulnerability to attack, that Prozac gave her. Here was a dilemma for me. Ought I to provide medication to someone who was not depressed? I could give myself reason enough—construe it that Tess was sliding into relapse, which perhaps she was. In truth, I assumed I would be medicating Tess's chronic condition, call it what you will: heightened awareness of the needs of others, sensitivity to conflict, residual damage to self-esteem—all odd indications for medication. I discussed the dilemma with her, but then I did not hesitate to write the prescription. Who was I to withhold from her the bounties of science? Tess responded again as she had hoped she would, with renewed confidence, self-assurance, and social comfort.

* * *

I believe Tess's story contains an unchronicled reason for Prozac's enormous popularity: its ability to alter personality. Here was a patient whose usual method of functioning changed dramatically. She became socially capable, no longer a wallflower but a social butterfly. Where once she had focused on obligations to others, now she was vivacious and fun-loving. Before, she had pined after men; now she dated them, enjoyed them, weighed their faults and virtues. Newly confident, Tess had no need to romanticize or indulge men's shortcomings.

Not all patients on Prozac respond this way. Some are unaffected by the medicine; some merely recover from depression, as they might on any antidepressant. But a few, a substantial minority, are transformed. Like Garrison Keillor's marvelous Powdermilk biscuits, Prozac gives these patients the courage to do what needs to be done.

What I saw in Tess—a quick alteration in ordinarily intractable problems of personality and social functioning— other psychiatrists saw in their patients as well. Moreover, Prozac had few immediate side effects. Patients on Prozac do not feel drugged up or medicated. Here is one place where the favorable side-effect profile of Prozac makes a difference: if a doctor thinks there is even a modest chance of quickly liberating a chronically stymied patient, and if the risk to the patient is slight, then the doctor will take the gamble repeatedly.

And of course Prozac had phenomenal word of mouth, as "good responders" like Tess told their friends about it. I saw this effect in the second patient I put on Prozac. She was a habitually withdrawn, reticent woman whose cautious behavior had handicapped her at work and in courtship. After a long interval between sessions, I ran into her at a local bookstore. I tend to hang back when I see a patient in a public place, out of uncertainty as to how the patient may want to be greeted, and I believe that, while her chronic depression persisted, this woman would have chosen to avoid me. Now she strode forward and gave me a bold "Hello." I responded, and she said, "I've changed my name, you know."

I did not know. Had she switched from depression to mania and then married impulsively? I wondered whether I should have met with her more frequently. She had, I saw, the bright and open manner that had brought Tess so much social success.

"Yes," she continued, "I call myself Ms. Prozac."

There is no Ms. Asendin, no Ms. Pamelor. Those medicines are quite wonderful—they free patients from the bondage of depression. But they have not inspired the sort of enthusiasm and loyalty patients have shown for Prozac.

* * *

No doubt doctors should be unreservedly pleased when their patients get better quickly. But I confess I was unsettled by Ms. Prozac's enthusiasm, and by Tess's as well. I was suspicious of Prozac, as if I had just taken on a cotherapist whose charismatic style left me wondering whether her magic was wholly trustworthy.

The more rational component to my discomfort had to do with Tess. It makes a psychiatrist uneasy to watch a medicated patient change her circle of friends, her demeanor at work, her relationship to her family. All psychiatrists have seen depressed patients turn manic and make decisions they later regret. But Tess never showed signs of mania. She did not manifest rapid speech or thought, her judgment remained sound, and, though

she enjoyed life more than she had before, she was never euphoric or Pollyannaish. In mood and level of energy, she was "normal," but her place on the normal spectrum had changed, and that change, from "serious," as she put it, to vivacious, had profound consequences for her relationships to those around her.

As the stability of Tess's improvement became clear, my concern diminished, but it did not disappear. Just what did not sit right was hard to say. Might a severe critic find the new Tess a bit blander than the old? Perhaps her tortured intensity implied a complexity of personality that was now harder to locate. I wondered whether the medication had not ironed out too many character-giving wrinkles, like overly aggressive plastic surgery. I even asked myself whether Tess would now give up her work in the projects, as if I had administered her a pill to cure warmheartedness and progressive social beliefs. But in entertaining this thought I wondered whether I was clinging to an arbitrary valuation of temperament, as if the melancholy or saturnine humor were in some way morally superior to the sanguine. In the event, Tess did not forsake the projects, though she did make more time for herself.

Tess, too, found her transformation, marvelous though it was, somewhat unsettling. What was she to make of herself? Her past devotion to Jim, for instance—had it been a matter of biology, an addiction to which she was prone as her father had been to alcoholism? Was she, who defined herself in contrast to her father's fecklessness, in some uncomfortable way like him? What responsibility had she for those years of thralldom to degrading love? After a prolonged struggle to understand the self, to find the Gordian knot dissolved by medication is a mixed pleasure: we want some internal responsibility for our lives, want to find meaning in our errors. Tess was happy, but she talked of a mild, persistent sense of wonder and dislocation....

* * *

I wondered what I would have made of Tess had she been referred to me just before Jim broke up with her, before she had experienced acute depression. I might have recognized her as a woman with skills in many areas, one who had managed to make friends and sustain a career, and who had never suffered a mental illness; I might have seen her as a person who had examined her life with some thoroughness and made progress on many fronts but who remained frustrated socially. She and I might suspect the trouble stemmed from "who she is"—temperamentally serious or timid or cautious or pessimistic or emotionally unexpressive. If only she were a little livelier, a bit more carefree, we might conclude, everything else would fall into place.

Tess's family history—the depressed mother and alcoholic father—constitutes what psychiatrists call "affective loading." (Alcoholism in men seems genetically related to depression in women; or, put more cautiously, a family history of alcoholism is moderately predictive of depression in near relatives.) I might suspect that, in a socially stymied woman with a familial predisposition to depression, Prozac could prove peculiarly liberating. There I would sit, knowing I had in hand a drug that might give Tess just the disposition she needed to break out of her social paralysis.

Confronted with a patient who had never met criteria for any illness, what would I be free to do? If I did prescribe medication, how would we characterize this act?

For years, psychoanalysts were criticized for treating the "worried well," or for "enhancing growth" rather than curing illness. Who is not neurotic? Who is not a fit candidate for psychotherapy? This issue has been answered through an uneasy social consensus. We tolerate breadth in the scope of psychoanalysis, and of psychotherapy in general; few people today would remark on a patient's consulting a therapist over persistent problems with personality or social interactions, though some might object to seeing such treatments covered by insurance under the rubric of illness.

But I wondered whether we were ready for "cosmetic psycho-pharmacology." It was my musings about whether it would be kosher to medicate a patient like Tess in the absence of depression that led me to coin the phrase. Some people might prefer pharmacologic to psychologic self-actualization. Psychic steroids for mental gymnastics, medicinal attacks on the humors, antiwallflower compound —these might be hard to resist. Since you only live once, why not do it as a blonde? Why not as a peppy blonde? Now that questions of personality and social stance have entered the arena of medication, we as a society will have to decide how comfortable we are with using chemicals to modify personality in useful, attractive ways. We may mask the issue by defining less and less severe mood states as pathology, in effect saying, "If it responds to an antidepressant, it's depression." Already, it seems to me, psychiatric diagnosis had been subject to a sort of "diagnostic bracket creep"— the expansion of categories to match the scope of relevant medications.

How large a sphere of human problems we choose to define as medical is an important social decision. But words like "choose" and "decision" perhaps misstate the process. It is easy to imagine that our role will be passive, that as a society we will in effect permit the material technology, medications, to define what is health and what is illness....

* * *

An indication of the power of medication to reshape a person's identity is contained in the sentence Tess used when, eight months after first stopping Prozac, she telephoned me to ask whether she might resume the medication. She said, "I am not myself."

I found this statement remarkable. After all, Tess had existed in one mental state for twenty or thirty years; she then briefly felt different on medication. Now that the old mental state was threatening to re-emerge—the one she had experienced almost all her adult life —her response was "I am not myself." But who had she been all those years if not herself? Had medication somehow removed a false self and replaced it with a true one? Might Tess, absent the invention of the modern antidepressant, have lived her whole life—a successful life, perhaps, by external standards—and never been herself?

When I asked her to expand on what she meant, Tess said she no longer felt like herself when certain aspects of her ailment—lack of confidence, feelings of vulnerability—returned, even to a small degree. Ordinarily, if we ask a person why she holds back socially, she may say, "That's just who I am," meaning shy or hesitant or melancholy or overly cautious. These characteristics often per-

sist throughout life, and they have a strong influence on career, friendships, marriage, self-image.

Suddenly those intimate and consistent traits are not-me, they are alien, they are defect, they are illness—so that a certain habit of mind and body that links a person to his relatives and ancestors from generation to generation is now "other." Tess had come to understand herself—the person she had been for so many years —to be mildly ill. She understood this newfound illness, as it were, in her marrow. She did not feel herself when the medicine wore off and she was rechallenged by an external stress.

On imipramine, no longer depressed but still inhibited and subdued, Tess felt "myself again." But while on Prozac, she underwent a redefinition of self. Off Prozac, when she again became inhibited and subdued—perhaps the identical sensations she had experienced while on imipramine—she now felt "not myself." Prozac redefined Tess's understanding of what was essential to her and what was intrusive and pathological.

This recasting of self left Tess in an unusual relationship to medication. Off medication, she was aware that, if she returned to the old inhibited state, she might need Prozac in order to "feel herself." In this sense, she might have a lifelong relationship to medication, whether or not she was currently taking it. Patients who undergo the sort of deep change Tess experienced generally say they never want to feel the old way again and would take quite substantial risks— in terms, for instance, of medication side effects—in order not to regress. This is not a question of addiction or hedonism, at least not in the ordinary sense of those words, but of having located a self that feels true, normal, and whole, and of understanding medication to be an occasionally necessary adjunct to the maintenance of that self.

Beyond the effect on individual patients, Tess's redefinition of self led me to fantasize about a culture in which this biologically driven sort of self-understanding becomes widespread. Certain dispositions now considered awkward or endearing, depending on taste, might be seen as ailments to be pitied and, where possible, corrected. Tastes and judgments regarding personality styles do change. The romantic, decadent stance of Goethe's young Werther and Chateaubriand's René we now see as merely immature, overly depressive, perhaps in need of treatment. Might we not, in a culture where overseriousness is a medically correctable flaw, lose our taste for the melancholic or brooding artists—Schubert, or even Mozart in many of his moods?

These were my concerns on witnessing Tess's recovery. I was torn simultaneously by a sense that the medication was too far-reaching in its effects and a sense that my discomfort was arbitrary and aesthetic rather than doctorly. I wondered how the drug might influence my profession's definition of illness and its understanding of ordinary suffering. I wondered how Prozac's success would interact with certain unfortunate tendencies of the broader culture. And I asked just how far we—doctors, patients, the society at large—were likely to go in the direction of permitting drug responses to shape our understanding of the authentic self.

My concerns were imprecisely formulated. But it was not only the concerns that were vague: I had as yet only a sketchy impression of the drug whose ef-

fects were so troubling. To whom were my patients and I listening? On that question depended the answers to the list of social and ethical concerns; and the exploration of that question would entail attending to accounts of other patients who responded to Prozac.

* * *

My first meeting with Prozac had been heightened for me by the uncommon qualities of the patient who responded to the drug. I found it astonishing that a pill could do in a matter of days what psychiatrists hope, and often fail, to accomplish by other means over a course of years: to restore to a person robbed of it in childhood the capacity to play. Yes, there remained a disquieting element to this restoration. Were I scripting the story, I might have made Tess's metamorphosis more gradual, more humanly comprehensible, more in sync with the ordinary rhythm of growth. I might even have preferred if her play as an adult had been, for continuity's sake, more suffused with the memory of melancholy. But medicines do not work just as we wish. The way neurochemicals tell stories is not the way psychotherapy tells them. If Tess's fairy tale does not have the plot we expect, its ending is nonetheless happy.

By the time Tess's story had played itself out, I had seen perhaps a dozen people respond with comparable success to Prozac. Hers was not an isolated case, and the issues it raised would not go away. Charisma, courage, character, social competency—Prozac seemed to say that these and other concepts would need to be re-examined, that our sense of what is constant in the self and what is mutable, what is necessary and what contingent, would need, like our sense of the fable of transformation, to be revised.

NO

Seymour Fisher and
Roger P. Greenberg

PRESCRIPTIONS FOR HAPPINESS?

The air is filled with declarations and advertisements of the power of biological psychiatry to relieve people of their psychological distress. Some biological psychiatrists are so convinced of the superiority of their position that they are recommending young psychiatrists no longer be taught the essentials of doing psychotherapy. Feature stories in such magazines as *Newsweek* and *Time* have portrayed drugs like Prozac as possessing almost a mystical potency. The best-selling book *Listening to Prozac* by psychiatrist Peter Kramer, M.D., projects the idyllic possibility that psychotropic drugs may eventually be capable of correcting a spectrum of personality quirks and lacks.

As longtime faculty members of a number of psychiatry departments, we have personally witnessed the gradual but steadily accelerated dedication to the idea that "mental illness" can be mastered with biologically based substances. Yet a careful sifting of the pertinent literature indicates that modesty and skepticism would be more appropriate responses to the research accumulated thus far. In 1989, we first raised radical questions about such biological claims in a book, *The Limits of Biological Treatments for Psychological Distress: Comparisons with Psychotherapy and Placebo* (Lawrence Erlbaum). Our approach has been to filter the studies that presumably anchor them through a series of logical and quantitative (meta-analytic) appraisals.

HOW EFFECTIVE ARE ANTIDEPRESSANT DRUGS?

Antidepressants, one of the major weapons in the biological therapeutic arsenal, illustrate well the largely unacknowledged uncertainty that exists in the biological approach to psychopathology. We suggest that, at present, no one actually knows how effective antidepressants are. Confident declarations about their potency go well beyond the existing evidence.

To get an understanding of the scientific status of antidepressants, we analyzed how much more effective the antidepressants are than inert pills called "placebos." That is, if antidepressants are given to one depressed group and a placebo to another group, how much greater is the recovery of those taking the active drug as compared to those taking the inactive placebo? Generous claims that antidepressants usually produce improvement in about 60 to 70 percent of patients are not infrequent, whereas placebos are said to benefit 25 to 30 percent. If antidepressants were, indeed, so superior to placebos, this would be a persuasive advertisement for the biological approach.

We found 15 major reviews of the antidepressant literature. Surprisingly, even the most positive reviews indicate that 30 to 40 percent of studies show no significant difference in response to drug versus placebo! The reviews indicate overall that one-third of patients do not improve with antidepressant treatment, one-third improve with placebos, and an additional third show a response to medication they would not have attained with placebos. In the most optimistic view of such findings, two-thirds of the cases (placebo responders and those who do not respond to anything) do as well with placebo as with active medication.

We also found two large-scale quantitative evaluations (meta-analyses) integrating the outcomes of multiple studies of antidepressants. They clearly indicated, on the average, quite modest therapeutic power.

We were particularly impressed by the large variation in outcomes of studies conducted at multiple clinical sites or centers. Consider a study that compared the effectiveness of an antidepressant among patients at five different research centers. Although the pooled results demonstrate that the drug was generally more effective than placebo, the results from individual centers reveal much variation. After six weeks of treatment, every one of the six measures of effectiveness showed the antidepressant (imipramine) to be

merely equivalent to placebo in two or more of the centers. In two of the settings, a difference favoring the medication was detected on only one of 12 outcome comparisons.

In other words, the pooled, apparently favorable, outcome data conceal that dramatically different results could be obtained as a function of who conducted the study and the specific conditions at each locale. We can only conclude that a good deal of fragility characterized the apparent superiority of drug over placebo. The scientific literature is replete with analogous examples.

Incidentally, we also looked at whether modern studies, which are presumably better protected against bias, use higher doses, and often involve longer treatment periods, show a greater superiority of the antidepressant than did earlier studies. The literature frequently asserts that failures to demonstrate antidepressant superiority are due to such methodological failures as not using high enough doses, and so forth.

We examined this issue in a pool of 16 studies assembled by psychiatrists John Kane and Jeffrey Lieberman in 1984. These studies all compare a standard drug, such as imipramine or amitriptyline, to a newer drug and a placebo. They use clearer diagnostic definitions of depression than did the older studies and also adopt currently accepted standards for dosage levels and treatment duration. When we examined the data, we discovered that the advantage of drug over placebo was modest. Twenty-one percent more of the patients receiving a drug improved as compared to those on placebo. Actually, most of the studies showed no difference in the percentage of patients significantly improved by drugs. There was no indication that these studies, using more careful methodology, achieved better outcomes than older studies.

Finally, it is crucial to recognize that several studies have established that there is a high rate of relapse among those who have responded positively to an antidepressant but then are taken off treatment. The relapse rate may be 60 percent or more during the first year after treatment cessation. Many studies also show that any benefits of antidepressants wane in a few months, even while the drugs are still being taken. This highlights the complexity of evaluating antidepressants. They may be effective initially, but lose all value over a longer period.

ARE DRUG TRIALS BIASED?

As we burrowed deeper into the antidepressant literature, we learned that there are also crucial problems in the methodology used to evaluate psychotropic drugs. Most central is the question of whether this methodology properly shields drug trials from bias. Studies have shown that the more open to bias a drug trial is, the greater the apparent superiority of the drug over placebo. So questions about the trustworthiness of a given drug-testing procedure invite skepticism about the results.

The question of potential bias first came to our attention in studies comparing inactive placebos to active drugs. In the classic double-blind design, neither patient nor researcher knows who is receiving drug or placebo. We were struck by the fact that the presumed protection provided by the double-blind design was undermined by the use of placebos that simply do not arouse as many body sensations as do active drugs. Research shows that patients learn to discriminate

between drug and placebo largely from body sensations and symptoms.

A substance like imipramine, one of the most frequently studied antidepressants, usually causes clearly defined sensations, such as dry mouth, tremor, sweating, constipation. Inactive placebos used in studies of antidepressants also apparently initiate some body sensations, but they are fewer, more inconsistent, and less intense as indicated by the fact that they are less often cited by patients as a source of discomfort causing them to drop out of treatment.

Vivid differences between the body sensations of drug and placebo groups could signal to patients as to whether they are receiving an active or inactive agent. Further, they could supply discriminating cues to those responsible for the patients's day-to-day treatment. Nurses, for example, might adopt different attitudes toward patients they identify as being "on" versus "off" active treatment—and consequently communicate contrasting expectations.

THE BODY OF EVIDENCE

This is more than theoretical. Researchers have reported that in a double-blind study of imipramine, it was possible by means of side effects to identify a significant number of the patients taking the active drug. Those patients receiving a placebo have fewer signals (from self and others) indicating they are being actively treated and should be improving. By the same token, patients taking an active drug receive multiple signals that may well amplify potential placebo effects linked to the therapeutic context. Indeed, a doctor's strong belief in the power of the active drug enhances the apparent therapeutic power of the drug or placebo.

Is it possible that a large proportion of the difference in effectiveness often reported between antidepressants and placebos can be explained as a function of body sensation discrepancies? It is conceivable, and fortunately there are research findings that shed light on the matter.

Consider an analysis by New Zealand psychologist Richard Thomson. He reviewed double-blind, placebo-controlled studies of antidepressants completed between 1958 and 1972. Sixty-eight had employed an inert placebo and seven an active one (atropine) that produced a variety of body sensations. The antidepressant had a superior therapeutic effect in 59 percent of the studies using inert placebo—but in only one study (14 percent) using the active placebo. The active placebo eliminated any therapeutic advantage for the antidepressants, apparently because it convinced patients they were getting real medication.

HOW BLIND IS DOUBLE-BLIND?

Our concerns about the effects of inactive placebos on the double-blind design led us to ask just how blind the double-blind really is. By the 1950s reports were already surfacing that for psychoactive drugs, the double-blind design is not as scientifically objective as originally assumed. In 1993 we searched the world literature and found 31 reports in which patients and researchers involved in studies were asked to guess who was receiving the active psychotropic drug and who the placebo. In 28 instances the guesses were significantly better than chance—and at times they were surprisingly accurate. In one double-blind study that called for administering either imipramine, phenelzine, or placebo to depressed patients, 78 percent of patients and 87 percent of psychiatrists correctly distinguished drug from placebo.

One particularly systematic report in the literature involved the administration of alprazolam, imipramine, and placebo over an eight-week period to groups of patients who experience panic attacks. Halfway through the treatment and also at the end, the physicians and the patients were asked to judge independently whether each patient was receiving an active drug or a placebo. If they thought an active drug was being administered, they had to decide whether it was alprazolam or imipramine. Both physicians (with an 88 percent success rate) and patients (83 percent) substantially exceeded chance in the correctness of their judgments. Furthermore, the physicians could distinguish alprazolam from imipramine significantly better than chance. The researchers concluded that "double-blind studies of these pharmacological treatments for panic disorder was not really 'blind.'"

Yet the vast majority of psychiatric drug efficacy studies have simply *assumed* that the double-blind design is effective; they did not test the blindness by determining whether patients and researchers were able to differentiate drug from placebo.

We take the somewhat radical view that this means most past studies of the efficacy of psychotropic drugs are, to unknown degrees, scientifically untrustworthy. At the least, we can no longer speak with confidence about the true differences in therapeutic power between active psychotropic drugs and placebos. We must suspend judgment until future studies are completed with more adequate controls for the defects of the double-blind paradigm.

Other bothersome questions arose as we scanned the cascade of studies focused on antidepressants. Of particular concern is how unrepresentative the patients are who end up in the clinical trials. There are the usual sampling problems having to do with which persons seek treatment for their discomfort, and, in addition, volunteer as subjects for a study. But there are others. Most prominent is the relatively high proportion of patients who "drop out" before the completion of their treatment programs.

Numerous dropouts occur in response to unpleasant side effects. In many published studies, 35 percent or more of patients fail to complete the research protocol. Various procedures have been developed to deal fairly with the question of how to classify the therapeutic outcomes of dropouts, but none can vitiate the simple fact that the final sample of fully treated patients has often been drastically reduced.

There are still other filters that increase sample selectivity. For example, studies often lose sizable segments of their samples by not including patients who are too depressed to speak, much less participate in a research protocol, or who are too disorganized to participate in formal psychological testing. We also found decisions not to permit particular racial or age groups to be represented in samples or to avoid using persons below a certain educational level. Additionally, researchers typically recruit patients whose depression is not accompanied by any other type of physical or mental disorder, a situation that does not hold for the depressed in the general population.

So we end up wondering about the final survivors in the average drug trial. To what degree do they typify the average individual in real life who seeks treatment? How much can be generalized from a sample made up of the "leftovers" from multiple depleting processes? Are we left with a relatively narrow band of those most willing to conform to the rather rigid demands of the research establishment? Are the survivors those most accepting of a dependent role?

The truth is that there are probably multiple kinds of survivors, depending upon the specific local conditions prevailing where the study was carried out. We would guess that some of the striking differences in results that appear in multicenter drug studies could be traced to specific forms of sampling bias. We do not know how psychologically unique the persons are who get recruited into, and stick with, drug research enterprises. We are not the first to raise this question, but we are relatively more alarmed about the potential implications.

RESEARCHER MOTIVATION AND OUTCOME

We recently conducted an analysis that further demonstrates how drug effectiveness diminishes as the opportunity for bias in research design wanes. This analysis seized on studies in which a new antidepressant is compared (under double-blind conditions) with an older, standard antidepressant and a placebo. In such a context the efficacy of the newer drug (which the drug company hopes to introduce) is of central interest to the researcher, and the effectiveness of the older drug of peripheral import. Therefore, if the double-blind is breached (as is likely), there would presumably be less bias to enhance the efficacy of the older drug than occurred in the original trials of that drug.

We predicted that the old drug would appear significantly less powerful in the newer studies than it had in earlier designs, where it was of central interest of the researcher. To test this hypothesis, we located 22 double-blind studies in which newer antidepressants were compared with an older antidepressant drug (usually imipramine) and a placebo. Our meta-analysis revealed, as predicted, that the efficacy rates, based on clinicians's judgments of outcome, were quite modest for the older antidepressants. In fact, they were approximately one-half to one-quarter the average size of the effects reported in earlier studies when the older drug was the only agent appraised.

Let us be very clear as to what this signifies: When researchers were evaluating the antidepressant in a context where they were no longer interested in proving its therapeutic power, there was a dramatic decrease in that apparent power, as compared to an earlier context when they were enthusiastically interested in demonstrating the drug's potency. A change in researcher motivation was enough to change outcome. Obviously this means too that the present double-blind design for testing drug efficacy is exquisitely vulnerable to bias.

Another matter of pertinence to the presumed biological rationale for the efficacy of antidepressants is that no consistent links have been demonstrated between the concentration of drug in blood and its efficacy. Studies have found significant correlations for some drugs, but of low magnitude. Efforts to link plasma levels to therapeutic outcome have been disappointing.

Similarly, few data show a relationship between antidepressant dosage levels and their therapeutic efficacy. That is, large doses of the drug do not necessarily have greater effects than low doses. These inconsistencies are a bit jarring against the context of biological explanatory framework.

We have led you through a detailed critique of the difficulties and problems that prevail in the body of research testing the power of the antidepressants. We conclude that it would be wise to be relatively modest in claims about their efficacy. Uncertainty and doubt are inescapable.

While we have chosen the research on the antidepressants to illustrate the uncertainties attached to biological treatments of psychological distress, reviews of other classes of psychotropic drugs yield similar findings. After a survey of anti-anxiety drugs, psychologist Ronald Lipman concluded there is little consistent evidence that they help patients with anxiety disorders: "Although it seems natural to assume that the anxiolytic medications would be the most effective psychotropic medications for the treatment of anxiety disorders, the evidence does not support this assumption."

BIOLOGICAL VERSUS PSYCHOLOGICAL?

The faith in the biological approach has been fueled by a great burst of research. Thousands of papers have appeared probing the efficacy of psychotropic drugs. A good deal of basic research has attacked fundamental issues related to the nature of brain functioning in those who display psychopathology. Researchers in these areas are dedicated and often do excellent work. However, in their zeal, in their commitment to the so-called biological, they are at times overcome by their expectations. Their hopes become rigidifying boundaries. Their vocabulary too easily becomes a jargon that camouflages over-simplified assumptions.

A good example of such oversimplification is the way in which the term "biological" is conceptualized. It is too often viewed as a realm distinctly different from the psychological. Those invested in the biological approach all too often practice the ancient Cartesian distinction between somatic-stuff and soul-stuff. In so doing they depreciate the scientific significance of the phenomena they exile to the soul-stuff category.

But paradoxically, they put a lot of interesting phenomena out of bounds to their prime methodology and restrict themselves to a narrowed domain. For example, if talk therapy is labeled as a "psychological" thing—not biological—this implies that biological research can only hover at the periphery of what psychotherapists do. A sizable block of behavior becomes off limits to the biologically dedicated.

In fact, if we adopt the view that the biological and psychological are equivalent (biological monism), there is no convincing real-versus-unreal differentiation between the so-called psychological and biological. It *all* occurs in tissue and one is not more "real" than the other. A patient's attitude toward the therapist is just as biological in nature as a patient's response to an antidepressant. A response to a placebo is just as biological as a response to an antipsychotic drug. This may be an obvious point, but it has not yet been incorporated into the world views of either the biologically or psychologically oriented.

Take a look at a few examples in the research literature that highlight the overlap or identity of what is so often split apart. In 1992, psychiatrist Lewis Baxter and colleagues showed that successful psychotherapy of obsessive-compulsive patients results in brain imagery changes equivalent to those produced by successful drug treatment. The brain apparently responds in equivalent ways to both the talk and drug approaches. Even more dramatic is a finding that instilling in the elderly the illusion of being in control of one's surroundings (by putting them in charge of some plants) significantly increased their life span compared to a control group. What could be a clearer demonstration of the biological nature of what is labeled as a psychological expectation than the postponement of death?

Why are we focusing on this historic Cartesian confusion? Because so many who pursue the so-called biological approach are by virtue of their tunnel vision motivated to overlook the psychosocial variable that mediate the administration of such agents as psychotropic drugs and electroconvulsive therapy. They do not permit themselves to seriously grasp that psychosocial variables are just as biological as a capsule containing an antidepressant. It is the failure to understand this that results in treating placebo effects as if they were extraneous or less of a biological reality than a chemical agent.

PLACEBO EFFECTS

Indeed, placebos have been shown to initiate certain effects usually thought to be reserved for active drugs. For example, placebos clearly show dose-level effects. A larger dose of a placebo will have a greater impact than a lower dose. Placebos can also create addictions.

Patients will poignantly declare that they cannot stop taking a particular placebo substance (which they assume is an active drug) because to do so causes them too much distress and discomfort.

Placebos can produce toxic effects such as rashes, apparent memory loss, fever, headaches, and more. These "toxic" effects may be painful and even overwhelming in their intensity. The placebo literature is clear: Placebos are powerful body-altering substances, especially considering the wide range of body systems they can influence.

Actually, the power of the placebo complicates all efforts to test the therapeutic efficacy of psychotropic drugs. When placebos alone can produce positive curative effects in the 40 to 50 percent range (occasionally even up to 70–80 percent), the active drug being tested is hard-pressed to demonstrate its superiority. Even if the active drug exceeds the placebo in potency, the question remains whether the advantage is at least partially due to the superior potential of the active drug itself to mobilize placebo effects because it is an active substance that stirs vivid body sensations. Because it is almost always an inactive substance (sugar pill) that arouses fewer genuine body sensations, the placebo is less convincingly perceived as having therapeutic prowess.

Drug researchers have tried, in vain, to rid themselves of placebo effects, but these effects are forever present and frustrate efforts to demonstrate that psychoactive drugs have an independent "pure" biological impact. This state of affairs dramatically testifies that the labels "psychological" and "biological" refer largely to different perspectives on events that all occur in tissue. At present, it is somewhat illusory to separate the so-called biological and psychological effects of drugs used to treat emotional distress.

The literature is surprisingly full of instances of how social and attitudinal factors modify the effects of active drugs. Antipsychotic medications are more effective if the patient likes rather than dislikes the physician administering them. An antipsychotic drug is less effective if patients are led to believe they are only taking an inactive placebo. Perhaps even more impressive, if a stimulant drug is administered with the deceptive instruction that it is a sedative, it can initiate a pattern of physiological response, such as decreased heart rate, that it is sedative rather than arousing in nature. Such findings reaffirm how fine the line is between social and somatic domains.

What are the practical implications for distressed individuals and their physicians? Administering a drug is not simply a medical (biological) act. It is, in addition, a complex social act whose effectiveness will be mediated by such factors as the patient's expectations of the drug and reactions to the body sensations created by that drug, and the physician's friendliness and degree of personal confidence in the drug's power. Practitioners who dispense psychotropic medications should become thoroughly acquainted with the psychological variables modifying the therapeutic impact of such drugs and tailor their own behavior accordingly. By the same token, distressed people seeking drug treatment should keep in mind that their probability of benefiting may depend in part on whether they choose a practitioner they truly like and respect. And remember this: You are the ultimate arbiter of a drug's efficacy.

How to go about mastering unhappiness, which ranges from "feeling blue" to despairing depression, puzzles everyone. Such popular quick fixes as alcohol, conversion to a new faith, and other splendid distractions have proven only partially helpful. When antidepressant drugs hit the shelves with their seeming scientific aura, they were easily seized upon. Apparently serious unhappiness (depression) could now be chemically neutralized in the way one banishes a toothache.

But the more we learn about the various states of unhappiness, the more we recognize that they are not simply "symptoms" awaiting removal. Depressed feelings have complex origins and functions. In numerous contexts —for example, chronic conflict with a spouse—depression may indicate a realistic appraisal of a troubling problem and motivate a serious effort to devise a solution.

While it is true that deep despair may interfere with sensible problem-solving, the fact is that, more and more, individuals are being instructed to take antidepressants at the earliest signs of depressive distress and this could interfere with the potentially constructive signaling value of such distress. Emotions are feelings full of information. Unhappiness is an emotion, and despite its negativity, should not be classified single-mindedly as a thing to tune out. This in no way implies that one should submit passively to the discomfort of feeling unhappy. Actually, we all learn to experiment with a variety of strategies for making ourselves feel better, but the ultimate aim is long-term effective action rather than a depersonalized "I feel fine."

CHALLENGE QUESTIONS

Have Antidepressant Drugs Proven to Be Effective?

1. Assume that "mood brighteners" such as Prozac are as effective as Kramer says they are for Tess and that they are also perfectly safe. What would be some of the problems and prospects of this "brightened" world?

2. Fisher and Greenberg say that "depressed feelings have complex origins and functions." What function could such feelings have? How would their removal by antidepressants be problematic?

3. How would you account for what Fisher and Greenberg term "the power of the placebo"? How could this be used in psychotherapy?

4. Draw up a list of recommendations for improving drug evaluation research.

5. How do you account for the seemingly phenomenal success of Prozac as seen by psychiatrists such as Kramer?

ISSUE 16

Is Electroconvulsive Therapy Safe?

YES: Raymond R. Crowe, from "Electroconvulsive Therapy: A Current Perspective," *The New England Journal of Medicine* (July 19, 1984)

NO: Leonard Roy Frank, from "Electroshock: Death, Brain Damage, Memory Loss, and Brainwashing," *The Journal of Mind and Behavior* (Summer/Autumn 1990)

ISSUE SUMMARY

YES: Psychiatrist Raymond R. Crowe argues that not only is electroconvulsive therapy (ECT) safe and effective, but it also acts quickly after many other treatments have failed.

NO: Leonard Roy Frank, who has been an outspoken advocate against psychiatric shock therapy since his involuntary commitment to the Twin Pines Psychiatric Hospital in Belmont, California, asserts that ECT only seems effective because of the brain damage it causes and that many practitioners of ECT underestimate its risks.

Electroconvulsive therapy (ECT) has been controversial since it was first introduced in 1938. Despite continued questions, approximately 100,000 people in the United States are treated with ECT each year. ECT is used for a variety of problems, including depression, schizophrenia, and obsessive-compulsive disorder. During ECT treatments, electrical current is applied to the patient's brain for one-half to two seconds, which produces a seizure. The number of seizures induced during a course of treatment varies from 6 to 35, depending on the disorder and the severity of the symptoms.

The controversy surrounding ECT originates from both its side effects and its questionable effectiveness. Common side effects include memory loss, confusion, disorientation, apathy, dizziness, and headaches. While most of these seem to subside several hours after treatment, critics of ECT argue that some of these effects—especially memory loss—are permanent and compromise ECT's effectiveness. Proponents of ECT claim that this is an outmoded view. They argue that changes in technology have reduced the side effects and risks formerly associated with the procedure and that outcome research has indicated its effectiveness as a treatment strategy.

Raymond R. Crowe argues that ECT is often the most effective treatment available. In treating depression, for example, ECT is especially useful to individuals who do not respond to medication. He cites evidence that 75 to

85 percent of depressed patients respond positively to this type of treatment. He also claims that the mortality rate for ECT is very low and that ECT is considered one of the safest medical procedures requiring general anesthesia. Part of the reason why ECT is now considered a relatively safe treatment is the introduction of new procedures—side effects have been dramatically reduced. Memory loss remains the most common complaint, but this can be at least partially a function of depression itself. Crowe reports that the majority of ECT patients proclaim the helpfulness of ECT and that most would undergo it again if it were recommended.

Leonard Roy Frank contends that ECT is just as harmful today as it was when it was first introduced. He describes his own experience with ECT and the long-term effects of this experience. He claims that the use of ECT is increasing due to the financial gains it provides the people who administer it. He further claims that the "effectiveness" of ECT comes from brain damage that is induced by the seizures. Frank explains that following ECT, patients have symptoms similar to those found in persons with head injuries. Psychiatrists simply redefine these symptoms as signs of improvement. Frank also cites evidence indicating that the death rate from ECT is much higher than that claimed by Crowe. In addition, other adverse effects are much more serious and occur more frequently than is typically reported by ECT practitioners. He concludes that ECT is analogous to brainwashing because both ECT and brainwashing produce changes in one's perception of reality.

POINT	COUNTERPOINT
• ECT is often more effective than drugs in treating depression.	• ECT's "effectiveness" is actually brain damage that is caused by the procedure.
• ECT therapy is among the safest of all medical procedures that require general anesthesia.	• Evidence suggests that those who administer ECT underestimate its dangers.
• Complaints of memory loss among depressed patients are the result of the depression.	• Memory loss is a common complaint after ECT, regardless of the diagnosis.
• Recent modifications in treatment techniques have reduced the occurrence of side effects.	• Although modifications have been made, the underlying destructive potential remains the same.
• The majority of ECT patients feel they were helped by the procedure.	• ECT changes an individual's perception of reality.

YES

Raymond R. Crowe

ELECTROCONVULSIVE THERAPY:
A CURRENT PERSPECTIVE

Electroconvulsive therapy has become a national issue. Attacks on it have appeared in movies and television documentaries, as well as in the popular and professional press. These criticisms have resulted in legislation restricting its use in several states and, more recently, in an attempt to ban its use altogether in Berkeley, California. Because of growing public concern, physicians are likely to be consulted by the public about the treatment; thus, it is surprising that a current review of the subject is not available in a major general medical journal. A considerable body of research has been carried out on electroconvulsive therapy and several comprehensive reviews have been published, but they appear in books and specialty journals that may not be readily available to the nonpsychiatrist. The purpose of this article is to review the current status of this type of treatment for the nonspecialist.

Electroconvulsive therapy induces a grand mal seizure by means of an electric current applied across scalp electrodes. In current practice a series of 8 to 12 treatments is given at a rate of 2 to 3 treatments per week. Although the mechanism of action is unknown, most investigators agree that the seizure rather than the electricity produces the therapeutic benefit.

INDICATIONS AND EFFECTIVENESS

The primary indication for electroconvulsive therapy is severe depression, with this diagnosis accounting for 77 per cent of cases in which the treatment is used in this country. Since electroconvulsive therapy is often more effective than drugs, it is indicated in depressions that are refractory to medication, and since it acts more rapidly, it is indicated in cases involving a serious risk of suicide.

In the early 1960s two large trials of treatment for depression included a comparison of electroconvulsive therapy with placebo. In the American study, electroconvulsive therapy resulted in "marked improvement" in 76 per cent of 63 depressed patients, as compared with a 46 per cent response rate among 39 controls given placebo. The difference between electroconvulsive therapy and placebo was even larger in patients who were manic–depressive

From Raymond R. Crowe, "Electroconvulsive Therapy: A Current Perspective," *The New England Journal of Medicine*, vol. 311, no. 3 (July 19, 1984), pp. 163–166. Copyright © 1984 by The Massachusetts Medical Society. Reprinted by permission. References omitted.

or had involutional depression: 78 to 85 per cent of such depressions responded to electroconvulsive therapy, and 25 to 37 per cent responded to placebo. This difference contrasts with the usually milder and more chronic "neurotic" depressions, 78 per cent of which responded to either treatment. In the British investigation 84 per cent of 58 patients treated with electroconvulsive therapy improved, and 71 per cent were rated as having "no or only slight symptoms." In contrast, the respective rates for 51 controls receiving placebo were 45 and 39 per cent.

Although these large studies were conducted in different countries by different investigators using different diagnostic criteria, the agreement in results is striking, and the findings are consistent with those of other studies comparing electroconvulsive therapy with a placebo. In short, the evidence suggests that 75 to 85 per cent of depressed patients will respond to this type of treatment, as compared with a placebo response rate of 25 to 45 per cent. Moreover, acute endogenous depressions are likely to show the largest effects from the treatment.

The effectiveness of electroconvulsive therapy in depression is further supported by 10 trials employing a sham-treatment group. Nine were double-blind and the same number used random assignment to treatment groups and objective outcome ratings. Nine of the 10 studies found electroconvulsive therapy to be superior to sham treatment at a statistically significant level. Two of the studies deserve further comment. The only study with negative results used low-energy stimulation, which may be less effective than stimulation with higher levels of electrical energy. Another study found electroconvulsive therapy to be superior to sham treatments at the end of the treatment course, but one month later no difference was evident. However, many of the patients in both groups received antidepressant drugs after the trial; therefore, the question this study raises is whether electroconvulsive therapy is superior to conventional antidepressant therapy.

The effectiveness of electroconvulsive therapy as compared with standard antidepressants can be judged from the results of the American and British trials of antidepressant therapy cited above. Both studies administered two classes of antidepressant medication (tricyclic antidepressants and monoamine oxidase inhibitors) in therapeutic doses over an adequate trial period. The American study was an eight-week trial of imipramine (200 to 250 mg), phenelzine (60 to 75 mg), isocarboxazid (40 to 50 mg), and electroconvulsive therapy (nine or more treatments). Marked improvement was observed in 49 per cent of the 73 patients receiving imipramine, in 50 per cent of the 38 receiving phenelzine, and in 28 per cent of the 68 receiving isocarboxazid, as compared with 76 per cent of the group treated with electroconvulsive therapy. The difference between the latter and every other treatment group was statistically significant at the 0.05 confidence level, by a Yates chi-square analysis.

In the British study 58 patients received a minimum of four weeks of imipramine treatment in doses adjusted up to 200 mg, 50 received up to 60 mg of phenelzine, and 58 received four to eight electroconvulsive treatments. The percentage of patients with "no or only slight symptoms" was 52 per cent in the imipramine group and 30 per cent in the phenelzine group, as compared with 71 per cent of those receiving electroconvulsive therapy. The difference between imipramine and electroconvulsive treatment was just short of statistical significance (P = 0.056) but the difference between phenelzine and electroconvulsive therapy was significant (P < 0.001).

Differences in the response rates between active treatments are more difficult to demonstrate than treatment–placebo differences, and it is not surprising that some studies have failed to show a difference between electroconvulsive therapy and either tricyclic antidepressants or monoamine oxidase inhibitors, although others have found such a difference. Assuming that the true response rates are 75 per cent for electroconvulsive therapy and 50 per cent for drugs, a power analysis reveals that at least 43 patients in each treatment group would be necessary to achieve a 50 per cent probability of detecting the difference at the 0.05 level of significance. Indeed, all four studies with sample sizes exceeding this minimum have shown a statistically significant superiority of electroconvulsive therapy over drug. Perhaps more telling, however, is the fact that no study has found drugs to be more effective than electroconvulsive treatment.

Thus, electroconvulsive therapy is clearly as effective as antidepressant medication; moreover, it has two advantages over drugs: its rapid onset of action and its effectiveness when drugs have failed. In a recent double-blind trial comparing electroconvulsive therapy and imipramine (150 mg), 11 patients received sham imipramine and electroconvulsive therapy, and 13 received imipramine and sham electroconvulsive therapy. Both groups responded well after four weeks, but the response to electroconvulsive therapy was significantly greater during the first three weeks. This rapid response has been noted by others as well. The effectiveness of electroconvulsive therapy in cases in which drugs have failed is illustrated by an investigation of 437 depressed patients who were treated with 200 to 350 mg of imipramine per day; when the 190 patients who did not respond after one month received electroconvulsive therapy, a 72 per cent improvement rate was observed.

Schizophrenia accounts for only 17 per cent of cases treated with electroconvulsive therapy. Common indications include unresponsiveness to drugs in an illness of less than 18 months' duration, the presence of a secondary depression, and a superimposed catatonic state. Manic excitement responds well to electroconvulsive therapy but is the indication in only 3 per cent of patients receiving this therapy, since it has largely been replaced by medication in the treatment of mania. Finally, catatonic stupor is a rare condition in which electroconvulsive therapy is often effective even when drug therapy fails. . . .

Mortality
The mortality rate from 3438 courses of electroconvulsive therapy administered in Denmark during 1972–1973 was 4.5 deaths per 100,000 treatments, or 2.9 deaths per 10,000 patients treated. Complications included six instances of endotracheal intubation due to secretions, several cases of laryngospasm, and a tooth fracture. The largest reported series of deaths included 62 from the years 1947 to 1952. The cause was cardiovascular in 55 per cent of the cases, pulmonary in 31 per cent, and cerebrovascular in 6 per cent, with miscellaneous causes accounting for the remaining 8 per cent. Although the mortality statistics are from Scandinavia, the treatment technique was comparable

to current American practice; therefore, the findings should also be representative of experience in the United States. If they are, these figures place electroconvulsive therapy among the safest of all medical procedures requiring general anesthesia.

Adverse Effects

Adverse effects can be divided into those occurring during treatment, those appearing on recovery from each treatment, and those persisting after the course of treatments is over.

Adverse effects occurring during treatment may result either from the seizure or from the drugs used to modify it. Examples of the former include hypotension, hypertension, and bradyarrhythmias and tachyarrhythmias. Although frequent, they are rarely serious. Fractures, the most frequent complication of unmodified electroconvulsive therapy, have practically been eliminated by the use of muscle-paralyzing agents. Prolonged seizures are rare and easily terminated with intravenous diazepam. Adverse effects secondary to medication include laryngospasm and prolonged apnea due to pseudocholinesterase deficiency.

In the immediate post-treatment period, all patients experience transient postictal confusion. The next most frequently reported effects are memory disturbance and headache, which were mentioned by 64 and 48 per cent, respectively, of patients interviewed about previous electroconvulsive therapy. Less frequent effects after treatment are nausea and muscle pain.

The most frequently reported long-term effect of electroconvulsive therapy is memory disturbance, which has led to concern that the treatment may cause permanent brain damage. The apparent simplicity of investigating this question is deceptive. Patients with depression often perform at an impaired level on cognitive testing, and their performance improves with electroconvulsive therapy, masking any cognitive impairment that may have resulted from the treatment. Conversely, patients who have a relapse or do not improve may perform poorly on follow-up testing, leading to an erroneous assumption of persistent deficits secondary to electroconvulsive therapy. Thus, the importance of an appropriate control group cannot be overstressed, and in this respect, much of the earlier research is inadequate. Fortunately, renewed concerns over possible brain damage have led to a number of properly controlled studies, so that the question can be answered more firmly today than it could a few years ago.

In a recent follow-up study 55 per cent of patients who had received bilateral electroconvulsive therapy reported memory loss three years later. However, memory complaints are common in depression, and many patients who report memory disturbance after electroconvulsive therapy are clinically depressed; thus, it may be misleading to attribute these complaints entirely to the treatment. Nevertheless, considerable evidence indicates that electroconvulsive therapy does affect memory. First of all, complaints after treatment differ from those voiced before treatment and are therefore not entirely due to depression. Secondly, the nature of the memory disturbance differs as well. Depressed patients have poor registration and normal retention, but after electroconvulsive therapy they have normal registration and poor retention. Finally, reports of memory disturbance are more frequent after bilateral than after unilateral electroconvulsive therapy.

Reports of memory disturbance can be verified objectively. Memory tests conducted seven months after a course of bilateral electroconvulsive therapy indicate that memory of events immediately before and during the course of treatments remains impaired, memory of events up to two years before treatment shows minimal impairment, and more remote memory returns to normal. On the other hand, anterograde memory tested six months after electroconvulsive therapy demonstrates no impairment, as compared with the performance of controls with affective disorders.

In contrast to retrograde memory, other cognitive functions return to normal after electroconvulsive therapy. Weeks et al. conducted a prospective study of 51 depressed patients who received electroconvulsive therapy, 51 depressed patients receiving other treatments, and 51 normal controls. The groups were assessed before and after treatment and again after four and seven months, with a battery of 19 cognitive tests. Before treatment the group receiving electroconvulsive therapy scored below the patient-controls on 9 of the 19 tests; no test score deteriorated with treatment, and after four months performance on only one test separated the two groups. By seven months the electroconvulsive-therapy group outperformed the patient-controls on one test, but both patient groups performed at a level somewhat below that of the normal controls on several tests, presumably because of persistent depression in some patients. The Northwick Park trial also found that by six months groups that had received electroconvulsive therapy or sham therapy did not differ on cognitive testing.

How are these findings to be reconciled with the frequent reports of memory disturbance by patients treated with electroconvulsive therapy? First of all, continuing depression undoubtedly accounts for some of the complaints, although it cannot explain all of them. Secondly, continuing retrograde amnesia for events around the time of treatment may sensitize the patient to the normal process of forgetting. These two explanations are supported by the finding that patients who have undergone electroconvulsive therapy perform as well on objective memory tests as patients with depression who have not undergone such therapy. Finally, it is possible that anterograde memory may be impaired after treatment in a small number of patients. One study enrolled patients on the basis of subjective memory impairment that had persisted after electroconvulsive therapy, and administered a battery of 19 cognitive tests on them. The patients scored significantly below controls on three tests of verbal and nonverbal anterograde memory, after the confounding effects of medication and residual depression had been eliminated. However, because of the way in which these patients were identified, it is difficult to attribute their memory impairment to electroconvulsive therapy. Moreover, as already noted, the same investigators prospectively administered an identical battery of tests to carefully matched groups of patients with affective disorders receiving electroconvulsive therapy or other treatments and found no difference on any memory functions seven months after treatment.

MODIFICATIONS

The fear and adverse effects associated with unmodified electroconvulsive therapy have led to a number of modifications in treatment technique, with the aim of reducing morbidity without sacrificing effectiveness.

First of all, pharmacologic modifications have been used, including a short-acting anesthetic such as methohexitol for general anesthesia, oxygen to prevent hypoxia, atropine to reduce secretions and bradyarrhythmias, and succinylcholine to attenuate the convulsion.

Secondly, unilateral electrode placement on the nondominant hemisphere has been found to reduce the volume of brain tissue exposed to electricity and to spare the language functions located in the dominant hemisphere. A large number of studies comparing unilateral with bilateral electrode placement have reported less memory impairment with the former, but the findings with respect to treatment effectiveness are less clear. The majority of studies have found the two forms of treatment to be equally effective, but a minority have found unilateral placement less effective.

Finally, brief-stimulus therapy has been used. This form of treatment uses a stimulus consisting of a train of brief electrical pulses rather than a continuous sinusoidal wave form. The brief stimulus is capable of inducing a seizure with half the electrical energy of a sine-wave stimulus, and often less. The hypothesis that a brief stimulus causes less cognitive impairment has been difficult to substantiate statistically, although two recent studies have found a trend in that direction. However, the therapeutic efficacy of this therapy has generally equalled that of sine-wave treatment.

PATIENT ACCEPTANCE

Perhaps the ultimate judge of a treatment should be the person who receives it. How do patients who have received a course of electroconvulsive therapy regard the experience? A recent survey found that 40 per cent remembered approaching the treatment with some degree of anxiety, but in retrospect 82 per cent considered it no more anxiety-provoking than a dental appointment. The most unpleasant aspects were premedication, waiting for treatment, waking up, and recovery—each considered unpleasant by 15 to 20 per cent of patients. Seventy-eight per cent felt they were helped by electroconvulsive therapy, and 80 per cent said they would not be reluctant to have it again.

CONCLUSION

Electroconvulsive therapy is a safe and effective treatment for severe depression. Its advantages are its rapid onset of action and its effectiveness when other treatments have failed. Recent follow-up investigations have found no evidence of damage to the central nervous system. The most troublesome adverse effect is a transient amnestic syndrome in some patients, which clears but leaves a mild deficit in retrograde memory. The frequency of this disorder can be reduced by treatment modifications, but its occurrence cannot be eliminated altogether. Although the majority of patients with amnestic symptoms do not find them bothersome, some do, and patients should be apprised of the common adverse effects, as well as the benefits, of electroconvulsive therapy.

NO

Leonard Roy Frank

ELECTROSHOCK: DEATH, BRAIN DAMAGE, MEMORY LOSS, AND BRAINWASHING

Since its introduction in 1938, electroshock, or electroconvulsive therapy (ECT), has been one of psychiatry's most controversial procedures. Approximately 100,000 people in the United States undergo ECT yearly, and recent media reports indicate a resurgence of its use. Proponents claim that changes in the technology of ECT administration have greatly reduced the fears and risks formerly associated with the procedure. I charge, however, that ECT as routinely used today is at least as harmful overall as it was before these changes were instituted. I recount my own experience with combined insulin coma-electroshock during the early 1960s.... I report on who is now being electroshocked, at what cost, where, and for what reasons.... I examine assertions and evidence concerning ECT's effectiveness and ECT-related deaths, brain damage, and memory loss. Finally, I... [draw] a parallel between electroshock and brainwashing.

In October 1962, at the age of 30, I had a run-in with psychiatry and got the worst of it. According to my hospital records (Frank, 1976), the "medical examiners," in recommending that I be committed, wrote the following: "Reportedly has been showing progressive personality changes over past 2 or so years. Grew withdrawn and asocial, couldn't or wouldn't work, & spent most of his time reading or doing nothing. Grew a beard, ate only vegetarian food and lived life of a beatnik—to a certain extent" (p. 63). I was labeled "paranoid schizophrenic, severe and chronic," denied my freedom for nine months and assaulted with a variety of drugs and 50 insulin-coma and 35 electroshock "treatments."

Each shock treatment was for me a Hiroshima. The shocking destroyed large parts of my memory, including the two-year period preceding the last

From Leonard Roy Frank, "Electroshock: Death, Brain Damage, Memory Loss, and Brainwashing," *The Journal of Mind and Behavior*, vol. 11, nos. 3 and 4 (Summer/Autumn 1990), pp. 489–504, 506. Copyright © 1990 by The Institute of Mind and Behavior, P.O. Box 522, Village Station, New York, NY 10014. Reprinted by permission. The original article includes 58 references and is also available from the author; address: 2300 Webster Street, San Francisco, CA 94115.

shock. Not a day passes that images from that period of confinement do not float into consciousness. Nor does the night provide escape, for my dreams bear them as well. I am back there again in the "treatment room"; coming out of that last insulin coma (the only one I remember); strapped down, a tube in my nose, a hypodermic needle in my arm; sweating, starving, suffocating, struggling to move; a group of strangers around the bed grabbing at me; thinking—where am I, what the hell is happening to me?

Well into the shock series, which took place at Twin Pines Hospital in Belmont, California, a few miles south of San Francisco, the treating psychiatrist wrote to my father:

> In evaluating Leonard's progress to date, I think it is important to point out there is some slight improvement but he still has all his delusional beliefs regarding his beard, dietary regime and religious observances that he had prior to treatment. We hope that in continuing the treatments we will be able to modify some of these beliefs so that he can make a reasonable adjustment to life. (p. 77)

During the comatose phase of one of my treatments, my beard was removed —as "a therapeutic device to provoke anxiety and make some change in his body image," the consulting psychiatrist had written in his report recommending this procedure. He continued, "Consultation should be obtained from the TP [Twin Pines Hospital] attorney as to the civil rights issue—but I doubt that these are crucial. The therapeutic effort is worth it—inasmuch that he can always grow another" (p. 76). Earlier, several psychiatrists had tried unsuccessfully to persuade me to shave off my beard. "Leonard seems to attach a great deal

of religious significance to the beard," the treating psychiatrist had noted at the time. He had even brought in a local rabbi to change my thinking (p. 75), but to no avail. I have no recollection of any of this: it is all from my medical records....

One day, about a week after my last treatment, I was sitting in the "day room," which was adjacent to the shock-treatment wing of the hospital building. It was just before lunch and near the end of the treatment session (which lasts about five hours) for those being insulin-shocked. The thick metal door separating the two areas had been left slightly ajar. Suddenly, from behind the door, I heard the scream of a young man whom I had recently come to know and who was then starting an insulin course. It was a scream like nothing I had ever heard before, an all-out scream. Hurriedly, one of the nurses closed the door. The screams, now less audible, continued a while longer. I do not remember my own screams; his, I remember.

> [The insulin-coma patient] is prevented from seeing all at once the actions and treatment of those patients further along in their therapy.... As much as possible, he is saved the trauma of ·sudden introduction to the sight of patients in different stages of coma—a sight which is not very pleasant to an unaccustomed eye. (Gralnick, 1944, p. 184)

During the years since my institutionalization, I have often asked myself how psychiatrists, or anyone else for that matter, could justify shocking a human being. Soon after I began researching my book *The History of Shock Treatment* (1978) I discovered Gordon's (1948) review of the literature in which he compiled 50 theories purporting to explain the "healing" mechanism of the various forms of shock therapy then in use, including insulin, Metrazol, and electroshock. Here are some excerpts:

> Because prefrontal lobotomy improves the mentally ill by destruction, the improvement obtained by all the shock therapies must also involve some destructive processes....
> They help by way of a circulatory shake up....
> It decreases cerebral function....
> The treatments bring the patient and physician in closer contact....
> Helpless and dependent, the patient sees in the physician a mother....
> Threat of death mobilizes all the vital instincts and forces a reestablishment of contacts with reality....
> The treatment is considered by patients as punishment for sins and gives feelings of relief....
> Victory over death and joy of rebirth produce the results....
> The resulting amnesia is healing....
> Erotization is the therapeutic factor....
> The personality is brought down to a lower level and adjustment is obtained more easily in a primitive vegetative existence than in a highly developed personality. Imbecility replaces insanity. (pp. 199–401)

One of the more interesting explanations I found was proposed by Manfred Sakel, the Austrian psychiatrist who in 1933 introduced insulin coma as a treatment for schizophrenia. According to Sakel (cited in Ray, 1942, p. 250),

> with chronic schizophrenics, as with confirmed criminals, we can't hope for reform. Here the faulty pattern of functioning is irrevocably entrenched. Hence we must use more drastic measures to silence the dysfunctioning cells and so liberate the activity of the normal cells. This time we must *kill* the too vocal dysfunctioning cells. But can we do this without

killing normal cells also? Can we *select* the cells we wish to destroy? I think we can. (italics in original)

Electroshock may be considered one of the most controversial treatments in psychiatry. As I document below, the last decade has witnessed a resurgence of ECT's popularity, accompanied by assertions from proponents concerning its effectiveness and safety—assertions which deny or obscure basic facts about the historical origins of ECT, the economic reasons behind its current popularity, as well as its potential for destroying the memories and lives of those subjected to it....

ELECTROSHOCK FACTS AND FIGURES

Since 1938 between 10 and 15 million people worldwide have undergone electroshock. While no precise figure is available, it is estimated that about 100,000 people in the United States are electroshocked annually (Fink, cited in Rymer, 1989, p. 68). Moreover, the numbers appear to be increasing. Recent media accounts report a resurgence of ECT interest and use. One reason for this is the well-publicized enthusiasm of such proponents as Max Fink, editor-in-chief of *Convulsive Therapy*, the leading journal in the field. Fink was recently cited as saying that "[ECT should be given to] all patients whose condition is severe enough to require hospitalization" (Edelson, 1988, p. 3).

A survey of the American Psychiatric Association (APA) membership focusing on ECT (APA, 1978) showed that 22% fell into the "User" category. Users were defined as psychiatrists who had "personally treated patients with ECT," or "recommended to residents under their supervision that ECT be used on patients," during the last six months (p. 5). If valid today, this figure indicates that approximately 7,700 APA members are electroshock Users.

A survey of all 184 member hospitals of the National Association of Private Psychiatric Hospitals (Levy and Albrecht, 1985) elicited the following information on electroshock practices from the 153 respondents (83%) who answered a 19-item questionnaire sent to them in 1982. Fifty-eight percent of the respondents used electroshock (3% did not use electroshock because they considered it to be "inappropriate treatment for any illness"). The hospitals using ECT found it appropriate for a variety of diagnoses: 100% for "major depressive disorder," 58% for "schizophrenia," and 13% for "obsessive-compulsive disorder." Twenty-six percent of the ECT-using hospitals reported no contraindications in the use of the procedure. Darnton (1989) reported that the number of private free-standing psychiatric hospitals grew from 184 in 1980 to 450 in 1988. In addition, nearly 2,000 general hospitals offer inpatient psychiatric services (p. 67). While the use of ECT in state hospitals has fallen off sharply over the last 20 years, the psychiatric wards of general hospitals have increased their reliance on ECT in the treatment of their adult inpatients (Thompson, 1986).

In cases of depression, an ECT series ranges from six to 12 seizures—in those of schizophrenia, from 15 to 35 seizures —given three times a week, and usually entails four weeks of hospitalization. In 72% of the cases, according to the APA (1978, p. 8) survey cited above, electroshock costs are paid for by insurance companies. This fact led one psychiatrist to comment, "Finding that the patient has insurance seemed like the most common indication for giving electroshock" (Viscott, 1972, p. 356). The overall cost for a series of electroshock in a private hospital ranges from $10,000 to $25,000. With room rates averaging $500 to $600 a day, and bed occupancy generally falling, some hospitals have obtained considerable financial advantage from their use of ECT. A regular ECT User can expect yearly earnings of at least $200,000, about twice the median income of other psychiatrists. *Electroshock is a $2–3 billion-a-year industry.*

More than two-thirds of electroshock subjects are women, and a growing number are elderly. In California, one of the states that requires Users to report quarterly the number and age categories of electroshock subjects, "the percentage 65 and over" being electroshocked increased gradually from 29% to 43% between 1977 and 1983 (Warren, 1986, p. 51). More recently, Drop and Welch (1989) reported that 60% of the ECT subjects in a recent two-year period at the Massachusetts General Hospital in Boston were over 60 years and 10% were in their eighties (p. 88). There are published reports of persons over 100 years old (Alexopoulos, Young, and Abrams, 1989) and as young as 34 1/2 months (Bender, 1955) who have been electroshocked. In the latter case, the child had been referred in 1947 to the children's ward of New York's Bellevue Hospital "because of distressing anxiety that frequently reached a state of panic. . . . The child was mute and autistic." The morning after admission he received the first of a series of 20 electroshocks and was discharged one month later. "The discharge note indicated a 'moderate improvement,' since he was eating and sleeping better, was more friendly with the other children, and he was toilet trained" (pp. 418–419).

Children continue to be electroshocked. Black, Wilcox, and Stewart (1985) reported on "the successful use of ECT in a prepubertal boy with severe depression." Sandy, 11 years old, received 12 unilateral ECTs at the University of Iowa Hospitals and Clinics in Iowa City. He "improved remarkably" and "was discharged in good condition. Follow-up over the next 8 years revealed five more hospitalizations for depression" (p. 98)....

In the early 1970s electroshock survivors—together with other former psychiatric inmates/"patients"—began forming organizations aimed at regulating or abolishing electroshock and other psychiatric practices which they believed were harmful. In 1975 one group, the Network Against Psychiatric Assault (San Francisco/Berkeley), was instrumental in the passage of legislation that regulated the use of electroshock in California. Since then more than 30 states have passed similar legislation.

In 1982 the Coalition to Stop Electroshock led a successful referendum campaign to outlaw ECT in Berkeley, California. Although the courts overturned the ban six weeks after it went into effect, this was the first time in American history that the use of any established medical procedure had been prohibited by popular vote.

The Committee for Truth in Psychiatry (CTIP), all of whose members are electroshock survivors, was formed in 1984 to support the Food and Drug Administration (FDA) in its original (1979) classification of the ECT device in the high-risk category of medical devices, Class III, which earmarks a device or its related procedure for a safety investigation. To prevent an investigation of ECT, the APA had petitioned the FDA in 1982 for reclassification of the ECT device to Class II, which signifies low risk. After many years of indecision, the FDA proposed in 1990 to make this reclassification—but has not yet done so....

CLAIMS OF ELECTROSHOCK EFFECTIVENESS

Virtually all the psychiatrists who evaluate, write about and do research on electroshock are themselves Users. This partially explains why claims regarding ECTs effectiveness abound in the professional literature—while the risks associated with the procedure are consistently understated or overlooked. User estimates of ECT's effectiveness in the treatment of the affective disorders (i.e., depression, mania, and manic-depression) usually range from 75% to 90%. Two important questions, however, need to be addressed: What is meant by effectiveness and how long does it last?

Breggin (1979, p. 135; 1981, pp. 252–253) has proposed a "brain-disabling hypothesis" to explain the workings of electroshock. The hypothesis suggests that ECT "effectiveness" stems from the brain damage ECT causes. As happens in cases of serious head injury, ECT produces amnesia, denial, euphoria, apathy, wide and unpredictable mood swings, helplessness and submissiveness. Each one of these effects may appear to offset the problems which justified the use of ECT in the first place. Amnesia victims, having forgotten their problems, tend to complain less. Denial serves a similar purpose: because of their embarrassment, ECT subjects tend to discount or deny unresolved personal problems as well as ECT-caused intellectual deficits. With euphoria, the subject's depression seems to lift. With apathy, the subject's "agitation" (if that had been perceived as part of the original problem) seems to diminish. Dependency and submissiveness tend to make what may have been a resistive, hostile subject more cooperative and friendly. In hailing the wonders of electroshock, psychiatrists often simply redefine the symptoms of psychiatrogenic brain damage as signs of improvement and/or recovery.

Electroshock advocates themselves unwittingly provide support for the brain-disabling hypothesis. Fink, Kahn, and Green (1958) offered a good example when describing a set of criteria for rating improvement in ECT subjects: "When a depressed patient, who had been withdrawn, crying, and had expressed suicidal thoughts, no longer is seclusive, and is jovial, friendly and euphoric, denies his problems and sees his previous thoughts of suicide as 'silly,' a rating of 'much improved' is made" (p. 117)....

On the question of duration of benefit from ECT, Weiner (1984)—in one of the most important review articles on ECT published during the last decade—was unable to cite a single study purporting to show long-term, or even medium-term, benefits from ECT. Opton (1985) drew this conclusion from the Weiner review: "In this comprehensive review of the literature, after fifty years of research on ECT, no methodologically sound study was found that reported beneficial effects of ECT lasting as long as four weeks" (p. 2). Pinel (1984), in his peer commentary on the Weiner article, accepted Weiner's conclusion that "the risks of ECT-related brain damage are slight" and then added, "it is difficult to jus-

tify any risks at all until ECT has been shown unambiguously to produce significant long-term therapeutic benefits" (p. 31)....

The underlying assumption of this approach ["maintenance" ECT] is that affective disorders are for the most part chronic and irreversible. There is a popular saying among psychiatrists, "Once a schizophrenic, always a schizophrenic." While not a maxim, "Once a depressive, always a depressive," is nevertheless a core belief among many ECT Users. It "explains" so much for them. From this perspective, there are hardly any ECT failures, only patients with recurring depressive episodes who require ongoing psychiatric treatment, intensive and maintenance by turns.

Proponents also claim, but cannot demonstrate, that ECT is effective in cases of depression where there is a risk of suicide. They often cite a study by Avery and Winokur (1976) to support their position. But this study makes no such claim, as we can see from the authors' own conclusion: "In the present study, treatment [ECT and antidepressants] was not shown to affect the suicide rate" (p. 1033). Nevertheless, Allen (1978), in the very first paragraph of his article on ECT observed, "Avery and Winokur showed that suicide mortality in patients afflicted with psychotic depression was lower in patients treated with ECT than in those who were not" (p. 47).

DEATH FROM ELECTROSHOCK

Proponents claim that electroshock-caused death is rare. Alexopoulos et al. (1989) cited studies published in 1979 and 1985 indicating that the death rate from ECT was between 1 and 3 per 10,000 persons treated (0.01%–0.03%)—

considerably lower than estimates for the early years of ECT and, according to the authors, "probably related to the introduction of anesthesia and muscular relaxants" (p. 80). On the other hand, Kalinowsky (1967), who reported a death rate of up to 1 per 1,000 for the period before the premedicative drugs were being routinely used, had "the definite impression that the anesthesia techniques increased the number of fatalities" (p. 1282). Crowe (1984a, p. 164) cited a study conducted during 1972–1973 in Denmark which reported a rate of 2.9 deaths per 10,000 cases (0.029%).

Can any of these figures be relied upon? In researching my book on shock treatment (Frank, 1978, p. 153–156), I found reports of 384 electroshock-related deaths published between 1941 and 1977 in English-language sources, among which were a number of reports and studies with much higher death rates than those cited above. For example: three deaths in 150 cases—2% (Lowinger and Huddleson, 1945); four deaths in 276 cases—1.4% (Gralnick, 1946); five deaths in 356 cases—1.4% (Martin, 1949); two deaths in 18 cases—11.1% (Weil, 1950); three deaths in 700 cases—0.4% (Gaitz, Pokorny, and Mills, 1956); three deaths in 90 cases—3.3% (Kurland, Hanlon, Esquibel, Krantz, and Sheets, 1959); three deaths in 1,000 cases—0.3% (McCartney, 1961); two deaths in 183 cases—1.1% (Freeman and Kendell, 1980).

In the broadest and most informative study on ECT-related deaths, Impastato (1957) reported 254 deaths: 214 from published accounts and 40 previously unpublished. Most of the fatalities had received unmodified ECT. He estimated an overall death rate of 1 per 1,000 (0.1%) and 1 per 200 (0.5%) in persons over 60 years of age. Impastato was able to

determine the cause of death in 235 cases. There were 100 "cardiovascular deaths" (43%), 66 "cerebral deaths" (28%), 43 "respiratory deaths" (18%), and 26 deaths from other causes (11%) (p. 34).

Impastato's estimate of an ECT death rate among elderly persons five times higher than the overall death rate—coupled with his finding that cardiovascular failure was responsible for 43% of the deaths—should be very troubling in light of the growing tendency toward shocking the elderly. To justify this practice, Users usually point to the serious risks of cardiac complications and death involved in treating the elderly depressed —particularly those with heart disease —with antidepressant drugs. In current standard psychiatric practice, these drugs constitute basically the only alternative to electroshock.

Whether ECT or antidepressants offer less risk of fatality for these persons remains an open question, but Users assume ECT is less risky....

The Impastato findings have embarrassed the electroshock camp. As a result, this essential research has been largely neglected in the literature on electroshock since then. Thus, in three key review books authored or co-authored by Kalinowsky (Kalinowky, 1959; Kalinowsky and Hippius, 1969; Kalinowsky and Hoch, 1961), the Impastato study was nowhere mentioned, although Impastato's other works were frequently cited. Kalinowsky is not alone in this regard. Crowe's (1984a) ECT-review article—because it was published in the influential New England Journal of Medicine—must be considered among the most important of the 1980s. Citing a paper by Maclay (1953), Crowe wrote that "the largest reported series of deaths included 62 from the years 1947–1952" (p.

164), but Crowe neither referred to the Impastato study in his ECT mortality section nor cited it among his 80 references....

BRAIN DAMAGE FROM ELECTROSHOCK

One does not need a medical degree to recognize the destructive potential of passing 100 to 150 volts of electricity through the human brain. The same amount of current used to produce a seizure in ECT, if applied to the chest, would be fatal (Task Force, 1977, p. 1).

Fifteen years before the Impastato study (1957) which reported 66 "cerebral deaths," and four years after the introduction of ECT, Alpers and Hughes (1942) commented on their findings in an autopsy performed on a woman who had died following electroshock:

> The foregoing case is the first reported instance, so far as we know, of hemorrhages in the brain attributable to electrical convulsion treatment.... [T]he importance of the case lies in that it offers a clear demonstration of the fact that electrical convulsion treatment is followed at times by structural damage of the brain. (p. 177)

Hoch (1948), a well-known ECT proponent, likening electroshock to lobotomy, claimed that the brain damage each produced was beneficial:

> This brings us for a moment to a discussion of the brain damage produced by electroshock.... Is a certain amount of brain damage not necessary in this type of treatment? Frontal lobotomy indicates that improvement takes place by a definite damage of certain parts of the brain. (pp. 48–439)

Psychiatrist and neurophysiologist Pribram commented in a 1974 interview:

> I'd much rather have a small lobotomy than a series of electroconvulsive shocks.... I just know what the brain looks like after a series of shocks—and it's not very pleasant to look at. (p. 9)

The American Psychiatric Association's (1978) ECT survey, cited earlier, reported that 41% of the psychiatrist-respondents agreed with the statement, "It is likely that ECT produces slight or subtle brain damage." Only 26% disagreed. In their review of the literature, Templer and Veleber (1982) concluded "that ECT caused and can cause permanent brain pathology" (p. 65). Sament (1983), a neurologist, published his views on ECT's brain-damaging effects in a letter to the editor of a professional journal:

> I have seen many patients after ECT, and I have no doubt that ECT produces effects identical to those of a head injury. After multiple sessions of ECT, a patient has symptoms identical to those of a retired, punch-drunk boxer.
>
> After one session of ECT the symptoms are the same as those of a concussion (including retrograde and anterograde amnesia). After a few sessions of ECT the symptoms are those of a moderate cerebral contusion, and further enthusiastic use of ECT may result in the patient functioning at a subhuman level. (p. 11)

Sackeim (1986) also describes in a straightforward manner the effects of ECT:

> The ECT-induced seizure, like spontaneous generalized seizures in epileptics and most acute brain injury and head trauma, results in a variable period of

disorientation. Patients may not know their names, their ages, etc. When the disorientation is prolonged, it is generally referred to as an organic brain syndrome. (p. 482)...

Despite evidence of ECT-caused brain damage, most fully documented by Breggin (1979), proponents continue to claim that ECT does not cause brain damage....

In a recent 216-page document, *The Practice of ECT: Recommendations for Treatment, Training and Privileging,* the Task Force on ECT (APA, 1989) dismissed the critical issue of electroshock-caused brain damage with two sentences. The first, "Cerebral complications are notably rare" (p. 63), is false. The second, which concluded the Task Force's recommendations for information to be provided in the formal consent document for ECT— "In light of the available evidence, 'brain damage' need not be included as a potential risk" (p. 77)—is falsely premised. From this latter statement we see that the report's authors not only denied the possibility of ECT-caused brain damage, but found the very notion of such damage so *unthinkable* that they placed the term in quotation marks.

MEMORY LOSS FROM ELECTROSHOCK

The most serious and common effect of electroshock as reported by survivors is memory loss. The loss stretching backward in time from the treatment period is called retrograde amnesia and may cover many months or years. The memory loss from the treatment period forward in time is called anterograde amnesia and usually covers several months, often including the treatment period itself. The amnesia may be global or patchy; some memories return, others are permanently lost. These losses affect one's entire personality and are often experienced as a diminution of self. They not only impair one's ability to function in everyday affairs but also higher realms of spiritual and creative activity.

Herskovitz (cited in Philadelphia Psychiatric Society, 1943) reported finding memory defects among 174 people treated with ECT at the Norristown State Hospital, Pennsylvania, "to be rather general and often prominent. Therefore, patients whose occupation requires intellectual ability are selected for treatment with caution" (p. 798). In 1973, at the age of 49 Marilyn Rice (cited as Natalie Parker, a pseudonym, in Roueché, 1974) underwent a series of eight ECTs at the Psychiatric Institute of Washington. Soon afterwards, ECT-caused disability forced her into early retirement from her job as an economist. She described her return to work following electroshock:

> I came home from the office after that first day back feeling panicky. I didn't know where to turn. I was terrified. All my beloved knowledge, everything I had learned in my field during twenty years or more was gone. I'd lost the body of knowledge that constituted my professional skill.... I'd lost my experience, my knowing. But it was worse than that. I felt I'd lost myself. (pp. 95–96)

Andre (1988) described her memory losses following a series of 15 ECTs at New York Hospital in New York City in 1984 when she was 24 years old:

> My behavior was greatly changed; in a brain-damaged stupor, I smiled, cooper-

ated, agreed that I had been a very sick girl and thanked the doctor for curing me. I was released from the hospital like a child just born. I knew where I lived, but I didn't recognize the person I lived with. I didn't know where I had gotten the unfamiliar clothes in the closet. I didn't know if I had any money or where it was. I didn't know the people calling me on the phone.... Very, very gradually—because you can't know what you don't remember—I realized that three years of my life were missing. Four years after shock, they are still missing. (p. 2)...

Abrams (1988a) summarized his chapter on memory functioning after ECT as follows: "A remarkable amount has been learned in the past decade about the effects of ECT on memory, and the day is now past when the physician administering bilateral ECT can blithely assure his patient that 'the memory-loss will only be temporary'" (p. 153). Abrams favors unilateral ECT, claiming that it causes little or no "memory disturbance" and that "whatever dysmnesia does occur will be transient and probably undetectable 6 months later" (p. 154).

Over the years, ECT Users have tried to discount the significance of amnesia reports from electroshock survivors. Kalinowsky and Hoch (1952) gave an early explanation: "All patients who remain unimproved after ECT are inclined to complain bitterly of their memory difficulties" (p. 139). Implicit in this remark is the suggestion to Users that an ECT series should continue until the subject's memory "complaints" cease. In the same vein, the APA's 1978 report on ECT lent its weight to the notion that ECT "might lead many individuals ... to have persistent illusion of memory impairment" (p. 68).

More recently, Users have been arguing that the culprit responsible for memory problems is more likely to be the depression, not the electroshock (Crowe, 1984a). They assert that memory loss is a component of depression. Where the ECT subject is elderly, Users are likely to regard reports of memory loss as a normal sign of the aging process and, in the more severe cases, as symptomatic of senility. It is interesting to note that the Janis (1950) study—which concluded that ECT caused persistent amnesia (p. 372) —included very few depressed persons (only 3 of 30 subjects). More significantly on this point, the control group of 19 "depressed patients" who had not undergone ECT in the Squire (1983) study... "reported no memory problems at all at follow-up" (p. 6)....

ELECTROSHOCK AND BRAINWASHING

The term "brainwashing" came into the language during the early 1950s. It originally identified the technique of intensive indoctrination developed by the Chinese for use on political dissidents following the Communist takeover on the mainland and on American prisoners of war during the Korean War. The method involves the systematic application of sleep and food deprivation, prolonged interrogation, brow-beating, and physical punishment to force captives to renounce their beliefs. Once "brainwashed," they are reprogrammed to accept the beliefs of their captors.

While electroshock is not overtly used against political dissidents, it is used against cultural dissidents, social misfits and the unhappy, whom psychiatrists diagnose as "mentally ill" in order to justify ECT as a medical intervention. Indeed, electroshock is a classic example of brainwashing in the most meaningful sense of the term. Brainwashing means washing the brain of its contents. Electroshock destroys memories and ideas by destroying the brain cells in which memories and ideas are stored. A more accurate name for what is now called electroconvulsive therapy (ECT) would be electroconvulsive brainwashing (ECB)....

While electroshock cannot, of course, be used to reshape reality, it—like brainwashing—can and has been used to reshape the subject's perception of reality. Warren (1988) reported on interviews with ten married women 26–40 years old, from the San Francisco Bay Area who had undergone ECT between 1957 and 1961. The salient feature of ECT for these women was memory loss: "Troubling life-events and relationships commonly forgotten by these women included the existence of their husbands and children, their own names, and their psychiatrists" (p. 292). Some of the husbands, Warren reported, "used their wives' memory loss to establish their own definitions of past situations in the marital relationship." Other relatives found they "could freely re-define past situations without challenge" (p. 294). Warren comments: "When the recollections of one [marital] partner are to some degree erased, the dynamic reconstruction of reality shifts a little, or a lot" (p. 297).

Those who define reality usually control it. What had shifted here was power —away from the electroshock survivor. Without referring to brainwashing as such, Warren shows that electroshock and brainwashing serve similar ends. Electroconvulsive brainwashing is psychiatry's cleansing ritual; its method for controlling painful, unhappy memories and false or unpopular beliefs by destroying them.

CONCLUSION

Mystification and conditioning have undoubtedly played an important role in shaping the public's tolerant attitude toward electroshock. But it is not only the uninformed and misinformed public that has stood by silently during the electroshock era. There has hardly been a voice of protest from the informed elite —even when one of its own has been victimized.

While undergoing a series of involuntary electroshocks at the famed Mayo Clinic in 1961, Ernest Hemingway told visitor A. E. Hotchner, "Well, what is the sense of ruining my head and erasing my memory, which is my capital, and putting me out of business? It was a brilliant cure but we lost the patient. It's a bum turn, Hotch, terrible..." (cited in Hotchner, 1967, p. 308). A few days after his release from the Mayo Clinic following a second course of ECT, Hemingway killed himself with a shotgun. With all that has been written about him since his death, no recognized figure from the world of literature, academia, law, religion or science has spoken out against those responsible for this tragedy. As might have been expected, the psychiatric profession has also been silent. Not only did the psychiatrist who electroshocked Hemingway escape the censure of his colleagues, but a few years later they elected him president of the American Psychiatric Association....

ECT User Robert Peck titled his book *The Miracle of Shock Treatment* (1974). Antonin Artaud (cited in Sontag, 1976), the French actor and playwright, who was electroshocked in the early 1940s, wrote afterwards: "Anyone who has gone through the electric shock... never again rises out of its darkness and his life has been lowered a notch" (p. 530). In which perspective—or at what point between these two perspectives —is the truth to be found? This is no trivia question. For some, it will be the gravest question they will ever have to answer.

CHALLENGE QUESTIONS

Is Electroconvulsive Therapy Safe?

1. If you or a close family member were severely depressed and had not responded to other treatments, would you support the use of ECT? Are the benefits worth the risks of treatment?

2. How can you evaluate and make sense of the widely varying claims and the supporting evidence cited in reference to this issue? Crowe is a medical professional, while Frank is a former mental health patient. Does this affect your interpretation of the data in any way? Why, or why not?

3. Is ECT a form of brainwashing? Why, or why not?

4. Frank states that signs of "effectiveness" are really symptoms of brain damage. Do you agree with this position? What evidence supports your position?

5. Frank quotes a psychiatrist as saying that the most common reason for administering ECT is the patient's having health insurance to cover its cost. Why might this be the case? Describe how economic considerations might be weighed into recommendations for treatment.

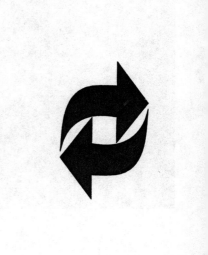

PART 6

Social Psychology

Social psychologists usually study the more "social" aspects of behavior, which include the influences of society upon the individual. One particularly controversial example is the question of whether or not pornography is harmful. Another example that is gaining more exposure is whether or not religious commitment can improve one's mental health. Both of these questions are addressed in this section.

■ Is Pornography Harmful?

■ Does Religious Commitment Improve
    Mental Health?

ISSUE 17

Is Pornography Harmful?

YES: Victor Cline, from "A Psychologist's View of Pornography," in D. E. Wildmon, ed., *The Case Against Pornography* (Victor Books, 1986)

NO: F. M. Christensen, from *Pornography: The Other Side* (Greenwood Press, 1990)

ISSUE SUMMARY

YES: Victor Cline, a professor emeritus of psychology and copresident of the seminar group Marriage and Family Enrichment, argues that pornography poses a great harm to viewers because it degrades women and desensitizes males to sexual violence.

NO: Professor of philosophy F. M. Christensen contends that there is little evidence that pornography is harmful and that pornography is only a scapegoat for other societal problems.

There is no denying that the amount of sexually explicit materials in our society has increased. Whereas movie directors and magazine photographers once feared photographing kisses and plunging necklines, they now do not hesitate to photograph simulated intercourse and nudity. Some consider this type of material pornography. Likewise, there is general agreement that the production of hard-core pornography has also increased. How does this affect our society? Does the proliferation of pornographic materials hurt people, particularly women and children?

In 1985 the U.S. Attorney General's Commission on Pornography, commonly referred to as the Meese commission, was appointed to answer these questions. In the course of the commission's work, many psychological studies were examined and many psychologists were consulted. Although the members of the commission did not agree unanimously on all the issues, they did conclude that pornography is harmful. Interestingly, a "shadow commission"—a citizen group that followed the commission to report on its theory and practice—immediately criticized this conclusion, claiming that it was politically motivated and that it ignored many important psychological investigations of the issues.

In the following selections, Victor Cline sides with and even adds to the Meese commission's findings. Cline argues that media portrayals of male aggression against women can have very harmful effects on women. He points to research documenting the potential harm of aggressive erotic materials to the male psyche, including studies on the effects of repeated exposure to sexual and violent materials. He believes that these studies show that viewing explicit sexual or violent material can decrease the inner controls that normally prevent violent behavior and increase the likelihood that an individual will act out what is viewed.

F. M. Christensen, in contrast, considers the various charges against pornography and concludes that there is little evidence confirming that it has ill effects. In refuting the charge that viewing pornography leads to wrongful behavior, Christensen argues that we assign too much power to the media. The media do not control our desires and actions, he asserts, but, as a form of media, pornography has nevertheless become a scapegoat for society's ills. Christensen concludes that society's problems related to sex and violence originate elsewhere.

POINT	COUNTERPOINT
• There is plenty of evidence that pornography is harmful.	• A careful interpretation of the evidence does not show any harm from pornography.
• Pornography creates a climate in which a rapist believes he is giving in to "natural urges."	• Sexual entertainment has little effect on a person's perceptions of reality.
• After repeated exposure to nonaggressive pornography, men show more callousness toward women.	• Pornography has become a scapegoat for the conflicts between men and women.
• Pornography can be a threat to marriages and families.	• Pornography can help preserve marriages.

YES

Victor Cline

A PSYCHOLOGIST'S VIEW OF PORNOGRAPHY

VIOLENT CRIME ON INCREASE

The United States is by far the most violent country in the world compared with all of the other advanced societies. For example, the U.S. rape rate is many times higher than that of the United Kingdom. We have more homicides annually on just the island of Manhattan than those reported in all of England, Scotland, and troubled Ireland combined. Our homicide rate is ten times that of the Scandinavian countries. At the present time crimes of violence in the U.S. are increasing at four to five times the rate of population growth.

Behavioral scientists recognize that there are many causes for any violent act, and it behooves us to investigate and understand those key triggers or contributors—if we care at all about the kind of society we want for ourselves and our children. Many lines of evidence have pointed to media influences such as commercial cinema and television as being especially suspect; as presenting inappropriate models and instigations of violent and antisocial behavior, especially for our young.

MENTAL HEALTH STUDY BLAMES TV VIOLENCE

In reviewing all of the scientific evidence relating to the effect TV violence has on behavior, the National Institute of Mental Health in 1984 issued a ten-year-report that concluded that there is in deed "overwhelming evidence of a causal relationship between violence on television and later aggressive behavior."

Some long-term studies and cross national studies also indicate that this learned aggressive behavior is stable over time—the victims stay aggressive. It is by no means just a transient kind of effect.

The reviewers of the research at the National Institute of Mental Health also note the role that TV (and by implication, commercial cinema) play as sex educators for our children. TV contributes significantly to sex role

From Victor Cline, "A Psychologist's View of Pornography," in D. E. Wildmon, ed., *The Case Against Pornography* (Victor Books, 1986). Copyright © 1986 by SP Publications, Inc., Wheaton, IL 60187. Reprinted by permission.

socialization as well as shaping attitudes and values about human sexuality. Various studies suggest that in TV presentations sex is commonly linked with violence. Erotic relationships are seldom seen as warm, loving, or stable. When sex is depicted it is almost always illicit. It is rather rare to suggest or depict sexual relations between a man and a woman married and who love each other. This agrees with similar results from my own research on the content of commercial cinema conducted several years ago.

RAPE RATE GROWS 700 PERCENT

Aggression against women is increasingly becoming a serious social problem. This can be seen in the escalation of wife battering, sexual molestation of female children, and sexual assaults on adult females.

Examining empirical data on the incidence of this type of thing is risky. This is because nearly all statistics on rape, for example, tend to underreport its actual occurrence. Many women for reasons of shame, humiliation, embarrassment, or seeking to avoid further trauma do not report these experiences. Data from many sources indicates that police get reports on one in four attempted or actual rapes. And of those reported less than 5 percent result in prosecution and conviction. Since 1933 the increase in the rape rate in the U.S. is in excess of 700 percent (this is in relation to population growth —in actual numbers the increase is much greater).

This means that the chances of a woman being sexually attacked are seven times greater now than in 1933. This clearly indicates major changes in male attitudes about sexual aggressiveness toward women. Obviously, more men today have a lower esteem of women. Why should this be in an age such as ours when women are being heard and winning rights?

PORNOGRAPHY DEGRADES WOMEN

Feminists such as Susan Brownmiller, Diana Russell, Laura Lederer, and Kathleen Barry point to the fact that our culture influences men to regard women as things—to be used. They note, for example, that nearly all pornography is created by males for a primarily male audience. Most of it is hostile to women. There is much woman hatred in it. It is devoid of foreplay, tenderness, caring, to say nothing of love and romance. They see its main purpose to humiliate and degrade the female body for the purpose of commercial entertainment, erotic stimulation, and pleasure for the male viewer. This is perceived as creating a cultural climate in which a rapist feels he is merely giving in to a normal urge and a woman is encouraged to believe that sexual masochism is healthy liberated fun.

Susan Brownmiller states, "Pornography, like rape, is a male invention designed to dehumanize women."

Many of the men's magazines such as *Hustler* are filled with antifemale messages both overt and covert. The victims in most "hard R" slasher movies are women—it is they who are most often sexually assaulted, tortured, and degraded. The feminist's concern is that these films sexually stimulate men while at the same time pairing this erotic arousal with images of violent assaults on women. The possibility of conditioning a potential male viewer into deviancy certainly has to be considered here.

MEN CONDITIONED TO SEXUAL DEVIATION

In a laboratory experiment using classical conditioning procedures at the Naudsley Hospital in London, England, Dr. Stanley Rachman conditioned a number of young males into being fetishists—a mild form of sexual deviation. A number of studies by such investigators as Davison, Bandura, Evans, Hackson, and McGuire suggest that deviant sexual fantasies through a process of masturbatory conditioning are related in many instances to later acted-out deviant sexual behavior. What happens here is that deviant sexual fantasies in the man's mind are paired with direct sexual stimulation and orgasm via masturbation. In this way the deviant fantasies acquire strong sexually arousing properties—which help sustain the sexual interest in the deviant behavior. Thus reinforced sexual imagery and thoughts (accompanied via masturbation) are a link in the acquisition and maintenance of new deviant sexual arousal and behavior. In the light of this, media portrayals of sex modeling male aggression against women logically can have a harmful effect on certain viewers. These portrayals, it would be concluded, facilitate deviant conditioning by providing new malignant fantasy material as well as increasing motivation for masturbatory experiences—leading to changes in the man's sexual attitudes, appetites, and behavior.

For example: A Los Angeles firm is currently marketing an 8mm motion picture film, available through the mails to anybody wishing it, which depicts two girl scouts in their uniforms selling cookies from door to door. At one residence they are invited in by a mature, sexually aggressive male who proceeds to subject them to a variety of unusual and extremely explicit sexual acts—all shown in great detail. This film is what is usually referred to as "hard-core" pornography. If the research of Rachman, McGuire, and others has any meaning at all, it suggests that such a film could potentially condition some male viewers, via masturbatory conditioning, into fantasies and later behavior involving aggressive sex with female minors.

Also, we might mention, that sex therapists have for years used carefully selected erotic material to recondition men with sexual deviations and help them out of their problems. In other words, the conditioning can go both ways using erotic materials. If all sexual deviations are learned, as psychologist Albert Bandura suggests, then one would assume that most deviations occur through "accidental conditioning"—which is exactly what many feminists have concerns about—especially as they see how they are treated in male-oriented media presentations.

At the present time in most urban areas of the U.S., there have arisen groups of women with concerns about what the media are doing to them—and especially about the social/sexual enculturation of males. Women Against Violence in Pornography and Media, based in San Francisco, is one example of this kind of group. Initially, their concerns were intuitive, moralistic, and emotional. They picketed various establishments—movie houses, adult bookstores, etc., selling or marketing highly sexist and antifemale materials—material that might tend to engender hate toward women. This includes the so-called "snuff films" in which women were supposedly murdered on-camera for the voyeuristic entertainment of male viewers.

However, in the last five years there has been a flood of well-done behavioral studies by researchers that appear to scientifically legitimize the concerns of these groups. These studies have repeatedly given documentation of potential harms to viewers of aggressive erotic materials, especially males.

These findings have been given very little attention by the popular press and are known only to a few scientists who are privy to the journals that these articles are showing up in. Thus, most ordinary citizens, journalists, as well as professionals in other disciplines, are not aware of these studies. For example, one of the editors of the *Utah Daily Chronicle* on March 1, 1985, in an editorial column discussing the cable TV bills before our state legislature, wrote, "Research has shown there is no demonstrable relationship between watching TV and increased aggressiveness . . . [and] regardless of what Utah legislators may believe, there is no scientific correlation between obscenity and antisocial conduct."

Both of these statements are totally incorrect. I am sure they were written as a result of ignorance, not as a conscious attempt at deception. In fact, quite ironically, on the day this editorial appeared, the Department of Psychology was sponsoring a widely publicized seminar featuring one of the nation's leading authorities on television effects, Dr. Raoul Huesmann, who discussed a pioneering 22-year study on the long-term negative effects of TV violence viewing.

WORLD'S MOST VIOLENT ADVANCED SOCIETY

I will not further belabor the issue of media violence and its potential negative effects on viewers. The evidence is really quite overwhelming on this issue. But let me briefly summarize what the literature suggests:

1. We are the most violent advanced society in the world.
2. We have the highest rates of media violence (in our entertainments) of any nation.
3. There are something like 20 years of behavioral studies linking exposure to media violence with violent behavior. These include both laboratory and field studies. And while there are many contributions to any particular violent act, I do not think that any fair reviewer of the literature can deny that the media are one important contributor to the violence problems in our society.

In my judgment repeated violence viewing also desensitizes the observer to the pathology in the film or material witnessed. It becomes with repeated viewing more acceptable and tolerable. We lose the capacity to empathize with the victim. Man's inhumanity to man (or woman) becomes a spectator sport. We develop and cultivate an appetite for it, no different than in early Rome, where people watched gladiatorial contests in which men fought to their deaths, dismembering their opponents' bodies. In other contests, others fought wild animals barehanded, eventually to be eaten alive. Again, a spectator sport. We become to some extent debased, even dehumanized, if you wish, by participating in these kinds of experiences. And, of course, approximations of what happened in the Roman arena nightly occur in some movie houses and on some TV screens —especially the cable variety where explicit violence is broadcast unedited. And usually—women are the victims.

INCREASING ASSAULTS IN MARRIAGE

Let us now move to the issue of linking aggressive pornography to increased aggressive behavior in marriage. It can be physical abuse, psychological abuse, or both. I see many couples in marital counseling. Violence between spouses is a common problem. Of course many women have learned to fight back. And this leads to an ever-escalating exchange of anger and hostility. Divorce usually doesn't solve the problem. If you don't know how to handle anger and aggressive feelings in one relationship, switching partners doesn't necessarily solve that problem for you in the next relationship.

There have been many experiments on aggressive pornography and its effects on consumers conducted by such capable investigators as Edward Donnerstein and Leonard Berkowitz at the University of Wisconsin; Neil Malamuth and James Check at the University of Manitoba; Dolf Zillman and Jennings Bryant at Indiana University; and Seymour Feshbach and his associates at UCLA.

SEXUAL AROUSAL, AGGRESSION LINKED

There has been a convergence of evidence from many sources suggesting that sexual arousal and aggression are linked or are mutually enhancing. Thus materials that are sexually exciting can stimulate aggressive behavior and, contrariwise, portrayals of aggression in books, magazines, and films can raise some people's levels of sexual arousal.

Thus it is not by accident that some four-letter words are frequently used in the context of an epithet or as part of a verbal attack on another.

Many theorists have noted the intimate relationship between sex and aggression —including Sigmund Freud, or more recently, Robert Stoler at UCLA who suggests that frequently it is hostility that generates and enhances sexual excitement.

A large number of research studies consistently and repetitiously keep coming to one conclusion—those subjects who are sexually aroused by strong erotic stimuli show significantly greater aggression than nonaroused controls.

The typical experiment will sexually arouse with pornographic stimuli a group of experimental subjects who will then be given an opportunity to punish a confederate with electric shock. Their aggressiveness will be compared to a neutral group who will have seen only a bland nonsexual film or reading material.

If the film combines both erotic *and* aggressive elements, this usually produces even higher levels of aggressiveness (as measured by the subjects' willingness to shock their partners at even higher and apparently more painful levels of shock intensity). If the erotic material is very mild—like pin-ups and cheesecake type photos—then it appears to have reverse effect on aggression—tending to dampen it.

In the situation of reading about or witnessing a filmed presentation of rape, if the female victim is seen as in great pain this can also have a dampening effect on aggressive arousal. It serves as an inhibitor. But if the portrayal showing the woman as finally succumbing to and enjoying the act (as is typical of most pornography), then the situation is reversed for males (but not females). It becomes very arousing. For men, the fantasy of a woman becoming sexually excited as a result of a sexual assault reverses any inhibitions that might have been initially mobilized by the coercive nature of the act and seeing the woman initially in pain.

This message—that pain and humiliation can be "fun"—encourages in men the relaxation of inhibitions against rape.

Doctors Gager and Schurr in their studies on the causes of rape note that a common theme in pornography is that women enjoy being raped and sexually violated. Sexual sadism is presented as a source of sexual pleasure for women. The Gager and Schurr studies note: "The pattern rarely changes in the porno culture.... After a few preliminary skirmishes, women invite or demand further violation, begging male masters to rape them into submission, torture, and violence. In this fantasy land, females wallow in physical abuse and degradation. It is a pattern of horror which we have seen in our examination of sex cases translated again and again into actual assaults."

UNIVERSITY STUDY SHOWS EFFECTS OF MOVIES

Going outside the laboratory, Neal Malamuth at the University of Manitoba sent hundreds of students to movies playing in the community. He wanted to see what the effects would be of their being exposed to films portraying sexual violence as having positive consequences. The movies they went to see were not pornography, but everyday "sex and violence" of the R-rated variety. The films included *Swept Away* (about a violent male aggressor and a woman who learns to crave sexual sadism; they find love on a deserted island). A second film, *The Get-*

away, tells about a woman who falls in love with the man who raped her in front of her husband, then both taunt the husband until he commits suicide.

A second group of students was assigned to see two control films, *A Man and a Woman,* and *Hooper,* both showing tender romance and nonexplicit sex. Within a week of seeing the films, Malamuth administered an attitude survey to all students who had participated in the experiment. The students did not know that the survey had anything to do with the films which they seen. Embedded within the survey were questions relating to acceptance of interpersonal violence and acceptance of such rape myths as "women enjoy being raped." Examples of questions asked also included: "Many women have an unconscious wish to be raped and may unconsciously set up a situation in which they are likely to be attacked."

The results of the survey indicated that exposure to the films portraying sexual violence significantly increased male subjects' acceptance of interpersonal violence against women. For females, the trend was in the opposite direction.

Dr. Malamuth concluded: "The present findings constitute the first demonstration in a nonlaboratory setting... of relatively long-term effects of movies that fuse sexuality and violence." And, of course, these were not hard-core pornography but rather R-rated type, edited films that have appeared on national commercial TV and unedited films shown on cable TV.

As I review the literature on media effects, it appears that in the areas of both sex and violence materials depicting these kinds of behaviors do several things: (1) they stimulate and arouse aggressive and sexual feeling—especially in males; (2) they show or instruct in detail *how* to do the acts—much of it antisocial; (3) when seen frequently enough have a desensitization effect which reduces feelings of conscience, guilt, inhibitions, or inner controls, the act is in a sense legitimized by its repetitious exposure; and finally, (4) there is increased likelihood that the individual will act out what he has witnessed.

Seymour Feshbach's research at UCLA has a direct bearing on this issue. After exposing a group of male college students to a sadomasochistic rape story taken from *Penthouse* magazine—telling of a woman's pleasure at being sexually mistreated—he asked these men if they would like to emulate what the rapist did to the woman. Seventeen percent said they would. When asked the same question but with the added assurance they would not get caught—51 percent indicated a likelihood of raping. This finding has been replicated in a number of other studies—though the percentages vary somewhat from research to research.

Doctors Edward Donnerstein and Neil Malamuth, in reviewing a large number of both field and laboratory experiments, found that exposure to media materials that mix both sex and violence causes six things to happen: (1) it sexually excites and arouses (especially) the male viewer; (2) it increases both his aggressive *attitudes* and *behavior*; (3) it stimulates the production of aggressive rape fantasies; (4) it increases men's acceptance of so-called rape myths (such as: "women ask for it"); (5) it produces a lessened sensitivity about rape (and increased callousness); and (6) it leads to men admitting an increased possibility of themselves raping someone—especially if they think they can get away with it.

PORNOGRAPHY REDUCES COMPASSION

What about exposure to nonaggressive erotic materials? Do these have any kind of effects on the consumer? Doctors Dolf Zillman and Jennings Bryant at Indiana University studied 160 male and female undergraduates who were divided into groups where they were exposed to: (1) massive amounts of pornography over a period of six weeks; (2) a moderate amount of pornography over that time period; and (3) no exposure over the same time period. Among their many findings were that being exposed to a lot of pornography led to a desensitization effect. The more they saw, the less offensive and objectionable it became to them. They also tended to see rape as a more trivial offense. They had an increasing loss of compassion for women as rape victims (even though no aggressive pornography was shown them).

Massive exposure to nonaggressive pornography clearly promoted sexual callousness in males toward women generally. This was measured by a scale where men agreed with such items as: "Pickups should expect to put out." Or, "If they are old enough to bleed, they are old enough to butcher" (referring to women).

The thrust of this presentation is to suggest that there is an abundance of scientific evidence suggesting social harms from some types of media exposure as has been previously discussed. The studies we have discussed are only illustrative. Many others have not been mentioned due to time limitations. Extensive documentation and lengthy bibliographies on this subject matter are available from the speaker on request.

CAN WE CONTROL PORNOGRAPHY?

We now come to the really hot issue—the bottom line. Does a community have a constitutional right through democratically enacted laws to censor or limit the public broadcast of these kinds of materials—because of their malignant nature? The recent controversy about the First Amendment of the Constitution? Where does or where can one draw the line? How bad or pathological does material have to be before it can be limited? Or should our position be: anything goes regardless of the consequences? Free speech is free speech.

Seymour Feshbach, the UCLA psychologist, states: "As psychologists, we would support community efforts to restrict violence in erotica to adults who are fully cognizant of the nature of the material and who choose knowingly to buy it. We are opposed to advertisements that have appeared in some popular magazines depicting sadomasochism; a recent fashion layout in *Vogue*, for instance, featured a man brutally slapping an attractive woman. We also oppose the practice of some therapists who try to help their patients overcome sexual inhibitions by showing them films of rape or by encouraging them to indulge in rape fantasies. Psychologists, in our judgment, ought not to support, implicitly or explicitly, the use and dissemination of violent erotic materials."

In reference to the First Amendment to our Constitution, we must recognize that today there are many kinds of democratically enacted prohibitions of speech and expression. These, of course, can be amended or repealed anytime we wish. Examples include libel, slander, perjury, conspiracy, false advertising, excitement to violence or speech that might create a "clear and present danger" such as yelling "Fire!" in a crowded theater. Still other examples include TV cigarette advertisements and also obscenity. In fact most of the people who went to jail in the Watergate scandal did so because of what they said—or for words they spoke (e.g., perjury and conspiracy).

In certain public broadcast mediums such as TV and radio, even obscene language can be proscribed without running afoul of the First Amendment.

At present, cable TV is the most controversial area about what is appropriate or inappropriate for broadcast. Currently there are virtually no restrictions on what can be aired. There are some channels in the U.S. broadcasting the roughest kind of hard-core pornography. There are others, including some in Utah, that are regularly broadcasting soft-core pornography mixed with violence. Last spring one of the local cable networks broadcast some 15 times *Eyes of a Stranger*. This film shows in explicit detail a young woman and her boyfriend being attacked by a sadist. He chops the boyfriend's head off, then proceeded to tear the girl's clothes off, strangle her, then rapes the dead body. The film continues with a series of attacks, rapes, and killings of other females. In my judgment this kind of programming, some of it in primetime, represents antisocial and irresponsible behavior on the part of the cable station owners.

Of course, there are many other similar type films which are being regularly broadcast. This is not an isolated incident. But along with this are films of great merit and quality which represent a major contribution to our cultural life as well as entertainment.

At present close to 30 percent of homes in the U.S. have cable. Industry analysts project that by 1985 this will be up to 50 percent and by the end of the decade 80–90 percent. This means that within a few years most all of us will have cable. This is not hard to understand when you consider that very shortly the cable networks will be able to outbid the regular networks for choice sporting events, fights, new Broadway musicals, etc. Even now all the latest movies come to cable before they reach regular commercial TV.

At present there is a double standard in television. The FCC (Federal Communications Commission) has control over the broadcast of appropriate materials by the regular commercial TV channels. They cannot air obscene or other objectionable material without threat of losing their licenses. Cable TV has no restrictions whatever. And, of course, cable firms are taking advantage of this. And there are some adults in our community who are delighted. Others are appalled and have concerns, especially about exposing their children to this kind of programming.

As with most controversial issues, there are no simple solutions which will please everybody. But somewhere a line must be drawn—if we care about the quality of life in our community. We have a right to protect ourselves in our own self-interest.

MEDIA SAVAGERY GROWS

George Elliot has commented: "If one is for civilization, for being civilized...,

then one must be willing to take a middle way and pay the price for responsibility. To be civilized, to accept authority, to rule with order, costs deep in the soul, and not the least of what it costs is likely to be some of the sensuality of the irresponsible." Some have argued, as Elliot notes, that since guilt reduces pleasure in sex, the obvious solution is to abolish all sexual taboos and liberate pornography, which in turn would supposedly free the human spirit —and the body.

This is a cheery optimistic view, not unlike the sweet hopefulness of the old-fashioned anarchist who thought that all we had to do in order to attain happiness was to get rid of governments so that we might all express our essentially good nature unrestrained. But sexual anarchism, or the aggressive impulse turned loose, like political anarchism before it, is a "lovely" but fraudulent daydream. Perhaps, before civilization, savages were noble, but if there is anything we have learned in this century, it is that those who regress from civilization become ignoble beyond all toleration. They may aspire to innocent savagery, but what they achieve too often is brutality and loss of their essential humanity.

The issue of how we should deal with the savagery which continues to escalate in our media presentations is just as much your problem as mine. I have shared with you some of the consequences of its presence on our culture. But the solution has to be a shared one—if we really believe in democracy.

NO
F. M. Christensen

ALLEGED ILL EFFECTS FROM USE

[T]he belief that pornography is evil in itself is simply wrong. This leaves open the important question of whether it has effects on the user's attitudes or behavior that are harmful to anyone. Charges that this is so are continually being made, so ... we will explore [a few aspects of] that issue [here]....

One particularly profound problem involves the issue of human agency. Now, some people are logically inconsistent in regard to this issue. In response to the suggestion that a violent criminal was made that way by a traumatic childhood, they invoke a notion of absolute free will: "His circumstances are not to blame; he *chose* to let them affect him!" But let the subject be something as comparatively minor as exposure to words or pictures, and suddenly the same people insist on a causal influence. The perennial debate over freedom of the will can hardly be discussed here. But one thing is perfectly clear from all the evidence: heredity and environment have a powerful influence on human behavior. The only room for rational debate is over whether that influence is total (deterministic) or not—and, once more, over just how much effect different types of causal factor exert....

THE DOMINO THEORY OF CHARACTER

The first of the claims we will discuss is usually expressed in vague generalities; it is basically the charge that use of pornography tends to produce all sorts of wrongful behavior. From the rhetoric some of its proponents employ, one would swear they believe sexual thoughts that are not strictly confined will create a desire to rush out and break windows or steal cars. It is as if they retained the primitive belief that individuals are motivated by only two basic desires—to do good or to do evil—rather than by a complex panoply of needs and emotions. In the minds of some, this idea seems to rest on the conviction that one sort of corruption just naturally leads to others. Few, if any, scientists take such ideas seriously today; "degeneracy theory," with its concept that physical, psychological, and moral defects are all bound together, was popular in the last century but died with the rise of psychology and scientific medicine. In the rest of the population, unfortunately, notions like this one linger on.

The more specific suggestion is sometimes made that "losing self-control" in regard to sex—as allegedly might be precipitated by the use of pornography—produces a general lack of self-discipline, hence a tendency toward selfish libertinism or worse. This sort of thinking has a long history. In Victorian times, married couples were advised to limit the frequency of their sexual activities strictly lest they lead to a weakening of the will and of general character. And the myth that sexual excess brought about the decline and fall of Rome has been around for centuries, having come down to us with those old suspicions about bodily pleasure. (Never mind the gladiators and slavery and brutal imperialism; sexual pleasure was Rome's real failing.) Part of what is involved in the thinking, evidently, is an inability to distinguish between the very specific matter of sexual "permissiveness" and the rejection of *all* restraints on behavior. Alternatively, it is a confusion between a strong interest in sex and a failure to care about any other sources of happiness, or else a tendency to be concerned only with one's own happiness or with the pleasures of the moment. Such tendencies are certainly bad; for example, a person or nation fixated on momentary satisfactions will lack the discipline to plan for and protect future happiness. But there is no reason to suppose that sexual desires are any more apt to have such consequences than are other strong desires.

... [I]t is revealing to point out the inconsistency between these concerns and the lack of fears associated with other needs and pleasures, say, those involving food, love, religious devotion, or the arts. How many are alarmed that our lack of eating taboos—so common in other cultures—will lead to a general obsession with the happiness of the moment? Perhaps we should ban the Wednesday food section in the newspaper, with its seductive pictures and emphasis on the pleasure of eating over its utilitarian function. How many suppose that getting great enjoyment from music or dance will lead to a general lack of self-discipline, or to a disregard for the welfare of others (say, of those who perform them)? The rhetoric about the perils of "pleasure-seeking" is remarkably selective in regard to which pleasures it notices. The real source of this belief, it seems clear, is the sexual anxiety with which so many are raised; it produces the fear that something terrible will happen if one should ever "let go."

The most important response to such charges, however, is that those who make them do not have a shred of genuine evidence. They have been accepted and repeated endlessly, like so many other cultural beliefs, without critical examination. In earlier times, when racism was more socially acceptable than it is now, mixing of the races was often alleged to have brought about the decline of Rome and other civilizations—on the basis of the same worthless *post hoc* reasoning.... Certain commentators have claimed to have evidence from one or two studies that reported finding a statistical association between exposure to sexual materials and juvenile delinquency in the United States. It could well be true that in this society, there has been a tendency for those who lack the traditional sexual attitudes to reject other social standards as well. The former is easily explained as a result of the latter, however: those who have been less well socialized into or have rebelled against the system as a whole will naturally be among the ones whose sexual behavior is less constrained. Alternatively, those whose needs have led them to break one social taboo will feel less threatened by other societal rules....

Of course, that a belief is held for bad reasons does not mean there are no good reasons for it. Nonetheless, it can be said without hesitation that the evidence available is strongly against the "domino theory" of character. One has only to consider the cross-cultural picture to begin to realize this, say, the promiscuous children and youth of Mangaia or the Trobriand Islands or the Muria villages, who grow up into hard-working adults who have internalized all of their society's moral standards. More generally, there is no indication that sexually positive cultures have greater amounts of antisocial behavior. In fact, one cross-cultural survey found significantly more personal crime in groups where premarital sex is strongly punished than in others. (The fact that the crime rate in permissive northern Europe is much lower than that in the United States may already be known to the reader—but beware of *post hoc* thinking.) The belief that gratifying sexual feelings tends somehow to turn into a general state of moral corruption, or even to damage one's capacity for self-discipline, is sheer superstition....

PERSONAL RELATIONSHIPS

A second variety of claim that pornography has ill effects is that its use tends to damage personal relationships between men and women. This charge takes several different forms, including some that are bizarre (e.g., the idea that many men prefer it to real women and hence will avoid relationships with them if given that option). The simplest of these allegations, however, just points out that numerous women are upset by their partners' interest in pornography, so that it becomes a source of conflict. Part of the problem here is jealousy: the mere biologically normal fact that the partner is attracted to other persons is threatening to some, even when it is all fantasy. But that is evidently not the main difficulty. Few men feel upset over their partners' interest in love stories, say, in soap operas, with their romantic hunks and adulterous love affairs. The real problem seems to be the woman's aversion to nudity and sexual openness.

That being so, this argument presupposes that pornography is hurtful rather than proving it. For it could equally well be said that it is the woman's prudishness, rather than the man's interest in pornography, that is "the real" source of the trouble; which it is would have to be argued for rather than just assumed. Mention to the feminists and religionists who employ this objection that women's liberation or religious devotion has broken up many relationships, and they will make the same basic point.... [M]oreover, it seems clear which one is the real culprit. In earlier years, the attitude that explicit sex is offensive to women led men to go off by themselves to watch "stag films"; what could have been an enjoyable shared experience became a source of alienation. Although female interest in such things might never approach that of males, the ones who divide the sexes are those who say, "My desires are noble and yours are nasty," not those who believe in the equal worth and dignity of the needs of both.

One special argument of this kind alleges that pornography harms relationships by its overemphasis on sex, and also by its underemphasis on companionship or romantic love. It is said to "teach men" to value the former too much and the latter too little. With its culture-bound and egocentric notions of how much emphasis is too much or too little, this claim ignores the possibility of keeping the sexes in harmony by teaching women to want sex in the same way. Its biggest error, however, lies in assigning to media depictions far more power to influence basic desires than is at all justified. As usual, those who make this claim express no similar beliefs about the persuasive powers of the constant barrage of love songs and love stories in all the entertainment media. If such exposure were really so effective, one would think, we would all be incurable love-junkies by now. In any case, there is certainly no lack of publicity promoting love and companionship in our society. Moreover, male sexuality is not detectably different in cultures without appreciable amounts of pornography; indeed, it is evidently very much the same the world over.

What really underlies this claim is an old problem: the unfortunate fact that, on average, men's and women's needs in regard to love/commitment and sex are not well matched. Unable—or perhaps just unwilling—to believe men could ultimately have such different needs than they themselves do, some women suppose it must be the different amount of stress on sex or love among men that does it. One common response is simply to deny that men are really different. For example, these women say men just *think* they have a strong need for sex because advertisers keep telling them they do. Others grant the reality of male sexual responses but do not want to believe they are natural. (Among feminists, this is just part of the wider conviction that

there are *no* innate differences between the sexes except anatomical ones.) Yet those who make both claims insist it is men who have been most affected by culture in this regard. Over and again, without offering any argument as to which is cause and which effect, they assert that men would not be so interested in sex, or so attracted to female bodies, if only there were not so much emphasis on those things in this society. Besides projecting their own responses onto male nature—responses that are themselves largely culture-conditioned—the women (and sometimes men) who make such claims are somehow blind to all the societal efforts to suppress male sexuality and promote female needs.

What is true is that a double standard is still taught to adolescents in our culture. But it is glaringly false to say that it encourages males to be sexual; it merely discourages them less. Consider the common charge that "this society" teaches young males they have to "score" to be real men, for example. In fact, you will not find this preached by any of the major socializing institutions, not by church, government, school, family, *or* the media. Even that small segment of the latter that celebrates sex overtly cannot really be said to do this—and it is standardly maligned and even banned by the society at large. The one place where such a thing is taught is in the peer groups of some young men as they themselves rebel against society's teaching on the subject, trying to justify their own needs and feelings. However all this may be, the point remains that pornography is not the cause of male sexuality. It has again become a scapegoat in connection with male-female conflicts whose real causes lie in biology, or at least much deeper in the socialization of men—or of women....

Some have claimed there is scientific evidence that standard pornography causes misperception of other people's sexual desires. In a certain type of experiment, volunteers are exposed to a presentation of some kind and then asked questions about their beliefs or attitudes. (A subterfuge is used to keep them from realizing the true purpose of the test.) In one version of this test, subjects who have been shown sexual materials indicated they regarded women (as well as men) as somewhat more sexually liberal than did subjects who had not been shown the materials. In itself, this is no evidence of misperception; the former might have been closer to the truth than the latter. In any case, the result is not in the least remarkable. A recent or extended experience of *any* kind looms large in one's consciousness. Hence just about any book or movie, *or* real person that one has recently met, would have a similar influence on one's other judgments, temporarily. For a more striking example, one who has just seen a scary movie is much more likely to look under the bed before retiring at night. The effect soon fades, however; it is swamped by that of subsequently encountered books or movies or real people. And most of the latter tend to promote the culture's current party line on sex, just as they do on other subjects. Except in unusual circumstances, the conclusion remains: sexual entertainment will have little effect on perceptions of reality.

A variant of this objection says that the ecstatic pleasure often portrayed in pornography will tend to make the readers or viewers disappointed with their own sexual experience and, hence, with their partners or their partners'

performance. (Although it is women who standardly complain about the latter, this new claim is usually framed in terms of male dissatisfaction.) It is not always clear whether those who present the argument believe ordinary tepid sex is really all that is possible—the half-hour orgasms of Mangaian women argue otherwise—or whether for some reason they just think it unwise to aspire to greater enjoyment. In any case, few people would be misled even by genuine exaggeration, which is an extremely common part of life. Does the hysterical euphoria of the consumers in commercials for hamburgers and soft drinks make anyone seriously expect them to taste different? Once again, the only reason for possibly being misled in the special case of sex is societally imposed ignorance. And it is people who use arguments like this one who often want to keep young people in that vulnerable state....

Most of the... claims about pornography's "effects" assume that too much stress on sex is dangerous to an intimate relationship. That can certainly be true, but the proper balance of emphasis between sex and other needs in that context is one that requires sensitive exploration, not dogma. In fact, those who give these fallacious arguments typically overlook the opposite problem. Surveys and clinical experience have long revealed that a high percentage of couples have unsatisfying sex lives. That is a major destroyer of relationships in itself. There are many reasons for this, but a serious one continues to be the sexual inhibition this society inculcates, with its *negative* stress on sex. Conversely,... countless women have discovered that sex could be a joy rather than a burden, and they have done so precisely by learning to become more sexually assertive and more adventurous in bed.

What is especially relevant to our purposes about the latter fact is that pornography has often aided in the process. Large numbers of people have reported that it has helped their sex lives and hence their relationships. In one survey of couples who went to sex movies together, for example, 42 percent made that claim. In her beautiful little book on female sexuality, *For Yourself*, Dr. Lonnie Barbach tells how women have overcome difficulty in getting sexually aroused, or in having orgasms, by learning to use fantasy and pornography. Indeed, it has become standard practice for therapists to use sex films to treat the sexual disabilities of individuals and couples. The ways in which they help are very revealing in light of what has just been discussed: they aid in overcoming inhibition, enhance arousal in preparation for sex, and introduce ideas and techniques that bring freshness to a stale routine. So far from harming intimate personal relationships, pornography can have the very opposite effect.

MARRIAGE AND THE FAMILY

A third general charge of social harm from pornography has been put forth, mostly by traditionalists. Its use is seen as a threat, not to love and personal relationships as such, but to marriage and the family. The basic claim is that by celebrating sex for its own sake, pornography entices people to leave or refrain from entering committed relationships—"Why be married if you can get sex without it?" —or else leads to their breakup by encouraging extramarital adventures that result in jealous conflicts. This is a seri-

ous charge indeed. The legalistic concern some have with marriage ceremonies is highly questionable; but the family, in its role of raising children, is of crucial importance. And divorce, with its adverse effects on children, has become increasingly common in recent decades. Such a large and complex topic can hardly be explored adequately here, but we can address two relevant questions: Is a positive attitude toward sex for its own sake necessarily a threat to marriage? And is pornography an appreciable factor in promoting that sort of attitude, hence itself such a threat?

The answer to the first question seems to be negative. For one thing, there have been many cultures with a stable family life and also an accepting attitude toward nonmarital sex. In fact, prior to the rise of the world religions and the empires that spread them, socially sanctioned premarital sex may well have been the cross-cultural norm. It has even been suggested that such behavior contributes to later marital stability by providing young people with experience on which to base a wiser choice of mate. In any case, it does not speak very well of marriage to suggest that, given a choice, people will reject it. As a matter of fact, most do have a strong inclination toward pair-bonding. Since they do not marry just for sex in the first place (and *shouldn't* do so), liberal sexual attitudes are not likely to dissuade them; only the timing is apt to be affected. In addition, there are many good reasons for not forcing young people to rush into marriage by making it the only way they can get sex.

As for the case of *extra*marital sex, where it has been socially sanctioned and controlled, it too has not been a serious threat to the stability of the family. It is true that jealousy is a powerful emotion. But it is also true that humans are far from being strictly monogamous in their feelings. Although our culture has traditionally taken jealousy as morally justified and condemned extramarital desires, others have done just the reverse: they have sought to mitigate the conflict between the two emotions by controlling the former more than the latter. And the anthropological reports indicate that they succeed rather well. It just may be, for all we know, that their system works better than ours in this respect. In fact, it can be argued that our unbending attitude toward sexual exclusivity contributes to marital breakup by creating unrealistic expectations. The offending party may not want such a break but feel it is necessary to satisfy other desires; and the offended one may fear loss of face in not avenging the act, or else think there must be something wrong with one of them or with the marriage for such a thing to have happened.

However all this may be, it is not the immediate question here. For us the issue is whether pornography is in any of the ways suggested a threat to the family in our culture. In spite of what many assume, it is far from obvious that it is. Indeed, it may be more likely to act as a "safety valve" for preventing marital breakup by providing a substitute way to satisfy nonmonogamous desires. Many cultures of the world have had special festival times and special locations in which the usual sexual taboos could be broken. (For just one example, consider the temple "prostitution" of the ancient Near East, in which all men and women took part.) The seeming value of such institutions in maintaining both monogamy and mental health has been noted by many students of the subject. The fact that such large numbers of strictly monogamous couples in the present time have come to use sexual entertainment together hints that it can serve the same purpose. Given the strong biological urge to have more than one sex partner, this may be an extremely important consideration.

Furthermore, pornography can help to preserve marriages by means of the positive effects listed earlier. As for the chance that it can also have the opposite effect, it might be suggested that romantic love stories present more of a danger to long-term pairing by awakening desires that many a marriage gone stale cannot satisfy. After all, falling in love with someone else is more likely to produce the wish for divorce than is a one-night stand. In any case, factors other than sexual fantasies have been vastly more influential in creating marital instability. The data indicate that such things as the following have been responsible for increasing divorce rates: greater independence for women (most female advocates of long-term commitment do not assail *this* causal factor), changes in laws and attitudes regarding divorce, unemployment and other financial troubles, and the greater mobility of the population, which has led to a loss of controls by the extended family and the community.

To really answer the question before us, however, we must consider the possible dynamics. Exactly how might pornography produce the allegedly destabilizing desires? Those who make the charge sometimes talk as if it is just a matter of arousing feelings that would not otherwise exist. But that is *their* fantasy, for biology can quite adequately do so. It does not take "outside agitators" like pornography to produce lust and wandering eyes. There is one thing, however, that pornography certainly can do, and that is to thwart attempts to suppress such feelings. Efforts to promote one moral point of view are indeed apt to be hampered when people are allowed to become aware of other views as genuine alternatives. This is just to say, however, that freedom and knowledge are an obstacle to attempts at thought control. "How're you gonna keep 'em down on the farm, after they've seen Paris?" asks an old song. It was not only the pill, but the loosening of restraints on sexual content in the media, that launched the reassessment of traditional sexual attitudes that occurred in the 1960s.

So there is a much broader point here that is very important. It is clear that formal and informal education—learning more about the world—tend to make people more tolerant and liberal in their views. For just one apparent example, surveys have revealed that half the readers of sex magazines are college educated, in contrast to a third of the readers of magazines in general. Ideologues, however, do not like such tolerance; what they are opposed to at bottom is the right of other people to make up their own minds. (From Moscow to Washington, they answer, "Don't *let* 'em see Paris.") But it cannot easily be argued that keeping people in ignorance of different ideas is best for them. As Carl Sagan pointed out in *Cosmos*, science has flourished at those times and places in history where there have been the greatest social openness and freedom. So it is for good reasons that we have our tradition of freedom of expression: aside from the great value of liberty itself, we have a better chance of discovering truth in a "free marketplace of ideas" than in conditions where only certain beliefs and attitudes may be extolled.

In particular, our best hope of working out the most viable social arrangement concerning sex and the family is to allow an open dialogue in which all human needs are given consideration. It is just as wrong to censor portrayals of alternative sexual lifestyles as it is to suppress those of different political or religious systems. In all likelihood, given the large range of human differences that exists, the best system in the present regard is a pluralistic one that allows individuals to discover the different modes of living that maximize their fulfillment. To rigidly impose the same kinds of relationships upon everyone (on homosexual and heterosexual, pair-bonder and non-pair-bonder and so forth) surely does not serve the best interests of individual people. And the common assumption that it is best for society as a whole is the product, not of a careful study of alternatives, but of the very prejudice that censors consideration of alternatives. Socially enforced error is self-perpetuating.

CHALLENGE QUESTIONS
Is Pornography Harmful?

1. How do you explain the increase of sexually explicit materials in our society? How does this affect our society?

2. Do you believe that today's more liberal attitudes toward sex have an effect on the incidence of rape, including date rape? Why, or why not?

3. Should policymakers pass legislation controlling or even banning pornography and other sexually explicit materials? Support your position.

4. Cline reports that viewing nonaggressive pornography can lead men to be more callous toward women. Do you agree? Do you think that other circumstances can lead to such attitudes? If so, what?

ISSUE 18

Does Religious Commitment Improve Mental Health?

YES: David B. Larson, from "Have Faith: Religion Can Heal Mental Ills," *Insight* (March 6, 1995)

NO: Albert Ellis, from "Dogmatic Devotion Doesn't Help, It Hurts," *Insight* (March 6, 1995)

ISSUE SUMMARY

YES: David B. Larson, president of the National Institute for Healthcare, maintains that religious commitment improves mental health and that spirituality can be a medical treatment.

NO: Albert Ellis, president of the Institute for Rational-Emotive Therapy, challenges Larson's studies and questions particularly whether a religious commitment of "fanatic" proportions is truly mentally healthy.

Before the modern forms of medicine and psychotherapy were ever formulated, many religious people were considered healers. The Judeo-Christian tradition and its literature are filled with claims about healing powers and reports of healing even psychological disorders. Part of the reason that these healing claims have been discounted is that some periods of history equated religious sin with psychological disorder. The people of these periods assumed that what we would now call "schizophrenia" and "depression" were really the results of sin or the indwelling of an evil spirit.

Recently, however, the healing claims of some religious people have gained a new hearing. Few of these people would contend that all psychological and emotional problems are simply sin or an evil spirit. But they caution us that although medical and living problems play an important role in psychological disorders, religious factors may also be influential. And although biological and psychological treatments have enjoyed some success, religious variables, such as spirituality, can also be important factors in alleviating mental or emotional problems. At the very least, they argue, this is an empirical rather than a religious question. Do religious factors, such as spirituality and religious commitment, improve one's mental health?

David B. Larson believes that this type of improvement has been demonstrated in numerous empirical studies. In the following selection, he presents research findings showing that spirituality is an effective treatment for drug and alcohol abuse and depression as well as an effective reducer of teen suicide and divorce. Larson explains how spirituality and religious commitment accomplish these results. Unfortunately, Larson says, psychologists' bias against religion has resulted in a continuing neglect of research on religious factors. Such bias has prevented therapists and policymakers from fully understanding the role of religion in health care. This, in turn, has deprived patients of a vital tool in coping with psychological disorders.

Albert Ellis, in contrast, questions how vital this "tool" really is. Ellis distrusts the objectivity of the studies that Larson cites. Nearly all the studies, he contends, were conducted by religious believers and published in religious journals. These people, according to Ellis, can hardly be considered to be dispassionate observers of "reality." Ellis also asserts that the more seriously people take their religious beliefs, the more fanatical they can become. Fanaticism, he suggests, is mentally and emotionally unhealthy. Therefore, the seriously religious—those who are committed and convinced—cannot be the psychologically healthy.

POINT

- The religiously committed report a higher rate of marital satisfaction than the nonreligious.

- Many mental health professionals resist positive findings on religious people because of antireligious views.

- Religious people have a greater sense of overall life satisfaction than nonreligious people.

- Mental health status improves for those who attend religious services on a regular basis.

- Studies show that religious commitment is the best predictor of a lack of substance abuse.

COUNTERPOINT

- Religious people are more likely than nonreligious people to respond in a socially desirable fashion.

- Many studies of religious people do not present a true picture of the mental health benefits of being religious.

- Many religious people have a tendency to claim happier and less stressful lives than they actually have.

- There is a high degree of correlation between dogmatic religiosity and mental disorder.

- Most of these studies are conducted by religious believers who are motivated to prove that religionists are healthier than nonreligionists.

YES
David B. Larson

HAVE FAITH: RELIGION CAN HEAL MENTAL ILLS

If a new health treatment were discovered that helped to reduce the rate of teenage suicide, prevent drug and alcohol abuse, improve treatment for depression, reduce recovery time from surgery, lower divorce rates and enhance a sense of well-being, one would think that every physician in the country would be scrambling to try it. Yet, what if critics denounced this treatment as harmful, despite research findings that showed it to be effective more than 80 percent of the time? Which would you be more ready to believe—the assertions of the critics based on their opinions or the results of the clinical trials based upon research?

As a research epidemiologist and board-certified psychiatrist, I have encountered this situation time and again during the last 15 years of my practice. The hypothetical medical treatment really does exist, but it is not a new drug: It is spirituality. While medical professionals have been privately assuming and publicly stating for years that religion is detrimental to mental health, when I actually looked at the available empirical research on the relationship between religion and health, the findings were overwhelmingly positive.

Just what are the correlations that exist between religion and mental health? First, religion has been found to be associated with a decrease in destructive behavior such as suicide. A 1991 review of the published research on the relationship between religious commitment and suicide rates conducted by my colleagues and I found that religious commitment produced lower rates of suicide in nearly every published study located. In fact, Stephen Stack, now of Wayne State University, showed that non-church attenders were four times more likely to kill themselves than were frequent attenders and that church attendance predicted suicide rates more effectively than any other factor including unemployment.

What scientific findings could explain these lower rates of suicide? First, several researchers have noted that the religiously committed report experiencing fewer suicidal impulses and have a more negative attitude toward suicidal behavior than do the nonreligious. In addition, suicide is a less-acceptable alternative for the religiously committed because of their belief in a moral accountability to God, thus making them less susceptible than the nonreligious to this life-ending alternative. Finally, the foundational religious beliefs in an afterlife, divine justice and the possibility of eternal condemnation all help to reduce the appeal of potentially self-destructive behavior.

If religion can reduce the appeal of potentially self-destructive behavior such as suicide, could it also play a role in decreasing other self-destructive behavior such as drug abuse? When this question has been examined empirically, the overwhelming response is yes. When Richard Gorsuch conducted a review of the relationship between religious commitment and drug abuse nearly 20 years ago, he noted that religious commitment "predicts those who have not used an illicit drug regardless of whether the religious variable is defined in terms of membership, active participation, religious upbringing or the meaningfulness of religion as viewed by the person himself."

More recent reviews have substantiated the earlier findings of Gorsuch, demonstrating that even when employing varying measures of religion, religious commitment predicted curtailed drug abuse. Interestingly, a national survey of 14,000 adolescents found the lowest rates of adolescent drug abuse in the most "politically incorrect" religious group—theologically conservative teens. The drug-abuse rates of teens from more liberal religious groups rose a little higher but still sank below rates of drug abuse among nonreligious teens. The correlations between the six measures of religion employed in the survey and the eight measures of substance abuse all were consistently negative. These findings lead the authors of the study to conclude that the amount of importance individuals place on religion in their lives is the best predictor of a lack of substance abuse, implying that "the (internal) controls operating here are a result of deeply internalized norms and values rather than fear ... or peer pressure." For teens living in a society in which drug rates continue to spiral, religion may not be so bad after all.

Just as religious commitment seems to be negatively correlated with drug abuse, similar results are found when examining the relationship between religious commitment and alcohol abuse. When I investigated this area myself, I found that those who abuse alcohol rarely have a strong religious commitment. Indeed, when my colleagues and I surveyed a group of alcoholics, we found that almost 90 percent had lost interest in religion during their teenage years, whereas among the general population, nearly that same percentage reported no change or even a slight increase in their religious practices during adolescence. Furthermore, a relationship between religious commitment and the nonuse or moderate use of alcohol has been extensively documented in the research literature. Some of the most intriguing results have been obtained by Acheampong Amoateng and Stephen Bahr of Brigham Young University, who found that whether or not a religion specifically proscribed alcohol use, those who were active in a religious group consumed substantially less than those who were not active.

Not only does religion protect against clinical problems such as suicide and drug and alcohol abuse, but religious commitment also has been shown to enhance positive life experiences such as marital satisfaction and personal well-being. When I reviewed the published studies on divorce and religious commitment, I found a negative relationship between church attendance and divorce in nearly every study that I located.

To what can these lower rates of divorce be attributed? Some critics argue that the religiously committed stay in unsatisfactory marriages due to religious prohibitions against divorce. However research has found little if any support for this view. In my review I found that, as a group, the religiously committed report a higher rate of marital satisfaction than the nonreligious. In fact, people from long-lasting marriages rank religion as one of the most important components of a happy marriage, with church attendance being strongly associated with the hypothetical willingness to remarry a spouse —a very strong indicator of marital satisfaction. Could these findings be skewed because, as is believed by some in the mental-health field, religious people falsify their response to such questions to make themselves look better? When the studies were controlled for such a factor the researchers found that the religiously committed were not falsifying their responses or answering in a socially acceptable manner and truly were more satisfied in their marriages.

Although the religiously committed are satisfied with their marriages, is this level of satisfaction also found in the sexual fulfillment of married couples? Though the prevailing public opinion is that religious individuals are prudish or even sexually repressed, empirical evidence has shown otherwise. Using data from *Redbook* magazine's survey of 100,000 women in 1975, Carole Tavris and Susan Sadd contradicted the longstanding assumption that religious commitment fosters sexual dysfunction. Tavris and Sadd found that it is the most religious women who report the greatest happiness and satisfaction with marital sex—more so than either moderately religious or nonreligious women. Religious women also report reaching orgasm more frequently than nonreligious women and are more satisfied with the frequency of their sexual activity than the less pious. Thus, while surprising to many, research suggests that religious commitment may play a role in improving rather than hindering sexual expression and satisfaction in marriage.

Not only has religious commitment been found to enhance sexual satisfaction, but overall life satisfaction as well. For example, David Myers of Hope College reviewed well-being literature and found that the religiously committed have a greater sense of overall life satisfaction than the nonreligious. Religion not only seems to foster a sense of well-being and life satisfaction but also may play a role in protecting against stress, with religiously committed respondents reporting much lower stress levels than the less committed. Even when the religiously committed have stress levels that are similar to the nonreligious, the more committed report experiencing fewer mental-illness problems than do the less committed.

Mental-health status has been found to improve for those attending religious services on a regular basis. Indeed, several studies have found a significant reduction in diverse psychiatric symptomatology following increased religious involvement. Chung-Chou Chu and colleagues at the Nebraska Psychiatric Institute in Omaha found lower rates of rehospitalization among schizophrenics who attended church or were given supportive aftercare by religious homemakers and ministers. One of my own studies confirmed that religious commitment can improve recovery rates as well. When my colleagues and I examined elderly women recovering from hip fractures, we found that those women with stronger religious beliefs suffered less from depression and thus were more likely to walk sooner and farther than their non-religious counterparts.

* * *

Yet, despite the abundance of studies demonstrating the beneficial effects of religious commitment on physical and mental health, many members of the medical community seem immune to this evidence. This resistance to empirical findings on the mental-health benefits of religious commitment may stem from the anti-religious views espoused by significant mental-health theorists. For example, Sigmund Freud called religion a "universal obsessional neurosis" and regarded mystical experience as "infantile helplessness" and a "regression to primary narcissism." More recently, Albert Ellis, the originator of rational-emotive therapy, has argued that "unbelief, humanism, skepticism and even thorough-going atheism not only abet but are practically synonymous with mental health; and that devout belief, dogmatism and religiosity distinctly contribute to, and in some ways are equal to, mental or emotional disturbance." Other clinicians have continued to perpetuate the misconception that religion is associated with psychopathology by labeling spiritual experiences as, among other things, borderline psychosis, a psychotic episode or the result of temporal-lobe dysfunction. Even the consensus report, "Mysticism: Spiritual Quest or Psychological Disturbance," by the Group for the Advancement of Psychiatry supported the long-standing view of religion as psychopathology; calling religious and mystical experiences "a regression, an escape, a projection upon the world of a primitive infantile state."

What is perhaps most surprising about these negative opinions of religion's effect on mental health is the startling absence of empirical evidence to support these views. Indeed, the same scientists who were trained to accept or reject a hypothesis based on hard data seem to rely solely on their own opinions and biases when assessing the effect of religion on health. When I conducted a systematic review of all articles published in the two leading journals of psychiatry, the *American Journal of Psychiatry* and the *Archives of General Psychiatry,* which assessed the association between religious commitment and mental health, I found that more than 80 percent of the religious-mental health associations located were clinically beneficial while only 15 percent of the associations were harmful—findings that run counter to the heavily publicized opinion of mental-health professionals. Thus, even though the vast majority of published research studies show religion as having a positive influence on mental health, religious commitment remains at best ignored or at worst, maligned by the professional community.

The question then begs to be asked: Why do medical professionals seem to ignore such positive evidence about religion's beneficial effect on mental health? One possible source of this tension could lie in clinicians' unfamiliarity with or rejection of traditional religious expression. For example, not only do mental-health professionals generally hold levels of religious commitment that diverge significantly from the general population, but they have much higher rates of atheism and agnosticism as well. The most recent survey of the belief systems of mental-health professionals found that less than 45 percent of the members of the American Psychiatric Association and the American Psychological Association believed in God—a percentage less than half that of the general population. When asked whether they agreed with the statement, "My whole approach to life is based on my religion," only one-third of clinical psychologists and two-fifths of psychiatrists agreed with that statement—again, a percentage that is nearly half that of the U.S. population. Indeed, more than 25 percent of psychiatrists and clinical psychologists and more than 40 percent of psychoanalysts claimed that they had abandoned a theistic belief system, compared with just less than 5 percent of the general population reporting the same feelings.

Science is assumed to be a domain that progresses through the gradual accumulation of new data or study findings, yet the mental-health community seems to be stalled in its understanding of the interface between religion and mental health. If a field is to progress in its knowledge and understanding of a controversial issue such as religion, empirical data and research must be relied upon more than personal opinions and biases. At a time when the rising cost of health care is causing so much discussion in our country, no factor that may be so beneficial to health can be ignored. The continuing neglect of published research on religion prevents clinicians and policymakers from fully understanding the important role of religion in health care and deprives patients as well as themselves of improved skills and methods in clinical prevention, coping with illness and quality of care. The mental health establishment needs to begin to recognize that it is treating a whole person—mind, body and, yes, even spirit.

NO
Albert Ellis

DOGMATIC DEVOTION DOESN'T HELP, IT HURTS

According to the psychological studies cited by David Larson, religious believers have more satisfying marriages, more enjoyable sex lives, less psychological stress, less depression and less drug and alcohol abuse than nonreligious people. Do these studies present a "true" picture of the mental health benefits of being religious? Probably not, for several reasons. First, the scientific method itself has been shown by many postmodernists to be far from "objective" and unassailable because it is created and used by highly subjective, often biased individuals. Scientists are never purely dispassionate observers of "reality" but frequently bring their own biases to their experiments and conclusions.

Second, practically all the studies that Larson cites were conducted by religious believers; some were published in religious journals. Many of the researchers were motivated to structure studies to "prove" that religionists are "healthier" than nonreligionists and only to publish studies that "proved" this.

None of the studies cited—as I noted when I read many of them myself —eliminated the almost inevitable bias of the subjects they used. I showed, in two comprehensive reviews of personality questionnaires that were published in the *Psychological Bulletin* in 1946 and 1948 and in several other psychological papers, that people often can figure out the "right" and "wrong" answers to these questionnaires and consequently "show" that they are "healthy" when they actually are not. I also showed, in an article in the *American Sociological Review* in 1948, that conservative and religious subjects probably more often were claiming falsely to have "happier" marriages on the Burgess-Locke Marriage Prediction Test than were liberal and nonreligious subjects.

This tendency of conservative, religious, job-seeking and otherwise motivated individuals to overemphasize their "good" and deemphasize their "poor" behavior on questionnaires has been pointed out by a number of other reviewers of psychological studies. Because all these studies included a number of strongly religious subjects, I would guess that many of these religionists had a distinct tendency to claim to be happier, less stressful and less addictive personalities than a good clinician would find them to be. I believe that this is a common finding of psychologists and was confirmed by my reviews mentioned previously.

Although Larson has spent a number of years locating studies that demonstrated that religious believers are healthier than nonreligious subjects, a large number of researchers have demonstrated the opposite. Several other studies have found that people who rigidly and dogmatically maintain religious views are more disturbed than less-rigid religious followers. But all these studies, once again, are suspect because none of them seem to have eliminated the problem of the biased answers of some of their subjects who consciously or unconsciously want to show how healthy they are.

Larson points out that many psychologists are sure that religionists are more disturbed than nonreligionists in spite of their having no real scientific evidence to substantiate their opinions. He is largely right about this, in view of what I have already said. Nonetheless, some reasonably good data back up the views of these psychologists that devout religionists often are disturbed.

Antiabortion killers such as Paul Hill have demonstrated that fanatical beliefs can have deadly consequences. But lesser-known fanatical religious believers have used ruthless tactics to oppose such "enlightened" views as birth control, women's liberation and even separation of church and state. Some religious zealots have jailed, maimed or even killed liberal proponents of their own religions. Nobel laureate Naguib Mahfouz is still recovering from stab wounds inflicted by Muslim extremists last October near his home in Cairo. (Mahfouz, considered by many to be a devout Muslim, frequently has ridiculed religious hypocrisy in his work.) Indian-born author Salman Rushdie has lived for seven years under a death sentence pronounced by the late Ayatollah Khomeini. Rushdie explained to the *New York Times* that dissidents within the Muslim world become "persons whose blood is unclean and therefore deserves to be spilled."

Religious persecution and wars against members of other religions have involved millions of casualties throughout human history Islamic fundamentalists from North Africa to Pakistan have established, or done their best to establish, state religions that force all the citizens of a country or other political group to strictly obey the rules of a specific religious group.

People diagnosed as being psychotic and of having severe personality disorders frequently have been obsessed with religious ideas and practices and compulsively and scrupulously follow religious teachings.

The tragic, multiple suicides of members of the Switzerland-based Order of the Solar Temple last October is only the most recent illustration of an extremist religious cult which manipulated its adherents and induced some of them to harm and kill themselves.

Do these manifestations of religious-oriented fanaticism, despotism, cultism and psychosis prove that religious-minded people generally are more disturbed than nonreligious individuals? Of course not. Many—probably most—religionists oppose the extreme views and practices I have just listed, and some actually make efforts to counteract them. One should not conclude, then, that pious religiosity in and of itself equals emotional disturbance.

However, as a psychotherapist and the founder of a school of psychotherapy called rational emotive behavior therapy, I have for many years distinguished between people who hold moderate religious views and those who espouse devout, dogmatic, rigid religious attitudes. In my judgment, most intelligent and educated people are in the former group and temperately believe God (such as Jehovah) exists, that He or She created the universe and the creatures in it, and that we preferably should follow religious, ethical laws but that a Supreme Being forgives us fallible humans when we do not follow His or Her rules. These "moderate" religionists prefer to be "religious" but do not insist that the rest of us absolutely and completely always must obey God's and the church's precepts. Therefore, they still mainly run their own lives and rarely damn themselves (and others) for religious nonobservance. In regard to God and His or Her Commandments, they live and let live.

The second kind of religious adherents —those who are devout, absolutistic and dogmatic—are decidedly different. They differ among themselves but most of them tend to believe that there absolutely has to be a Supreme Being, that He or She specifically runs the universe, must be completely obeyed and will eternally damn all believers and nonbelievers who deviate from His or Her sacred commands.

Another devout and absolutistic group of people do not believe in anything supernatural, but do rigidly subscribe to a dogmatic, secular belief system— such as Nazism, Fascism or Communism —which vests complete authority in the state or in some other organization and which insists that nonallegiance or opposition to this Great Power must be ruthlessly fought, overthrown, punished and annihilated.

As an advocate of mental and emotional health, I have always seen "moderate" religious believers as reasonably sound individuals who usually are no more neurotic (or otherwise disturbed) than are skeptical, nonreligious people. Like nonbelievers, they are relatively open-minded, democratic and unbigoted. They allow themselves to follow and experience "religious" and "secular" values, enjoyment and commitments. Therefore, they infrequently get into serious emotional trouble with themselves or with others because of their religious beliefs and actions.

This is not the case with fanatical, pietistic religionists. Whether they are righteously devoted to God and the church or to secular organizations and cults (some of which may be atheistic) these extreme religionists are not open-minded, tolerant and undamning. Like nonreligious neurotics and individuals with severe personality disorders, they do not merely wish that other religionists and nonbelievers agree with them and worship their own Supreme Being and their churchly values. They insist, demand and command that their God's and their church's will be done.

Since the age of 12, I have been skeptical of anything supernatural or god-like. But I always have believed that undogmatic religionists can get along well in the world and be helpful to others, and I relate nicely to them. Many, if not most, of the mental-health professionals with whom I have worked in the field of rational emotive behavior therapy are religious. A surprisingly large number of them have been ordained as Protestant ministers, Catholic priests or nuns or Jewish rabbis. A few have even been fundamentalists! So some forms of psychotherapy and moderate religious belief hardly are incompatible.

The important question remains: Is there a high degree of correlation between devout, one-sided, dogmatic religiosity and neurosis (and other personality disorders)? My experience as a clinical psychologist leads me to conclude that there well may be. Some of the disturbed traits and behaviors that pietistic religionists tend to have (but, of course, not always have) include these:

A dearth of enlightened self-interest and self-direction. Pietistic religionists tend to be overdevoted, instead, to unduly sacrificing themselves for God, the church (or the state) and to ritualistic self-deprivation that they feel "bound" to follow for "sacred" reasons. They often give masochistic and self-abasing allegiance to ecclesiastical (and/or secular) lords and leaders. Instead of largely planning and directing their own lives, they often are mindlessly overdependent on religious-directed (or state-directed) creeds, rules and commandments.

Reduced social and human interest. Dogmatic religionists are overly focused on godly, spiritual and monastic interests. They often give greater service to God than to humanity and frequently start holy wars against dissidents to their deity and their church. Witness the recent murders by allegedly devout antiabortionists!

Refusal to accept ambiguity and uncertainty. In an obsessive-compulsive fashion, they hold to absolute necessity and complete certainty, even though our universe only seems to include probability and chance. They deny pliancy, alternative-seeking and pluralism in their own and other people's lives. They

negate the scientific view that no hypothesis is proved indisputably "true" under all conditions at all times.

Allergy to unconditional self-acceptance. Emotionally healthy people accept themselves (and other humans) unconditionally—that is, whether they achieve success and whether all significant others approve of them. Dogmatic religionists unhealthily and conditionally accept themselves (and others) only when their God, their church (or state) and similar religionists approve of their thoughts, feelings and behaviors. Therefore, they steadily remain prone to, and often are in the throes of, severe anxiety guilt and self-condemnation.

In rational-emotive therapy we show people that they "get" emotionally disturbed not only by early or later traumas in their lives but mainly by choosing goals and values that they strongly prefer and by unrealistically, illogically and defeatingly making them into one, two or three grandiose demands: (1) "I absolutely must succeed at important projects or I am an utterly worthless person"; (2) "Other people must treat me nicely or they are totally damnable"; (3) "Life conditions are utterly obligated to give me everything that I think I need or my existence is valueless."

When people clearly see that they are largely upsetting themselves with these godlike commandments, and when they convert them to reasonable—but often still compulsive—desires, they are able to reconstruct their disturbed thoughts, feelings and actions and make themselves much less anxious, depressed, enraged and self-hating and much more self-actualizing and happy.

Being a philosophical system of psychotherapy, rational emotive behavior therapy has much to learn from theological and secular religions. But individuals who choose to be religious also may learn something important from it, namely: Believe whatever you wish about God, the church, people and the universe. But see if you can choose a moderate instead of a fanatical form of religion. Try to avoid a doctrinal system through which you are dogmatically convinced that you absolutely must devote yourself to the one, only, right and unerring deity and to the one, true and infallible church. And try to avoid the certitude that you are God. Otherwise, in my view as a psychotherapist, you most probably are headed for emotional trouble.

CHALLENGE QUESTIONS

Does Religious Commitment Improve Mental Health?

1. Explain why Ellis feels that the data concerning the benefits of religion are not objective. Could his explanation be applied to other types of psychological research?

2. Ellis is the founder of a major school of psychotherapy— rational-emotive therapy. Find a description of this therapy, and discuss how Ellis's own nonreligious values might influence his formulation of this therapy.

3. If it were generally agreed that religious factors were beneficial for mental health, how might psychotherapists use these factors? What problems might a person encounter in employing these factors?

4. How does Ellis distinguish between those who adopt moderate forms of religion and those who adopt fanatical forms of religion? How is this distinction different from the distinction between those who consider their religion relatively superficially and those who take their religious beliefs seriously?

5. For the last few centuries, religion and science have been considered completely separate endeavors. How might this historical separation play into the controversy between Larson and Ellis?

CONTRIBUTORS
TO THIS VOLUME

EDITOR

BRENT SLIFE is a clinical psychologist and a professor of psychology at Baylor University in Waco, Texas. A fellow of the American Psychological Association, he has authored over 60 articles and books, his most recent being *Time and Psychological Explanation* (State University of New York Press, 1993), which describes the overlooked influence of linear time on mainstream psychology. Recently designated the Outstanding Research Professor at Baylor University, he is also the editor of the *Journal of Theoretical and Philosophical Psychology* and serves in editorial capacities on the *Journal of Mind and Behavior* and *Theory and Psychology*. He received a Ph.D. from Purdue University, where he and Joseph Rubinstein, his coeditor in the first seven editions of *Taking Sides: Clashing Views on Controversial Psychological Issues,* began the dialogue approach to psychology that is the basis of this volume.

STAFF

Mimi Egan   Publisher
David Dean   List Manager
David Brackley   Developmental Editor
Brenda S. Filley   Production Manager
Libra Ann Cusack   Typesetting Supervisor
Juliana Arbo   Typesetter
Lara Johnson   Graphics
Diane Barker   Proofreader
Richard Tietjen   Systems Manager

AUTHORS

ALAN C. ACOCK is a professor in and the chair of the Department of Human Development and Family Sciences at Oregon State University in Corvallis, Oregon.

NANCY E. ADLER is a professor in the Department of Psychology at the University of California, San Francisco.

MARCIA ANGELL is a pathologist and a lecturer in the Department of Social Medicine at the Harvard Medical School.

ELIZABETH BALDWIN is research ethics officer for the American Psychological Association's Science Directorate. Her work involves a broad range of research ethics issues, including those relating to the use of animals in research. She has also worked at the Congressional Research Service in the Division of Science Policy. She holds a B.A. in biology, an M.S. in entomology, and an M.A. in science, technology, and public policy.

ELLEN BASS is a nationally recognized counselor, lecturer, and professional trainer who works with survivors of child sexual abuse.

NAZLI BAYDAR is a researcher with the Battelle Human Affairs Research Center in Seattle, Washington.

ALAN D. BOWD is a professor of educational psychology and director of the School of Education at Lakehead University in Thunder Bay, Ontario, Canada. He received an M.A. in psychology from the University of Sydney and a Ph.D. in educational psychology from the University of Calgary. His main interest is in the ethical treatment of animals, and his published research has focused on the development of beliefs and attitudes about animals during childhood.

JEANNE BROOKS-GUNN is the Virginia and Leonard Marx Professor in Child Development and Education at Columbia University's Teachers College in New York City and director of the university's Center for Young Children and Families. She is a member of the National Institute of Child Health and Human Development's Consortium on Child and Family Well-Being and of the National Institutes of Mental Health's Family Research Consortium. She is on the editorial boards of the *Journal of Research on Adolescence,* the *Journal of Youth and Adolescence,* and *Psychosomatic Medicine.*

WILLIAM BYNE is a research associate in the Albert Einstein College of Medicine at Yeshiva University in New York City, where he investigates the brain structure of humans and other primates, as well as an attending psychiatrist at the New York State Psychiatric Institute. His research focuses on the ways in which biological and social factors interact to influence behavior. He received his Ph.D. in 1985 from the University of Wisconsin–Madison and his M.D. in 1989 from Yeshiva University.

BRANDON S. CENTERWALL is an assistant professor of epidemiology in the School of Public Health and Community Medicine at the University of Washington in Seattle, Washington.

F. M. CHRISTENSEN is a professor in the Department of Philosophy at the University of Alberta in Edmonton, Alberta, Canada.

VICTOR CLINE is a professor emeritus of psychology at the University of Utah in Salt Lake City, Utah. His research interests include media effects and person perception issues.

LEE COLEMAN is a psychiatrist in Berkeley, California, and a critic of the role of mental health professionals in legal settings. His current research interests focus on false accusations of child sexual abuse.

RAYMOND R. CROWE is a clinical psychiatrist and a professor in the Department of Psychiatry at the University of Iowa College of Medicine in Iowa City, Iowa.

LAURA DAVIS is an expert on healing from child sexual abuse and a nationally recognized workshop leader.

PATRICK H. DeLEON, a psychologist and a lawyer, is a staff member for Senator Daniel K. Inouye (D) of Hawaii.

DAVID H. DEMO is an associate professor in the Department of Sociology at Virginia Polytechnic Institute and State University in Blacksburg, Virginia. His research focuses on the influences of family structure and family relations on parents and children.

GARLAND Y. DENELSKY is head of the psychology section and director of the Psychology Training Program at the Cleveland Clinic, where he provides training and supervision for psychology fellows and psychiatry residents. His clinical and research interests include the enhancement of coping skills, facilitation of smoking cessation, and treatment of performance anxiety. He received his Ph.D. from Purdue University in 1966 and was recently awarded the Outstanding Alumni Award from Grinnell College, where he received his bachelor's degree.

BERNARD DIXON is vice president of the General Section of the British Association for the Advancement of Science and chair of the Programme Planning Committee of the Edinburgh International Science Festival.

ALBERT ELLIS, founder of rational-emotive therapy, is president of the Institute for Rational-Emotive Therapy, located in New York City. He received his Ph.D. in clinical psychology from Columbia University, and he has authored or coauthored more than 600 articles and over 50 books on psychotherapy, marital and family therapy, and sex therapy, including *Why Some Therapies Don't Work: The Dangers of Transpersonal Psychology* (Prometheus Books, 1989), with Raymond Yaeger.

SEYMOUR FISHER is a professor of psychology and coordinator of research training in the Department of Psychiatry and Behavioral Sciences at the University of New York Health Science Center at Syracuse. He has published 16 books and approximately 200 scientific papers. His scholarly work has focused on such areas as body image, sexual behavior, the validity of psychoanalytic theory, the psychodynamics of comedians, and the efficacy of psychotropic drugs.

LEONARD ROY FRANK is cofounder of the Network Against Psychiatric Assault (NAPA) in San Francisco and Berkeley, California, and a member of Concerned Citizens Opposing Electroshock in San Francisco.

ROGER P. GREENBERG is a professor in and head of the Division of Clinical Psychology, as well as director of psychology internship training, at the State University of New York Health Science Center at Syracuse. His more than 150 publications and presentations include the award-winning books *The Scientific Credibility of Freud's Theories and Therapy* (Columbia University Press, 1985) and *A Critical Appraisal of Biological Treatments for Psychological Distress: Comparisons With Psychotherapy and Placebo* (Lawrence Erlbaum, 1989), both coauthored with Seymour Fisher.

DEAN H. HAMER received his Ph.D. in biological chemistry from Harvard University in 1977. For the past 17 years, he has held positions at the National Institutes of Health, where he is currently chief of the section on gene structure and regulation at the National Cancer Institute. His studies focus on the role of genes in sexual orientation and in complex medical conditions, including the progression of HIV and Kaposi's sarcoma.

ARTHUR R. JENSEN is a professor of educational psychology at the University of California, Berkeley. His research interests focus on psychometrics, behavioral genetics, and theories of intelligence.

EVE C. JOHNSTONE is a professor in the Department of Psychiatry at the University of Edinburgh.

PETER D. KRAMER is a psychiatrist and the author of *Moments of Engagement: Intimate Psychotherapy in a Technological Age* (W. W. Norton, 1989).

DAVID B. LARSON is an assistant secretary of planning at the Department of Health and Human Services in Washington, D.C.

SIMON LeVAY earned a doctorate in neuroanatomy at the University of Göttingen in Germany. His work in the early 1970s at Harvard University focused on the brain's visual system. He

has worked as head of the vision center of the Salk Institute for Biological Studies in San Diego, and he is the founder of the Institute of Gay and Lesbian Education.

JOAN McCORD is a professor of criminal justice at Temple University in Philadelphia, Pennsylvania, where she has been teaching since 1987. She has received the Prix Emile Durkheim Award from the International Society of Criminology and the Edwin H. Sutherland Award from the American Society of Criminology for her research. A former president of the American Society of Criminology, she has authored or coauthored more than 100 articles, books, and essays on theory, treatment effects, crime, alcoholism, protective factors, and socialization.

JANAKI RAMANAN is an instructor at the University of Texas in Dallas, Texas.

D. L. ROSENHAN (b. 1929) is a professor of law and psychology at Stanford University and a social psychologist whose focal concern has been clinical and personality matters. He has also been a faculty member at Princeton University, the University of Pennsylvania, and Swarthmore College.

VINCENT M. RUE is codirector of the Institute for Pregnancy Loss in Portsmouth, New Hampshire.

THEODORE R. SARBIN is an emeritus professor of psychology and criminology at the University of California, Santa Cruz.

KENNETH J. SHAPIRO is executive director of Psychologists for the Ethical Treatment of Animals and editor of the academic biannual *Society and Animals*. His background is in clinical psychology, phenomenological psychology, and intellectual history. He has published scholarly work in phenomenological psychology, developing and applying methods for the study of both human and nonhuman animals.

BRIAN SIANO is a writer and researcher based in Philadelphia, Pennsylvania. His column "The Skeptical Eye" appears regularly in *The Humanist.*

ANNE C. SPECKHARD is a clinician, a researcher, and a consultant practicing in Alexandria, Virginia, who has consulted on several postpartum stress research projects.

ROBERT L. SPITZER is affiliated with the New York State Psychiatric Institute in New York City. He is a former chairman of the American Psychiatric Association and its Task Force on Nomenclature and Statistics.

ROBERT J. STERNBERG is the IBM Professor of Psychology and Education at Yale University and a member of the Educational Testing Service Board of Visitors.

MURRAY A. STRAUS is a professor of sociology and codirector of the Family Research Laboratory at the University of New Hampshire in Durham, New Hampshire. He has held academic appointments at Cornell University, the University of Minnesota, the University of Wisconsin, and Washington State University, as well as at universities in England, India, and Sri Lanka. He is the author or coauthor of over 150 articles and 15 books on the family, research methods, and South Asia, including *Physical Violence in American Families: Risk, Factors,* *and Adaptations to Violence in 8,145 Families* (Transaction, 1989), coauthored with Richard J. Gelles.

DEBORAH LOWE VANDELL is a professor in the Department of Educational Psychology at the University of Wisconsin–Madison in Madison, Wisconsin. She is the author of numerous articles on the effects of child care and maternal employment on children's development.

JUDITH S. WALLERSTEIN is an internationally recognized authority on the effects of divorce on children and their parents. Her current research interests focus on successful marriage. Before her retirement, she was executive director of the Center for the Family in Transition —a research, training, and clinical center in Corte Madera, California, which she founded in 1980—and a senior lecturer in the School of Social Welfare at the University of California, Berkeley. She is the coauthor, with Sandra Blakeslee, of *Second Chances: Men, Women, and Children a Decade After Divorce* (Ticknor & Fields, 1989). She received a Ph.D. in psychology from Lund University in Sweden in 1978.

RICHARD N. WILLIAMS is a member of the psychology department at Brigham Young University.

ROBERT WRIGHT is senior editor at *New Republic.* He is the author of *The Moral Animal: Evolutionary Psychology and Everyday Life.*

STEPHEN C. YANCHAR is a doctoral student in the theoretical psychology program at Brigham Young University in Provo, Utah, where he specializes in theories of the mind.

INDEX